The Future of International Human Rights

Burns H. Weston
Stephen P. Marks

Editors and Contributors

 Transnational Publishers, Inc.
Ardsley, New York

This book may be cited as follows:
THE FUTURE OF INTERNATIONAL HUMAN RIGHTS
(Burns H. Weston & Stephen P. Marks eds. & contribs., 1999).

Library of Congress Cataloging-in-Publication Data

The future of international human rights / edited by Burns H. Weston,
  Stephen P. Marks.
     p.   cm.
  Includes bibliographical references, appendices, and index.
  ISBN 1-57105–098–1
  1. Human rights. I. Weston, Burns H. II. Marks, Stephen P.
  JC571.F79 1999
  341.4'81—dc21   99-19909
                                                          CIP

Manufactured in the United States of America.

For
Marta
and
Kathleen

Contents

Contributors

M. Cherif Bassiouni
Professor of Law, De Paul University; President of the International Institute of Higher Studies in Criminal Sciences, Siracusa, Italy. J.D., 1964, Indiana University; LL.M., 1966, John Marshall Law School; S.J.D., 1973, George Washington University; LL.D. 1981. Chairman, U.N. Commission of Experts Established Pursuant to 1992 Security Council Resolution 780 to Investigate Violations of International Humanitarian Law in the Former Yugoslavia (1993); Vice-Chairman, U.N. General Assembly Ad Hoc Committee on the Establishment of an International Criminal Court (1995); Vice-Chairman, U.N. General Assembly Preparatory Committee on the Establishment of an International Criminal Court (1996); Chairman, Drafting Committee of the U.N. Diplomatic Conference on the Establishment of an International Criminal Court (July 1998); Special Rapporteur on The Rights to Restitution, Compensation, and Rehabilitation for Victims of Grave Violations of Human Rights and Fundamental Freedoms (Summer 1998). Professor Bassiouni is also the author and editor of many books and articles on U.S. criminal law, international and comparative criminal law, and international human rights law, published in Arabic, English, French, Italian, and Spanish.

Upendra Baxi
Professor of Law and Development, University of Warwick. B.A. (Honors), 1958, University of Gujarat; L.L.B. and L.L.M., 1962 and 1964, University of Bombay; L.L.M. and J.S.D., 1965 and 1972, University of California at Berkeley. Professor of Law, University of Delhi (1973–96); Vice Chancellor, University of South Gujarat (1982–85); Vice Chancellor, Delhi University (1990–1994). President of the Indian Society of International Law (1992–95) and Honorary Director of Research, The Indian Law Institute, New Delhi (1985–89), Professor Baxi's many publications include THE CRISIS OF INDIAN LEGAL SYSTEM (1982), COURAGE, CRAFT AND CONTENTION: THE INDIAN SUPREME COURT IN THE EIGHTIES (1986), LIBERTY AND CORRUPTION (1990), MARX, LAW AND JUSTICE (1993), MAMBRINO'S HELMET: HUMAN RIGHTS FOR A CHANGING WORLD (1994), INHUMAN WRONGS AND HUMAN RIGHTS (1994), and THE FUTURE OF HUMAN RIGHTS (forthcoming). Having worked for over two decades with peoples' groups in India and elsewhere relative to the strategic uses of law for human amelioration, Professor Baxi's current work, relating to globalization and law, especially with regard to the future of human rights, is focused on ways of combating mass impoverishment.

John Dugard

Professor of Public International Law, Leiden University; Professor of Law Emeritus, University of the Witwatersrand. B.A., 1956, University of Stellenbosch; LL.B., 1958, University of Stellenbosch; LL.B. and Diploma in International Law, 1965, Cambridge University; LL.D., 1980, Cambridge University. Dean of the Faculty of Law (1975–77) and Director of the Centre for Applied. Legal Studies (1978–90), University of Witwatersrand; Member, U.N. International Law Commission; Arthur Goodhart Visiting Professor of Legal Science and Director of the Lauterpacht Research Centre for International Law, Cambridge (1997–98). Professor Dugard specializes in international law and human rights law and has published widely in these fields. Among his many publications are THE SOUTH WEST AFRICA/NAMIBIA DISPUTE (1973), HUMAN RIGHTS AND THE SOUTH AFRICAN LEGAL ORDER (1978), RECOGNITION AND THE UNITED NATIONS (1987), THE LAST YEARS OF APARTHEID: CIVIL LIBERTIES IN SOUTH AFRICA (1992), and INTERNATIONAL LAW: A SOUTH AFRICAN PERSPECTIVE (1994). In 1995, Professor Dugard served as a technical adviser in the drafting of the Bill of Rights in the 1996 South African Constitution.

Richard A. Falk

Albert G. Milbank Professor of International Law and Practice, Princeton University. B.S., 1952, Wharton School, University of Pennsylvania; LL.B., 1955, Yale University; S.J.D., 1962, Harvard University. A member of the editorial boards of numerous scholarly journals, including *Alternatives—Social Transformation and Humane Governance*, the *American Journal of International Law, The Nation, Third World Quarterly*, and *World Politics*, Professor Falk is the author of many articles and books. His most recent books include HUMANE GOVERNANCE: TOWARD A NEW GLOBAL POLITICS (1995) and LAW IN AN EMERGING GLOBAL VILLAGE: A POST-WESTPHALIAN PERSPECTIVE (1998). A forthcoming book, tentatively entitled HUMAN RIGHTS HORIZONS, will be published in 2000.

Kamal Hossain

Barrister-at-law, Dhaka; Senior Advocate, Supreme Court of Bangladesh. B.A (Honors in Jurisprudence), 1957, Oxford University; B.C.L., 1957, Oxford University; Ph.D. (International Law), 1964, Oxford University. Service to the Government of Bangladesh as Member of Parliament (1972–75), Minister of Law (1972), Minister of Foreign Affairs (1973–75), and Minister of Petroleum and Minerals (1974–75). Chairman, Bangladesh Legal Aid and Services Trust; Member of the Board, International Centre for Human Rights and Democratic Development (Montreal); Chairperson, Commonwealth Human Rights Advisory Commission (1993–98); U.N. Special Rapporteur of the human rights situation in Afghanistan (1998–); Vice-Chairman, Forum for Democratic Leaders of the Asia-Pacific; Vice-Chairman, Transparency International. The Dom Helder Camara Visiting Professor at the Free University of Amsterdam in 1997, Dr. Hossain is the author of LAW AND POLICY IN PETROLEUM DEVELOPMENT (1979), editor of LEGAL ASPECTS OF THE NEW

INTERNATIONAL ECONOMIC ORDER (1980), and co-editor of PERMANENT SOVEREIGNTY OVER NATURAL RESOURCES IN INTERNATIONAL LAW (1984). In addition to his human rights law practice, Dr. Hossain writes and lectures extensively, currently about globalization and human rights.

Stephen P. Marks

François-Xavier Bagnoud Professor of Health and Human Rights, Harvard School of Public Health; formerly Director, United Nations Studies Program, Co-director of the Human Rights and Humanitarian Affairs Concentration at the School of International and Public Affairs (SIPA) and Lecturer in the School of Law, Columbia University. B.A., 1964, Stanford University; Diplôme, 1971, University of Law, Economics and Social Sciences of Paris; Diplôme, 1972, University of Humanities of Strasbourg; Doctor of Laws, 1979, University of Nice. Stephen Marks has taught also as Visiting Professor of Law and Director of the Program in International Law and Human Rights, Benjamin N. Cardozo School of Law (1989–91), on the Faculty of Law at the University of Phnom Penh (1992), and as Lecturer of Public and International Affairs, Woodrow Wilson School of Public and International Affairs, Princeton University (1995). President of the U.S. Committee for International Service for Human Rights; Senior Programme Specialist, UNESCO (1973–83); Program Officer, Human Rights and Social Justice Program, The Ford Foundation (1983–88); Chief of Section, Human Rights Component, United Nations Transitional Authority in Cambodia (1992–93). A consultant to various foundations and international organizations, Dr. Marks' scholarship emphasizes international law and organizations, peacekeeping, development, democratic transition, and human rights.

Julie A. Mertus

Professor of Law, Ohio Northern University. B.S., 1985, Cornell University; J.D., 1988, Yale University. Visiting Human Rights Fellow, Harvard University (1986–87); Peace Fellow, MacArthur Foundation (1994–95); Fulbright Scholar and Professor, University of Bucharest (1996). Clerk to the Honorable John Walker, Second Circuit Court of Appeals (1988–89); Attorney, American Civil Liberties Union (1990–91); Counsel, Helsinki Watch/Human Rights Watch (1993–94). A consultant on gender and refugee issues for humanitarian and human rights organizations, Professor Mertus' books include OPEN WOUNDS: HUMAN RIGHTS ABUSES IN KOSOVO (1994), THE SUITCASE: REFUGEES' VOICES FROM BOSNIA AND CROATIA (1997), KOSOVO: HOW MYTHS AND TRUTHS STARTED A WAR (1999), and LOCAL ACTION/GLOBAL CHANGE: LEARNING ABOUT THE HUMAN RIGHTS OF WOMEN AND GIRLS (1999).

Rein Müllerson

Professor and Chair of International Law, King's College, London. Candidate of Law, 1979, Moscow University; LL.D., 1985, Moscow University. Deputy Foreign Minister of Estonia (1991-92); Head, Department of International Law, Institute of

State and Law, Academy of Sciences, Moscow (1987–91); Visiting Centennial Professor, London School of Economics and Political Science (1992–94). A member of the U.N. Human Rights Committee from 1988 to 1992, Professor Müllerson is also the author of several books on international law and politics. His last book, HUMAN RIGHTS DIPLOMACY, was published in 1997. Since 1995 Professor Müllerson has been an *Associé* of the *Institut de Droit International*.

Martha C. Nussbaum

Ernst Freund Distinguished Service Professor of Law and Ethics, University of Chicago (with appointments in the School of Law, the Divinity School, and the Department of Philosophy, and an associate appointment in the Department of Classics). B.A., 1969, New York University; M.A., 1971, New York University; Ph.D., 1975, Harvard University. Pen Spielvogel-Diamondstein Prize (1990). Member, American Academy of Arts and Sciences; Chair, U.N. Commission on the Status of Women (1994–97). From 1986 to 1993, Professor Nussbaum worked as a Research Advisor for the World Institute for Development Economics Research in Helsinki (a division of the United Nations University). In connection with that appointment, she edited (with Amartya Sen) THE QUALITY OF LIFE (1993) and (with Jonathan Glover) WOMEN, CULTURE, AND DEVELOPMENT (1995). Among her many books and articles are THE FRAGILITY OF GOODNESS (1986), LOVE'S KNOWLEDGE (1990), THE THERAPY OF DESIRE (1994), CULTIVATING HUMANITY (1997), and SEX AND SOCIAL JUSTICE (1998).

Anne Orford

Senior Lecturer, Faculty of Law, University of Melbourne. B.A., 1987, University of Queensland; LL.B. (Honors), 1988, University of Queensland; LL.M. (Merit), 1992, University of London. Associate Lecturer, School of Law and Legal Studies, La Trobe University (1993–95); Lecturer, Faculty of Law, Australian National University (1995–1998); Visiting Lecturer, Human Rights Session of the Academy of European Law, European University Institute, Florence (1998). Secretary, Australian and New Zealand Society of International Law; Member, Board of Editors, *Australian Feminist Law Journal*. Ms. Orford has published widely in the areas of international economic law, international human rights law, collective security, feminist theory, postcolonial theory and legal education. She currently is working on a major project funded by the Australian Research Council exploring the impact of IMF programs on human rights and democratic governance in Asia.

Mary Robinson

United Nations High Commissioner for Human Rights. B.A., 1967, Trinity College, University of Dublin; LL.M., 1968, Harvard University; M.A., 1970, Trinity College, University of Dublin. Reid Professor of Constitutional and Criminal Law and Lecturer in European Community Law, Trinity College, Dublin (1969–75);

Senator, Irish Parliament (1969–89); President, Republic of Ireland (1990–97). Member, Advisory Commission of Inter-Rights (1984–90); Member, International Commission of Jurists (1987–90), Founder and Director, Irish Centre for European Law (1988–90). In 1993, Mrs. Robinson was Special Rapporteur to the Interregional Meeting organized by the Council of Europe on the theme "Human Rights at the Dawn of the 21st Century," as part of its preparation for the 1993 Vienna World Conference on Human Rights. Also, she delivered the keynote address at the Council of Europe preparatory meeting for the 1995 Beijing Fourth World Conference on Women. Mrs. Robinson was the first Head of State to visit Somalia (1992) and Rwanda (1994) in the aftermath of the crises in those countries, and the first Head of State to visit the International Criminal Tribunal for the Former Yugoslavia.

Dinah Shelton

Professor of Law, Center for Civil and Human Rights, School of Law, University of Notre Dame. B.A., 1967, University of California at Berkeley; J.D., 1970, University of California at Berkeley. Graduate Fellow, International Institute of Human Rights, Strasbourg (1970–72); Member, Faculty of Law, University of Santa Clara (1975–87); Director of the staff attorneys for the United States Court of Appeals for the Ninth Circuit (1987–89); Visiting Professor of Law, Stanford University (Spring 1991); Visiting Professor of Law, Université Robert Schumann, Strasbourg (1991-92). Professor Shelton is a member of the executive councils of the International Institute of Human Rights, the Marangopoulos Foundation for Human Rights, and Redress International. Her many books and articles focus primarily upon international human rights law and international environmental law, including the award-winning PROTECTING HUMAN RIGHTS IN THE AMERICAS (with Thomas Buergenthal and Robert Norris, 1982, and with Thomas Buergenthal, 1996), INTERNATIONAL ENVIRONMENTAL LAW (with Alexandre Kiss, 1991), and EUROPEAN ENVIRONMENTAL LAW (with Alexandre Kiss, 1993).

Burns H. Weston

Bessie Dutton Murray Distinguished Professor of Law and Associate Dean for International and Comparative Legal Studies, The University of Iowa. B.A., 1956, Oberlin College; LL.B., 1961, Yale University; J.S.D., 1970, Yale University. Director, Center for World Order Studies, The University of Iowa (1972–76); Senior Fellow and Director, Transnational Academic Program, Institute for World Order, New York City (1976–78). Vice-President, American Society of International Law (1992–94); Fellow, World Academy of Art and Science; Member, Board of Trustees, Procedural Aspects of International Law Institute; Member, Advisory Council, International Human Rights Law Group; Member, Council on Foreign Relations. Editor of the Procedural Aspects of International Law Book Series and a member of the Board of Editors of the *American Journal of International Law*, Professor Weston's recent books include ALTERNATIVE SECURITY: LIVING WITHOUT NUCLEAR

DETERRENCE (1990); HUMAN RIGHTS IN THE WORLD COMMUNITY: ISSUES AND ACTION (with Richard P. Claude, 2nd ed., 1992); PREFERRED FUTURES FOR THE UNITED NATIONS (with Saul Mendlovitz, 1995); INTERNATIONAL LAW AND WORLD ORDER: A PROBLEM-ORIENTED COURSEBOOK (with Richard Falk and Hilary Charlesworth, 3rd ed., 1998); and INTERNATIONAL ENVIRONMENTAL LAW AND WORLD ORDER: A PROBLEM-ORIENTED COURSEBOOK (with Jonathan Carlson, Lakshman Guruswamy, and Sir Geoffrey Palmer, 2d ed., 1999).

Yozo Yokota
Professor of Law, The University of Tokyo. B.A., 1964, International Christian University; LL.M., 1966, The University of Tokyo; LL.D., 1969, The University of Tokyo, 1969. Professor of International Law and Organization, International Christian University (1979–95); Visiting Professor of Law at the University of Adelaide, the University of Michigan, and Columbia University (1983–85). Alternate Member, U.N. Sub-Commission on Prevention of Discrimination and Protection of Minorities; Member of the International Commission of Jurists; Legal Counsel of the World Bank (1974–76); Special Rapporteur of the U.N. Commission on Human Rights for Myanmar (Burma) (1992–96). Author of many books and articles, including INTERNATIONAL LAW AND SOCIETY (1986), THE TWENTIETH CENTURY AND INTERNATIONAL ORGANIZATION (1989), and INTRODUCTION TO INTERNATIONAL LAW (1996).

Preface

This volume, commemorating the fiftieth anniversary of the Universal Declaration of Human Rights and graced by a Foreword by U.N. High Commissioner for Human Rights Mary Robinson, seeks to envisage the future of international human rights through both an analysis of existing human rights norms, institutions, and procedures, and the projection of preferred future trends in these realms. The thirteen essays that make it up, however, are as diverse as the origins and identities of their authors, representing eight different nationalities. And this is as it should be. The future of human rights is not writ in any one culture or outlook, and certainly it will depend on many different voices from many different lands and peoples.

At the same time, the essays comprising this volume possess important features in common. Whatever the origins and identities of their authors, they are the product of a community of scholars and activists for whom the Universal Declaration of Human Rights charted a valued course, one that is as relevant for the next fifty years as it has been for the last fifty. Accordingly, this book underscores the common commitment of its diverse authorship to the human global quest of a legal, moral, and political culture that is based on universal respect for internationally-recognized human rights.

In so doing, however, it may be accused of unduly emphasizing experience and scholarship in one discipline—international law—with all the advantages and disadvantages that the predominance of one discipline represents. Being international lawyers ourselves, this may be seen as only natural, and we plead guilty; but it is not surprising given that the Universal Declaration is itself the work primarily of international lawyers. Furthermore, several of the essays go beyond the confines of the legal sciences and consider international human rights from the perspective of political and social thought generally.

We editors acknowledge also another arguable deficiency: few of the references are from languages and publications that prevail outside the English-speaking world. Yet, neither we nor any of our co-authors underestimate the value of thinking and writing in other languages, especially when it comes to the future of international human rights, which of course is the exclusive domain of no country or culture. To the contrary, it is our hope that the authors' understanding of the issues through the prism of their own cultures and languages as well as through the prism of other cultures and languages with which they are familiar will at least partially compensate for this weakness.

In any event, by this collection we seek to make the future of international human rights a subject of active discourse among and across a wide range of people, including, of course, students and teachers of international law, international relations, and political science at both the undergraduate and graduate levels. We believe it will be helpful, too, to governmental officials, international civil servants, nongovernmental organizations, and, not least, the general reader with an interest in world affairs, both to fix the state of international human rights at the turn of the century and to anticipate the normative, institutional, and procedural challenges —legal, moral, and political—that confront states and peoples' movements in the coming decades. It is, we believe, a volume fit not only for the classroom but for readers generally.

We of course are deeply indebted to the wonderful team of authors who contributed so richly to this endeavor. That they would give so generously of their vast knowledge and experience is humbling beyond what words can express. Likewise are we indebted to Mrs. Robinson for her most gracious Foreword. Her role at the forefront of the U.N.'s human rights diplomacy and action will be critical to the realization of the prescriptions advocated by the essays in this volume.

In addition, we are indebted to a number of people for clearly invaluable assistance: to our research assistants Brian D. Grogan, Nicholas G. Hansen, and Andrea S. Pappan at Columbia University and Bassel El-Kasaby, Du Guangming, and Eugene D. Krass at The University of Iowa, not least for their tolerance of our professional eccentricities; to the editors of *Transnational Law & Contemporary Problems (TLCP)* who generously authorized our use of all or part of the Bassiouni, Baxi, Dugard, and Orford essays from *TLCP's* Fall 1998 issue; likewise to the editors of the *Australian Journal of International Affairs* and the *Fordham Law Review* for large segments of, respectively, the Falk and Nussbaum essays; and to Professor Weston's secretary, Grace E. Newby, for her customary adroit skills and unfailing good humor.

Finally, we wish to record our deep appreciation for the commitment, competence, and courtesy of Heike Fenton, President of Transnational Publishers, Inc., and her ever so gracious staff, especially Maria Angelini, our editor.

Burns H. Weston
Iowa City, Iowa

Stephen P. Marks
New York, New York

February 15, 1999

Foreword
Human Rights in Transformation:
From the Last Fifty Years to the Next Fifty

Mary Robinson

A half century after the adoption of the Universal Declaration of Human Rights (UDHR),[1] we stand at a crossroads that affords a contrasting panorama, a view at once beautiful and horrifying which forces anyone concerned about human rights to experience intensely mixed feelings.

On the one hand, the last fifty years of human rights have taken us far beyond where we were in the previous fifty. Prior to the Second World War, except for a few sundry minority rights guarantees in international peace agreements, concluded in the aftermath of World War I, human rights were considered to be matters entirely of domestic legal concern, and in that sense there were no *international* human rights. Today, human rights issues figure prominently in the political rhetoric of the day; the basic rights and freedoms of individuals and groups cannot be ignored no matter where around the world they may be endangered.

In the last fifty years, the level of consciousness as to the inherent dignity of the human being and the imperative upon everyone to respect it, within the larger framework of democratic governance and the rule of law, have risen remarkably. The self-awareness of individuals of their rights and freedoms and the spread of a culture of tolerance for others, continue to manifest themselves in the growth of nongovernmental organizations devoted to human rights, the elaboration of national structures and institutions to promote and protect human rights, and the rise of impressive human rights systems within the United Nations and regional intergovernmental organizations. Indeed, in an increasingly interdependent world, violent conflict, whether at an interpersonal, interethnic, intercultural, or international level, is more and more recognized to entail consequential damage. Thus, the *internationalization* of human rights standards and the *institutionalization* of mechanisms at all levels to implement them count as major advances since the end of the Second World War. And human rights as a symbol for the future betterment of all should not be underestimated.

All this can appear as little more, however, than abstract concepts unless and until these standards are implemented effectively. Without concrete and effective implementation, the horrors of genocide, war crimes, crimes against humanity, and

---

[1]   *See infra* Appendix I.

other serious violations of human rights shall continue as terrible stains on the universal moral fabric of humankind.

Peering into the future of human rights law is akin to sizing up the promise and failings of the human soul. To understand the past and present of human rights can be a way of understanding what collectively we may become in the future, a profoundly important task to which this book is dedicated.

I commend the editors and contributors of this volume for the excellent work they have done in identifying the problems and promise of human rights for the next fifty years.

Prologue

The Dead Have Nothing to Lose by Telling the Truth*

*On the Fiftieth Anniversary of the Adoption of the
Universal Declaration of Human Rights*

He sees the leaves fly free.
She sees the wild horse and the sparrow.
Free to labor, to consort with their kind, to choose or be chosen.
He sees them fed and feeding, mindful of the season.
She hears the continents shifting, he smells the air of change.
He tastes the wind-borne soot of rebirth.
She feels the human cry in her bones.

What can they do to gain our attention?
Shall he dance, shall he spin in the air, shall he vote with his feet, with his voice, with the
    shells of his burning ears?
Shall she tell the world to hear the world's crying?
Shall she number the bodies, the prisons, the pyres, shall he mark the graves,
    display the bloody shackles?
How many pairs of disembodied heads will it take?
How many detached hands and feet?
How many hollow cheeks, empty stomachs, vacant eyes?
How many skulls without memory?
He has been there, she has seen it, they have lived and died a long time.
He has something to say about who did what.
She has something to say about the living.
Let history honor the murmurs of conscience that are heard above ground.
Let praise flow to those who unclenched a fist.
Who granted men and women the freedom of the sparrow.
Who taught us to think twice.
Who showed us that famine is not a fast.
That exile is the last step.
That the rights of the few must be written down by the many.

She sees the leaves fly free.
He sees the wild horse and the sparrow.
Free to work, to consort with their kind, to choose or be chosen.
She sees them fed and feeding, mindful of the season.
He hears the continents shifting, she smells the air of change.
She tastes the wind-borne soot of rebirth.
He feels the human cry in his bones.

— Marvin Bell

• Copyright © 1998 by Marvin Bell. Marvin Bell is the Flannery O'Conner Professor of Letters at
The University of Iowa's Writers' Workshop. He is the author of fifteen books of poetry and essays,
the latest of which are *Ardor (The Book of the Dead Man,* Vol. 2), *Poetry for a Midsummer's Night*
(with paintings by Mary Powell), and *Selected Poems* to appear in Ireland. The present poem was
commissioned by *Global Focus: Human Rights '98,* a campus-wide initiative of the The University of
Iowa's International and Comparative Law Program and the University's Office of International
Programs commemorating the 50th anniversary of the Universal Declaration of Human Rights.

A Half Century of Human Rights: Geopolitics and Values*

Richard A. Falk

I. Fifty Years of Background: A Tentative Balance Sheet

Although human rights are affirmed in the United Nations Charter in very general language, their operative reality was not specified therein and their overall role in international political life was deemed marginal in the aftermath of World War II.[1] This marginality existed in 1945 in the face of the vivid disclosures of the Nazi era as well as in a vague aura of guilt that hovered over Western liberal democracies, associated with their prolonged forbearance in relation to Nazi Germany so long as Hitler's atrocious crimes were directed at his own citizenry. Despite this mood, the foundation of world order continued to rest very much on the territorial logic of territorial states, in conjunction with the supportive doctrine of sovereignty and the ideology of nationalism.[2] A major

---

* An earlier version of this essay appeared under the title *A Half Century of Human Rights* in 52 AUSTL. J. INT'L AFF. 255 (1998). Reprint permission granted.

1 *See* DAVID H. OTT, PUBLIC INTERNATIONAL LAW IN THE CONTEMPORARY WORLD 143 (1987); Burns H. Weston, *Human Rights*, 20 ENCYCLOPAEDIA BRITANNICA 714 (15th ed. 1998 prtg.), *updated and revised in* ENCYCLOPAEDIA BRITANNICA ONLINE (visited Dec. 1, 1998) <http://www.eb.com:180/cgi-bin/g?DocF=macro/5002/93.html>. Prior to World War II, practices associated with protecting aliens and their property could be considered in some respects as antecedents to the emergence of the international protection of human rights. These practices, known as "the diplomatic protection of aliens abroad" and "capitulations" were explicitly associated with the colonial era, providing interventionary support for individuals whose rights were endangered by the "independent" countries in Latin America or by exempting Europeans from territorial applications of criminal law in Asia. Status of Forces Agreements that partially exempt U.S. military personnel from territorial application of criminal law have been criticized for these reasons. The main point here is that international law made some effort to uphold the economic, political, and social rights of individuals, and even if Eurocentric in its implementation, initiated a rights discourse in international relations. Additionally, as such individuals were generally supported by their governments, enforcement capabilities existed, although their application was not a right of the individual, but dependent on a policy assessment by the state.

2 Of course, nationalism and statism are not identical, although the state has done its best to co-opt nationalist identities both by the embrace of secularism and through control over the status of juridical nationality. It is obvious that tensions persist between dominant and subordinate nationalisms caught within the boundaries of a given state. These tensions have strong human rights implications that will be discussed later.

1

implication of this logic was that the internal arrangements and policies of states were never properly subject to external accountability.[3] The U.N. Charter confirmed this statist feature of world order in Article 2(7) by reassuring its members that it lacked the authority to intervene in matters that were "essentially within the domestic jurisdiction" of states, a prohibition that was subject only to qualification relating to the overriding responsibility of the U.N. acting under Chapter VII of the Charter to maintain international peace and security.

Even the original articulation of international human rights in the form of the Universal Declaration of Human Rights (UDHR)[4] fifty years ago was not *initially* perceived to be a significant development. The norms affirmed in the Declaration contributed a comprehensive compilation of various legal and moral ideas about state/society/individual relationships. But this enumeration of standards was at most conceived as an admonishment to governments and, more relevantly, as a kind of heterogeneous wish list cobbled together by representatives of liberal individualism and collectivist socialism. In effect, at birth, the UDHR amounted to a rather innocuous and syncretist statement of consensus about desirable societal goals and future aspirations for humanity as a whole, but formulated as if self-regarding states in a world of gross material disparities did not exist. Also, it should be appreciated that by using the language of "declaration" and by avoiding all pretensions of implementation, a clear signal was given that the contents were not to be treated as necessarily authoritative and binding.[5]

Perhaps more damaging was the patent hypocrisy manifest with respect to the issuance of the UDHR. Many of the endorsing governments were at the time imposing control over their societies in a manner that systematically ignored or repudiated the standards being affirmed by the Declaration. And it was not only

---

[3]   The internal accountability of a government for abuses of the rights of its citizens goes back at least as far as the American and French Revolutions in the late Eighteenth Century. The French Revolution's rhetoric of "the rights of man," leaving aside its gendered formulation, most directly anticipates the thinking that underlies "human rights" as the foundation of external accountability. If even a conservative thinker such as Hobbes acknowledged a right of revolution in reaction to tyrannical government, the rationale for humanitarian intervention in response to genocidal practices and widespread crimes against humanity becomes more readily understandable as a limitation upon territorial sovereignty.

[4]   See *infra* Appendix I [hereinafter UDHR].

[5]   Over time, this legal status has changed as a result of the widespread acceptance of the norms contained in the UDHR as authoritative. The incorporation of the Declaration in the constitutions of many newly independent developing countries, its frequent citation, and its treatment by scholars as expressive of *jus cogens* endowed it with an obligatory character in international law with the passage of time. Such an evolution occurred without any very careful scrutiny of its specific standards and of the degree to which they were accepted by states as obligatory. A second step in this evolution was the reformulation of human rights standards in a treaty form, and their broad separation reflecting East/West ideological differences.

the Soviet Union and the countries under its sway that seemed resolutely opposed to upholding the main thrust of the UDHR as it pertained to the rights of individuals in relation to the state. The participation of the colonial powers of Europe was also beset by contradiction, given their role at the time in holding most of the peoples of Asia and Africa under their dominion by means of oppressive rule. Furthermore, the military dictatorships that then dotted the political landscapes in Latin America never could have intended to take seriously a series of human rights standards, which, if even loosely applied, would undermine their authoritarian style of rule.

So from the outset of these moves fifty years ago to make the observance of human rights a matter of international law, there were strong grounds for skepticism as to whether to regard the development as nominal rather than substantive. A note of skepticism could not be avoided given the patterns of governance that existed around the world. Only the most naive legalist would avoid the implication of an obvious rhetorical question—why did oppressive governments agree to such an elaborate framework for human rights unless their leaders were convinced that the UDHR was nothing more than a paper tiger?

In fact, the resistance to this process of internationalization of human rights is even more deeply rooted and pervasive than the considerations so far mentioned. A country like the United States, with its strong domestic constitutional and ideological commitment to human rights, has several awkward skeletons in its closet, including slavery (and racial discrimination) and ethnocidal policies pursued against Native American peoples. As well, the U.S. Government has been notably laggard with respect to formal adherence to the very international legal framework that it invokes against others. It has generally viewed human rights standards as important for the South, but superfluous for the countries of the North (at least, in the post-Cold War era), and certainly unnecessary with respect to the internal political life of the United States. The confusingly one-sided message that has been sent by the most powerful state in the world is that human rights are conceived as almost exclusively an instrument of *foreign* policy (that is, a series of obligations for others) although their concerns purport to be mainly domestic (that is, the relations of state and society).

Official spokespersons for China took evident satisfaction in pointing out several years ago that it was strange for Washington to present itself as the world champion of international human rights, considering that the record showed that China had ratified seventeen major human rights treaties while the U.S. had managed to ratify only fifteen. There are, in other words, strong sources of sovereignty-oriented resistance to the internationalization of human rights even on the part of major liberal democracies, based on the idea that a sovereign people should never confer any legal authority on an international body external to the state.[6] This sub-

---

[6]   Such concerns have united the U.S. Government and that of China in their resistance to the establishment of a truly independent International Criminal Court; major geopolitical

ordination of human rights to the abstraction of sovereignty has been systematically challenged only within the comfortable confines of the European Union. In this setting, the commonality of outlook among the members and a long-standing alliance underpinning has produced a political community that upholds human rights in a form that anticipates their implementation by recourse to the European Court of Human Rights. Such a breakthrough in the internationalization of the protection of human rights is conceptually irreconcilable with the Westphalian logic of world order.

European exceptionalism aside, for the rest of the world, regardless of its commitment to constitutional democracy as the foundation of domestic public order, the internationalization of human rights remains minimal, and its prospect is still to varying degrees problematic.[7] For one thing, it is an incomplete process even in states that claim the identity of being a constitutional democracy and generally are governed according to such an outlook; there are powerful cultural practices that are difficult to overcome by reliance on law enforcement, especially relating to the treatment of women and children, and to social differentiations among classes, castes, and religions. For another, supplementing the political and juridical aspects of sovereignty and the prohibition on intervention that get in the way, there are a variety of other types of resistance that reflect the characteristics of state/society relation that pertain to the particular country. While adherence to the framework of international human rights is a widely shared sentiment around the world that definitely informs the conduct of diplomacy and the language of statecraft, departures and resistances are evident in all parts of the world. Their special features vary from state to state, reflecting differences in history, culture, stage of development, domestic public order, and many other factors as well.

Additionally, it is important to take account of some influential general patterns of criticism that are directed at the claim that the norms of international human rights law deserve unconditional respect. For example, several anti-hegemonic discourses have been challenging the authoritativeness of human rights claims from a variety of perspectives. These critical discourses are particularly persuasive in the post-colonial circumstances of many countries in the countries of the South. Their general orientation is one of calling to mind the history of prior Western colonial abuse and exploitation, including intrusions on territorial space justified by international law doctrines of protection of nationals abroad and capitulatory regimes. This line of analysis contends that, despite the end of colonialism, this structure of dominance has been essentially maintained, assuming more indirect and disguised forms. These discourses argue accordingly that the promotion of human rights needs

---

actors, regardless of their seeming commitment to law and humane governance, are very worried about diluting traditional notions of sovereignty in relation to the external accountability of their own citizens.

7   *See* RETHINKING HUMAN RIGHTS: CHALLENGES FOR THEORY AND ACTION (Smitu Kothari & Harsh Sethi eds., 1989) [hereinafter Kothari & Sethi].

to be understood in its primary role as an instrument of choice to validate renewed claims and innovative modalities of intervention by the North in the South, although equally damaging and no less objectionable. In effect, current patterns of intervention are allegedly being shaped by the realities of post-colonialism, including the techniques, priorities, and dominant ideas associated with the theory and practice of economic globalization. Further, it is argued along a quite independent line of reasoning, that adherence to international human rights standards is not entirely warranted from either a substantive or procedural viewpoint. If due account is taken of the facts surrounding the Western origins and biases of international human rights standards, then their universal applicability is drawn into question.[8]

Perhaps the most serious of all constraints bearing on the application of international human rights norms is in most respects unappreciated, or at least seldom articulated. It arises directly from the realist orientation of political élites that have continued to control the shaping of foreign policy on behalf of most states, and especially on behalf of those states that play the most active geopolitical roles. The realist frame of reference entertains extremely serious, *principled* doubts about the relevance of law and morality to the proper operation of the state system. Realism is not easily reconciled with the human rights tradition unless such concerns are *pragmatically* invoked as an instrument of foreign policy, and even then only in a selective and opportunistic manner.

Alleging human rights violations has become a useful means for realists to indict foreign adversaries in a manner that generates media attention; exposing human rights violations often helps to prepare the ground for a later imposition of sanctions and geopolitical recourse to other forms of hostile action. The realist outlook is reasonably forthright about subordinating any international human rights commitment to its strategic priorities, including patterns of alignment and conflict, and in many circles, this deference to the interests of the state often has given human rights a bad name inasmuch as their invocation and evasion by prominent governments seems opportunistic, lacking in substance and values-driven convictions. In this manner, the human rights rhetoric used by political leaders and diplomats causes an impression similar to that created when a film substitutes dubbed voices in another language. A foreign language is superimposed on the sound track, but the lips of the actors on the screen are "out of sync," moving with the rhythms of the spoken language; reverting to our concerns, the superimposed language is that of human rights, but the lips of political authority still are moving according to the discordant logic of geopolitics. It is this core interaction between different approaches to the action and identity of the state that causes so much of the confusion and uncertainty about the significance of human rights and its future

---

[8]   *See, e.g.,* Chandra Muzaffar, Human Rights and the New World Order (1993); Richard Falk, *False Universalism and the Geopolitics of Exclusion: The Case of Islam,* 18 Third World Q. 7 (1997). *See also* Burns H. Weston, *The Universality of Human Rights in a Multicultured World: Toward Respectful Decision-Making, infra* in this volume at p. 65.

prospects. To the extent that the mission of the state is to make the world more receptive to neoliberal ideas, then the promotion of human rights in the sense of constitutionalism becomes a new type of "strategic interest." However, if upholding human rights interferes with important market access and investment opportunities, then pressures mount to overlook the human rights abuses of trading partners. In the first context the state is acting on behalf of the overall neoliberal program, while in the second it is furthering the more mercantilist goals of its citizens. This is an unfortunate state of affairs as it encourages the formation of misleading polar attitudes as to the significance of human rights: either the exaggerated expectations of human rights activists or the cynical dismissal of power-wielders.

In many respects, both of the opposing faces of realist manipulation of human rights have been exemplified by the approach taken by the Clinton Administration in its relationship with China.[9] So long as the issue of respect for human rights was one of domestic ideological posturing within the United States, it seemed beneficial to highlight China's responsibility for the bloody crackdown of the democracy movement in Tiananmen Square in June 1989 and, as well, as China's overall miserable human rights record. But the attention of American political leaders began in 1997 to shift to China's successful recovery from the Asian crisis and as an economic superpower, as well as its status as a major trading partner. At that point it became desirable to downplay China's human rights abuses and to focus instead on the benefits arising from what is now being called "cordial engagement," to distinguish it from a colder diplomatic approach that had been known generally as "constructive engagement."

This shift in emphasis gave rise to extensive and often intemperate commentary relative to President Clinton's visit to China in June 1998. On the one side were those who felt bitterly disappointed, a viewpoint strongly expressed by the former Chinese political prisoner, Wei Jingsheng:

> America has become the leader of a full Western retreat from the human rights cause in China. Clinton's decision to go to Beijing at this time sends a very clear signal that he is more concerned with supporting the autoc-

---

9   The U.S. approach to human rights has exhibited various forms of contradiction over the years. Human rights began to assume a high-profile role in American foreign policy during the early years of the Carter presidency, 1976–78, partly as an expression of liberal conviction, but also because, at the time, it served to restore national self-esteem in the aftermath of the Vietnam War. By so highlighting human rights, whatever the initial motivations, encouragement was given to human rights activists throughout the world, given the US leadership role. As well, it strengthened permanently the role of human rights within the federal bureaucracy of the United States. This convergence of political circumstances and support for human rights is what has periodically pushed implementation beyond the limits of earlier expectations.

racy than with the democratic movement in China. The timing of the West's abandonment of China's democratic movement could not be worse.[10]

The realist counter-attack was equally vigorous, and as uncompromising. Charles Freeman, Jr., First Assistant Secretary of State of Defense for International Security Affairs, insisted that it was time to approach China from a strategic viewpoint rather than persist with the feel-good human rights agenda: "[T]he administration accepted that it was going to have to deal seriously with China, that China was more than a theme park for the human rights advocates and the Dalai Lama's followers."[11] The unfortunate impression created by this remark strongly suggested that the earlier insistence on human rights was an essentially frivolous way for the United States to approach a state of such size and importance as China. The moment had now arrived when the U.S. needed to abandon a foreign policy commitment in support of human rights so as to pursue its *real* interests, which meant a mature approach that was based on economic opportunity and the calculus of power relations in Asia.

Because realist priorities impinge, human rights activists often are disappointed by their recurrent inability to gain the commanding heights of policymaking, especially when strong strategic interests appear to point in an opposite direction. Those making the policy choices are generally trying hard to diminish the impact of what they believe to be sentimental and ideological concerns that should not in most circumstances be given too much weight if the practice of international relations is going to proceed in a rational manner. Confusion arises because realists themselves "use" human rights from time-to-time to accentuate positions of hostility or to appease domestic pressure groups in relation to a particular country, raising expectations about its influence, and then abandon human rights concerns just as easily when strategic winds change direction. In these respects, the impact of the realist outlook in geopolitics produces results that often are confusing and uncertain. Realism has given human rights an important push from time to time, as occurred in the latter phases of the Cold War, but realists are ever ready to shove human rights aside if the domestic mood changes or strategic interests point in a different direction, contending that what is needed is a rational assessment of interests relating to wealth and power. In some respects, what is required for an understanding of both the achievement and limits of international human rights is a "Hindu sensibility"— that is, forms of consciousness that are much more comfortable in the presence of contradiction than is the case for the Western mind that has been caught up in a dualistic worldview since the time of ancient Greece that insists that something is "this" *or* "that." The Hindu perspective is attractive because it is so much more comfortable in saying that "this" *and* "that" are both true.

---

[10]   Wei Jingsheng, *The "Brutal Cynicism" of the West's Defection*, INT'L HERALD TRIB., June 20–21, 1998.

[11]   Barton Gellman, *New U.S. China Ties Are the Fruit of '96 Shift in Policy*, INT'L HERALD TRIB., June 23, 1998.

It should be appreciated that my discussion so far has proceeded within the conventional framework of a statist world order, with the impetus for norms and their implementation coming from governmental and intergovernmental action. As is now widely appreciated, such a focus on state action tells far from the whole story of the worldwide emergence of human rights on the global agenda. This emergence owes much to the rise of transnational human rights activism, which deserves major credit for avoiding a stillborn Universal Declaration of Human Rights. It also is relevant to note the success over time in making human rights a major dimension of activity within the setting of the United Nations.[12] The U.N. system has become much more firmly committed to the promotion of human rights than was the case in 1948 when the UDHR was first made public. This rising curve of attention to human rights was dramatized by the 1993 U.N. World Conference on Human Rights in Vienna, and followed shortly by the creation of the new U.N. post of High Commissioner for Human Rights, a position now held by the former president of Ireland, Mary Robinson.[13]

This background raises two main questions: Why did governments ever agree in the first instance to subvert their own territorial sovereignty?[14] And why, despite massive obstacles, has the field of international human rights evolved to the point where it is widely acknowledged to be of substantive importance and growing salience in the contexts of foreign policy and world order? In an introductory manner brief responses can be put forward. I think governments accepted the UDHR in the first instance precisely because they thought that it would amount to nothing at all. This calculation turned out to be wrong because of the unanticipated activism of voluntary citizens associations, the emergence of a global visual media, and the contending ideological claims of the superpowers in the various arenas of the Cold War. Human rights became more politically potent than could have been anticipated fifty years ago.

As we stand poised on the threshold of a new millennium, a further question for careful scrutiny concerns the future of human rights. Is it likely that the next fifty years are likely to witness the further inclusion of international human rights standards and implementing authority within both formal and informal structures of global governance? Current trends seem contradictory in many respects. This allows those who believe in the strengthening of international human rights to find encouraging signs in growing attention and institutionalization. Similarly, those who believe that self-interest and power are the persisting mainsprings of international

---

12   Regarding the United Nations and human rights, see Stephen P. Marks, *The United Nations and Human Rights: The Promise of Multilateral Diplomacy and Action, infra* in this volume at p. 291.

13   *See* Mary Robinson, *Human Rights in Transformation: From the Last Fifty Years to the Next Fifty, supra* in this volume at *xv*.

14   For a brief discussion of this question, see Stephen P. Marks & Burns H. Weston, *International Human Rights at Fifty: A Foreword*, 8 Transnat'l L. & Contemp. Probs. 113, 117–18 (1998).

relations find confirmation in the opportunistic evasions of human rights considerations by political leaders and market forces.

In the next section of this essay, the relation between upholding international human rights and geopolitical priorities is discussed with an eye toward a partial acceptance of their co-existence. A later section then evaluates several of the main human rights initiatives of the last fifty years. On these bases, the final section offers tentative thoughts on what to expect with regard to human rights, given the deepening process of economic globalization.

II. Geopolitics and International Human Rights: Unresolved and Unresolvable?

As suggested earlier, there exist two clusters of views about how best to interpret the last fifty years of international experience with respect to human rights. One cluster is normatively driven, perceiving the attention given to human rights as indicative of the growing importance of law and morality in the world. The second cluster is power driven, perceiving an essential continuity of geopolitics over time based on the retention by sovereign states of the capacity to wage war and mobilize resources, along with their consistent neglect of legal and moral considerations when these are seriously challenged by strategic interests.

The first view, as might be expected, is generally satisfied with the progress made to protect international human rights during the last fifty years. It finds support for its positive assessment in the large number of multilateral treaties devoted to human rights, the increased activity on behalf of human rights in various arenas of the United Nations and at regional levels, and the greater attention being given to questions of human rights in the media and on the part of policy-makers. Adherents of this rights-oriented view are, to be sure, frequently disappointed in specific instances, but such failures of performance are usually explained as lapses in leadership or as unfortunate concessions to domestic pressure groups. There is no doubt on the part of those who endorse the first view that human rights will continue to increase in influence over time; further, that it is desirable to subordinate other goals of foreign policy to this overriding effort to achieve as full an implementation of human rights standards on a worldwide basis as is feasible at any given time.

In contrast, the second view finds that geopolitical factors remain the decisive forces moving history. From this perspective, the greater visibility of human rights is heavily discounted as a new kind of window-dressing that has come to the fore in recent years because the winners of the Cold War have remained somewhat trapped within the confines of their own earlier anti-Communist propaganda; further, that the promotion of values at the expense of interests is a dangerous indulgence in international political life that often is likely to intensify conflict among states without really helping the victims of human rights abuses. A rational foreign policy is based on calculations of gains and losses, not on a comparison of rights and wrongs, and if progress is to be made in the way governments treat individuals and groups within their borders, it will be as a result of internal struggle and reform.

These polar ways of thinking about the relations between human rights norms and geopolitics involve a clash of preferences and worldviews that have been sharpened by the realization that recent decades are the background of a period of transition in the structure of world order.[15] It is possible that the promotion of human rights and the realist pursuit of interests will increasingly converge in the future. It also is possible that one or the other will displace its rival and become the uncontested view of how things do and should work in the relation of power to values.

But some sort of reconciliation also is possible. There are several political and ideological trends that are encouraging partial reconciliation between geopolitics and human rights. The widespread and severe denial of human rights in a country beset by strife and poverty has increasingly become an occasion causing refugees and transnational migrations that can be a major source of trouble for neighboring states. When the United States led the U.N. effort in 1995 to preserve the democratic process in Haiti and protect Haitians against the brutalities of the military junta, it was strongly motivated by its interest in curtailing the outflow of refugees who were at the time unwelcome entrants to American society, threatening to provoke an angry domestic political reaction. The U.S. Government had earlier been dealing with this problem, in pre-Clinton years, by intercepting the refugees at sea and putting them in detention centers; but this, too, provoked a damaging political backlash among African-Americans in and out of government. The Clinton presidency did not want to alienate this constituency, and so it was faced with finding a policy that *both* avoided an influx of refugees from Haiti and abandoned the policies of the Bush presidency that were seen as cruel to the escaping victims of Haitian oppression. Establishing civilian, moderate government in Haiti had the intended beneficial side effect of curtailing the outflow of Haitians, thereby overcoming Clinton's refugee dilemma (neither accept, detain, or return) by "imposing" democracy and human rights.[16] Whether the internal play of forces in Haiti will accept this solution is subject to considerable doubt, especially given signs of social and economic deterioration, and the renewed threat of challenges from the militarist right wing. In this respect, what may appear as a reconciliation of geopolitics and human rights may turn out to be temporary and quite limited. However, the pattern is broader.

Many internal struggles around the world have produced these massive outflows that can be ended and reversed only by political moderation and stability, which usually entails an overall improvement in the human rights situation. This

---

15   *See generally* RICHARD FALK, ON HUMANE GOVERNANCE: TOWARD A NEW GLOBAL POLITICS (1995).

16   *See* Richard Falk, *The Haitian Intervention: A Dangerous World Order Precedent for the United Nations*, 36 HARV. INT'L L.J. 341 (1995).

pattern also influenced the European and American decision to support NATO initiatives relative to ending the war in Bosnia and underpin the willingness to exert pressure on Belgrade to restore autonomy and human rights to Kosovo. Part of the geopolitical motivation is an anxiety about the potential of the conflict to spread in the Balkan region, even threatening to embroil NATO members, Greece and Turkey, on opposite sides. It is not relevant to appraise the plausibility of these concerns. The point is that there exists a positive link between insisting upon human rights for the Kosovars and the geopolitical interest in avoiding a wider European conflict. It should be noted that such a geopolitical link is not pervasive with respect to such separatist movements, as the responses to the situations in Tibet or Chechnya confirm. But it should also be appreciated that the protection of human rights now often provides a functional alternative to the sort of bloc stability that had been a feature of the Cold War era, and was achieved partly by ignoring the well-being of oppressed peoples and nations.

The problems of internal chaos and strife have grown far more common in the years since 1989, as the unraveling of Yugoslavia most revealingly illustrated. This unraveling, if it occurs outside the domain of strategic interests, as in sub-Saharan Africa, is not likely to mount strong pressure for humanitarian diplomacy. Such is "the lesson of Mogadishu," the learning experience that followed upon the abandonment of the U.S./U.N. effort at humanitarian peacemaking in Somalia during 1992–94. The unwillingness of the U.S./U.N. to take steps to avoid humanitarian disasters in Rwanda, Burundi, and Zaire in the mid-1990s, in the absence of perceived geopolitical incentives, is also a revealing part of the emerging intertwined relationship of human rights and geopolitics.

In sum, the polarization of human rights and geopolitics evident in the two standard positions is increasingly misleading. International developments have created important sectors of mutuality in which geopolitical incentives exist for the implementation of human rights standards by international action. At the same time, such a convergence should not be exaggerated or generalized. Everything depends on context and the perceived interests of the major political actors. Captive "nations" have been struggling in many settings where the main geopolitical interests seem to be associated with maintaining the unity of existing states, leading the organized world community to turn a blind eye to their resolution by force to the extent necessary. Perhaps the most extreme example is the U.S./U.N. relationship to the internal situation in Iraq since the Gulf War where, despite unprecedented intrusions on Iraqi sovereignty to ensure compliance with duties to abolish weaponry of mass destruction, there has been no willingness to contest Saddam Hussein's oppressive rule for fear of fragmenting Iraq. This failure to include the human rights of the Iraqi people in the goals of the U.S./U.N. in Iraq since the cease-fire in 1991 is further aggravated by the maintenance of sanctions over a period of more than seven years despite overwhelming evidence of their devastating impact upon the well-being of the Iraqi civilian society, especially the very young. In this respect, the U.N. seems complicit in a policy that has had the effect on a massive scale of depriving innocent Iraqis of their most basic right to life, and in a setting where there is no evidence that the Baghdad government or its leaders have been weakened or significantly curtailed in their capacity to rule; indeed, by so alienating the people of Iraq, it has been argued that the sanctions have strengthened the government's grip on the society.

The final aspect of the situation is disclosed by a comparison of the response to Bosnia and Kosovo with that in relation to human tragedies of great magnitude in Africa. It is only when geopolitical interests are present that some substantial international effort to protect the human rights of a deeply threatened citizenry is likely to be forthcoming.[17] The absence of geopolitical incentives is likely to result in reducing international responses to a nominal form. Such a complex interplay of human rights and geopolitics suggests the inappropriateness of the two prevailing views identified at the outset of this section, and the need for a third view that is more nuanced. This third view formulates the relationship on the basis of a partial and limited reconciliation of human rights and geopolitics.

III. Human Rights and Neo-Liberalism: Closing the Ideological Gap

A closely related development, in some respects supportive of human rights, has been occurring on an ideological front in recent years, contrasting with the approaches adopted during the Cold War. The earlier view in conservative political circles had been that non-Communist forms of authoritarian rule in the South was either the lesser of evils or a necessary, if temporary, expedient in relation to the rivalry with the Soviet Union. The West, which operationally meant the United States in most instances, not only supported repressive governments on the basis of such reasoning, but actually relied upon interventionary diplomacy (often in the form of covert operations to disguise the sponsorship of an anti-democratic "solution") to disrupt or overthrow governments that appeared to be democratic, especially if compared to what preceded or what followed. Among the more celebrated instances of anti-democratic intervention are the restoration to power of the Shah in Iran (1953), the overthrow of the Arbenz government in Guatemala (1954), and the efforts to destabilize the Allende government in Chile (1970–73). Although it is conceptually possible for a benign autocrat to protect human rights more successfully than an incompetent or paralyzed democrat, it is usually the case that the displacement of democratic governance is accompanied by a dramatic deterioration in human rights. Such was certainly the case in the instances given above.

---

[17]   Even then, however, the difficulties of humanitarian intervention should not be underestimated, especially if the geopolitical incentives are not very pronounced, as was the case in Bosnia. Shallow humanitarian intervention may have the main effect of intensifying the internal conflict and adding to the human suffering. *See generally* Richard Falk, *The Complexities of Humanitarian Intervention*, 17 MICH. J. INT'L L. 491 (1996).

The new political ideology that has taken hold in the West since 1989 insists that only democratic forms of governance are fully legitimate, with "democracy" being presented as including a fair measure of human rights.[18] This advocacy of democracy is tied very closely to the endorsement of neoliberal ideas about state/society relations, especially the reliance on the market to guide economic priorities, the minimization of the social role of government, and the encouragement of maximum privatization of economic life. In its more progressive interpretations, there is evident the conviction that marketization is not enough. Indeed, this was the main theme of Bill Clinton's 1998 message to the Chinese people and their leaders, but also meant to be heard back home by the U.S. Congress and the media that had been critical of his visit on human rights grounds. Clinton's formulations suggested to China that it would not achieve "the prosperity and social stability that it is seeking until it embraces greater individual freedoms."[19]

This linkage between the market and human rights started to influence world order thinking during the period that Margaret Thatcher and Ronald Reagan were the political leaders of their respective countries. Its formulation as "market-oriented constitutionalism" began to be evident in the final documents of the annual economic summits of the Group of Seven, an outlook that achieved a certain canonical form in the Charter of Paris for a New Europe, adopted at an important meeting of the Conference (now Organization) on Security and Co-operation in Europe at Paris on November 21, 1991.[20] This formulation signaled the ideological break between the mentality of the Cold War and that of the dawning era of globalization.

Although an affirmation of human rights is integral to these neoliberal perspectives, it is partial in relation to the corpus of rights protected under international law. Human rights are understood to encompass exclusively the civil and political rights of the individual, with economic, social, and cultural rights being put aside. Indeed, the neoliberal repudiation of a socially activist government and public sector approaches to human well-being is an implicit rejection of many of the standards of human rights that are present in the UDHR and the two covenants which, together with the UDHR, comprise the "International Bill of Human Rights."[21] It

---

[18] *See generally* Thomas M. Franck, *The Emerging Right to Democratic Governance*, 86 AM. J. INT'L L. 46 (1992).

[19] J. F. Harris, *Clinton's Message to China: Individual Freedom Is Vital*, INT'L HERALD TRIB., June 29, 1998, at 1, col. 4.

[20] *See* Charter of Paris for a New Europe and Supplementary Document to Give Effect to Certain Provisions Contained in the Charter of Paris for a New Europe, *reprinted in* 30 I.L.M. 190 (1991) *and* 1 INTERNATIONAL LAW AND WORLD ORDER: BASIC DOCUMENTS I.D.13 (Burns H. Weston ed., 5 vols., 1994–).

[21] *See* International Covenant on Economic, Social and Cultural Rights, *infra* Appendix II [hereinafter ICESCR]; International Covenant on Civil and Political Rights, *infra* Appendix III [hereinafter ICCPR].

is relevant to note that many of the provisions of the UDHR that are regarded as of utmost importance in countries of the South are those that are treated as nonexistent by the North. In a more journalistic vein, William Pfaff has indicted "unregulated capitalism" of the sort that is occurring under neoliberal banners of globalization for its cruel and dangerous disregard of human well-being; he dismisses the invocation of democracy and human rights by neoliberal champions of globalization as a "complacent and unhistorical argument" that refuses to take account "of the moral nihilism of an unregulated capitalism" that is making livelihood and employment a "byproduct of the casino."[22]

It is too early to assess the full impact of economic globalization of a neoliberal character upon the pursuit of economic and social rights, and even in relation to civil and political rights. Until the Asian economic crisis of 1997, it seemed that globalization was bringing economic relief to tens of millions of previously impoverished peoples, and providing a prospect for sustained economic improvement with a gradual spillover effect enhancing political and civil rights as well.[23] Geopolitically, as well, globalization seemed to be having a leveling up effect, giving a global voice to those countries that were not only independent, but economically dynamic.

It is now more difficult to be so confident about the contributions of economic globalization. What the crisis managers within and without the International Monetary Fund have done in reaction to the Asian financial crisis is exactly what one would expect, namely, to prescribe neoliberal medicines in varying dosages, which means in the short-run a hardening of the life circumstances of the poorer sectors of society and a placement of the burden of adjustment costs during the process of recovery on those least able to bear it. It was reported in July 1998 that half of the Indonesian population has fallen back into a condition of destitution, and that some of the villages are eating insects to survive.[24] The IMF approach is also spreading the neoliberal model of governance as a substitute for the now discredited Asian model of capitalist development. The Asian model, which itself had many diversities, included a larger role for the state in actively promoting employment, welfare, and anti-poverty efforts. Unfortunately, it also created the conditions for the flourishing of crony capitalism. To the extent that the text of the UDHR authoritatively identifies the scope of human rights, neoliberal ideology amounts to a drastic foreshortening with no legal or moral mandate. Human rights are narrowed to the point that only civil and political rights are affirmed, or in the more

---

22   William Pfaff, *Gambling with Nihilo-Capitalism*, INT'L HERALD TRIB., May 18, 1998, at 1.

23   I have explored this theme in Richard Falk, *An Inquiry into the Political Economy of World Order*, 1 NEW POL. ECON. 13 (Mar. 1996) and Richard Falk, *Resisting "Globalization-from-above" through "Globalization-from-below,"* 2 NEW POL. ECON. 17 (Mar. 1997).

24   M. W. Brauchli, *Indonesia's Downfall Casts a Long Shadow Over the World Bank*, WALL ST. J. EUR., July 14, 1998, at 1, col. 10.

general normative language of the day, "individual freedom" and "democracy" are asserted as beneficial, and indeed necessary, to the attainment of economic success via the market. By implication, moves to uphold social and economic rights by direct action are seen as generally dangerous to the maintenance of civil and political rights because of their tendency to consolidate power in the state and to undermine individualism.

In conclusion, the relationship between the realization of human rights and the ideological orientation of neoliberal globalization is ambiguous in conception and behavioral effects. To the extent that neoliberal perspectives are anti-authoritarian, they tend to encourage the implementation of human rights in state/society relations, especially through the argument that an economistic approach to development will be frustrated if such rights are not upheld. However, the neoliberal outlook ruptures a sense of human solidarity within a given political community by effectively rejecting any commitment of responsibility for those members who are economically and socially disadvantaged. And in times of difficulty this weakening of community bonds tends to impose the most difficult burdens of adjustment on those who are least able to bear them, including those with marginal jobs or unemployed. As such, it represents a *de facto* repeal of the broad scope of human rights as initially specified by the UDHR and carried forward in the International Covenant on Economic, Social and Cultural Rights,[25] and so far most of the better known human rights NGOs have not focused their attention on this weakening of the human rights commitment.

IV. A Note on the Universal Declaration and Civilizational Values

The evolution of human rights as a self-conscious tradition was principally associated with Western patterns of thought and practice, although formulated as if metaphysically grounded on principles of universal validity. There were many echoes and parallel ideas in scriptures and philosophical writings of other civilizations, but no coherent and consistent reliance on a rhetoric of rights. The appearance of the UDHR on the normative scene fifty years ago was at a triumphalist moment for the humanist claims of the West, having recently prevailed in the struggle against fascism and yet retaining a large measure of control over non-Western civilizations. As such, the UDHR was never effectively challenged at the time as being Western in origin and outlook, and therefore falling far short of its pretension of offering a *universal* foundation for human rights. This challenge came much later, preceded by non-Western preoccupations with carrying the various anticolonial struggles to completion and then engaging in the daunting tasks of state-building and economic development. To the extent that a challenge was asserted at all, it was largely indirect and implicit, premised on the idea that human rights (and democracy) were not a priority for newly independent societies confronting massive poverty and

---

25   ICESCR, *infra* Appendix II.

underdevelopment. It was often argued that order, more than freedom, was the precondition for sustained economic development, which in turn was necessary if massive poverty was to be reduced in the face of a rapidly expanding population.

To the extent there was seen to be a cleavage concerning human rights it was regarded as essentially intra-Western, pitting the liberalism of individualist rights against the Marxist stress on social or collective rights. The UDHR provides a framing of human rights that encompasses both traditions, allowing each side to stress its own ideological interpretation. This division was acknowledged to a greater extent during the second major stage of evolution when the human rights covenants divided human rights in two: political and civil on one side and economic, social, and cultural on the other.[26] The West, led by the United States, made it quite clear, especially from the time in the early 1980s when it went on the offensive in support of private capital and the market ethos, that it was committed to upholding the first covenant as providing the basis for legitimate governance at the level of the state; but nothing more. At the same time, its diplomats were increasingly outspoken in their insistence that the second covenant was virtually irrelevant to the presence or absence of a good society, and as having no universally obligatory content under international law. Thus, disguised beneath the original universal framing was the ideological debate that was carried on during the cold war years about the nature of human rights. The debate was always a bit fraudulent as the Soviet bloc suppressed their population economically as well as politically. In this fundamental sense, Soviet ideological postures were not reinforced by policies and practices. In any event, the debate over rights quickly faded into oblivion with the fall of the Berlin Wall in 1989 and the general discrediting of socialist thinking about state/society relations thereafter.

Another challenge to universality of a more genuine sort (that is, concerning practices and policies) emanated from the global network of indigenous peoples, who became internationally active already in the 1970s. Their profound grievances about the evolving international law of human rights assumed salience with the formation of the Working Group on Indigenous Populations as a project of the Sub-Commission on the Prevention of Discrimination and Protection of Minorities of the U.N. Commission on Human Rights. The sessions of the Working Group made it clear that for indigenous peoples, despite their many differences one from another, they were agreed that their world views and circumstances had been simply left out of consideration when the UDHR was drafted. The UDHR had proceeded from the alien assumptions of modern and modernizing societies and did not speak to the conditions and needs of peoples intent on preserving traditional ways of life in the face of modernity. As well, the ameliorative efforts of the International Labour Office to remedy this failure were unsatisfactory, despite 1989 ILO Convention No. 169[27]

---

26   *See supra* note 21.

27   International Labour Organisation Convention (No. 169) Concerning Indigenous and Tribal Peoples in Independent Countries, June 27, 1989, International Labour Conference Draft Report of the Committee on Convention No. 107, App. I, C.C. 1–7/D 303 (June 1989),

being a big step forward when compared to the embarrassedly paternalistic 1957 Convention No. 107.[28]

What has emerged from the more authentic undertaking by indigenous peoples acting for themselves is a document crafted with the input of representatives of indigenous peoples over a period of more than a decade. Called the 1994 Draft Declaration on the Rights of Indigenous Peoples[29] and built around the idea of indigenous peoples as distinct and separate from other peoples yet equal and fully entitled to claim a right of self-determination, this Declaration is locked in controversy within the United Nations system, and its future is in doubt. Whether such a document can survive intergovernmental scrutiny, especially with respect to the claimed right of self-determination, seems uncertain even after more than four years of consideration within the U.N. system. It also is far from clear that the network of indigenous peoples will go along with a sanitized version of what their lengthy deliberations produced, especially if the symbolic affirmation of the right of self-determination is removed or curtailed. What is not in doubt is the perception of the 1948 Universal Declaration of Human Rights as utterly failing to encompass the circumstances and world views of indigenous peoples, and as having never conceived of their participation in the norm-creating processes as essential to establish the claim of universality. In this regard, the challenge to universality comes from a vertical, nongeographical perspective as well as from a horizontal, spatial perspective. Indigenous peoples, often seeking to have the right to a separate existence based on their traditional patterns of organization and governance, do not necessarily share the foundational secularist, modernist, and statist assumptions of the human rights mainstream. At the very least, they insist that the traditionalist alternative be legitimized and, to the extent necessary, safeguarded. Such a concern is far from ritualistic, as indigenous peoples currently are being displaced and their lands plundered in many parts of the world, perhaps most flagrantly in Amazonia and South Asia. The importance attached by representatives of indigenous peoples to self-determination is bound up with their status as nations with claims of autonomy and with the history of their encounters with settlers who set out to destroy their way of life and often their lives as well.

The inter-civilizational critique of human rights that has gained the most notoriety has involved reactions against the West by parts of the world formerly colo-

---

reprinted in 28 I.L.M. 1382 (1989) *and* 3 INTERNATIONAL LAW AND WORLD ORDER: BASIC DOCUMENTS III.F.2 (Burns H. Weston ed., 5 vols., 1944–   ) [hereinafter 3 Weston].

[28]   International Labour Organisation Convention (No. 107) Concerning the Protection and Integration of Indigenous and Other Tribal and Semi-Tribal Populations in Independent Countries, June 26, 1959, 328 U.N.T.S. 247, *reprinted in* 3 Weston III.F.1, *supra* note 27.

[29]   Draft Declaration on the Rights of Indigenous Peoples, adopted by the U.N. Commission on Human Rights Sub-Commission on the Prevention of Discrimination and Protection of Minorities, Aug. 26, 1994, U.N. Doc. E/CN.4/1995/2, E/CN.4/Sub.2/1994/56 (Oct. 28, 1994), *reprinted in* 34 I.L.M. 541 (1989) *and* 3 Weston III.F.4, *supra* note 27.

nized by European countries. These reactions are associated both with the norms and with their implementation, especially by coercive or interventionary means. The critique advances both the case on behalf of cultural relativism (that the UDHR is distinctively Western and as such is inconsistent with the beliefs and values of non-Western civilization) and the argument about Western post-colonial geopolitics (that human rights are a new pretext for intervention and encroachment upon sovereign rights).[30] Critics of the critics argue that the claims of Islamic exceptionalism and Asian values are largely diversionary efforts by brutal and arbitrary governments to evade fundamental responsibilities to their own peoples, and represent very cynical efforts to excuse authoritarian abuses of various kinds that are condemned by the moral teachings of all civilizations.[31] There also is a tendency to suggest that civilizational objections to human rights standards can be reconciled with the claimed universalism of the UDHR if interventionary implementation is avoided and ample space is provided for societal interpretation. Such a trend has been understood in the West as a reluctant affirmation of the authenticity of the international human rights tradition, and as evidence of the power of the human rights idea.[32]

Widespread public attention to these issues arose in relation to the Islamic response to the publication of Salman Rushdie's *Satanic Verses*, especially the *fatwa* issued in 1989 by Ayatollah Khomeini imposing a death sentence on Rushdie, despite his residence and citizenship in the United Kingdom, and reinforcing this act by a large bounty that would be given to whoever managed to kill Rushdie. There are many issues bound up together here. The first involves the imposition of a death sentence without trial or defense upon an absent individual over whom there is no authority. The second involves the use of religion to provide the basis for condemning and restricting the distribution of a literary work, and justifying the punishment of its author. And the third involves differing views about protecting freedom of expression in the face of community sensitivities. These are complex matters, but the potential for international conflict arising from apparent differences based on civilizational outlook was vividly disclosed. Such a disclosure opens the way for dangerously inflammatory views of impending culture wars, of which the

---

[30]   *See generally* MUZAFFAR, *supra* note 8; Kothari & Sethi, *supra* note 7. *See also* Weston, *supra* note 8.

[31]   *See* Amartya K. Sen, *Human Rights and Asian Values* (Sixteenth Morgenthau Memorial Lecture on Ethics and Foreign Policy, Carnegie Council on Ethics and International Affairs, 1997).

[32]   Ann Mayer so presents the reaction of Sudan to U.N. censure of its human rights record and the participation of representatives of the Islamic government of Saudi Arabia at the 1993 U.N. World Conference on Human Rights along these lines. This is, in effect, an acknowledgment of the authority of the norms, but a contention that Islamic violations are either unjustified and slanderous, or the claim that, with appropriate interpretative freedom to take account of Islamic tradition, the appearance of a violation would quickly disappear. *See* ANN E. MAYER, ISLAM AND HUMAN RIGHTS: TRADITION AND POLITICS 182–83 (3d ed. 1999).

notorious projections of Samuel Huntington about an impending "clash of civilizations" were the most spectacular and widely discussed. On further reflection, it became evident that there were almost as many differences within Islam as between Islam and the West; as Edward Said has so persuasively written, all civilizations and cultures exhibit an extraordinary heterogeneity.[33]

In other words, there are certainly differences in belief and values that can be given a civilizational expression, but such differences are not consistent enough across civilizational boundaries to be by themselves the basis of a new geopolitics, especially given the strength of global market forces and their tendency to establish a global counter-civilization.

What may turn out to be the case is that the further elaboration and implementation of human rights could take on a regional character. In part, this follows upon the European example, but it also parallels the rise of regionalism in relation to economic and security relations. It is, as well, a reaction to the decline of the United Nations, although so far this overall decline has not affected the U.N.'s role in relation to human rights, which actually has increased in the 1990s. To the extent that regional initiatives in relation to human rights are advanced, a part of the rationale, as in Europe, will be on the basis of shared values and traditions. In this sense, the cultural critique of the UDHR might in the near future become less polemical and take on a more substantive and specific character. Of course, in such a setting, intra-regional differences are likely to gain greater attention, especially in Asia where the diversities are so evident.

There is a final point. The main energy associated with the assertion of "Asian values" accompanied "the Asian economic miracle." The successful achievement of sustained economic growth in an atmosphere of political stability apparently gave Asian leaders the confidence to defend against international criticism by recourse to civilizational arguments, including critiques of the West as arrogant and as itself suffering the adverse social consequences of decadence and permissiveness. The Asian crisis, which shows no signs of an early abatement, has seemingly diverted attention from the cultural dimensions of its relations with the West.

The Universal Declaration of Human Rights has definitely survived the civilizational critique mounted against the claim that the international human rights tradition deserves adherence in all parts of the world. At the same time, the Western origins and evolution of the tradition have exposed some important weaknesses. Undoubtedly, the claims of inadequacy associated with the efforts of indigenous peoples will persist. Controversy over implementation will undoubtedly continue to raise concerns about whether human rights are a vehicle for intervention or whether opposition to intervention is a pretext for shielding abusive behavior from international accountability. If the UDHR had been drafted in 1998 rather than in 1948, it likely would exhibit far greater sensitivity to cultural diversity and to the

---

[33] EDWARD W. SAID, CULTURE AND IMPERIALISM xx–xxvii (1993).

relations between politics and religion, but possibly far less empathy for the economically and socially disadvantaged. And so the UDHR enters the next century, as do the two covenants, having been somewhat bypassed by historical developments, yet still commanding such widespread respect by governments and civil society as to remain authoritative in relation to the substance of international human rights standards.

V. Achievements, Prospects, and Priorities

The Universal Declaration of Human Rights was celebrated in 1998 not only because of its own textual reality, but also because it initiated a process that has had an extraordinary cumulative impact on the role of human rights in international political life in the course of the last fifty years. This cumulative impact has exhibited ebbs and flows, and has reflected considerable selectivity in emphasis, as well as being subject to the foreign policy agendas of the major geopolitical actors. Nevertheless, the achievements have been impressive and can be briefly summarized.

1. *Changing the discourse of international relations.* To a considerable extent, invoking human rights standards has come to replace moralizing in statecraft. As such, it has been effective in establishing an objective, shared set of standards as the foundation for legitimate resistance by civil society to abuses of power by the state and for the display of international concern within the United Nations and elsewhere. The parameters of this human rights discourse are not at all firmly established as yet. Still, as compared to a half century ago, this internationalization of the manner by which a government exercises its authority within its territory has challenged the idea of sovereignty in a crucial respect. The outcomes of this challenge are not yet clear, and the results are quite uneven at this point. The internationalization of human rights is one aspect of globalization and nascent global governance that is still at an early stage of evolution. And yet, even at this point, this discourse on human rights has altered the language of diplomacy. In so doing, it also has narrowed the gaps between state and society, between state and world, by providing a common normative currency that is invoked by governments, international institutions, and civil society.

2. *The elaboration of normative architecture.* Starting with the UDHR, there has been a steady stream of law-making treaties that have elaborated human rights standards in many areas of international life and started to move the process from law-making to implementation. The most dramatic step in this direction was the transformation of the UDHR into treaty form by way of the two covenants in 1966.[34] Because these covenants included reporting requirements, the monitoring of compliance was a further step forward and formally brought within the scope of activity assigned to the U.N. Economic and Social Council. Subsequently, many additional human rights treaties were negotiated, signed, and so widely rat-

---

[34] *See supra* note 21.

ified as to stake reasonable claims for qualifying as customary international law. These include the 1951 Convention on the Status of Refugees,[35] the 1953 Convention on the Political Rights of Women,[36] the 1966 International Convention on the Elimination of all Forms of Racial Discrimination,[37] the 1979 Convention on the Elimination of All forms of Discrimination Against Women (CEDAW),[38] the 1984 Convention Against Torture and Other Cruel Inhuman or Degrading Treatment or Punishment,[39] and the 1989 Convention on the Rights of the Child.[40] In addition, there have been many declarations endorsed by the U.N. General Assembly that have had the effect of adding further dimension to the human rights discourse. Among the most important of these are the following: the 1960 Declaration on the Granting of Independence to Colonial Countries and Peoples,[41] the 1974 Universal Declaration on the Eradication of Hunger and Malnutrition,[42] the 1981 Declaration on the Elimination of All Forms of Intolerance Based on Religion or Belief,[43] the 1986 Declaration on the Right to Development,[44] the 1992 Declaration of the Rights of Persons Belonging to National or Ethnic, Religious and Linguistic Minorities,[45] and the 1993 Declaration on the Elimination

---

[35]   Concluded, July 28, 1951 (entered into force, Apr. 22, 1954), 189 U.N.T.S. 150, *reprinted in* 3 Weston III.G.4, *supra* note 27.

[36]   Concluded, Mar. 31, 1953 (entered into force, June 7, 1954), 193 U.N.T.S. 135, *reprinted in* 3 Weston III. F.1, *supra* note 27.

[37]   Concluded, Mar. 7, 1966 (entered into force, Jan. 4, 1969), 660 U.N.T.S. 195, *reprinted in* 5 I.L.M. 352 (1966) *and* 3 Weston III.I.1, *supra* note 27.

[38]   Concluded, Dec. 18, 1979 (entered into force, Sept. 3, 1981), 1249 U.N.T.S. 13, *reprinted in* 19 I.L.M. 33 (1980) *and* 3 Weston III.C.13, *supra* note 27.

[39]   Concluded, Dec. 10, 1984, (entered into force, June 26, 1987), G.A. Res. 39/46 (Annex), U.N. GAOR, 39th Sess., Supp. No. 51, at 197, U.N. Doc. A/RES/39/51 (1985), *reprinted in* 23 I.L.M. 1027 (1984) *and* 3 Weston III.K.2, *supra* note 27.

[40]   Concluded, Nov. 20, 1989 (entered into force, Sept. 2, 1990), G.A. Res. 44/25 (Annex), U.N. GAOR, 44th Sess., Supp. No. 49, at 166, U.N. Doc. A/RES/44/49 (1990), *reprinted in* 30 I.L.M. 1448 (1989) *and* 3 Weston III.D.3, *supra* note 27.

[41]   Adopted by the U.N. General Assembly, Dec. 14, 1960. G.A. Res. 1514, U.N. GAOR, 15th Sess., Supp. No. 16, at 667, U.N. Doc. A/4684 (1961), *reprinted in* 3 Weston III.Q.2, *supra* note 27.

[42]   Adopted by the U.N. World Food Conference, Nov. 16, 1974. Report of the World Food Conference, U.N. Doc. E/CONF. 65/20 (1974), *reprinted in* 3 Weston III.N.1, *supra* note 27.

[43]   Adopted by the U.N. General Assembly, Nov. 25, 1981. G.A. Res. 36/55, U.N. GAOR, 36th Sess., Supp. No. 51, at 171, U.N. Doc. A/RES/36/51 (1981), *reprinted in* 3 Weston III.I.3, *supra* note 27.

[44]   Adopted by the U.N. General Assembly, Dec. 4, 1986. G.A. Res. 41/128 (Annex), U.N. GAOR, 41st Sess., Supp. No. 53, at 186, U.N. Doc. A/RES/41/53 (1987), *reprinted in* 3 Weston III.R.2, *supra* note 27.

[45]   Adopted by the U.N. General Assembly, Dec. 18, 1992. G.A. Res. 47/135 (Annex), U.N. GAOR, 47th Sess., Supp. No. 49, at 210, U.N. Doc. A/RES/47/135 (1992), *reprinted in* 3 Weston III.I.5, *supra* note 27.

of Violence Against Women.[46] In addition, there have been a series of very important regional initiatives with respect to the establishment of human rights standards and procedures, most extensively in Europe, but also significantly in the Inter-American setting of the Western Hemisphere, Africa, and—although not yet institutionalized—Asia.

3. *Enhancing the role of human rights within the U.N. system.* The references to human rights within the U.N. Charter did not suggest a major role for the U.N. Over the years, however, the U.N. has come to play a more and more significant part in evolving human rights standards and providing an institutional capacity for monitoring compliance and censuring serious violations.[47] The 1993 U.N. World Conference on Human Rights was a milestone in this regard, and provided also an arena for civil society to assert its particular concerns about the abused circumstances of women and indigenous peoples. One important outcome of this event was the mandate to establish a High Commissioner for Human Rights, ensuring both budgetary support and agenda salience for human rights within the U.N. despite downsizing pressures.

4. *Historical struggles against oppressive circumstances.* On several dramatic occasions human rights have been at the very center of popular struggles for emancipation from oppressive circumstances. These occasions also exhibited the remarkable effects of converging popular movements for change in civil society with strong international support for the implementation of human rights. The most dramatic instances of this convergence are the anti-colonial struggles of the Asian and African peoples, the movements for freedom and rights in the countries of Eastern Europe and the Soviet Union during the 1980s, and, of course, the anti-apartheid campaign in South Africa. In each case, a significant internal political dynamic was reinforced symbolically and diplomatically by international action based on fundamental human rights.

5. *The engagement of civil society.* From the outset, the effectiveness of human rights within the United Nations and elsewhere has reflected the rise of transnational and indigenous human rights associations of citizens. These associations have regarded the realization of human rights as a political project with legal backing and the strongest possible moral support. The voices of civil society were also filling a vacuum created by realist patterns of statecraft that often wanted to give lip service to human rights commitments or to restrict the relevance of the human rights discourse to the channels of hostile propaganda. In many respects, the growth of global civil society was based on human rights activism in civil society that originated in the Western democracies, but gradually spread to all parts of the world.

---

[46]   Adopted by the U.N. General Assembly, Dec. 20, 1993. G.A. Res. 48/104, U.N. GAOR, 48th Sess., Supp. No. 49, at 217, U.N. Doc. A/RES/48/104 (1993), *reprinted in* 33 I.L.M. 1049 (1994) *and* 3 Weston III.C.14, *supra* note 27.

[47]   *See generally* 7 THE UNITED NATIONS AND HUMAN RIGHTS (1945–1995) (U.N. Publications, Blue Book Series, 1995).

6. *Extensions to the humanitarian law of war and crimes against humanity.* Increasingly, the domain of human rights has been extended to include wartime behavior that is violative of fundamental rights of the person.[48] This effort to encompass what Ken Booth has termed "human wrongs" within our sense of human rights[49] has gone forward in the form of the establishment of *ad hoc* tribunals charged with the indictment and prosecution of individuals accused of crimes against humanity and genocide in the former Yugoslavia and Rwanda. This revival of the effort associated with the post-World War II trials of surviving German and Japanese leaders also has led to a strong movement to establish an independent international penal tribunal that resulted in the adoption of the July 1998 Rome Statute giving jurisdiction, once it enters into force, to the International Criminal Court to deal with accusations of extreme abuses of human rights.[50] The struggle to criminalize extreme abuse has produced a coalition of governments committed to this type of global reform and supportive elements in civil society that have mounted a massive global campaign. It has also produced a geopolitical backlash that has united several powerful states in resistance, including the United States, China, and France.

Looking forward to the next century, it seems safe to predict that human rights will continue to provide a focus for normative energy within global civil society, the U.N. system, and in the foreign policy of leading states. At the same time, the friction between realist orientations toward statecraft and the commitment to human rights is likely to persist for the foreseeable future, producing inconsistent expressions of concern and allegations of double standards. It also is certain that efforts at implementation will be resisted by invoking claims of sovereign rights and by mounting arguments against reliance on interventionary techniques to advance human rights.

In the near future, it is likely that human rights will be seen as producing mixed results. The two major civic campaigns underway are the ratification of the treaties banning anti-personnel landmines and the creation of the International Criminal Court. Both involve innovative coalitions with like-minded governments and both have generated geopolitical resistance. Their outcome will provide short-run litmus tests of the relative potency of the global human rights constituency, but these results are likely to be provisional. The past fifty years demonstrates, above all else, that the great human rights victories have occurred when grassroots activism converges with geopolitical opportunism in a context of favorable historical circumstance. It also demonstrates that the biggest frustrations and disappointments with respect to human rights are associated with the absence of civic momentum and the presence of geopolitical resistance.

---

48   *See, e.g.*, M. Cherif Bassiouni, *Strengthening the Norms of International Humanitarian Law to Combat Impunity, infra* in this volume at p. 245.

49   Ken Booth, *Human Wrongs and International Relations*, 71 INT'L AFF. 103 (1995).

50   Rome Statute of the International Criminal Court, U.N. Doc. A/CONF.183/9 (1998).

As with many matters of global policy, the orientation of the United States government plays a very influential role in relation to human rights. In one sense, it was the first two years of the Carter presidency that raised human rights to a high place in the global policy agenda by making human rights a primary foreign policy goal. This emphasis had extremely important secondary effects, such as encouraging greater risk-taking by opposition movements in oppressive societies and giving human rights a stronger voice in national bureaucracies, including that of the U.S. government.

The Universal Declaration of Human Rights continues to provide an inspirational foundation for human rights although its substantive authority seems to have been mainly transferred to subsequent documents with more specific focus and a more obligatory status. The utopian provisions of the UDHR, such as the promise of a standard of living for every person sufficient to meet basic human needs[51] and the commitment to establish an international order capable of realizing this goal and the overall program of human rights, are likely to remain important reminders of the work that remains to be done.[52] As with almost all aspects of the human rights subject, the achievements over the course of the last fifty years are extraordinary, but the obstacles to full realization seem as insurmountable as ever.

---

[51]   UDHR, *infra* Appendix I, art. 25.

[52]   UDHR, *id.* art. 28.

Capabilities, Human Rights, and the Universal Declaration*

Martha C. Nussbaum

I. Introduction

Fifty years ago, on December 10, 1948, forty-eight states voted for the Universal Declaration of Human Rights (UDHR),[1] while South Africa, Saudi Arabia, and six states in the Soviet bloc abstained. The rhetorical consensus on this enunciation of human aspirations in the language of rights was consolidated on the Universal Declaration's twentieth anniversary, when the first United Nations International Conference on Human Rights, meeting in Teheran in 1968, proclaimed by consensus the Declaration to express "a common understanding of the peoples of the world concerning the inalienable and inviolable rights of all members of the human family and constitutes an obligation for the members of the international community."[2] For the Universal Declaration's forty-fifth anniversary, the second U.N. World Conference on Human Rights, meeting in Vienna in 1993, proclaimed the text to constitute "a common standard of achievement for all peoples and all nations."[3] More significant than international conference instruments is the vast array of international conventions and national constitutions that refer explicitly to the Declaration and purport to give legally binding character to the propositions it contains. The governments and international agencies engaged in this process express people's basic political and economic entitlements in the language of rights, singling out a group of particularly urgent interests that deserve special protection. The language of rights, especially of human rights, is regularly preferred.

The language of rights has a moral resonance that makes it hard to avoid in contemporary political discourse. But it is certainly not on account of its theoreti-

---

* Adapted and substantially revised from Martha C. Nussbaum, *Capabilities and Human Rights*, 66 FORDHAM L. REV. 273 (1997). Reprint permission granted.

1 *See infra* Appendix I [hereinafter UDHR].

2 Final Act of the United Nations International Conference on Human Rights at Teheran, May 13, 1968, pmbl., *in* HUMAN RIGHTS: A COMPILATION OF INTERNATIONAL INSTRUMENTS 43 (1988), *reprinted in* 3 INTERNATIONAL LAW AND WORLD ORDER: BASIC DOCMENTS III.U.1 (Burns H. Weston ed., 5 vols., 1944–) [hereinafter 3 Weston].

3 Vienna Declaration and Programme of Action, adopted by the U.N. World Conference on Human Rights, June 25, 1993, pmbl., U.N. Doc. A/CONF.157.24 (pt. I), at 20 (1993), at 20, *reprinted in* 32 I.L.M. 1661 (1993) *and* 3 Weston III.U.2, *supra* note 2.

cal and conceptual clarity that it has been preferred. There are many different ways of thinking about what a right is, and many different definitions of "human rights."[4] For example, rights are often spoken of as entitlements that belong to all human beings simply because they are human, or as especially urgent interests of human beings as human beings that deserve protection regardless of where people are situated.[5] Within this tradition there are differences. The dominant tradition has typically grounded rights in the possession of rationality and language, thus implying that non-human animals do not have them, and that mentally impaired humans may not have them.[6] Some philosophers have maintained that sentience, instead, should be the basis of rights; thus, all animals would be rights-bearers.[7] In contrast to this entire group of natural-rights theorists, there are also thinkers who treat all rights as artifacts of state action.[8] The latter position would seem to imply that there are no human rights where there is no state to recognize them. Such an approach appears to the holders of the former view to do away with the very point of rights language, which is to point to the fact that human beings are entitled to certain types of treatment whether or not the state in which they happen to live recognizes this fact.

There are many other complex unresolved theoretical questions about rights. One of them is the question whether the individual is the only bearer of rights, or whether rights belong, as well, to other entities, such as families, ethnic, religious, and linguistic groups, and nations. Another is whether rights are to be regarded as

---

[4] For one excellent account, with discussion of other views, see ALAN GEWIRTH, THE COMMUNITY OF RIGHTS (1996). *See also* Burns H. Weston, *Human Rights*, 20 ENCYCLOPAEDIA BRITANNICA 714 (15th ed. 1998 prtg.), *updated and revised in* ENCYCLOPAEDIA BRITANNICA ONLINE (visited Dec. 1, 1998) <http://www. eb.com:180/cgi-bin/g?DocF=macro/5002/93.html>.

[5] This is the view of Thomas Paine. For just one example, see COMMON SENSE, THE RIGHTS OF MAN, AND OTHER ESSENTIAL WRITINGS OF THOMAS PAINE 186–90 (Sidney Hook ed., 1994) (1792) (quoting and discussing the French Declaration of the Rights of Man and of Citizens) (hereinafter THOMAS PAINE); *id.* at 226 (insisting that rights, so conceived, should be the foundation of a nation's prosperity). Such views ultimately derive from ancient Greek and Roman Stoic views of natural law. *See* Weston, *supra* note 4. The Latin word *ius* can be translated either as "right" or as "law;" Grotius already discussed the manifold applications of *ius. See* HUGO GROTIUS, DE IURE BELLI AC PACIS (ON THE LAW OF WAR AND PEACE) (P.C. Molhuysen ed. 1919) (1625).

[6] The most influential exemplar of such a view, followed by most later theorists, is Cicero. *See* M. TULLI CICERONIS, DE OFFICIIS (ON DUTIES) bk. 1, paras. 11–14 (Oxford Univ. Press 1994) (distinguishing humans from beasts by reference to rationality and language); *id.* paras. 20–41 (deriving duties from this).

[7] *See* PETER SINGER, ANIMAL LIBERATION (2d ed. 1990).

[8] This view is most influentially found in Kant. *See* Immanuel Kant, *The Metaphysics of Morals, in* KANT: POLITICAL WRITINGS 132–35 (Hans Reiss ed. & H. B. Nisbet trans., 2d enlarged ed. 1991) (1798) (defining right and the theory of right with reference to law and the state).

side-constraints on goal-seeking action, or as parts of a goal that is to be promoted.[9] Still another unresolved question is whether rights—thought of as justified entitlements—are correlated with duties. If A has a right to S, then it would appear there must be someone who has a duty to provide S to A. But it is not always clear who has these duties—especially when we think of rights in the international context. The Universal Declaration, for example, stipulates that the aim of its proclamation is "that every individual and every organ of society, keeping this Declaration constantly in mind, shall strive . . . to secure their universal and effective recognition and observance. . . ."[10] Even accepting that specific obligation of a legal character was supposed to await what eventually became the two 1966 international covenants,[11] this text reveals ambiguity as to who is the duty-holder. The reference to "organs of society" suggests that state agents have duties to secure observance of the declared rights. But so do ordinary citizens and probably noncitizens since the text is directed also at "every individual." Thus the vagueness of these terms could be interpreted to create obligation both on agents of the state in dealing with individuals and on individuals in their relations with other individuals.[12] Furthermore, it is unclear whether all duties are correlated with rights. One might hold, for example, that we have a duty not to cause pain to animals without holding that animals have rights—if, for example, one accepted one of the classic accounts of the basis of rights that makes reference to the abilities of speech and reason as the foundation, and yet still believed that we have other strong reasons not to cause animals pain.

Finally, there are difficult theoretical questions about what rights are to be understood as "rights to." When we speak of human rights, do we mean, primarily,

---

[9]   An influential example of the first approach is in ROBERT NOZICK, ANARCHY, STATE, AND UTOPIA 26–53 (1974) (Chapter 3: Moral Constraints and the State, arguing that rights supply moral constraints on state action). *See also* SAMUEL SCHEFFLER, THE REJECTION OF CONSEQUENTIALISM (rev. ed. 1994) (developing a theory of rights as side constraints). For the second approach, see, for example, Amartya Sen, *Rights as Goals, in Equality and Discrimination, in* ESSAYS IN FREEDOM AND JUSTICE (S. Guest & A. Milne eds., 1985) [hereinafter *Rights as Goals*], developing an account of rights as among the goals of public action.

[10]   UDHR, *infra* Appendix I, at pmbl.

[11]   International Covenant on Economic, Social and Cultural Rights, *infra* Appendix II; International Covenant on Civil and Political Rights, *infra* Appendix III.

[12]   This all-encompassing approach to identifying the duty-holder is confirmed in Article 29 of the Universal Declaration, according to which "[e]veryone has duties to the community in which alone the free and full development of his personality is possible." The ambiguity is not eliminated in the more specific enunciation of rights. Article 9, for example, posits that "[n]o one shall be subjected to arbitrary arrest, detention or exile." One would normally think that law enforcement officials have the principal duty to respect this right; however, the duty not to commit any of the three prohibited acts could also apply to private parties who might sequester or kidnap other private parties.

a right to be treated in certain ways? A right to a certain level of achieved well-being? A right to certain resources with which one may pursue one's life plan? A right to certain opportunities and capacities with which one may, in turn, make choices regarding one's life plan? Political philosophers who debate the nature of equality commonly tackle a related question head on, asking whether the equality most relevant to political distribution should be understood primarily as equality of well-being, or equality of resources, or equality of opportunity, or equality of capabilities.[13] The language of rights to some extent cuts across this debate and obscures the issues that have been articulated, particularly in distinguishing between "positive" and "negative" rights.[14]

Thus, one might conclude that the language of rights, including that of the Universal Declaration, is not especially informative, despite its uplifting character, unless its users link their references to rights to a theory that answers at least some of these questions.[15] It is for this reason, among others, that a different language has begun to take hold in talk about people's basic entitlements. This is the language of capabilities and human functioning which was in some ways anticipated in the Universal Declaration even though its authors came from diverse cultural backgrounds and did not use this language per se.[16] As this essay seeks to demonstrate, rethinking the Universal Declaration in terms of human capabilities and functioning enhances rather than questions the validity of most of the normative pronouncements of that text and suggests public policy directions for the Declaration's second fifty years.

---

13   See Amartya K. Sen, Equality of What?, in I THE TANNER LECTURES ON HUMAN VALUES 195 (Sterling M. McMurrin ed., 1980), reprinted in AMARTYA K. SEN, CHOICE, WELFARE AND MEASUREMENT 353 (1982) [hereinafter Equality of What?] (arguing that the most relevant type of equality for political purposes is equality of capability). See also AMARTYA K. SEN, INEQUALITY REEXAMINED passim (1992) [hereinafter INEQUALITY REEXAMINED] (making the same case in more detail); Richard J. Arneson, Equality and Equal Opportunity for Welfare, 56 PHIL. STUD. 77 (1989) (defending equality of opportunity for welfare); G. A. Cohen, On the Currency of Egalitarian Justice, 99 ETHICS 906, 920–21 (1989) (arguing that the right thing to equalize is "access to advantage"); Ronald Dworkin, What Is Equality? Part 1: Equality of Welfare, 10 PHIL. & PUB. AFF. 185 (1981) (discussing distributional equality); Ronald Dworkin, What Is Equality? Part 2: Equality of Resources, 10 PHIL. & PUB. AFF. 283 (1981) (arguing that the right thing to equalize are resources, and defining a suitable conception of equality of resources); John E. Roemer, Equality of Resources Implies Equality of Welfare, 101 Q. J. ECON. 751 (1986) (arguing that, suitably understood, equality of resources implies equality of welfare).

14   See Weston, supra note 4.

15   See, e.g., Bernard Williams, The Standard of Living: Interests and Capabilities, in THE STANDARD OF LIVING 94, 100 (Geoffrey Hawthorn ed., 1987) (arguing for an approach to basic human rights through basic capabilities).

16   See Stephen P. Marks, From "That Single Confused Page" to the "Decologue for Six Billion Persons": The Legacy of the French Revolution in the Universal Declaration of Human Rights, 20 HUM. RTS. Q. 459 (1998).

The application of the capabilities approach to international human rights standards has accelerated in recent years. Since 1993, the Human Development Reports of the United Nations Development Programme (UNDP)[17] have assessed the quality of life in the nations of the world using the concept of people's capabilities, or their abilities to do and to be certain things deemed valuable.[18] Under the influence of economist/philosopher and Nobel laureate Amartya Sen, they have chosen that conceptual framework as basic to inter-country comparisons and to the articulation of goals for public policy. In 1997, this concern with human capabilities merged into a new policy of a rights-based approach to development, approved in November 1997, and set out in the UNDP publication *Integrating Human Rights with Sustainable Human Development*.[19] The Director of the Human Development Report herself expressed an approach to human rights based on capabilities and functioning: "While human rights are rooted in the concept of human dignity, human development is rooted in the concept of 'capability and functionings'—the valuable things that a person can do."[20] She adds: "These are not identical concepts but they share much in common. In particular, they both have the same point of departure—the concern with people as the central purpose of development efforts."[21] My contention is that human rights are also rooted in the concept of capability and functionings.

Along with Sen, I have been one of the people who have pioneered what is now called the "capabilities approach," defending its importance in international debates about welfare and quality of life. My own use of this language was originally independent, and reflected the fact that Aristotle used a notion of human capability (Greek *dunamis*) and functioning (Greek *energeia*) to articulate some of the goals

---

[17]   *See, e.g.,* UNITED NATIONS DEVELOPMENT PROGRAMME, HUMAN DEVELOPMENT REPORT 1993 [hereinafter HUMAN DEVELOPMENT REPORT 1993] UNITED NATIONS DEVELOPMENT PROGRAMME, HUMAN DEVELOPMENT REPORT 1996.

[18]   The reports' primary measure of quality of life is the "human development index" ("HDI"). HUMAN DEVELOPMENT REPORT 1993, *supra* note 17, at 10. HDI is a composite of three basic components of human development: longevity (measured by life expectancy), knowledge (measured by a combination of adult literacy and mean years of schooling), and standard of living (measured by income relative to the poverty level). *Id.* at 100. For a standard definition of capabilities, see Amartya K. Sen, *Capability and Well-Being, in* THE QUALITY OF LIFE 30–31 (Martha C. Nussbaum & Amartya K. Sen eds., 1993), explaining the choice of the term and its relationship to other basic concepts.

[19]   The Administrator of UNDP, James Gustave Speth, communicated this policy to all resident representatives in "Direct Line 17" of January 30, 1998, in which he suggested, as one of UNDP's roles, human rights advocacy which "may include encouragement of the country's acceding to international human rights treaties and/or the development of the capacity to implement its treaty obligations."

[20]   Sakiko Fukuda-Parr, *Towards a Wholistic Approach to Human Rights*, 1 SOCIAL DEV. REV. 3, 5 (1997).

[21]   *Id.*

of good political organization.[22] But the projects soon became fused: I increasingly articulated the Aristotelian idea of capability in terms pertinent to the contemporary debate,[23] while Sen increasingly emphasized the ancient roots of his idea.[24] In a variety of contexts, we argued that the capabilities approach was a valuable theoretical framework for public policy, especially in the international development context.[25] We commended it to both theoreticians and practitioners as offering certain advantages over approaches that focus on opulence—GNP per capita, or welfare—construed in terms of utility or desire-satisfaction, or even the distribution of basic resources.[26] Similar efforts using different theoretical starting-points have been articulated in the public policy approach of the so-called New Haven School of Jurisprudence[27] and research on the intersection of basic needs and human rights.[28]

---

22   *See* Martha C. Nussbaum, *Nature, Function, and Capability: Aristotle on Political Distribution, in* [SUPPLEMENTARY VOLUME] OXFORD STUDIES IN ANCIENT PHILOSOPHY 145 (Julia Annas & Robert Grimm eds., 1988) [hereinafter *Nature, Function, and Capability*].

23   *See* Martha C. Nussbaum, *Aristotelian Social Democracy in* LIBERALISM AND THE GOOD 203 (R. Bruce Douglass et al. eds., 1990) [hereinafter *Aristotelian Social Democracy*]; Martha C. Nussbaum, *Aristotle on Human Nature and the Foundations of Ethics, in* WORLD, MIND, AND ETHICS: ESSAYS ON THE ETHICAL PHILOSOPHY OF BERNARD WILLIAMS 86 (E.J. Altham & Ross Harrison eds., 1995) [hereinafter *Human Nature*]; Martha C. Nussbaum, *Human Capabilities, Female Human Beings, in* WOMEN, CULTURE, AND DEVELOPMENT 61 (Martha C. Nussbaum & Jonathan Glover eds., 1995) [hereinafter *Human Capabilities*]; Martha C. Nussbaum, *Non-Relative Virtues: An Aristotelian Approach, in* THE QUALITY OF LIFE, *supra* note 18, at 242; Martha C. Nussbaum, *Human Functioning and Social Justice: In Defense of Aristotelian Essentialism*, 20 POL. THEORY 202 (1992) [hereinafter *Human Functioning*]; Martha C. Nussbaum, *The Good as Discipline, The Good as Freedom, in* THE ETHICS OF CONSUMPTION AND GLOBAL STEWARDSHIP 312 (D. Crocker & T. Linden eds., 1998) [hereinafter *The Good as Discipline, The Good as Freedom*]; MARTHA C. NUSSBAUM, SEX AND SOCIAL JUSTICE (1998) (Chapter 1: *Women and Cultural Universals*) [hereinafter *Women and Cultural Universals*].

24   *See, e.g.*, INEQUALITY REEXAMINED, *supra* note 13 (containing his most recent formulation of the approach).

25   A good summary of our approaches, and the similarities and differences between Sen's and my views, is found in David A. Crocker, *Functioning and Capability: The Foundations of Sen's and Nussbaum's Development Ethic*, 20 POL. THEORY 584 (1992) [hereinafter *Functioning and Capability: Part 1*] and David A. Crocker, *Functioning and Capability: The Foundations of Sen's and Nussbaum's Development Ethic, Part 2, in* WOMEN, CULTURE, AND DEVELOPMENT, *supra* note 23, at 153 [hereinafter *Functioning and Capability: Part 2*].

26   *See* Amartya K. Sen, *Capability and Well-Being, in* THE QUALITY OF LIFE, *supra* note 18, at 30; AMARTYA K. SEN, COMMODITIES AND CAPABILITIES (1985); *Equality of What?, supra* note 13; Amartya K. Sen, *Gender Inequality and Theories of Justice, in* WOMEN, CULTURE, AND DEVELOPMENT, *supra* note 23, at 259 [hereinafter *Gender Inequality*]; Amartya K. Sen, *Well-Being, Agency and Freedom: The Dewey Lectures 1984*, 82 J. PHIL. 169 (1985) [hereinafter *Well-Being*].

27   *See, e.g.*, MYRES S. MCDOUGAL, HAROLD D. LASSWELL & LUNG-CHU CHEN, HUMAN RIGHTS AND WORLD PUBLIC ORDER: THE BASIC POLICIES OF AN INTERNATIONAL LAW OF HUMAN DIGNITY (1980)

28   *See, e.g.*, JOHAN GALTUNG, HUMAN RIGHTS IN ANOTHER KEY (1994); Johan Galtung &

Both Sen and I stated from the start that the capabilities approach needs to be combined with a focus on rights. Sen wrote about rights as central goals of public policy throughout the period during which he developed the approach.[29] I stressed from the start that Aristotle's theory was grossly defective because it lacked a theory of the basic human rights, especially rights to be free from government interference in certain areas of choice.[30] More recently, responding to communitarian critics of rights-based reasoning and to international discussions that denigrate rights in favor of material well-being, both Sen and I have even more strongly emphasized the importance of rights to our own capabilities approach. We stressed the various roles liberty plays within our respective theories and emphasized the closeness of our approach to liberal theories such as that of John Rawls.[31]

Moreover, rights play an increasingly large role inside the account of what the most important capabilities are. Unlike Sen, who prefers to allow the account of the basic capabilities to remain largely implicit in his statements, I have produced an explicit account of the most central capabilities that should be the goal of public policy. The list is continually being revised and adjusted, in accordance with my methodological commitment to cross-cultural deliberation and criticism. But another source of change has been an increasing determination to bring the list down to earth, so to speak, making the "thick vague conception of the good"[32] a little less vague, so that it can do real work guiding public policy. At this point, the aim is to come up with the type of specification of a basic capability that could figure in a constitution,[33] or perform, apart from that, the role of a constitutional guarantee.

Anders H. Wirak, *Human Needs, Human Rights and the Theories of Development, in* INDICATORS OF SOCIAL AND ECONOMIC CHANGE AND THEIR APPLICATIONS (UNESCO, Reports and Papers in Social Science No. 37, 1976). *See also* HUMAN RIGHTS IN THE WORLD COMMUNITY: ISSUES AND ACTION ch. 3 (Richard P. Claude & Burns H. Weston eds., 2d ed. 1992); Stephen P. Marks, *The Peace-Human Rights-Development Dialectic*, 11 BULL. PEACE PROPOSALS No. 4, at 339 (1980).

29   *See* Amartya Sen, *Rights and Capabilities, in* MORALITY AND OBJECTIVITY: A TRIBUTE TO J. L. MACKIE 130 (Ted Honderich ed., 1985), *reprinted in* AMARTYA K. SEN, RESOURCES, VALUES AND DEVELOPMENT 307 (1984) [hereinafter *Rights and Capabilities*]; *Rights as Goals, supra* note 9; Amartya K. Sen, *Rights and Agency*, 11 PHIL. & PUB. AFF. 3 (1982) [hereinafter *Rights and Agency*].

30   *See Aristotelian Social Democracy, supra* note 23, at 239.

31   *See* JOHN RAWLS, POLITICAL LIBERALISM (1993) [hereinafter POLITICAL LIBERALISM]; JOHN RAWLS, A THEORY OF JUSTICE (1971) [hereinafter A THEORY OF JUSTICE]. Sen discusses, and supports, the Rawlsian notion of the priority of liberty in *Freedoms and Needs*, THE NEW REPUBLIC, Jan. 10 & 17, 1994, at 31–38 [hereinafter *Freedoms and Needs*]. I discuss the relationship between my own version of the capabilities view and Rawls' theory in *Aristotelian Social Democracy, supra* note 23, and *The Good as Discipline, The Good as Freedom, supra* note 23. In *The Good as Discipline, The Good as Freedom*, I emphasize the liberal roots of my own Aristotelianism, contrasting my view with two nonliberal forms of Aristotelianism.

32 This is my term from *Aristotelian Social Democracy, supra* note 23, at 217, contrasting with Rawls' "thin theory of the good" in A THEORY OF JUSTICE, *supra* note 31, at 395–99.

33   *See Human Capabilities, supra* note 23, at 85.

In the process, I have increasingly used the language of rights, or the related language of liberty and freedom, in fleshing out the account of the basic capabilities. Thus, in *Human Capabilities*, I speak of "legal guarantees of freedom of expression . . . and of freedom of religious exercise"[34] as aspects of the general capability to use one's mind and one's senses in a way directed by one's own practical reason. I also speak of "guarantees of non-interference with certain choices that are especially personal and definitive of selfhood," and of "the freedoms of assembly and political speech."[35] In *Women and Cultural Universals*,[36] I actually use the language of rights itself in articulating the capability to seek employment outside the home, and several of the other important capabilities. In part, this is a rhetorical choice, bringing the list of capabilities into relation with international human rights instruments that have a related content, in particular the Universal Declaration and the two covenants which purported to transform the rights of the Declaration into what I call "side constraints."[37] But in part it also reflects a theoretical decision to emphasize the affiliations of the approach with liberal rights-based theories, in an era of widespread reaction against the Enlightenment and its heritage.[38]

But there still are some large questions to be answered. The relationship between the two concepts remains as yet underexplored. Does the capabilities view supplement a theory of rights, or is it intended to be a particular way of capturing what a theory of rights captures? Is there any tension between a focus on capabilities and a focus on rights? Are the two approaches competitors? On the other hand, is there any reason why a capabilities theorist should welcome the language of rights—that is, is there anything in the view itself that leads naturally in the direction of recognizing rights? Would a natural-law Catholic theorist who used an Aristotelian language of capability and functioning, but rejected liberal rights-based language, be making a conceptual error?[39] Does the capabilities view help us to answer any of the difficult questions that I sketched above, which have preoccupied theorists of rights? Does the capabilities view incline us to opt for any particular

---

[34] *Id.* at 84.

[35] *Id.* at 84–85.

[36] *Supra* note 23.

[37] *Id.* at 25–26.

[38] For the close relationship between the capabilities approach and Enlightenment liberalism, see *Freedoms and Needs, supra* note 31, and *The Good as Discipline, The Good as Freedom, supra* note 23.

[39] I put things this way because the most prominent anti-liberal natural law theorists do not explicitly reject rights language. *See* JOHN FINNIS, NATURAL LAW AND NATURAL RIGHTS (1980) and ROBERT P. GEORGE, MAKING MEN MORAL: CIVIL LIBERTIES AND PUBLIC MORALITY (1993). And the most prominent Catholic opponent of rights language does not endorse the capabilities approach. *See* Mary Ann Glendon, RIGHTS TALK: THE IMPOVERISHMENT OF POLITICAL DISCOURSE (1991). But the combination is easy enough to imagine.

set of answers to the various questions about rights, or any particular conception of rights? For example, is Sen justified in thinking that the capabilities view supports a conception of rights as goals, rather than as side-constraints?[40] Finally, is there any reason, other than a merely rhetorical one, why we should continue to use the language of rights in addition to the language of capabilities?

In short, the conceptual relationship needs further scrutiny.[41] Commenting on Sen's Tanner Lectures in 1987, Bernard Williams expressed sympathy with the capabilities approach, but called for a conceptual investigation:

> I am not very happy myself with taking rights as the starting point. The notion of a basic human right seems to me obscure enough, and I would rather come at it from the perspective of basic human capabilities. I would prefer capabilities to do the work, and if we are going to have a language or rhetoric of rights, to have it delivered from them, rather than the other way around. But I think that there remains an unsolved problem: how we should see the relations between these concepts.[42]

In a precursor to this essay, in a paper that I contributed to a 1997 symposium on "Human Rights on the Eve of the Next Century—Beyond Vienna and Beijing: Rights in Theory," I attempted to illuminate some of the issues that must be faced when one does attempt to connect the two ideas, some of the options one has, some of the problems that arise, and some of the positive dividends one may reap.[43] This chapter is a further contribution to that project, focusing on the implications of the capabilities approach relative to the enumeration of rights in the Universal Declaration and its progeny over the years. The principal difference between this chapter and the above-mentioned symposium is that I am proposing here that the interpretation of human rights as formulated in international texts by reference to capabilities and functioning is a tool for understanding and applying the concepts of the obligations stated therein to "respect, protect and fulfill."[44] In other words,

---

[40]   *See Rights and Capabilities, supra* note 29, at 310–12.

[41]   A valuable beginning, bringing together all that Sen and I have said on the topic, is in *Functioning and Capability: Part 2, supra* note 25, at 186–91.

[42]   Williams, *supra* note 15, at 100.

[43]   Martha C. Nussbaum, *Capabilities and Human Rights*, 66 Fordham L. Rev. 273 (1997).

[44]   The Maastricht guidelines, adopted in January 1997 by a group of experts and subsequently published as a United Nations document, distinguished these obligations as follows:

> Like civil and political rights, economic, social and cultural rights impose three different types of obligations on States: the obligations to respect, protect and fulfil. Failure to perform any one of these three obligations constitutes a violation of such rights. The obligation to *respect* requires States to refrain from interfering with the enjoyment of economic, social and cultural rights. Thus, the right to housing is violated if the State engages in arbitrary forced evictions. The obligation to

the capabilities approach requires that international human rights standards be conceived and received as more than "formal" rights, that they become more deeply informed by social reality. Beyond that, I shall not be able to answer all the outstanding questions, and I shall certainly not be able to offer a theory of rights that solves all the problems I have outlined. But I hope to illuminate some of the issues that must be faced when one does attempt to connect the two ideas, some of the options one has, some of the problems that arise, and some of the positive dividends one may reap.

I begin by describing the capabilities approach and the motivations for its introduction: what it was trying to do in political philosophy, how it commended itself by contrast to other standard ways of thinking about entitlements. Then I shall briefly clarify the connection between the capabilities approach and liberal theories of justice. Finally, I shall turn to my central topic, the relationship between rights and capabilities.

II. The Capabilities Approach: Antecedents and Argument

Why, then, should there be a theory of human capabilities? What questions does it answer, and what is its practical point? Why should an international agency such as the UNDP use a measure of quality of life based on human capability and functioning, rather than other more traditional measures: for example, those based on opulence, utility, or a distribution of resources that satisfies some constraint, whether it be a social minimum, or the Rawlsian Difference Principle, or some more exacting egalitarian condition?

The account of human capabilities has been used as an answer to a number of distinct questions, such as: What is the living standard?[45] What is the quality of life?[46] These questions are crucial to the interpretation of Article 25 of the Universal Declaration, according to which "[e]veryone has the right to a standard of living adequate for the health and well-being of himself and of this family, including food, clothing, housing and medical care and necessary social services, and the rights to

---

protect requires States to prevent violations of such rights by third parties. Thus, the failure to ensure that private employers comply with basic labour standards may amount to a violation of the right to work or the right to just and favourable conditions of work. The obligation to *fulfil* requires States to take appropriate legislative, administrative, budgetary, judicial and other measures towards the full realization of such rights. Thus, the failure of States to provide essential primary health care to those in need may amount to a violation.

The Maastricht Guidelines on Violations of Economic, Social and Cultural Rights, 20 HUM. RTS. Q. 691, 693–94 (1998).

[45] Williams, *supra* note 15, at 100–02 (discussing Sen's proposal that the living standard should be defined in terms of capabilities).

[46] *See* THE QUALITY OF LIFE, *supra* note 18.

security in the event of unemployment, sickness, disability, widowhood, old age or other lack of livelihood in circumstances beyond his control." These fifty-seven words summarize welfare state policy in virtually its entirety, but what do they mean as the articulation of a human right? The Committee on Economic Social and Cultural Rights, in interpreting the component right to housing as further elaborated in Article 11 of the International Covenant on Economic, Social and Cultural Rights, has stated that this right

> should be seen as a right to live somewhere in security, peace and dignity ... [which] should be ensured to all persons irrespective of income or access to economic resources. ... [Article 11.1] must be read as referring not just to housing but to adequate housing, [which means] adequate privacy, adequate space, adequate security, adequate lighting and ventilation, adequate basic infrastructure and adequate location with regard to work and basic facilities—all at a reasonable cost.[47]

The concept of an adequate standard of living clearly responds to considerations of distributive justice and equality.

As Stephen Marks has pointed out, however, it would be erroneous to attribute such considerations in the international human rights texts exclusively to the socialist thinking of European social democracies and communist party states and to the New Deal in the United States.[48] The egalitarian ideas of the Universal Declaration are the legacy also of Rousseau among the Enlightenment philosophers and of several influential members of the French National Assembly—for example, the Abbé Sieyès who elaborated over two-hundred years ago a theory of human rights based on the fulfillment of human needs: "Man is, by nature, subject to *needs*; but, by nature, has the *means* to satisfy them. ... Individual means are linked by nature to individual needs. Whoever is responsible for needs must therefore freely dispose of the means."[49] Sieyès further explains various forms of inequality and declares that a purpose of society is to develop the moral and physical capacities of its members which it augments through the "inestimable collaboration of public works and assistance."[50] This antecedent to the capabilities approach properly underscores the essential element of equality.

---

[47] Committee on Economic, Social and Cultural Rights, General Comment 4 [the right to adequate housing (art. 11(1)] of the Covenant (Sixth Sess., 1991), COMPILATION OF GENERAL COMMENTS AND GENERAL RECOMMENDATIONS ADOPTED BY HUMAN RIGHTS TREATY BODIES, U.N. Doc. HRI/GEN/1/Rev.12, at 53 (1994), para. 7.

[48] *Supra* note 16, at 503.

[49] Abbéy Sieyès, *Préliminaire de la Constitution, Reconnaissance et Exposition raisonnée des droits de l'homme et du Citoyen, quoted in* Marks, *supra* note 16, at 503 (emphasis in the original).

[50] *Id.*

What is the relevant type of equality that we should consider in political planning?[51] What does it mean when the Universal Declaration affirms that "[e]veryone is entitled to all the rights and freedoms set forth in this Declaration, without distinction of any kind, such as race, colour, sex, language, religion, political or other opinion, national or social origin, property, birth or other status"?[52] Equality has also been closely linked to discussion of a theory of justice, because such a theory has a need for an account of what it is trying to achieve for people. I believe that the most illuminating way of thinking about the capabilities approach is that it is an account of the space within which we make comparisons between individuals and across nations as to how well they are doing. This idea is closely linked with the idea of a theory of justice, since one crucial aim of a theory of justice typically is to promote some desired state of people; and in *Aristotelian Social Democracy*[53] I linked it very closely to an account of the proper goal of government, to bring all citizens up to a certain basic minimum level of capability. But up to a point, the approach is logically independent of a theory of justice, since a theory of justice may acknowledge many constraints with regard to how far it is entitled to promote people's well-being. For example, Robert Nozick could grant that capabilities are the relevant space within which to make comparisons of well-being while denying that this has anything at all to do with a theory of justice, since he rejects theories of justice based on a "patterned end-state" conception, preferring to define justice solely in terms of procedures and entitlements.[54]

The capabilities idea is also closely linked to a concern with equality, in that Sen has always used it to argue that people are entitled to a certain level of rough material and social equality. But, strictly speaking, these two concerns of Sen's are logically independent. One might agree that capabilities are the relevant space within which to compare lives and nations, and yet hold that equality of capability is not the appropriate goal. Capabilities inform us as to what type of equality might be thought pertinent; they do not by themselves tell us whether we should value an equal distribution or some other distribution.

As a theory of the relevant space within which to make comparisons, the capabilities approach is best understood by contrasting it with its rivals in the international development arena. The most common method of measuring the quality of life in a nation and making cross-national comparisons used to be simply to enumerate GNP per capita. This crude method is reminiscent of the economics lesson imagined by Charles Dickens in *Hard Times*, and used by Sen and me to introduce our volume on *The Quality of Life*:

---

51   *See* INEQUALITY REEXAMINED, *supra* note 13.

52   UDHR, *infra* Appendix I, art. 2.

53   *Supra* note 23.

54   NOZICK, *supra* note 9, at 150–64 (criticizing patterned end-state conceptions in favor of procedural conceptions).

"And he said, Now this schoolroom is a Nation. And in this nation, there are fifty millions of money. Isn't this a prosperous nation? Girl number twenty, isn't this a prosperous nation, and a'n't you in a thriving state?"

"What did you say?" asked Louisa.

"Miss Louisa, I said I didn't know. I thought I couldn't know whether it was a prosperous nation or not, and whether I was in a thriving state or not, unless I knew who had got the money, and whether any of it was mine. But that had nothing to do with it. It was not in the figures at all," said Sissy, wiping her eyes.

"That was a great mistake of yours," observed Louisa.[55]

In short, the crude approach does not even tell us who has the money, and thus typically gave high marks to nations such as South Africa, which contained enormous inequalities. Still less does it provide any information at all about elements of human life that might be thought very important in defining its quality, but that are not always well-correlated with Gross National Product (GNP) per capita: educational opportunities, health care, life expectancy, infant mortality, the presence or absence of political liberties, the extent of racial or gender inequality.

Somewhat less crude is an economic approach that measures quality of life in terms of utility, understood as the satisfaction of preference or desire.[56] This approach at least has the advantage of concerning itself to some degree with distribution, in the sense that it does look at how resources are or are not going to work to make people's lives better. But it has severe shortcomings. First, there is the familiar problem that utilitarianism tends to think of the social total, or average, as an aggregate, neglecting the salience of the boundaries between individual lives.[57] As Rawls pointed out, this approach means that utilitarianism can tolerate a result in which the total is good enough, but where some individuals suffer extremely acute levels of deprivation, whether of resources or of liberty.[58] In that sense, it does not tell Sissy "who has got the money and whether any of it is mine," any more than does the GNP-based approach. (Indeed, Sissy's teacher was clearly a Benthamite Utilitarian.) Rawls was convinced that the failure of utilitarianism to justify adequately strong protections for the basic political liberties, given this propensity to aggregate, was by itself sufficient reason to reject it.[59] Bernard Williams, similarly,

---

[55] CHARLES DICKENS, HARD TIMES 74–75 (Oxford, 1989) (1854).

[56] For a discussion of this approach, see *Equality of What?*, *supra* note 13, at 358–64.

[57] *See* A THEORY OF JUSTICE, *supra* note 31; Amartya K. Sen & Bernard Williams, *Introduction*, UTILITARIANISM AND BEYOND 1, 4–5 (Amartya K. Sen & Bernard Williams eds., 1982) (arguing that utilitarianism views persons simply as locations of their respective utilities).

[58] *See* A THEORY OF JUSTICE, *supra* note 31, at 179–83 (arguing that utilitarianism treats people as means, rather than as ends).

[59] *Id.* at 207 (arguing that it is unacceptable to take chances with basic liberties).

has considered utilitarianism's neglect of the "separateness of persons" to be a cardinal failure, and a reason why the theory cannot give an adequate account of social well-being.[60]

A second problem with utilitarianism is its commitment to the commensurability of value, the concern to measure the good in terms of a single metric and thus to deny that there are irreducibly plural goods that figure in a human life.[61] Both Sen and I have pursued this question extensively, apart from our work on capabilities.[62] But it has also had importance in justifying the capabilities approach, since the quality of life seems to consist of a plurality of distinct features—features that cannot be simply reduced to quantities of one another. This recognition limits the nature of the tradeoffs it will be feasible to make.[63]

But a third feature of utilitarianism has been even more central to the capability critique. As Sen has repeatedly pointed out, people's satisfactions are not very reliable indicators of their quality of life. Wealthy and privileged people get used to a high level of luxury, and feel pain when they do not have delicacies that one may think they do not really need. On the other hand, deprived people frequently adjust their sights to the low level they know they can aspire to, and thus actually experience satisfaction in connection with a very reduced living standard. Sen gave a graphic example: In 1944, the year after the Great Bengal Famine, the All-India Institute of Hygiene and Public Health did a survey.[64] Included in this survey were a large number of widows and widowers.[65] The position of widows in India is

---

[60] Here I am combining arguments from Williams' essay, *A Critique of Utilitarianism*, *in* UTILITARIANISM: FOR AND AGAINST 77 (1973) (arguing that utilitarianism cannot give an adequate account of a person's special connection to his or her own actions, and therefore of personal integrity) with his *Persons, Character and Morality*, *in* THE IDENTITIES OF PERSONS 197 (Amelie O. Rorty ed., 1969) (arguing that the separateness of persons is a central fact of ethical life).

[61] *See* the discussion in Martha C. Nussbaum, *Plato on Commensurability and Desire*, *in* MARTHA C. NUSSBAUM, LOVE'S KNOWLEDGE 106 (1990) [hereinafter *Commensurability and Desire*], and Martha C. Nussbaum, *The Discernment of Perception: An Aristotelian Conception of Private and Public Rationality, id.* at 54 [hereinafter *Discernment of Perception*], arguing that the plurality and distinctness of the valuable things in life make any single metric a damaging distortion.

[62] *See Discernment of Perception, supra* note 61; *Plato on Commensurability and Desire, supra* note 61. *See also* MARTHA C. NUSSBAUM, THE FRAGILITY OF GOODNESS 290–317 (1986) (arguing that Aristotle was right to recognize a type of deliberation that does not rely on a single metric); AMARTYA K. SEN, ON ETHICS AND ECONOMICS 62–63 (1987) [hereinafter ON ETHICS AND ECONOMICS] (discussing plurality and noncommensurability); Amartya K. Sen, *Plural Utility*, 81 PROC. ARISTOTELIAN SOC'Y 193 (1981) [hereinafter *Plural Utility*] (arguing that the right way to think of utility is as a plurality of vectors).

[63] *See Human Capabilities, supra* note 23, at 85–86; ON ETHICS AND ECONOMICS, *supra* note 62, at 63–64.

[64] *Rights and Capabilities, supra* note 29, at 309.

[65] *Id.*

extremely bad, in all kinds of ways but notoriously in terms of health status.[66] But in the survey, only 2.5 percent of widows, as against 48.5 percent of widowers, reported that they were either ill or in indifferent health. And when the question was just about "indifferent health," as opposed to illness—for which we might suppose there are more public and objective criteria—45.6 percent of widowers said their health was "indifferent," as opposed to zero percent of the widows.[67] The likely explanation for this discrepancy is that people who have regularly been malnourished, who have in addition been told that they are weak and made for suffering, and who, as widows, are told that they are virtually dead and have no rights, will be unlikely to recognize their fatigue and low energy as a sign of bodily disease; but not so for males, who are brought up to have high expectations for their own physical functioning. Sen concludes: "Quiet acceptance of deprivation and bad fate affects the scale of dissatisfaction generated, and the utilitarian calculus gives sanctity to that distortion."[68]

This phenomenon of "adaptive preferences"—preferences that adjust to the low level of functioning one can actually achieve—has by now been much studied in the economic literature,[69] and is generally recognized as a central problem, if one wants to use the utilitarian calculus for any kind of normative purpose in guiding public policy.[70]

We are especially likely to encounter adaptive preferences when we are studying groups that have been persistent victims of discrimination, and who may as a result have internalized a conception of their own unequal worth. It is certain to be true when we are concerned with groups who have inadequate information about their situation, their options, and the surrounding society—as is frequently the case, for example, with women in developing countries. For these reasons, then, the utility-based approach seems inadequate as a basis for offering comparisons of quality of life.

Far more promising is an approach that looks at a group of basic resources and then asks about their distribution, asking, in particular, how well even the worst off

---

66 *Id.*

67 *Id.*

68 *Id.*

69 *See* Jon Elster, *Sour Grapes—Utilitarianism and the Genesis of Wants, in Utilitarianism and Beyond, in* UTILITARIANISM AND BEYOND, *supra* note 57, at 219 (defining adaptive preferences and arguing that their existence poses insuperable problems for utilitarianism); Amartya K. Sen, *Gender and Cooperative Conflicts, in* PERSISTENT INEQUALITIES 123 (Irene Tinker ed., 1990) (arguing that women frequently adjust their expectations to the low level of well-being they can achieve, and that on this account a bargaining model of the family is superior to a utilitarian account).

70 *See* Gary S. Becker, *Nobel Lecture: The Economic Way of Looking at Behavior, in* THE ESSENCE OF BECKER 633, 636–37 (R. Febrero & P. Schwartz eds., 1995) (arguing that the beliefs of employers, teachers, and others that minorities are less productive can be self-fulfilling, causing minorities to underinvest in education and work skills, thus becoming less productive than they would otherwise have been).

citizens are doing with respect to the items on the list. Such is the approach of John Rawls, who, in *A Theory of Justice* and subsequent works, advanced a list of the "primary goods" intended to be items that all rational individuals, regardless of their more comprehensive plans of life, would desire as prerequisites for carrying out those plans.[71] These items include liberties, opportunities, and powers, wealth and income, and the social basis of self-respect. More recently, Rawls has added freedom of movement and the free choice of occupation.[72] The idea is that we measure who is better off and less well-off by using such a list of primary resources; that information is used, in turn, by the parties who are choosing principles of justice. Notice that this list is heterogeneous. Some of its items are capacities of persons such as liberties, opportunities, and powers; and the social basis of self-respect is a complex property of society's relation to persons, but income and wealth are pure resources. And income and wealth frequently play a central role in the measurement of who is better and worse off.[73] Rawls was at pains, moreover, to state that this list of "primary goods" is not a comprehensive theory of what is good or valuable in life.[74] For Rawls, the attraction of operating with a list of resources is that it enables the approach to steer clear of prescribing the basic values of human life, which individuals must be able to select for themselves, in accordance with their own more comprehensive religious or ethical conceptions.

Sen's basic argument against Rawls, for the past twenty years, has been that the space of resources is inadequate as a space within which to answer questions about who is better and who is worse off.[75] The inadequacy derives from the fact that individuals vary greatly in their need for resources and in their ability to convert resources into valuable functionings. Some of these differences are physical. Nutritional needs vary with age, occupation, and sex. A pregnant or lactating woman needs more nutrients than a nonpregnant woman. A child needs more protein than an adult. A person whose limbs work well needs few resources to be mobile, whereas a person with paralyzed limbs needs many more resources to achieve the same level of mobility. Many such variations escape our notice if we live in a prosperous nation that can afford to bring all individuals to a high level of physical

---

71   A THEORY OF JUSTICE, *supra* note 31, at 62, 90–95, 396–97. More recently, Rawls has qualified his view by stating that the primary goods are to be seen not as all-purpose means, but as the needs of citizens understood from a political point of view, in connection with the development and expression of their "moral powers." He has stressed that the account of the moral powers—of forming and revising a life plan—is itself an important part of the political theory of the good. *See* POLITICAL LIBERALISM, *supra* note 31, at 178–90.

72   POLITICAL LIBERALISM, *supra* note 31, at 181.

73   A THEORY OF JUSTICE, *supra* note 31, at 97–98 (discussing different ways of defining the least well off—both favored approaches focus on income and wealth as indicators).

74   POLITICAL LIBERALISM, *supra* note 31, at 187–88.

75   *See Equality of What?*, *supra* note 13, at 364–67; *Gender Inequality*, *supra* note 26, at 263–66.

attainment; in the developing world we must be highly alert to these variations in need. Some of the variations, again, are social, and have to do with traditional social hierarchies. If we wish to bring all citizens of a nation to the same level of educational attainment, we will need to devote more resources to those who encounter obstacles from traditional hierarchy or prejudice. Thus, women's literacy will prove more expensive than men's literacy in many parts of the world. This means that if we operate only with an index of resources, we will frequently reinforce inequalities that are highly relevant to well-being. An approach focusing on resources does not go deep enough to diagnose obstacles that can be present even when resources seem to be adequately spread around, causing individuals to fail to avail themselves of opportunities that they in some sense have, such as free public education, the right to vote, or the right to work.

For this reason, we argue that the most appropriate space for comparisons is the space of capabilities. Instead of asking "How satisfied is person A," or "How much in the way of resources does A command," we ask the question: "What is A actually able to do and to be?" In other words, about a variety of functions that would seem to be of central importance to a human life, we ask: Is the person capable of this, or not? This focus on capabilities, unlike the focus on GNP, or on aggregate utility, looks at people one by one, insisting on locating empowerment in this life and in that life, rather than in the nation as a whole. Unlike the utilitarian focus on satisfactions, it looks not at what people feel about what they do, but about what they are actually able to do.[76] Nor does it make any assumptions about the commensurability of the different pursuits. Indeed, this view denies that the most important functions are all commensurable in terms of a single metric and it treats the diverse functions as all important, and all irreducibly plural.[77] Finally, unlike the focus on resources, it is concerned with what is actually going on in the life in question: not how many resources are sitting around, but how they are actually going to work in enabling people to function in a fully human way.[78]

The distinction just made between the subjective acceptance of a given level of satisfaction and a more objective standard of empowerment for each individual to understand and achieve capabilities has practical implications for human rights action strategies. Recent approaches to human rights education, drawing on Frierian concepts of the pedagogy of the oppressed,[79] stress the distinction between the

---

[76]   Sen has insisted, however, that happiness is "a momentous functioning," in *Well-Being, supra* note 26, at 200, and I have insisted that emotional functioning is one of the important types of functioning that we should consider. *See* Martha C. Nussbaum, *Emotions and Women's Capabilities, in* WOMEN, CULTURE, AND DEVELOPMENT, *supra* note 23, at 360.

[77]   *See Human Capabilities, supra* note 23, at 85–86; *Plural Utility, supra* note 62.

[78]   In this sense, the approach takes its inspiration from Marx's discussion of fully human functioning in several early works in which he was, in turn, much influenced by Aristotle. For discussion of these links, see *Human Nature, supra* note 23, at 119–20.

[79]   *See* PAOLO FREIRE, PEDAGOGY OF THE OPPRESSED (1973).

static teaching of abstract human rights concepts and the transformative pedagogy that engages learners in analyzing the causes of their deprivation and in taking control of the transformation of that reality until they attain a higher level of capability. This idea was captured in a definition agreed upon as a regional workshop on human rights education in the Asia-Pacific region in 1994: "Human rights education is a participative process of developing knowledge, values and skills that will enable people to develop their potentials and emancipate themselves from oppressive social realities."[80] Similarly, Richard Claude defines human rights education as "a process through which people and/or communities increase their control or mastery of their lives and the decisions that affect their lives."[81] Such transformative pedagogies have been developed and applied especially in community based human rights education[82] and for the secondary level as well.[83] Their aim is the practical realization of the theoretical potential revealed by the capabilities approach to human rights insofar as they teach affected populations to reject as inadequate the utilitarian goal of the greatest good and even the liberal goal of Rawls's primary goods and advocate instead the empowerment of each individual to become capable of actually functioning in the fully human way defined in the international human rights texts. Enabling people to develop their potential captures the essence of the capabilities approach.

III. The Central Human Capabilities and Their Correlation to Human Rights

Sen has focused on the general defense of the capability space, and has not offered any official account of what the most central human capabilities are, although in practice he has to some extent done so, by focusing on some areas of human life and not others in constructing the measures used in the Human Development Reports.[84] Again, his recent book on India gives many concrete

---

[80] *Quoted in* RICHARD P. CLAUDE, EDUCATING FOR HUMAN RIGHTS: THE PHILIPPINES AND BEYOND 198 (1996).

[81] RICHARD P. CLAUDE, THE BELLS OF FREEDOM—WITH RESOURCE MATERIALS FOR FACILITATORS OF NON-FORMAL EDUCATION AND 24 HUMAN RIGHTS ECHO SESSIONS 7 (Action Professionals Association for the People, Addis Ababa, Ethiopia, 1996).

[82] In addition to the works cited in notes 80 and 81, *supra*, see numerous examples in RICHARD P. CLAUDE & GEORGE ANDREOPOULOS, HUMAN RIGHTS EDUCATION FOR THE TWENTY-FIRST CENTURY (1997). Other sources on the community education approach include COMMITTEE FOR THE PROTECTION OF DEMOCRATIC RIGHTS (CPDR), KNOW YOUR RIGHTS: A HANDBOOK FOR POLITICAL ACTIVISTS, SOCIAL WORKERS, TRADE UNIONISTS (1980) and INITIATING HUMAN RIGHTS EDUCATION AT THE GRASSROOTS: ASIAN EXPERIENCES, BANGKOK: ASIAN CULTURAL FORUM ON DEVELOPMENT (Clarence J. Dias ed., 1992).

[83] *See, e.g.*, BETTY REARDON, EDUCATING (Denver, Center for Teaching International Relations, 1988).

[84] *See supra* notes 17–18 and accompanying text.

examples of the importance and the interrelationships of various concrete human capabilities.[85] I, by contrast, have focused on the task of producing such a working list, describing a methodology by which we might both generate and justify such a list[86] and defending the whole project of giving such a list against the objections of relativists and traditionalists.[87] The list is supposed to be a focus for political planning, and it is supposed to select those human capabilities that can be convincingly argued to be of central importance in any human life, whatever else the person pursues or chooses. The central capabilities are not just instrumental to further pursuits; they are held to have value in themselves, in making a life fully human. But they are held to have a particularly central importance in everything else we plan and choose. In that sense, central capabilities play a role similar to that played by primary goods in Rawls's more recent account; they support our powers of practical reason and choice, and have a special importance in making any choice of a way of life possible. They thus have a special claim to be supported for political purposes in societies that otherwise contain a great diversity of views about the good. I do not think of the political sphere in exactly the way that Rawls conceives it, since I do not make the assumption that the nation-state should be the basic deliberative unit,[88] and the account is meant to have broad applicability to cross-cultural deliberations. Nonetheless, the basic point of the account is the same: to put forward something that people from many different traditions, with many different fuller conceptions of the good, can agree on as the necessary basis for pursuing their good life.[89]

The list is an attempt to summarize the empirical findings of a broad and ongoing cross-cultural inquiry. As such, it is open-ended and humble; it can always be contested and remade. It does not claim to read facts of "human nature" off of biological observation, although it does of course take account of biology as a relatively constant element in human experience. Nor does it deny that the items on the list are to some extent differently constructed by different societies. Indeed, part of the idea of the list is that its members can be more concretely specified in accordance with local beliefs and circumstances. In that sense, the consensus it hopes to

---

[85] See, e.g., JEAN DRÈZE & AMARTYA K. SEN, INDIA: ECONOMIC DEVELOPMENT AND SOCIAL OPPORTUNITY 13–16, 109–39 (1995) (discussing the relationship between health and education and other capabilities); id. at 155–178 (discussing the relationship between gender inequality and women's functioning and capability). For an enumeration of all the examples Sen has given in a variety of different works, see Functioning and Capability: Part 1 and Functioning and Capability: Part 2, supra note 25.

[86] This is especially evident in Human Nature, supra note 23, at 90–95.

[87] See Human Capabilities, supra note 23, at 67–72, 93–95; Human Functioning, supra note 23; Women and Cultural Universals, supra note 23, at 12–20.

[88] For an excellent discussion of this question, and a critique of Rawls with which I largely agree, see THOMAS W. POGGE, REALIZING RAWLS 211–80 (1989).

[89] See The Good as Discipline, The Good as Freedom, supra note 23, at 324, where I have stressed this political-liberal role of the capabilities list more than in previous papers.

evoke has many of the features of the "overlapping consensus" described by Rawls.[90]

Here is the current version of the list,[91] revised as a result of my recent visits to development projects in India.[92] Most of the central capabilities correspond to the essence of the rights proclaimed in the Universal Declaration which, in turn, have been reaffirmed by the expanding membership of the international community and resoundingly reaffirmed in their entirety on the fiftieth anniversary of the Universal Declaration.[93] Their mention in the international texts contributes to the cross-cultural basis of the list, and in this sense the Declaration becomes a source, an evidentiary element, in defining the good. To illustrate this correlation, the following table records both the basic capabilities that I have identified and the corresponding article of the Universal Declaration.

1. *Life.* Being able to live to the end of a human life of normal length; not dying prematurely, or before one's life is so reduced as to be not worth living.	Article 3 on right to life.
2. *Bodily Health.* Being able to have good health, including reproductive health; to be adequately nourished; to have adequate shelter.	Article. 25, further defined in Article 12 of the ICESCR as the "highest attainable level of physical and mental health."
3. *Bodily Integrity.* Being able to move freely from place to place; to be secure against violent assault, including sexual assault and domestic violence; having opportunities for sexual satisfaction and for choice in matters of reproduction.	Articles 3, 4, 5 and 13, although domestic violence, sexual satisfaction, and reproductive choice were not sufficiently well-established in 1948 for the overwhelmingly male drafters to include them.

---

90   POLITICAL LIBERALISM, *supra* note 31, *passim.*

91   The list is compatible with, but less abstract and more detailed than, the four "welfare values" (wealth, well-being, skills, enlightenment) and four "deference values" (power, respect, rectitude, affection) upon which the so-called New Haven School of Jurisprudence is premised. *See* MCDOUGAL ET AL., *supra* note 27.

92   The primary changes are a greater emphasis on bodily integrity, a focus on dignity and non-humiliation, and an emphasis on control over one's environment. Oddly, these features of human "self-sufficiency" are the ones most often criticized by Western feminists as "male" and "Western"—one reason for their more muted role in earlier versions of the list. *See* MARTHA C. NUSSBAUM, THE FEMINIST CRITIQUE OF LIBERALISM, THE LINDLEY LECTURE (University of Kansas, 1997); *see also* SEX AND SOCIAL JUSTICE, *supra* note 23.

93   *See* Commission on Human Rights Res. 1998/56, adopted Apr. 17, 1998 (declaring "solemnly its commitment to the fulfillment of the Universal Declaration of Human Rights as a common standard of achievement for all peoples and all nations. . . .").

4. *Senses, Imagination, and Thought.* Being able to use the senses; being able to imagine, to think, and to reason, and to do these things in a "truly human" way, a way informed and cultivated by an adequate education, including, but by no means limited to, literacy and basic mathematical and scientific training. Being able to use imagination and thought in connection with experiencing and producing expressive works and events of one's own choice, religious, literary, musical, and so forth. Being able to use one's mind in ways protected by guarantees of freedom of expression with respect to both political and artistic speech and freedom of religious exercise. Being able to have pleasurable experiences and to avoid non-beneficial pain.

Articles 18 on freedom of thought, conscience, and religion; Article 19 on freedom of opinion and expression; Article 26 on the right to education, which "shall be directed to the full development of the human personality"; Article 27 on participation in cultural life.

5. *Emotions.* Being able to have attachments to things and people outside ourselves; to love those who love and care for us, to grieve at their absence; in general, to love, to grieve, to experience longing, gratitude, and justified anger. Not having one's emotional development blighted by fear and anxiety. Supporting this capability means supporting forms of human association that can be shown to be crucial in their development.

Articles 12 and 16, although privacy, non-interference with family and the right to marry and found a family are manifestations of a much broader idea of capabilities regarding emotions.

6. Being able to form a conception of the good and to engage in critical reflection about the planning of one's life. This entails protection for the liberty of conscience and religious observance.

Article 18 on freedom of thought, conscience, and religion.

7. *Affiliation.*

   A. *Friendship.* Being able to live for and to others, to recognize and show concern for other human beings, to engage in various forms of social interaction; to be able to imagine the situation of another and to have compassion for that situation; to have the capability for

Article 1, mentioning "spirit of brotherhood[sic.]"; Article 18 on thought and conscience; Article 19 on opinion and expression; Article 20 on peaceful assembly and association; Article 29 on duties to the community and respect for the rights of others and

both justice and friendship. Protecting this capability means, once again, protecting institutions that constitute such forms of affiliation, and also protecting the freedoms of assembly and political speech.

    B. *Respect*. Having the social bases of self-respect and non-humiliation; being able to be treated as a dignified being whose worth is equal to that of others. This entails provisions of non-discrimination on the basis of race, sex, ethnicity, caste, religion, and national origin.

"just requirements of morality, public order and general welfare in a democratic society."

Article 1 on equality in dignity and rights; Article 2 on non-discrimination.

8. *Other Species*. Being able to live with concern for and in relation to animals, plants, and the world of nature.

This concern is found in international environmental instruments and in several draft texts on human rights and the environment, but not in the Universal Declaration, except by implication in Article 28.

9. *Play*. Being able to laugh, to play, and to enjoy recreational activities.

Article 24 relative to rest and leisure

10. *Control Over One's Environment*.
    A. *Political*. Being able to participate effectively in political choices that govern one's life; having the right of political participation, protections of free speech and association.

Article 21 on political participation; Article 19 on speech; Article 20 on association

    B. *Material*. Being able to hold property (both land and movable goods); having the right to employment; having freedom from unwarranted search and seizure.

Article 17 on property; Article 23 on right to work and free choice of employment; Article 12 on non-interference in privacy, family, home or correspondence

    This list is, emphatically, a list of separate and indispensable components. We cannot satisfy the need for one of them by giving a larger amount of another. All are of central importance and all are distinct in quality and thus may be understood, in the official language of rights of the United Nations, as "universal, indivisible and interdependent and interrelated,"[94] which is often ritualized rhetoric in compromise resolutions on human rights but which, in the context of central human capabilities, acquires practical significance. Practical reason and affiliation, I argue

---

[94]   Vienna Declaration and Programme of Action, *supra* note 3, para. 5.

elsewhere, are of special importance because they both organize and suffuse all the other capabilities, making their pursuit truly human. The individual importance of each component limits the trade-offs that it will be reasonable to make, and thus limits the applicability of quantitative cost-benefit analysis. At the same time, the items on the list are related to one another in many complex ways. One of the most effective ways of promoting women's control over their environment, and their effective right of political participation, is to promote women's literacy. Women who can seek employment outside the home have more resources in protecting their bodily integrity from assaults within it.

IV. Capability of Goal: Rights as Entitlements and Rights as Policy Objectives

"Reflecting varying environmental circumstances, differing world views, and inescapable interdependencies within and between value processes," writes Burns Weston, "human rights refer to a wide continuum of value claims ranging from the most justiciable to the most aspirational. Human rights partake of both the legal and the moral orders, sometimes indistinguishably. They are expressive of both the 'is' and the 'ought' in human affairs."[95] In practice, depending upon observational perspective, human rights are viewed either as legal entitlements that are immediately justiciable before courts or as guiding aspirational principles that all branches of government should keep in mind as general propositions even if not as specific prescriptions to resolve specific cases.[96] Commonly, the issue of these competing approaches to human rights is erroneously reduced to the distinction—made at the time of the elaboration of the two 1966 covenants[97]—between, on the one hand, civil and political rights which supposedly are freedoms from state interference and immediately applicable and justiciable, and, on the other hand, economic, social, and cultural rights which are claims against the state for benefits to be provided progressively as resources allow. Rightist thinkers have attempted a philosophical justification of this approach.[98] A more recent development assumes that all human

---

[95] Weston, *supra* note 4.

[96] In the United States, courts tend to regard human rights treaties as "non-self-executing"—i.e., as not automatically justiciable—and the Senate commonly attaches reservations, understandings, and declarations (RUDs) to the ratification of human rights treaties so as to ensure that they will not create automatically justiciable rights. The most pertinent and, in my view, outrageous example is the set of RUDs attached to the U.S. ratification of the 1966 International Covenant on Civil and Political Rights, *supra* note 11. See Louis Henkin, *U.S. Ratification of Human Rights Conventions: The Ghost of Senator Bricker*, 89 AM. J. INT'L L. 341 (1995).

[97] *See infra* Appendices II and III.

[98] The distinction was used to rationalize the position of the U.S. government during the Reagan and Bush administrations to the effect that economic, social, and cultural rights are not rights properly so-called, but, rather, laudable social goals that governments should pur-

rights—civil, cultural, economic, political, and social—are not only interdependent but of equal legal and moral validity, and thus focuses on the nature of obligations to realize rights. According to this view, the duty-holder (usually the state) has the triple obligation to "respect" (not to commit a violation), to "ensure respect" or to "protect"(not to allow others to violate), and to "fulfill" (provide the means to realize).[99] Depending on the object of the right (freedom from torture or access to education, for example), one or the other of these obligations predominates. Without all three, human rights remain abstractions that the right-holder possesses in theory but does not enjoy in practice. The distinction between capability and functioning underlies this approach to obligation in the human rights field.

But how are capability and functioning related? Understanding this relationship is crucial in defining the relation of the "capabilities approach" to both liberalism and human rights theories. For if we were to take functioning itself as the goal of public policy, the liberal would rightly judge that we were precluding many choices that citizens may make in accordance with their own conceptions of the good, and perhaps violating their human rights. A deeply religious person may prefer not to be well-nourished, but instead prefer to engage in strenuous fasting. Whether for religious or for other reasons, a person may prefer a celibate life to one containing sexual expression. A person may prefer to work with an intense dedication that precludes recreation and play. Am I declaring, by my very use of the list, that these are not fully human or flourishing lives? And am I instructing government to nudge or push people into functioning of the requisite sort, no matter what they prefer?

It is important that the answer to these questions is no. Capability, not functioning, is the political goal. Capability must be the goal because of the great importance the capabilities approach attaches to practical reason, as a good that both suffuses all the other functions, making them human rather than animal,[100] and figures itself as a central function on the list. It is perfectly true that functionings, not simply capabilities, are what render a life fully human: if there were no functioning of any kind in a life, we could hardly applaud it, no matter what opportunities it contained. Nonetheless, for political purposes it is appropriate for us to strive for capabilities, and those alone. Citizens must be left free to determine their course after they have the capabilities. The person with plenty of food may always choose to fast, but there is a great difference between fasting and starving, and it is this difference that we wish to capture. Again, the person who has normal opportunities

---

sue but to which the citizen possesses no entitlement. *See* U.S. Dep't State, Country Reports on Human Rights Practices for 1992, at 5 (1993).

[99] On the distinction, see Adbjørn Eide, *Economic, Social and Cultural Rights as Human Rights, in* 2 Economic, Social and Cultural Rights: A Textbook 37–40 (A. Eide et al. eds., 1995). It was recently applied in the Maastricht Guidelines on Violations of Economic, Social and Cultural Rights, *supra* note 44. *See also* text accompanying *supra* note 44.

[100] *See Human Nature, supra* note 23, at 119–20 (discussing Marx).

for sexual satisfaction can always choose a life of celibacy, and we say nothing against this. What I speak against, for example, is the practice of female genital mutilation, which deprives individuals of the opportunity to choose sexual functioning, and indeed, the opportunity to choose celibacy as well.[101] A person who has opportunities for play can always choose a workaholic life. Again, there is a great difference between that chosen life and a life constrained by insufficient maximum-hour protections and/or the "double day" that make women unable to play in many parts of the world.

I can make the issue clearer, and also prepare for discussion of the relationship between capabilities and rights, by pointing out that there are three different types of capabilities that figure in my analysis.[102] First, there are what I call *basic capabilities*: the innate equipment of individuals that is the necessary basis for developing the more advanced capability. Most infants have from birth the basic capability for practical reason and imagination, though they cannot exercise such functions without a lot more development and education. Second, there are *internal capabilities*: that is, states of the person herself that are, so far as the person herself is concerned, sufficient conditions for the exercise of the requisite functions. A woman who has not suffered genital mutilation has the internal capability for sexual pleasure; most adult human beings everywhere have the internal capability to use speech and thought in accordance with their own conscience. Finally, there are *combined capabilities*,[103] which I define as internal capabilities combined with suitable external conditions for the exercise of the function. A woman who is not mutilated but is secluded and forbidden to leave the house has internal but not combined capabilities for sexual expression—and work, and political participation. Citizens of repressive nondemocratic regimes have the internal but not the combined capability to exercise thought and speech in accordance with their conscience.

The aim of public policy is the production of combined capabilities. This idea means promoting the states of the person by providing the necessary education and care, as well as preparing the environment so that it is favorable for the exercise of practical reason and the other major functions.[104] The Universal Declaration

---

101 See Martha C. Nussbaum, *Religion and Women's Human Rights, in* RELIGION AND CONTEMPORARY LIBERALISM 93, 107–10 (Paul J. Whiteman ed., 1997) [hereinafter *Religion and Women's Human Rights*]; Martha C. Nussbaum, *Double Moral Standards?*, BOSTON REV., Oct.–Nov. 1996, at 28, 30 (replying to Yael Tamer's *Hands Off Clitoridectomy*, BOSTON REV., Summer 1996, at 21-22).

102 See *Human Capabilities, supra* note 23, at 88 (discussing the basic capabilities); *Nature, Function, and Capability, supra* note 22, at 160–64 (referring to Aristotle's similar distinctions). Sen does not use these three levels explicitly, although many things he says assume some such distinctions.

103 In earlier papers I called these "external capabilities." *See, e.g., Nature, Function, and Capability, supra* note 22, at 164. But Crocker has suggested to me that this suggests a misleading contrast with "internal."

104 This distinction is related to Rawls's distinction between social and natural primary

expresses this idea clearly in Article 28: "Everyone is entitled to a social and international order in which the rights and freedoms set forth in this declaration can be fully realized."[105] The most philosophically coherent interpretation of this article, and potentially the most powerful exhortation of the Universal Declaration for the second half century of its life, is based on the capabilities approach. Specifically, the human rights of the Universal Declaration and its progeny cannot be realized unless and until the social, economic, and political conditions prevailing domestically and internationally ensure each rights-holder the combined capability to exercise the rights he or she may desire. This means that their internal capabilities (called "human potential" in many human rights texts) are combined with the social order, including the legal regime and the economic and social conditions, so that they can express a controversial idea, attain sexual pleasure, secure free public education, or escape from poverty if they wish.

This explanation of the types of capability clarifies the link between capabilities and human rights. I am not saying that public policy should rest content with internal capabilities, but remain indifferent to the struggles of individuals who have to try to exercise these capabilities in a hostile environment. In that sense, my approach is highly attentive to the goal of functioning, and instructs governments to keep functioning always in view. On the other hand, I am not pushing individuals into the function; once the stage is fully set, the choice is up to them. My approach clarifies the international human rights formulation "Everyone has the rights to" or "States Parties recognize the right of everyone to". It is implicit in each such proposition that the right in question shall be exercised only if the right-holder so chooses.

The matter is confused when human rights texts also enumerate duties, thus shattering the distinction between capabilities and functioning. Once a text purporting to affirm rights stipulates duties, the factor of choice is eliminated. The expression of duties in the Universal Declaration does not suffer this defect as it states that "[e]veryone has duties to the community in which alone the free and full development of his personality is possible."[106] The problem arises more commonly in constitutional texts that enumerate a set of duties along with rights, usually to pay taxes, to defend the fatherland, to support the government's development policy or socialist system, to protect the constitution against all enemies foreign and domestic, etc. The idea of a declaration of duties is not new. Thomas Paine wrote

---

goods. A Theory of Justice, *supra* note 31, at 62. Whereas he holds that only the social primary goods should be on the list, and not the natural (such as health and imagination), we say that the social basis of the natural primary goods should most emphatically be on the list.

105 The drafters had in mind a democratic society domestically and the United Nations Charter internationally. Ideological East-West confrontations at the beginning of the Cold War, however, precluded a more explicit definitions the vague "social and international order."

106 UDHR, *infra* Appendix I, art. 29.

disapprovingly of recommendations for a *separate* declaration of duties to accompany the 1789 French Declaration of the Rights of Man and the Citizen when that Declaration was before the French National Assembly: "A Declaration of Rights is, by reciprocity, a Declaration of Duties also. Whatever is my right as a man is also the right of another; and it becomes my duty to guarantee as well as to possess."[107] This approach to duties, maintained in the Universal Declaration, may be interpreted as meaning that everyone has the duty to allow others to exercise the choice implicit in the concept of functionings. The enumeration of other "duties" goes beyond the "duty to guarantee" to which Paine referred. From this perspective, it was a particularly unhelpful initiative of the InterAction Council of former heads of state to draft and recommend for adoption on the occasion of the fiftieth anniversary of the Universal Declaration a "Universal Declaration of Human Responsibilities."[108] The task for human rights and for sustainable human development is to realize combined capabilities, not restrict the choices open to each individual by confusing rights with responsibilities.

The approach of basic, internal, and combined capabilities is very close to Rawls's approach using the notion of primary goods.[109] We can see the list of capabilities as like a long list of opportunities for life-functioning, such that it is always rational to want them whatever else one wants. If one ends up having a plan of life that does not make use of all of them, one has hardly been harmed by having the chance to choose a life that does. Indeed, in the cases of fasting and celibacy it is the very availability of the alternative course that gives the choice its moral value. The primary difference between this capabilities list and Rawls's list of primary goods is its length and definiteness, and in particular its determination to include the social basis of several goods that Rawls has called "natural goods," such as "health and vigor, intelligence and imagination."[110] Since Rawls has been willing to put the social basis of self-respect on his list, it is not at all clear why he has not made the same move with imagination and health.[111] Rawls's evident concern is that no society can guarantee health to its individuals—in that sense, saying that the goal is full external capability may appear unreasonably idealistic. Some of the

---

[107] THOMAS PAINE, *supra* note 5, at 189.

[108] The text proposed by the InterAction Council is available on the Internet at <http://www.asiawide.or.jp/iac/declara 1/.> (visited Jan. 5, 1999).

[109] A THEORY OF JUSTICE, *supra* note 31, at 62, 90–95.

[110] *Id.* at 62.

[111] Rawls comments that "although their possession is influenced by the basic structure, they are not so directly under its control." *Id.* This is of course true if we are thinking of health, but if we think of the social basis of health, it is not true. It seems to me that the case for putting these items on the political list is just as strong as the case for the social basis of self-respect. In *The Priority of Right and Ideas of the Good*, 17 PHIL. & PUB. AFF. 251, 257 (1988), Rawls suggests adding leisure time and the absence of pain to the list. He makes the same suggestion in POLITICAL LIBERALISM, *supra* note 31, at 181–82. For Rawls' current treatment of health, see *id.* at 184.

capabilities—for example, some of the political liberties—can be fully guaranteed by society, but many others involve an element of chance and cannot be so guaranteed. My response to this concern is that the list—whether of basic capabilities or of rights in the Universal Declaration—is a list of political goals that should be useful as a benchmark for aspiration and comparison. Even though individuals with adequate health support often fall ill, it still makes sense to compare societies by asking about actual health-capabilities, since we assume that the comparison will reflect the different inputs of human planning, and can be adjusted to take account of more and less favorable natural situations. Sometimes, however, it is easier to get information on health achievements than on health capabilities; to some extent we must work with the information we have, while not forgetting the importance of the distinction.

In saying these things about the political goal, we focus on adults who have full mental and moral powers—what Rawls calls "normal cooperating members of society."[112] Children are different, since we are trying to promote the development of adult capabilities. We may in some cases be justified in requiring functioning of an immature child, as with compulsory primary and secondary education, but we must always justify coercive treatment of children with reference to the adult-capability goal. This is precisely what the Universal Declaration does by including as part of the "right to education" free, *compulsory* primary education.[113] A balance between recognizing the choice to functioning by a child in areas where the child's internal capabilities are developed and withholding such choice to allow the development of those capabilities is struck also in the 1989 Convention on the Rights of the Child.[114] The careful elaboration of that text over a ten-year period resulted in the recognition of a considerable degree of children's capability and therefore of their rights.

Earlier versions of the list appeared to diverge from the approach of Rawlsian liberalism by not giving as large a place to the traditional political rights and liberties—although the need to incorporate them was stressed from the start.[115] This version of the list corrects that defect of emphasis. These political liberties have a central importance in rendering well-being human. A society that aims at well-being while overriding these liberties has delivered to its members a merely animal level of satisfaction.[116] As Sen has recently written: "Political rights are important not only for the fulfillment of needs, they are crucial also for the formulation of needs. And this idea relates, in the end, to the respect that we owe each other as fellow

---

112 POLITICAL LIBERALISM, *supra* note 31, at 183.

113 UDHR, *infra* Appendix I, art. 26. The right in question is further elaborated in Article 13 of the International Covenant on Economic, Social and Cultural Rights, *infra* Appendix II.

114 G.A. Res. 44/25 (Annex), U.N. GAOR 44th Sess., Supp. No. 49, at 166, U.N. Doc. A/44/49 (1990), *reprinted in* 3 Weston III.D.3, *supra* note 2.

115 *See Aristotelian Social Democracy, supra* note 23, at 239–40.

116 *See Human Nature, supra* note 23, at 110–120.

human beings."[117] This idea of freedoms as need has recently been echoed by Rawls: primary goods specify what citizens' needs are from the point of view of political justice.[118] It also is present in the first twenty articles of the Universal Declaration which, along with the elaborate set of subsequent, related international standards, cover all the political and civil rights more thoroughly than either Rawls's list or my own.

The capability view justifies its elaborate list by pointing out that choice is not pure spontaneity, flourishing independently of material and social conditions. If one cares about people's powers to choose a conception of the good, then one must care about the rest of the form of life that supports those powers, including its material conditions. Thus, the approach claims that its more comprehensive concern with flourishing is perfectly consistent with the impetus behind the Rawlsian project. Rawls has always insisted that we are not to rest content with merely formal equal liberty and opportunity, but that we must pursue their fully equal worth by ensuring that unfavorable economic and social circumstances do not prevent people from availing themselves of liberties and opportunities that are formally open to them.[119]

The guiding thought behind this form of Aristotelianism is, at its heart, a profoundly liberal idea,[120] and one that lies at the heart of Rawls's project and the Universal Declaration as well: the idea of the citizen as a free and dignified human being, a maker of choices.[121] Politics here has an urgent role to play, providing citizens with the tools that they need, both in order to choose at all and in order to have a realistic option of exercising the most valuable functions. The idea that civil and political rights are a necessary but not sufficient condition for economic, social, and cultural rights expresses the same relationship. The choice of whether and how to use the tools, however, is left up to the citizens, in the conviction that this choice is an essential aspect of respect for their freedom. They are seen not as passive recipients of social patterning, but as dignified free beings who shape their own lives.[122]

V. Rights and Capabilities: Two Different Relationships

How, then, are capabilities related to human rights? We can see, by this time, that there are two rather different relations that capabilities have to the human rights

---

117 *Freedoms and Needs, supra* note 31, at 38.

118 POLITICAL LIBERALISM, *supra* note 31, at 187–88.

119 A THEORY OF JUSTICE, *supra* note 31, at 83–90, 224–27.

120 Though in one form Aristotle had it too. *See Human Nature, supra* note 23, at 110–120.

121 *See* A THEORY OF JUSTICE, *supra* note 31, at 251–57; *Freedoms and Needs, supra* note 31, at 38.

122 *Cf. Freedoms and Needs, supra* note 31, at 38 ("The importance of political rights for the understanding of economic needs turns ultimately on seeing human beings as people with rights to exercise, not as parts of a 'stock' or a 'population' that passively exists and must be looked after. What matters, finally, is how we see each other.").

traditionally recognized by international human rights instruments. In what follows, I shall understand a human right in the same way as the Universal Declaration, namely as involving an especially urgent and morally justified claim that a person has, simply by virtue of being a human,[123] and independently of membership in a particular nation, or class, or sex, or ethnic or religious or sexual group.[124]

First, there are some areas in which the best way of thinking about rights is to see them as combined capabilities to function in various ways. The right to political participation, the right to religious free exercise, the freedom of speech, the freedom to seek employment outside the home, and the freedom from unwarranted search and seizure are all best thought of as human capacities to function in ways that we then go on to specify. The further specification will usually involve both an internal component and an external component: a citizen who is systematically deprived of information about religion does not really have religious liberty, even if the state imposes no barrier to religious choice. On the other hand, internal conditions are not enough: women who can think about work outside the home, but who are going to be systematically denied employment on account of sex, or beaten if they try to go outside, do not have the right to seek employment. In short, to secure a right to a citizen in these areas is to put them in a position of capability to go ahead with choosing that function if they should so desire. This understanding of what securing rights means should be part of the interpretation of the underlying aim of the Universal Declaration, set out in its final preambular paragraph: "to secure their universal and effective recognition and observance." To "secure . . . effective . . . observance" can be and should be interpreted to mean that the rights-holder must be put in a position of capability to choose the function expressed by the essence of each of the rights proclaimed.

Of course, there is another way in which we use the term "right" in which it could not be identified with a capability. We say that A has "a right to" seek employment outside the home, even when her circumstances obviously do not secure such a right to her. When we use the term "human right" this way, we are saying that just by virtue of being human, a person has a justified claim to have the capability secured to her: so a right in that sense would be prior to capability, and a ground for the securing of a capability. "Human rights" used in this sense lie very close to what I have called "basic capabilities," since typically human rights are thought to derive from some actual feature of human persons, some untrained power in them

---

[123] The reference to "human" does not take into account the relatively minor limitations on the rights recognized for children.

[124] *Cf.* Weston, *supra* note 4 ("if a right is determined to be a human right it is understood to be quintessentially general or universal in character, in some sense equally possessed by all human beings everywhere, including in certain instances even the unborn. In stark contrast to "the divine right of kings" and other such conceptions of privilege, human rights extend in theory to every person on earth without discriminations irrelevant to merit, simply for being human").

that demands or calls for support from the world. Rights theories differ about which basic capabilities of the person are relevant to rights, but the ones most commonly chosen are the power of reasoning, generally understood to be moral reasoning, and the power of moral choice.[125]

On the other hand, when we say, as we frequently do, that citizens in country C "have the right of free religious exercise," what we typically mean is that this urgent and justified claim is being answered, that the state responds to the claim that they have just by virtue of being human. It is in this sense that capabilities and rights should be seen to be equivalent: As I have said, combined capabilities are the goals of public planning.

Why is it a good idea to express rights, so understood, in terms of capabilities? I think this approach is a good idea because we then understand that what is involved in securing a right to people is usually a lot more than simply putting it down on paper. We see this very clearly in India, for example, where the Constitution is full of guarantees of Fundamental Rights that are not backed up by effective state action. Thus, since ratification women have had rights of sex equality—but in real life they are unequal not only *de facto*, but also *de jure*. This inequality results from the fact that most of the religious legal systems that constitute the entire Indian system of civil law have unequal provisions for the sexes, very few of which have been declared unconstitutional.[126] So we should not say that women have equal rights, since they do not have the capabilities to function as equals. Again, women in many nations have a nominal right of political participation without really having this right in the sense of capability: for they are secluded and threatened with violence should they leave the home. This is not what it is to have a right. In short, thinking in terms of capability gives us a benchmark in thinking about what it is really to secure a right to someone.

There is another set of rights, largely those in the area of property and economic advantage, which seem to me analytically different in their relationship to capabilities. Take, for example, the right to a certain level of income, or the right to shelter and housing, expressed in the Universal Declaration as the "right to a stan-

---

[125]   This way of thinking derives from the ancient Stoic tradition, continued through Cicero and on into Grotius and Kant. *See* Martha C. Nussbaum, *Kant and Stoic Cosmopolitanism*, 5 J. POL. PHIL. 1 (1997) [hereinafter *Kant and Stoic Cosmopolitanism*]; Martha C. Nussbaum, *The Incomplete Feminism of Musonius Rufus: Platonist, Stoic, and Roman*, Paper presented at the Conference on Gender and Sexual Experience in Ancient Greece and Rome, Finnish Academy in Rome (June 22–25, 1997) (on file with the author).

[126]   *See Religion and Women's Human Rights, supra* note 101, at 121–26 (reviewing this situation). Typically, only small and unpopular religions get their laws thrown out. Thus, the Christian inheritance law—or one of them, since Christians in India are governed by a bewildering variety of different systems of Christian law—was declared unconstitutional on grounds of sex equality, but the attempt to set aside a part of the Hindu marriage act on these grounds was reversed at the Supreme Court level. *Id.* at 108.

dard of living adequate for the health and well-being of himself and of his family, including food, clothing, housing and medical care. . . ."[127] These are rights that can be analyzed in a number of distinct ways, in terms of resources, or utility, or capabilities. We could think of the right to a decent level of living as a right to a certain level of resources; or, less plausibly, as a right to a certain level of satisfaction; or as a right to attain a certain level of capability to function.

Once again, we must distinguish the use of the term "right" in the sentence "A has a right to X," from its use in the sentence "Country C gives citizens the right to X." All human beings may arguably have a right to something in the first sense, without being in countries that secure these rights. If a decent living standard is a human right, then American citizens have that right although their state does not give them, or secure to them, such a right. So far, then, we have the same distinctions on our hands that we did in the case of the political liberties. But the point I am making is that at the second level, the analysis of "Country C secures to its citizens the right to a decent living standard" may plausibly take a wider range of forms than it does for the political and religious liberties, where it seems evident that the best way to think of the secured right is as a capability. The material rights may, by contrast, plausibly be analyzed in terms of resources, or possibly in terms of utility.

An interesting controversy erupted during the Second United Nations Conference on Human Settlements (Habitat II) in Istanbul, in June 1996. The United States delegation strongly resisted efforts to include in the final document any reference to the "right to housing" as such. It proposed instead that the text refer to "adequate shelter for all" and "enablement."[128] While the concept of "enablement" may be seen as an element of the concept of capabilities and functionings, it does not address the responsibility of the state when the real estate industry, acting under the law of supply and demand, fails to make a significant dent in the problem of homelessness. It is here that the link between the human rights language and capabilities makes practical sense. The concept of "enabling environment" leaves open the possibility that an environment that holds out the potential for alleviating homelessness fails to do so in fact. The state is off the hook because the enabling environment—here the free operation of the real estate industry—exists. The concept of capabilities restores the obligation of result and makes it possible to talk of a right to housing.

Indeed this is the approach of the International Covenant on Economic, Social and Cultural Rights.[129] The right in question is expressed in language similar to the Universal Declaration: the "right of everyone to an adequate standard of living for

---

[127] UDHR, *infra* Appendix I, art. 25 (1).

[128] Draft Statement of Principles and Commitment and Global Plan of Action, The Habitat Agency, Preparatory Committee for the United Nations Conference on Human Settlements (Habitat II), U.N. Doc. A/CONF.165/PC.3/4, paras. 13, 24–25, 28–29 (Oct. 24, 1995).

[129] *See infra* Appendix II.

himself and his family, including adequate food, clothing and housing, and to the continuous improvement of living conditions."[130] However, the Covenant further stipulates that the "States Parties will take appropriate steps to ensure the realization of this right, recognizing to this effect the essential importance of international co-operation based on free consent."[131] The first part of this provision suggests that states parties must place persons within their jurisdiction in the position of being capable of having shelter, while suggesting, in the second part, that voluntarily-given foreign aid and technical cooperation through Specialized Agencies is most likely going to be necessary for poor countries to realize this right. Moreover, the entire Covenant is conditioned by the general obligation of each state party

> to take steps, individually and through international assistance and cooperation, especially economic and technical, to the maximum of its available resources with a view to achieving progressively the full realization of the rights recognized in the present Covenant by all appropriate means, including particularly the adoption of legislative measures.[132]

The reference to resources is crucial. The adoption of legislative measures, except with regard to legislation allocating resources for the national budget, is only marginally relevant to the issue of capabilities expressed in terms of allocation of resources.

Here again, however, I think it is valuable to understand these rights, insofar as we decide we want to recognize them, in terms of capabilities. That is, if we think of a right to a decent level of living as a right to a certain quantity of resources, then we get into the very problems I have pointed to; that is, giving the resources to people does not always bring differently situated people up to the same level of functioning. If you have a group of people who are traditionally marginalized, you are probably going to have to expend more resources on them to get them up to the same living standard—in capability terms—than you would for a group of people who are in a favorable social situation.

Analyzing economic and material rights in terms of capabilities would thus enable us to understand, as we might not otherwise, a rationale we might have for

---

130 *Id.* art. 11 (1).

131 *Id.*

132 *Id.* art. 2 (1). On the interpretation of this general obligation, see Philip Alston & Gerard Quinn, *The Nature and Scope of States Parties' Obligations under the International Covenant on Economic, Social and Cultural Rights*, 9 HUM. RTS. Q. 156 (1987). The Committee on Economic, Social and Cultural Rights has interpreted this obligation in its General Comment No. 3. *See* Committee on Economic, Social and Cultural Rights, General Comment 3 [the nature of states parties' obligations (art. 2(1))] of the Covenant, Fifth Sess., 1990), COMPILATION OF GENERAL COMMENTS AND GENERAL RECOMMENDATIONS ADOPTED BY HUMAN RIGHTS TREATY BODIES, U.N. Doc. HRI/GEN/1/Rev.12, at 45 (1994).

spending unequal amounts of money on the disadvantaged, or creating special programs to assist their transition to full capability. The Indian government has long done this. In fact, affirmative action in this sense for formerly despised caste and tribal groups was written into the Constitution itself, and it has played a crucial role in creating the situation we have today, in which lower-caste parties form part of the ruling government coalition. Indeed, one could also argue that even to secure political rights effectively to the lower castes required this type of affirmative action. If we think of these economic rights asking the question—"What are people actually able to do and to be?"—then I think we have a better way of understanding what it is really to put people securely in possession of those rights, to make them able really to function in those ways, not just to have the right on paper. This way of thinking has also practical implications for understanding what states parties must do to comply with their obligations under the International Covenant on Economic, Social and Cultural Rights. The acknowledgment on paper of the right is not sufficient; securing the right as a capability is closer to meeting the duties imposed on the state by the Covenant.

If we have the language of capabilities, do we still need, as well, the language of rights? The language of rights still plays, I believe, four important roles in public discourse, despite its unsatisfactory features. When used in the first way, as in the sentence "A has a right to have the basic political liberties secured to her by her government," rights language reminds us that people have justified and urgent claims to certain types of urgent treatment, no matter what the world around them has done about that. I have suggested that this role of rights language lies very close to what I have called "basic capabilities," in the sense that the justification for saying that people have such natural rights usually proceeds by pointing to some capability-like feature of persons that they actually have, on at least a rudimentary level, no matter what the world around them has done about that. And I actually think that without such a justification the appeal to rights is quite mysterious. On the other hand, there is no doubt that one might recognize the basic capabilities of people and yet still deny that this entails that they have rights, in the sense of justified claims, to certain types of treatment. We know that this inference has not been made through a great deal of the world's history, though it is false to suppose that it only was made

---

[133] On Indian discussions of religious pluralism and liberty, see Amartya K. Sen, *Human Rights and Asian Values*, NEW REPUBLIC, July 14 & 21, 1997, at 33–40. For a related discussion of Indian conceptions of pluralism, see Amartya K. Sen, *Tagore and His India*, N.Y. REV. BOOKS, June 26, 1997, at 55–56. For other non-Western perspectives, see Marks, *supra* note 16, at 480–86, and references *supra* at note 3. On the Greek and Roman origins of ideas of human rights, see Fred D. Miller, Jr., *Nature, Justice, and Rights*, in ARISTOTLE'S POLITICS (1995) (arguing that Aristotle's political theory contains the basic ingredients of a theory of rights); *Nature, Function, and Capability, supra* note 22 (arguing that Aristotle's political theory contains the view that the job of politics is to distribute to citizens the things that they need for a flourishing life); *Kant and Stoic Cosmopolitanism, supra* note 125, (arguing that Kant's view of basic human rights is in many ways indebted to the views of the Greek and Roman Stoics).

in the West, or that it only began in the Enlightenment.[133] So, appealing to rights communicates more than appealing to basic capabilities: it says what normative conclusions we draw from the fact of the basic capabilities.

Even at the second level, when we are talking about rights guaranteed by the state, the language of rights places great emphasis on the importance and the basic role of these things. To say, "Here's a list of things that people ought to be able to do and to be" has only a vague normative resonance. To say, "Here is a list of fundamental rights," means considerably more. It tells people right away that we are dealing with an especially urgent set of functions, backed up by a sense of the justified claim that all humans have to such things, by virtue of being human. This is the essence of the role of the Universal Declaration; it reaffirms in a list of normative propositions the claims that people may consider fundamental to their human-ness.

Third, rights language has value because of the emphasis it places on people's choice and autonomy. The language of capabilities, as I have said, was designed to leave room for choice, and to communicate the idea that there is a big difference between pushing people into functioning in ways you consider valuable and leaving the choice up to them. At the same time, if we have the language of rights in play as well, I think it helps us to lay extra emphasis on this very important fact: that what one ought to think of as the benchmark are people's autonomous choices to avail themselves of certain opportunities, and not simply their actual functionings.

Finally, in the areas where there is disagreement about the proper analysis of right talk—where the claims of utility, resources, and capabilities are still being worked out—the language of rights preserves a sense of the terrain of agreement, while we continue to deliberate about the proper type of analysis at the more specific level. Rights language thus limits the areas that can be bargained away in a policy compromise. For example, a wide range of justifiable limitations may be placed on freedom of speech for reasons of public safety, order, morals, national security and other reasons, but rights language precludes the policy option of replacing freedom of speech with a residual principle of censorship.

One further point should be made. I have discussed one particular view about human capabilities and functioning, my own, and I have indicated its relationship to Sen's very similar view. But of course there are many other ways in which one might construct a view based on the idea of human functioning and capability without bringing capabilities nearly so close to rights. As I have suggested, the view Sen and I share is a liberal view of human capabilities, which gives a strong priority to traditional political and religious liberties, and which focuses on capability as the goal precisely in order to leave room for choice. In addition, as I have more recently stressed, the items on my list of basic capabilities are to be regarded as the objects of a specifically political consensus, rather like a Rawlsian list of primary goods, and not as a comprehensive conception of the good. The Universal Declaration and its many progeny are manifestation of such a specific political consensus. In spite of the tendency to call them immutable and inalienable, the fact is that the lists of rights in these texts are the result of political bargaining. Other lists are possible and other formulations of the rights reaffirmed are conceivable. They are not the exhaustive, definitive definition of the good expressed in terms of rights; they are a very good approximation of a consensus about what capabilities should be provided by every society to its citizens.

A capabilities theorist might construct a view that departed from our view in all of these ways. First, the content of the list might be different: it might not give the same importance to the traditional liberal freedoms. Second, government might be given much more latitude to shoot directly for functioning as a goal, and to penalize people who do not exhibit the desired mode of functioning. Such, indeed, is the strategy of some natural-law thinkers in the Catholic tradition, and in this regard they are closer to Aristotle himself than I am.[134] In that sense, as I have written, they construe the account of the human good as a source of public discipline on the choices of citizens, whereas we construe the good as an account of freedoms citizens have to pursue a variety of different plans of life. Finally, one might think of the account of human functioning as a comprehensive conception of human flourishing for both public and private purposes, rather than as the object of a specifically political consensus. Again, natural law theorists sometimes understand the view this way, as does Aristotle himself—although some Catholic thinkers have themselves adopted a political-liberal interpretation of their tradition.[135] Insofar as any of these alternatives are pursued, the relationship between capabilities and rights will shift accordingly.

VI. Rights as Goals and Side-Constraints

One final question remains to be discussed. Sen has argued that thinking of rights in terms of capabilities should lead us to opt for a particular way of thinking about rights and to reject another way. Specifically, it should encourage us to think of rights as goals, and thus as part of a more general account of social goals that it is reasonable to promote, rather than to think of them as "side-constraints," or as justified claims of individuals that should be respected no matter what, and that thus constrain the ways in which we may promote our social goals.[136] Since Sen's target here is the libertarian theory of Robert Nozick, and since I believe his critique has force primarily *ad hominem* against Nozick, and not against all versions of a side-constraints view, I must describe Nozick's position.

---

134 *See* FINNIS, *supra* note 39; GEORGE, *supra* note 39. For a detailed discussion of differences between the Sen/Nussbaum view and those views in a range of areas of public policy, see *The Good as Discipline, The Good as Freedom, supra* note 23.

135 For an eloquent example, see Jacques Maritain, *Truth and Human Fellowship, in* JACQUES MARITAIN, ON THE USE OF PHILOSOPHY: THREE ESSAYS 16, 24–29 (1961). It is significant from our perspective to recall that Maritain was influential in placing the Universal Declaration in a philosophical context and in supporting the text. *See* JACQUES MARITAIN, AU TOUR DE LA DÉCLARATION UNIVERSELLE DES DROITS DE L'HOMME (UNESCO, 1948).

136 *Rights and Capabilities, supra* note 29; *Rights as Goals, supra* note 9; *Rights and Agency, supra* note 29.

Nozick's basic argument, in *Anarchy, State, and Utopia*,[137] is that people have rights, in the sense—apparently, since no account of rights is presented—that these rights should not be overridden for the sake of the greater good. The rights people have are a function of their initial entitlements, together with a theory of just transfer. One of the notoriously frustrating aspects of Nozick's theory is that he refuses to present his own account of initial entitlements, although he alludes to a controversial interpretation of Locke, in order to illustrate the type of thing he has in mind. Through this process, he derives the view—which must be advanced tentatively, since the account of initial entitlement has not been given—that people have a right to the property they hold, just in case they acquired it by a series of just transfers from the original owners. It is wrong of the state to take any of this property away from them for redistributive purposes. Nozick focuses on property throughout the book, and says little about political, religious, and artistic liberty.

Nozick's theory has been criticized in a number of ways. First of all, in the absence of a theory of initial entitlement, it is very difficult to see what the upshot will be, and thus impossible to know whether a procedural conception of justice like Nozick's will produce results that are acceptable or quite bizarre and unacceptable. And of course one might answer questions about entitlement very differently from the way in which Nozick seems inclined to answer them, saying, for example, that individuals are never entitled to any property they do not need for their own use, or that they are never entitled to accumulate a surplus. Such, for example, was Aristotle's view of entitlement, and this meant that for Aristotle the very existence of private ownership of land was a highly dubious business.[138] In Aristotle's ideal city, fully half of the land is publicly owned, and the rest is "common in use," meaning its produce can be taken by anyone who is in need.[139] So Aristotle's view of entitlement, combined with his strong moral distaste for hoarding and accumulation, would certainly not yield the Nozickian conclusion that: "Capitalist acts between consenting adults are no crime."

Second, it has been pointed out that even if individuals do have entitlements to what they have acquired in a just transfer, it does not follow that they are entitled to the surplus value of these goods, when for contingent reasons they rise in value during the time they hold them. In fact, even the Lockean tradition is much divided on this question.[140]

Third, one might point out that the economic inequalities apparently tolerated in Nozick's minimal state would erode the meaningful possession of other rights that Nozick apparently thinks people have, such as the right to political participation. Nozick nowhere confronted possible tensions between two parts of his libertarian

---

[137] *Supra* note 9.

[138] *See Aristotelian Social Democracy, supra* note 23, at 203–06, 231–32.

[139] *See id.* at 205.

[140] Barbara Fried, *Wilt Chamberlain Revisited: Nozick's "Justice in Transfer" and the Problem of Market-Based Distribution*, 24 Phil. & Pub. Aff. 226 (1995).

view, so we do not even know whether he would be willing to tax people in order to get the money to support the institutions that make meaningful political and religious liberties for all a social reality. In these ways, his attitude toward rights remained obscure.

Fourth, the view of self-ownership on which much of Nozick's argument rested was both rather obscure and somewhat questionable.[141] What does it mean to say of people that they own themselves, and how, precisely, does and should this affect arguments on a variety of topics, from the morality of slavery to the legality of prostitution?

These are only some of the ways in which one might criticize Nozick's view. Let me now describe Sen's critique. Sen argues that if we allow rights to function the way Nozick says they should, as "side-constraints" that can almost never be overridden for the sake of the general good, then we will be led to tolerate an unacceptable level of misery.

The question I am asking is this: if results such as starvation and famines were to occur, would the distribution of holdings still be morally acceptable despite their disastrous consequences? There is something deeply implausible in the affirmative answer. Why should it be the case that rules of ownership, etc., should have such absolute priority over life-and-death questions? But once it is admitted that consequences can be important in judging what rights we do or do not morally have, surely the door is quite open for taking a less narrow view of rights, rejecting assessment by procedures only.[142]

Sen seems to be saying two things not easily made compatible. First, that Nozick has given the wrong account of what rights people have: they do not have the right to keep their surplus when others are dying. Second, that the consideration of consequences shows that the type of view of rights Nozick advances must be wrong: a side-constraints view is implausible, and we should think of rights as parts of a total system of social goals. But if the first point is correct, as I believe it certainly is, then we have had as yet no reason to accept the second claim. If we question the whole way Nozick thinks about what people's rights and entitlements are, as we most certainly should, then we have no reason to think that a correct list of rights should not be used as side-constraints.

This realization is important, since a list of human rights typically functions as a system of side-constraints in international deliberation and in internal policy debates. That is, we typically say to and of governments, let them pursue the social good as they conceive it, so long as they do not violate the items on this list. I think this is a very good way of thinking about the way a list of basic human rights should function in a pluralistic society, and I have already said that I regard my list of basic capabilities this way, as a list of very urgent items that should be secured to people

---

141 G.A. COHEN, SELF-OWNERSHIP, FREEDOM, AND EQUALITY 1–115 (1995).

142 *Rights and Capabilities, supra* note 29, at 312.

no matter what else we pursue. In this way, we are both conceiving of capabilities as a set of goals—a subset of total social goals—and saying that they have an urgent claim to be promoted, whatever else we also promote. Indeed, the point made by Sen, in endorsing the Rawlsian notion of the priority of liberty, was precisely this.[143] We are doing wrong to people when we do not secure to them the capabilities on this list. The traditional function of a notion of rights as side-constraints is to make this sort of anti-utilitarian point, and I see no reason why rights construed as capabilities—or analyzed in terms of capabilities—should not continue to play this role.

The theory of democratic constitutionalism, which is at the foundation of liberalism, focuses on that same balancing of utilitarian choices made by a democratic legislature, on the one hand, and side-constraints in the form of constitutional protected rights—including by extension applicable international human rights instruments—on the other. Jürgen Habermas considers that "[d]emocracy and human rights form the universalist core of the constitutional state. . . ."[144] The capabilities approach enriches the concept of liberal, constitutional democracy. The expression of the popular will does not extend to violating constitutionally protected human rights. If those rights are understood as capabilities, the democratic function would not include the taking of measures that reduce the capabilities of citizens to exercise their rights. It would include the duty to adopt legislation that goes beyond the formal recognition of constitutionally—or internationally—protected rights and contributes to putting citizens in the position of enjoying the rights in practice.

Of course there will be circumstances in which we cannot secure to all the citizens the capabilities on my list. Sen and I have argued that the political liberties and liberties of conscience should get a high degree of priority within the general capability set.[145] But we also conceive of the capabilities as a total system of liberty, whose parts support one another. Thus we also hold that there is something very bad about not securing any of the items. The precise threshold level for many of them remains to be hammered out in public debate; but there are surely levels easy to specify, beneath which people will have been violated in unacceptable ways if the capabilities are not secured. Viewing capabilities as rather like side-constraints also helps here: for it helps us to understand what is tragic and unacceptable in such situations, and why individuals so treated have an urgent claim to be treated better, even when governments are in other ways pursuing the good with great efficiency.

---

[143] *See Freedoms and Needs, supra* note 31, at 32 (defending the Rawlsian priority of liberty).

[144] JÜRGEN HABERMAS, BETWEEN FACTS AND NORMS: A CONTRIBUTION TO A DISCOURSE THEORY OF LAW AND DEMOCRACY 465 (1996).

[145] *See Religion and Women's Human Rights, supra* note 101, at 113–14 (religious liberty); *Freedoms and Needs, supra* note 31, at 32–38; *The Good as Discipline, The Good as Freedom, supra* note 23, at 314–21 (defending the general liberal approach); *id.* at 332–33 (political liberty).

The capabilities approach discussed in this essay builds on an understanding of human rights only vaguely alluded to in the Universal Declaration of Human Rights. Nevertheless, it fits well within the normative framework of the Declaration and offers a valuable tool for assessing compliance with the rights it reaffirms and that are set out in the numerous instruments that have built upon it. The array of national and international procedures and programs for the implementation of those human rights standards are public policy aimed at the production of combined capabilities, as understood in this essay.

The Universality of Human Rights in a Multicultured World: Toward Respectful Decision-Making

Burns H. Weston*

I. Delimitation of the Problem

Values are preferred events, "goods" we cherish; and, as pointed out by McDougal, Lasswell, and Chen in their germinal treatise on *Human Rights and World Public Order*,[1] the value of respect, "conceived as the reciprocal honoring of freedom of choice about participation in value processes,"[2] is "the core value of all human

---

* I am greatly indebted to my former research assistant, Mark Teerink, for invaluable creative thought and friendship, and to my wife, Marta Cullberg Weston, and several admired friends for perceptive comments: David Baldus, Upendra Baxi, Stephen Burton, John Dugard, Richard Falk, Michael Reisman, Jerome Shestack, Serena Stirer, and Andrew Willard. I thank them all. For documentation of divese cultural practices and related tasks, I thank also my present research assistant, Bassel El-Kasaby, and my former reasearch assistant, the late Erich D. Mathias, who tragically lost his life in a winter storm on January 8, 1999. I dedicate this essay to Erich's memory, which resonates with intellect, compassion, and a fierce commitment to social justice worldwide.

1 *See* MYRES S. MCDOUGAL, HAROLD D. LASSWELL & LUNG-CHU CHEN, HUMAN RIGHTS AND WORLD PUBLIC ORDER: THE BASIC POLICIES OF AN INTERNATIONAL LAW OF HUMAN DIGNITY (1980). My indebtedness to this treatise is apparent throughout.

2 *Id.* at 7. A subsequent elaboration on this brief definition reveals that the authors impose an individualistic perspective on the meaning of the value of "respect." They write: "In the fundamental sense with which we are here concerned [*i.e*, with respect as the core value of human rights], respect is defined as an interrelation *among individual human beings* in which they reciprocally recognize and honor each other's freedom of choice about participation in the value processes of the world community or any of its component parts." *Id.* at 451 (emphasis added). They continue, at 452 (emphasis again added):

> In more precise specification, respect may be said to entail four particular outcomes:
>
> 1. A fundamental freedom of choice for all *individuals* regarding participation in all value processes;
>
> 2. An equality of opportunity for all *individuals* to have experiences that enable them to enjoy the widest range of effective choice in their interactions with others and to participate in all value processes in accordance with capability, that is, without discrimination for reasons irrelevant to capability;

rights."[3] In a world of diverse cultural traditions that is simultaneously distinguished by the widespread universalist claim that "human rights extend in theory to every person on earth without discriminations irrelevant to merit,"[4] the question thus unavoidably arises: when, in international human rights decision-making, are cultural differences to be respected and when are they not?

A decade ago, this question was greeted, at least initially, with a surprising perplexity when Iran's Ayatollah Khomeini issued a death threat against British novelist Salman Rushdie for publication of *The Satanic Verses*[5] and, as well, a *fatwa* to suppress its distribution. Outrage at this theocratic salvo, condemned by Western leaders as "deeply offensive to the norms of civilized behavior,"[6] was duly recorded, to be sure. But a palpable hesitancy and timidity in its expression at the time, discernible especially at the beginning of the episode, suggested a concern for more than diplomatic niceties. It suggested also a haunting uncertainty as to whether the forceful advocacy of free conscience and speech was not simply giving voice to a set of idiosyncratic biases of one's own, neither wanted nor relevant in a faraway Islamic land shaken by claimed apostasy. Perhaps haunted by the absolute that there are no absolutes, supposed universal human rights ran up against the variability of human culture.

Of course, the Rushdie affair is only one of a long history of occasions in which the universal validity of moral judgments has been called into question. The following table, listing (according to the physical and behavioral dimensions of human

---

3. Additional rewards in deference to *individuals* who make preeminent contribution to common interests; and

4. An aggregate pattern of social interactions in which all *individuals* are protected in the utmost freedom of choice and subjected to the least possible governmental and private coercion.

No explanation or justification is given by the authors for this individualistic skew. And just as well. I see no reason why this otherwise useful definition of the value of respect cannot and should not apply to *groups* of human beings as well as to individual members of the human family. To the contrary, a more inclusive definition, even one that extends to animate and inanimate nature, is more in keeping with the very idea of human rights, certainly of *universal* human rights.

3   *Id.* at xvii.

4   Burns H. Weston, *Human Rights*, 20 ENCYCLOPAEDIA BRITANNICA 714 (15th ed. 1998 prtg.), *updated and revised in* ENCYCLOPAEDIA BRITANNICA ONLINE (visited Dec. 1, 1998) <http://www.eb.com:180/cgi-bin/g?DocF=macro/5002/93.html>. Reconsidering this phrase, I am today inclined to add "capability" to "merit" (and possibly also "basic need" insofar as is not a function of "capability") as potentially a permissible basis for discrimination in otherwise equal arenas of claim and decision.

5   SALMAN RUSHDIE, THE SATANIC VERSES (1988).

6   Statement of President George Bush, *quoted in* N.Y. TIMES, Feb. 22, 1989, at 1, col. 6. For equivalent comments by the Ministers of Foreign Affairs of the European Community, including reference to "the universal values of tolerance, freedom and respect for international law," see N.Y. TIMES, Feb. 21, 1989, at 6, col. 1.

Physical Practices	Behavioral Practices

1. Abortion
  a. Mandatory
  b. Permitted, prohibited
2. Cannibalism
3. Corporal disfigurement
  a. Foot binding
  b. Genital cutting
    (1) Male (*e.g.*, circumcision)
    (2) Female genital cutting
    (FGC, a/k/a "FGM" and
    "FGS")[7]
  c. Scarring, tatooing
4. Corporal punishment
  a. Public (state imposed/
    sanctioned)
    (1) Amputation
    (2) Caning, flogging, lashing,
      spanking, whipping
    (3) Death/Execution
      (a) Electric chair
      (b) Firing squad
      (c) Hanging
      (d) Lethal injection
      (e) Stoning
  b. Private (*e.g.*, familial)
    (1) Spanking, slapping,
      whipping
    (2) "Honor killing"
5. Euthanasia
6. Genocide, "ethnic cleansing"
7. Imprisonment
  a. Life
  b. Solitary
  c. Hard labor
8. Infanticide
9. Torture (physical, mental)
	1. Banishment, "ethnic cleansing,"
	  ostracization
	2. Discrimination, segregation
	  a. Age
	  b. Caste/Class
	  c. Ethnicity
	  d. Gender, sexual orientation
	  e. Health (*e.g.*, HIV, lepers)
	  f. Merit/Basic Need
	  g. Nationality
	  h. Political opinion
	  i. Race
	  j. Religion
	3. Divorce, separation
	  a. Unilateral
	4. Dress codes
	  a. Body covering
	  b. Veil wearing
	5. Marriage
	  a. Arranged child marriage
	  b. Bride price, dower
	  c. Forced marriage
	  d. Homosexual
	  e. Polygamy/polygyny
	6. Slavery, forced labor
	7. State-sponsored deprivations
	  a. Civil/political deprivations
	    (1) Assembly, association
	    (2) Expression, opinion, speech
	    (3) Other
	  b. Economic/social deprivations
	    (1) Education
	    (2) Employment
	    (3) Other

---

7   "Female genital cutting" (FGC) is a value-neutral term that I borrow from *The New York Times* and other newspapers to avoid the pre-judgment bias of the expression "female genital mutilation" or "FGM." I choose the term in lieu of "female genital surgery" or "FGS" because this latter expression implies a greater degree of precision and refinement in the

existence,[8] and in alphabetical order) cultural practices well-known for the cross-cultural controversies they generate or might generate, demonstrates how this is so (although it is not presumed that the two lists comprising the table are exhaustive or altogether unambiguous[9]). And the more the process of global modernization unfolds and accompanying "culture contact" grows, the more are such occasions likely to arise in the future and to insist upon answers.

By way of illustration, consider the practices of child betrothal and fixed marriage widespread in the "Third World." Sooner or later one must ponder Article 16 of the Universal Declaration of Human Rights (UDHR) proclaiming that "[m]en and women of full age, without any limitation due to race, nationality or religion, have the right to marry and found a family" and "only with the free and full consent of the intending spouses."[10] Similarly, in light of the communitarian traditions prevalent in sub-Saharan Africa of defining an individual's existence and status primarily with reference to birthright, sex, age, and group membership, or, alternatively, the occasional Hindu and Muslim traditions of segregating women (*Harem, Purdah*), one must puzzle over the reach of the Universal Declaration's guarantees of equality and nondiscrimination irrespective of "race, colour, sex, language, religion, political or other opinion, national or social origin, property, birth or other status."[11] Such illustrations of the possible nonuniversality of alleged universal human rights are of course many and in no way restricted to "Third World" settings. The long-standing resistance of the capitalist countries, particularly the United States, to economic and social rights, and of the communist countries, past and present, to civil and political rights, even if less intense today than in earlier times,

---

practice than I believe is empirically warranted overall. I thus do not follow entirely in the footsteps of two very insightful essays on the subject that likewise have sought linguistic neutrality in discourse about it: Isabelle Gunning, *Arrogant Perception, World Traveling and Multi-Cultural Feminism: The Case of Female Genital Surgeries*, 23 COLUM. HUM. RTS. L. REV. 189, 227 (1991) and Hope Lewis, *Between Irua and "Female Genital Mutilation": Feminist Human Rights Discourse and the Cultural Divide*, 8 HARV. HUM. RTS. J. 1 (1993). Lewis usefully distinguishes between three types of "female genital surgery" or "FGS" (her terms): (1) circumcision, known as "Sunna" ("traditional"), "is the mildest but also rarest form" of FGS, involving "the removal of the clitoral prepuce"; (2) excision which entails the amputation of the clitoris, and most (or all) of the labia minora; and (3) infibulation, known as Pharoanic circumcision, entailing "the amputation of the clitoris, the whole of the labia minora" and most of the labia majora. *Id*. at 5.

8   The inner existential (spiritual) dimension of human existence does not seem apt for separate categorization inasmuch as all cultural practices for which relativist claims have been or might be made appear to affect the human psyche in some way, mental or psychological torture most directly of course.

9   It is believed, however, that behaviors not expressly identified here will fit comfortably into one or the other of the groupings comprising the table above.

10   *See infra* Appendix I [hereinafter UDHR].

11   *Id*. art. 2.

attest to this fact. So too does the fact that the "right to life" set forth in Article 3 of the UDHR is challenged as much by abortion and nuclear weapons policies in the industrialized world as it is by the practices of infanticide and female sacrifice (*e.g.*, Sati) in "pre-modern" societies. And when one adds to the mix the fact that disagreements over claimed universal human rights exist not only in respect of their substantive identification but, as well, and probably more frequently, with regard to their interpretation and enforcement, the argument of cultural relativism, a term borrowed from anthropology and moral philosophy[12] to claim that there are no overarching moral truths and that local customs and traditions therefore fundamentally determine the existence and scope of rights in any given society,[13] may be seen to loom rather large.

The issue remains with us today. Since 1989 especially, when cultural variabilities were freed from the silencing grip of Cold War loyalties, it has been forcefully argued in several—particularly Asian—quarters that, as Pascal observed some three centuries ago, what may be truth on one side of the Pyrenées may be error on the other ("Verité au-deçà des Pyrenées, erreur au-delà.");[14] and in the wake of such assertions, there ensued not a little debate among governmental officials, scholars, and others about the extent to which, if at all, cultural particularities should be allowed to determine the existence and scope of rights promised to individuals and groups by the UDHR[15] and related universalist human rights instruments[16]—for

---

[12]   For helpful explication, see Fernando R. Tesón, *International Human Rights and Cultural Relativism*, 25 VA. J. INT'L L. 869, 885–88 (1985).

[13]   "Relativists make an argument of the following kind: for too long western civilization has been obsessed with finding concrete and objective truths. Yet no consensus has formed around the various offerings. This is so precisely because there have never been truths to be found. Therefore, we should recognize that there is no truth beyond ourselves and the institutions we create; and, in admitting this, we should recognize the limitations of our convictions." John F. G. Hannaford, *Truth, Tradition, and Confrontation: A Theory of International Human Rights*, 31 CAN. Y.B. INT'L L. 151, 152 (1993).

[14]   BLAISE PASCAL, PENSÉES 135 (Garnier-Flammarion ed. 1976) (1897).

[15]   UDHR, *infra* Appendix I.

[16]   Anticipating this debate, see especially JACK DONNELLY, UNIVERSAL HUMAN RIGHTS IN THEORY AND PRACTICE (1989); RELATIVISM: INTERPRETATION AND CONFRONTATION (Michael Krausz ed., 1989); ADAMANTIA POLLIS & PETER SCHWAB, HUMAN RIGHTS: CULTURAL AND IDEOLOGICAL PERSPECTIVES (1979); RETHINKING HUMAN RIGHTS: CHALLENGES FOR THEORY AND ACTION (Smithu Kothari & Harsh Sethi eds., 1989); Howard R. Berman, *Are Human Rights Universal?*, INTERCULTURE 83 (Jan.–June 1984); Jack Donnelly, *Cultural Relativism and Human Rights*, 6 HUM. RTS. Q. 400 (1984); Cornelius F. Murphy, Jr., *Objections to Western Conceptions of Human Rights*, 9 HOFSTRA L. REV. 433 (1981); Raimundo Pannikar, *Is the Notion of Human Rights a Western Concept?*, 120 DIOGENES 75 (1982); Tesón, *supra* note 12, at 869. Among the many post-Cold War contributions to the debate should be noted at least the following: ASIAN PERSPECTIVES ON HUMAN RIGHTS (Claude E. Welch & Virginia Leary eds., 1990); DONALD BROWN, HUMAN UNIVERSALS (1991); WILLIAM THEODORE DE

example, the International Covenant on Economic, Social and Cultural Rights (ICE-SCR)[17] and its companion International Covenant on Civil and Political Rights

BARY, ASIAN VALUES AND HUMAN RIGHTS: A CONFUCIAN COMMUNITARIAN PERSPECTIVE (1998); HUMAN RIGHTS AND CHINESE VALUES (Michael C. Davis ed., 1995); HUMAN RIGHTS IN CROSS-CULTURAL PERSPECTIVE: A QUEST FOR CONSENSUS (Abdullahi A. An-Na'im ed., 1992); RHODA E. HOWARD, HUMAN RIGHTS AND THE SEARCH FOR COMMUNITY (1995); HUMAN RIGHTS IN AFRICA: CROSS-CULTURAL PERSPECTIVES (Abdullahi A. An-Na'im & Francis M. Deng eds., 1990); AKIRA IRIYE, CULTURAL INTERNATIONALISM AND WORLD ORDER (1997); CHANDRA MUZAFFAR, HUMAN RIGHTS AND THE NEW WORLD ORDER (1993); ALISON D. RENTELN, INTERNATIONAL HUMAN RIGHTS: UNIVERSALISM VS. RELATIVISM (1990); THE EAST ASIAN CHALLENGE FOR HUMAN RIGHTS (Joanne R. Bauer & Daniel A. Bell eds., 1999); Anne E. Bayefsky, *Cultural Sovereignty, Relativism, and International Human Rights: New Excuses for Old Strategies*, 9 RATIO JURIS 42 (1996); Daniel A. Bell, *The East Asian Challenge to Human Rights: Reflections on an East-West Dialogue*, 18 HUM. RTS. Q. 641 (1996); Christina M. Cerna, *Universality of Human Rights and Cultural Diversity: Implementation of Human Rights in Different Socio-Cultural Contexts*, 16 HUM. RTS. Q. 740 (1994); Michael C. Davis, *Constitutionalism and Political Culture: The Debate over Human Rights and Asian Values*, 11 HARV. HUM. RTS. J. 109 (1998); Richard A. Falk, *False Universalism and the Geopolitics of Exclusion: The Case of Islam*, 18 THIRD WORLD Q. 7 (1997); Carolyn Fluehr-Lobban, *Cultural Relativism and Universal Rights*, CHRON. HIGHER EDUC., June 9, 1995, at B1; Thomas M. Franck, *Is Personal Freedom a Western Value?*, 91 AM. J. INT'L L. 593 (1997); Yash Ghai, *Human Rights and Governance: The Asia Debate*, 15 AUSTL. Y. B. INT'L L. 1 (1994); Hannaford, *supra*, note 13, at 151; Rhoda E. Howard, *Dignity, Community, and Human Rights*, in HUMAN RIGHTS IN CROSS-CULTURAL PERSPECTIVE: A QUEST FOR CONSENSUS (Abdullahi A. An-Na'im ed., 1992); Bilahari Kausikan, *East and Southeast Asia and the Post-Cold War International Politics of Human Rights*, 92 FOR. POL'Y 24 (1993); Bilahari Kausikan, *An Asian Approach to Human Rights*, 89 AM. SOC'Y INT'L L. PROC. 152 (1995); Kim Dae Jung, *Is Culture Destiny?*, 73 FOR. AFF., No. 6, at 189 (Nov./Dec. 1994); Ann E. Mayer, *Universal vs. Islamic Human Rights: A Clash of Cultures or a Clash with a Construct?*, 15 MICH. J. INT'L L. 307 (1994); Dianne Otto, *Rethinking the "Universality" of Human Rights Law*, 29 COLUM. HUM. RTS. L. REV. 1, 11 (1997); Adamantia Pollis, *Cultural Relativism Revisited: Through the State Prism*, 18 HUM. RTS. Q. 316 (1996); Prabhakar, *Values? Whose Values?*, GLOBAL TIMES 14 (May 1996); Arati Rao, *The Politics of Gender and Culture in International Human Rights Discourse*, in WOMEN'S RIGHTS, HUMAN RIGHTS 167 (Julie Peters & Andrea Wolper eds., 1995); Alison D. Renteln, *A Cross-Cultural Approach to Validating Human Rights*, in HUMAN RIGHTS: THEORY AND MEASUREMENT 7 (David L. Cingranelli ed., 1988); Amartya K. Sen, *Human Rights and Asian Values* (Sixteenth Morgenthau Memorial Lecture on Ethics and Foreign Policy, Carnegie Council on Ethics and International Affairs, 1997); Jennifer Schirmer, *The Dilemma of Cultural Diversity and Equivalency in Universal Human Rights Standards*, in HUMAN RIGHTS AND ANTHROPOLOGY (Theodore E. Downing & Gilbert Kirschner eds., 1998); George Weigel, *Are Human Rights Universal?*, COMMENTARY, Feb. 1995, at 43; Burns H. Weston, *The Extension of Human Rights in a Divided World*, in LES DROITS DE L'HOMME: UNIVERSALITÉ: 1789–1989, at 363 (Guy Braibant & Gérard Marcou eds., 1990). Fareed Zakaria, *A Conversation with Lee Kuan Yew*, 73 FOR. AFF., No.2, at 109 (Apr./May 1994).

17   See *infra* Appendix II [hereinafter ICESCR].

(ICCPR)[18] which, together with the Universal Declaration, constitute what has come to be called the "International Bill of Human Rights." To be sure, as the Rushdie affair alone suggests, the issue is not a new one. As Jerome Shestack has correctly observed, "[f]rom time to time during the nineteenth and early twentieth centuries, the claims of *Volkgeist* arose . . . in the European political context of ultranationalism versus universalist principles of Enlightenment philosophy."[19] Also, the debate appears to have slackened somewhat since 1997 when the collapse of certain Asian economies helped to propagate a heightened awareness of fundamental interdependencies and thus to lessen a bit "the clash of civilizations"[20] in some at least temporary measure.[21] Nevertheless, given the riot of ideological, philosophical, and religious divisions that prevail worldwide even as the globalization of capital renders us ever more homogenous, the issue remains contentious and therefore important. The interplay between the landmark 1993 Vienna Declaration and Programme of Action[22] adopted by acclamation by 172 states participating in the U.N. World Conference on Human Rights that produced it and the provocatively relativist Bangkok Declaration that emanated from the 1993 Regional Meeting of Asian and Pacific States preparatory to the Vienna Conference[23] makes this clear. The

---

[18]   *See infra* Appendix III [hereinafter ICCPR].

[19]   Jerome J. Shestack, *The Philosophical Foundations of Human Rights*, 20 HUM. RTS. Q. 201, 229 (1998).

[20]   The phrase belongs to SAMUEL P. HUNTINGTON, THE CLASH OF CIVILIZATIONS AND THE REMAKING OF WORLD ORDER (1996). For a lyrical critique of Professor Huntington's "clash of civilizations" thesis, see Frederick S. Tipson, *Culture Clash-ification: A Verse to Huntington's Curse*, 76 FOR. AFF. No. 2, at 166, 167 (Mar.–Apr. 1997).

[21]   Writes Richard Falk:

> The main energy associated with the assertion of "Asian Values" accompanied "the Asian economic miracle." The successful achievement of sustained economic growth in an atmosphere of political stability apparently gave Asian leaders the confidence to defend against international criticism by recourse to civilizational arguments, including critiques of the West as arrogant and as itself suffering the adverse social consequences of decadence and permissiveness. The Asian crisis, which shows no signs of an early abatement, has seemingly diverted attention from the cultural dimensions of its relations with the West.

Richard A. Falk, *A Half Century of Human Rights: Geopolitics and Values, supra* in this volume, at p. 1, 19. *Cf.* Amitai Etzioni, *The End of Cross-Cultural Relativism*, 22 ALTERNATIVES—SOCIAL TRANSFORMATION AND HUMANE GOVERNANCE 177 (1997) (arguing that cultural relativism is—and should be—in full-scale retreat).

[22]   Adopted June 25, 1993, the Declaration may be found in REPORT OF THE WORLD CONFERENCE ON HUMAN RIGHTS, U.N. Doc. A/CONF.157/24 (pt. I) (Oct. 13, 1993), at 20–46, *reprinted in* 32 I.L.M. 1661 *and* 3 INTERNATIONAL LAW AND WORLD ORDER: BASIC DOCUMENTS III.U.2 (Burns H. Weston ed., 5 vols., 1994–   ) [hereinafter 3 Weston].

[23]   Adopted Mar. 29–Apr. 3, 1993, U.N. Doc. A/CONF/93, *reprinted in* 14 HUM. RTS. L. J. 370 (1993). The Declaration was based heavily on a proposal authored by China. *See* Jin Yongjian, *Asia's Major Human Rights Concerns*, BEIJING REV. (April 19–25, 1993).

Bangkok Declaration, after reaffirming a "commitment to principles contained in the Charter of the United Nations and the Universal Declaration of Human Rights,"[24] stresses "the urgent need to . . . ensure a positive, balanced and non-confrontational approach to addressing and realizing all aspects of human rights";[25] emphasizes "the principles of respect for national sovereignty and territorial integrity as well as non-interference in the internal affairs of States, and the non-use of human rights as an instrument of political pressure";[26] and recognizes that "while human rights are universal in nature, they must be considered in the context of a dynamic and evolving process of international norm-setting, bearing in mind the significance of national and regional particularities and various historical, cultural and religious backgrounds. . . ."[27] In language renunciative but reminiscent of this Bangkok Declaration, the 1993 Vienna Declaration provides that

> [a]ll human rights are universal, indivisible and interdependent and inter-related. The international community must treat human rights globally in a fair and equal manner, on the same footing, and with the same emphasis. While the significance of national and regional particularities and various historical, cultural and religious backgrounds must be borne in mind, it is the duty of States, regardless of their political, economic and cultural systems, to promote and protect all human rights and fundamental freedoms.[28]

This outcome, Dianne Otto observes, "can be read as supporting either the universalist or relativist position."[29] It "reflects the paralysis of the debate," she adds, "and leaves the issue firmly on the international human rights agenda for another day."[30] While Otto exaggerates, I think, the impact of the relativist position on the Vienna Declaration, judging from recent lectures, conferences, and symposia honoring the fiftieth anniversary of the UDHR she correctly opines that the relativist-universalist debate itself remains strong on the human rights agenda.[31]

A survey of the literature reveals that the vast majority of commentators choose not an analytically neutral position but, rather, one that champions one side of the debate or the other. It also reveals that the greatest number, most of them intellectually indebted or otherwise sympathetic to Western thought and tradition (doubtless because they are the most likely to have ready access to the relevant journals,

---

24   *Id.* pmbl.

25   *Id.* para. 3.

26   *Id.* para. 5.

27   *Id.* para 8.

28   *Supra* note 22, para. 5

29   Otto, *supra* note 16, at 11. *Cf.* Hannaford, *supra* note 13, at 151.

30   Otto, *supra* note 16, at 11.

31   *See, e.g., Symposium, International Human Rights at Fifty*, 8 TRANSNAT'L L. & CONTEMP. PROBS. No. 2 (Fall 1998).

etc.), come down, therefore not surprisingly, on the side of universalism. Cultural relativism, if it is not being criticized for preventing transnational moral judgments altogether when pushed to the extreme, is repeatedly denounced as "a new excuse for an old strategy,"[32] used "to justify limitations on speech, subjugation of women, female genital mutilation,[33] amputation of limbs and other cruel punishment, arbitrary use of power, and other violations of international human rights conventions."[34] Where once the old Adam of territorial sovereignty served generally to prevent outside intervention into "the domestic jurisdiction" such as might offset major abuse, now, in a world where state sovereignty is becoming more and more porous, cultural relativism is seen increasingly to substitute in this role, invoked to prevent transnational judgments and policies, both legal and moral, about genocide, ethnic cleansing, torture, rape, and other such acts of human violation wherever they occur.

Are these choices and conclusions unequivocally favoring universalism over relativism legitimate? In a critical sense, I think not, although not because they are the result of simplistic *a priori* reasoning or even that they are wrong. To the contrary, as Martha Nussbaum has pointed out, relativism, as a normative thesis about how we should make moral judgments, suffers from major conceptual problems of its own making:

> First, it has no bite in the modern world, where the ideas of every culture are available, internally, to every other, through the internet and the media. . . . Many forms of moral relativism . . . use an unrealistic notion of culture. They imagine homogeneity where there is really diversity. . . . Second, it is not obvious why we should think the normative thesis true. Why should we follow the local ideas, rather than the best ideas we can find? Finally, normative relativism is self-subverting; for, in asking us to defer to local norms, it asks us to defer to norms that in most cases are strongly non-relativistic. Most local traditions take themselves to be absolutely, not relatively true. So in asking us to follow the local, relativism asks us not to follow relativism.[35]

Furthermore, sympathetic (Westerner) as I am to the expansion and invigoration of universal human rights norms and practices, I personally am much taken by the idea that universalist international human rights law can and should serve as a basis for rendering cross-cultural normative judgments. My concern is that, without

---

³² Bayefsky, *supra* note 16.

³³ *See supra* note 9.

³⁴ Shestack, *supra* note 19, at 231.

³⁵ Martha C. Nussbaum, *In Defense of Universal Values* (unpublished manuscript, on file with the author and forthcoming from Cambridge University Press in 2000 under the title MARTHA C. NUSSBAUM, WOMEN AND HUMAN DEVELOPMENT: THE CAPABILITIES APPROACH (based on the Seeley Lectures in Political Theory delivered at Cambridge University, Mar. 1998)).

an analytically neutral approach to deciding when cultural differences are to be respected and when they are not, the pro-universalist choices and conclusions undermine the credibility and defensibility of their own particularistic objectives and thus make the idea of international human rights law as a basis for rendering moral judgments very difficult, perhaps even unworkable on occasion. One-sided assertions of legitimacy and priority, by definition discounting the centrality of the value of respect in human rights, invite countervailing charges of cultural imperialism (defending against real or imagined claims of cultural superiority—"colonizing") and cultural ethnocentrism (defending against real or imagined claims of cultural bias—"Westernizing"), and thus defeat the core goals they seek to achieve. True, cultural relativists also often express themselves in ways that contradict and therefore subvert their own credo—as when, for example, non-Western and sometimes even Western proponents of cultural pluralism evince absolutist outrage at the supposed moral decay of the West.[36] But this is only to prove my point. Any human rights orientation that is not genuinely in support of the widest possible embrace of the value of respect in the prescription and application of human rights norms in a multicultured world is likely to provoke substantial and widespread skepticism if not unreserved hostility.

It is of course tempting to argue that international human rights law itself settles the issue. Indeed, I hinted in this direction in an earlier foray into this treacherous cross-cultural domain a number of years ago.[37] In human rights convention after human rights convention, after all, states have committed themselves to the universality of human rights, both regionally and globally. Therefore, given the rudimentary—indeed foundational—international law principle *pacta sunt servanda*, they are duty bound to uphold that universality, inconsistent cultural practices notwithstanding.

The argument, however, falls woefully short of the cross-cultural challenge. There are at least four reasons why.

First, not all states, certainly not all "relativist states," have ratified even some of the core international human rights instruments, thus thwarting the *pacta sunt servanda* argument *ab initio* in many if not most instances of relativist-universalist contestation. Furthermore, given that the vast majority of international human rights law is conventional in kind (a powerful reminder of the resilience of the state sovereignty principle despite its increasing permeability), the instances in which cus-

---

36 *See, e.g.*, Kishore Mahbubani, *The Dangers of Decadence*, 72 FOR. AFF. No. 4, at 10 (Sept.–Oct. 1993). Writing about "massive social decay" in the United States, the author declares that "[m]any a society shudders at the prospects of this happening on it is shores." *Id.* at 14. *See also* Mohamed Elhachmi Hamdi, *The Limits of the Western Model*, 7 J. DEMOCRACY No. 2, at 82 (Apr. 1996) (insisting that "Western democracy appears . . . to be running amok. It is hard to see why lax Western mores that weaken or destroy the family . . . should be exported to the rest of the world") *Id.* at 82.

37 *See* Weston, *supra* note 16, at 366.

tomary international human rights law, binding on all states, may be said to apply, are bound to be, let us be candid, exceedingly rare.

Second, while many cultures share common values, much of international human rights law, particularly as it relates to such "first generation" or "negative" rights as are reflected in the ICCPR, may be said to be Western inspired,[38] thus fueling the conflict rather than resolving it.[39] That sometimes "[t]he universalist position completely denies that the existing universal standards may themselves be culturally specific and allied to dominant regimes of power"[40] does not alter this fact. So, when Jack Donnelly writes that "[l]ife, social order, protection from arbitrary rule, prohibition of inhuman and degrading treatment, the guarantee of a place in the life of the community, and access to an equitable share of the means of subsistence are central *moral aspirations* in nearly all cultures,"[41] we must be careful to read him and other keen observers like him precisely; the language of morality is not be confused with the language of law even though the former invariably shapes the latter and *vice versa*.

Third, all human rights instruments are filled with ambiguity and indeterminacy, sometimes deliberately to ensure signature and ratification. Thus they require interpretation to inform the *content* of universalism even when the *concept* of it has been accepted.[42] When, for example, does a cultural practice—say, caning in Singapore or death by electrocution, firing squad, hanging, or lethal injection in the United States—run afoul of formal promises that "[n]o one shall be arbitrarily deprived of his [*sic*] life"[43] or "subjected to torture or to cruel, inhuman or degrading treatment or punishment"?[44] As Philip Allot reminds us, "in all societies governments have been reassured in their arrogance by the idea that, if they are not proved actually to be violating the substance of particularized human rights, if they can bring their willing and acting within the wording of this or that

---

[38]   On human rights and the Western tradition, see JOHAN GALTUNG, HUMAN RIGHTS IN ANOTHER KEY (1994) (ch. 1).

[39]   One recent observer is unambiguously blunt about this Western influence and what to do about it: "[T]he 1948 UDHR should be treated as a Western document; . . . other cultures and religions should produce their own similar documents and . . . out of these a genuinely universal declaration may then be forged." Arvind Sharma, *Human Wrongs and Human Rights, in* HUMAN RIGHTS: POSITIVE POLICIES IN ASIA AND THE PACIFIC RIM 29, 40 (John D. Montgomery ed., 1998).

[40]   Otto, *supra* note 16, at 3.

[41]   Donnelly, *supra*, note 16, at 414–15 (emphasis added).

[42]   Even relativists agree, Rhoda Howard points out, that "the *concept* of human rights is universal, but the *content* (what, substantively, are or ought to be rights) varies among different societies." HOWARD, *supra* note 16, at 54.

[43]   ICCPR, *infra* Appendix III, art. 6(1).

[44]   *Id.* art. 7.

formula with its lawyerly qualifications and exceptions, then they are doing well enough."[45]

Finally, when their plenipotentiaries are not signing human rights treaties and voting for human rights resolutions "as mere gestures for temporary public relations purposes,"[46] states, including states that profess the universality of human rights, typically hedge their bets by resort to reservations, statements of understanding, and declarations so as to ensure that certain practices deemed central to their legal or other cultural traditions will not be rendered unlawful or otherwise anachronistic. In this way, formal commitments to the universality of particular human rights doctrines, principles, and rules are commonly qualified by the operational codes of everyday life.[47] As Upendra Baxi observes, "[a]ny international human rights lawyer worth her or his calling knows the riot of reservations, understandings, and declarations that parody the texts of universalistic declarations. The 'fine print' of reservations usually cancels the 'capital font' of universality. In this sense, claims concerning the universality of human rights are diversionary, embodying the politics *of*, rather than *for*, human rights."[48]

In sum, the invocation of international human rights law does not of itself settle the relativist-universalist debate. There is, thus, no escaping that claims of cultural relativism demand and deserve thoughtful responses. Given the centrality of the value of respect in human rights, the onus is on the human rights advocate to provide a reasoned and intelligent—respectful—response to them.

But how, one may ask, is this to be done, not in the abstract but in the particular case? Granted that, after thoughtful consideration, a particular claim of universalism may be deemed to trump a competing claim of cultural relativism or *vice versa*, what is the content of the "thoughtful consideration" that permits us to reach this or that result?

The remainder of this essay explores this question. Starting from the belief that there is nothing quite so practical as a good theory, my project is a *methodology of respect* according to which competing relativist-universalist claims can be assessed more objectively than subjectively, thereby hopefully to escape charges of cultural imperialism and ethnocentrism. While I expect to elaborate upon it particularistically in the future, I limit myself now to its broad contours, resorting to concrete illustrations where necessary to help make matters clear. Relying upon my training in the "New Haven" or "configurative policy science" approach to legal analysis,[49] I begin

---

45 PHILIP ALLOTT, EUNOMIA: NEW ORDER FOR A NEW WORLD 288 (1990).

46 Stephen P. Marks & Burns H. Weston, *International Human Rights at Fifty: A Foreword*, 8 TRANSNAT'L L. & CONTEMP. PROBS. 112, 119 (1998).

47 *Cf.* W. MICHAEL REISMAN, FOLDED LIES: BRIBERY, CRUSADES, AND REFORMS (1979) (ch. 1: "Myth System and Operational Code").

48 Upendra Baxi, *Voices of Suffering, Fragmented Universality, and the Future of Human Rights, infra* in this volume, at p. 101, 131.

49 For the central initiatives of this approach, see MYRES S. MCDOUGAL & ASSOCIATES,

by delineating what I see to be the observational standpoint that is needed to render human rights judgments about particular cultural practices in transnational settings in an objectively respectful manner. Next I postulate the world public order goals that would likely result from that observational standpoint. I then outline the intellectual tasks—five of them—that I believe are required to facilitate such goals. Thereafter I conclude with an appraisal and recommendation. Be it noted, however, that I approach this multiple task with humility, recognizing my own vulnerability to cultural bias at least insofar as I rely upon analytical concepts that derive from my own culture to describe and assess realities in others.

II. Delineating the Objective Observational Standpoint

The observational standpoint to which one should aspire when faced with the necessity of relativist-universalist choice about different cultural practices around the world is, I believe, that of rational persons of diverse identity (creed, gender, race, etc.) acting privately (*i.e.*, not as state representatives) and in their personal self-interest relative to the policies or values they believe should define the world public order of which they are a part, but behind a "veil of ignorance" as to the

---

STUDIES IN WORLD PUBLIC ORDER (1960, 1986); MYRES S. MCDOUGAL & WILLIAM T. BURKE, THE PUBLIC ORDER OF THE OCEANS: A CONTEMPORARY INTERNATIONAL LAW OF THE SEA (1962, 1987); MYRES S. MCDOUGAL & FLORENTINO P. FELICIANO, LAW AND MINIMUM WORLD PUBLIC ORDER: THE LEGAL REGULATION OF INTERNATIONAL COERCION (1961, 1994); MYRES S. MCDOUGAL & HAROLD D. LASSWELL, JURISPRUDENCE FOR A FREE SOCIETY: STUDIES IN LAW, SCIENCE AND POLICY (1992); MYRES S. MCDOUGAL, HAROLD D. LASSWELL & LUNG-CHU CHEN, *supra* note 1; MYRES S. MCDOUGAL, HAROLD D. LASSWELL & JAMES C. MILLER, THE INTERPRETATION OF AGREEMENTS AND WORLD PUBLIC ORDER (1967, 1994); and MYRES S. MCDOUGAL, HAROLD D. LASSWELL & IVAN A. VLASIC, LAW AND PUBLIC ORDER IN SPACE (1963). *See also* ROSALYN HIGGINS, THE DEVELOPMENT OF INTERNATIONAL LAW THROUGH THE POLITICAL ORGANS OF THE UNITED NATIONS (1963); DOUGLAS M. JOHNSTON, THE INTERNATIONAL LAW OF FISHERIES: A FRAMEWORK FOR POLICY-ORIENTED INQUIRIES (1965, 1987); DOUGLAS M. JOHNSTON, CONSENT AND COMMITMENT IN THE WORLD COMMUNITY: THE CLASSIFICATION AND ANALYSIS OF INTERNATIONAL INSTRUMENTS (1997); B.S. MURTY, THE IDEOLOGICAL INSTRUMENT OF COERCION AND WORLD PUBLIC ORDER (1968, 1989); B.S. MURTY, THE INTERNATIONAL LAW OF DIPLOMACY: THE DIPLOMATIC INSTRUMENT AND WORLD PUBLIC ORDER (1989); W. MICHAEL REISMAN, NULLITY AND REVISION: THE REVIEW AND ENFORCEMENT OF INTERNATIONAL JUDGMENTS AND AWARDS (1971); W. MICHAEL REISMAN & ANDREW R. WILLARD, INTERNATIONAL INCIDENTS: THE LAW THAT COUNTS IN WORLD POLITICS (1988); JAN SCHNEIDER, WORLD PUBLIC ORDER OF THE ENVIRONMENT: TOWARDS AN INTERNATIONAL ECOLOGICAL LAW AND ORGANIZATION (1979); BURNS H. WESTON, INTERNATIONAL CLAIMS: POSTWAR FRENCH PRACTICE (1971); John Norton Moore, *Prolegomenon to the Jurisprudence of Myres McDougal and Harold Lasswell*, 54 VA. L. REV. 662 (1968); Eisuke Suzuki, *The New Haven School of International Law: An Invitation to a Policy-Oriented Jurisprudence*, 1 YALE STUD. IN WORLD PUBLIC ORDER 1 (1974); Frederick S. Tipson, *The Lasswell-McDougal Enterprise: Toward a World Public Order of Human Dignity*, 14 VA. J. INT'L L. 535 (1974).

particular circumstances of their own personal condition within that order. Persons familiar with legal philosophy will recognize the influence here of neo-Kantian legal theorist John Rawls.[50] The true principles of justice, Rawls argues, are those of "fairness"—to wit, those that "free and rational persons concerned to further their own interests would accept in an *initial position* of equality as defining the fundamental terms of their association."[51] While hypothetically presupposing—unrealistically—an egalitarian and procedurally just starting point, and while not affording access to transcendent truth (in part because of its unrealistic hypothetical premise), this intellectual device does greatly minimize, even if it does not eliminate altogether, the influence of the biases and prejudices of the observer or decision-maker.[52] The assumption is of thinking men and women who, come together in their private capacity in some original social setting, but without knowledge of the details of their own physical and social environments, freely choose a public order that is fair to all in its distribution of benefits (rights) and burdens (duties) because, rationally contemplating their own self-interests, they choose a public order that will not cause anyone, including of course themselves, to end up in a position of disadvantage in the real world; they choose principles of governance that will be good for all and not simply for some or a few. The result is a set of public order value preferences that transcend parochial interest and selfish motive, a map of basic values or blueprint of fundamental laws that can win the assent of persons everywhere, and thereby facilitate respectful decision when it comes to legal and moral judgments about particular cultural practices across national boundaries.

Is this proposed observational standpoint subject to criticism for being too Western inspired, too individualistically oriented? After all, Rawls comes from a long tradition of discourse, dating back to the so-called Enlightenment, that, at an earlier time of flourishing, had no apparent conceptual difficulty in promoting rights and the rule of law in the West (more or less) while colonizing and subjugating

---

[50]   *See* JOHN RAWLS, A THEORY OF JUSTICE §§1–4, 9, 11–17, 20–30, 33–35, 39–40 (1971) (explaining the essence of the author's theory of justice) (emphasis added).

[51]   *Id.* at 11 (emphasis added). I adopt the expression "initial position" throughout the remainder of this essay because of its appearance in this much-quoted phrase even though Rawls uses the expressions "initial situation" and "original position" as frequently if not more so.

[52]   While Rawls himself acknowledges, in *id.* at 12, that his "initial position" device, "a purely hypothetical situation" corresponding to the state of nature in traditional social contract theory, "is not . . . thought of as an actual historical state of affairs, much less a primitive condition of culture," intentionally his "initial position" device does not concede the unequal and otherwise unjust realities of the "real world." This failing, it might be said, undermines the usefulness of the "initial position" device in the present "real world" context of cross-cultural decision-making; and it is apparently for such reasons that Rawls has since modified his observational standpoint so that his "original position" has yielded to a system of "overlapping consensus." *See* JOHN RAWLS, POLITICAL LIBERALISM (1993). However, one does not have to agree with Rawls' original premises (or, for that matter, his conclusions) to find heuristic utility in his "initial position" contrivance. *Cf.* Shestack, *supra* note 19, at 223: "Critics of Rawls' theory maintain that it was designed to support the institutions of modern

much of the rest of the world.[53] The fact is that a subtext can be discerned here of *rational* (not spiritual) persons making *atomistic/ deductive* (not holistic/dialectic) choices in their *individual* (not group) capacity and self-interest, unaware of the particularities of their *idiosyncratic* (not general) situation in the world, including their potential for membership in some social group. The skeptic might therefore contend that a Western/individualistic skew has been insinuated into the "initial position" decision-makers' role. By assuming ignorance as to class, ethnicity, nationality, race, religion, tribe, sex, and other such indicia of social position, it might be argued, and thus ignorance as to actual membership in a social group, we preclude the spiritual/dialectic or collectivist/communitarian person from participating in the evaluation of a cultural practice and thus make the above-defined observational standpoint for cross-cultural decision-making questionable at best. But this argument, I submit, misses an important point. Merely because Rawls' "initial position" decision-makers may be acting individually and behind a "veil of ignorance" as to their *actual* positions does not mean that they are acting individually and behind a "veil of ignorance" as to their *potential* positions; and thus we can assume that, as with anything else that rational people are capable of anticipating, they can foresee the possibility that they will belong to social groups that espouse spiritual/dialectic and collectivistic/communitarian as well as Western/individualistic values, and that therefore they may belong to a public order that embraces all of these community values. The essential thrust of the observational standpoint thus remains valid: the rational "initial position" decision-maker will choose the world public order that will most guarantee the fairest distribution of benefits (rights) and burdens (duties) among all social groups as well as all individuals and thereby ensure that groups as well as individuals will benefit as much as possible and suffer the least possible disadvantage.

Of course, whatever one may conclude about the influence of Western individualism upon the observational standpoint recommended here— to wit, the perspective of free and rational persons acting in their own self-interest in an "initial position" of equality behind a "veil of ignorance" as to the precise terms of their societal circumstance—the actual attainment of such an observational standpoint is most likely impossible in the real world. No social psychologist would vouchsafe a person's capacity, be he or she individualistically or collectivistically inclined, for complete objectivity in legal and moral decision-making. The legal realists long ago and the proponents of critical legal studies more recently certainly have taught us that.

---

democracy in a *domestic* context. But even if that were the case, the criticism does not refute his moral thesis, nor an international extension of it."

[53] *Cf.* Upendra Baxi, *From Human Rights to the Right to be Human: Some Heresies, in* RETHINKING HUMAN RIGHTS, *supra* note 16, who writes that "John Rawls, at the end of a spectacularly cogent and massive analysis in *Theory of Justice* [sic], is able to say, without a frown on his face, on page 543 of his well-acclaimed work, that the lexical priority of liberty, after all, may not apply to societies where basic wants of the individual are not fulfilled." *Id.* at 182.

In other words, an observational standpoint that identifies more with the human species as a whole than with the primacy of any of its individual or group parts remains, at least for anyone committed to global justice, an ideal to be pursued even if it is never to be fully realized. Hence the observational standpoint recommended here. Absent the core value of respect at the center of all inquiry into the relativist-universalist debate—which is to say objectivity, at a minimum—there will be no extending human rights values of any kind without rancor, possibly even violence. Needed is an objective guidepost for community-wide decision-making that will at least facilitate a fair—just—world public order in both individualistic and collectivistic or communitarian terms. As stated above, one-sided characterizations of legitimacy and priority, by definition discounting the centrality of the value of respect in human rights, are likely, over the long term at least, to undermine the moral credibility of their proponents and the defensibility of their particularistic objectives.[54]

III. The Postulation of Basic World Public Order Goals

So what map of basic values, what fundamental principles of decision-making, ones that can at least facilitate a just world public order in individualist, collectivist, spiritual, or other terms, should our "initial position"decision-makers choose to guide their transnational judgments about particular cultural practices? If they are to be consistent with the observational standpoint for respectful decision recommended above, surely such values or principles cannot be representative only of the exclusive interests of a particular segment of the world community; surely they must reflect an inclusive approach to humankind's great diversity.

Rawls argues that his "initial position" decision-makers would choose two "principles of justice," each intuitively derived: a "First Principle" that "each person is to have an equal right to the most extensive total system of equal basic liberties compatible with a system of liberty for all"[55] (ergo, essentially, the value of liberty); and a "Second Principle" that "[s]ocial and economic inequalities are to be arranged so that they are . . . to the greatest benefit of the least advantaged . . . and . . . attached to offices and positions open to all under conditions of fair equality and opportunity"[56] (ergo, essentially, the value of equality). Together these principles achieve, with help from others that compensate for comparative disadvantages (a "Difference Principle") and ensure the common interest when the values of liberty and equality clash (a "Reconciliation Principle"), Rawls' general conception of justice: fairness for all. A difficulty with Rawls' argument, however, is that, as explained below in a discussion of the community policies that are actually and potentially at stake in all or most relativist-universalist controversies,[57] cultural prac-

---

[54] *See* text nearly following note 35, *supra*.

[55] RAWLS, *supra* note 50, at §46 generally, p. 302 specifically.

[56] *Id*. at §11 generally, p. 63 specifically.

[57] *See infra* Section III(A).

tices for which relativist claims have been or might be made commonly reach beyond the values of liberty and equality that Rawls stresses. Accordingly, neither liberty nor equality are sufficient to serve adequately as the exclusive determinants of relativist-universalist contests.

An alternative choice, emphasizing the *postulation of empirically-premised* public order goals in contradistinction to their *intuitive* derivation in the manner of Rawls, is, as proposed by McDougal, Lasswell, and Chen, "the greatest production and widest possible distribution of *all* important values, with a high priority accorded persuasion rather than coercion in such production and distribution"[58]— that is, "[t]he comprehensive set of goal values . . . which are commonly characterized as the basic values of human dignity or of a free society,"[59] "those [values] which have been bequeathed to us by all the great democratic movements of humankind and which are being more insistently expressed in the rising common demands and expectations of peoples everywhere."[60] The phrasing of this choice, however, while appealing to a confirmed believer in the "free society" and "great democratic movements," betrays a distinct Western bias that appears, in all objective candor, to prejudge the outcome of the very issues and policy concerns that often are at stake in relativist-universalist controversies in the first place; and this bias seems not at all dispelled by the authors' subsequent acknowledgment of the "many different cultural and institutional modalities"[61] by which their proposed goal values might be formulated and accepted worldwide. Indeed, as evidenced by their invocation of the United Nations Charter,[62] the UDHR,[63] the two covenants born of the UDHR,[64] and "their host of ancillary expressions"[65] to lend authoritative support to their postulate, it seems clear that their bias, heavily favoring universalist international human rights law (which, as observed above, cannot of itself settle the relativist-universalist debate[66]), is not just Western but also universalist, clearly not a neutral posture in the relativist-universalist debate under scrutiny here.

Thus, a compromise seems in order, drawing from both Rawls and McDougal-Lasswell-Chen. We must conclude, I believe, that the map of basic values or fundamental decision-making principles that should guide transnational judgments about particular cultural practices should be one that is both more expansive or

---

58 McDougal et al., *supra* note 1, at 90 (emphasis added).

59 *Id.*

60 *Id.*

61 *Id.*

62 Concluded June 26, 1945 (entered into force, Oct. 24, 1945), 1 U.N.T.S. xvi, 1976 Y.B.U.N. 1043, *reprinted in* 1 International Law and World Order: Basic Documents I.A.1 (Burns H. Weston ed., 5 vols., 1994–).

63 *See infra* Appendix I.

64 *See infra* Appendices II and III .

65 McDougal et al., *supra* note 1, at 90.

66 *See* text accompanying notes 37–48, *supra*.

inclusive than that proposed by Rawls and, consistent with the observational stand-point from which they would be postulated, simultaneously less vulnerable than the McDougal-Lasswell-Chen formulation to accusations of Western/universalist bias, ergo one chosen by Rawls' "initial position" decision-makers that embraces the following self-interested *desiderata*:

- the widest possible shaping and sharing of *all* the values of human dignity, including but not limited to (political) liberty and (socioeconomic) equality,

- without discrimination of any kind save that of merit and basic need (*e.g.*, physical/mental handicap, rank poverty) in many though not necessarily all instances,

- consistent with the truism that in a world of finite possibility, as I have written elsewhere, "most assertions of human rights . . . are qualified by the limitation that the rights of any particular individual or group in any particular instance are restricted as much as is necessary to secure the comparable rights of others and the aggregate common interest."[67]

It need here be added only that, in choosing this policy guide to respectful relativist-universalist decision, our "initial position" decision-makers might substitute Martha Nussbaum's (and Amartya Sen's) language of "capabilities" for the more commonly used language of "rights"—which is to say that they then would think upon all the values of human dignity that are to be shaped and shared inclusively not in terms of *abstract goals* but, rather, in terms of the concrete and more readily *measurable needs* that all people must have satisfied to fulfill the requirements of human dignity (however defined).[68]

IV. The Intellectual Tasks of Relativist-Universalist Decision

Having delimited the relativist-universalist problem, delineated the objective observational standpoint from which to appraise cultural practices in respectful terms, and then postulated the world public order goals that optimally should define and govern such appraisal, emphasizing the widest possible shaping and sharing of *all* the values (or capabilities) of human dignity, it is tempting to argue that local practices that are indisputably destructive of the values (or capabilities) of human dignity must be altogether rejected and that such rejection should not be confused with disrespect for cultural differences or the principles of nonintervention and self-deter-

---

[67] Weston, *supra* note 4.

[68] *See* Martha C. Nussbaum, *Capabilities, Human Rights, and the Universal Declaration, supra* in this volume, at p. 25. *See also* AMARTYA K. SEN, COMMODITIES AND CAPABILITIES (1985); Martha C. Nussbaum, *Capabilities and Human Rights*, 66 FORDHAM L. REV. 273 (1997); Amartya K. Sen, *Capability and Well-Being, in* THE QUALITY OF LIFE 30–31 (Martha C. Nussbaum & Amartya K. Sen eds., 1993).

mination that afford them protection. I have in mind such policies and practices as genocide, ethnic cleansing, imposed starvation, physical and mental torture, arbitrary arrest, detention, and execution, slavery, forced labor, and racial *apartheid*. If they are not entirely without cultural basis in the first place, the threshold question in all instances of relativist/universalist decision-making, these policies and practices are now so widely condemned that they no longer can be justified by any local custom or rationale.

Or so it might be initially argued. In an earlier essay, I took this starting position, arguing that "[i]f cultural relativism is to function in these and like instances it does so only as a cloak for despotism, stripping international human rights law from all expectation of assuring . . . 'basic decencies'."[69] And I was not alone.[70] These observations, intuitively reached, remain valid, in my view precisely because the practices mentioned appear to be without cultural basis in the first place. But, without having first subjected each of them to the intellectual tasks of policy-oriented inquiry for the purpose of facilitating fully respectful decision when cross-cultural legal and moral judgments are being rendered, they were intellectually premature. It is, I believe, incumbent upon fully respectful cross-cultural judgment to enter first upon *all* the intellectual tasks that seem required when having to resolve, from an "initial position" policy-oriented perspective, a particular relativist-universalist controversy: (1) the clarification of community policies relevant to the specific cultural practice at issue, (2) the description of past trends in decision relevant to that practice, (3) the analysis of the factors affecting these decisional trends, (4) the projection of future trends in decision relevant to the specific cultural practice in question, and (5) the invention and evaluation of policy alternatives to that practice. An analytical flow chart of these intellectual tasks looks as follows:

Clarification of Community Policies

↕

Description of Past Trends in Decision

↕

Analysis of Factors Affecting Decision

↕

Projection of Future Trends in Decision

↕

Invention and Evaluation of Policy Alternatives

Although they are presented in a logically sequenced order here, they must be applied configuratively (as the two-way arrows suggest) and not in isolation from one another, each task informing and being informed by the others, to achieve as comprehensive a contextual analysis as possible. The goal is to test each of these dimensions of policy-oriented inquiry for their ability to contribute to rational but respectful choice in decision, and to obtain guidance in the development of inter-

---

[69]   Weston, *supra* note 16, at 366.

[70]   *See, e.g.*, Donnelly, *supra* note 16, at 112–15.

national community policy relative to the practices in question. Of course, as already intimated, a preliminary issue is the threshold question of whether or not the practice in question is a *cultural* practice as distinct from one that might be, say, *idiosyncratic* to the particular governing elite involved. If the latter, then the relativist-universalist issue is by definition not implicated, and a decision about the practice may be taken according to potentially different policy criteria. If, however, the practice in question can be properly denominated a cultural one, then it is incumbent upon us, from the standpoint of our "initial position" decision-makers, to pursue the policy-oriented inquiry outlined.

A. Clarification of Community Policies

In Section I above ("Delimitation of the Problem"), I listed according to human life's physical and behavioral dimensions, as many cultural practices as I could think of that are well known for the cross-cultural controversies they generate or might generate.[71] The policy issue most fundamentally underlying each of these two existential categories concerns the intensity and scope of power being exercised —more particularly, the necessity of the intensity and scope of power being exercised—by one group of people (public or private) in relation to another in the administration of the practice in question. This comes as no surprise, of course, because it is alleged abuses or excesses of power that characterize most if not all human rights controversies.

Spanning these two existential categories, however, though not coextensive with them (and thus not jointly to serve as an alternate typology, particularly in a world social process of ever-shifting elements), are at least two other dimensions of human experience that merit attention because they hint at still more precise ways of identifying at least the principal policies that are at stake when cross-cultural normative judgments are being attempted: the societal functions of (1) punishment and (2) social differentiation. Regarding punitive practices, relativist-universalist disagreement centers essentially on the severity of the punishment in question or, alternatively, its proportionality *vis-à-vis* the alleged precipitating social transgression, and thus, more precisely, on community policies that regulate resort to coercion in the administration of cultural practices. Regarding socially differentiating practices, relativist-universalist disagreement centers mainly on the justification given for the differentiation in question, and thus, again more precisely, on community policies that regulate the legal and moral rationales of cultural administration—which, as it happens, tend to be, significantly, gender-based and favoring men over women (patriarchy) in many if not most instances. Women's issues lie at the heart of many relativist-universalist controversies, both directly and indirectly, particularly at the intersection between masculine hegemony and women's sexual and reproductive identities. As feminist

---

71   *See* table, *supra* p. 67.

scholar Arati Rao has observed, "[n]o social group has suffered greater violation of its human rights in the name of culture than women."[72]

From a policy-clarifying standpoint, some of these practices are less easily diagnosed than others. Exceedingly difficult, for example, even though obviously involving power relationships, is the matter of abortion. This is so not because of the emotional politics that surround the practice (in the United States at least) but, rather, because central to it is fundamental disagreement on what it means to be human, ergo fundamental disagreement on whether it is the human rights of the fetus that are at stake (the right to life, the "pro-life" position) or the human rights of the mother (the right to liberty, the "pro-choice" position) when the practice is confronted. Adding to the complexity is the matter of mandatory or forced abortion as a function of population control. It is likely that both "pro-life" and "pro-choice" proponents would agree that forcing a woman to have an abortion without her consent is a clear violation of human rights—but whose human rights espoused by whom?

Also complicating policy clarification are the competing philosophical traditions of individualism (liberty) and collectivism/communitarianism (equality) that, as already intimated, have greatly influenced at least Western moral thought and action throughout most of the last two to three centuries. In addition to being invoked to prioritize civil and political ("first generation" or "negative") rights, on the one hand, or economic and social ("second generation" or "positive") rights, on the other, even to the complete denial of one generation in favor of the other, and thus to the disregard of the fundamental indivisibility that exists between each, they have served to rationalize most, perhaps even all, of the physical and behavioral practices that have proved controversial in the cross-cultural setting. Exalting liberty and equality to the disregard of other principles or values, they have diverted responsible attention from the centrality of respect in human rights decision-making and thus thwarted clear-headed thinking about the relativist-universalist choice.

Consider, for example, a cultural practice that privileges one group of people over another. As such, it contradicts the collectivist/communitarian value of equality (as commonly understood to mean the same measure/quantity or privilege/status as another) and therefore, *a fortiori*, such human rights (individual or group) as are premised on the value of equality. If, then, equality as commonly understood is to serve as our policy guide (a not unreasonable universalist inference given the egalitarian content of the world's existing human rights instruments[73]), it follows that relativist defenses of the practice must be rejected. All of which will seem reasonable enough if the local differentiation is based on, say, gender or race and we shun gender- or race-based discrimination or segregation as incompatible with

---

[72]   Rao, *supra* note 16, at 169.

[73]   *See, e.g.*, ICCPR, *infra* Appendix III, art. 2(1): "Each State Party to the present Covenant undertakes to respect and to ensure to all individuals within its territory and subject to its jurisdiction the rights recognized in the present Covenant, without distinction of any kind. . . ."

equality. But what if it is based on, say, age, basic need, capability, or merit? What decision then? The point is, of course, that the answer is not self-evident from the standpoint of equality, that notions of equality do not of themselves provide a reliable exit from the relativist-universalist conundrum. Caught up in a swirl of normative tautology in which we find ourselves providing answers according to the very questions that are at issue in the first place, we are not any closer to the objective understanding we seek. For this we must be guided by something else.

Similar confusion sometimes accompanies the cross-cultural assessment of physical practices, at least in theory. Consider, for example, the Islamic (*Qisas*) practice of hand amputation for thievery in theocratic Afghanistan and imprisonment for thievery in the secular United States. Clearly each practice contradicts the individualist value of liberty (as commonly understood to mean the condition of being free from restriction and especially governmental control). But surely, given the widespread acceptance of deprivations of liberty for socially deviant behavior, it is not this contradiction or infringement that inclines us to reject a relativist defense of the theocratic culture in the first instance and possibly accept a relativist defense (depending on other variables) *vis-à-vis* the secular culture in the second instance. The issue here is not whether liberty may be infringed, but, as earlier suggested, to what extent, in what proportion. Thus, just as notions of equality do not of themselves provide a reliable exit from the relativist-universalist conundrum, neither do notions of liberty. For this we must be guided again by something else.

This "something else," this guide to respectful decision, is, of course, that map of basic values or fundamental principles of decision-making that our hypothetical "initial position" decision-makers would choose behind a "veil of ignorance" to ensure the greatest possible equal distribution of benefits (rights) and burdens (duties) within the public order of which they are a part, to wit, *all* the values (or capabilities) of human dignity postulated to be appropriate and necessary for transnational judgments about particular cultural practices. Only by relating these broad postulated goals to specific instances of relativist-universalist controversy— be it hand amputation in Afghanistan or outright execution in the United States— will it be possible to ensure respectful decision about the competing values of cultural pluralism, on the one hand, and of universalist principle, on the other. True, the task of relating these broad goals to specific cultural practices is no easy one; and it is not made easier by the fact that behind the relativist-universalist debate, particularly evident in the "Asian values" controversy, there lurks a desire, evident on *both* sides of the debate, less to ensure cultural pluralism than to further the interests of the private and public governing elites who, in the post-Cold War phenomenon we inadequately call "globalization," currently are engaged in a grand struggle for economic and political influence—to the shameful disregard, it regrettably must be added, of the interests of the "Other," the "huddled masses, yearning to breathe free,"[74] who typically are the victims of globalization's highly uneven, indeed unjust,

---

[74]   Emma Lazarus, from the inscription on the Statue of Liberty in New York Harbor.

distribution of economic benefits and burdens[75] and whose pain always must be central to human rights discourse and action.[76] In fact, it is precisely this hidden or unstated agenda that requires vigilance in judging cross-cultural human rights controversies in a respectful manner. The relativist-universalist debate is not merely a conflict between differing cultural and universal norms. It is on many an occasion a high-level confrontation between competing conservative and liberal versions of capitalism, none of which is *a priori* superior to the other, especially when expressed in cultural terms. Neither the relativist nor the universalist thus may dismiss the other's claims without a reasoned response. The policies that underwrite their claims must be understood for what they are and properly measured for their compatibility with the wider public order goals that our neutral "initial position" decision-makers would have chosen to ensure respectful decision when rendering cross-cultural moral judgments.

B. Description of Past Trends in Cross-Cultural Decision

A key task in any international or transnational case where a concrete cross-cultural judgment must be rendered is to describe the past trends in cross-cultural decision that are relevant to the particular practice that is in question. This is so for the very important reason that an understanding of past cross-cultural decision-making can reveal the extent to which the world community, in its many different modes of expression, has actively denounced/supported, passively opposed/tolerated, or otherwise disapproved/condoned the particular practice across space and time, and therefore help to reveal the extent to which one should or should not take seriously the immediate objection to it. The essentially passive official response to the caning of a young U.S. national for alleged vandalism in Singapore in the mid-1990s, for example, might usefully be examined from this perspective. In addition, assuming a desire to repeal or reform a local practice in keeping with some legal/moral universalist perspective, past trends can instruct us on the cross-cultural difficulties that are likely to be encountered when subjecting provisional formulations of the desirable to the discipline of the possible, and thus encourage sensitivity to the potential for excessively burdensome demands for change, a particularly important concern where developing "Third World" countries may be involved. Our concern, it bears re-emphasizing, is the tension between the core value of respect, on the one hand, and, on the other hand, all other values (or capabilities) that may be espoused in any particular relativist-universalist controversy, and our policy challenge is to figure out how to reconcile this tension objectively, how to promote and protect the values (or capabilities) that reflect the unity of human aspiration and, simultaneously, cultural diversity.

---

[75] For insightful commentary, see, *e.g.*, GLOBALIZATION: CRITICAL REFLECTIONS (James H. Mittelman ed., 1996); Kamal Hossain, *Globalization and Human Rights: Clash of Universal Aspirations and Special Interests, infra* in this volume, at p. 187. *See also* John Gray, False Dawn: The Delusions of Global Capitalism (1998).

[76] Writes Upendra Baxi, *supra* note 48, at 126. "To give language to pain, to experience the pain of the Other inside you, remains the task, always, of human rights narrative and discourse."

C. The Analysis of Factors Affecting Cross-Cultural Decision

Once having clarified the community policies that are at stake in any given relativist-universalist contest and then identified the past trends in decision that are relevant to it, it is important to analyze the factors that have influenced those decisional trends and thus also the case at hand. It is important because such analysis helps us to understand not only how and why relevant precedents were reached, but also, and arguably more importantly, what factors are likely to serve as useful indicators for present and future decisions, particularly as they may prove useful in guiding our evaluation and recommendation of policy alternatives. The following considerations, organized around the principal elements of social process (derived from the compound question: who does what to whom, why, when and where, with what capabilities, how, and with what short- and long-term results?), are among the many that doubtless have arisen intuitively in cross-culturally controversial practices in the past and that therefore doubtless should be asked in the present and future as well whenever a particular cultural practice is challenged by universalist principle. Respectful decision in this realm demands as much. Only by such contextually oriented questions is a truly objective decision-maker likely to be able to so sift fact from fiction and cause from consequence as to permit sharp delineation of the critical public order policies that are at stake and thereby acquire the comprehensive understanding of a given cultural practice that is necessary to reach a respectful decision about it. The following impressionistic forays, *by no means exhaustive*, should help to clarify what I have in mind, understanding that it is seldom the investigation of one conditioning factor alone but, rather, the in-depth exploration of all of them that is going to provide the cumulative—comprehensive—knowledge that is needed to achieve the respectful decision that is our objective.

1. Participants

In all cultural practices, individual human beings are the ultimate actors, either because they are themselves the *masters* of the practice or its *servants*, or because they are affiliated with a group that is either way directly involved.[77] If only just to comprehend the practice, therefore, it is important to ask, as an anthropologist or historian might do, such descriptively-oriented questions as: Who are the key participants in the practice (*e.g.*, individuals, families, clans, ecclesiastical organizations, private associations, pressure groups, political parties, governments,

---

77 There are no perfect words of common usage to identify the key participants in cultural practices. Therefore, for lack of more suitable alternatives and for purely descriptive purposes (*i.e.*, free of bias or preference), I adopt the term "master" to refer to those persons who define, execute, administer, and otherwise govern cultural practices, and the term "servant" to refer to those persons who follow or who are expected to follow such practices. It must be understood, however, that neither the masters nor servants of cultural practices are restricted to their most distinctive participatory characteristics. On many occasions, the same participant or participants will perform both roles simultaneously.

international institutions)? Who is responsible for the practice, who are its principal masters? Who is the object of it, who are its primary servants? What biological characteristics (race, sex, age, sexual orientation), culture (ethnicity, nationality), class (wealth, power), interest (group membership), or personality (authoritarian, submissive) may be attributed to each? And so forth. But participatory questions such as these, helping us to understand the identity and roles of the different participants involved, can also greatly assist the issue of whether or not to honor a cultural practice, particularly where the resolution of that issue turns on the legal and moral rationales given for social differentiation. Indeed, together with other considerations, they may, in such instances, prove decisive in the given case. Consider, for example, the practice of racial *apartheid* in pre-1990 South Africa. In addition to its violating our general "initial position" public order postulate of nondiscrimination in the shaping and sharing of all values,[78] the fact that it privileged minority whites of European origin over majority blacks of indigenous origin obviously had much to do with the world's having outlawed it. Might similar conclusions be reached vis-à-vis the Hindu and Muslim traditions in Central and South Asia and in the Middle East of segregating women (*Harem, Purdah*)? Of veil wearing (*Chador, Hijab, Niqab*) and total body covering (per the *Shari'a* doctrine of *Urf*)? Of the erstwhile Chinese practice of female foot binding were it still exercised today? In light of our nondiscrimination postulate, surely the participatory (patriarchal) dynamics of such practices (privileging men over women) are important, sometimes perhaps even decisive, to the issue of whether they should or should not be honored in cross-cultural judgment. For example, if the practice can be shown to involve a broad cross-section of society participating in decision-making about it, including its servants as well as its masters, we might tentatively conclude that the practice has some at least *prima facie* legitimacy. If, on the other hand, it can be found that only privileged persons make the relevant decisions about it (*e.g.*, men, people from elite castes/races, etc.), we would apply, in light of the postulated public order goal values of our "initial position" decision-makers, a higher level of scrutiny to the cultural practice. Likewise, if only one group benefits—particularly if the benefit is at the expense of another group or if only one group "loses"—the practice, according to the same criteria, should be called into question.

2. Perspectives

Persons who participate in cultural practices, whether individually or as members of a group, bring to them predispositional variables or perspectives—objectives (value demands), identities (for whom values are demanded), and expectations (about the fulfillment or nonfulfillment of demanded values)—which, together with environmental factors, affect cross-cultural judgment about the legitimacy or not of a given practice from the standpoint and postulated goal values of our "initial position" decision-makers. Thus, questions pertaining to the objectives and per-

---

[78] *See supra* Section II, at 77–80.

spectives of such persons, be they the masters or the servants of the cultural practice in question, are important in the relativist-universalist judgmental setting as well: What are the objectives, identities, and expectations of the master(s) of the practice? The servant(s)? To what extent do the former affect the fulfillment or nonfulfillment of the latter and vice versa? Are the perspectives of the master(s) constructive and expansionist, believed to increase aggregate values for all, or are they defensive, intended to protect the existing values of exclusive groups? Are the perspectives of the servant(s) opposed to the given practice, or are they in support of it? Does the master of a given practice seek power, wealth, or some other value at the expense of the servant? Does the servant willingly acquiesce to such demands? Unwillingly? Do the identities of the participants relate to the common interest of all members of the culture or only to the interests of a few? Do all or some of the participants, masters and servants alike, perceive an intrinsic value in fulfilling one's role in the cultural practice? If so, which ones? Are they conditioned to personal or social security or insecurity as part of their daily routine? Consider in these lights the death threat and literary suppression imposed by Iran's theocratic government upon Salman Rushdie for his Shiite apostasy, claimed necessary for the promotion and protection of religious rectitude; or the imposition of the death penalty in the United States, professedly to deter crime and otherwise promote civic virtue.

It is of course not only the express or stated perspectives of the participants that must be taken into account. As recent events in the Balkans and the Great Lakes region of sub-Saharan Africa bear witness, such inherent or quasi-inherent identities as ethnicity, race, color, sex, religion, political or other opinion, language, nationality, age, and life-style are commonly the victims of policies officially proclaimed and justified by their masters on the grounds of, but bearing no real relation to, capability or merit. An example from United States history is the closing of public nursing homes and swimming pools allegedly for economic reasons, concerns for public safety, or health purposes when the real objective was to deny access to minorities.[79] Similarly, in a world where processes of socialization commonly promote the internalization and toleration of patterns of inequality and, in so doing, subordinate the objectives, identities, and expectations of the servants of cultural practices to the demands of those who enforce them, it is of utmost importance to question the extent to which acquiescence to the given practice in

---

[79] *See, e.g.,* Wood v. Vaughan, 209 F. Supp. 106 (W.D. Va. 1962) (affirming the integration of public swimming pools, nursing homes, and other municipal facilities). *But see* Palmer v. Thompson, 403 U.S. 217 (1971), where, in a 5–4 decision, the city of Jackson, Mississippi was upheld as not violating the equal protection clause of the Fourteenth Amendment in its claim that it could not "safely and economically" operate integrated public swimming pools. This decision has never been expressly overruled. However, later cases, holding that a law valid on its face may still violate equal protection, may be said to have significantly limited if not altogether abrogated *Palmer. See, e.g.,* Hernandez v. Woodward, 714 F. Supp 963, (N.D. Ill. 1989); Church of Scientology v. Clearwater, 2 F.3d 1514 (11th Cir. 1993) (*rehearing and cert. denied*).

issue is freely given. While by no means the exclusive determinant of cross-cultural judgment, it is in this light that one should assess, for example, the female dress codes of veil wearing (*Chador, Hijab, Niqab*) and total body covering (per the *Shari'a* doctrine of *Urf*) in certain Islamic societies and the tradition of arranged child betrothal in South Asia and elsewhere. In such cases, if we are to be consistent with the postulated public order goals of our "initial position" decision-makers, a high level of scrutiny is warranted.

3. Situations

Spatial, temporal, institutional, and crisis-level features of social process also set the parameters within which cultural practices must be judged. Is the practice confined to a single country or subnational unit or does it extend across national frontiers to embrace whole regions or continents? Is it of long-standing or short duration, sporadic or continuous, thriving or dying out? Does it operate exclusively in the private sphere—say, as part of the institution of the nuclear family or clan—or is it initiated and/or sanctioned by governmental, religious, or other institutions of national scope and sway? Is it a function of emergency situations or is it an everyday organic occurrence? Consider in these lights, for example, resort to the death penalty in the United States; female genital cutting (FGC)[80] recently outlawed in Egypt[81] and reportedly on the decline in Kenya and the Côte d'Ivoire;[82] female "honor killings" in Jordan (to protect one's family's reputation) in violation of

---

[80]   *See supra* note 7.

[81]   *See Egypt Ends Female Genital Mutilation*, INTER PRESS SERV., *available in* 1998 WL 5988706 (reporting the banning of female genital cutting by the Egyptian Council of State after a period of controversial debate in Egypt). *See also* Barbara Crossette, *Court Backs Egypt's Ban on Mutilation*, N.Y. TIMES, Dec. 29, 1997, § A, at 4; *Court Reinstates Ban on Female Circumcision*, MIDDLE EAST TIMES, Jan. 4, 1998; Inter-African Committee (IAC) Newsletter, No. 22, at 5, Dec. 1997 (c/o ECA/ACW, P.O. Box 3001, Addis Ababa, Eth., 147, rue de Lausanne, 1202 Geneva, Switz.), *available in* 1998 WL 5045178; *Egyptian Health Minister Defends Female Circumcision Ban*, AGENCE-FRANCE PRESSE, Feb. 13, 1998; *Egypt Continues Ban on Genital Mutilation*, WASH. POST, July 12, 1997.

[82]   Regarding Kenya, *see, e.g.*, Cesar Chelala, *An Alternative Way to Stop Female Genital Mutilation*, 352 THE LANCET (UMI), No. 9122, Jul. 11, 1998, *available in* 1998 WL 14104178, at 1; Cesar Chelala, *New Rite Is Alternative to FGM*, S.F. CHRON., Sept. 16, 1998, *available in* 1998 WL 3923069; Judy Mann, *From Victims to Agents of Change*, WASH. POST, Apr. 29, 1994, at E3; Judy Mann, *Rituals: Replacing the Bad with Good*, WASH. POST, June. 15, 1994, at E15; Malik Stan Reaves, *Alternative Rite to Female Circumcision Spreading in Kenya*, AFR. NEWS SERV., Nov. 19, 1997, *available in* 1997 WL 15137606. Re the Côte d'Ivoire, see, *e.g.*, Melvis Dzisah, *FGM Practitioners Start to Abandon the Trade*, INTER PRESS SERV., *available in* 1998 WL 19900917; *Female Genital Mutilation*, 24 WIN NEWS No. 1, *available in* 1998 WL 15486015; Melvis Dzisah, *Ivorian MPs Split on How to Tackle Genital Cutting*, INTER PRESS SERV., *available in* 1998 WL 5986408.

Jordanian public policy;[83] and the curtailment of civil liberties in the presence of civil conflicts or in the wake of national disasters. If the practice extends broadly geographically, or has been around for centuries or is growing in use, or is sponsored or actively supported by national governmental or religious institutions, or is a function of normal everyday life, might it not deserve at least *prima facie* deference? By the same token, if it is geographically confined, relatively new or dying out, carried out without church/state participation or approval, and/or implemented only or mainly during "manufactured crises," surely greater skepticism regarding claims of "cultural tradition" would be warranted. Guiding our assessment of the answers to these questions are, of course, the public order goals postulated by our "initial position" decision-makers.

4. Bases of Power

Potentially, all values (the "welfare values" of wealth, well-being, skills, and enlightenment, on the one hand, and the "deference values" of power, respect, rectitude, and affection, on the other[84]) may be, alone or in combination, bases of power to ensure the continuity or discontinuity of given cultural practices. They are, indeed, the essential components of power in any social process, and thus the need for careful scrutiny of those that are available to the masters and servants of a cultural practice in any given case seems axiomatic. Notably requiring attention, for example, is the availability or nonavailability of particular values to the respective parties in the absolute sense, as often this will explain both the intensity and the character of selected courses of action or inaction—that is, the enforcement (execution or maintenance) of a cultural practice, on the one hand, and/or its reception (acceptance or toleration), on the other—and thus the cross-cultural deference that should or should not be extended to it. Even more important, perhaps, is the need to delineate the relative value positions of the masters and servants of a cultural practice inasmuch as significant disparities between them, relative to each other and to the

---

[83] As reported by Christiane Amanpour in "Blood for Honor" on CNN, Jan. 10, 1999. For the transcript of this broadcast report, see <http://cnn.com/TRANSCRIPTS/9901/10/impc. 00.html> (visited Jan. 11, 1999). *See also* Mary Curtius, *Paying a High Price for Honor: An Arab Tribal Custom Obliges a Man to Kill a Female Relative If He Thinks She Has Sullied the Family Name; Palestinian Women Hope that in the New Mideast Tolerance of Such Murders Will End*, L.A. TIMES, Mar. 12, 1995, at 1; Irene R. Prusher, *Spotlight on Killing of Women for "Family Honor": Jordanian Journalist Rana Husseini Broke a Job Barrier to Probe a Deadly Tradition*, CHRIST. SCI. MONITOR, Oct. 23, 1998, at 6.

[84] For this typology, I am intellectually indebted to the germinal work: HAROLD D. LASS-WELL & ABRAHAM KAPLAN, POWER AND SOCIETY: A FRAMEWORK FOR POLITICAL INQUIRY (1950). Lasswell and Kaplan write, at 55–56: "By 'welfare values' we mean those whose possession to a certain degree is a necessary condition for the maintenance of the physical activity of the person. . . . Deference values are those that consist in being taken into consideration (in the acts of others and of the self)."

wider community of which they are a part, might well tip the scales of cross-cultural judgment. It is well known, for example, that such masters of cultural practices as family clans, ethnic and religious groups, and governments commonly possess greater effective influence (power) and control more resources and personnel (wealth, enlightenment, skill) than the servants of such practices. In such circumstances, it logically would seem, one's evaluative guard must be up. Bearing in mind the postulated public order goals of our "initial position" decision-makers, a cultural practice that continues mostly or exclusively because those with the most resources are able to force others to submit to it irrespective of their own perspectives about it should be subject to intense scrutiny, as in the case, for example, of caste-based social organization in which only "upper" caste members may hold high positions of power and influence while "lower" caste members are relegated to laborious jobs and poor living conditions. The examples are of course legion and require no pedant's footnotes here.

5. Strategies

The strategies employed by both the masters and the servants of cultural practices, in support of their respective perspectives and qualified by the bases of power that they can bring to bear in this regard, commonly embrace, in varying degree, combination, and sequence, the whole range of instruments of policy—diplomatic, ideological, economic, and military[85]—that invariably are available to public and private officials. The masters of cultural practices will resort to some or all of them, typically, to ensure the vitality and continuity of such practices, and the servants of them will do likewise either for the same reasons or, alternatively, to resist their continued exercise. Thus, because the type of strategy employed may sometimes shape cross-cultural judgment about the support of, or opposition to, a given practice and thus its acceptability within the social framework within which it is exercised, it is useful to ask what strategies the participants employ to secure their objectives. For example, again recalling the public order goals postulated by our "initial position" decision-makers, one might legitimately look askance at cultural practices whose continued maintenance depends upon, say, bribery and other cor-

---

[85] I use these terms as they are defined in MCDOUGAL ET AL., *supra* note 1, at 135:

Diplomacy in the broadest sense depends primarily upon symbols in the form of offers, counter-offers, and agreements (deals) among elite figures. Ideological strategy also uses symbols as the principal means of action, its distinctiveness being communications directed to large audiences. Economic instruments involve goods and services; military strategy employs means of violence and destruction. While diplomacy and ideology are especially concerned with perspectives, economic and military instruments are based upon capabilities. No instrument, however, is restricted to its most distinctive modality.

rupt measures (economic instrument) or resort to the use of force (military instrument). However, particularly relevant for decision-making regarding given cultural practices is, as implied, less the type of strategy that is employed than the differing degrees of coerciveness and persuasiveness with which they are employed. From the standpoint of the masters of cultural practices, this calls for responsible attention to alleged abuses or excesses of power that commonly manifest coercive or disproportionate means of enforcing cultural practices. All other things being equal, and once more recalling the postulated public order goals of our "initial position" decision-makers, a practice that is implemented largely through highly coercive or arguably disproportionate uses of power—amputation and stoning in the Middle East? the death penalty and solitary confinement in the United States?—should come under greater scrutiny than those that are characterized mainly by persuasion and with all or most of the participants freely choosing to take part in the practice in question. From the standpoint of the servants of cultural practices, it is well to consider the intensity of commitment or resistance to the practice and thus to the degree of persuasiveness or coerciveness with which it is greeted by them. Relying upon the same judgmental criteria, if a practice is carried out or served voluntarily, all other things being equal, it warrants at least *prima facie* deference or respect in cross-cultural decision-making. By the same token, if it is violently resisted, say to the point of provoking widespread riots or other civil disturbances, surely its legitimacy must be seen as in doubt.

6.   Outcomes and Effects

Perhaps most important to cross-cultural judgment about given cultural practices are the short-term outcomes and long-term effects (or consequences) of the interactions between the masters and servants of the cultural practice in question. When all is said and done, it is the balance sheet of net value gains and losses, both short- and long-term, absolute and relative, that results from the exercise of the practice that commonly determines whether that practice is to be honored or dishonored in cross-cultural judgment, for hovering over that balance sheet is, as stressed in Section IV(A) above, the issue of necessity—that is, the necessity of the value losses relative to the gains for cultural diversity or pluralism.

Thus, the following kinds of "outcome" questions are exceedingly pertinent: Does the continued exercise of the practice spell a "win-win" outcome for the participants involved? A "win-lose" outcome? If the latter, who "wins" and who "loses," and in what ways? In other words, if the continued exercise of the cultural practice can be seen essentially to reflect the shared aspirations of persons engaged in a cooperative community enterprise (a "win-win" outcome), then surely at least preliminary deference should be shown that practice. If on the other hand, its continued exercise may be concluded to benefit only a small group of "winners," say, at the expense of a large group of "losers," then surely also a high degree of scrutiny relative to it is warranted, particularly when the "losers" manifest distinctive "minority" identity. Even if the masters of a cultural practice do not intend a discriminatory result, the postulated public order goals of our "initial position" decision-makers compel us to account for the fact of discriminatory deprivation or nonfulfillment as such.

As for the long-term effects that can be observed to result from the exercise of the cultural practice in dispute, which potentially can impact not only the immediate participants involved but, as well, all the actors in the larger global system, again cross-cultural decision-making must take heed. Suppose, for example, that the continued exercise of a given cultural practice were to result in racially discriminatory outcomes that, in turn, would spark instability and violent uprisings in large parts of the country involved and perhaps even beyond—as indeed occurred in pre-1990 South Africa in response to the continued exercise of the then claimed cultural practice of racial *apartheid*.[86] What then? If we are to be faithful to the postulated public order goals of our "initial position" decision-makers, then, logically, cross-cultural decision-making should look upon the practice with not a little skepticism. Suppose, however, that the opposite were true, *i.e.*, that the continued exercise of the cultural practice—say, discriminations based on merit or basic need—were to have a net positive effect for the society in question as a whole. Then, just as logically and based on the same criteria, cross-cultural decision-making should display at least initial great deference.

The point is, of course, that cultural practices can have both beneficial and detrimental outcomes and effects relative to the postulated public order goals of our "initial position" decision-makers. Precise characterization of them and therefore cross-cultural judgment about them will hinge at least in part on whether and how one appraises their short- and long-term consequences.

7. General Conditions

It takes little imagination to see that if cross-cultural decision-making is to respond adequately to the vicissitudes of our times, it must be made to account not only for the primary characteristics of the particular relativist-universalist case, but also for those influential general conditions of the larger global context within which those characteristics live. Of course, the wider influential context within which such decision-making operates is ever-changing. Moreover, what may be relevant in the wider context for one relativist-universalist controversy may not be germane for another. Nevertheless, certain features of the current world scene, many of them contradictory, seem especially significant and therefore worthy of at least pass-

---

[86]   One is reminded, in this regard, of the question attributed to former U.S. President John F. Kennedy: "Is not peace, in the last analysis, basically a matter of human rights?" *Quoted in* Arthur J. Goldberg, *Our Concern for Human Rights*, 32 Congress Bi-Weekly, No. 13, at 8, 8 (Nov. 15, 1965) (an article excerpted from Ambassador Goldberg's address at the Stephen Wise Awards Dinner in New York City, Oct. 31, 1965).

ing consideration when attempting cross-cultural judgment at the present time:

- the United States as the sole superpower, the disappearance (however temporary) of serious normative rivalry, and thus an ambiguous geopolitical environment for global decision-making of all kinds, fundamentally influencing, *inter alia*, the United Nations and other experiments at international, cross-cultural collaboration;

- the accelerating socio-economic "globalization" of the world, commonly on unequal terms as between "modern" and "traditional" peoples and cultures;

- a consequent expanding interpenetration and interdependence of the world's peoples and their cultures (however uneven) and simultaneous decline of state power (the United States included);

- increased resort to intercultural civil conflict (ethnic, religious, tribal) together with increased even if hesitant resort to external "humanitarian intervention," on the one hand, and decreasing resort to major aggressive international warfare, on the other;

- a growing fragility of national and international controls over weapons of mass destruction and, at the same time, a marked tendency toward inter-civilizational/inter-cultural national and international terrorism (both state and non-state) of the most violent sort;

- an enlarging trend toward democratization and the rule of law midst widespread disillusionment with democratic processes born of, *inter alia*, inter-civilizational/inter-cultural tensions and unrewarded experiment;

- a widening disparity in economic position between the world's "haves"and "have-nots" (both between and within the North and South) and simultaneously declining public funds for economic development, thus deepening and expanding the culture of poverty and the formidable obstacles to progressive change that inhere in it; and

- mounting ecological emergencies of regional and global—indeed, extraterrestrial—dimension and hesitant support for environmental protection and the cultures that are ecologically dependent.

Comprehensive assessment of these and other "secondary" contextual conditions would seek richer indication of their specific relevance to diverse cultural practices and to the fundamental policies that are deemed pertinent in relation to them.

D. The Projection of Future Trends in Cross-Cultural Decision

The projection of probable future developments relative to given cultural practices—in the sense of the broad trend, not the particular instance—is an important variable to take into account in cross-cultural decision-making for at least two reasons. First, it can help us to see whether continuation of the given practice will reveal movement toward or away from the postulated public order goals of our "initial position" decision-makers. If so, then the practice should be seen as deserving at least *prima facie* deference; if not, then the opposite. Second, to minimize the diminishment of cultural pluralism where continuation of the given practice will reveal movement away from the postulated public order goals of our "initial position" decision-makers, it can help to stimulate creativity in the invention and evaluation of alternatives to the manner in which the given cultural practice is currently being exercised so as simultaneously to preserve the essence of the practice and make it consistent with our postulated public order goals. This is no easy decisional task. Certainly it cannot be done on the basis of some simpleminded extrapolation of the past. It requires a disciplined analysis of all the relevant features of the practice under scrutiny and of the primary and secondary contextual factors that condition it.

E. The Invention and Evaluation of Alternatives

The final intellectual task of respectful decision-making in relativist-universalist controversies, already hinted at, relates to the deliberate search for, and assessment of, alternatives either to the continuation of the given cultural practice itself or to the manner in which it is exercised in cases where it may be found that the practice or, more precisely, its manner of exercise is at odds with the postulated public order goals of our "initial position" decision-makers. It is, one might say, the task of last resort in as much as it is the one towards which all the preceding intellectual tasks accumulate and therefore the one to be pursued after all of its predecessors have been credibly exhausted. The point is that the ultimate goal of respectful decision-making in the relativist-universalist context is to provide not a basis for declaring victory by one side of the debate over the other, but, rather, to enhance the possibility of ensuring the world's rich diversity (cultural pluralism) while at the same time serving the values of *human* dignity as defined by the postulated public order goals of our "initial position" decision-makers. Thus, where, on final analysis, a particular cultural practice is found to conflict with those postulated public order goals in the manner of its exercise but not necessarily in its innate purpose or social function, one would look to encourage or reward initiatives that would make the practice consistent with the values of human dignity embedded in the postulated public order goals of our "initial position" decision-makers. A recent case in point is found in the rites of female passage and sexual purification in sub-Saharan Africa where, for generations, these rites have been administered via female genital cutting (FGC).[87] Recently in Kenya and the Côte d'Ivoire, however, the focus of responsible attention has shifted to emphasize the innate purpose of the occasion rather than the modality of its implementation and thus to preserve the occasion and simultaneously lessen or eliminate its severity.[88] To the extent feasible, in other words, respectful decision-making in cross-cultural context should seek integrative

---

[87]   *See supra* note 7.

[88]   *See supra* note 82.

solutions characterized by maximum gains and minimum losses for all sides of the relativist-universalist debate; it should seek diversity in unity.

V. Appraisal and Recommendation

In the preceding pages, I have attempted to outline, in at least impressionistic fashion, the key intellectual tasks and inquiries that I believe are required to serve respectful decision in relativist-universalist contests. To say that they are the *key* intellectual tasks and inquiries, however, is not to say that they constitute *all* the study that is needed. Additionally critical to respectful cross-cultural decision is an honest assessment of the very decision process pursuant to which that judgment is being rendered. As any sophisticated law student knows, who decides what, why, when, where, and how often has as much and sometimes more to do with the resolution of legal controversies as the facts and pertinent doctrines, principles, and rules themselves. Indeed, for precisely this reason, a thorough "policy science" approach to respectful decision in the relativist-universalist context would identify and analyze that process just as it would identify and analyze the process of decision in any controversy—that is, not simply as just one more factor generally conditioning the controversy, but, rather, as a separate yet intimately interrelated central part of the total social process surrounding the controversy that merits discrete analysis in its own right.

For reasons of efficiency and space, however, I leave this further exploration to another day. For present purposes, suffice it to say that questions concerning the identity, perspectives, decisional arenas, bases of power, strategies, and other attributes that help to define those who render cross-cultural judgments about relativist-universalist controversies have also to be seen as indispensable factors to be taken into account if genuinely respectful decision is to be rendered. Especially is this true in the highly decentralized world of the contemporary international legal order where authoritative and controlling decisions commonly are rendered on a horizontal or one-to-one, foreign office-to-foreign office basis where officials typically serve in a dual capacity as claimant and judge at the same time—what French jurist Georges Scelle has called the "dédoublement fonctionnel."[89] In such settings, less immune to "external" political influences than ordinarily are highly developed judicial systems on the national plane, and especially in inter-civilizational disputes, the motivations and bases of power of the decision-maker, for example, can have powerful—even illegitimate—influence upon the outcome of relativist-universalist decision and thus should be subject to rigorous objective scrutiny—really self-scrutiny in the horizontal inter-office setting—when trying to weigh the authenticity and validity of competing relativist and universalist claims. The core value of respect demands at a minimum that the process of cross-cultural decision-making

---

[89] Georges Scelle, *Théorie et Pratique de la Fonction Executive en Droit International*, 55 Recueil des Cours (Hague Acad. Int'l L.) 87, 93–96 (1936).

itself prove its own legitimacy when it comes to challenging, possibly eliminating altogether, a demonstration of cultural pluralism.

In any event, one thing is certain: if one is to take seriously the proposition that respect is "the core value of all human rights,"[90] there is no escaping that cross-cultural decision-making about relativist-universalist controversies cannot be a simpleminded affair. Necessarily, it must reflect the complexity of life itself, implicating a whole series of interrelated activities and events that are indispensable to effective inquiry and therefore to rational and respectful choice in decision. And to this end, I therefore join other human rights theorists and activists in advocating the importance of dialogue across cultures and societies.[91] But not only ethical or moral dialogue. Also needed is that kind of cross-cultural dialogue that can yield substantial detailed consensus on the many factual and policy-oriented questions that absolutely need to be asked—hopefully systematically in keeping with the *methodology of respect* that I have urged here—so as to guarantee that the core value of respect will be present in all relativist-universalist decision-making. This essay is offered as a modest preliminary contribution to that end.

---

[90]   *Supra* note 1, at xvii. *See also id.* ch. 6.

[91]   *See, e.g.*, Abdullahi An-Na'im, *Islamic Law and the Dilemma of Cultural Legitimacy for Universal Human Rights, in* HUMAN RIGHTS IN CROSS-CULTURAL PERSPECTIVE: A QUEST FOR CONSENSUS (Abdullahi Ahmed An-Na'im ed., 1995); Etzioni, *supra* note 21, at 183–88; Gunning, *supra* note 7, at 227; Otto, *supra* note 16, at 31–36.

Voices of Suffering, Fragmented Universality, and the Future of Human Rights*

Upendra Baxi

I. Introduction

A. An Age of Human Rights?

Much of the Christian twentieth century, especially its later half, will be recalled as an "Age of Human Rights." No preceding century of human history[1] has been privileged to witness a profusion of human rights enunciations on a global scale. Never before have the languages of human rights sought to supplant all other ethical languages. No preceding century has witnessed the proliferation of human rights norms and standards as a core aspect of what may be called the politics of intergovernmental desire. Never before has there been a discourse so varied and diverse that it becomes necessary to publish and update regularly, through the unique discursive instrumentality of the United Nations system, in ever-exploding volumes of fine print, the various texts of instruments relating to human rights.[2] The Secretary-General of the United Nations was perhaps right to observe (in his inaugural remarks at the 1993 Vienna Conference on Human Rights) that human rights constitute a "common language of humanity."[3] Indeed, it would be true to say that, in some ways, a human rights "sociolect" has emerged, in this era of the end of

---

*   Copyright © 1999 by Upendra Baxi. This essay anticipates some themes and formulations from my work THE FUTURE OF HUMAN RIGHTS (forthcoming). A less refined version appears under a somewhat different title in 8 TRANSNAT'L L. & CONTEMP. PROBS. 125 (1998). Reprint permission granted.

[1]   I use the term "human" as an act of communicational courtesy. Human is marked by the presence of *man*; so is per*son*. My preferred non-sexist version is, therefore, a combination of the first letters of both words: *huper*. I await the day when the word "huper" will replace the word "human."

[2]   *See* THE UNITED NATIONS, HUMAN RIGHTS: A COMPILATION OF INTERNATIONAL INSTRUMENTS (1997).

[3]   Boutros Boutros-Ghali, *Human Rights: The Common Language of Humanity, in* UNITED NATIONS: WORLD CONFERENCE ON HUMAN RIGHTS, THE VIENNA DECLARATION AND PROGRAMME OF ACTION (1993).

ideology, as the only universal ideology in the making, enabling both the legitimation of power and the *praxis* of emancipatory politics.[4]

At the same time, the Christian twentieth century has been tormented by its own innovations in catastrophic politics. The echoes of Holocaust and Hiroshima-Nagasaki suffering vibrate in the Universal Declaration of Human Rights (UDHR)[5] as well as in the millennial dream of turning swords into ploughshares. But the politics of cruelty continue even as sonorous declarations on human rights proliferate. A distinctively European contribution to recent history, the politics of organized intolerance and ethnic cleansing, has been universalized in the "killing fields" of post-colonial experience. The early, middle, and late phases of the Cold War[6] orchestrated prodigious human suffering as well as an exponential growth of human rights enunciations. And if Cold War practices were deeply violative of basic human rights, post-Cold War practices—for example the "ethnic wars"—are no less so.[7]

Still, though not radically ameliorative of here-and-now suffering, international human rights standards and norms empower peoples' movements and conscientious policy-makers everywhere to question political practices. That, to my mind, is an inestimable potential of human rights languages, not readily available in previous centuries. Human rights languages are perhaps all that we have to interrogate the barbarism of power, even when these remain inadequate to humanize fully the barbaric practices of politics.

---

4   For the notion of ideology as a set of languages characterized by reflexivity—or as "sociolect," see ALVIN GOULDNER, THE DIALECTIC OF IDEOLOGY AND TECHNOLOGY: THE ORIGINS, GRAMMAR AND FUTURE OF IDEOLOGY 61–65 (Oxford University Press 1982); J.B. THOMPSON, STUDIES IN THE THEORY OF IDEOLOGY (1984). A more recent variant is the use of the phrase "dialects of human rights." *See* MARY ANN GLENDON, RIGHTS TALK: THE IMPOVERISHMENT OF POLITICAL DISCOURSE (1991). *See also* DAVID JACOBSON, RIGHTS ACROSS BORDERS: IMMIGRATION AND THE DECLINE OF CITIZENSHIP 2–3 (1996) (the state, Jacobson rightly stresses, is becoming less constituted by sovereign agency and more by "a larger international and constitutional order based on human rights." Human rights provide a "vehicle and object of this revolution."); Upendra Baxi, *Human Rights Education: The Promise of the Twenty-first Century?, in* HUMAN RIGHTS EDUCATION 142 (George J. Andreopoulos & Richard Pierre Claude eds., 1997) (for a full version, *see* <http://www.pdhre.org> (visited Dec. 1, 1998)).

5   *See infra* Appendix I [hereinafter UDHR].

6   Periodization of "cold war" is crucial to any understanding of how the intergovernmental politics of desire pursued its own distinctive itineraries. The "cold war" condenses many a moment of practices of cruelty while simultaneously registering innovation in human rights enunciations. For an overall account of the politics of cruelty, see CLIVE PONTING, PROGRESS AND BARBARISM: THE WORLD IN THE TWENTIETH CENTURY (1998).

7   For an insightful analysis, see ANATOLY M. KAZANOV, AFTER THE USSR: ETHNICITY, NATIONALISM, AND POLITICS IN THE COMMONWEALTH OF INDEPENDENT STATES (1995).

In this essay, I ponder the future of human rights, a future that is periclated by a whole variety of developments in theory and practice. I do so by addressing seven critical themes:

- *first*, the genealogies of human rights, both "modern" and "contemporary," their logics of exclusion and inclusion, and the construction of ideas about "human";

- *second*, the realities of the overproduction of human rights norms and standards and their significance for human rights futures;

- *third*, the politics of difference and identity, which views human rights as having not just an emancipative potential but also a repressive one;

- *fourth*, the post-modernist suspicion of the power to tell large global stories (the "meta-narratives") which carries the potential of converting human rights languages into texts or tricks of governance;

- *fifth*, the resurfacing of arguments about ethical and cultural relativism interrogating the politics of universality of human rights, making possible, in good conscience, toleration of vast stretches of human suffering;

- *sixth*, the danger of conversion of human rights movements into human rights markets; and

- *seventh*, the emergence, with the forces and relations of "globalization" (attested to by such dominant ideologies as "economic rationalism," "good governance," and "structural adjustment"), of a trade-related, market-friendly paradigm of human rights seeking to supplant the paradigm of the UDHR.

In addressing these themes, I take it as axiomatic that the historic mission of "contemporary" human rights is *to give voice to human suffering*, to make it visible and to ameliorate it. The notion that human rights regimes may, or ought to, contribute to the "pursuit of happiness" remains the privilege of a miniscule segment of humanity. For hundreds of millions of the "wretched of the earth,"[8] human rights enunciations matter, if at all, only if they provide shields against torture and tyranny, deprivation and destitution, pauperization and powerlessness, desexualization and degradation.

Contrary to the range of expectations evoked by the title of this essay, I do not make explicit the actual voices of human suffering to assist our sense of the reality of human rights. But I try to do the next best thing: to relate the theory and practice of human rights to the endless varieties of preventible human suffering. Recovery of the sense and experience of human anguish provides the only hope that there is for the future of human rights.

---

8   *See* Frantz Fanon, The Wretched of the Earth (1963).

B. Some De-Mystifications

At the outset, some approaches to keywords may be helpful. I shun the self-proclaimed post-modernist virtue that, even at its best moment, celebrates incomprehensibility as a unique form of intelligibility.

True, the worlds of power and resistance to power are rife with complexity and contradiction. True also, the production of human rights "truths" contesting those of power is marked by a surplus of meaning. For those who suffer violation, an appeal to public virtue, no matter how creatively ambiguous, remains a necessity. In contrast, brutal clarity characterizes regimes of political cruelty. All the same, I also believe that clarity of conviction and communication is a crucial resource for promoting and protecting human rights. Success in this performance is never assured, but the struggle to attain it is by itself a human rights task.

1. Human Rights

The very term "human rights" is deeply problematic.[9] It straddles several universes of discourse. Moral philosophers signify by it a set of ethical imperatives that contribute to making the basic structure of society and state to be and remain overall "just." International lawyers regard the term as a set of norms and standards produced juridically (as having some sort of binding effect on the behavior of states and regional and international organizations). Architects and administrators of regional governance (such as the European Union) regard "human rights" promotion and protection as symbolic of the syndrome of shared sovereignty. For national power-elites, "human rights" provides vocabularies of legitimation of governance. For those who regard practices and structures of governance as deeply unjust or morally flawed, "human rights" represent a rallying cry against oppression and sites for practices of "counter-power."

The abundance of its meanings may not be reduced to a false totality such as "basic human rights" inasmuch as all human rights are basic to those who are deprived, disadvantaged, and dispossessed. Nor may we succumb to an anthropomorphic illusion that the range of human rights is limited to human beings; the new rights to a clean and healthy environment (or what is somewhat inappropriately, even cruelly, called "sustainable development"[10]) take us far beyond such a narrow

---

[9] The human rights discourse is not bloodless. Devout Nazis, or their lineal neo-Nazi descendants, are rarely affected by the afflictions of erudite discourse concerning properties of "human rights" (their universality, interdependence, indivisibility, and inalienability). They claim logics and paralogics of human rights as the weaponry that would destroy the very notion! The esoteric human rights discourse is at worst an ecological threat (forests have to be felled in order that human rights discourses thrive worldwide).

[10] See ANDREW ROWELL, GREEN BACKLASH: GLOBAL SUBVERSION OF THE ENVIRONMENTAL MOVEMENT 4–41 (1996). For the extraordinary relation between Nazism and deep ecology, see LUC FERRY, THE NEW ECOLOGICAL ORDER 91–107 (Carol Volk trans., 1995).

notion. Nor should one reduce the forbiddingly diverse range of human rights enunciations or totality of sentiments that give rise to them to some uniform narrative that seeks family resemblance in such ideas as "dignity," "well-being," or human "flourishing." The expression "human rights" shelters an incredibly diverse range of *the politics of desire-in-dominance* and *the politics of desire-in-insurrection*. These forms of politics resist encapsulation in any formula. The best one may hope for is to let the contexts of domination and resistance articulate themselves as separate but equal perspectives on the meaning of "human rights."

2. Discursivity

By "discursivity" I refer to both erudite and ordinary practices of "rights-talk." Rights-talk (or discursive practice) occurs within traditions (discursive formations).[11] Traditions, themselves codes for power and hierarchy, allocate competences (who may speak), construct forms (how one may speak, what forms of discourse are proper), determine boundaries (what may not be named or conversed about), and structure exclusion (denial of voice). What I call "modern" human rights offers powerful examples of the power of the rights-talk tradition.

What I call "contemporary" human rights discursivity illustrates the power of the subaltern discourse. When that discourse acquires the intensity of a discursive insurrection, its management becomes a prime task of human rights diplomacy. Dominant or hegemonic rights-talk seeks but does not ever fully achieve the suppression of subaltern rights-talk. Human rights discursivity, to invoke a Filipino template, is marked by complexity and contradiction between the statist discourse of the educated (*illustrados*) and the subversive discourse of the indigenous (*indio*).[12]

Discourse theorists often maintain that discursive practice constitutes social reality; there are no violators, violated, and violations outside discourse. But all this ignores or obscures nondiscursive or material practices of power and resistance. The nondiscursive order of reality, the materiality of human violation, is just as important, if not more so, from the standpoint of the violated.[13]

---

[11] For example, rights-talk (discursive practice) gives rise to distinct, even if related, regimes (discursive formations): the civil and political rights regime in international law is distinct from the social, cultural, and economic rights regime. The ways in which discursive formations occur determine what shall count as a violation of human rights. The prohibition against torture, cruel, inhuman, degrading punishment or treatment in the civil and political rights formation also prohibits rights-talk which equates starvation or domestic violence as a violation of human rights. The latter gets constituted as *violation* only when discursive boundaries are transgressed.

[12] See ANTHONY WOODIWISS, GLOBALISATION, HUMAN RIGHTS AND LABOR LAW IN THE PACIFIC ASIA 104 (1998).

[13] This point is cruelly established, for example, by the "productive" technologies entailed in the manufacture and distribution of landmines or weapons and instruments of mass

3. Logics and Paralogics of Human Rights

By the use of the notion of "paralogics," I conflate the notions of logic and rhetoric. Paradigmatic logic follows a "causal" chain of signification to a "conclusion" directed by major and minor premises. Rhetorical logic does not regard argument as "links in the chain," but rather, as legs to a chair.[14] What matters in rhetorical logic is the choice of *tópoi*, literary conventions that define sites from which the processes of suasion begin. These sites are rarely governed by any pre-given *tópoi*; rather, they dwell in that which one thinks one ought to argue about.[15] "Human rights" logic or paralogics are all about how one may or should construct *"techniques of persuasion [as] a means of creating awareness."*[16]

The human rights "we-ness" that enacts and enhances these techniques of suasion is multifarious, contingent, and continually fragmented. That "we-ness" is both an artifact of power as well as of resistance. Human rights discourse is intensely partisan; it cannot exist or endure outside the webs of impassioned commitment and networks of contingent solidarities, whether on behalf and at the behest of dominant or subaltern ideological practice. Both claim the ownership of a transformative vision of politics, of anticipation of possible human futures. The historic significance of human rights (no matter what we perform with this potter's clay) lies in the denial of administered regimes of disarticulation, even when this amounts only to the perforation of the escutcheon of dispersed sovereignty and state power.

---

destruction. It would be excessive to say that these are constituted by discursive practices and do not exist outside of these practices. The materiality of nondiscursive practices, arenas, and formations is relatively autonomous of discourse theories. It is another matter that human rights discursive practices are able, at times, to highlight victimage caused by the deployment of these technologies as violative of human rights.

14   *See* JULIUS STONE, LEGAL SYSTEM AND LAWYERS' REASONINGS 327 (1964).

15   This is expressed brilliantly by Umberto Eco:

For example, I can argue as follows: "What others possess having taken it away from me is not their property; it is wrong to take from others what is their property; but it is not wrong to restore the original order of property, putting back into my hands what was originally in my hands." But I can also argue: "Rights of property are sanctioned by the actual possession of a thing; if I take from someone what is actually in their possession, I commit an act against the rights of property and therefore theft." Of course a third argument is possible, namely: "All property is *per se* theft; taking property from property-owners means restoring the equilibrium violated by original theft, and therefore taking from the propertied the fruits of their thefts is *not just right but a duty*."

UMBERTO ECO, APOCALYPSE POSTPONED 75–76 (Robert Lumley ed., 1994) (emphasis added).

16   *Id.* at 77. I borrow Eco's phrase explaining the task of rhetoric in general (emphasis added).

4. Future of Human Rights

A sense of unease haunts my heavy invocation of "the future of human rights." In a sense, this future is already the past of human rights time, manner, and circumstance. What may constitute the future history of human rights depends on how imaginatively one defines, both in theory and movement, the challenges posed by the processes of globalization. Already we are urged to appreciate the "need to relocate" human rights in the "current processes of change."[17] From this perspective, what is mandated is the mode of structural adjustment of human rights reflexivity itself. The prospects of recycling the moral languages of human rights appear rather bleak in our globalizing human condition in ways that they did not to the forerunners and founders of human rights, from a Grotius to a Gandhi.

A contrasting vision stresses "rooted Utopianism."[18] It conceives of human rights futures as entailing nontechnocratic ways of imaging futures. The technocratic imaging takes for granted "the persistence of political forms and structures, at least short of collapse through catastrophe."[19] In contrast, the nontechnocratic ways derive sustenance from exemplary lives of citizen-pilgrims "at work amidst us" who embody a "refusal to be bound by either deference or acquiescence to statism" and "relate fulfillment to joy in community, not materialist acquisition."[20]

This essay hovers uncertainly between the globalization (doomsday) anticipation of the human future and the vision of utopian transformation animated by exemplary lives of countless citizen-pilgrims.[21] Yet it must be acknowledged that "human rights" have not one but many futures.

5. Suffering

Save when expedient, statist human rights discourse does not relate to languages of pain and suffering in its enunciations. In contrast, peoples' struggles against

---

[17]   *The Realization of Economic, Social and Cultural Rights: Final Report on the Question of the Impunity of Perpetrators of Human Rights Violations (Economic, Social and Cultural Rights)* (El Hadji Guissé, Special Rapporteur) (on file with the author).

[18]   RICHARD FALK, EXPLORATIONS AT THE EDGE OF TIME: THE PROSPECTS FOR WORLD ORDER 101–03 (1995).

[19]   *Id.*

[20]   *Id.*

[21]   Professor Falk mentions Mother Teresa, Bishop Desmond Tutu, Paulo Friere, Lech Walesa, Kim Dae Jung, and Petra Kelly. But alongside these charismatic figures exist "countless other women and men we will never know." Behind every legendary human rights life lie the lives of hundreds of human beings, no less exemplary. The task of historiography of human rights is to roll back the orders of anonymization. This task gets complicated in some troublesome ways by many a media-porous, U.N.-accredited, and self-certified NGO that obscures from view the unsurpassed moral heroism embodied in everyday exemplary lives. FALK, *supra* note 18.

regimes practicing the politics of cruelty are rooted in the direct experience of pain and suffering.

Even so, it remains necessary to problematize notions of suffering. Suffering is ubiquitous to the point of being natural, and is both creative and destructive of human potential. Religious traditions impart a cosmology to human suffering[22] towards which secular human rights traditions bear an ambivalent relationship. Additionally, recent social theory understanding of human suffering evinces many ways of enacting a boundary between "necessary" and "unnecessary" suffering,[23] sensitive to the problématique of the cultural/professional appropriation of human suffering.[24]

Crucial for present purposes is the fact that even human rights regimes enact an hierarchy of pain and suffering. Statist human rights regimes seek to legitimate capital punishment (despite normative trends signaling its progressive elimination); provide for the suspension of human rights in situations of "emergency" (howsoever nuanced); and promote an obstinate division between the exercise of civil and political rights, on the one hand, and social, economic, and cultural rights, on the other. Similarly, some global human rights regimes, policing via emergent post-Cold War sanctioning mechanisms, justify massive, flagrant, and ongoing human rights violations in the name of making human rights secure. Even non-statist human rights discursivity (at first sight "progressive") justifies the imposition of human suffering in the name of autonomy and identity movements. The processes of globalization envision a new dramaturgy of "justifiable" human suffering.

In sum, relating the future of human rights to human suffering is fateful for the futures of human rights.

II. Two Notions of Human Rights: "Modern" and "Contemporary"

The contrasting paradigms of "modern" and "contemporary" human rights mask forms of continuity within the framework of *raison d'état*. The basic contrasts seem to me to be four. First, in the "modern" paradigm of rights the logics of exclusion are pre-eminent, whereas in the "contemporary" paradigm, the logics of inclusion are paramount. Second, the relationship between human rights languages and governance differ markedly in the two paradigms. Third, the "modern" enunciation of human rights was almost ascetic; in contrast, "contemporary" enunciations present

---

22 *See, e.g.*, THOMAS AQUINAS, THE LITERAL EXPOSITION ON JOB: A SCRIPTURAL COMMENTARY CONCERNING PROVIDENCE (Anthony Damico trans., Martin D. Yaffe Interpretive Essay and Notes, Scholars Press 1989).

23 MAURICE GLASMAN, UNNECESSARY SUFFERING: MANAGING MARKET UTOPIA (1996).

24 *See, e.g.*, Arthur Kleinman & Joan Kleinman, *The Appeal of Experience; The Dismay of Images: Cultural Appropriation of Suffering in Our Times*, *in* SOCIAL SUFFERING 1 (Arthur Kleinman et al. eds., 1997).

a carnival. Finally, the "contemporary" paradigm inverts the inherent modernist relationship between human rights and human suffering.

The terms I use, *faute de mieux*, may mislead. What I call, "modern" also embraces a Hugo Grotius with his memorable emphasis on *temperamenta belli* (insistence on the minimization of suffering in war) and a Francisco Vittoria who valiantly proselytized, against the Church (to the point of heresy) and the Emperor (to the point of treason) the human rights of the New World. What I call the "contemporary" human rights paradigm is marked in some of its major moments by practices of *realpolitik*, above all the conscripting of human rights languages to brutal ends in former superpower Cold War rivalry and in emergent post-Cold War politics.

In any event, my description of the two paradigms is distinctly oriented to the European imagination about human rights. An adequate historiography will, of course, locate the originating languages of human rights far beyond European space and time. I focus on the "modern" precisely because of its destructive impact, in terms of both social consciousness and organization, on that which may be named—clumsily and with deep human violation—"pre-" or "non-" modern.

A. The Logics of Exclusion and Inclusion

The notion of human rights—historically the rights of *men*—is confronted with two perplexities. The first concerns the nature of human nature (the *is* question). The second concerns the question: who is to count as human or fully human (the *ought* question). While the first question continues to be debated in both theistic and secular terms,[25] the second—"Who should count as 'human'?"—occupies the center stage of the "modern" enunciation of human rights. The criteria of individuation in the European liberal traditions of thought[26] furnished some of the most powerful ideas in constructing a model of human rights. Only those beings were to be regarded as "human" who were possessed of the capacity for reason and autonomous moral will, although what counted as reason and will varied in the long development of the European liberal tradition. In its major phases of development, "slaves," "heathens," "barbarians," colonized peoples, indigenous populations, women, children, the impoverished, and the "insane" have been, at various times

---

25 The theistic responses trace the origins of human nature in the Divine Will; the secular in contingencies of evolution of life on earth. The theistic approaches, even when recognizing the holiness of all creation, insist on Man being created in God's image, and therefore capable of perfection in ways no other being in the world is. The secular/scientific approaches view human beings as complex psychosomatic systems co-determined by both genetic endowment and the environment and open to experimentation, like all other objects in "nature." These differences could be (and have been) described in more sophisticated ways, especially by various *ius naturalist* thinkers. *See, e.g.*, STONE, *supra* note 14.

26 *See* Bhikhu Parekh, *The Modern Conception of Rights and Its Marxist Critique, in* THE RIGHT TO BE HUMAN 1 (Upendra Baxi et al. eds., 1987). *See also* RAYMOND WILLIAMS, KEYWORDS 161–65 (1983).

and in various ways, thought unworthy of being bearers of human rights. In other words, these discursive devices of Enlightenment rationality were devices of exclusion. The "Rights of Man" were the human rights of all *men* capable of autonomous reason and *will*. While by no means the exclusive prerogative of "modernity,"[27] a large number of human beings were excluded by this peculiar ontological construction.[28]

Exclusionary criteria are central to the "modern" conception of human rights. The foremost historical role performed by them was to accomplish the justification of the unjustifiable, namely, colonialism and imperialism.[29] That justification was inherently racist; colonial powers claimed a collective human right of superior races to dominate the inferior ones ("the Other"). The Other in many cases ceased to exist before imperial law formulations such as the doctrine of *terra nullius*, following Blackstone's scandalous distinction between the inhabited and uninhabited colonies.[30] Since the Other of European imperialism was by definition not human or fully human, "it" was not worthy of human rights; at the very most, Christian compassion and charity fashioned some devices of legal or jural paternalism. That Other, not being human or fully human, also was liable to being merchandised in the slave market or to being the "raw material" of exploitative labor within and across the colonies. Not being entitled to a right to be and remain a human being, the Other was made a stranger and an exile to the language and logic of human rights being fashioned slowly but surely in (and for) the West. The classical liberal theory and practice of human rights, in its formative era, thus was innocent of the notion of universality of rights though certainly no stranger to its rhetoric.

The only *juristic* justification for colonialism/imperialism, if any is possible, is the claim that there is a *natural collective human right* of the superior races to rule the inferior ones, and the justification comes in many shapes and forms. One has but to read the "classic" texts of Locke or Mill to appreciate the range of talents that are devoted to the justification of colonialism.[31] The related but different logics combined to instill belief in the collective human right of the well-ordered

---

27 Religious traditions specialized, and still do, in ontological constructions that excluded, for example, Untouchables, rendering them beyond the pale of the *varna* system. *See* Upendra Baxi, *Justice as Emancipation: The Legacy of Babasaheb Ambedkar, in* CRISIS AND CHANGE IN CONTEMPORARY INDIA 122–49 (Upendra Baxi & Bhikhu Parekh eds., 1995).

28 *See* PETER FITZPATRICK, THE MYTHOLOGY OF MODERN LAW 92–145 (1992); MAHMOOD MAMDANI, CITIZEN AND SUBJECT: CONTEMPORARY AFRICA AND THE LEGACY OF LATE COLONIALISM 62–137 (1996).

29 Francisco de Vittoria, remarkably ahead of his times, made out a most cogent case for the human rights of the inhabitants of the "New World." *See* FRANCISCO DE VITTORIA, DE INDIS ET DE IVRE BELLI RELECTIONES (J. Bate trans., 1917) (1557).

30 *See* FITZPATRICK, *supra* note 28, at 72–91.

31 Bhikhu Parekh, *Liberalism and Colonialism: A Critique of Locke and Mill, in* THE DECOLONIZATION OF IMAGINATION: CULTURE, KNOWLEDGE AND POWER 81–88 (Jan Nederveen Pieterse & Bhikhu Parekh eds., 1995).

societies to govern the wild and "savage" races. All the well-known devices of the formative era of classical liberal thought were deployed: the logics of rights to property and progress; the state of nature and civil society; and social Darwinism, combining the infantalization and maturity of "races" and stages of civilization. The collective human right to colonize the less well-ordered peoples and societies for the collective "good" of both as well as of humankind was by definition indefeasible as well, and not in the least weakened in the curious logical reasoning and contradictions of evolving liberalism.

B. Human Rights Languages and the Power of Governance

The languages of human rights are integral to tasks and practices of governance, as exemplified by the constitutive elements of the "modern" paradigm of human rights—namely, the collective human right of the colonizer to subjugate "inferior" peoples and the absolutist right to property. The manifold though complex justifications offered for these "human rights" ensured that the "modern" European nation-state was able to marshal the right to property, as a right to world-wide *imperium* and *dominium*.

The construction of a collective human right to colonial/imperial governance is made sensible by the co-optation of languages of human rights into those of governance abroad and class and patriarchal domination at home. The hegemonic function of rights languages, in the service of governance at home and abroad, consisted in making whole groups of people socially and politically invisible. Their suffering was denied any authentic voice, since it was not constitutive of human suffering. "Modern" human rights, in their original narrative, entombed masses of human beings in shrouds of necrophilic silence.

In contrast, the "contemporary" human rights paradigm is based on the premise of radical self-determination. Self-determination insists that every person has a right to a voice, the right to bear witness to violation, and a right to immunity against "disarticulation" by concentrations of economic, social, and political formations. Rights languages, no longer exclusively at the service of the ends of governance, thus open up sites of resistance.

C. Ascetic versus Carnivalistic Rights Production

The "contemporary" production of human rights is exuberant.[32] This is a virtue compared with the lean and mean articulations of human rights in the "modern" period. In the "modern" era, the authorship of human rights was both state-centric

---

[32] For an insightful overview, see Burns H. Weston, *Human Rights*, 20 ENCYCLOPEDIA BRITANNICA 714 (15th ed. 1998 prtg.), *revised and updated in* ENCYCLOPAEDIA BRITANNICA ONLINE (visited Dec. 1, 1998) <http://www.eb.com:180/cgi-bin/g?DocF=macro/5002/93. html>.

and Eurocentric; in contrast, the formulations of "contemporary" human rights are increasingly inclusive and often marked by intense negotiation between NGOs and governments. The authorship of contemporary human rights is multitudinous, and so are the auspices provided by the United Nations and regional human rights networks. As a result, human rights enunciations proliferate, becoming as specific as the networks from which they arise and, in turn, sustain. The "modern" notion of human rights forbade such dispersal, the only major movement having been in the incremental affirmation of the rights of labor and minority rights. The way collectivities are now constructed in human rights enunciations is radically different. They do not merely reach out to "discrete" and "insular" minorities;[33] they extend also to wholly new, hitherto unthought of, justice constituencies.[34]

D. Human Suffering and Human Rights

Even at the end of the Second Christian Millennium we lack a social theory about human rights. Such a theory must address a whole range of issues,[35] but for present purposes it is necessary only to highlight the linkage between human suffering and human rights.

---

[33] This historic phrase comes from the famous footnote 4 in Carolene Products v. United States, 323 U.S. 18, 21 n. 4 (1944).

[34] Contemporary enunciations thus embrace, to mention very different orders by way of example, the rights of the girl-child, migrant labor, indigenous peoples, gays and lesbians (the emerging human right to sexual orientation), prisoners and those in custodial institutional regimes, refugees and asylum-seekers, and children.

[35] By the phrase "a social theory of human rights," a term frequently invoked in this essay, I wish to designate bodies of knowledge that address: (a) genealogies of human rights in "pre-modern," "modern" and "contemporary" human rights discursive formations; (b) contemporary dominant and subaltern images of human rights; (c) tasks confronting projects of engendering human rights; (d) exploration of human rights movements as social movements; (e) impacts of high science and "hi-tech" on the theory and practice of human rights; (f) the problematic of the marketization of human rights; (g) the economics and the political economy of human rights.

The listing is illustrative of bodies of reflexive knowledges. In select areas, these knowledges are becoming incrementally available but remain as yet in search of a new genre in social theory. Even as the era of "grand theory" in the imagination of social thought seems to begin to disappear, a return to it seems imperative if one is to make sensible a whole variety of human rights theory and practice. Daunting difficulties entailed in acts of totalization of human rights stand aggravated by this aspiration, but I continue to feel that the endeavor is worthy. Valuable beginnings in some of these directions have been made by FALK, *supra* note 18; WENDY BROWN, STATES OF INJURY: POWER AND FREEDOM IN LATE MODERNITY (1995); BOAVENTURA DE SOUSA SANTOS, TOWARDS A NEW COMMON SENSE: LAW, SCIENCE AND POLITICS IN THE PARADIGMATIC TRANSITION (1995); ROBERTO MANGABERIA UNGER, WHAT SHOULD LEGAL ANALYSTS BECOME? (1996). *See also* UPENDRA BAXI, THE FUTURE OF HUMAN RIGHTS (forthcoming).

The "modern" human rights cultures, tracing their pedigree to the Idea of Progress, Social Darwinism, racism, and patriarchy (central to the "Enlightenment" ideology), justified a global imposition of cruelty as "natural," "ethical," and "just." The "modern" liberal ideology that gave birth to the very notion of human rights, howsoever Euro-enclosed and no matter how riven with contradiction between liberalism and empire,[36] regarded the imposition of dire and extravagant suffering upon individual human beings as wholly justified. Practices of politics, barbaric even by the standards of the theological and secular thought of the Enlightenment, were somehow considered justified overall by ideologues, state managers, and the political unconscious that they generated (despite, most notably, the divergent struggles of the working classes). This "justification" boomeranged in the form of the politics of genocide of the Third Reich, often resulting in cruel complicity by "ordinary" citizens, unredeemed by even Schindler's list, in the worst foundational moments of present-day ethnic cleansing.[37]

In contrast, the post-Holocaust and post-Hiroshima angst registers a normative horror at human violation. The "contemporary" human rights movement is rooted in the illegitimacy of all forms of the politics of cruelty. No doubt what counts as cruelty varies enormously even from one human rights context/instrument to another.[38] Even so, there now are in place firm *jus cogens* norms of international human rights and humanitarian law, which de-legitimate and forbid barbaric practices of power in state as well as civil society. From the standpoint of those violated, this is no small gain; the community of perpetrators remains incrementally vulnerable to human rights cultures, howsoever variably, and this matters enormously for the violated. In a non-ideal world, human rights discursivity appears to offer an "ideal even if a second best" option.

---

[36] See UDAY MEHTA, LIBERALISM AND EMPIRE: A STUDY IN NINETEENTH-CENTURY LIBERAL THOUGHT (1999).

[37] Is this standpoint any more contestable in the wake of DANIEL JONAH GOLDHAGEN, HITLER'S WILLING EXECUTIONERS: ORDINARY GERMANS AND THE HOLOCAUST (1996) and RICHARD WEISBERG, POETHICS: AND OTHER STRATEGIES OF LAW & LITERATURE (1992)?

[38] For example: Is capital punishment in any form and with whatever justification a practice of cruelty? When does discrimination, whether based on gender, class, or caste, assume the form of torture proscribed by international human rights standards and norms? When may forms of sexual harassment in the workplace be described as an aspect of cruel, inhuman, and degrading treatment forbidden under the current international human rights standards and norms? Do nonconsensual sex practices within marriage relationships amount to rape? Do all forms of child labor amount to cruel practice, on the ground that the confiscation of childhood is an unredressable human violation? Are mega-irrigation projects that create eco-exiles and environmental destruction/degradation acts of developmental cruelty? Are programs or measures of structural adjustment an aspect of the politics of imposed suffering? This range of questions is vast and undoubtedly more may be added. For an anthropological mode of interrogation of torture, see Talal Asad, *On Torture, or Cruel, Inhuman and Degrading Treatment, in* SOCIAL SUFFERING, *supra* note 24, at 285–308.

No matter how many contested fields are sustained by the rhetoric of the universality, indivisibility, interdependence, and inalienability of human rights, contemporary human rights cultures have constructed new criteria relative to the legitimation of power. These criteria increasingly discredit any attempt to base power and rule on the inherent violence institutionalized in imperialism, colonialism, racism, and patriarchy. "Contemporary" human rights make possible, in most remarkable ways, discourse on human suffering. No longer may practices of power, abetted by grand social theory, justify beliefs that sustain willful infliction of harm as an attribute of sovereignty or of a good society. Central to "contemporary" human rights discourse are visions and ways of constructing the ethic of power which prevent the imposition of repression and human suffering beyond the needs of regime-survival no matter how extravagantly determined. The illegitimacy of the languages of immiseration becomes the very grammar of international politics.

Thus, the distinction between "modern" and "contemporary" forms of human rights is focused on *taking suffering seriously*.[39] Outside the domain of the laws of war among and between the "civilized" nations, "modern" human rights regarded large-scale imposition of human suffering as just and right in pursuit of a Eurocentric notion of human progress. It silenced the discourses of human suffering. In contrast, "contemporary" human rights are animated by a politics of international desire to render problematic the very notion of the politics of cruelty.

III. Critiques of "Contemporary" Human Rights

Many critiques of human rights have gained wide currency. Unmitigated skepticism about the possibility and/or desirability of human rights is frequently promoted. Unsurprising when stemming from autocratic or dictatorial leaders or regimes who criticize human rights norms and standards on the grounds of their origin, scope, and relevance (almost always reeking of expediency and bad faith), such critiques, when they emanate from the foremost social thinkers, require response.

I sample here two overarching criticisms of the idea of human rights. Talking about "contemporary" human rights in the "normal U.N. practice," Alasdair MacIntyre, in his widely acclaimed *After Virtue*, says that it thrives on "not giving

---

[39] *See* Upendra Baxi, *Taking Suffering Seriously: Social Action Litigation Before the Supreme Court of India, in* LAW AND POVERTY: CRITICAL ESSAYS 387 (Upendra Baxi ed., 1988). How may one explain this paradigm shift? At least six historic processes are entailed, which are both complex and contradictory. First, the many phases of the Cold War marked the birth and career of "contemporary" human rights, giving rise to fragmented "universality" of human rights. Second, the Cold War simultaneously "problematized" as well as naturalized human suffering. Third, within the fragmented universality emerged the outlawry of racism. Fourth, also within that fragmented universality emerged new forms of global solidarity for human rights. Fifth, the universalization of the Marxian critique of bourgeois human rights began to reshape these traditions. Sixth, all this created an endowment of practices of politics *of* and *for* human rights. I dwell on these features in BAXI, *supra* note 35, ch. 2.

good reasons for *any* assertion whatsoever;"[40] he even is moved to conclude that there are no natural or self-evident human rights and that belief in them is one with belief in witches and unicorns![41] Additionally Zygmunt Bauman asserts that human rights have "become a war-cry and blackmail weapon in the hands of aspiring 'community leaders' wishing to pick up powers that the state has dropped."[42] These eminent thinkers present their *ipse dixit*, however, as manifest truths. In contrast, responsible critiques of human rights are concerned with: (a) the modes of production of human rights; (b) the problems posed by the politics of universality of human rights and the politics of identity/difference; and (c) the arguments from relativism and multiculturalism. I examine each of these briefly.[43]

A. Too Many Rights or Too Few?

Is it the case that the late Christian twentieth century "suffers" from an overproduction of human rights standards and norms, entailing a policy and resource overload that no government or regime, however conscientious, can bear? Should every human need find an embodiment in a human rights norm? Does overproduction entail a belief that each and every major human/social problem is best defined and solved in terms of human rights, in terms of the talismanic property of human rights enunciations? Should concentrations of economic power be allowed to harness these talismanic properties?[44]

I address here only the issue of overproduction. The important question concerns, perhaps not the *quantity* but the *quality* of human rights norms and standards since the UDHR, with insistence on their universality and interdependence. Even more striking is the redefined scope of human rights, which now extends to material as well as nonmaterial needs. This conversion of needs into rights, however problematic, is the hallmark of "contemporary" human rights. It results in waves or "generations" of rights enunciations, at times characterized by a "blue," "red," and "green" rights color scheme.[45] Being color-blind, I do not know which color best signifies the emerging recognition of the collective rights of the foreign

---

40 ALASDAIR MACINTYRE, AFTER VIRTUE 69 (1984).

41 *Id.* at 66.

42 ZYGMUNT BAUMAN, POSTMODERN ETHICS 64 (1993).

43 For a fuller elaboration, see BAXI, *supra* note 35, ch. 3.

44 As is the case with the assorted interest groups of international airlines, hotels, and travel agents who assiduously lobby the U.N. to proclaim a universal human right of tourism? And when a group of predatory investment organizations produces a Draft Multilateral Agreement on Investment (MAI)? *See* the OECD web site (visited Oct. 24, 1998) <http://www.oecd.org/daf/cmis/mai/maitext.pdf>. Must the aggregations of capital and technology (the *proprietariat*) always be disabled from acting upon the capitalist belief that the protection of its rights as human rights is the best assurance there is for the amelioration of the life-condition of the proletariat?

45 *See* JOHAN GALTUNG, HUMAN RIGHTS IN ANOTHER KEY 151–56 (1994).

investor, global corporations, and international financial capital-in short, of global capitalism. But this much is compellingly clear: the emergent collective human rights of global capital presents a formidable challenge to the human rights paradigm inaugurated by the UDHR.

The astonishing quantity of human rights production generates various experiences of skepticism and faith.[46] Some complain of exhaustion (what I call "rights-weariness"). Some suspect sinister imperialism in diplomatic maneuvers animating each and every human rights enunciation (what I call "rights-wariness"). Some celebrate human rights as a new global civic religion which, given a community of faith, will address and solve all major human problems (what I call "human rights evangelism"). Their fervor is often matched by those NGOs that tirelessly pursue the removal of brackets in pre-final diplomatic negotiating texts of various United Nations' summits as triumphs in human solidarity (what I call "human rights romanticism"). Some other activists believe that viable human rights standards can best be produced by exploiting contingencies of international diplomacy (what I call "bureaucratization of human rights"). And still others insist that the real birthplaces of human rights are far removed from the ornate rooms of diplomatic conferences and are found, rather, in the actual sites (acts and feats) of resistance and struggle (what I call "critical human rights realism"[47]).

All these ways of "reading" the production of human rights are implicit discourse on "contemporary" human rights. I review, cursorily, five principal approaches.

First, an organizational way of reading this profusion, within the United Nations system, concerns hierarchical control over the normative contingency of rights production. Increasing autonomy by agencies within the system is seen as a hazard to be contained, as poignantly illustrated by the debate over the right to development.[48] Similarly, the manner in which treaty bodies formulate, through the distinctive device of the "General Comment," somewhat unanticipated treaty obligations upon state parties now begins to emerge as a contested process.

Second, some question the value and the utility of the inflation of human rights. Does this endless normativity perform any useful function in the "real world"? Is there an effective communication among (to invoke Galtung's trichotomy) the norm-senders (the U.N. system), norm-receivers (sovereign states), and the norm-objects

---

[46] BAXI, *supra* note 35.

[47] Also, some human rights activists believe in "aborting," as it were, global instruments favoring the rights of global capital as opposed to the human rights of human beings (what I call *free choice* politics *for* human rights).

[48] *See* Philip Alston, *Revitalizing United Nations Work on Human Rights and Development,* 18 MELB. U.L. REV. 216 (1991); Jack Donnelly, *In Search of the Unicorn: The Jurisprudence and Politics of the Rights to Development,* 15 CAL. W. INT'L J. 473 (1985). *But see* Upendra Baxi, *The Development of the Right to Development, in* HUMAN RIGHTS (Janus Symonides ed., forthcoming from UNESCO in 1999). *See also* the essay by Stephen Marks, *infra* in this volume at pp. 291, 339–43.

(those for whose benefit the rights enunciations are said to have been made)?[49] Who stands to benefit the most by the overproduction of human rights norms and standards? Is it merely a symptom of a growing democratic deficit, sought to be redressed by "legitimation traffic" between norm-senders (the U.N. system) and norm-receivers (the member states)?

A third reading, from the standpoint of high moral theory, warns us against the danger of assuming that the languages of human rights are the only, or the very best, moral languages we have. Rights languages, after all, are languages of claims and counter-claims that typically entail mediation through authoritative state instrumentalities, including contingent feats of adjudicatory activism. The overproduction of rights locates social movements on the grid of power, depriving human communities of their potential for reflexive ethical action. Being ultimately state-bound, even the best of all rights performances typically professionalize, atomize, and de-collectivize energies for social resistance, and do not always energize social policy, state responsiveness, civic empathy, or political mobilization. Not altogether denying the creativity of rights languages, this perspective minimizes its role, stressing instead the historic role of lived relations of sacrifice, support, and solidarity in the midst of suffering.

A fourth orientation views the production of human rights as perhaps the best hope there is for inclusive participation in the making of human futures. It assumes a world historic moment in which neither the institutions of governance nor the processes of the market, singly or in combination, is equipped to fashion just futures. It thrives on the potential of "peoples politics" (not as a system but as chaos) which may emerge only by a convergence of singular energies of dedication by (local, national, regional, and global NGOs). No other understanding of women's movements celebrating the motto "Women's Rights are Human Rights," for example, is possible except the one that regards as historically necessary and feasible the overthrow, by global praxis, of universal patriarchy in all its vested and invested sites. This viewpoint seeks to combat patriarchy, persistent even in the making of human rights, and to explore ways of overcoming the limits of human rights languages that constitute very often the *limits* of human rights action.

A fifth perspective questions the very notion of the overproduction of human rights norms and standards. Not only does the global enunciation of rights entail a long, often elephantine, gestation period;[50] it also produces mainly "soft" human

---

[49]   *See* GALTUNG, *supra* note 45, at 56–70.

[50]   As is the case with the Declaration of the Rights of Indigenous Peoples, which emerges as a last frontier of contemporary human rights development. *See* Draft Declaration of the Rights of Indigenous Peoples, adopted by the U.N. Commission on Human Rights Sub-Commission on the Prevention of Discrimination and Protection of Minorities, Aug. 24, 1994, U.N. Doc. E/CN.4/1995/2; E/CN.4/Sub.2/1994/56 (Oct. 28, 1994), *reprinted in* 34 I.L.M. 541 (1995) *and* 3 INTERNATIONAL LAW AND WORLD ORDER: BASIC DOCUMENTS III.F.4 (Burns H. Weston ed., 5 vols., 1994–) [hereinafter 3 Weston]. M. Cherif Bassiouni offers a use-

rights law (exhortative resolutions, declarations, codes of conduct, etc.), that does not reach, or even at times aspire, to the status of operative norms of conduct. The "hard law" enunciations of human rights, which become enforceable norms, are very few and low in intensity of application. Contemporary human rights production remains both sub-optimal (whatever may be said in comparison with the "modern" period) and inadequate. The task is, from this perspective, to achieve an optimal production of internationally enforceable human rights.

These ways of reading the profusion of human rights norms and standards carry within them all kinds of impacts on the nature and future of human rights. A fuller understanding of these impacts is an important aspect of a social theory of human rights.

B. Politics of Identity/Difference

Informed by post-modernist mood, method, and message, critics of "contemporary" human rights, which champions the universality of human rights, remain anxious at the re-emergence of the idea of "universal reason," a legacy of the Age of Enlightenment that helped to perfect justifications for classical colonialism and racism and for universal patriarchy.[51] The notion of universality invokes not merely new versions of essentialism about human nature but also the notion of meta-narratives: global stories about power and struggles against power. In both of these tropes, do we return to "totalization" modes of thought and practice?

Critics of essentialism remind us that the notion "human" is not pre-given (if, indeed, anything is) but constructed, often with profound rights-denying impacts. Post-modernist critiques now lead us to consider that the idiom of the universality of human rights may have a similar impact. For example, the motto "Women's Rights are Human Rights" masks, often with grave costs, the heterogeneity of women in their civilizational and class positions.[52] So does the appellation "indigenous" in the search for a commonly agreed declaration of indigenous people's rights.[53] Similarly, the human

---

ful approach to the normative stages, which he classifies into the enunciative, declarative, prescriptive, enforcement, and criminalization stages. *See* M. Cherif Bassiouni, *Enforcing Human Rights through International Criminal Law*, in THROUGH AN INTERNATIONAL CRIMINAL COURT IN HUMAN RIGHTS: AN AGENDA FOR THE NEXT CENTURY 347 (Louis Henkin & John L. Hargrove eds., 1994). For a more extended analysis of these modes of reading, see BAXI, *supra* note 35.

51   Concerning patriarchy, see Sally Sedgwick, *Can Kant's Ethics Survive the Feminist Critique?*, in FEMINIST INTERPRETATIONS OF IMMANUEL KANT 77–110 (Robin May Schott ed., 1997). *See also* FEMINISTS READ HABERMAS: GENDERING THE SUBJECT OF DISCOURSE (Johanna Meehan ed., 1995).

52   *See* ELIZABETH V. SPELMAN, INESSENTIAL WOMAN: PROBLEMS OF EXCLUSION IN FEMINIST THOUGHT ix (1988) (maintaining that the endeavors of defining "women as women" or "sisterhood across boundaries" is the "trojan-horse of western feminist ethnocentrism").

53   *See* Russell Barsh, *Indigenous Peoples in the 1990s: From Object to Subject of International Law?*, 7 HARV. HUM. RTS. J. 33 (1994); Stephan Marquardt, *International Law and Indigenous Peoples*, 3 INT'L J. GROUP RTS. 47 (1995).

rights instruments on child rights ignore the diversity of children's circumstances. In many societies, the passage between the first and second childhood or the distinction between "child" and "adult" is brutally cut short, as with child labor, the girl child, or children conscripted into insurrectionist-armed warfare.

Are then identities, universalized all over again in positing a *universal* bearer of human rights, obscuring the fact that identities may themselves be vehicles of power, all too often inscribed or imposed? And do the benign intentions that underlie such performative acts of power advance the cause of human rights as well as they serve the ends of power?

Students of international law, knowingly or not, are familiar with post-modernisms. They know well the problematic of identity as vehicles of power, from the Kelsenite "constitutive" theory of recognition of states (under which states may be said not to exist unless "recognized" by others) to the travails of the right to self-determination. They know how that "self" is constructed, deconstructed, and reconstructed by the play of global power,[54] with attendant legitimations of enormous amounts of human misery. The evolution of the right to self-determination of states and people signifies no more than the power of hegemonic or dominant states to determine the "self" which then has the right to "self-determination." In sum, that right is only a right to access a "self" pre-determined by the play of hegemonic global powers.

Is it any longer true that, outside the contexts of self-determination, the shackles of state sovereignty no longer determine, even when they condition, the bounds of identity? Increasingly, the de-territoralization of identity is said to be a *global* social fact or human condition.[55] Identities are becoming fluid, multiple, contingent, perhaps even to the point where an individual (or the subject) is viewed, in Chantal Mouffe's words, as "the articulation of an ensemble of subject positions, constructed within specific discourses and always precariously sutured at the

---

[54] *See* Hurst Hannum, *Rethinking Self-Determination*, 34 VA. J. INT'L L. 1 (1993). He contrasts effectively the reservation by India confining the right to self-determination in Article 1 of the International Covenant on Civil and Political Rights, *infra* Appendix III [hereinafter ICCPR], "only to peoples under foreign rule" with the German objection to it insisting on the availability of this right to "all peoples." The zeal with which the developed countries have sought to expand the range of self-determination rights arises from their unique capability for organizing the collective amnesia of their ruthless prowess in suppressing (not too long ago) even the softest voice urging freedom from the colonial yoke. This said, it also must be stated that the Indian reservation based on "national integrity" creatively mimes the very same order of enclosure of the politics of identity and difference, in vastly different postcolonial conditions, and the social imagery of colonial/imperial representation of European nation-states.

[55] For a vivid account of the processes, see ARJUN APPADURAI, MODERNITY AT LARGE: CULTURAL DIMENSIONS OF GLOBALIZATION 27–65 (1996).

intersection of subject positions";[56] and the community appears as "a discursive surface of inscriptions."[57] There is a great appeal in Mouffe's notion of a "non-individualistic conception of the individual," a notion that rejects, relative to human rights, the idea of the individual in terms of "possessive individualism" and that, furthermore, conceives of the individual as "the intersection of a multiplicity of identifications and collective identities that constantly subvert each other."[58]

In any event, this kind of thinking raises several questions from the standpoint of those who are engaged in actual human rights struggles. Four are noted here.

First, are *all* the identities being made, by processes of globalization, "fluid," "multiple," and "contingent"? If we were to place ourselves in the (non-Rawlsian) position of a person belonging to an untouchable community (say, in a remote area of Bihar, India), would we agree that caste and patriarchal identity are fluid, multiple, and contingent? As an untouchable, no matter how you perceive your identity (as a mother, wife, or daughter), you still are liable to be raped; still will be denied access to water in the high caste village well; still will be subjected to all kinds of forced and obnoxious labor; still have your huts set ablaze; still have your adult franchise regularly confiscated at elections by caste Hindu militia.[59] Human rights logic and rhetoric, fashioned by historic struggles, simply and starkly assert that such imposition of primordial identities is morally wrong and legally prohibited. Discrimination on the grounds of birth, sex, domicile, ethnicity, disability, or sexual orientation, for example, counts as a violation of internationally proclaimed human rights. It is the mission of human rights logics and paralogics to dislodge primordial identities that legitimate the orders of imposed suffering, socially invisible at times even to the repressed. But it is a mission that is fraught with grave difficulties. When the imposition of primordial identities occurs in civil society, human rights logic and rhetoric require the state to combat it, raising liberal anxieties about augmenting the New Leviathan. In addition, the state and the law can oppose such imposition only by a reconstruction of that collective identity. The "untouchables" in India, constitutionally christened the "scheduled castes," will have to be burdened by this reconstitution because, in law and society, they necessarily will be either untouchables or ex-untouchables. Justifications of affirmative action programs worldwide, for example, depend on maintaining the integrity of their narratives of millennial histories of collective hurt. It is true that these narratives essentialize historic identities as new sites of injury. But is there a way out of embattled histories, shaped by the dialectics of human rights?

Second, what is there to subvert if identities are "fluid," "multiple," or "contingent"; if the individual or collective self no longer exists as a unified, discursive,

---

[56] Chantal Mouffe, *Democratic Citizenship and the Political Community, in* DIMENSIONS OF RADICAL DEMOCRACY: PLURALISMS AND CITIZENSHIP 237 (Chantal Mouffe ed., 1992).

[57] Chantal Mouffe, *Democratic Politics Today, in id.* at 14.

[58] CHANTAL MOUFFE, THE RETURN OF THE POLITICAL 97, 100 (1993).

[59] For a devastatingly accurate account, see ROHINTON MISTRY, A FINE BALANCE (1996).

or semiotic object that can be said to be a bearer of human rights? If the subject is no more, and only subject-positions exist, how are we to construct or pursue politics for human rights? Put another way, how may one theorize repression and violation? It would unduly burden this essay to sharpen these questions, attend to their genealogy, and salvage the possibility of conversation about human rights from the debris of post-identity discourse. I attempt it elsewhere.[60]

Third, how does this diaspora of identity narratives empower those who are haunted by practices of flagrant, massive, and ongoing violations of human rights? For the gurus of post-modern ethics, this is not a seriously engaged concern compared to the preoccupation of defining and contesting all that is wrong with liberalism and socialism.[61]

Fourth, is this human rights path (requiring us to internalize a primordial identity) counter-productive when, in particular, it casts the state and law "as neutral arbiters of injury rather than themselves invested with the power to injure?"[62] Emancipatory in origin, human rights, in the course of enunciation and administration, may become "a regulatory discourse, a means of obstructing or co-opting more radical political demands, or simply the most hollow of empty promises."[63] It is ironic that "rights sought by a politically defined *group* are conferred upon depoliticized *individuals*; at the moment a particular "we" succeeds in obtaining rights, it loses its 'we-ness' and dissolves into individuals."[64] Indeed, in certain moments, human rights development yields itself to tricks of governance; the

---

[60] *See* BAXI, *supra* note 35.

[61] Jacques Derrida properly assails the heady optimism of the liberalism of Fukuyama, asking, rightly, whether it is credible to think that "all these cataclysms (terror, oppression, repression, extermination, genocide *and so on*)" constitute "contingent or insignificant limitations" for the messianic and triumphant post-Cold War moment of liberalism." JACQUES DERRIDA, SPECTERS OF MARX: THE STATE OF THE DEBT, THE WORK OF MOURNING & THE NEW INTERNATIONAL 57 (Peggy Kamuf trans., 1994) (emphasis added). Note the gesture of exhaustion in the words italicized here! At the same time, Derrida asserts, "[o]ur aporia here stem from the fact that there is no longer any *name* or *technology* for determining the Marxist *coup* and its subject." *Id.* at 98. What follows? Derrida, after a fascinating detour on the work of mourning and narcissism, enjoins us thus: " [O]ne must constantly remember that the impossible . . . is, alas, possible. One must constantly remember that this absolute evil . . . can take place. One must constantly remember that it is even on the basis of the terrible possibility of the impossible that justice is desirable. . . ."; though beyond what Derrida calls "right and law." *Id.* at 175.

Who is this "one" addressed by Derrida? The avant-garde theorist or the being of those subjected continually to the absolute order of evil? No doubt, it is important to sensitize theoretical fellow travelers to the dangers of amnesia. But what does it or should it mean to the victims of orders of absolute evil?

[62] BROWN, *supra* note 35, at 27.

[63] *Id.*

[64] *Id.* at 98.

pillar of emancipation turns out to be the pillar of regulation,[65] as seen in some striking detail in the next section. Were this the only moment of human rights, every triumphal attainment would also be its funerary oration. But does not often a regulatory discourse, at one moment, also become, at another moment, an arena of struggle?

If international human rights lawyers and movement people need to attend to the type of interrogation thus raised, post-modernist ethical thinkers need to wrestle with the recent history of the politics of cruelty, which has constructed, as it were, new primordial communities. These are the communities of the tortured and tormented, the prisoners of conscience across the world, represented with poignancy and unequaled moral heroism by Amnesty International. Would it be true to say that their identity as victims is random, contingent, rather than caused by the play of global politics? Until this question is seriously pursued, can it not be said that human rights enunciations and movements commit no mortal sin of essentialism or foundationalism in insisting upon a universal norm that de-legitimates this invention?

Nor does the post-essentialism that achieves many a rhetorical *tour de force* for a Derrida respond to the problematic posed by the archetypal Aung San Suu Kyi. She embodies human rights essentialism. So do the Afghan women who, under dire straits, protest the Taliban regime. So do UNICEF and Save the Children, which, thanks in part to the globalized media, seek at times to do the impossible, moving the atrophied conscience of the globalized middle classes to an occasional act of charity, even of genuine compassion, thanks to the unbearable CNN and equivalent depictions of cruelly starved children in Sudan midst a well-earned *aperitif* or first course of dinner.[66] No matter how flawed to the Parisian and neo-Parisian cognitive fashions, human rights discourse furnishes potential for struggle that the post-modernist discourse on the politics of identity as yet does not. These cognitive fashion parades must not be allowed to drain emergent solidarities in struggle unless the post-modernist, anti-essentialist critique demonstrates that human rights are *a mistake.*

Indeed, engaged human rights discourse makes possible a deeper understanding of the politics of difference insofar as it is an act of suffering rather than sanitized thought. It insists that the Other is *not* dispensable; it sensitizes us to the fact

---

[65] I adapt here Santos' analysis of dialectic of regulation and emancipation. *See* SANTOS, *supra* note 35, at 7–55.

[66] But perhaps suffering as a *spectacle* can do no more. For the very act of mass media producing the spectacle of suffering needs to divest it of any structural understanding of the production of suffering itself. In a way, the community of gaze can be only instantly constructed by the erasure of the slightest awareness of complicity. Thus, the mass media must obscure the fact that "all those weapons used to make far-away homelands into killing fields have been supplied by our own arms factories, jealous of their orderbooks and proud of their productivity and competitiveness—the life-blood of our own cherished prosperity." ZYGMUNT BAUMAN, GLOBALIZATION: THE HUMAN CONSEQUENCES 75 (1998).

that the politics of Otherhood is not ethically sensible outside the urgency of the maxim: "Ask not for whom the bell tolls; it tolls for thee." It insists, with Rabbi Israeli Salanter, that the *"the material needs of my neighbor are my spiritual needs."*[67] Critically engaged human rights discourse refuses to de-essentialize human suffering, even under the banner of dispersed identities.

C. The Summons for the Destruction of Narrative Monopolies

The post-modernist critique of human rights further maintains that the telling of large *global* stories ("meta-narratives") is less a function of emancipation than an aspect of the politics of intergovernmental desire that ingests the politics of resistance. Put another way, meta-narratives serve to co-opt into mechanisms and processes of governance the languages of human rights such that bills of rights may, with impunity, adorn many a military constitutionalism and that so-called human rights commissions may thrive upon state/regime sponsored violations. Not surprisingly, the more severe the human rights violation, the more the power elites declare their loyalty to the regime of human rights. The near-universality of ratification of the Convention on the Elimination of Discrimination Against Women (CEDAW), for example, betokens no human liberation of women. Rather, it endows the state with the power to tell more Nietschzean lies. "State is the name of the coldest of all cold monsters. Coldly, it tells lies, too; and this lie grows out of its mouth: 'I, the state, am the people'."[68]

All too often, human rights languages become stratagems of imperialistic foreign policy through military invasions as well as through global economic diplomacy. Superpower diplomacy at the United Nations is not averse to causing untold suffering through sanctions whose manifest aim is to serve the future of human rights.[69] The United States, the solitary superpower at the end of the millennium, has made sanctions for the promotion of human rights abroad a gourmet feast at the White House and on Capitol Hill.[70]

What is more, the post-modernist critique may rightly insist that the classic paradigm of universal human rights contains contradictory elements. The UDHR

---

[67] *Cited in* EMMANUEL LEVINAS, NINE TALMUDIC READINGS 99 (Annette Aronwicz trans., 1991) (emphasis added).

[68] WALTER KAUFMANN, THE PORTABLE NIETZSCHE 160–61 (1954).

[69] *See* Noam Chomsky, *Great Powers and Human Rights: The Case of East Timor, in* NOAM CHOMSKY, POWERS AND PROSPECTS: REFLECTIONS ON HUMAN NATURE AND THE SOCIAL ORDER 169–221 (1996). *See also* CHANDRA MUZAFFAR, HUMAN RIGHTS AND THE NEW WORLD ORDER (1993); GUSTAVO ESTEVA & MADHU SURI PRAKASH, GRASSROOTS POSTMODERNISM: REMAKING THE SOIL OF CULTURE (1998); WININ PEREIRA, INHUMAN RIGHTS: THE WESTERN SYSTEM AND GLOBAL HUMAN RIGHTS ABUSE (1997).

[70] American Association for World Health, *Denial of Food and Medicine, the Impact of the U.S Embargo on Health and Nutrition in Cuba* (visited Oct. 24, 1998) <http://www.usenagage.org./studies/cuba.html>.

provides for the protection of the right to property[71] and thereby makes possible its conversion, in these halcyon days of globalization, into a paradigm of trade-related, market-friendly human rights, (beginning its career with the World Trade Organization (WTO),[72] now maturing in obscene progression in the Multilateral Agreement on Investment (MAI) of the Organization for Economic Cooperation and Development (OECD).[73] Global trade relations now resonate with the moral rhetoric of human rights (witness, for example, the discourse on the "social clauses" of the WTO as well as many a bilateral/regional economic/trade arrangement). More to the point, many southern NGOs that merely critiqued globalization now look upon international financial institutions as instrumentalities of deliverance from the pathologies of the nation-state.

The range and depth of post-modernist critiques of human rights is not dissimilar to Karl Marx's critique *On the Jewish Question*,[74] though the unique idiom of post-modernism was not historically available to him. The summons for the destruction of "narrative monopolies"[75] in human rights theory and practice is of enormous importance, as it enables us to recognize that the authorship of human rights rests with communities in the struggle against illegitimate power formations and the politics of cruelty. The "local," not the "global," it needs to be emphasized, remains the crucial locus of struggle for the enunciation, implementation, and enjoyment of human rights. Almost every global institutionalization of human rights has been preceded by grassroots activism.[76]

---

[71] UDHR, *infra* Appendix I, art. 17. Article 17 protects individual as well as associational rights to property, a provision which for all practical purposes negates the radical looking assurances in Articles 23–26. Not surprisingly, intellectual property rights are fully recognized in Article 27(2).

[72] Agreement Establishing the World Trade Organization, Apr. 15, 1994, *reprinted in* 33 I.L.M. 1144 *and* 4 INTERNATIONAL LAW AND WORLD ORDER: BASIC DOCUMENTS IV.C.2a (Burns H. Weston ed., 5 vols., 1994–) (hereinafter 4 Weston).

[73] For the text of the MAI, see *supra* note 44.

[74] For a post-modernist revisitation, see BROWN, *supra* note 35, at 97–114.

[75] Lyotard insists: "Destroy all narrative monopolies. . . . Take away the privileges the narrator has granted himself." JEAN FRANÇOIS LYOTARD, THE LYOTARD READER 153 (Andrew Benjamin ed., 1989).

[76] To quote myself, immodestly:

  After all it was a man called Lokmanya Tilak who in the second decade of this century gave a call to India: *swaraj (independence) is my birthright and I shall have it*, long before international human rights proclaimed a right to self-determination. It was a man called Gandhi who challenged early this century racial discrimination in South Africa, which laid several decades later the foundations for international treaties and declarations on the elimination of all forms of racial discrimination and apartheid. Compared with these male figures, generations of legendary women martyred themselves in prolonged struggles against patriarchy and for gender equality. The current campaign based on the motto "Women's

From this perspective, claims of "Western" authorship of human rights are sensible only within a meta-narrative tradition that in the past served the domineering ends of colonial/imperial power formations and that now serve these ends for the Euro-Atlantic community or the "triadic states" (the U.S., the EC, and Japan). In this dominant discourse, both "modern" and "contemporary" notions of human rights emerge, though in different modes, as a "vision of a *novus ordo selcorum* in the world as a whole."[77] And this discourse prevents recognition of the fact that communities in struggle are the primary authors of human rights. As the golden dust of UDHR festivities settles, no task is more important than tracing the history of human rights from the standpoint of communities united in their struggle midst unconscionable human suffering.

Various feminists have rightly contested the destruction of meta-narratives as inimical to the politics of difference.[78] At the same time, they maintain that the telling of stories of everyday violation and resistance that recognize the role of women as authors of human rights is more empowering in terms of creating solidarity than weaving narratives of universal patriarchy or theorizing repression only as a discursive relation.[79] The feminization of human rights cultures begins only when one negotiates this conflict between meta- and micro-narratives of women in struggle. One may even call the task or mission as one of *humanizing human rights* —going beyond rarefied discourse on the variety of post-modernisms and post-structuralisms to histories of individual and collective hurt. Narratives of concrete ways in which women's bodies are held *in terroram*[80] do not pre-eminently feature or figure in human rights theory, and theorizing repression does not, to my mind,

---

Rights *Are* Human Rights" is inspired by a massive history of local struggles all around.

Upendra Baxi, *The Reason of Human Rights and the Unreason of Globalization*, Address at The First A.R. Desai Memorial Lecture, University of Bombay (1996), wherein I also note that "[t]he historic birthplaces of all human rights struggles are the hearth and the home, the church and the castle, the prison and the police precinct, the factory and the farm."

[77]   JACOBSON *supra* note 4, at 1.

[78]   *See* CHRISTINE DI STEFANO, DILEMMAS OF DIFFERENCE IN FEMINISM & POSTMODERNISM 76 (Linda Nicholson ed., 1990).

[79]   *See* ERNESTO LACLAU & CHANTAL MOUFFE, HEGEMONY AND SOCIALIST STRATEGY: TOWARDS A RADICAL DEMOCRATIC POLITICS 87–88, 115–16 (1985).

[80]   Mary Jo Frug, *A Postmodern Feminist Legal Manifesto, in* AFTER IDENTITY: A READER IN LAW AND CULTURE 7–23 (Dan Danielson & Karen Engle eds., 1995). The lived reality of sex-trafficking, sweat labor, agrestic serfdom, workplace discrimination, sexual harassment, dowry murders, rape in peacetime as well as in war as a means of doing "politics," torture of women and medicalization of their bodies—all these and related devices of state and society—present problems of routinization of terror. While feminist scholarship has demonstrated the power of story telling, social theory of human rights has yet to conceive of ways and means of investing individual biographies of the violated with the power of social texts.

best happen by contesting a Lacan, a Derrida, or a Foucault; it happens when the theorist shares both the nightmares and dreams of the oppressed. To give language to pain, to experience the pain of the Other inside you, remains the task, always, of human rights narrative and discourse. If the varieties of post-modernisms help us to accomplish this, there is a better future for human rights; if not, they constitute a dance of death for all human rights.

D. Arguments from Relativism

1. The Universality Thesis

The "historical forms in which the relationship between universality and particularity have been thought" are many and diverse.[81] It would take this work far afield to survey the discursive scene, even from the standpoint of Western metaphysics. Yet the thesis that "contemporary" human rights are "universal" remains firmly imbricated within this discursive field.

If human rights are said to be "universal" in the very same sense as a property or relation that may be "instantiated" by a whole variety of particular things, phenomena, or state of affairs, may one say that that to be "human" is to be possessed of certain kinds of rights? If "universality" is said to exist independently of things, phenomena, or states of affairs, is it conceivable that human rights exist independently of political things, phenomena, or states of affairs? Or does the universality of human rights exist in and through these things, phenomena, or states of affairs, that is rights "manifest" themselves through these? Or are universals nominal: just a matter of naming these under one linguistic practice? Or are these ultimately justifiable, capable of being grounded, in a comprehensive ethical feats of theorizing?[82] Or is the construction of universal human rights no more than an exercise in reification, the ideological praxis of converting the multitude of diversity under the totalizing banner of a unity? Or is the expression "human rights" merely an "empty signifier," a "signifier without a signified"?[83]

The questions are compounded by the different constructions of "human rights." Quite clearly, thinkers within the Enlightenment traditions of discourse were preoccupied with the problematic of "natural rights."[84] Leading contemporary ethical thinkers construct "human rights" either in social contractarian or communi-

---

81   ERNESTO LACLAU, EMANCIPATIONS 22 (1996).

82   Of which Alan Gewirth is the foremost exemplar. See ALAN GEWIRTH, THE COMMUNITY OF RIGHTS (1996).

83   See LACLAU, supra note 81, at 36–46. I derive some of the questions here raised, though not their formulation in relation to human rights, from this work of Laclau as well as from Ernesto Laclau & Lilian Zac, Minding the Gap: The Subject of Politics, in THE MAKING OF POLITICAL IDENTITIES 11–39 (Ernesto Laclau ed., 1994).

84   For a recent exposition, see STEVEN B. SMITH, HEGEL'S CRITIQUE OF LIBERALISM: RIGHTS IN CONTEXT (1989) (hereinafter SMITH).

tarian terms, terms that relate to ways of thinking about rights that make "just" the basic structure of a society.[85] The context of rights principles thus articulated is that of justice through rights within individual societies or cultures, even when the this notion is presented as universalizable. "Contemporary" human rights discursivity addresses, however, the problematic of a just international order, that is a world order based on the promotion and protection of "human rights" *within* and *across* human societies, traditions, and cultures. Respect for "human rights," or the right to be and remain human, entails a complex, interlocking network of meanings that have to be sustained (and renovated and replenished) at *all* levels; individuals, associations, markets, states, regional organizations of states, and international agencies and organizations constitute a new totality that now stands addressed by the logics and paralogics of human rights. This difference raises it own distinctive problems when we address the issue of "universality."

Indeed, it marks a break, a radical discontinuity with previous Enlightenment modes of thought.[86] The epistemological break is of the same order as that which occurred in the seventeenth century European tradition. If "prior to the seventeenth century, governments made no reference to rights as a standard of legitimacy,"[87] prior to the mid-twentieth century the world international order did not regard respect for human rights as a standard for legitimacy of international relations or affairs. This epistemological break complicates recourse to the Enlightenment discursivity on human rights as natural rights; for, as we have seen, the notion of being "human" was all along constructed on Eurocentric, or racist, lines.

The notion of "universality" of "human rights" raises heavy and complex questions that may seem distant from the real world of human rights praxis. But these erupt constantly in that "real" world where the lack of approaches to a response make the enterprise of promoting and protecting human rights even more difficult than, perhaps, it actually need be.

In a sense, these issues relate to how one may construct the "universal" in the proclaimed "universality" and which interpretive community, if any, may feel privileged to so do. The way the "universality" of human rights is constructed and contested, as we see later, matters a great deal. But Hegel states with finality (if such things can be!) the modes of construction when he distinguishes between three "moments": *abstract universality, abstract particularity*, and *concrete*

---

[85] See, e.g., MacIntyre, *supra* note 40; John Rawls, A Theory of Justice (1971); Michael Sandel, Liberalism and the Limits of Justice (1982); Michael Walzer, Spheres of Justice: A Defense of Pluralism and Equality (1983).

[86] Thus, for example, when Hegel maintained that "the right to recognition," that is "respect for the person or 'free personality' as such," is the "core of the modern state," he was neither critiquing colonialism or imperialism, patriarchy or racism. *Quoted in* Smith, *supra* note 84, at 112.

[87] Smith, *supra* note 84, at 61.

universality.[88] The first moment stands for "undifferentiated identity;" the second for "the differentiation of identity and difference;" and the third for "concrete universality, which is the full realization of individuality."[89]

The claim of universality of human rights may be constructed through these three moments. Its *abstract universality* addresses the undifferentiated identity of all bearers of human rights, regardless of history or future.[90] The second moment of *abstract particularity* occurs when the identity of the bearers of human rights cognizes that bearer by gender, indigeniety, vulnerability or persecution attributes. The third moment of *concrete universality* becomes possible of attainment when the first two moments prevail: the moment of identity of all beings as "fully" human and the moment of internal differentiation of that "human."

Should we chose to distinguish these three moments, many of the objections or difficulties with the "universality" of human rights recede or need to be recast. The UDHR proceeds on the basis of abstract universality through its enunciatory referents: "all human beings," "everyone," "all," and "no one." All these entities have human rights; the only occasion when the moment of abstract particularity stands comprehsively cognizant is in its very last article.[91] Subsequent rights-enunciations increasingly address abstract particularities: for example, women's rights as human rights, the rights of indigenous peoples, the rights of children and migrants, including migrant labor. These are particularities because they differentiate the *abstract human* in the UDHR. They are abstract because, as yet, the identities they constitute still do not address the specificity of subject-positions/locations of the constituencies of human rights/obligations constituencies. But this is what must be addressed in the third moment of concrete universality where rights come home, as it were, in lived and embodied circumstances of being human in time and place marked by finite individual existence. In the moment of the concrete universal, while structures of domination and power are cross-generational (though liable to disruption and collapse) individual life spans are not merely finite in the abstract but governed by the vagaries and whims of practices of politics of cruelty and of *catastrophic politics.*

The relation between the first two and the third form of universality of human rights remains deeply problematic. The moment of concrete universality appears, on one reading of human rights, contingent on the performative acts of the first two

---

[88]   *See* Mark C. Taylor, Altarity 16–17 (1987).

[89]   *Id.*

[90]   "[T]he mutual recognition of one another's rights," according to Hegel, "must take place at the expense of nature, by abstracting or denying all the individual differences between us until we arrive at a pure *I*, the free will or 'universal consciousness' which is at the root of these differences," Smith, *supra* note 84, at 124.

[91]   UDHR, *infra* Appendix I, art. 30: "Nothing in this Declaration may be interpreted as implying for any *State, group or person* any rights to engage in any activity or to perform any act aimed at the *destruction* of any of the rights and freedoms set forth herein" (emphasis added). I take the reference to *persons* as embracing *corporate persons* in addition to *natural persons*, that is, individual human beings.

moments. The concrete universality of human rights presupposes the movement of both abstract universality and abstract particularity. On the other hand, the moments are *reversible, entailing no logic of a hierarchy or progression of moments*, in the sense that often enough (as explained earlier) it is the here-and-now assertion of human rights that lack a *being in the world* that in turn creates the other two moments. The concrete universality of human rights often consists in the acts of prefigurative praxis. No theory of moments of human rights guided struggles for decolonization or Mohandas Gandhi's protests against the incipient but still vicious forms of an early regime of apartheid. Much the same may be truly said of the civil rights movements led by Martin Luther King, Jr., or of women's or environmental rights movements.

This suggests the possibility of two types of distinctions: first, between the *universality* of human rights and their *universalizability*; and second, between *globalization* and the *universality* of human rights as a mode of actualizing *preferred* conceptions. The first distinction concerns the dialectic among the three moments; the second concerns the power of the play of hegemons. The hegemon may *globalize* human rights without *universalizing* them. Globalization of human rights consists in those practices of governance by the dominant states that selectively target the enforcement of certain set of rights or sets of interpretation of rights upon the "subaltern" state actors in the world system. Such practices need no ethic of "universality" of human rights; these constitute an amoral exercise or enforcement of dominant, hegemonic power because the hegemon does not accept as a universal norm that its sovereign sphere, rife with human and human rights violations, ought to be equally liable to similarly based intrusion. Even when construed as ultimately designed to "serve," without their consent and against their will, the human rights of the peoples, the unilateral and ultimately unaccountable use of military force (as, yet again illustrated in the recent strikes against Iraq and the Federal Republic of Yugoslavia or the armed covert and overt operations by the United States in Chile and Nicaragua) remains an instance of globalization of human rights. Sometimes the globalization of human rights proceeds on moral maxims as yet not enunciated, because they are not acceptable to the hegemons themselves. The public discourse concerning the removal of President Saddam Hussain, for example, reiteratively explicit in statements by the U.S. President and the British Prime Minister in December 1998, seems based on the notion of justified tyrannicide, a notion as yet not articulated by "contemporary" human rights enunciations. The globalization of human rights is also marked by moral duplicity. People in struggle are denied the same order of impunity for committing tyrannicide as the incumbent heads of states "enjoy" in relation to the commission of genocide. The first constitutes "treason" at home and "terrorism" abroad; the second is thought essential to preserve structures of global power against themselves.

Much the same has to be said concerning aid conditionalities, whether under the auspices of the international financial institutions or of trade sanctions for violation of labor and associated human rights norms and standards. The hegemon insists that these standards may be enforced selectively against vulnerable and dependent states, denying that the same justification may extend to its promotion of the right of global capital to exploit workers at home and abroad. In contrast, the logics/paralogics of "universal" human rights are deeply ethical, *tormented by reflexivity all the way*.

These summary observations commend the distinction I make between two orders of discursivity: *globalization* and *universality* of human rights. The latter ought to "problematize" the former. In this sense, the discourse concerning "relativism" seems, from at least the standpoint of those violated, deeply diversionary. In any case, the inability to problematize this distinction, in theoretical and activist critique about the "universality" of human rights and their globalization casts a long shadow over their future.

2. Antifoundationalism

"Contemporary" human rights paradigms constantly invite interrogation when they stress the universality of human rights. It is maintained by many, and in various ways, that universal human rights are simply impossible because what counts as "human" and as "rights" belonging to humans are context-bound and tradition-dependent. There is no transcultural fact or being that may be called "human" to which universal human rights may be attached. Argentine jurist Eduardo Rabossi has recently urged that the "human rights phenomenon renders human rights foundationalism outmoded and irrelevant."[92] By human rights phenomenon, I believe that Rabossi means what I describe as the fact of the enunciative explosion of human rights. For him, that fact is all that matters; it is unnecessary to revisit the philosophical grounds on which human rights may be based.

Antifoundationalism is a close post-modernist cousin of relativism; each urges us to pay heed to contexts of culture and power. Both insist, though in somewhat different ways that matter, that whatever may be the agenda of human rights is best performed without the labors of grounding rights in any transcultural fact or "essence" named as "human being." The claim here is that such labors of theoretical practice are either futile or dangerous. They are futile because who or what counts as being "human" is always being socially deconstructed and reconstructed and cannot be legislated by any ethical imperative, no matter how hard and long one may try to so do. They are dangerous because under the banner of the universality of "human nature," regimes of human violation actually thrive and prosper. The danger for human rights is in the very construction of "human," which then allows the power of what Erick Erickson called "pseudospeciation," a process by which different regimes of psychopathic practices of the politics of cruelty may erect the dichotomy between "humans" and "nonhumans," "people" and "non-

---

[92]   *Quoted in* Richard Rorty, *Human Rights, Rationality, and Sentimentality, in* ON HUMAN RIGHTS: THE OXFORD AMNESTY LECTURES 1993, at 112, 116 (Stephen Shute & Susan Hurley eds., 1993).

people."[93] My own critique of what I call the "modern" human rights paradigm commits me to an acknowledgment of the power of this very danger.

The danger is compounded when we attend the mission of the Dead White Males, or what earlier was called the "White Man's Burden," drawing sustenance from the mission of universality of human rights. The American Anthropological Association, in its 1947 critique of the draft declaration of the UDHR, stated, memorably, that doctrines of "the white man's burden"

> have been employed to implement economic exploitation and to deny the right to control their own affairs to millions of peoples over the world, where the expansion of Europe and America has not meant . . . the literal extermination of the whole populations. Rationalized in terms of ascribing cultural inferiority to these peoples, or in conceptions of backwardness in development of their "primitive mentality," that justified their being held in the tutelage of their superiors, the history of the expansion of the western world has been marked by demoralization of human personality and the disintegration of human rights among the people over whom hegemony has been established.[94]

This was stated with elegant clarity in the pre-post-modern era! And even today critiques of the universality of human rights enact only variations on this theme.

The issues involved here relate to ways in which human rights logics and paralogics have been deployed for the ends of historic forms of domination and to ways through which practices of governance everywhere legitimate themselves through recourse to the languages of "human rights." The language game of human rights is also a power game, that phenomenon that I call "the politics *of* human rights."

3. The "Histories" of Human Rights "Universality"

It is at this juncture that one may raise the issue of how the histories of the "universality" of human rights may be narrated. I have endeavored to demonstrate through the distinction between "modern" and "contemporary" human rights paradigms the ways in which the "universality" notions get constructed in radically different ways. Apart from the unfolding of the politics *of* human rights, there arises also the need to trace the interaction between two forms of human rights politics: the politics *of* and *for* human rights.

From this perspective, whatever may have been the case with the UDHR, the argument concerning "relativism" is curious in terms of the actual history of author-

---

[93]   Tu Wei-Ming, *Maoism as a Source of Suffering in China, in* SOCIAL SUFFERING 149, 166–67 (Arthur Kleinman et al. eds., 1996).

[94]   The Executive Board, American Anthropological Association, *Statement on Human Rights*, 49 AM. ANTHROPOLOGIST 539 (1947).

ing contemporary international human rights standards and norms. If we were to accept the view that "contemporary" human rights authorship lies with the communities of states, no recourse to a grand theory or to a gourmet diet of a whole variety of "post-isms" or endologies[95] is required to maintain a just anxiety about the universality of human rights. Any international human rights lawyer worth her or his calling knows the riot of reservations, understandings, and declarations that parody the texts of universalistic declarations.[96] The "fine print" of reservations usually cancels the "capital font" of universality. In this sense, claims concerning the universality of human rights enunciations are diversionary, embodying the politics *of*, rather than *for*, human rights. What is "universal" about human rights is that they become binding on sovereign states when such states consent to treaty obligations or demonstrate by their belief and practice that certain enunciations are binding as the customary law of human rights. And in the making of these "universal" norms, states do articulate a measure of cultural and civilizational diversity. Even in respect of such "universal" human rights norms, the universality abides in the purported logic of aspiration, not always in the reality of attainment. Obviously, this petty detail concerning the making of internationally binding human rights gets wholly ignored in the high discourse of relativism, antifoundationalism, and "postmodernisms."

The dominant discourse wishes us to believe that the anticolonial struggles relied upon and wholly mimed the typical human rights discourse of the "West." This mode of thought relies upon catachresis, signifying the lack of an "adequate historical referent" in the cultures of the Other.[97]

If, on the other hand, we were to entertain a more "radical" view of authorship of human rights (which I have elaborated thus far) where peoples and communities are the primary authors of human rights, the argument from relativism falls. This is because, on this view, resistance to power has a creationist role in the making of "contemporary" human rights, which then, at a second-order level, get translated into standards and norms by the community of states. In the making of human rights, it is the "local" that translates into "global" languages the reality of its aspiration for a just world.

The context bears a moment's reflection, too, upon the world without rights. I refer to "modern" human rights enunciations that enacted—cruelly—many a vari-

---

95 Upendra Baxi, *The "Reason" of Human Rights and the "Unreason" of Globalization: The First Akshay Desai Memorial Lecture*, University of Bombay 1996 (forthcoming in 1999 in Economic and Political Weekly).

96 Upendra Baxi, *"A Work in Progress?": Reflections on the United States Report to the United Nations Human Rights Committee*, 36 Ind. J. Int'l L. 34 (1996); Ann Elizabeth Mayer, *Reflections on the Proposed United States Reservations to CEDAW*, 23 Hastings Const. L.Q. 727–823 (1996).

97 Gayatri Chakravorty Spivak, *Constitutions and Culture Studies, in* Legal Studies as Cultural Studies: A Reader in (Post) Modern Critical Theory 155 (Jerry D. Leonard ed., 1995).

ety of exclusionary theory/practice. The "modern" epoch of human rights enunciation was unabashedly relativistic; it claimed individual and collective rights for some peoples and regimes and denied these wholesale to others. These latter were denied rights either because they were not fully human or the task of making them fully human required denial of rights to them. Do not the colonial practices of power provide a full repository for the practices of relativism?

Human rights universalism somehow begins to become problematic at the beginning of the end of colonialism, in association with the principle of self-determination proclaimed in the two covenants.[98] True, the UDHR also occurs at the onset of the Cold War. Also true, it embodies, in its Articles 17 and 27(2), exceptional regard for the right to property. But it contains also vital social rights (education, work, and health) that can, and have been used to impose an array of reasonable restrictions on the rights to property. The values repressed by empire, by the doctrines of the White Man's Burden, are no longer considered legitimate. Were not the anticolonial struggles partly about the realization of the right to a just "international and social order," respectful of the dignity and human rights of all people (art. 28)? Or about rights to freedom of opinion and expression (art.19)? Or about the right to peaceful assembly and association (art. 20) and a right to democracy (art. 21)?

And if these were typically "Western" values, how do we explain their resonance in the regional human rights instruments—for example, the 1948 American Declaration of the Rights and Duties of Man,[99] the 1969 American Convention on Human Rights,[100] and the 1988 Additional Protocol to the American Convention on Human Rights in the Area of Economic, Social and Cultural Rights[101] amplifying on the American Convention? Or the 1981 African Charter on Human and Peoples' Rights?[102] Or the Cairo Declaration on Human Rights in Islam?[103] Unquestionably, these instruments are innovative in their

---

[98]   The right to self-determination is expressly enunciated in Article 1 of the International Covenant on Economic, Social and Cultural Rights, *infra* Appendix II [hereinafter ICESCR]; also in Article 1 of the ICCPR, *infra* Appendix III.

[99]   Adopted May 30, 1948, OAS, BASIC DOCUMENTS PERTAINING TO HUMAN RIGHTS IN THE INTER-AMERICAN SYSTEM [hereinafter BASIC DOCUMENTS], OAS Res. OAS Off. Rec. OEA/Ser. L/V/I.4 Rev. (1965), OEA/Ser.L/VII.92, Doc. 31, Rev. 3 at 17 (1996), *reprinted in* 3 Weston III.B.23, *supra* note 50.

[100]   Concluded, Nov. 22, 1969, OASTS No. 36, OAS Off. Rec. OEA/Ser.L/V/IL.23, Doc. 21, Rev. 6 (1979), 1144 U.N.T.S. 123, *reprinted in* 9 I.L.M. 673 (1970) *and* 3 Weston III.B.24, *supra* note 50.

[101]   Concluded, Nov. 17, 1988 (not yet in force). OASTS No. 69, OAS Doc. OEA/Ser.A/42 (SEPF), *reprinted in* 28 I.L.M. 156 (1989) *and* 3 Weston III.B.25, *supra* note 50. The Protocol is not yet in force.

[102]   Concluded June 27, 1981 (entered into force Oct. 21, 1986). OAU Doc. CAB/LEG/67/3 Rev. 5, *reprinted in* 21 I.L.M. 58 (1982) *and* 3 Weston III.B.I, *supra* note 50.

[103]   For an English translation, see *World Conference on Human Rights*, U.N. GAOR, 4th

human rights enunciations (by their emphasis on the rights of peoples or on human duties). But a close comparison with the UDHR would also show that they converge on many a crucial human rights value as well.

Indeed, this historical evidence of *normative consensus* over the universality of some human rights norms and standards becomes all the more striking when discourse on relativism pauses to notice subsequent developments occurring, undoubtedly, under the auspices of Third World leadership during the 1960s and 1970s crystallizing its distinctive conceptions of global justice and human rights. Human rights norms and standards proliferate, extending to the collective rights of de-colonized states and peoples, from the 1962 Resolution on Permanent Sovereignty over Natural Resources[104] (to take a long leap!) to the 1986 Declaration on the Right to Development.[105] I suggest that the discourse on "relativism" remains afflicted by its very own political unconscious (to borrow Fredrick Jameson's fecund notion[106]).

That political unconscious, in relation to human rights discursivity, assumes many forms of historic, cultural, civilizational, and even epistemic racial arrogance toward the Other of Enlightenment and even post-Enlightenment thought and political action. That arrogance, which regards all human rights imagination as the estate of the West, which others can at best only mime, prevents recognition of authorship of human rights by states and peoples of the Third World. Must all the history of the latter be reduced to the thesis that the "universality" of human rights is the pervasive syndrome of Western hegemony? Does not, after all, this "cultural" or ethical" relativism talk, ostensibly directed to the recognition of diversity, perform, in reality, the labors of reinstalling the "Myth of Origins" about human rights in the West?

What is of interest here is the fact that the practices of the politics *of* human rights converge here with those of the politics *for* human rights. The very regimes and cliques that deny freedom and dignity and canons of political accountability by denouncing human rights "universality" as a sinister imperial conspiracy find support from intellectual and social activists critiquing the "universality" in the same prose. Undoubtedly, human rights rhetoric has been conspicuously consumed by the United States and its normative cohorts, most brutally in moves to "make the

---

Sess., Agenda Item 5, U.N. Doc. A/CONF. 157/PC/62/Add.18 (1993), *reprinted in* 11 HUMAN RIGHTS: A COMPILATION OF INTERNATIONAL INSTRUMENTS 478 (1997). *See also* Arab Charter on Human Rights, Sept. 15, 1994, Council of the League of Arab States, 102d Sess., Res. 5437. An unofficial translation of the Charter appears at 56 REV. INT'L COMM. JURISTS 57 (1996) and 4 INT'L HUM. RTS. REP. 850 (1997).

104 Adopted Dec. 14, 1962, G.A. Res. 1803, U.N. GAOR, 17th Sess., Supp. No. 17, at 15, U.N. Doc. A/5217 (1963), *reprinted in* 2 I.L.M. 223 (1963) *and* 4 Weston IV.F.1, *supra* note 72.

105 Adopted Dec. 4, 1986, G.A. Res. 41/128 (Annex), U.N. GAOR, 41st Sess., Supp. No. 53, at 186, U.N. Doc. A/41/53 (1987), *reprinted in* 3 Weston III.R.2, *supra* note 50.

106 *See* FREDERICK JAMESON, THE POLITICAL UNCONSCIOUS NARRATIVE AS A SOCIALLY SYMBOLIC ACT (1981).

world safe for democracy" (read global capital) during the Cold War and beyond. An exposé of this horrible practice of the politics *of* human rights is continually necessary and desirable. It is but natural that peoples and states that believe in "manifest destiny" to lead the world deploy all available normative resources, including the languages of human rights, to pursue it. But does that necessarily constitute the indictment of the very notion of universal human rights? Or, the notion of the universality of human rights? Should this ineluctable critique of the politics *of* human rights become also the *norm* of the politics *for* human rights?

Free-floating historians of ideas keep telling us that Asian, African, or other "non-Western" traditions had no analogue to the expression "human rights."[107] But neither had the "Western tradition" even the phrase "rights" until the mid-nineteenth century.[108] And the invention of the phrase "human rights" is very recent indeed. Apart from the socio-linguistic discovery of novelty, nothing much follows! No doubt, words and phrases carry burdens of histories. But histories also give rise to regimes of phrases that mold the future. Surely, the discourse on human struggles and movements that empower human beings in time, place, and circumstance to resist oppression (whether in East Timor or Myanmar) are also entitled to the same order of privilege that historians of ideas or cultural anthropologists claim for themselves!

This essay does not address the daunting tasks of tracing these scattered hegemonies of "relativist" desires, a task crucial for a social theory of human rights. But as a preliminary step towards it I undertake a critical overview of the agendum of relativism in relation to contemporary human rights discursive formation.

And in so doing I transgress simple logic. A logical way, exposing the fault line of relativism, is to present it as an axiom that maintains that there are no truths save the truth that all truths are relative! You may substitute for "truth" in this axiom "values," "human rights," notions of being "human" (or whatever the context requires) It is well known by now that logically such a position is simply incoherent.

4. Multiculturalism

In complete disregard of the fact that contemporary human rights norms and standards are not monologically but dialogically produced and enacted (and stand brokered and mediated by global diplomacy, including that of the NGOs), it still is maintained that human rights enunciations ignore cultural and civilizational diversity. This is bad, even wicked, sociology. The pro-choice women's groups at the U.N.

---

107   Interested readers may pursue the relevant literature via massive footnote 3 in Stephen P. Marks, *From the "Single Confused Page" to the "Declaration for Six Billion Persons": The Roots of the Universal Declaration of Human Rights in the French Revolution,* 20 HUM. RTS. Q. 459, 460 (1998) or equally massive note 16 in Burns Weston's essay *supra* in this volume at pp. 65, 69–70.

108   MACINTYRE, *supra* note 40, at 69.

Beijing Conference, for example, confronted by His Holiness the Pope's Open Letter to the Conference, or the participants at the U.N. Cairo summit on population planning, know this well.

The enactment of human rights into national social policies is even more heavily mediated by the multiplicity of cultural, religious, and even civilizational traditions. The American feminists on every anniversary of *Roe v Wade*[109] know this. So does the African sisterhood modulating public policy on female genital mutilation, and the Indian sisterhood in its moves to outlaw dowry murders. No engaged human rights theory or practice, to the best of my knowledge, enacts, in real life, pursuit of universal human rights without any regard for cultural or religious traditions. Nor does it completely succumb to the virtues and values of "theoretical" ethical relativism.

In ways that relativist arguments do not, the logic of the universality of rights is one that opens up for interrogation settled habits of representation of "culture" and "civilization." It makes problematic that which was regarded as self-evident, natural, and true and makes possible to friendly human rights reading of tradition or scripture[110] and, indeed, even the claim that some contemporary human rights were anticipated by these.

Of course, as is well known, conflicts over interpretation of tradition are conflicts not just over values but about power as well. In turn, both the "fundamentalists" and the human rights evangelists become prisoners of a new demonology. Both tend to be portrayed in the not always rhetorical warfare[111] that follows as *fiends*, not fully human and therefore unworthy of dignity of discourse. Practices of the politics of intolerance begin to thrive all around. Practices of solidarity among human rights activists, national and transnational, begin to be matched by powerful networks of power and influence at home and abroad. The politics of the universality of human rights becomes increasingly belligerent. And the martyrdom count of human rights activists registers an unconscionable increase.

At this point, the universality of human rights ceases to be an abstract idea with its history of doctrinal disputations, but, instead, a living practice, a form of struggle, a practice of transformative vision. Its truths of resistance, in constant collision with the truths of power, seek to universalize themselves. And its truths are formed not in the comfort of contemplative life but in and through the gulags.

---

[109] 410 U.S. 113 (1973).

[110] Readings of scriptural traditions yield repressive as well as emancipative consequences. As is well known (or ought to be), long before feminism happened, the Koranic verse on polygamy generated a two century-old debate, before the doors of *ijehad* were declared to be closed in the 10th century A.D. on the verse on polygamy which was construed to *prohibit* the practice of polygamy which on established reading it permitted. Similarly, rights to sexual orientation-friendly readings have been discovered in major religious texts of the world by the hermeneutic labors of human rights praxis.

[111] Those who proselytize "radical" readings of the scriptural traditions, though no longer burnt at the stake, are relentlessly subjected to territorial, and even extra-territorial, repression and punishment.

In this sense, the claim to the universality of human rights signifies an aspiration and movement to bring new civility to power among states and human societies. That civility consists in making power increasingly accountable. Does the dialogue over the relativity of values matter much *when so much* is at stake?

5. "Westoxification"

Although the complex history of the notion of "Westoxification" cannot be pursued here,[112] the critique insists that human rights enunciations and cultures represent secular versions of the Divine Right to rule the "Unenlightened." It demonstrates that the West seeks to impose standards of right and justice, which it has all along violated in its conduct towards Islamic societies and states.[113] It rejects the notion that the outpourings and actions of the U.S. Department of State and their normative cohorts are exhaustive of the totality of "contemporary" human rights discourse. It seeks to locate the politics of human rights within the tradition of the *shari'a*.[114] As Muhammad Shykh Fadalla has eloquently stated: "As Moslems, we consider politics to be part of our whole life, because the Koran emphasizes the establishment of justice as a divine mission. . . . *In this sense, the politics of the faithful is a kind of prayer.*[115] At the heart of the critique lies the epochal politics of difference, which of course does not regard Islam, in the image of "the recurrent Western myth," as a "monolithic" tradition.[116]

Responsible "Westoxification" notions seek to bring an element of piety within the logics and paralogics of the construction of human rights. If the politics *for* human rights is a kind of "prayer of the faithful" for pious Muslims, so it is also for the secular congregation of a civic religion called "human rights." The contribution that this kind of understanding brings for the future of human rights (of a very different order than that provided by post-modernisms or recrudescent forms of relativism) calls for inter-faith dialogue. A dialogue that will yield a sense of justice to the worlds of power provides invaluable resource to the universalization of human rights.

6. The Types of Relativism

Relativism, a coat of many colors,[117] indicts the logic of universality of human rights (as noted) on the ground that different cultural and civilizational traditions have

---

[112] For a rich account of the history of origins, see JOHN L. ESPOSITO, THE ISLAMIC THREAT: MYTH OR REALITY? 188–253 (2d ed. 1995). Also see the provocative analysis by Booby Sayyid, *Sign O'Times: Kaffirs and Infidels Fighting the Ninth Crusade, in* THE MAKING OF POLITICAL IDENTITIES 233 (Ernesto Laclau ed., 1994).

[113] *See* MUZAFFAR, *supra* note 69.

[114] *See Cairo Declaration on Human Rights in Islam, supra* note 103.

[115] *Quoted in* ESPOSITO, *supra* note 112, at 149 (emphasis added).

[116] *Id.* at 201.

[117] See the superb analysis in CHRISTOPHER NORRIS, RECLAIMING TRUTH: CONTRIBUTION TO A

diverse notions of what it means to be human and for humans to have rights. While this is true, it is also trivial[118] and simply does not make impossible cross- or inter- or trans-cultural understandings.

If, on the other hand, relativism is a claim that what people believe to be right or wrong determines what is wrong or right for them,[119] then universal standards of human rights (such as the prohibition of genocide, torture, racial discrimination, and violence against women) remain "universal" only for the groups of people who believe themselves to be so. The insistence on universality is also mistaken when it erects the notion that moral judgments apply not just to "a particular action but to a class of actions;"[120] that "these judgments apply to everybody,"[121] and that "others besides the speakers are assumed to share [them]."[122] That this form of relativism turns out to be logically or analytically flawed is, unfortunately, good news that does not travel fast! The fatal flaw lies in the fact that even when some people believe it to be good or moral to kill, torture, or rape, they may not claim a duty on the part of others (who believe otherwise) not to interfere with their practices of "virtue" (as seen, I must add, by them).[123] The bad news is that even so gifted a philosopher as Richard Rorty could base his entire Oxford-Amnesty Lectures meditation on human rights on the following initial statement:

> Serbian murderers and rapists do not think of themselves as violating human rights. For they are not doing these things to fellow human beings but to *Muslims*. They are not being inhuman, but rather are discriminating between the true humans and pseudo-humans. They are making the same sorts of distinction as the Crusaders made between humans and infidel

---

CRITIQUE OF CULTURAL RELATIVISM (1996). Of course, "relativism" is a vacuous word. We need to distinguish between several types relativism. See the useful effort by Fernando R. Tesón, *International Human Rights and Cultural Relativism*, 25 VA. J. INT'L L. 869 (1985). *See also* Adamantia Pollis, *Cultural Relativism Revisited: Through a State Prism*, 18 HUM. RTS. Q. 316 (1996). A more sustained analysis of relativism is offered by R. G. PEFFER, MARXISM, MORALITY AND SOCIAL JUSTICE 268–316 (1990) (hereinafter PEFFER) who distinguishes between four types of relativism.

118 Because what people may believe is an important social datum, nothing follows from this on the issue of what they *ought* to believe. *Cf.* PEFFER, *supra* note 117, at 272–73.

119 For the elaboration of the notion of "normative ethical relativism" as entailing two distinct positions, see PEFFER, *supra* note 117, at 273–74, and the literature cited there. Does the normative ethical relativistic position refer to an individual's criteria of moral rightness or does it refer to criteria accepted by a society or culture as a whole?

120 BERNARD R. MAYO, ETHICS AND MORAL LIFE 91–92 (1958), *quoted in* PEFFER, *supra* note 117, at 276.

121 *Id.*

122 *Id.*

123 See the logical demonstration of this in PEFFER, *supra* note 117, at 275.

dogs, and Black Muslims make between humans and blue-eyed devils. The founder of my university was able both to own slaves and to think it self-evident that all men were created equal. . . . Like the Serbs, Mr. Jefferson did not think of himself as violating *human rights*.[124]

What follows? Does it follow that the "murderers and rapists" are justified? From the relativist position so far canvassed they could so maintain. But Professor Rorty suggests that the way out of all this lies in "making our own culture—the human rights culture—more self-conscious and powerful," not in "demonstrating its superiority to other cultures by an appeal to something transcultural."[125] By "our culture," "the culture of human rights," Rorty means primarily the United States culture (and more broadly the Euro-Atlantic culture). The Other has to be educated in human rights sensibility, not by any allegiance to the UDHR values (since these are transcultural). The acknowledgement about Jefferson and the Crusaders suggests heavily that there has been a progress in moral sentiments in the United States (and allied Northern cultures) which has yet to reach the benighted Serbs.[126] Probably what Rorty exemplifies is not so much a variety of normative ethical relativism but either, or even both, "meta-ethical" and "meta-evaluative" forms of relativism. Probably there are no "sure" or "objective" ways to prove to everyone's satisfaction that something is morally right or wrong or just that something is right or wrong. But who is that "everyone?" This is apparently a vexed question for ethical theorists[127] and may well remain so for the better part of the next millennium.

But both of these forms of relativism rely on, or at any rate invoke, the possibility of "intrasubjective consensus" on at least the *prima facie* validity of certain moral norms. Neither prevents us from claiming that "a certain moral principle (*e.g.*, slaughtering of defenseless infants) is *prima facie* wrong."[128] If so, "human rights" constitute at least the burden of ethical justification on those who engage in practices of "pseudospeciation" or indulge in catastrophic practices of the politics of cruelty. And if serious-minded relativism suggests that construction of such *onus probandi* is itself a complex moral affair, and accordingly requires great care in the enunciation of human rights norms and standards, this message is of considerable importance for those who would steer the future of human rights.

---

[124] Rorty, *supra* note 92, at 112.

[125] *Id.* at 117.

[126] It is remarkable that Rorty collapses the "pre-modern" (Crusades), the "modern" (colonial/imperial), and "contemporary" (human rights era) into one master narrative! On the paradigm offered in this work, Jefferson was consistent with the logics and paralogics of "modern" human rights practices of exclusion. Rorty's Serbs are, however, located in a world that *invented human rights*, including perhaps the basic human right against (to invoke Eric Erickson's term again) "pesudospeciation." *See* Tu Wei-Ming, *supra* note 93.

[127] *See* WILLIAM K. FRANKENA, ETHICS (1963); KURT BATER, THE MORAL POINT OF VIEW (1965); and the discussion in PEFFER *supra* note 117, at 281–85, 305–13.

[128] PEFFER, *supra* note 117, at 273.

Anyone familiar with the Asian, Arab, African and Latin American charters or conventions on human rights (and at the spawning NGO re-articulation of the UDHR on its golden jubilee) surely knows that human rights enunciations are marked by such moral agonizing, though not always in languages that comfort moral philosophers. Arguments from relativism that remain willfully ignorant or dismissive of the histories of construction of the "universality" of human rights are altogether unhelpful. From the perspectives of sociology of knowledge, they may even appear to some as exercises in unconscious *realpolitik*, which it is the task of "contemporary" human rights to render problematic.

7. What Is Living and Dead in Argument from Relativism?

What, perhaps, is helpful in relativism regarding the "contemporary" human rights movement is the notion that human suffering is not wholly legible outside cultural scripts. Since suffering, whether defined as individual pain or as social suffering is egregious, different religions and cultural traditions enact divergent hierarchies of "justification" of experience and imposition of suffering, providing at times and denying at others, language to pain and suffering.

The universality of human rights, it has been argued recently by Talal Asad, extravagantly forfeits cultural understanding of social suffering[129] and alienates human rights discourse from the lived experience of culturally/civilizationally constituted humanness. Professor Asad highlights the fact that the Western colonial discourses on suffering valorized "[p]ain endured in the movement of becoming 'fully human'. . . [and] was seen as necessary because social or moral reasons justified why it must be suffered."[130] He shows the ways by which the very idea of cruelty and degradation becomes and remains "unstable, mainly because the aspirations and practices to which it is attached are themselves contradictory, ambiguous, or changing."[131] This instability, he argues, is scarcely remedied by neither the "attempt by the Euro-Americans to impose their standards by force on others nor the willing invocation of these standards by the weaker peoples in the Third World."[132] He alerts us to the fact that "cruelty can be experienced and addressed *in ways other than violation of rights*—for example, as a failure of specific virtues or as an expression of particular vices."[133]

This is, indeed, a responsible practice of cultural relativism, because, while maintaining skepticism concerning the "universalistic discourses" around the 1984 U.N. Convention Against Torture and Other Cruel Inhuman or Degrading Treatment

---

129 Asad, *supra* note 38, at 285.

130 *Id.* at 295.

131 *Id.* at 304.

132 *Id.*

133 *Id.* (emphasis added).

or Punishment,[134] it does not attack its norm on any ethical grounds. Rather, it shows us how ethnographies of cruelty may assist the progressive promotion and protection of human rights there enshrined, in ways that respect discursive traditions other than those of human rights.

Similarly, the ethnography of suffering summons us to focus on the difficult relationship between violence and rights. The promotion and protection of rights always has entailed regimes or practices of *justified* or legitimate violence, although rights-talk habituates us to the idea that violence is the very antithesis of rights. Moreover, human rights discursivity rarely concedes that violence of the oppressed often can be rights-generative. It can also be horrendously destructive.

Veena Das, in her pioneering exploration, expresses the latter. Her construction of violence brings to us the "unnamable" phenomenon (when the horrors of the partition of India inscribed on the bodies of women) led to the birth of citizen-monsters: "[I]f men emerged from colonial subjugation as autonomous citizens of an independent nation, they emerged simultaneously as monsters."[135] Her precious, anguished insights invite us to consider what Walter Benjamin called the *foundational violence of the law*[136] and, one may add, of historic practice of the human right to self-determination. The citizen-monster dialectic is reiterative as well, in the everyday life of modern Indian experience of women's suffering, despite law, policy, and administration, even when human rights-oriented.

The challenge that this genre of writing, which exposes writing as violence, poses for human rights logic and paralogics is simply enormous and cannot be captured by the unfeeling and dense prose of relativism. It directs attention to ways in which human rights languages lie at the surface (and not in any Foucaldian sense that treats *depth* as a mere fold on the surface) of lived and embodied human anguish and suffering. It interrogates distinctions between forms of suffering as an aspect of state-imposed and "people"/ "civil society" inflicted, or even self-chosen and imposed suffering, and hierarchies or "transactions in construction of suffering."

The practices of promotion and protection of universal human rights entail construction of moral or ethical hierarchies of suffering.[137] Such construction takes place when certain rights (such as civil and political rights) stand priorized over other human rights (such as social, economic, and cultural rights). It occurs when even the former set of rights are subjected to the reason of the state (as when their

---

[134] Concluded, Dec. 10, 1984 (entered into force, June 26, 1987) G.A. Res. 39/46 (Annex), U.N. GAOR, 39th Sess., Supp. No. 51, at 197, U.N. Doc. A/RES/39/51 (1985), *reprinted in* 23 I.L.M. 1027 (1984) *and* 3 Weston III.K.2, *supra* note 50.

[135] Veena Das, *Language and Body: Transactions in Construction of Pain, in* SOCIAL SUFFERING 67, 86 (Arthur Kleinman et al. eds., 1996). *See also* Stanley Cavell, *Comments on Veena Das, id.* at 93.

[136] *See* Jacques Derrida, *The Force of Law: The Mystical Foundation of Authority, in* DECONSTRUCTION AND THE POSSIBILITY OF JUSTICE 3, 29–67 (Drucilla Cornell et al. eds., 1992).

[137] I derive this notion from Veena Das, *Moral Orientations to Suffering, in* HEALTH AND SOCIAL CHANGE 139 (L.C. Chen, et al. eds., 1994).

suspension is legitimated in "time of public emergency which threatens the life of the nation"[138]. It occurs when solemn treaties prohibiting genocide and torture, cruel, and degrading treatment or punishment allow scope for reservations and derogations that eat out the very heart of remedies otherwise declared available for the violated.

Not merely does the community of states construct such transactional hierarchies. Even human rights praxis does this.[139] This makes human rights praxis at best *global* but not *universal*, with deep implications for the future of human rights.

IV. Human Rights Movements and Human Rights Markets

A. Human Rights Movements as Social Movements

Human rights struggles are among the most defining characteristics of the second half of the Christian twentieth century; indeed, more often than not, we think of human rights praxis in terms of social movements. But the latter notion raises many perplexing issues concerning how one may define, classify, and evaluate them, and all remain apposite to a social theory of human rights yet in its infancy. Among the first necessary steps is understanding of how movements define their identity, their antagonists, and their teleology (visions of transformation).[140] Social theory about social movements stresses the importance of either the Weberian value-neutrality or the postmodern suspicion of "predetermined directionality." Thus writes Manuel Castells:

Social movements may be socially conservative, socially revolutionary or both or none. After all, we now have concluded (and I hope for ever) that there is no predetermined directionality in social evolution, that the *only*

---

138   ICCPR, *infra* Appendix III, art. 4.

139   The way in which human rights mandates are fashioned or formed within the United Nations agencies and across the NGOs illustrates this problem rather strikingly. As concerns the former, it often is argued that specialized agencies claim a version of human rights for themselves rather than for the violated. Katarina Tomaševski has shown recently that much of the discourse of the U.N. High Commission for Refugees (UNHCR) has been focused on the *right of access* by intergovernmental agencies to victims of "wars of hunger" rather than on human rights of access by the violated to ameliorative agencies. *See* Katarina Tomaševski, *Human Rights and Wars of Starvation, in* WAR AND HUNGER: RETHINKING INTERNATIONAL RESPONSE TO COMPLEX EMERGENCIES 70–91 (Joanna Macrae & Anthony Zwi eds., 1994). As concerns the sculpting of human rights mandates, the activist grapevine all too often condemns Amnesty International for focusing too heavily on violations of civil and political rights at the expense of fully understanding the importance of the protection of economic, social, and cultural rights. Human rights NGOs who adopt a special mandate for themselves (*e.g.*, "sustainable development," "population planning") often are charged for neglecting other bodies of crucial human rights. It is pointless to multiply instances. In each such situation, the criticism is justified only from the standpoint of different constructions of hierarchy of suffering or evil, rarely made theoretically explicit.

140   *See* MANUEL CASTELLS, THE POWER OF IDENTITY 71 (1997).

sense of history is the history we sense. Therefore, from an analytical perspective, there are no "bad" and "good" social movements. They are all symptoms of our societies and all impact social structures, with variable intensities and outcomes that must be established by social research.[141]

Human rights movements as social movements demand such research.[142] But a social theory of human rights may have considerable difficulty with the demand that even the manifestly rights-denying social or human rights movements should escape moral evaluation pending social research. A willing suspension of ethical beliefs, deferring human rights action to sustained social science research, can have impacts on the power of human rights movements to name an evil and to create public concern and capacity to contain or eliminate it. For example, some social movements may defend as just traditions that confine women to home and hearth, or may find justifications for reinventing apartheid and genocide. Indeed, they may claim the protection of extant human rights regimes to do so. Hate speech missionaries seek to "justify" racism as an aspect of freedom of speech and expression. The protagonists of human life invoke the fetal human right to life even to justify aggression on abortion clinics and professionals. The recent Rawlsian notion valorizing the defense of "well-ordered societies" is eminently suitable to justify regimes of military intervention or superpower sanction against the less well-ordered societies.[143]

Such movements turn upside down the very power of human rights rhetoric to identify certain regimes of human rights! The power of human rights discourse to name an order of evil is used to name human rights as the very order of evil! Perhaps, to evoke Castells' phrase, this standpoint emerges as a "symptom" of our societies. No doubt, as he says, these symptoms "impact social structures, with variable intensities and outcomes,"[144] inviting a prolific growth of cognitive social science knowledge to empower us with some understanding. At the same time, human rights praxis (whether through movements or markets) may generate scientific knowledge rather than await it; the history of human rights praxis, from Mohandas Gandhi to Ken Saro-Wiwa, from Joan of Arc to Petra Kelly, is truly prefigurative of future knowledges about freedom and fulfillment.

A social theory of human rights must find bases for ethical judgment concerning "good" and "bad" social movements; howsoever contestable, human rights movements cannot take as axiomatic the notion that "the only sense of history is

---

141   *Id.* at 70 (emphasis added).

142   Upendra Baxi, *The State and Human Rights Movements in India, in* PEOPLE'S RIGHTS: SOCIAL MOVEMENTS AND THE STATE IN THE THIRD WORLD 335–52 (Manoranjan Mohanty et al. eds., 1998).

143   John Rawls, *The Law of Peoples, in* ON HUMAN RIGHTS: THE OXFORD AMNESTY LECTURES 1993, at 41 (Stephen Shute et al. eds., 1993).

144   CASTELLS, *supra* note 140.

the history we sense." It must seek to provide a "pre-determined directionality" in human social development by articulating an ethic of power, whether in state, civil society, or the market. It must contest the notion that certain human interactions and transactions constitute moral free-zones.[145]

B. From "Movements" to "Markets

Increasingly, human rights movements organize themselves in the image of markets. Of course, the use of terms like "market" and "commoditization" may be deeply offensive to human rights practitioners, and the analogy with markets may turn out, on closer analysis not to be too strong. Moreover, we should distinguish between the discourse of social movements and the "social processes with which they are associated: for example, globalization, informationalization, the crisis of representational democracy, and the dominance of symbolic politics in the space of media."[146] From this standpoint, and quite rightly so, "movements" are analytically distinguishable from "markets." A reductionist analysis, which disregards the relative autonomy of movements from markets, does not advance clarity or conviction. At the same time, the idiom of the "market" brings more sharply into view the complexity and contradiction of human rights movements.

Human rights markets consist of a network of transactions that serve the contingent and long-term interests of human rights investors, producers, and consumers. These transactions rely upon the availability, which they in turn seek to reinforce, of symbolic capital[147] in the form of international human rights norms, standards, doctrines, and organizational networks. Furthermore, since grids of power are globalized, human rights markets also create and reinforce global networks, each of which seek to influence the conduct of those actors who violate human rights norms and standards and the behavior of those who resist such violations. Human rights market rationality requires the production and re-production of human rights skills and competences, which enable negotiation of tolerably acceptable outcomes between and among the violators and the violated such that market failures do not erode the legitimacy of the network of overall transactions. Human rights markets thus share the salient features of service industries.

C. The Investor and Consumer Markets in Human Rights

Human rights movements at all levels (global, regional, national, and local) have tended to become "capital-intensive." That is, the praxis of promoting and protect-

---

[145] DAVID GAUTHIER, MORALS BY AGREEMENT 13, 83–112 (1986).

[146] *See* CASTELLS, *supra* note 140, at 70.

[147] *See generally* PIERRE BOURDIEU, THE FIELD OF CULTURAL PRODUCTION: ESSAYS ON ART AND LITERATURE 74–142 (1993); PIERRE BOURDIEU, OUTLINE OF A THEORY OF PRACTICE (Richard Nice trans., 1977).

ing human rights now entails entrepreneuership in raising material resources, including funding, from a whole variety of governmental, inter-governmental, and philanthropic sources. These sources are organized in terms of management imperatives, both of line-management and upward accountability. Any human rights NGO or NGI (nongovernmental individual) involved in programs for the celebration of the golden jubilee of the UDHR surely knows this! The promotion and protection of human rights is an enterprise that entails access to organized networks of support, consumer loyalty, efficient internal management, management of mass media and public relations, and careful crafting of mandates.

A full analysis of these variables would unconscionably burden this essay; but it needs to be acknowledged that both consumer NGOs and funding agencies compete *inter se* for scarce resources and that this scramble for support generates forms of investor rationality, which generally may be defined as seeking a tangible return on investment.[148] That rationality must negotiate the Scylla of mobilization of support of governmental, corporate, and community conscience-money contributions and the Charybidis of their "legitimation" in host societies and governments. This negotiation, in turn, requires the marshaling of high entrepreneurial talent suffused with a whole range of negotiating endowments. Understandably, investor rationality in human rights markets is constantly exposed to a crisis of "nervous rationality." Both the "inputs" and "outputs" in human rights portfolio investment protection remain indeterminate; nevertheless, these must be ledgered, packaged, sold, and purchased on the most productive terms.

The crisis of "nervous rationality" is replicated in consumer rationality. Human rights NGOs, especially in the Third World, must negotiate the dilemmas of legitimacy and autonomy. The ever so precarious legitimacy of human rights networks seems forever threatened by allegations of foreign funding orchestrated both by interested governments and by rival NGOs that want to do better than their "competitors." There exists, too, competition to capture the beneficiary groups who measure the legitimacy of human rights networks not in terms of any "cargo cult" or messianic rationality but according to what these networks bring to people in terms of here-and-now accomplishments or results.

At the same time, NGOs seek a free enterprise market relative to the agenda of their semi-autonomous human rights concerns. They seek to define their markets for human rights promotion and protection not merely in terms of what the markets of human rights investment will bear at any given moment but also in terms of how these markets may be re-orientated in terms of consumer power. This may partly explain the populous presence and participation of the best and the brightest of NGOs and NGIs in this decade and half of the United Nations summits in Vienna, Cairo, Copenhagen, Beijing, and Istanbul. By their determined participa-

---

148 *See* DAVID GILLIES, BETWEEN PRINCIPLE AND PRACTICE: HUMAN RIGHTS IN NORTH-SOUTH RELATIONS (1996); KATARINA TOMAŠEVSKI, BETWEEN SANCTION AND ELECTIONS: AID DONORS AND HUMAN RIGHTS (1997).

tion at these summits (and the inevitably mandated "plus-5" meetings), they seek to re-orient the global investment markets in human rights. The interests of civil servants (national and international) intermesh, in this process, with those of the NGOs and the NGIs.

D. Techniques of Commodification of Human Suffering

The raw material for human rights investment and consumer markets is provided by here-and-now human misery and suffering. However morally deplorable, it is a social fact that the overall human capacity to develop a fellowship of human suffering is awesomely limited. It is a salient fact about the "contemporary" human scene that individual and associational life-projects are rarely disturbed, let alone displaced, by the spectacle of human suffering or human suffering as a spectacle. In such a milieu, human rights markets, no matter whether investor or consumer, are confronted with the problem of "compassion fatigue." This is a moral problem, to be sure, but it is also a material problem. Of necessity, markets for human rights concentrate on this aspect of the problem if only because when compassion fades, the resources for the alleviation of human suffering through human rights languages are depleted. This intersection registers the necessity for human rights entrepreneurs to commodify human suffering, to package and sell it in terms of what the markets will bear. Human rights violations must be constantly commoditized to be combated. Human suffering must be packaged in ways that the mass media markets find it profitable to bear overall.

But the mass media can commodify human suffering only on a dramatic and contingent basis. Injustice and human rights violations are headline news only as the "porn of power" and its voyeuristic potential lies in the reiterative packaging of violations that titillate and scandalize, for the moment at least, the dilettante sensibilities of the globalizing classes. The mass media plays also a creationist role in that they "in an important sense 'create' a disaster when they decide to recognize it. . . . [T]hey give institutional endorsement or attestation to bad events which otherwise will have a reality restricted to a local circle of victims."[149] Such institutional endorsement poses intractable issues for the marketization of human rights. Given the worldwide patterns of mass media ownership, and the assiduously cultivated consumer cultures of "info-entertainment," the key players in human rights markets need to manipulate the media into authentic representations of the suffering of the violated. They must marshal the power to mold the mass media, without having access to resources that the networks of economic/political power so constantly command, into exemplary communicators of human solidarity. So far, this endeavor has rested in the commodification of human suffering, exploiting the markets for instant news and views.

---

[149] JONATHAN BENTHALL, DISASTERS, RELIEF AND THE MEDIA 3–4 (1993); *quoted in* STANLEY COHEN, DENIAL AND ACKNOWLEDGMENT: THE IMPACT OF INFORMATION ABOUT HUMAN RIGHTS VIOLATIONS 90 (1995). *See also* Kleinman et al., *supra* note 24.

In a germinal monograph, Stanley Cohen has brought home the daunting tasks entailed in the commodification of human suffering. The commodification of human suffering has as its task (according to Cohen, with whom I agree) the conversion of the "politics of denial" into that of the "politics of acknowledgment." Cohen brings to attention an entire catalogue of perpetrator-based techniques of denial of human violation and the variety of responses that go under the banner of "bystanderism," whether internal or external.[150]

The various techniques of marketing human suffering in the name of "human rights" succeed or fail according to the standpoint one chooses to privilege. Efficient market rationality perhaps dictates a logic of excess. The more human rights producers and consumers succeed in diffusing horror stories, the better it is, on the whole, for the sustenance of global human rights cultures. The more they succeed in establishing accountability institutions (truth commissions, commissions for human rights for women, indigenous peoples, children, and the urban and rural impoverished) the better commerce there is. Giving visibility and voice to human suffering is among the prime function of human rights service markets. But it is an enterprise that must overcome "compassion fatigue"[151] and an overall desensitization to human misery. When the markets are bullish, the logic of excess does seem to provide the most resources for the disadvantaged, dispossessed, and deprived human communities. But in situations of recession, serious issues arise concerning the ways in which human suffering is or should be merchandized; and when those who suffer begin to counter these ways, we witness crises in human rights market management.

Human rights markets are crowded with an assortment of actors, agencies, and agendas. But they seem united in their operational techniques. A standard technique is that of reportage: several leading organizations specialize in services providing human rights "watch" and "action alerts." A related market technique is that of lobbying, whereby official or popular opinion is sought to be mobilized around human rights situations, events, or catastrophes.

A third technique is that of cyberspace solidarity, spectacular uses of instant communication networks across the world. Manuel Castells has recently provided stunning examples of how cyber-technologies have made a dramatic difference in networking solidarities; but, as his analysis itself suggests, these solidarities may work for human rights advancement (as in the case of the Zapatistas) or, more

---

[150]   These consist of: (a) denial of injury; (b) denial of victims; (c) denial of responsibility; (d) condemnation of the condemners; and (e) appeal to higher loyalty. These "neutralization" techniques are firmly in place and violators only play variations on a theme. Professor Cohen also offers a typology of bystander passivity or effect, consisting of: (a) diffusion of responsibility; (b) inability to identify with the victim; and (c) inability of conceiving an effective intervention. *See* COHEN, *supra* note 149, at 32–35.

[151]   *Id.* at 89–116.

importantly, against the nascent human rights cultures (as in the case of the American militia or Japanese *Aum Shinrikyo* movements).[152] Apparently the days of the pre-cyberspace creation of mass movement solidarity are numbered or over, at least if one is to believe that the cyberspace markets for human rights provide the only or best creative spaces. In any case, once we recognize the danger of an historical cyberspace romanticism, it remains a fact that cyberspace offers a useful marketing technique. A fourth technique consists in converting the reportage of violation in the idiom and grammar of judicial activism. An exemplary arena is provided by the invention of social action litigation, pursuant to which Indian appellate courts, including the Supreme Court of India, have been converted from the ideological and repressive apparatuses of the state and global capital into an institutionalized movement for the promotion and protection of human rights.[153] The resonance of this movement extends to many a third world society.

A fifth technique is to sustain the more conventional networks of solidarity of which the facilitation of inter-NGO dialogue is a principal aspect. Usually done through conferences, colloquia, seminars, and the facilitation of individual visits by victims or their next of kin, this technique has in recent times extended to the holding of hearings/listenings of victim groups, a device that seeks to bring unmediated the voices and texts of suffering to empathetic observers across the world. The various U.N. summits have provided a spectacular illustration of this technique, but there are more institutionalized arrangements as well. All bring the raw material of human suffering for further processing and packaging in the media and related human rights markets.

A sixth technique is rather specialized, comprising various acts of lobbying of the treaty bodies of the United Nations. This form of human rights marketing specializes in providing legislative or policy inputs in the norm-creation process, with NGO entrepreneurs assuming the roles of quasi-international civil servants and quasi-diplomats for human rights, although it is the thinking and conduct of the *de jure* international diplomats and civil servants that they seek to influence. By this specialized intervention, this activity runs the risks of co-optation and alienation from the community of the violated, especially when the NGO activity becomes the mirror-image of inter-governmental politics. However, this sort of intervention does offer, when invested with integrity, substantial gains for the progressive creation of human rights norms.

A seventh, and here final, technique is that of global direct action against imminent or actual violations of human rights. Apart from the solitary though splendid example of Greenpeace, however, this technique is not considered sustainable by the leading global and regional NGOs. Of course, there are less spectacular and sustained examples furnished in the narratives of resistance to such global events, such

---

[152] *See* CASTELLS, *supra* note 140, at 68–109.

[153] *See supra* note 39.

as the G-7 and Asia-Pacific Economic Cooperation (APEC) conferences where methods of "citizen arrest" of global leadership are enacted, or when celebrations of the golden jubilee of international financial institutions are sought to be converted into events of embarrassment. Not to be ignored in this context are recourses to direct action by the Argentine mothers against "disappearances" or of the British women's movements against the sites of civilian or military nuclear operations. At the end of the day, however, the dominant market cost-benefit rationality does not legitimate such recourse to direct action in the dramaturgy of human rights.

This sort of illustrative listing is to suggest the variety and complexity of human rights market initiatives, which entail high quotients of managerial and entrepreneurial talent and the ability to boost market or investor confidence in human rights ventures. It also is partly my intention to suggest that the "science" of risk-analysis and risk-management is as relevant to the markets of promotion and protection of human rights as it is to those that perpetrate violations.

It is true that as human suffering intensifies, markets for human rights grow. But to say this does not entail any ethical judgment concerning the commodification of human suffering, although the reader may feel justified in treating some anguished sub-texts in this paper as warranting a wholesale moral critique of human rights markets. The future of human rights praxis is linked with, as always, the success or failure of human rights missions and their latent or patent capability to scandalize the conscience of humankind. The modes of scandalization will, of course, remain contested among the communities of the violators and the violated. The task for those who find the commodification of human suffering unconscionable lies in the contested ways of its accomplishment, not in lamenting the global fact of the very existence of human rights markets.

E. The Problem of "Regulation" of Human Rights Markets

State regulation of human rights markets is fraught with complexities. When may it be said to be invasive of human rights? How far, if at all, should states regulate the very existence or modes of operation of the NGOs involved? Should the regime of accreditation of NGOs in the United Nations system be liberal or conservative? How and by whom is this process to be determined?

The problem of regulation of human rights markets is not just state-centric. Human rights investor as well as consumer communities are stakeholders, with investor-based regulation taking myriad forms of channeling and controlling human rights agendas and transactions, generating a product mix that is the very essence of an audit culture (of upward accountability and line management). But the investors in human rights themselves may be regulated and, in this regard, must establish their legitimacy with the host society and government in ways that are propitious for cross-border markets in human rights promotion and protection.

The operators of the local/global human rights markets, primarily NGOs, confront related but distinct problems in devising self-regulatory and other-oriented regulatory frameworks. Self-regulatory frameworks must address the crises of investor rationalities in a highly competitive scramble for resourcing. Other-directed regulatory approaches are no less complex. On the one hand, there is a need to maintain acceptable patterns of consumer solidarity in the global investor markets; on the other hand, there exists the historic need, from the standpoint of the ultimate beneficiaries, to keep a watch on sister NGOs that are exposed to corruption, co-optation, or subversion by the forces of global capitalism, a problem recently illustrated in the now happily aborted case of the Bangla Desh Grameen Bank, which initially proposed a "deal" with Monsanto for their terminator seed technology. If there is no peer group regulation of occasions of co-optation, human rights markets can undergo substantial downturns.

But forms of peer-group regulatory interventions raise difficult if not intractable issues. When are NGO communities entitled to sound the alarm? Which modes of alleviation of human suffering are more progressively "just" from the standpoint of human rights communities that otherwise do not contest the existence of human rights markets in the name of human suffering? What superogatory ethics are at play here? Put another way, what standards of critical morality are furnished by extant human rights instruments (addressed primarily to state morality) for NGO critiques of sister NGOs? Are human rights markets per se more sensibly moral than all other markets?

Just as surely as there is an ideology of human rights, abundantly illustrated by the discourse on human rights, so is there a materiality to it, ever present in cross-border transactions in the symbolic capital of human rights. The usefulness of the market metaphor therefore should be apparent.

V. The Emergence of an Alternate Paradigm of Human Rights

A. The Paradigm Shift

My thesis herein requires a brutally frank statement. I believe that the paradigm of the UDHR is being steadily supplanted by a trade-related, market-friendly, human rights paradigm. This new paradigm reverses the notion that universal human rights are designed for the dignity and well-being of human beings and insists, instead, upon the promotion and protection of the collective rights of global capital in ways that "justify" corporate well-being and dignity over that of human persons. The UDHR model assigned human rights responsibilities to states; it called upon the state to construct, progressively and within the community of states, a just social order, both national and global, that could meet at least the basic needs of human beings. The new model denies any significant redistributive role for the state. It calls upon the state (and world order) to free as many spaces for capital as possible, initially by fully pursuing the "Three-Ds" of contemporary globalization: de-regulation, de-nationalization, and disinvestment. Putting an end to national regulatory and redistributive potentials is the *leitmotif* of present-day economic globalization, as anyone who has read several drafts of the Multilateral Agreement on Investment (MAI) knows.[154] But the program of rolling back the state aims at the same time for vigorous state action when the interests of global capital are at stake. To this extent, de-regulation signifies not an end of the nation-state but an end to the redistributionist state.[155]

Recent history has shown that multinational capital needs at one and the same time a "soft" state and a "hard" one.[156] The production of soft states is a high priority for multinational capital and its normative cohorts, as exemplified by the continuing reports of Ms. Fatima-Zohra Ksentini, Special Rapporteur to the Commission on Human Rights, on the adverse effect of the illicit movement and dumping of toxic and dangerous wastes on the enjoyment of human rights.[157] The biggest waste exporters are, of course, the most "developed" countries, and wastes continue to be dispatched to regions lacking the political and economic power to refuse it.[158] This deficit is not innate, but caused, in the last instance, by the formations of the global economy.

All kinds of unfortunate business practices abound: use of falsified documents; bribing of officials in the "country of origin, the transit country, or . . . the country of final destination,"[159] and private contracts "between Western companies and African countries whereby the companies paid a pittance for the land on which to dump toxic products. . . ."[160] The latter scandal brought forth an anguished resolution from the Organization of African Unity a decade ago, declaring toxic dumping to be a "crime against Africa and African people."[161] The Special Rapporteur had no difficulty in cataloging a large number of violations that these practices knowingly—and criminally—entail.[162] Soft states and regimes need to be continually constituted for the benefit of global capital, benefiting a few communities of people. That this imposes the cost of incredible human suffering on the impoverished nations[163] is irrelevant to the ruling standards of global capital, which must

---

[154] *See* Multilateral Agreement on Investment, *supra* note 73.

[155] *See* JANE KELSEY, THE NEW ZEALAND EXPERIMENT: A WORLD MODEL FOR STRUCTURAL ADJUSTMENT? (1995).

[156] *See* GUNNAR MYRDAL, ASIAN DRAMA: AN INQUIRY INTO THE POVERTY OF NATIONS (1968). Myrdal's concern was to portray South Asian states as lacking in social or institutional discipline and vulnerable to high levels of corruption.

[157] *Adverse Effects of the Illicit Movement and Dumping of Toxic and Dangerous Products and Wastes on the Enjoyment of Human Rights*, U.N. GAOR, Hum. Rts. Comm, U.N. Doc. E/CN.4/1998/10 (1998) [hereinafter *Adverse Effects*].

[158] *Id.* paras. 54 and 56.

[159] *Id.*

[160] *Id.*

[161] *Id.* para. 57.

[162] *Adverse Effects, supra* note 157, paras. 77–107.

[163] If you find this too metaphorical, please recall children being exposed to radiation by

measure the excellence of economic entrepreneuership by standards other than those provided by seemingly endless human rights normativity.

The contextuality of this enterprise bids a moment of reflection. The multinational corporations may not perform toxic dumping projects, for example, without the active support of the international financial institutions, and such support causes some Third World countries, ridden by "over-indebtedness and collapse of raw material prices," to view the import of hazardous wastes as "attractive" as a last resort to improve their liquidity.[164] In this context, one is talking about no more bad business practice that international codes of conduct may prohibit but, rather, of genocidal corporate and international financial institutional regimes of governance. These are, to coin a neologism (a barbarism in language that is insufficient to cope with the savagery of the "free market"), *rightsicidal* practices of management of governance.

Hard-headed international business practices require also proliferation of "hard" states and regimes which must be market-efficient in suppressing and delegitimating human rights practices of resistance or the pursuit of alternate politics. Rule of law standards and values need to be enforced by the state on behalf and at the behest of formations of the global economy and global technology. When, to this end, it is necessary for the state to unleash a reign of terror, it must be empowered, locally and globally, to do so. The state must remain, at all times, sufficiently active to ensure maximal security to the global or foreign investor, who has corresponding duties to assist the state in managing or refurbishing any democratic deficit that might thus arise. The flagrant, massive, and ongoing violations of human rights thus entailed must be denied a voice by state-of-the-art management of public and political opinion, nationally and globally.

The new paradigm will succeed if it can render problematic the voices of suffering. This occurs primarily through "rationality reform"—that is, by the production of epistemologies that normalize risk (there is no escape from risk), ideologize it (some grave risks are justified for the sake of "progress," "development," and "security"); problematize causation (in ways that the catastrophic impacts may not be traced to the activity of global corporations); raise questions (so dear to law and economics specialists concerning the efficiency of legal regimes of liability); and interrogate even a modicum of judicial activism (compensating rights-violation and suffering, favoring unprincipled and arbitrary extra-judicial settlement when risk management and damage containment strategies fail). It is not surprising that some of the most important questions in globalization discourse relate to how we conceptualize "victim," who may authentically speak about victimage and what, indeed, may be said to constitute "suffering."

---

playing on irradiated nuclear waste dump sites in the Marshall Islands or the victims of Bhopal still suffering from the lethal impact of catastrophic exposure to 47 tons of MIC.

[164] *See Adverse Effects, supra* note 157, para. 57.

The new paradigm asks us to shed the fetishism of human rights and to appreciate that, in the absence of economic development, human rights have no future at all. Some behavioral scientists urge us to believe in a quantitative methodology that "produces results," (certainly for them), that demonstrates a positive co-relation between foreign direct investment, multinational capital, and the observance of human rights. It is easier to combat dictatorial regimes that suspend human rights on the grounds of priority of economic development than to contest the gospel of economic rationalism, which is mystified by a new scholasticism with the assertion that, for example, "meso-development" is best promoted under conditions of authoritarianism. *Faute de mieux*, human rights communities must now work within the languages and imperatives of "economic rationalism"; they need to focus not on a conceptually elevated plateau of post-modern political theory, but, rather, on the new institutional economics, maintaining at the same time constant conversation with human suffering.

B. The Paradigms in Conflict

The paradigm of universal human rights has progressively sought normative consensus on the integrity of human rights, albeit expressed in different idioms. The diverse bodies of human rights found their highest summation with the Declaration on the Right to Development,[165] insisting that the individual is a subject of development, not its object.

The emergent paradigm reverses this trend. It seeks to make not just the individual human being but whole nations into the objects of development, as defined by global capital embodied in the "economic rationalism" of the supra-statal networks of the World Bank and the IMF, which are not democratically composed nor accountable to any constituency save investors. Their prescriptions for re-orientating the economic structures and polices of indebted and impoverished Third World societies, far from being designed to make the world order equitable, are addressed to the overall good of the world's hegemonic economies, in all their complexity and contradiction. Prescriptions of good governance are discriminatorily—and viciously —addressed only to states and communities outside the core Euro-Atlantic states. Even so, good governance is articulated as a set of arrangements, including institutional renovation, that primarily privileges and disproportionately benefits the global producers and consumers.

The paradigm of universal human rights enabled the emergence of the United Nations system as a congregation of faith. Regarded as no omnipotent deity but only as a frail, crisis-ridden arena, it became the privileged historic site for co-operative practices of reshaping the world through the idiom and grammar, as well as the vision, of human rights. This arena is being captured by the votaries of economic globalization who proselytize that free markets offer the best hope for human

---

[165] *Supra* note 105.

redemption. But the residue of the past cultures of universal human rights remains nonetheless, as recently manifested in a U.N. document that dares to speak about perverse forms of globalization, namely, those that abandon any degree of respect for human rights standards and norms.[166] A moment's reflection on the WTO agreements and the proposed Multilateral Agreement on Investment (MAI)[167] should demonstrate the truth of this assertion. But, of course, no United Nations formulation would go this far, given its own diplomacy on resourcing the system and emerging global economic realities. The Vienna Conference on Human Rights summed it all up with its poignant preambulatory reference to "the spirit of our age" and the "realities of our time."[168] The "spirit" is human rights vision; the "realities" are furnished by the headlong and heedless processes of globalization that are creating in their wake cruel logics of social exclusion and enduring communities of misfortune.

Of course, the continuing appropriation by the forces of capital of hard-won human rights for its own ends is not a *sui generis* event. Long before slavery was abolished and before women won the right to contest and vote at elections, corporations had appropriated rights to personhood, claiming due process rights for regimes of property but denied to human beings. The unfolding of what I call "modern" human rights is the story of the near-absoluteness of the right to property, as a basic human right. So is the narrative of colonization/imperialism which began its career with the archetypal East India Company (which ruled India for a century) when corporate sovereignty was inaugurated. Politics was commerce and commerce became politics.

So, it may be said, is this the case now. Some would even maintain that it was the case even during the halcyon days of human rights enunciations (from the Declaration on Permanent Sovereignty over Resources[169] to the Declaration on the Right to Development[170]). Peel away the layers of human rights rhetoric, they would maintain, and you will find a core of historic continuity where heroic assertions of human rights remained, in fact and effect, the insignia of triumphant economic interests.

This continuity thesis deserves its moment. It directs attention to facts and feats of global diplomacy over human rights in ways that moderate or even cure the celebrationist approach to human rights (whether human rights romanticism, mysticism, triumphalism, or hedonism). It alerts us to the fact that within the modalities of human rights enunciation beats the regular heartbeats of hegemonic interests.

---

166   *See Adverse Effects, supra* note 157.

167   *See* proposed Multilateral Agreement on Investment, *supra* note 73.

168   *See* Upendra Baxi, *"The Spirit of Our Age, The Realities of Our Time": The Vienna Declaration on Human Rights, in* MAMBRINO'S HELMET? HUMAN RIGHTS FOR A CHANGING WORLD 1–18 (1994).

169   *Supra* note 104.

170   *Supra* note 105.

It directs us towards a mode of thought that relocates the authorship of human rights away from the politics of inter-governmental desire to the multitudinous struggles of people against human violation.

If all this be so, is there a paradigm shift or merely an extension of latent capitalism that always has moved (as the readers of *Das Kapital* surely know) in accordance with bourgeois human rights trajectories? This is an important and difficult question raised by Burns Weston in his indefatigable editorial labors. My short answer for the present is that, while the appropriation by the capital of human rights logic and rhetoric is not a distinctively contemporary phenomenon, it is the scale of reversal now manifest that marks a radical discontinuity. Global business practices cancel, for example, many normative gains of the "contemporary" human rights movement through techniques of dispersal of these evils. The exploitation of child and sweat labor through free economic zones, and accompanying sex-based discrimination even in subsistence wages, is the hallmark of contemporary economic globalization. So is the creation of a "global risk society"[171] through hazardous industry and the very legible scripts of "organized irresponsibility" and "organized impunity" for corporate offenders, of which the Bhopal catastrophe furnishes a mournful reminder.[172]

What distinguishes the paradigm shift is the "legitimation" of extraordinary imposition of human suffering in the cause and the course of the present contemporary march of global capital. In the "modern" epoch of human rights, such suffering was considered *per se* legitimate. "Contemporary" human rights logics and paralogics challenged, and at times denied, this self-evident axiom. The paradigm shift seeks to cancel the historic gains of the progressive universal human rights movement in seemingly irreversible ways. It seeks to mute the voices of suffering and, in the process, regress human rights futures.

VI. Toward a Conclusion?

History, especially current history, presents always confused pathways. It is difficult to foretell with any degree of assurance, despite advances in futurology, where the future of human rights or indeed any future may lie. In this situation, the only reflexive task open to human rights communities consists in "planning ahead." The CEOs of leading multinationals are preoccupied with planning the futures of global capital movements in 2025 A.D. even as, remarkably, they confine the energies of human rights activists to perfidious instances of the "local-in-the-global" causation of human suffering (as, for example, in Bhopal and Ogoniland). The *fin-de-siècle* need and ordeal for human rights communities, worldwide, is to develop an agenda of action to arrest the paradigm-shift, without them converting themselves into new

---

[171] *See* ULRICH BECK, THE RISK SOCIETY: TOWARD A NEW MODERNITY (1992).

[172] *See* Upendra Baxi, *Introduction, in* VALIANT VICTIMS AND LETHAL LITIGATION: THE BHOPAL CASE (Upendra Baxi & Amita Dhandha eds., 1990).

bureaucrats or technocrats of human suffering. To some, this may seem an insensible challenge, as nothing seems more ludicrous than sailing against the wind. What is necessary is to combat this kind of mind-set. Human rights futures, dependent as they are upon imparting an authentic voice to human suffering, must engage in a discourse of suffering that moves the world.

Over a century and half ago, Karl Marx put the notion of human futures presciently when he urged that they are best born when the following twin tasks occur: when suffering humanity reflects and when thinking humanity suffers. I know of no better way to unite the future of human rights to human suffering.

Contesting Globalization: A Feminist Perspective on the Future of Human Rights*

Anne Orford

I. Introduction

The changes in international politics resulting from the break-up of the Soviet Union pose significant challenges to international human rights law. In particular, the increased trade and financial liberalization enabled by newly effective international economic institutions and the consequent speeding up of the process of economic globalization, have impacted upon sovereignty, self-determination, statehood, democracy, and the protection of human rights. The 50th anniversary of the Universal Declaration of Human Rights (UDHR) affords a valuable opportunity to reflect upon the place of human rights in the new world order that has emerged since the end of the Cold War.

This essay offers a feminist analysis of the challenges facing international human rights law at the end of the twentieth century. Feminists have been critical of international human rights law because of its narrow focus. In particular, feminist analyses have pointed to the failure of international human rights law to address violations of human rights that take place outside the "public" sphere or that are carried out by non-state actors.[1] Such criticisms of human rights have been fueled by the apparent inability of the international human rights system to address what many feminists see as the major human rights issue facing women in the post-Cold War era: the threat posed to human rights by economic globalization. The effect of globalization is a feminist issue for a number of reasons.

First, women often bear a disproportionate burden of the costs of economic globalization. The restructuring of economies, the contraction of the public sector, and cuts to government services accompanying macroeconomic reforms result in an increased burden on those who labor in the invisible economy outside the market, largely women. Women, for example, have been described as the "shock

* An earlier version of this essay was published under the same title in 8 TRANSNAT'L L. & CONTEMP. PROBS. 171 (1998). Reprint permission granted.

[1] See Charlotte Bunch, *Women's Rights as Human Rights: Toward a Re-Vision of Human Rights*, 12 HUM. RTS. Q. 486 (1990); Hilary Charlesworth, *The Mid-Life Crisis of the Universal Declaration of Human Rights*, 55 WASH. & LEE L.R. 781(1998); Hilary Charlesworth et al., *Feminist Approaches to International Law*, 85 AM. J. INT'L L. 613 (1991).

absorbers" of so-called shock therapy and structural adjustment programs imposed by the International Monetary Fund (IMF) and the World Bank, often the first to face the loss of employment when the public sector fires workers or when the workforce is casualized.[2] Women are likely to be required to pick up the burden of caring for sick, homeless, or mentally ill family or community members when the state divests itself of those responsibilities.[3] In many parts of the world, rural women are engaged in "hard-core economic resistance," fighting to protect ways of life under threat from the trade and financial liberalization promoted by the World Trade Organization (WTO).[4]

Second, the increased inequality produced by economic globalization is an issue for feminists who seek to resist the practices of exploitation and division of people against each other that are inherent in notions of competition, comparative advantage, free trade, and the international division of labor. As Andrea Rhodes-Little suggests:

> For feminists . . . the further challenge thrown down by "other" women is that of how to resist those social practices which produce inequality and divide women against each other within a global context as well as in local contexts. In short, feminists search for ethical practices which are answerable for the power relations they produce. We also search for law which acknowledges its position in the organizations of power relations between women and men and between white and "other."[5]

Third, feminist scholars have argued that economics is a means of imagining the world that is premised upon denigrating that which is understood as "feminine." Economic analyses assume a world in which nature and women have no creative power. The gendered metaphors of productivity that underlie economics idealize and valorize masculine activity as active, inspirational, generative, and creative.[6]

---

2   *See* Helen Hill, *From Nairobi to Beijing, in* BACK TO BASICS FROM BEIJING: AN AUSTRALIAN GUIDE TO THE INTERNATIONAL PLATFORM FOR ACTION 104, 106 (Suzette Mitchell & Rima Das Pradhan eds., 1997) [hereinafter BACK TO BASICS FROM BEIJING].

3   *See* Bharati Sadasivam, *The Impact of Structural Adjustment on Women: A Governance and Human Rights Agenda,* 19 HUM. RTS. Q. 630 (1997).

4   *See* Julie Stephens, *Running Interference: An Interview with Gayatri C. Spivak,* 7 AUSTL. WOMEN'S BOOK REV. 19, 20 (1995). *See also* Vandana Shiva, *The effects of the WTO on women's rights* (visited Oct. 27, 1998), <http://www.southbound.com.my/souths/twn/title/women-ch.htm>.

5   Andrea Rhodes-Little, et al., *In Search of the Ethics of Company Law,* 2 AUSTL. FEMINIST L.J. 180 (1994).

6   On the gendered code that makes sense of economic narratives, see Judith E. Grbich, *The Form of the Tax Reform Story: Marshall, Ordinary Meanings and the City Men,* 5 GRIFFITH L. REV. 40 (1996); Judith E. Grbich, *Taxation Narratives of Economic Gain: Reading Bodies Transgressively,* 5 FEMINIST LEGAL STUD. No. 2, at 131 (1997).

Nature, understood as feminine, is represented as a passive "container of raw materials waiting to be transformed into inputs for commodity production" rather than a creative, self-regenerating, powerful, and productive source of life.[7] The economic method of dividing the world into productive and unproductive spheres treats as invisible and without value much that is necessary to ecological survival and human existence.[8] As Judith Grbich argues, economics, like other forms of male knowledge, places women "in relations in which their laboring skills are devalued in different ways."[9]

Finally, as Grbich points out, "[w]omen have always been incredulous about the naturalness of power."[10] As a result, many women remain skeptical about the claims that the sacrifice and suffering inflicted by economic restructuring are a consequence of an inevitable and irresistible process of globalization somehow outside the control of human intervention. Feminists and other critical scholars remind us that the global markets driving globalization are after all social institutions, giving effect to the wishes and desires of the most privileged people in the world.[11]

For those reasons, this essay will explore whether feminist concerns about economic globalization can be addressed within a human rights framework. If they cannot, international human rights law may have little to offer many feminists for the future. My aim is to consider both what international human rights law can offer women in the post-Cold War era and what international human rights law can learn from feminism and women's activism as it faces the challenges of the next fifty years.

Part I outlines the changed conditions in which international human rights law operates in the late twentieth century. It argues that, as feminists and women's organizations have shown, the state no longer poses the principal threat to human rights. Instead, the processes of militarism, economic restructuring, and trade and financial liberalization are the primary causes of human rights abuses. In the post-Cold War era, those processes are conducted largely under the auspices of international law and international institutions. Part I argues that the exercise of power by actors other than states raises serious questions for international human rights law.

Part II considers the extent to which international human rights law has been able to address the forms of human rights abuse identified by feminists. The

---

7   Shiva, *supra* note 4.

8   *See generally* MARILYN WARING, COUNTING FOR NOTHING: WHAT MEN VALUE & WHAT WOMEN ARE WORTH (1988).

9   Judith E. Grbich, *The Body in Legal Theory, in* AT THE BOUNDARIES OF LAW: FEMINISM AND LEGAL THEORY 61, 75 (Martha A. Fineman & Nancy S. Thomadsen eds., 1991).

10   *See id.*

11   *See* J. K. GIBSON-GRAHAM, THE END OF CAPITALISM (AS WE KNEW IT): A FEMINIST CRITIQUE OF POLITICAL ECONOMY 263 (1996); DOUG HENWOOD, WALL STREET: HOW IT WORKS AND FOR WHOM 7 (1997).

development of international legal mechanisms that recognize and seek to protect the human rights of women does provide a response to some of the rights abuses identified by women.[12] That development in international human rights law, however, has not been sufficient to address the issues raised by those seeking an international system that fully protects and promotes all human rights. In particular, states have refused to respond to the feminist argument that militarism and economic globalization are often the causes of human rights abuses, and have treated the areas of security and economics as non-negotiable in the context of dealing with women's human rights. Part II concludes by considering what international human rights lawyers might learn from feminists and women's organizations to assist those engaged in resisting the destructive effects of globalization. It analyzes whether international human rights law can offer adequate responses to the threats posed by economic liberalization, particularly where it is conducted under the auspices of international institutions in the post-Cold War era.

II. International Human Rights Law and Globalization

The changes to the international system that have taken place since the breakup of the Soviet Union have significantly altered the capacity of international law to protect and promote human rights. In particular, the increase in the speed and scale of trade and financial liberalization poses challenges to international human rights law. Before addressing more detailed questions about the utility of international human rights law from a feminist perspective, it is necessary to come to terms with some of those changes.

A. Threats to Human Rights

International human rights law has been traditionally conceived as a means of constraining one form of power, that exercised by the state. Every tradition upon which the UDHR draws treats international human rights norms as binding upon states. The protection of civil and political rights, for example, draws on the liberal philosophies that fueled the revolutions in France and the United States at the end of the eighteenth century.[13] Liberalism was premised on the idea that all propertied men

---

[12] Throughout this article, I refer to the human rights of women, rather than women's rights. As Hilary Charlesworth has noted, the concept of women's human rights can have two possible meanings. First, women's rights can be taken to refer simply to those international instruments that deal specifically with women. Most of these elaborate the norm of formal nondiscrimination. Second, and Charlesworth's preferred sense, is to use women's international human rights to refer to taking women seriously across the entire spectrum of human rights. *See* Hilary Charlesworth, *What Are "Women's International Human Rights?," in* HUMAN RIGHTS OF WOMEN: NATIONAL AND INTERNATIONAL PERSPECTIVES 58, 59–60 (Rebecca J. Cook ed., 1994).

[13] For feminist analyses of the place of women in that liberal story, see generally Anne

were born free and equal, meaning that the governance of one such man by another could only be legitimate by agreement. That agreement, imagined as a contract, created two opposed realms: the public realm, where men agreed to be governed by the state; and the private realm, where the state could not interfere with a man's liberty. The liberal state could not legitimately regulate behavior understood to be properly in the realm of individual liberty. The protection of economic, social, and cultural rights in turn draws on a tradition that sees the state as the principle source of power that must be constrained and harnessed. This aspect of human rights protection is shaped by the socialist view that as the state participates in determining the economic system within which its people live, it must guarantee adequate standards of health, education, and food in order to prevent poverty, inequality, and suffering.

The international human rights law regime that developed after 1945 draws on those traditions, and treats the state as the principal threat to the freedom of the individual, human dignity, and human well-being. The human rights enshrined in the UDHR and in later international covenants are largely designed to restrain the ability of the state to infringe upon the liberty of the citizen, to guarantee the participation of all citizens in government, and to ensure that the state promotes the economic, social, and cultural rights of those living within its borders. International human rights law imposes obligations on states to respect, promote, and protect certain human rights of persons within their territories and makes provisions for remedies for violations of human rights and reports upon their progress in protecting and promoting rights.

Human rights law thus envisages states as the principal violators of human rights, and depends upon states being vested with human rights obligations. Yet economic restructuring is a process conducted at many different levels, and is made possible by the actions of many different actors—some constituted as national, some international, some public, and some private. For human rights to offer any useful response to the process of economic restructuring, a flexible approach to identifying which actors are exercising power and potentially violating human rights is necessary. Feminist scholars and women's nongovernmental organizations (NGOs), for example, have argued that other actors in addition to states, such as international economic institutions and transnational corporations (TNCs), are capable of violating human rights.[14] In particular, feminist networks active at the United Nations (U.N.) world conferences on women held in Nairobi in 1985 and Beijing in 1995 fought to place economic globalization, the power of TNCs, and the effects of the

---

Orford, *Liberty, Equality, Pornography: The Bodies of Women and Human Rights Discourse*, 3 AUSTL. FEM. L.J. 72 (1994); Margaret Davies, *The Heterosexual Economy*, 5 AUSTL. FEM. L.J. 27 (1995).

[14] *See* sources cited *supra* note 13 (providing information on sources for broader feminist critiques which argue that human rights law misrepresents the operation of power in ways that reinscribe and celebrate a particular version of "humanity" as the subject of rights).

activities of international economic institutions at the center of campaigns to achieve peace, human rights, or security. Concerns about economic globalization were central to the 1995 NGO Forum held in Beijing alongside the United Nations Fourth World Conference on Women. As one activist notes:

> [W]hat I heard passionately repeated like a mantra from many feminist networks of the South and a few from the North was that the critical issues which feminists must urgently address were the increasing globalization of the economy, the unbridled power of transnational corporations and the recolonising effects of international institutions and agreements such as the World Bank, the International Monetary Fund (IMF) and, most particularly, the Uruguay Round of the General Agreement on Tariffs and Trade (GATT). Only within this global economic web could other conference themes (governance, peace, human rights, personal violence) be meaningfully mapped.[15]

A more flexible approach to considering the capacity of actors other than states to violate human rights is evident in some areas of international human rights law. Indeed, Philip Alston argues that Article 28 of the UDHR, which recognizes that "[e]veryone is entitled to a social and international order in which the rights and freedoms set forth in this Declaration can be fully realized," itself establishes the principle that respect for human rights "is not a narrowly focused obligation applying only within strict limits to relations between individuals and their states, but rather is an open-ended obligation applying to all societal relations whether at the local, national or international level."[16] The area of economic, social, and cultural rights is one in which attention has been paid to the responsibility of international organizations in the human rights field.[17] In addition, collective rights, such as the right to development, focus on actors other than states as responsible both for protecting human rights, and for human rights violations.[18] Over the past fifty years, the focus of international human rights activism also has broadened in response to the recognition that actors other than states can be responsible for human rights violations. NGOs such as Amnesty International and Human Rights Watch, for

---

[15] Krysti J. Guest, *Post-Modernism/Pre-Modernism: Alive and Well in Beijing, in* BACK TO BASICS FROM BEIJING, *supra* note 2, at 110.

[16] Philip Alston, *The Shortcomings of a "Garfield the Cat" Approach to the Right to Development*, 15 CAL. W. INT'L L.J. 510, 515 (1985).

[17] *See, e.g., Globalization and Economic, Social and Cultural Rights*, Statement by the Committee on Economic, Social and Cultural Rights, May 1998 (visited Oct. 30, 1998) <http://www.unhchr.ch/html/menu2/6/cescrnote.htm#note18h>.

[18] Declaration on the Right to Development (1987), G.A. Res. 41/128 U.N. GAOR, 41st Sess. (Annex), Supp. No. 53, at 186, U.N. Doc. A/41/53, arts. 2(2), 3(3), 4(1), 4(2), *reprinted in* 3 INTERNATIONAL LAW AND WORLD ORDER: BASIC DOCUMENTS III.R.2 (Burns H. Weston ed., 5 vols., 1994–) [hereinafter 3 Weston].

example, have begun to consider actors other than states as potential violators of human rights. In 1991, Amnesty International announced that it would begin to report on abuses by "non-governmental entities with a political character, such as groups in a civil war or armed oppositions to governments exercising control over territory or population."[19] In 1995, the Commission on Global Governance called for recognition that "governments are only one source of threats to human rights" and that "all citizens . . . should accept that obligation to recognize and help protect the rights of others."[20] A growing number of human rights scholars also have begun to consider the effect that the activities of international institutions and TNCs can have on human rights.[21]

Despite such moves towards acknowledging that actors other than states are potentially capable of human rights abuses, the post-Cold War human rights literature has evidenced a new enthusiasm for treating states as the principal violators of rights. The assumption that states, and increasingly, nongovernmental entities with a political character within states pose the major threat to human rights continues to be made by those advocating a move away from state sovereignty towards increased international intervention in the interests of human rights protection.[22] In

---

[19]   HENRY J. STEINER & PHILIP ALSTON, INTERNATIONAL HUMAN RIGHTS IN CONTEXT: LAW, POLITICS, MORALS 484 (1996).

[20]   *Id.* at 488.

[21]   For examples of human rights scholars who have addressed the impact of economic institutions or of multinational corporations, see Philip Alston, *The Myopia of the Handmaidens: International Lawyers and Globalizations*, 8 EUR. J. INT'L L. 435 (1997); Hilary Charlesworth, *The Public/Private Distinction and the Right to Development in International Law*, 12 AUSTL. Y.B. INT'L L. 190 (1992); David P. Forsythe, *The United Nations, Human Rights, and Development*, 19 HUM. RTS. Q. 334 (1997); Krysti Justine Guest, *Exploitation Under Erasure: Economic, Social and Cultural Rights Engage Economic Globalizations*, 19 ADEL. L. REV. 73 (1997); WORLD DEBT AND THE HUMAN CONDITION: STRUCTURAL ADJUSTMENT AND THE RIGHT TO DEVELOPMENT (Ved P. Nanda et al. eds., 1993); Sadasivam, *supra* note 3.

[22]   Those commentators stressing the need to rethink state sovereignty in order to protect human rights include Tom J. Farer, *Collectively Defending Democracy in a World of Sovereign States: The Western Hemisphere's Prospect*, 15 HUM. RTS. Q. 716 (1993); Louis Henkin, *An Agenda for the Next Century: The Myth and Mantra of State Sovereignty*, 35 VA. J. INT'L L. 115, 118 (1994); Mark R. Hutchinson, *Restoring Hope: U.N. Security Council Resolutions for Somalia and an Expanded Doctrine of Humanitarian Intervention*, 34 HARV. INT'L L.J. 624 (1993); Max M. Kampelman, *Foreword, in* ENFORCING RESTRAINT: COLLECTIVE INTERVENTION IN INTERNAL CONFLICTS vii–viii (Lori Fisler Damrosch ed., 1993) (arguing that "there is a growing awareness of the need to look beyond state boundaries to the sources of instability within states. It is surely not now possible—if indeed it ever was—to take at face value claims of ruling elites that whatever goes on within state boundaries is solely a matter of domestic jurisdiction"); LARRY MINEAR & PHILLIPE GUILLOT, SOLDIERS TO THE RESCUE: HUMANITARIAN LESSONS FROM RWANDA 19 (1996) (arguing that there is growing support for the notion of a "global humanitarian imperative" requiring a "duty to interfere" in countries "in

the debate about the legitimacy of collective humanitarian intervention, for example, those who argue that Security Council actions taken since 1990 demonstrate the utility of intervening to protect human rights and democracy, suggest that state or local leaders pose the major challenges to human rights and democracy.[23] According to those commentators, humanitarian crises are largely caused by actions and developments initiated and carried out by local or government actors or institutions. On this analysis, international lawyers should abandon outmoded notions of sovereignty in order to enable states acting collectively to reach those who need their help. An assumption that the principal threats to human rights emanate from the state or local leaders is also apparent in the post-Cold War resurgence of interest in issues of democratic governance and election monitoring.[24] If human rights law is to provide tools for addressing the effects of economic globalization, it must be capable of constraining the actions of actors other than states, particularly inter-

which there is widespread suffering or abuse"); W. Michael Reisman, *Humanitarian Intervention and Fledgling Democracies*, 18 FORDHAM INT'L L.J. 794 (1995); and Fernando R. Tesón, *Collective Humanitarian Intervention*, 17 MICH. J. INT'L L. 323 (1996) (arguing that the domain reserved to the exclusive jurisdiction of the state is quite small).

23   *See, e.g.*, Domingo E. Acevedo, *The Haitian Crisis and the OAS Response: A Test of Effectiveness in Protecting Democracy*, in ENFORCING RESTRAINT: COLLECTIVE INTERVENTION IN INTERNAL CONFLICTS, *supra* note 22, at 119, 140–41 (arguing that "[i]n the past, authoritarian regimes that would otherwise have enjoyed no legitimacy among the people they purported to govern, and that retained power only through a pervasive infrastructure of internal coercion and intimidation, were often shielded against collective action by an extremely narrow interpretation of the principle of nonintervention"); Leon Gordenker & Thomas G. Weiss, *The Collective Security Idea and Changing World Politics*, in COLLECTIVE SECURITY IN A CHANGING WORLD 3, 14 (Thomas G. Weiss ed., 1993) (treating "ethnic particularism" as a threat to peace and security); SEAN D. MURPHY, HUMANITARIAN INTERVENTION: THE UNITED NATIONS IN AN EVOLVING WORLD ORDER (1996); W. Michael Reisman, *Some Lessons from Iraq: International Law and Democratic Politics*, 16 YALE J. INT'L L. 203, 213 (1991) (arguing that "tinhorn dictators" and "contemporary tyrants" threaten post-Cold War peace and security); Michael Stopford, *Locating the Balance: The United Nations and the New World Disorder*, 34 VA. J. INT'L L. 685, 686, 698 (1994) (suggesting that the breakdown of internal state structures and ancient ethnic and religious tensions are the major challenges to peace and security); Tesón, *supra* note 22, at 342 (treating state or local leaders or governments as the actors likely to threaten democracy and human rights).

24   *See* Christina M. Cerna, *Universal Democracy: An International Legal Right or the Pipe Dream of the West?*, 27 N.Y.U. J. INT'L L. & POL. 289 (1995); Jon M. Ebersole, *The United Nations' Response to Requests for Assistance in Electoral Matters*, 33 VA. J. INT'L L. 91 (1992); Gregory H. Fox, *The Right to Political Participation in International Law*, 17 YALE J. INT'L L. 539 (1992); Thomas M. Franck, *The Emerging Right to Democratic Governance*, 86 AM. J. INT'L L. 46 (1992); Melida N. Hodgson, *When to Accept, When to Abstain: A Framework for U.N. Election Monitoring*, 25 N.Y.U. J. INT'L L. & POL. 137 (1992); W. Michael Reisman, *International Election Observation*, 4 PACE Y.B. INT'L L. 1 (1992); David Stoelting, *The Challenge of UN-Monitored Elections in Independent Nations*, 28 STAN. J. INT'L L. 371 (1992).

national economic institutions. In the next section, I consider the significant role played by the institutions of the IMF, the World Bank, and the WTO in contributing to human rights violations.

B. Economic Globalization as a Threat to Human Rights

Critics of the economic "development" model that was imposed on the "Third World" during the decolonization era argue that it has served to protect and promote the property interests of foreign investors, particularly transnational corporations, while purporting to further the interests of local peoples.[25] Women have argued that economic globalization has resulted in increased unemployment and an increase in casual and part-time work, as the quality of employment offered by TNCs is often "precarious."[26] As Avega Bishop has observed, the end result of the narrow economic model of liberalization and development adopted by international economic institutions has resulted in the "overall monopolization of wealth, technology and resources in the hands of a few."[27] The consequence of the imposition of that model of development has been a net capital flow from those states subject to conditions imposed by international economic institutions to those states whose governments or banks act as lenders.[28]

Many analyses of the implications of economic globalization for human rights protection begin with the policies of the IMF and the World Bank. Those institutions have strongly influenced the direction of domestic policy in many states. During the 1980s and 1990s, the IMF and the World Bank required states to comply with certain conditions in order to make use of the resources of those institutions. In particular, the conditions imposed by "structural adjustment" and "shock therapy" programs included the requirements that states privatize public sector activities, move from a socialist to a capitalist political and economic system, liberalize investment and financial sectors, cut minimum wage levels, lower spending on health and education, increase exports and thereby reduce production for local markets, limit the provision of social security and subsidies, engage in constitutional

---

25   See ARTURO ESCOBAR, ENCOUNTERING DEVELOPMENT: THE MAKING AND UNMAKING OF THE THIRD WORLD (1995). For feminist alternatives to the model of development underlying the policies of international economic institutions, see the essays in CLOSE TO HOME: WOMEN RECONNECT ECOLOGY, HEALTH AND DEVELOPMENT WORLDWIDE (Vandana Shiva ed., 1994) [hereinafter CLOSE TO HOME]; ROSI BRAIDOTTI ET AL., WOMEN, THE ENVIRONMENT AND SUSTAINABLE DEVELOPMENT (1993).

26   See Guest, supra note 21, at 111.

27   Avega Bishop, Section A: Poverty, in BACK TO BASICS FROM BEIJING, supra note 2, at 10, 11.

28   See generally, SUSAN GEORGE, THE DEBT BOOMERANG: HOW THIRD WORLD DEBT HARMS US ALL xiv–xvi (1992); BRUCE RICH, MORTGAGING THE EARTH: THE WORLD BANK, ENVIRONMENTAL IMPOVERISHMENT AND THE CRISIS OF DEVELOPMENT 109–10, 175, 309 (1994); Patricia Stamp, Foucault and the New Imperial Order, 3 ARENA J. 11, 14 (1994).

reform, and increase levels of foreign investment.[29] At the NGO Forum accompanying the Third World Conference on Women in Nairobi in 1985, women criticized the effects of those structural adjustment programs, including cutbacks to public spending on health and education.[30] Again at Beijing, women's NGOs focused on the effects of structural adjustment programs, while most African NGOs called for the cancellation of multilateral debt.[31]

The conditions imposed by the IMF and the World Bank lead directly and indirectly to human rights violations. This is evident in several ways.

The imposition of structural adjustment and shock therapy programs, for example, directly impacts upon rights to political participation and self-determination. Decision-making over ever larger areas of what was once considered to be central to popular sovereignty and substantive democracy is now treated as legitimately within the province of economists in institutions such as the IMF and the World Bank.[32] The supposedly economic and technocratic changes required by these institutions shape the policy choices available to governments, alter existing constitutional and political arrangements, determine the extent to which people in many states can access health care, education, pensions and social security, shape labor markets, and thus affect functions that go to the heart of political and constitutional authority. The detail of the prescriptions imposed by the IMF and the World Bank makes it impossible for the people of target states to determine the nature of the economic and political system in which they live. People in such states are not free to choose forms of economic or social arrangements that differ from the models chosen by those who work for the IMF or the World Bank.

The failure of these institutions to develop mechanisms by which they can be held accountable to local people further limits the rights of political participation and self-determination of the peoples of target states. Critics have called for the establishment of an independent appeals and review commission with power to investigate complaints against the World Bank, full access to internal files, power

---

29   For detailed analyses of the nature and effects of such programs, see Anne Orford, *Locating the International: Military and Monetary Interventions After the Cold War*, 38 HARV. INT'L L.J. 443 (1997); Anne Orford & Jennifer Beard, *Making the State Safe for the Market: The World Bank's "World Development Report 1997,"* 22 MELB. U. L. REV. 195 (1998).

30   *See* Hill, *supra* note 2, at 106.

31   *See id.* For arguments in favor of debt reduction or cancellation, see GEORGE, *supra* note 28, at 171; RICH, *supra* note 28, at 175–76 (arguing that the Bank should at least forgive the alarming number of debts relating to projects that, according to its own reviews, have failed, and that it could write down other loans if assisting the poor were really a priority).

32   That is not to say that *states* are weakened through economic restructuring. Indeed, certain areas of state activity must be strengthened in order to provide secure and stable conditions for foreign investment. Instead, many aspects of what we once understood as *sovereignty* is now vested, not with "the people," however understood, but with economic experts.

to review and investigate violations of international law in World Bank-funded projects, and power to issue findings and recommendations that are binding unless reversed by a significant majority of the Bank's directors.[33] Instead, in 1993 the World Bank established an Inspection Panel, which can investigate and review complaints from any group of two or more people who allege that they have been harmed by breaches of the Bank's operating procedures, including breaches of guidelines relating to resettlements or environmental impact assessments.[34] While the Panel is independent of Bank management, it has few resources, no power to enforce compliance with its recommendations, and its reports are not made public until after the World Bank's response to the advice of the Panel is determined.[35] As the World Bank has no procedures for dealing with human rights, complaints about the human rights effects of projects are theoretically inadmissible before the Panel.[36] The constitution of the Panel is a step in the direction of greater accountability, but much more needs to be done to ensure that a truly independent process of challenge to World Bank policies and projects is available. No similar mechanism is available for bringing complaints against the IMF.

The model of development imposed by the IMF and the World Bank also impacts upon economic, social, and cultural rights. That model privileges the imposition of a narrow version of economic theory over any commitment to ensuring that people have access to food, health, education, social security, or employment. Structural adjustment conditions requiring the cutting of public expenditure on health and education, labor market deregulation, export-oriented production and privatization have led to increased income disparity and the marginalization of women, the poor, and rural populations in many countries.[37] Economic, social, and cultural rights, such as the right to health or the right to adequate food, are made significantly less relevant in states required to engage in those forms of economic restructuring.

---

[33] See the discussion of NGO proposals for a review body in SUSAN GEORGE & FABRIZIO SABELLI, FAITH AND CREDIT: THE WORLD BANK'S SECULAR EMPIRE 237–38 (1994).

[34] *See* Daniel D. Bradlow, *International Organizations and Private Complaints: The Case of the World Bank Inspection Panel*, 34 VA. J. INT'L L. 553 (1994); Daniel D. Bradlow & Claudio Grossman, *Limited Mandates and Intertwined Problems: A New Challenge for the World Bank and the IMF*, 17 HUM. RTS. Q. 411, 432–33 (1995).

[35] For criticisms of the limited powers of the panel, see RICH, *supra* note 28, at 307.

[36] *See* Sigrun I. Skogly, *The Position of the World Bank and the International Monetary Fund in the Human Rights Field, in* AN INTRODUCTION TO THE INTERNATIONAL PROTECTION OF HUMAN RIGHTS 193, 198 (Raiji Hanksi & Markku Suksi eds., 1997).

[37] *See* Sadasivam, *supra* note 3; *The Realization of Economic, Social and Cultural Rights: Final Report Submitted by Danilo Türk*, U.N. ESCOR Comm'n on Hum. Rts., 44th Sess., Provisional Agenda Item 8, at 1–37, U.N. Doc. E/CN.4/Sub.2/1992/16 (1992) (outlining human rights violations, including an increase in infant and child mortality rates as a result of Bank-IMF policies and projects).

The imposition of "structural adjustment" and "shock therapy" programs also creates a climate in which abuses of human rights, such as the right to freedom from torture or the right to life, are more likely to occur. Such programs have led to increased levels of insecurity and political destabilization in target states.[38] The effect of IMF and World Bank policies is to strip the state of most of its functions, except maintaining law and order and facilitating private investment. At the same time, when the interests of investors are protected and secured in situations where the state appears to address only the interests of international economic institutions and corporate investors, the insecurity, vulnerability, and frustration of people increases. Violent protests, political destabilization, attempted secession, and populist nationalism emerge as responses to governments that appear to be accountable only to foreign investors; and the increase in insecurity in states targeted by structural adjustment and shock therapy programs is further exacerbated by the refusal of the IMF and the World Bank to require cuts to military budgets.[39] According to Vito Tanzi of the IMF, excessive military budgets place a heavy burden on countries, leading to increases in budget deficits and a decline in public investment. Yet while IMF advice "often calls for reviewing military expenditures to identify potential fiscal savings," the Fund is "cautious not to claim expertise in evaluating the proper level of military spending in a given country."[40] That caution is quite remarkable given the detailed nature of the advice that the IMF and the World Bank are prepared to offer in other areas. As recent events in Indonesia have shown, the dangerous practice of imposing conditions that increase poverty, food scarcity, unemployment, and insecurity, while failing to recommend cuts to military budgets, is a recipe for human rights abuses. The "myopia" of international lawyers means that international legal debate fails to address the ways in which the destructive consequences of coercive economic restructuring create instability, leading to further violence and denials of human rights.[41]

A third institution targeted by women's rights activists is the WTO.[42] Those who attended the 1995 NGO Forum argued that the WTO is "less gender-sensitive,

---

[38] For analyses of the ways in which World Bank and IMF activities have contributed to increased levels of insecurity and destabilization, see generally Jochen Hippler, *Democratizations of the Third World After the End of the Cold War, in* THE DEMOCRATIZATIONS OF DISEMPOWERMENT: THE PROBLEM OF DEMOCRACY IN THE THIRD WORLD 1, 25 (1995); Orford, *supra* note 29; PETER UVIN, DEVELOPMENT AID AND CONFLICT REFLECTIONS FROM THE CASE OF RWANDA 1–3, 13–35 (1996).

[39] *See* DAVISON L. BUDHOO, ENOUGH IS ENOUGH: DEAR MR. CAMDESSUS . . . OPEN LETTER OF RESIGNATION TO THE DIRECTOR OF THE INTERNATIONAL MONETARY FUND 69–72 (1990).

[40] Vito Tanzi, *The Changing Role of Fiscal Policy in Fund Policy Advice,* paper presented at an IMF Seminar on "Asia and the IMF," Hong Kong, China, Sept. 19, 1997 (visited Sept. 29, 1998) <http://www.imf.org/external/np/apd/asia/TANZI.HTM>.

[41] On the "myopia" of international lawyers, see Alston, *supra* note 21. *See also* sources cited *supra* note 37 (discussing the political destabilization caused by World Bank and IMF policies).

[42] *See* Hill, *supra* note 2, at 106.

more threatening, and more outside of democratic control than even the widely criticized World Bank."[43] Criticisms of the potential impact of the agenda for trade, financial, and investment liberalization pursued by the WTO began to surface in the aftermath of the Uruguay Round of GATT trade negotiations.[44] The Uruguay Round outcomes significantly expanded the range of activities brought within the scope of the GATT regime to include trade-related aspects of intellectual property,[45] trade in services,[46] and trade- related investment measures,[47] and greatly increased the enforcement powers of the regime through the establishment of the WTO.[48] The new agenda of the WTO significantly narrows the areas of political, economic, and social life over which people can participate in making decisions, and infringes upon human rights. The trade and investment liberalization furthered by the Uruguay Round agreements entrenches a relationship between states and transnational corporations that privileges the property interests of those corporations over the human rights of local peoples and communities. According to Chakravarthi Raghavan, such agreements "curb the right of governments to intervene in the economy for the benefit of their people while expanding the 'space' for TNCs."[49]

One agreement that received little attention from human rights lawyers in the aftermath of the Uruguay Round, the *Agreement on the Application of Sanitary and Phytosanitary Measures* (the SPS Agreement),[50] provides a good illustration of the way in which highly technical free trade agreements impact upon human rights obligations. The SPS Agreement sets out obligations and procedures relating to the

---

[43] *Id.*

[44] The Final Act Embodying the Results of the Uruguay Round of Multilateral Trade Negotiations was ratified by over 120 countries at Marrakesh on April 15, 1994, *reprinted in* 4 INTERNATIONAL LAW AND WORLD ORDER: BASIC DOCUMENTS IV.C.2 (Burns H. Weston ed., 5 vols., 1994–) [hereinafter 4 Weston].

[45] *See* Agreement on Trade-Related Aspects of Intellectual Property Rights, Apr. 15, 1994, Marrakesh Agreement Establishing the World Trade Organization, Annex 1C, Legal Instruments—Results of the Uruguay Round vol. 31, (1994) [hereinafter TRIPS], *reprinted in* 33 I.L.M. 81 (1994) *and* 4 Weston, IV.A.2d, *supra* note 44.

[46] *See* General Agreement on Trade in Services, Apr. 15, 1994, 108 Stat. 4809, 4815, (1994), *reprinted in* 33 I.L.M. 1167 (1994) *and* 4 Weston, IV.C.2c, *supra* note 44.

[47] *See* Agreement on Trade-Related Investment Measures, Apr. 15, 1994, 108 Stat. 4809, 4815, *in* LAW AND PRACTICE OF THE WORLD TRADE ORGANIZATION, TREATIES BOOKLET 1, RELEASE 95–1, at 161 (Joseph F. Denin ed., 1995).

[48] *See* Agreement Establishing the World Trade Organization, Apr. 15, 1994, 108 Stat. 4809, 4815, *reprinted in* 33 I.L.M. 1144 (1994). *See also* Understanding on Rules and Procedures Governing the Settlements of Disputes, Apr. 15, 1994, 108 Stat. 4809, 4815 (1994), *reprinted in* 33 I.L.M. 1226 (1994) *and* 4 Weston, IV.C.2a, *supra* note 44.

[49] CHAKRAVARTHI RAGHAVAN, RECOLONIZATION, GATT, THE URUGUAY ROUND AND THE THIRD WORLD 40 (1990).

[50] Dec. 15, 1993, MTN/FA II–A1A–4 (1994) (visited Oct. 10, 1998) <http://www.wto.org/wto/goods/spsagr.htm> [hereinafter SPS Agreement].

use of sanitary and phytosanitary measures, including those aimed at protecting human or animal life or health, and applies to all sanitary and phytosanitary measures that may directly or indirectly affect international trade.[51] Members of the WTO are obliged to ensure that any such measure is applied only to the extent necessary to protect human, animal, or plant life or health, is based on scientific principles, and is not maintained without scientific evidence.[52] The only exception to the obligation to base such measures upon scientific evidence occurs where relevant scientific evidence is insufficient. In that situation, WTO Members can provisionally adopt measures on the basis of pertinent information, but must seek to obtain additional information necessary for a more objective assessment of risk within a reasonable period of time.[53] Under the Agreement, Members also agree to base their measures on international standards, guidelines, or recommendations where they exist.[54] Members may introduce or maintain standards which result in a higher level of protection than would be achieved by measures based on such international standards if there is a scientific justification for such increased protection or where the Member has engaged in a process of risk assessment as laid down in Article 5 of the Agreement.[55]

The 1998 decision of the Appellate Body of the WTO in the *EC Measures Concerning Meat and Meat Products (Hormones)* dispute provides a good example of the reach of the SPS agreement into areas of domestic policy-making and of its impact upon human rights protection.[56] That dispute involved parallel complaints brought against the European Community (EC) by Canada and the United States. The complaints concerned an EC ban on the sale of meat from animals that had been treated with any of six growth hormones.[57] Three of the banned growth hormones were "natural" hormones derived from animals, and the other three were synthetic hormones. A series of EC directives operated to ban the sale of such meat within the EC, and included a ban on the importation of meat treated with such

---

[51]   Such measures had theoretically been allowable as exceptions to the nondiscrimination provisions of GATT under Art. XX, particularly under Art. XX(b). The aim of the Agreement was, *inter alia*, to establish a framework of rules within which such exceptions would apply.

[52]   *See* SPS Agreement, *supra* note 50, art. 2.

[53]   *Id.* art. 5(7).

[54]   *Id.* art. 3(1).

[55]   *Id.* art. 3(3). According to a footnote to art. 3, there is a scientific justification for adopting a higher standard if, on the basis of an examination and evaluation of available scientific information, a member determines that the relevant international standards, guidelines, or recommendations are not sufficient to achieve the appropriate level of protection.

[56]   Appellate Body Report, *EC Measures Concerning Meat and Meat Products (Hormones)*, adopted Jan. 16, 1998, WT/DS26/AB/R, WT/DS26/AB/R [hereinafter Meat Hormones Report].

[57]   The hormones at issue were the "natural" hormones oestradiol-17J, progesterone and testosterone, as well as the "synthetic" hormones trenbolone acetate, zeranol, and melengestrol acetate (MGA).

growth hormones.[58] The complainants argued that the EC had introduced measures that differed from the voluntary standards proposed by the relevant international body, the Codex Alimentarius (the Codex).

The EC argued that the standards developed by the Codex were out of date, that it wished to maintain standards that resulted in a higher level of protection than would be achieved by measures based on the Codex standards, and that for one of the hormones, no Codex standards existed. The decision by the EC to ban the use of such hormones resulted from wide-ranging discussion and debate over a ten-year period. Consumers had become worried about the effects on human health of residues of growth hormones in meat, and consumer confidence in meat had suffered as a result. Accordingly, the EC commissioned a series of scientific inquiries into the issue, culminating in a 1995 roundtable on the use of growth hormones with scientists, consumer groups, industry workers, and other interested parties.[59] While most scientists agreed that use of the "natural" hormones in controlled conditions under veterinary supervision appeared to pose no threat to human health, the EC decided that it was not possible to monitor and regulate the conditions under which hormones were administered, nor was it possible to stop the black market trade in such hormones without imposing a total ban on their use. Accordingly, three directives were passed by the European Parliament enacting a ban on the use of those hormones. Those directives applied both to meat produced within the EC and that imported from third countries.[60]

The Appellate Body of the WTO found that the ban on importation of meat treated with hormones was in breach of the SPS Agreement. It held that the EC was not entitled to regulate the use of growth hormones as its decision to do so was not based on sufficient scientific evidence. With respect to the synthetic hormone MGA, for which there was no relevant international standard, the Appellate Body held that

---

[58]   The import prohibition was set out in three Directives of the Council of Ministers enacted before the SPS Agreement came into effect. *See* Council Directive 81/602/EEC of July 31, 1981; Council Directive 88/146/EEC of March 7, 1988; and Council Directive 88/299/EEC of May 17, 1988. As of July 1, 1997, those Directives were repealed and replaced with Council Directive 99/22/EC of April 29, 1996. The effect of those Directives was to prohibit the administration of substances having hormonal or thyrostatic action to farm animals. The Directives prohibited the placement on the market, or the importation from third countries, of meat and meat products from animals to which such substances, including the six hormones at issue in the dispute, were administered. Member States were allowed to authorize the administration, for therapeutic or zootechnical purposes, of certain substances having a hormonal or thyrostatic action, and under certain conditions meat and meat products treated in that way could be placed on the market or imported from third countries. *See* Meat Hormones Report, *supra* note 56, at paras. 1–5.

[59]   For a history of events, see Panel Report, *EC Measures Concerning Meat and Meat Products (Hormones)*, complaint by Canada, adopted August 18, 1997, WT/DS48/R/CAN, paras. II.26–II.33.

[60]   *See* Meat Hormones Report, *supra* note 56.

there was not sufficient scientific evidence to support the maintenance of provisional measures to protect human health. With respect to the other five growth hormones, the Appellate Body held that there was not sufficient scientific evidence to support the maintenance of food safety standards that were higher than those set by the Codex. There must be a risk assessment based on detailed scientific data in order for such measures to be enacted, even where there is no clear scientific opinion regarding the risks posed by a product.

The effects of that decision can be characterized in terms of both civil and political rights and of economic, social, and cultural rights. The SPS agreement, for example, has a significant impact on the right to health, particularly the health of women. In the *Meat Hormones* dispute, the EC relied upon scientific opinion that ingestion of the banned growth hormones is potentially carcinogenic. In particular, the EC presented scientific evidence that the synthetic hormone MGA increases the risk of breast cancer.[61] Although the EC was not able to produce scientific research conducted on the narrower question of the relationship between breast cancer and residues of MGA in meat when used as a growth promoter, it did produce scientific evidence relating to the relationship between levels of progesterone, the hormone MGA mimics, and increased rates of breast cancer.[62]

While the complainants, Canada and the United States, had scientific data relating to the health risks posed by MGA residues, the report of the Appellate Body notes that those parties "declined to submit any assessment of MGA upon the ground that the material they were aware of was proprietary and confidential in nature."[63] That information was presumably owned as intellectual property by the company producing the hormone.[64] The Appellate Body found that, as "there was an almost complete absence of evidence on MGA in the panel proceedings," the EC could *not* justify banning the use of that hormone.[65] While the EC had provided evidence relating to the general question of the carcinogenic potential of the hormones at issue, the Appellate Body held that the scientists upon whose opinion the EC was relying had not evaluated the carcinogenic potential of those hormones

---

61   See the discussion of the evidence of Dr. Lucier in the Meat Hormones Report, *supra* note 56, para. 198.

62   The EC provided evidence that included studies of the carcinogenic properties of the category of progestins of which the hormone progesterone is a member. The EC argued that because MGA is an anabolic agent which mimics the action of progesterone, those studies were relevant to its risk assessment regarding MGA. *See id.* para. 201.

63   *Id.*

64   Giant multinational corporation Monsanto, dubbed "the Microsoft of biotechnology," was one of the companies involved in manufacturing the growth hormones in question in the dispute. There has been heated debate over the accuracy of the scientific evidence Monsanto's scientists did provide regarding the safety of its growth hormone Posilac. *See* George Monbiot, et al., *How Monsanto Reaps a Rich Harvest*, GUARDIAN WKLY., Dec. 21, 1997, at 19.

65   Meat Hormones Report, *supra* note 56, para. 201.

when used specifically as growth promoters.[66] In an extraordinary footnote, the Appellate Body held that even if the scientific evidence concerning the risk to women was correct, only 371 women in the European Union would die from breast cancer as a result of eating meat treated with growth hormones, while the total population in 1995 was 371 million.[67] The reader is left to assume that the health risk posed to those women is considered minimal and insignificant by the members of the Appellate Body.

The EC argued unsuccessfully that, when dealing with a risk to public health of such a serious nature, and when faced with conflicting and inadequate scientific research, states should be permitted to take a cautious approach to allowing the unregulated use of such hormones. As a result of the *Meat Hormone* decision, however, the onus of proof as to the safety of a particular growth hormone rests not with the agri-chemical corporations who profit from the use of such hormones, but with the consumers in the states where the resulting products are to be sold.[68] Under the SPS Agreement, the lack of scientific research into the health risks posed by a novel product, process or technology acts as a barrier to consumer protection legislation, rather than as an indication that such legislation is necessary. A more cautious approach would suggest that states should be free to regulate such products or processes until the corporation seeking to profit from new technologies can show by reliable scientific studies that such products or processes are safe. The history of corporate carelessness about consumer safety suggests that governments are well advised to adopt a precautionary approach that privileges human and animal health and welfare over corporate profits where possible.[69] Instead, under the SPS Agreement, the right to health is subordinated to the imperatives of TNCs. In such

---

[66] *See id.* paras. 199–200.

[67] *See id.* para. 182.

[68] The Appellate Body formally held that the evidentiary burden of showing that the measure adopted was consistent with the SPS Agreement does not rest with the member imposing the measure, but with the member bringing the complaint. *See id.* para. 253(a). Nevertheless, it is clear from the Report that, in practice, the burden of proving the existence of scientific evidence sufficient to justify the measures in dispute rested with the EC. As noted above, the complainants, for example, were not even required to make available the scientific data to which they had access relating to the health risks posed by one of the hormones in question.

[69] The EC argued that the precautionary principle had emerged as a principle of customary international law, or at least as a general principle of law, and as such should be taken into account in determining its obligations regarding risk assessment. The EC argued that in the context of interpreting arts. 5.1 and 5.2 of the SPS Agreement, the precautionary principle meant that it was not necessary for all scientists to agree on the possibility or magnitude of the risk against which a measure was designed to protect consumers, nor was it necessary for all members of the WTO to perceive the risk in the same way. For the Appellate Body's discussion and rejection of that argument, see Meat Hormones Report, *supra* note 56, paras. 120–25.

a way, the investment liberalization agenda of the WTO shifts the boundary between public good and private interest in favor of the private interests of TNCs, a shift that has profound implications for the utility of liberal concepts of democracy and human rights operating in the public sphere.[70]

The right to food is also affected by the SPS Agreement. That right is dependent upon a state's capacity to ensure that economic conditions exist in which food can be provided, and upon the state's willingness to regulate industries engaged in food production. Decisions such as that of the Appellate Body, combined with moves by agri-corporations to make "eco-labelling" illegal, mean that it will be more difficult for small-scale farmers producing organic meat or dairy products to maintain a market for those products.[71] Such farming is labor intensive, requires small-scale production, and must be matched to "the peculiarities of the land."[72] As such, it is not an activity for which big agricultural producers are well suited. By limiting the extent to which consumers in the EC can demand meat that has not been treated by hormones, corporations can limit the means available to those consumers to resist the dominance of large-scale farming by TNCs in other parts of the world.[73]

The *Meat Hormone* decision also impacts upon civil and political rights. The effect of the SPS Agreement is to require states to base all public policy decisions about human or animal health or welfare on a narrowly defined form of scientific evidence, which excludes from consideration any other community concerns or knowledge. Scientific data is privileged as the only legitimate basis upon which states can decide matters relating to human, animal, or plant life or health. The privileging of science as a basis for decision-making is itself premised upon a gendered and racialized hierarchy of knowledges, in which Western science is treated as value-free, objective, impartial, and rational, while other forms of knowledge are dismissed as emotive, partial, subjective, and irrational.[74] The requirement that states

---

[70] John Frow, *Information as Gift and Commodity*, 219 NEW LEFT REV. 89, 105 (1996).

[71] According to one report, organic farming poses a threat to the globalized operation of monopolistic agrichemical firms. The consumption of organic produce is rising by 20 to 30 percent each year. *See* George Monbiot, *Give Us This Day Our Daily Toxic Bread*, GUARDIAN WKLY., Mar. 22, 1998, at 14.

[72] *Id.*

[73] Multinational corporations have increased their control over agriculture through increasing the integration of seeds with chemicals and animal products with hormones. As a result, farmers are becoming increasingly dependent on biotechnology corporations. For analyses of that process and its effects, see Shiva, *The Seed and the Earth: Biotechnology and the Colonizations of Regeneration, in* CLOSE TO HOME, *supra* note 25, at 128; Vandana Shiva, *Biotechnological Development and the Conservation of Biodiversity, in* BIOPOLITICS: A FEMINIST AND ECOLOGICAL READER ON BIOTECHNOLOGY 193 (Vandana Shiva & Ingunn Moser eds., 1995).

[74] *See generally* DONNA J. HARAWAY, SIMIANS, CYBORGS, AND WOMEN: THE REINVENTION OF NATURE (1991).

privilege the interests of scientists, who often are paid and employed by interested corporations, over the knowledge of local consumers, workers, industry groups, or farmers operates to limit the scope for contesting and debating particular policies and laws. Civil and political rights such as the right to political participation and the right to self-determination are weakened where international agreements operate to remove such decisions from the political arena. By denying civil and political rights such as the right to participate in decision-making to people in one part of the world, TNCs can more easily deny the economic, social and cultural rights of those people in other parts of the world seeking to develop sustainable means of producing food. Food production becomes increasingly tied to the profits and interests of monopolistic corporations.

The protection and promotion of human rights is similarly limited by the operation of agreements such as the General Agreement on Trade-Related Aspects of Intellectual Property Rights (TRIPS). That agreement obliges states to introduce patent and copyright laws and to provide infrastructure to support such regulatory schemes. The nature of the intellectual property regime embodied in TRIPS is such that traditional, community-based knowledge about seeds and plants is not patentable, while innovative, individually-based knowledge produced by scientific researchers but derived from traditional knowledge *is* patentable.[75] Corporations patent the genetic properties of seeds developed over generations as insect resistant or for medical properties, and are then able to exploit the intellectual property rights to that genetic material as a commodity in the countries from which the knowledge and seeds were first taken.[76] That practice is particularly widespread in the agrochemical and pharmaceutical industries. As a result, access to information about food and medicines is privatized and those goods are made more expensive.[77] Human rights such as the right to health or the right to adequate food thus become significantly less relevant.[78]

As can be seen from this survey, the policies, projects, and actions of the IMF, the World Bank, and the WTO shape the economic and political systems of many states. In turn, the actions of those institutions have a significant impact upon the promotion and protection of human rights in such states. I am not suggesting that those institutions always impose conditions upon states in situations where governments or elites are unwilling to accept such conditions. Often economic liberals or self-interested political leaders in such states support and stand to benefit from trade liberalization or structural adjustment programs. Nonetheless, international economic institutions are the key agents of economic restructuring in the

---

[75]   *See* Frow, *supra* note 70, at 98.

[76]   *See id.*

[77]   *See* Bruce Lindsay, *GATT: Development and Intellectual Property*, 3 ARENA J. 33, 38 (1994).

[78]   *See also* Orford, *supra* note 29, at 473 (discussion of the impact of TRIPS upon human rights).

post-Cold War era. A focus on their activities and goals reveals the challenges posed to international human rights law by the broader project of economic globalization.

C. The Utility of International Human Rights Law

Human rights law appears at first glance to provide a language for resisting the processes of globalization described above. While civil and political rights, for example, have been criticized for furthering the individualism that is a necessary condition of the capitalist state,[79] such rights offer some scope for challenging the authoritarian climate of the new world order, in which economic fundamentalists teach that economic restructuring can be imposed without consideration of its impact on human rights.[80] Economic, social, and cultural rights pose a more significant challenge to the premises of possessive individualism underlying globalization. Those rights question the logic according to which the world can be imagined as property owned by particular individuals. Rights can thus potentially act as a counterweight the coercive means of imposing economic restructuring, and offer an alternative to the ends of such restructuring. Yet there are serious limitations in the current formulations of human rights.

The capacity of civil and political rights to represent broader needs is limited by a history of being granted only to property-owners. In their analysis of the failure of domestic and international legal systems to provide mechanisms for averting the Bhopal disaster or for compensating those who were injured and killed as a result, Indira Jaising and C. Sathyamala argue that the "the origin of rights continues to spring from ownership of property" rather than from a recognition of the needs of human beings and their dependence upon the communities and environment in which they live.[81] The language of civil and political rights provides limited tools for attempting to "change the terms of the discourse from that of private rights vested in individuals, to public rights over common resources, vested in communities, and from individual ownership to collective control."[82] The language of individual rights, paradoxically, makes it easier for the state to wrest control of resources from communities.

The failure to apply human rights to the sphere of economics means that large areas of decision-making are now exempt from any need to account for state action in the old human rights terms. The unwillingness of elites to lose on issues of eco-

---

[79] *See* Karl Marx, *On the Jewish Question, in* NONSENSE UPON STILTS: BENTHAM, BURKE AND MARX ON THE RIGHTS OF MAN 137, 144–50 (Jeremy Waldron ed., 1987).

[80] The notion of economic fundamentalism is taken from JANE KELSEY, ECONOMIC FUNDAMENTALISM: THE NEW ZEALAND EXPERIMENT—A WORLD MODEL FOR STRUCTURAL ADJUSTMENT? (1995).

[81] *See* Indira Jaising & C. Sathyamala, *Legal Rights . . . and Wrongs: Internationalising Bhopal, in* CLOSE TO HOME, *supra* note 25, at 88, 95.

[82] *Id.*

nomic restructuring, a fundamental premise of democracy, means that any other values or principles that act as a barrier to economic visions of "the good life" can be ignored. Any measures are justified and any level of human suffering is reasonable to achieve the goals set by economic experts or by the "markets." In a world where people have ceased to recognize that economics, like law and politics, is a product of the human imagination, premised upon metaphors and myths, new organizational structures or methods of constraining state power may have little to offer feminist resistance. Those people who make up the investor class in major states appear to have ceased to imagine themselves in terms of the old liberal or even conservative stories based on respect for tradition or for the individual, and now are inhabiting a world in which old claims based on rights or the dangers of change have no purchase.

The involvement of powerful international or transnational actors complicates the usual responses of human rights lawyers calling for the abandonment of sovereignty in favor of international intervention. While there can be no doubt that states continue to violate the human rights of those living within their borders, human rights are also regularly infringed by a range of other actors. To date, international legal processes have provided few mechanisms for constraining human rights abuses carried out by such actors. Those violations are thus harder to redress. The extent to which the state is or is not an ally of those whose human rights are being violated in any given instance cannot be determined in advance, but depends upon the particular circumstances giving rise to the violations in question.[83]

Changes in the location of threats to human rights raise issues for the way that international law and international organizations are portrayed. Many progressive actors look to international law as a source of positive norms. International lawyers suggest that increased engagement by international institutions is a useful response to abuses of human rights, democratic norms, or humanitarian law. Focusing too readily on international law as the source of solutions to human rights problems, however, ignores the role played by international law and international organizations in contributing to human rights abuses.

III. Feminism, Globalization, and the Human Rights of Women

Feminists and women's NGOs have shown that the international project of economic liberalization poses significant challenges for human rights. This Part analyzes the extent to which international human rights law has met those challenges to date.

---

[83]   *See* Gayatri C. Spivak & David Plotke, *A Dialogue on Democracy, in* RADICAL DEMO-CRACY: IDENTITY, CITIZENSHIP, AND THE STATE 209, 215 (David Trend ed., 1996). Spivak argues that "non-elite Southern NGOs" have a "robustly contradictory" relationship to the state, standing behind the state where it is being subverted by transnational agencies exerting economic influence, but opposing the state where it is collaborating with the agents of economic restructuring.

It concludes by exploring what international law might offer to those engaged in challenging and resisting the threats to human rights in the post-Cold War era.

A. Taking the Risk out of Women's Human Rights

To date, human rights law has provided a limited response to feminist challenges, offering some recognition to the rights of women. The activism of women's groups and feminist challenges to international law have succeeded in placing the human rights of women on the international agenda. The recognition, protection, and promotion of the human rights of women has been strengthened by their inclusion in international legal instruments. The Convention on the Elimination of All Forms of Discrimination Against Women 1979 (CEDAW), for example, has 161 signatory parties as of this writing.[84] As a result of sustained criticism of the weakness of the procedures established to monitor CEDAW, some steps have been taken to strengthen that regime.[85] The Commission on the Status of Women is considering a draft optional protocol allowing individual and group complaints to be made to the CEDAW, and the General Assembly has approved an amendment to Article 20 to allow the CEDAW Committee to meet for three rather than two weeks each year.[86]

Feminists have also succeeded in having opposition to violence against women incorporated into legal instruments. Feminist campaigns to have gender-based violence recognized as a legal issue led to the appointment of Radhika Coomaraswamy as a Special Rapporteur on Violence Against Women in 1994,[87] and the adoption by the General Assembly of the Declaration on the Elimination of Violence Against Women.[88] However, states continue to refuse to recognize violence against women as a human rights issue,[89] and ignore some forms of violence against women alto-

---

[84]   1249 U.N.T.S. 80–120.

[85]   *See, e.g.*, Noreen Burrows, *International Law and Human Rights: The Case of Women's Rights, in* HUMAN RIGHTS: FROM RHETORIC TO REALITY 80, 95 (Tom Campbell et al. eds., 1986); Hilary Charlesworth et al., *Feminist Approaches to International Law*, 85 AM. J. INT'L L. 613, 631–34 (1991); Elizabeth Evatt, *Eliminating Discrimination Against Women: The Impact of the UN Convention*, 18 MELB. U.L. REV. 435, 447–49 (1991); Laura Reanda, *Human Rights and Women's Rights: The United Nations Approach*, 3 HUM. RTS. Q. 11, 22–23 (1981).

[86]   *See also* Andrew Byrnes & Jane Connors, *Enforcing the Human Rights of Women: A Complaints Procedure for the Women's Convention*, 21 BROOK. J. INT'L L. 779 (1996); Christine Chinkin, *Feminist Interventions Into International Law*, 19 ADEL. L. REV. 13, 15 (1997); Hilary Charlesworth, *Women as Sherpas: Are Global Summits Useful for Women?* in BACK TO BASICS FROM BEIJING, *supra* note 2, at 88, 93.

[87]   C.H.R. Res. 1994/45, U.N. Doc. E/CN.4/1994/132, at 143 (1994).

[88]   G.A. Res. 104, 48 U.N. GAOR, U.N. Doc. A/Res/48/104 (1993), *reprinted in* 33 I.L.M. 1049 (1994).

[89]   On the refusal of states to characterize violence against women as a human rights issue,

gether.[90] Thus, Yumi Lee argues that states refuse to recognize the violence done to women who are injured while working for TNCs, who develop cancer or suffer miscarriage as a result of toxic products banned in Europe but targeted at Third World women, who die of starvation or live in poverty as a result of an exploitative global economy, or whose environment is damaged with impunity by foreign investors. She writes:

> While it is simple to frame laws to charge husbands who abuse their wives, it is not as simple to deal with the economic violence of capitalism. When the . . . World Bank and the IMF . . . [impose] economic policies which perpetuate violence against women, the challenge is to broaden the way "violence against women" is represented.[91]

Both at the Vienna World Conference on Human Rights in 1993 and the Beijing Fourth World Conference on Women, the general proposition that the human rights of women are part of universal human rights was accepted, although not without controversy.[92] Women's human rights have thus to some extent been furthered by the series of women's summits held under the auspices of the UN. The utility of the official outcomes of those summits has been the subject of much debate. However, feminists point out that recognition of the rights of women continues to be resisted in areas that address causes of women's exploitation and oppression; many problems identified by women have not been placed on the international agenda.

In particular, states have refused to act on links identified by women's NGOs between militarism, economic liberalization, and women's human rights. That refusal has led to the sense amongst feminists that the commitment to women's human rights is a matter of "form over substance."[93] As Christine Chinkin argues:

> There has been some broader use of women-inclusive language in international instruments, but little changed practice. This language has neither

---

see Dianne Otto, *Holding up Half the Sky, but for Whose Benefit?: A Critical Analysis of the Fourth World Conference on Women*, 6 AUSTL. FEM. L.J. 7, 17 (1996).

[90] *See* Yumi Lee, *Violence Against Women: Reflections on the Past and Strategies for the Future—An NGO Perspective*, 19 ADEL. L. REV. 45 (1997).

[91] *Id.* at 50.

[92] *See* Beijing Declaration and Platform for Action, Report of the Fourth World Conference on Women, Beijing, Sept. 1995, U.N. Doc. A/CONF.177/20, para. 14, *reprinted in* 35 I.L.M. 401 (1996); World Conference on Human Rights, Vienna Declaration and Programme of Action, adopted on June 25, 1993, U.N. Doc. A/CONF.157/24, pt. I, para. 9 (1993), *reprinted in* 32 I.L.M. 1661 (1993) *and* 3 Weston, III.C.15, *supra* note 18. (stating that "the human rights of women and of the girl-child are an inalienable, integral and indivisible part of universal human rights"). The Beijing Declaration affirmed that "women's rights are human rights," but that statement was not included in the human rights section of the Platform for Action.

[93] Chinkin, *supra* note 86, at 26.

demanded nor facilitated transformation. All this activity has not really challenged gendered assumptions about the structures of global political and economic power, nor of the construction of knowledge in the rapidly changing environment of international law. . . . [T]he steps taken to bring women's human rights into mainstream UN activities have in most, although not all, instances been limited to placing women on the agenda, a traditional "add women and stir" approach that does not demand any radical rethinking of programmes or gender-awareness.[94]

Perhaps for this reason, a despondent tone has marked much scholarship reflecting upon the outcomes of feminist engagement with international law and international organizations in the aftermath of Beijing. Commentators express frustration with state leaders who purport to support women's human rights narrowly conceived, while jealously guarding power, obsessively building up weaponry, and accumulating ever greater monetary reserves. Feminists argue that the international legal recognition of women's rights is insufficient to address the human rights violations experienced by women as a result of globalization.[95] Indeed, states have tended to treat those areas of militarism and monetarism as non-negotiable in the context of dealing with women's human rights. Those who attended the NGO conferences at Nairobi and Beijing noted that while women's groups had developed sophisticated analyses of those processes, governments refused to treat their contributions as relevant.[96] Hilary Charlesworth describes women as "sherpas" at international summits, required to carry the heavy baggage but not yet "allowed the privileges of mountaineers who define the rules of the game."[97]

It seems that a sexual division of labor persists in the international arena, with women and feminists expected to remain concerned only with personal and familial issues deemed to be relevant to women, rather than with globalization and its

---

[94] *Id.*

[95] For arguments that the impact of militarism and economic restructuring on the human rights of women has not been addressed to date by international law, see Bishop, *supra* note 27; Chilla Bulbeck, *Less Than Overwhelmed by Beijing: Problems Concerning Women's Commonality and Diversity*, 6 AUSTL. FEM. L.J. 31, 32–33 (1996) (dealing with income inequality); Chinkin, *supra* note 86, at 23 (discussing economic restructuring and poverty); Guest, *supra* note 15, at 112–13 (dealing with economic issues); Hill, *supra* note 2, at 106–108 (discussing both military and economic issues); Janet Hunt, *Reflections on Beijing*, 6 AUSTL. FEM. L.J. 39, 40–41 (1996) (discussing both military and economic issues); Yumi Lee, *Section E: Armed Conflict, in* BACK TO BASICS FROM BEIJING, *supra* note 25, at 25, 27–28 (discussing militarism); Gillian Moon, *"Breakfast Money": Institutional and Financial Arrangements in the Beijing Platform for Action*, 6 AUSTL. FEM. L.J. 43, 45 (1996) (discussing aid, trade and development issues); Otto, *supra* note 89, at 20, 24, 27–28 (discussing both military and economic issues).

[96] *See* Chinkin, *supra* note 86, at 22; Hunt, *supra* note 95, at 40.

[97] *See generally* Charlesworth, *supra* note 85.

effects. Is the failure of international human rights law to address sufficiently the abuses experienced by women inevitable? What future is there for a dialogue between international human rights law and feminism?

B. Feminism and Globalization

International human rights lawyers can learn some useful lessons from the varied forms of resistance offered by feminist theorizing and organizing. Feminism provides a number of useful strategies for engaging economic globalization.

First, feminist scholars have begun to reflect upon the ways in which writing about processes like globalization can in fact be implicated in producing a world in which globalization appears irresistible. It is not possible to imagine alternatives to forms of social organizations and processes like capitalism or globalization when critics are complicit in representing those processes as all-powerful.[98] By reproducing the image of a "massive or monolithic" state, patriarchy, international organizations, or global capitalism, academics risk creating a feeling of hopelessness and passivity.[99] Reflecting a sense of omnipotence back to those whose sense of self is based precisely on that idea of power over others simply strengthens their self-image. As Doug Henwood notes:

> It's a cliche of the daily press that the markets are now more powerful than governments. . . . The cliche contains a partial truth: these markets are tremendously powerful. But they are social institutions, instruments of power, that derive their power in part from the sense of powerless awe they inspire among non-initiates. Say "the markets won't like" a minimum wage increase or a public jobs program, and critical scrutiny often evaporates, like wishes crushed by the unfriendly voice of God.[100]

Thus, critics of globalization often describe a world governed by global capitalism, with few options for resistance. Feminist economist J. K. Gibson-Graham writes of coming to realize that the image of global capitalism that she was pro-

---

[98]   *See* GIBSON-GRAHAM, *supra* note 11, at 263.

[99]   *See id.* In contrast, the New Right has profited from creating a subject position from which people can feel power and agency. Stuart Hall argued that one of the reasons that the Labour Party in Britain lost the 1987 election was that, while Labour politicians were addressing voters' needs in the areas of health, unemployment, and education, Margaret Thatcher offered such voters a fantasy in which all could "identify with the enterprise culture as the way of the future," and could "see themselves in their political imaginations as likely to be lucky in the next round." According to Hall, Thatcher's symbolic majority "forms an 'imaginary community' around Thatcherism's political project." *See* STUART HALL, THE HARD ROAD TO RENEWAL 262 (1988). *See also* RENATA SALECL, THE SPOILS OF FREEDOM: PSYCHOANALYSIS AND FEMINISM AFTER THE FALL OF SOCIALISM 33–36 (1994).

[100]   HENWOOD, *supra* note 11, at 11.

ducing in her work "was actively participating in consolidating a new phase of capitalist hegemony."[101] When she heard union leaders telling members to "accept the realities of the new global economy" and limit their demands, she felt partly responsible "for the note of inevitability in their voices."[102] Gibson-Graham suggests that activism concerning globalization, while designed to make the dominance of global capital visible and challengeable, has also produced a sense of fear in many people. The sense that globalization is inevitable and "normal" has constrained strategies for resisting global capitalism. The capacity of multinational corporations to control and dominate is treated as a fact, with those corporations discursively positioned as more powerful than people. To accept and reproduce that script as reality is to limit the actions that might be taken to counter globalization.[103]

Accordingly, feminists like Gibson-Graham are attempting to develop ways of talking about globalization that weaken "its ability to instill fear and thereby garner cooperation."[104] Gibson-Graham, for example, proposes rewriting the globalization script, "denying the inevitability and 'reality' of [multinational corporation] power over workers and communities and exploring ways in which the hard and penetrating body of the MNC can be seen as soft, fragile and vulnerable."[105] The challenge is to find ways to write about globalization that do not reproduce its image as all-powerful and irresistible, thus limiting strategies for resistance. In particular, it is useful to rescript globalization so that those who are on its receiving end are not presented as passive, vulnerable, and open, while the body of the multinational corporation is presented as hard, violent, aggressive, and virile. Instead, critics need to concentrate on representing the agency of those targeted by globalization, and the vulnerability of corporations. Women organizing around issues of economic justice, labor standards, public health, occupational safety, and environmental protection, for example, do have the capacity to exploit the vulnerable bodies of multinational corporations. That vulnerability is a product of the fact that corporations may be spread out across state boundaries, subject to many different forms of politics and social organizations as well as being "vulnerable to being punched in the underbelly by changes in political leadership or trade policy."[106]

Second, feminist activism and organization provides examples of the ways in which political action to resist globalization can be developed. Women have exploited possibilities for resistance at the local level, and have begun to link globally such forms of action to achieve change. Krysti Guest writes that she was inspired at Beijing by the "extent to which feminist organizations throughout the

---

[101] GIBSON-GRAHAM, *supra* note 11, at ix.

[102] *Id.*

[103] *Id.* at 126.

[104] *Id.* at 126–27.

[105] *Id.* at 146.

[106] *Id.* at 128.

South were both extremely articulate about, and actively organizing against, this phenomenon [of economic globalization]."[107] While states clearly are not yet willing to take the demands of women seriously, feminists have been nonetheless successful in using global summits to develop women's networks around issues of economic globalization. Feminists from states subjected to intervention by international economic institutions have educated and politicized women who previously had not thought about the interconnectedness of issues like violence, exploitation, economic restructuring, the activities of TNCs, insecurity, and women's rights. In part as a result of such networks, women from industrialized states have begun to learn from NGOs in Asia, Africa, Latin America, and Eastern Europe. These women have learned to look behind the rhetorical commitments of governments to human rights and to join the fight against economic globalization.

C. Feminist Futures for International Human Rights Law

In conclusion, what can international human rights law learn from the varied forms of resistance and hope offered by feminist theorizing and organizing? What can international human rights law offer to feminists and others engaged in resisting economic exploitation and military domination?

First, international human rights law can contribute to the process of resisting the current exploitative model of economic globalization by attempting to develop methods for holding non-state actors accountable for human rights abuses.[108] Human rights lawyers need to develop an approach to human rights protection that is sufficiently subtle to deal with situations where state functions are privatized in order to limit accountability for the effects of particular activities,[109] or where actions are carried out covertly or in private. One example of a secretive activity that has an impact on human rights is derivatives trading.[110] Commentators have argued that such trading was implicated in the Mexican and related Latin American currency crises of 1994.[111] Given the increases in the trade in derivatives in Asia during the 1990s,[112] the contribution of investors and currency speculators to the

---

[107] Guest, *supra* note 15, at 113. *See also* Spivak & Plotke, *supra* note 83, at 215 (commenting that organizations like the Third World Network and the Asian Women's Human Rights Council concentrate on issues like GATT: "[y]ou have no idea of the degree of expertise on GATT that exists among near-illiterate rural workers in these collectives").

[108] Orford & Beard, *supra* note 29, at 216.

[109] *Id.* at 208–12; Chinkin, *supra* note 86, at 21; Ian Duncanson, *Unchartered Lands in an Age of "Accountability,"* 3 RES REPUBLICA No. 1, at 3 (1997).

[110] For a discussion of the secretive nature of over-the-counter derivatives trades, see HENWOOD, *supra* note 11, at 34–37.

[111] *See* STEPHANY GRIFFITH-JONES, THE MEXICAN PESO CRISIS 21–25 (1996); FRANK PARTNOY, F.I.A.S.C.O.: BLOOD IN THE WATER ON WALL STREET 189–205 (1997).

[112] INTERNATIONAL MONETARY FUND, INTERNATIONAL CAPITAL MARKETS: DEVELOPMENTS,

destabilization of Southeast Asian economies should be discussed seriously. While the crises arguably fueled by derivatives trading have human rights impacts, the difficult challenge facing human rights lawyers is to envisage ways of holding particular actors accountable for human rights abuses in such instances.

Second, human rights lawyers can learn from the arguments made by feminist activists and explore the links between militarism, monetarism, and human rights abuses in their work. Any such exploration must include an analysis of the human rights abuses that occur as the result of the actions of international institutions. International lawyers seeking to contribute to the promotion and protection of human rights need to address the destructive effects of international law and multilateralism as they operate in much of the world today. Lawyers are well placed to make the links that are within their areas of expertise, such as those between the obligations imposed by the Uruguay Round agreements, the narrowed scope of the operation of human rights in many states, or between the conditions imposed by IMF programs and the increased denial of economic, social, and cultural rights to those living in states subjected to such conditions.

Third, international human rights lawyers can address the extent to which human rights are appropriated to facilitate economic liberalism. Some destructive forms of intervention are conducted in the name of human rights, yet contribute to human rights abuses.[113] For example, those who support the IMF's expanded role in the Southeast Asian crisis, including the United States government, have begun to link economic liberalization with the achievement of greater democracy and freedom in states subject to IMF conditions.[114] Yet the forms of economic restructuring required of states like Indonesia and South Korea by the IMF may well have led to the violation of human rights. Human rights lawyers therefore need to resist the tendency to subordinate human rights to economic theory, and to challenge the use

---

PROSPECTS, AND KEY POLICY ISSUES 72 (1996) (noting that "market participants report that the largest future growth area for derivatives is in the emerging markets, particularly Southeast Asia, as government restrictions on foreign exchange and stock ownership are eased"); David Lynch, *Growth in Asia-Pacific Markets, in* DERIVATIVES: THE RISKS THAT REMAIN 3, 16–24 (Elizabeth Sheedy & Sheelagh McCracken eds., 1997); Elizabeth Sheedy, *The Risks that Remain, in id.* at 332, 333. *See also* WILLIAM R. CLINE, INTERNATIONAL DEBT REEXAMINED 423–64 (1995).

113   The need to establish standards of good governance, for example, is used by the World Bank and the IMF as a basis for increasing intervention into political and constitutional arrangements, yet that increased intervention itself breaches fundamental human rights norms. The need to protect and promote human rights and democratic governance has been used as a justification for increased military intervention under the auspices of the Security Council. Such intervention has also led to serious human rights abuses. For further development of those arguments, see generally Orford, *supra* note 29; Anne Orford, *The Politics of Collective Security*, 17 MICH. J. INT'L L. 373 (1996).

114   *See, e.g.*, David Lague, *Embrace Democracy, Clinton Exhorts Asia*, SYDNEY MORNING HERALD, July 4, 1998, at 1.

of human rights to justify exploitative forms of international intervention. In other words, human rights lawyers need to be vigilant about the dangers of appropriation of human rights to further projects that are less than clearly humanitarian in effect.

Finally, despite the limitations of international human rights law, a commitment to human rights offers the promise of a global future built on something other than militarized economics. As the dictates of international economic institutions backed by military intervention become the basis of a state-sponsored new world order, the promise of human rights becomes increasingly valuable. International human rights law potentially offers a language for resisting the dictatorship of global capitalism. Human rights lawyers positioned to resist the destructiveness of economic globalization can learn to work with those activists seeking to envision and work towards alternate, nonexploitative ways of being.[115] Perhaps then the promise of human rights will not elude the generation of women who come to reflect upon the role played by international human rights law over the next fifty years.

---

[115] Marjorie Agosin argues that one effect of the Chilean dictatorship on those who lived under it was "the lack of trust among ourselves, the fear of learning alternate ways of being." That fear seems to be apparent in the highly competitive, economically correct, restructured world of the late twentieth century, and for similar reasons. *See* Marjorie Agosin, *The Generation of Disenchantment*, 14 HUM. RTS. Q. 135, 141 (1992).

Globalization and Human Rights: Clash of Universal Aspirations and Special Interests

Kamal Hossain

I. Introduction

In the fifty years since the adoption of the Universal Declaration of Human Rights (UDHR),[1] the world's population has doubled, the number of states more than trebled, and the world real GNP quadrupled.[2] The success of decolonization, the end of apartheid, the dissolution of the Soviet Union, and concomitant changes in Eastern Europe have resulted in an on-going process of global transformation. A critical aspect of this process is that it has raised expectations of a better life among ordinary women and men. It would not be an oversimplification to describe these expectations as widely-shared aspirations for a life of human dignity, as envisaged by the UDHR.

The process of globalization, of the integration of the global economy through liberalization, has been accelerating over the last two decades. The volume of foreign direct investment nearly quadrupled during the 1980s, reaching $2 trillion in the 1990s; the entire global volume of publicly traded financial assets (around $24 trillion) now turns over every twenty-four days; and the major multinationals grew in sales from $721 million in 1971 to $5.2 trillion in 1991.[3] These trends have been facilitated by the dismantling of trade barriers, the liberalization of currency regimes, privatization, deregulation, and an enhancement of the role of multinational corporations and banks, as national governments have lost ground in an increasingly borderless world insofar as finance and trade are concerned.

As a consequence, there is a growing body of literature that explores the wide range of impacts of the complex process of globalization, including the term "globalization" itself, a much-contested word. As a recent study has noted, "[g]lobalisation is neither a singular condition nor a linear process. Rather, it is best thought of as a multidimensional phenomenon involving diverse domains of activity and interaction

---

[1]   See infra Appendix I [hereinafter UDHR].

[2]   See PAUL KENNEDY, PREPARING FOR THE TWENTY-FIRST CENTURY 23, 48 (1993).

[3]   See WILLIAM GREIDER, ONE WORLD, READY OR NOT 21–23 (1997).

including the economic, political, technological, military, legal, cultural, and environmental. Each of these spheres involves different patterns of relations and activity."[4]

In the economic sphere, the impact of recent trends in globalization on developing countries has been uneven. A limited number of developing countries have been able to take advantage of economic globalization, attracting large inflows of external private capital and experiencing significant export-led growth and acceleration of growth in per capita gross domestic product (GDP). Many other countries, however, in particular African countries and the least-developed countries elsewhere, have shown slow or negative growth and continue to be marginalized. As a result, they generally have experienced stagnating or falling per capita GDP through 1995.[5]

Even those developing economies that have managed to integrate into the global economy and thereby achieve a certain level of dynamism have found themselves vulnerable to severe currency fluctuations and the rigors inflicted by international financial markets moving large amounts of capital in and out of countries, often with staggering speed. Recent events in East and Southeast Asia have demonstrated that, given such volatility, economic structures assiduously built over decades through painful adjustments and sound fiscal and monetary policies can crumble in the span of a few weeks. Through its contagion effect, this upheaval in one region can spill over to other parts of the world where even the developed countries are bound to feel its shock.[6]

The apprehended shock is now being felt across the globe. The president of the World Bank, addressing the 1998 Joint Annual Bank-IMF meeting, recognized that those assembled were meeting "under the shadow of a global crisis" and that since the previous meeting there had been "a year of turmoil and travail" causing adverse effects in different parts of the world.[7] He reported that

> [in] East Asia, estimates suggest that more than 20 million fell back into poverty last year, and where, at best, growth is likely to be halting and hesitant for several years to come. Russia [is] beset by economic and political crisis—caught between two worlds, two systems, comfortable with neither. Japan, the world's second largest economy, so crucial to East Asian recovery, with a government committed to economic reform, [is] yet still in recession, with a profound impact not just in Asia but around the world.[8]

All of this has profound implications for human rights. To this we now turn.

---

4   David Held, *Democracy and Globalization*, 3 GLOBAL GOVERNANCE 251, 252–53 (1997).

5   U.N. GENERAL ASSEMBLY, PROGRAMME FOR THE FUTURE IMPLEMENTATION OF AGENDA 21, at 3, para. 7 (1997).

6   *See* Ali Alatas, *Globalization and International Financial Markets*, 1 SOUTH LETTER No. 30, at 11 (1988).

7   James D. Wolfensohn, *Address to the Board of Governors* 1–2 (Oct. 6, 1998).

8   *Id.*

II. Impact of Globalization on Human Rights

The 1998 Human Development Report of the United Nations Development Programme (UNDP) records as follows:

> Globalization is integrating not just trade, investment and financial markets. It is also integrating consumer markets. This has two effects—economic and social. Economic integration has accelerated the opening of consumer markets with a constant flow of new products. There is fierce competition to sell to consumers worldwide. . . . On the social side, local and national boundaries are breaking down in the setting of social standards and aspirations in consumption. Market research identifies "global elites" and "global middle classes" who follow the same consumption styles, showing preferences for "global brands". . . . What are the consequences? First, a host of consumption options have been opened for many consumers—but many are left out in the cold through lack of income. . . . Second, protecting consumer rights to product safety and product information has become complex. Increasingly, new products with higher chemical content, such as foods and medicines, are coming on the market. When information is not adequate, or safety standards are not strictly enforced, consumers can suffer—from pesticides that are poisonous, from milk powder that is contaminated. . . ."[9]

Consider also a recent study of the United Nations Research Institute for Social Development (UNRISD) which reports:

> The social and economic consequences of free-market reforms have been dramatic. In general, the primary incomes of the poor are down, the number of people living in poverty is up, and social income—access to public services—has decreased. Targeted interventions meant to protect the poor and vulnerable groups from the worst aspects of adjustment never reach all of the poor, and seldom reach most of the poor. In addition, a range of other social impacts are associated with free-market reform. There has been a "desocialization" of social actors, as people from community to national levels turn their attention to coping with growing economic hardship in their individual capacities. Previous social bonds have been disrupted and social tensions have increased, leading to new or intensified forms of inter- and intra-group conflict. In many cases, the impact of restructuring on women is especially pronounced, as the household provides the primary safety net for those economically displaced by restructuring. Women's reproductive work has thus intensified just as they are increasingly joining the labor forces themselves.[10]

---

9   UNDP, Human Development Report 6–7 (1998).

10   UNRISD, Adjustment, Globalization and Social Development 2 (1995).

The vigorous promotion of market forces inherent in the process of the globalization of the world economy thus has social and economic consequences that can undermine or impede the promotion and realization of human rights, in particular social and economic rights.

The existing reality is, in other words, a world in which there are "growing social gaps—gaps, for example, between rich and poor; between those with means to cope with technological change and those without; between skilled and unskilled workers; between genders in terms of burdens and opportunities; between generations as social urbanization, change, and poverty weaken the family, disillusion youth, and create new generations of "street children"; and gaps between ethnic, cultural, and religious groups as diversity becomes a basis for differentiation and divisiveness. There are gaps, too, in many countries between native and migrant populations in a world of increasing transnational movements of people generated by social disintegration, poverty, and unemployment as well as political oppression.[11]

Over the past 25 years, consumption per capita has increased steadily in industrial countries (about 2.3 percent annually), spectacularly in East Asia (6.1 percent), and at a rising rate in South Asia (2 percent). Yet these developing regions are far from catching up to the industrial countries, and consumption growth has been slow or stagnant in others. The average African household today consumes 20 percent less than it did twenty-five years ago. The poorest 20 percent of the world's people and more have been left out of the consumption explosion. Well over a billion people are deprived of basic consumption needs. Of the 4.4 billion people in developing countries, nearly three-fifths lack basic sanitation. Almost a third have no access to clean water. A quarter do not have adequate housing. A fifth have no access to modern health services. A fifth of children do not attend school to grade five. About a fifth do not have enough dietary energy and protein. Micronutrient deficiencies are even more widespread. Worldwide, two billion people are anaemic, including 55 million in industrial countries. In developing countries only a privileged minority has motorized transport, telecommunications, and modern energy.

These statistics presented in the *1998 UNDP Human Development Report*[12] unambiguously document these enormous and widening inequalities. The UNDP report concludes:

> Inequalities in consumption are stark. Globally, the 20 percent of the world's people in the highest-income countries account for 86 percent of total private consumption expenditures—the poorest 20 percent a minuscule 1.3 percent. More specifically, the richest fifth:

---

[11]   *See, e.g.,* JOHN J. PAUL, INCORPORATING HUMAN RIGHTS IN THE WORK OF THE WORLD SUMMIT FOR SOCIAL DEVELOPMENT (ASIL 1995).

[12]   *Supra* note 9.

- Consume 45 percent of all meat and fish, the poorest fifth 5 percent.

- Consume 58 percent of total energy, the poorest fifth less than 4 percent.

- Have 74 percent of all telephone lines, the poorest fifth 1.5 percent.

- Consume 84 percent of all papers, the poorest fifth 1.1 percent.

- Own 87 percent of the world's vehicle fleet, the poorest fifth less than 1 percent."[13]

Thus, whatever good may be said about economic globalization, growing global disparities is today's stark reality for the majority of humankind. Nonetheless, in an increasingly competitive global economy, developing countries have been encouraged to undertake export promotion and to establish export processing zones where multinational corporations were offered exemptions not only from fiscal levies but from the obligation to comply with laws that protect the rights of workers. Unregulated markets fostered "no-holds-barred" competition in which low wages and unsafe working conditions were not only permitted but encouraged because they could generate higher profits. Economic liberalization which ignored the need for laws and social policies to regulate the operations of the market promoted a tendency to maximize profits by any means. Corruption in large international business transactions, and fraudulent financial transactions involving banks and stock exchanges, were some of the disturbing manifestations.

Against this backdrop, after reviewing widely divergent views regarding the impact of globalization, one observer has sought to provide a "balanced" summing up:

> One need not be alarmed by globalization, but neither should one take a Panglossian view of it. Globalization greatly enhances the opportunities available to those who have the skills and mobility to flourish in world markets. It can help poor countries to escape poverty. It does not constrain national autonomy nearly as much as popular discussions assume. At the same time, globalization does exert downward pressure on the wages of underskilled workers in industrialized countries, exacerbates economic insecurity, calls into question accepted social arrangements, and weakens social safety nets.[14]

The optimistic view of globalization thus sees the structural transformation of the world now occurring as holding out great promise for widening the range of choice for peoples by making available to them the best and the cheapest goods and services from around the world.[15] The removal of barriers to trade and investment,

---

[13]   *Id.* at 1–2.

[14]   Dani Rodrik, *Sense and Nonsense in the Globalization Debate*, FOREIGN POL'Y 19, 33 (Summer 1997).

[15]   *See* John H. Dunning, *The Advent of Alliance Capitalism, in* THE NEW GLOBALISM AND DEVELOPING COUNTRIES 32 (John H. Dunning & Khalil A. Hamdani eds., 1997).

and to financial flows, it is argued, can enable economies to achieve efficiency on the basis of an international division of labor based on comparative advantage. This maximizes consumer welfare by enabling persons to buy a better, cheaper, and larger variety of goods and services in the best markets. The negative impacts, however, are the down-sides of globalization—"the global paradox." The most immediate and visible consequences of the down-side, which currently all countries of the world are experiencing, is an increase in structural unemployment brought about by competitive pressures, the implementation of new technologies and the introduction of more market-oriented systems of governance. Across the globe, for developed and developing countries alike, change is bringing economic hardship.[16]

The expectation grounded in market ideology that the greatest good for the greatest number can be achieved through the capacity of the market for self-adjustment and self-regulation must contend with the reality of market failures and distortions brought about as a result of the disparities in economic power which characterize the actors in the global economy. The universal aspirations for a better life for all promised by a global free-market economy continues to be impeded by the manipulations and self-serving strategies of powerful special interests. They wield enormous economic power that is further enhanced through monopolistic concentration or strategic transnational alliances. Within nations, law and social policies were developed to regulate markets so as to ensure a level playing field, to sustain competition, and to curb monopolistic and restrictive practices. These regulations and social policies were designed to moderate the negative impacts of market failure and to provide a safety net for the losers from market forces by assisting them in adjusting to the changes wrought by the operations of the market. But, as Peter Drucker has perceptively observed, "yesterday's world order is going fast, while tomorrow's world order has yet to emerge. . . . The nation state has begun to come apart. . . . Increasingly the new challenges facing every government are challenges that simply cannot be dealt with by national or even international action. . . ."[17] Drucker continues: "No central bank any longer controls money flows. The amounts of money traded every day on the trans-national markets (the New York foreign exchange market or the London interbank market) [is of such magnitude] that the flows escape any attempts to control or limit them, let alone manage them."[18]

Equally, states find it difficult to regulate the operations of global corporations effectively on the national level. This is due to the corporations' extensive network of decision-making and operational structures formed by their headquarters, branches, subsidiaries, and other forms of investment in independent units throughout the world; and to their flexibility in moving seats of production as well as profits within the framework of the organization as a whole. Attempts to regulate the operations of multinational corporations by nonbinding international "codes of con-

---

[16] *Id.*

[17] PETER DRUCKER, POST-CAPITALIST SOCIETY 113, 142–43 (1993).

[18] *Id.*

duct" have produced little result and, due to changed circumstances, are thought by some to be no longer politically relevant.[19]

These developments have transformed the nature and prospects of democratic political communities. Observes David Held:

> First, the locus of effective political power can no longer be assumed to be national governments—effective power is shared and bartered by diverse forces and agencies at national, regional, and international levels. Second, the idea of a political community of fate—of a self-determining collectivity—can no longer be meaningfully located within the boundaries of a single nation-state alone.[20]

"Stateless" capitalism and more integrated investment and trade thus by-pass state control. At the same time, they require international "public goods" that go beyond the province of the nation-state, including the set of rules, standards, dispute-settlement institutions, and procedures that international lawyers consider their province. International markets require regimes for telecommunication and transportation, rules and procedures for financial stability and performance of contractual obligations, industrial and product standards, environmental protection rules, and much more.[21]

Almost a decade ago it was urged that

> [a] better management of interdependence requires stronger emphasis on policy, less on institutions; stronger focus on differentiation, between countries and within each one; more attention for the private sector, less exclusive emphasis on Governments; finally a clearer link between macro and micro, between growth, distribution and sustainable welfare. What is needed is a strong international public sector, which can correct international market process where necessary, and prevent uncontrolled concentration of economic power. An international public sector which would act against degradation of the environment, would ensure equitable distribution of resources, would provide a minimum international social protection against poverty, an international public sector within a mixed international economic order, and an international state of social protection based on principles of international law.[22]

---

19   *See, e.g.,* Peter Malanczuk, *Globalization and the Future Role of Sovereign States, in* INTERNATIONAL ECONOMIC LAW WITH A HUMAN FACE 45, 56 (Friedl Weiss et al. eds., 1998).

20   Held, *supra* note 4, at 260–61.

21   Oscar Schachter, *The Erosion of State Authority and its Implications for Equitable Development, in* INTERNATIONAL ECONOMIC LAW WITH A HUMAN FACE 31, 35 (Friedl Weiss et al. eds., 1998).

22   Jan Pronk, *Applying Lessons of the Past in Order to Improve the Future, in* TOWARDS A SYSTEM OF RESPONSIBLE GLOBAL GOVERNANCE FOR DEVELOPMENT 13 (Netherlands Royal Ministry of Foreign Affairs 1991).

More recently, the 1997 *Trade and Development Report* of the United Nations Conference on Trade and Development (UNCTAD) argued that

[t]he shift towards reliance on market forces as the primary means for the allocation of resources and the organization of economic activity as a whole means a new, but not necessarily less relevant, role for the State in promoting development. . . . Appropriate government policies or interventions may also be required to deal with market failures or deficiencies associated with the consistent inability of markets to deal with the phenomenon of externalities. An important example in this regard is the inability of markets to ensure on their own the environmental sustainability of economic activity. . . . Government also has an increased role to play in combating the unwanted accompaniments of liberalization and globalization. In particular, there is a need for public policy to address issues related to poverty and income distribution. Many economic actors, such as poor and vulnerable groups, are unable to seize market opportunities to achieve even minimum income levels. To assist these groups to gain access to, and to exploit, market opportunities, governments have a critical role to play in promoting social human development and in providing the poor with the necessary working skills. Adequate safety-net provisions for the unemployed are also important.[23]

Today there is a sense of urgency in the quest for a framework of global governance that could enable humane global objectives to be effectively pursued and cause the negative impacts of unregulated market forces to be curbed.

III. Promoting Globalization With a Human Face: Strategies to Protect Human Rights

There is increasing questioning about the adequacy of existing political and institutional structures and of normative legal frameworks to protect human rights and the social objectives valued by ordinary women and men. The same may be said about the validity of allowing impersonal market forces, manipulated by self-serving special interests, to take control over the destinies of nations and the lives of people. All of which is consistent with the universal aspirations for a better life that were articulated in the Universal Declaration of Human Rights fifty years ago, and that have found powerful reiteration and re-affirmation both in the 1992 Rio Declaration on Environment and Development[24] and in the 1993 Vienna Declaration

---

[23] UNCTAD, TRADE AND DEVELOPMENT REPORT 12–13 (Ch. I: Trade and Development in a Liberalized and Globalizing World Economy) (1997).

[24] Adopted by the U.N. Conference on Environment and Development at Rio de Janeiro, June 13, 1992, U.N. Doc. A/CONF.151/26 (Vol. I) (1992), *reprinted in* 31 I.L.M. 874 (1992) *and* 5 INTERNATIONAL LAW AND WORLD ORDER: BASIC DOCUMENTS V.B.16 (Burns H. Weston ed., 5 vols., 1994–) [hereinafter 5 Weston].

of the World Conference on Human Rights,[25] the former having proclaimed that "[h]uman beings are at the centre of concerns for sustainable development"[26] and having recognized the right to development.[27]

A normative framework is thus sought to be developed around the core concept of "sustainable human development." A recent UNDP policy document spells out how a normative framework can be developed from this concept. It explains that sustainable human development seeks to expand choices for all people—women, men, and children, current and future generations—while protecting the natural systems on which all life depends. Moving away from a narrow, economy-centered approach to development, sustainable human development places people at the fore, and views human beings as both a means to and an end of development. Thus, promoting sustainable human development involves a commitment to eliminate poverty, to promote human dignity and rights, and to provide equitable opportunities for all through good governance, thereby promoting the realization of all human rights—economic, social, cultural, civil, and political. The promotion of human rights is of particular relevance in the context of globalization and its potential for excluding and marginalizing weak members of the international community and people with limited resources. Human rights afford protection against such exclusion and marginalization.[28]

How is globalization to be directed towards the goal of sustainable development? Ordinary women and men who gathered in the NGO Forum held parallel to the 1992 Rio Conference on Environment and Development addressed this issue. They expressed their shared concern over the damaging consequences of a development model that is grounded in the pursuit of economic growth and consumption to the exclusion of human and environmental concerns. They judged that the current thought and action that dominates economic policy (of the kind that result in the negative impacts of globalization) is "a path to collective self-destruction, not to sustainable development." In the People's Earth Declaration adopted by the Forum,[29] it is candidly acknowledged that there are no clear models, but that a beginning towards crafting an alternative can be made by declaring a commitment to principles on which there was a broadly shared consensus. These included the following:

- the fundamental purpose of economic organization is to meet the community's basic needs, such as for food, shelter, clothing, education, health, and

---

25   Adopted by the U.N. World Conference on Human Rights, June 25, 1993, U.N. Doc. A/CONF.157/24 (pt. I) (Oct. 13, 1993), at 20–46, *reprinted in* 32 I.L.M. 1661 (1993) *and* 3 INTERNATIONAL LAW AND WORLD ORDER: BASIC DOCUMENTS III.U.2 (Burns H. Weston ed., 5 vols., 1994–) [hereinafter 3 Weston].

26   *Supra* note 24, Principle 1.

27   *Id.* Principle 3.

28   *Integrating Human Rights with Sustainable Human Development*, UNDP POLICY DOCUMENT 2–3 (Jan. 1998).

29   The People's Earth Delaration (Rio de Janeiro, 1992), *reprinted in* DAVID C. KORTON, WHEN CORPORATIONS RULE THE WORLD 239 (1996) *and* 5 Weston V.K.2, *supra* note 24.

the enjoyment of culture; this purpose must take priority over all other forms of consumption, particularly wasteful and destructive forms of consumption such as consumerism and military spending;

- the quality of human life depends more on the development of social relationships, creativity, cultural and artistic expression, spirituality, and opportunity to be a productive member of the community than on the ever increasing consumption of material goods;

- organizing economic life around decentralized, relatively self-reliant local economies that control and manage their own productive resources, provide all people an equitable share in the control and benefits of productive resources, and preserve their right to safeguard their own environmental and social standards is essential to sustainability; trade between such local economies, as between nations, should be just and balanced; where the rights and interests of corporations conflict with the rights and interests of the community, the latter must prevail;

- all elements of society, irrespective of gender, class, or ethnic identity, have a right and obligation to participate fully in the life and decisions of the community; the presently poor and disenfranchised, in particular, must become full participants; women's roles, needs, values, and wisdom are especially central to decision making on the fate of the Earth; there is an urgent need to involve women at all levels of policy making, planning, and implementation on an equal basis with men;

- knowledge is humanity's one infinitely expandable resource; beneficial knowledge in whatever form, including technology, is a part of the collective human heritage and should be freely shared with all who might benefit from it;

- transparency must be the fundamental premise underlying decision making in all public institutions, including at the international levels.

With these principles in mind, I have put forward a strategy for mobilizing the forces of international society in pursuit of just, sustainable, and participatory societies.[30] Three key components of that strategy are the following:

- a massive commitment to education: new understanding, values and skills must be developed at all levels and across all elements of society;

- a commitment by women and men to use their votes, their moral authority, and their purchasing power to remove from positions of authority those who insist on advancing socially and ecologically destructive policies that serve

---

[30] *See* Kamal Hossain, *Promoting Human Rights in the Global Market Place, in* REFLECTIONS ON INTERNATIONAL LAW FROM THE LOW COUNTRIES 101 (Erik Denters & Nico Schrijver eds., 1998).

short-term elite interests; this calls for the empowerment of women and men at the grassroots so that they can liberate the electoral process and representative institutions from the control of powerful and exclusive elites.

• coalition-building across boundaries—between members of civil society, including the business community, and government—in order to broaden and deepen consensus through "countless dialogues and negotiations throughout the world"[31] to refine the agreements adopted in Rio and to enlarge the growing global movement to promote sustainable development centered around the realization of human rights.

It is significant that in the address of the World Bank President at the Joint Bank-IMF Meeting of 1998 there were powerful echoes of the views expressed by the people assembled at Rio. President Wolfensohn drew attention to the need for a new holistic approach to development as follows:

[I]n a global economy, it is the *totality* of change in a country that matters. . . .

Development is about getting the macroeconomics right—yes; but it is also about building the roads, empowering the people, writing the laws, recognizing the women, eliminating the corruption, educating the girls, building the banking systems, protecting the environment, inoculating the children.

Development is about putting *all* the component parts in place—together and in harmony.

The notion that development involves a totality of effort—a balanced economic and social program—is not revolutionary, but the fact remains that it is not the approach that we in the international community have been taking.

While we have had some extraordinary success over the many years with individual programs and projects, too often we have not related them to the whole. Too often we have been too narrow in our conception of the economic transformations that are required—while focusing on micro-economic numbers, or on major reforms like privatization, we have ignored basic institutional infrastructure, without which a market economy simply cannot function. Rather that incentives for wealth creation, there can be misplaced incentives for asset stripping.[32]

Having identified the weaknesses of the existing approaches to development, the World Bank President went on to spell out the key elements of a new development framework which he said was urgently needed:

---

[31] *Id.* at 114.

[32] Wolfensohn, *supra* note 7, at 11–12.

We need a new development framework. What might countries look for in such a development framework?

First, the framework would outline the essentials of good governance—transparency, voice, the free flow of information, a commitment to fight corruption, and a well trained, properly remunerated civil service.

Second, it would specify the regulatory and institutional fundamentals essential to a workable market economy—a legal and tax system that guards against caprice, secures property rights, and that ensures that contracts are enforced, that there is effective competition and orderly and efficient processes for resolving judicial disputes and with supervision free of favor, and with internationally recognized accountancy and auditing standards for the private sectors.

Third, our framework would call for policies that foster inclusion—education for all, especially women and girls. Health care. Social protection for the unemployed, elderly, and people with disabilities. Early childhood development. Mother and child clinics.

Fourth, our framework would describe the public services and infrastructure necessary for communications and transport. Rural and trunk roads. Policies for livable cities and growing urban areas so that problems can be addressed with urgency—or in 25 years when they become overwhelming. And alongside an urban strategy, a program for rural development which provides not only agricultural services, but capacity for marketing and for financing and for the transfer of knowledge and experience.

Fifth, our framework would set forth objectives to ensure environmental and human sustainability—so essential to the long-term success of development and the future of our shared planet—water, energy, food security, issues which must also be dealt with at the global level. And we must ensure that the culture of each country is nurtured and enriched so that development is firmly based and historically grounded. All of these five, of course, within a supportive and effective macroeconomic plan and open trade relations.

This may not be a comprehensive list. It will of course vary from country to country depending on the views of government, parliamentary assemblies and civil society. But I submit it gets at the essentials.[33]

The people's consensus in Rio when it is reflected in a policy statement of the President of the World Bank shows a widening and deepening of consensus on the essential components of a "human rights"-friendly development strategy. Human rights provides a universally-acknowledged basis on which to build a normative

---

[33] *Id.* at 13–15.

framework for development. While recognizing the global reality of a clash of competing interests and the tensions created by it, this framework can aim to regulate the process of globalization and to direct it towards the realization of human rights and the fulfillment of the universal aspiration of humankind for freedom, equality and justice.[34]

---

[34] While the need for a rule-based global economic order is generally agreed, upon there is a continuing and active debate as to the approach and the type of legal architecture that would be appropriate. *See, e.g.,* ERNST-ULRICH PETERSMANN, THE GATT/WTO DISPUTE SETTLEMENT SYSTEM 4–6 (1997) (seeing "the modern evolution of human rights into world-wide constitutional law" as meeting the need for long-term constitutional rules to protect equal rights of persons against abuses of the policy-making process). Another approach sees "an international co-operative mechanism" being developed "to achieve optimal government response to market failures," pointing out that "when the economy becomes globalized, concepts of market failure and ideas of government responses can shift quite dramatically." JOHN J. JACKSON, THE WORLD TRADING SYSTEM 339–51 (1997), especially at 348.

Reflections on the Future of Economic, Social, and Cultural Rights

Yozo Yokota

I. Introduction

It has become a common practice to classify various human rights into three categories. The first is "civil and political rights," the second "economic, social and cultural rights," and the third "a new set of rights such as the right of self-determination, the right to development and the right to peaceful coexistence." In accordance with their historical appearances, they often are referred to as "first generation" (eighteenth century), "second generation" (late nineteenth and early twentieth centuries), and "third generation" (late twentieth century) rights.[1]

The generally subscribed characteristics of the first category are that the rights in this category are (a) negative and (b) immediately enforceable. They are negative in the sense that the rights of this kind are most often violated by positive actions of governments and that the best way to ensure the enjoyment of such rights is to require the governments to refrain from interfering with the life and freedoms of individuals. The rights in this category are also said to be immediately enforceable. If such rights are violated (most likely by governments), the victims may bring the matter to an appropriate authority (commonly a court) for immediate and effective relief and redress.

The rights in the second category, which are the main focus of this paper, are often described as (a) positive and (b) "programmatic" or "promotional."[2] They are

---

[1] MATTHEW C. R. CRAVEN, THE INTERNATIONAL COVENANT ON ECONOMIC, SOCIAL AND CULTURAL RIGHTS: A PERSPECTIVE ON ITS DEVELOPMENT 8 (1995). For a detailed analysis of the three generations of human rights and a useful description of the historical development of the notion of human rights, see Burns H. Weston, *Human Rights*, 20 ENCYCLOPAEDIA BRITANNICA 714 (15th ed. 1998 prtg.), *updated and revised in* ENCYCLOPAEDIA BRITANNICA ONLINE (visited Dec. 1, 1998) <http://www.eb.com:180/cgi-bin/g?DocF=macro/5002/93.html>.

[2] The words "programmatic" and "promotional" are used to describe the special feature of the rights stipulated in the Covenant on Economic, Social and Cultural Rights, *infra* Appendix II [hereinafter ICESCR]. *See* Scott Leckie, *Another Step Towards Indivisibility: Identifying the Key Features of Violations of Economic, Social and Cultural Rights*, 20 HUM. RTS. Q. 88 (1998); E. W. Vierdag, *The Legal Nature of the Rights Granted by the International Covenant on Economic, Social and Cultural Rights*, 9 NETH. Y.B. INT'L L. 83 (1978); and A. H. ROBERTSON, HUMAN RIGHTS IN THE WORLD: AN INTRODUCTION TO THE STUDY OF THE INTERNATIONAL PROTECTION OF HUMAN RIGHTS 230 (J. G. Merrills ed., 3d rev. ed. 1992).

considered positive because the role of governments has to be positive in order to realize these rights. For instance, the right to education, one of the typical examples of economic, social and cultural rights, cannot be realized unless governments provide school buildings, teachers and textbooks. The rights in this category are also said to be programmatic in the sense that they represent aspirations or policy objectives rather than justiciable rights whose violations can be remedied immediately.[3]

Many writers who try to distinguish economic, social and cultural rights, on the one hand, and civil and political rights, on the other, would refer to the different languages used in the two covenants regarding the obligations of states parties. Article 2, paragraph 1 of the International Covenant on Economic, Social and Cultural Rights (ICESCR)[4] provides: "Each State Party to the present Covenant undertakes to take steps, with a view to achieving progressively the full realization of the rights recognized in the present Covenant." The wording of this provision is contrasted with the relevant provision of the International Covenant on Civil and Political Rights (ICCPR).[5] Its Article 2, paragraph 1, stipulates: "Each State Party to the present Covenant undertakes to respect and to ensure to all individuals within its territory and subject to its jurisdiction the rights recognized in the present Covenant."

The third category rights are different from the first and second category rights in that the first and second category rights are individual rights whereas the rights in the third category are said to be people's rights and group rights.[6] For instance, the right of self-determination and the right to development, two typical rights in

---

3   *See* Mario Gomez, *Social Economic Rights and the Human Rights Commission*, 17 HUM. RTS. Q. 155, 161 (1995).

4   *See infra* Appendix II.

5   *See infra* Appendix III [hereinafter ICCPR].

6   For a detailed description of the third generation rights, see Stephen Marks, *Emerging Human Rights: A New Generation for the 1980s?*, 33 RUTGERS L. REV. 435, 439 (1981). The proposition that all human rights, whether civil, political, economic, social or cultural, are "interconnected and interdependent" already found expression in the U.N. General Assembly resolution of 1950. *See on this Economic, Social and Cultural Human Rights*, Advisory Committee on Human Rights and Foreign Policy of the Netherlands, Advisory Report No. 18, at 3 (1993). It is noteworthy also that the concept of the indivisibility and interdependence of human rights was explicitly mentioned in art. 6, para. 2, of the Declaration on the Right to Development, adopted by the U.N. General Assembly on Dec. 4, 1986, G.A. Res. 41/128 (Annex), U.N. GAOR, 41st Sess., Supp. No. 53, at 186, U.N. Doc. A/41/53 (1987), *reprinted in* 3 INTERNATIONAL LAW AND WORLD ORDER: BASIC DOCUMENTS III.R.2. (Burns H. Weston ed., 5 vol., 1994–) [hereinafter 3 Weston]. Article 6(1) reads: "All human rights and fundamental freedoms are indivisible and interdependent; equal attention and urgent consideration should be given to the implementation, promotion and protection of civil, political, economic, social and cultural rights."

this category, belong to "peoples" rather than individuals.[7] While admitting that such collective rights are rights clearly recognized and established under international law, it is not yet generally agreed whether they belong to "human rights". Human rights stem from human dignity. Groups usually do not share the same dignity with individuals. It is absolutely correct to talk about peoples' rights, but to argue that they are a part of human rights, more theoretical elaboration may be needed in order to obtain general support.

As many writers claim, and as we shall discuss in detail later, the above classification of human rights is not at all accurate nor practical. For instance, there are certain economic, social, and cultural rights, such as equal treatment of men and women in the enjoyment of such rights as stipulated in Article 3 of the ICESCR,[8] which are not programmatic but immediately enforceable.[9] On the other hand, certain civil and political rights need positive Governmental action for their effective implementation. For example, when persons belonging to a certain ethnic group are discriminated against at their workplace, the Government concerned must act positively to stop such practice and protect the victims.

Furthermore, some third category rights, such as the right to development, have individual as well as collective implications. Article 1, paragraph 1, of the Declaration on the Right to Development, adopted by the U.N. General Assembly on December 4, 1986,[10] provides: "The right to development is an inalienable human right by virtue of which every human person and all peoples are entitled to participate in, contribute to, and enjoy economic, social, cultural and political development, in which all human rights and fundamental freedoms can be fully realized". As this provision clearly attests, the right to development is: (a) individual as well as collective; and (b) programmatic as well as enforceable immediately. Such a right also has both positive and negative elements in the sense that: (a) states are required to refrain from interfering with the enjoyment of individuals' right to development, such as the right to participate in political development (negative aspect, see Art. 1, para. 1, of the Declaration on the Right to Development), on the one hand; and (b) states "have the primary responsibility for the creation of national and

---

[7]   Both covenants contain a provision (art. 1, para. 1), worded exactly the same in each, regarding the right of self-determination. It reads: "All peoples have the right of self-determination."

[8]   ICESCR, *infra* Appendix II.

[9]   The general comment (1990) of the Committee on Economic, Social and Cultural Rights states: "any suggestion that the provisions indicated are inherently non-self-executing would seem to be difficult to sustain." It further notes that some provisions of the Social and Economic Covenant "would seem to be capable to immediate application by judicial and other organs in many legal systems," and lists such immediately enforceable provisions as follows: art. 3 (equal rights of men and women), art. 7, para. (a), sub-para. (i) (equal pay for equal work), art. 8 (rights of trade unions), art. 10 (rights related to family), art. 13 (rights related to education), and art. 15 (rights related to scientific and cultural activities).

[10]   Declaration on the Right to Development, *supra* note 6.

international conditions favourable to the realization of the right to development" (positive aspect, see Art. 3, para. 1, of the Declaration), on the other.

Thus, the above three categories of rights represent mere classification for the purpose of convenience rather than based on distinctive characteristics of the respective rights. Yet, it is still useful to classify human rights into different groups for analytical convenience. It should also be pointed out that the characteristics of each category described above do show certain aspects of rights more or less commonly shared by the rights belonging to the same category. As long as we are aware that these characteristics are only superficial and represent only relatively stronger aspects of the rights belonging to the same category, we should not put aside the usefulness of such classification. With this basic understanding in mind, we shall proceed in analyzing the future of economic, social and cultural rights.

II. The Future of the Concept of Economic, Social and Cultural Rights

The World Conference on Human Rights in Vienna in 1993 adopted a declaration which clearly affirms that: "[a]ll human rights are universal, indivisible and interdependent and interrelated."[11] This concluded the debate about the issue of which human rights are more important and therefore be given priority. More specifically, there had been an assertion, which is still made today in some discourses on human rights, that, to realize economic, social, and cultural rights through economic development, certain civil and political rights would have to be restricted. This is in fact one of the reasons given by the Myanmar (Burmese) authorities for not giving political freedoms to people immediately.[12] It is well-known that similar contentions have also been advanced by some South East Asian leaders such as Former

---

[11] The Vienna Declaration and Programme of Action, adopted June 24, 1993 by the U.N. World Conference on Human Rights in Vienna, U.N. Doc. A/CONF.157/24 (pt. I) (Oct. 13, 1993), at 20–46, *reprinted in* 32 I.L.M. 1661 (1993) *and* 3 Weston III.U.2, *supra* note 6. As mentioned in note 6, *supra*, the "interconnectedness" and "interdependence" of all human rights were already mentioned by the U.N. General Assembly in 1950, and the "indivisibility" and "interdependence" of all human rights were referred to in the Declaration on the Right to Development of 1986, *supra* note 6. The only new word added in Vienna is "universality," if we understand that "interconnectedness" in the 1950 UNGA resolution and "interrelatedness" in the Vienna Declaration of 1993 mean basically the same thing.

[12] When the author of this paper, acting as U.N. Special Rapporteur, met Lt. Gen. Khin Nyunt of Myanmar, Secretary One of the State Law and Order Restoration Council, on Oct. 15, 1995, in Yangon, the latter explained that "the stability of the State was the most basic requirement for the development of the Union of Myanmar." In particular, he stressed the Government's efforts in the areas of economic, social and cultural development. He then added that "it was not the appropriate moment for the country to open up to democracy." For more detail, see *Report on the Situation of Human Rights in Myanmar*, U.N. Doc. E/CN.4/1995/65 (1996).

President Suharto of Indonesia, Prime Minister Mahatir of Malaysia, and former Prime Minister Lee Kuan Yew of Singapore.[13]

However, the delegates who gathered in Vienna in 1993 were in agreement that all human rights, irrespective of whether they are civil, political, economic, social, or cultural, are applicable anywhere in the world (universal), equally important (indivisible), mutually reinforcing (interdependent), and closely linked (interrelated). So, conceptually, economic, social, and cultural rights are of equal value with civil and political rights. This may lead to a conclusion that there may be no more need for studying economic, social, and cultural rights separately from civil and political rights. There is, however, an historical and practical reason for emphasizing the importance of economic, social, and cultural rights without, of course, undermining the value of civil and political rights.

First, as Audrey Chapman points out, "[d]espite a rhetorical commitment to the indivisibility and interdependence of human rights, the international community, including the international human rights movement, has treated civil and political rights as more significant and has consistently neglected economic, social, and cultural rights."[14] Consequently, in the debates particularly under the item "violation of human rights," both at the Commission on Human Rights and the Sub-Commission on Prevention of Discrimination and Protection of Minorities, most accusations of serious human rights violations, often made by Western-based human rights nongovernmental organizations (NGOs) are related to civil and political rights. The pleas made by the delegates or experts coming from the developing world to focus more on the tragic situations of violations of basic economic, social, and cultural rights, often stemming from extreme poverty, are largely ignored.

Secondly, because of their relative novelty, economic, social, and cultural rights have not yet been well and clearly defined. Gomez writes that "[t]he norms [of economic, social and cultural rights] are vague and lack the precision of their counterparts in the Civil and Political Rights Covenant."[15] He reasons: "[T]he norms are vague because they have not yet received sufficient attention from the courts, academics, or other agencies. Civil and political rights, on the other hand, have long

---

[13]   See, e.g., Fareed Zakaria, Culture Is Destiny: A Conversation with Lee Kuan Yew, 73 FOREIGN AFF. 109, 111, 114 (1994). The whole tone of Lee Kuan Yew's statement is that Singapore succeeded in achieving fast economic growth by creating a "well-ordered society" by some limitation imposed upon "the right of the individual to behave or misbehave as he pleases."

[14]   Audrey R. Chapman, A New Approach to Monitoring the International Covenant on Economic, Social and Cultural Rights, 55 REV. INT'L COMM. JURISTS 23, 24 (Special Issue, 1995). Gomez, supra note 3, also states, at 160, that "violations of civil and political rights have continued to be treated as though they are far more serious, and more patently intolerable, than are massive and direct denials of economic, social and cultural rights."

[15]   Gomez, supra note 3, at 161.

been the subject of interpretation by courts and other agencies, and have thus acquired a degree of clarity."[16]

It is interesting to note that the Universal Declaration of Human Rights (UDHR), adopted by the U.N. General Assembly on December 10, 1948,[17] without distinguishing explicitly between civil and political rights, on the one hand, and economic, social, and cultural rights, on the other, does provide for both categories of rights quite extensively. It includes traditional human rights, largely categorized as civil and political rights: equality (Art. 1); nondiscrimination (Art. 2); right to life (Art. 3); prohibition of slavery (Art. 4); prohibition of torture (Art. 5); right to recognition (Art. 6); equality before the law (Art. 7); right to effective remedy (Art. 8); prohibition of arbitrary arrest (Art. 9); right to a fair trial (Art. 10); assumption of innocence until final trial and no retroactivity of criminal charges (Art. 11); right to privacy (Art. 12); freedom of movement (Art. 13); right of asylum (Art. 14); right to nationality (Art. 15); right related to marriage and family (Art. 16); right to property (Art. 17);[18] freedom of thought, conscience and religion (Art. 18); freedom of speech and expression (Art. 19); freedom of peaceful assembly and association (Art. 20); and right to participate in the government (Art. 21). It also includes six further articles to provide for economic, social, and cultural rights: right to social security (Art. 22); various labor rights (Art. 23); right to leisure (Art. 24); right to minimum standard of living (Art. 24); right to education (Art. 25); and the right to cultural life (Art. 26).

What is striking in the above long list of provisions in the UDHR is that: (a) there is no distinction between civil and political rights and economic, social and cultural rights in the way they are provided for, in terms of legal or political weight and in the method of realization; (b) in spite of (a), the rights regarded as civil and political rights are grouped more or less together from Articles 1 through 21 and the rights broadly classified as economic, social and cultural rights are grouped thereafter from Articles 22 through 26, suggesting that the drafters of the Declaration consciously or unconsciously had two categories of human rights in mind; and (c) all the substantive provisions of the ICESCR are already conceived

---

[16]   *Id.*

[17]   *See infra* Appendix I [hereinafter UDHR].

[18]   As Eide and Rosas write, property rights are difficult to classify as to which category of human rights they belong. *See* Asbjørn Eide & Allan Rosas, *Economic, Social and Cultural Rights: A Universal Challenge, in* ECONOMIC, SOCIAL AND CULTURAL RIGHTS: A TEXTBOOK 15, 16 (Eide et al. eds., 1995) [hereinafter Eide]. Here, the right to property is classified, for convenience and also for historical development, into civil and political rights. Other writers, however, classify it as an economic right. *See, e.g.,* Lajos Lorincz, *Economic, Social and Cultural Rights, in* SOCIALIST CONCEPTS OF HUMAN RIGHTS 213 (I. Gombos ed., 1966).

of in the UDHR.[19] These points reinforce our position regarding the two categories of human rights that they are useful classification for convenience of analysis rather than finding any substantive differences in their characteristics. They further strengthen the position taken at Vienna that all human rights are universal, indivisible and interdependent and interrelated.

It is therefore regrettable that two covenants instead of one had to be adopted by the U.N. General Assembly in 1966,[20] providing different wording for the obligations of states parties to ensure and realize the respective rights recognized therein (Art. 2 of both covenants) and stipulating different procedures for reporting and monitoring (Arts. 16 to 22 of the ICESCR and Arts. 28 to 45 of the ICCPR).[21] The position of the UDHR as described above is more reflective of the actual situation of human rights; the different treatment given by the two covenants to civil and political rights, on the one hand, and economic, social, and cultural rights, on the other, is only the position of the two covenants, binding upon, and applicable to, only the states parties to them. This indeed means that all the economic, social, and cultural norms established independently, even antecedent to, the two covenants

---

[19]   See the comparison chart below of the various rights stipulated in the ICESCR, *infra* Appendix II, and the UDHR, *infra* Appendix I. As shown, practically all the major rights found in the ICESCR are also recognized by the UDHR. The difference is that the provisions in the Covenant are more detailed than those in the Declaration.

Right	*Covenant*	*Declaration*
To work	6	23 (1)
To fair and favourable conditions of work	7	23 (1)
To form and join trade unions	8	23 (4)
To social security	9	22
To protection of the family	10	25 (1), (2)
To adequate standard of living	11	25 (1)
To health and medical care	12	25 (1)
To education	13	26
To participate in cultural life	15	27

[20]   The history of preparing an internationally binding treaty for economic, social, and cultural rights goes back to 1950, when the U.N. General Assembly decided to produce a single Covenant to include such rights. Two years later, it decided to have two separate Covenants, one for civil and political rights and the other for economic, social and cultural rights. *See* ROBERTSON, *supra* note 2, at 229, and Advisory Committee on Human Rights and Foreign Policy of the Netherlands, *supra* note 6, at 3.

[21]   For historical discussions and the development of reporting and monitoring mechanisms under the ICESCR, *supra* note 4, as well as its problems and restrictions, see generally Philip Alston, *The Committee on Economic, Social and Cultural Rights, in* THE UNITED NATIONS AND HUMAN RIGHTS: A CRITICAL APPRAISAL (Philip Alston ed., 1992) [hereinafter ALSTON].

under customary international law, and in some domestic constitutional laws,[22] as expressed in the UDHR, are equally binding and enforceable.

Some efforts have been made to demonstrate that the existence of the two covenants and their different ways of stipulating governmental obligations should not be emphasized too much. The narrowing of the gaps found in the wording of the two instruments is being attempted by leading scholars and practitioners and indeed by the Committee on Economic, Social and Cultural Rights itself. But we may nonetheless conclude: (a) that there should be, and in fact will be, more attention given to economic, social, and cultural rights in the future; and (b) that there will be no distinction drawn between civil and political rights, on the one hand, and economic, social, and cultural rights, on the other, relative to the legal and political nature of these rights, the obligations of states to respect, protect, and fulfil them, and actual ways to achieve their full realization.

III. The Future of the Legal Provisions for Economic, Social, and Cultural Rights

In this section, we shall not attempt to analyze in detail all the provisions of the ICESCR nor shall we analyze similar provisions of regional conventions such as the European Social Charter.[23] Such efforts would require another major paper or even a volume. Here we would rather consider the question of how to define the various norms of economic, social, and cultural rights more clearly and precisely so as to make them legally binding and immediately enforceable under international and domestic laws.

Philip Alston and Gerard Quinn have endeavored to define more precisely several key provisions of the ICESCR, particularly Articles 2, 4 and 5 (all of them being general provisions related to the obligations of the states parties, restrictions upon limitations of the rights and relations with other laws and regulations), by applying the treaty interpretation clauses of the 1969 Vienna Convention on the Law

---

22   Lorincz's study, *supra* note 18, shows, at 197–200, that, after the First World War, the Mexican, German (Weimar), Spanish, and other Latin American and Central European constitutions contained provisions regarding certain economic, social, and cultural rights. This trend found firmer foundations when new constitutions in France (1946), Brazil (1946), Italy (1947), and Japan (1947), among others, included more comprehensive lists of economic, social, and cultural rights.

23   European Social Charter, Oct. 18, 1961, 529 U.N.T.S., *reprinted in* 3 Weston III.B.4, *supra* note 6; European Social Charter (Revised), May 3, 1996, Europe. T.S. No. 163, *reprinted in* 36 I.L.M. 31 (1997) *and* 3 Weston III.B.16d, *supra* note 6. For a general description of the European Social Charter, see 25 YEARS, EUROPEAN SOCIAL CHARTER (A. Ph. C. M. Jaspers & Lammy Betten eds., 1988); DAVID J. HARRIS, THE EUROPEAN SOCIAL CHARTER (1984); David J. Harris, *The European Social Charter and Social Rights in the European Union, in* THE PROTECTION OF FUNDAMENTAL SOCIAL RIGHTS IN THE EUROPEAN UNION 107 (Lammy Betten & Delma MacDevitt eds., 1996).

of Treaties (Arts. 31 and 32).[24] This is a very useful and helpful effort which can be extended to other, more substantive provisions of the ICESCR.[25]

In this regard, detailed analyses of the rights recognized in the European Social Charter,[26] which are contained in a study by Gomien, Harris, and Zwaak,[27] are very instructive. The authors give useful commentaries to each provision of the Charter, starting from the right to work (Art. 1), going further to the right to just conditions of work (Art. 2), the right to safe and healthy working conditions (Art. 3), the right to a fair remuneration (Art. 4), the right to organize (Art. 5), the right to bargain collectively (Art. 6), the right of children and young persons to protection (Art. 7), the right of employed women to protection (Art. 8), the right to vocational guidance (Art. 9), the right to vocational training (Art. 10), the right to protection of health (Art. 11), the right to social security (Art. 12), the right to social and medical assistance (Art. 13), the right to benefit from social welfare services (Art. 14), the right of physically or mentally disabled persons to vocational training, rehabilitation, and social resettlement (Art. 15), the right of the family to social, legal, and economic protection (Art. 16), the right of mothers and children to social and economic protection (Art. 17), the right to engage in a gainful occupation in the territory of other Contracting Parties (Art. 18), and finally, the right of migrant workers and their families to protection and assistance.

Such analyses can be undertaken for the provisions of economic, social, and cultural rights contained in universal human rights instruments such as the UDHR[28] and the ICESCR.[29] In the case of the provisions of the UDHR, the task of writing commentaries would be carried out by the Sub-Commission on Prevention of Discrimination and Protection of Minorities.[30] In the case of the provisions of the ICESCR, it is natural that the Committee on Economic, Social and Cultural Rights would undertake such a task.

---

[24] Vienna Convention on the Law of Treaties, May 23, 1969, 1155 U.N.T.S. 331, *reprinted in* 1 INTERNATIONAL LAW AND WORLD ORDER: BASIC DOCUMENTS I.E.1 (Burns H. Weston ed., 5 vols., 1994–).

[25] Indeed, Alston and Quinn analyze the meaning of art. 8 (labor rights) in relation to the limitations clause. *See* Philip Alston & Gerard Quinn, *The Nature and Scope of States Parties' Obligations under the International Covenant on Economic, Social and Cultural Rights*, 9 HUM. RTS. Q. 209 (1987).

[26] *Supra* note 23.

[27] DONNA GOMIEN ET AL., LAW AND PRACTICE OF THE EUROPEAN CONVENTION ON HUMAN RIGHTS AND THE EUROPEAN SOCIAL CHARTER 382–406 (1996).

[28] UDHR, *infra* Appendix I.

[29] ICESCR, *infra* Appendix II.

[30] If this were to be done by the Sub-Commission on Prevention of Discrimination and Protection of Minorities, it is likely that the Sub-Commission would create a new working group to draft such a new convention. On the work of the Sub-Commission through its working groups, see Asbjørn Eide, *The Sub-Commission on Prevention of Discrimination and Protection of Minorities, in* ALSTON, *supra* note 21, at 232–39.

In doing so, the above-mentioned analyses of the provisions of the European Social Charter offer helpful guidance. However, we must note that the above analyses reflect special European political, economic, social, and cultural conditions and contexts. Therefore, care must be given when applying the analyses of the European Social Charter to the provisions of economic, social, and cultural rights in more universal instruments. Also, we must be aware that the above listing of provisions are not complete lists of economic, social, and cultural rights recognized in the ICESCR—for instance, the right to education, the right to an adequate standard of living, and the right to participate in cultural life are missing in the above list. These missing provisions must be analyzed carefully also in preparing commentaries on the provisions of the ICESCR.

Another useful effort was made by a group of experts who met at the University of Limburg, Maastricht, The Netherlands, in 1986, and who succeeded in producing an agreed document often referred to as "The Limburg Principles," clarifying some interpretative principles to be applied to some provisions of the ICESCR.[31] The Limburg Principles clarify, for example, the following phrases or provisions of the Covenant:

Art. 2(1):   "to take steps by all appropriate means, including particularly the adoption of legislation".

"to achieve progressively the full realization of the rights"

"to the maximum of its available resources"

"individually and through international assistance and co-operation, especially economic and technical"

Art. 2(2):   Non-discrimination

Art. 2(3):   Non-nationals in developing countries

Art. 3:   Equal rights for men and women

Art. 4:   Limitations

"determined by law"

---

[31]   The Limburg Principles are the successful product of a symposium ("The Implementation of the International Covenant on Economic, Social and Cultural Rights") held at the University of Limburg on June 2–6, 1986, under the sponsorship of the International Commission of Jurists, the Faculty of Law of the University of Limburg and the Urban Morgan Institute for Human Rights (University of Cincinnati, Ohio). It was attended by twenty-nine participants from Australia, the Federal Republic of Germany, Hungary, Ireland, Mexico, the Netherlands, Norway, Senegal, Spain, the United Kingdom, the United States of America, Yugoslavia, the U.N. Centre for Human Rights, the ILO, UNESCO, WHO, the Commonwealth Secretariat, and the sponsoring organizations. Four members of the Committee on Economic, Social and Cultural Rights also participated. The Limburg Principles on the Implementation of the International Covenant on Economic, Social and Cultural Rights are reproduced in 9 HUM. RTS. Q. 122 (1987).

"promoting the general welfare"

"in a democratic society"

"compatible with the nature of these rights"

Art. 5: Prohibition of activity aimed at the destruction of the rights recognized in the Covenant

Art. 8: "prescribed by law"

"necessary in a democratic society"

"national security"

"public order (ordre public)"

"rights and freedoms of others"

The Limburg Principles certainly can serve as a useful guideline for preparing commentaries on the provisions of the ICESCR.

In this connection, it is submitted that, however precisely one may try to interpret a particular substantive provision which is vague, it may not be possible to establish its authoritative interpretation in a manner that is acceptable to all the states parties. For instance, Article 11(1) stipulates that: "[t]he States Parties to the present Covenant recognize the right of everyone to an adequate standard of living for himself and for his family." How might we clarify the meaning of "an adequate standard of living" applicable to all states parties, rich or poor?

This provision may be binding and immediately applicable, and in a concrete situation a state party might be found guilty of violating this provision by not providing an adequate standard of living to a person or her/his family. For example, if in a rich country the government were to provide only ten dollars a day to a person who is unemployed and with no savings, no assets, and no family that could support her/him, that government clearly would be regarded as violating this provision. On the other hand, if the government involved were of a developing country with average per capita income of $360 a year (or one dollar a day), how could we blame the government?

As the above example suggests, it is impossible to give precise interpretation to "an adequate standard of living" applicable to all countries in all situations. Thus, another more flexible, more contextual approach should be sought, and in this connection we have the following two suggestions that would place economic, social, and cultural rights in a more central position in international human rights discourse.

First is the suggestion to draft and adopt a new declaration or convention on a specific provision of the ICESCR or the relevant provision of the UDHR. In the case of the former, the task of initial drafting would rest with the Committee on Economic, Social and Cultural Rights which then would be sent for approval to the Economic and Social Council, then finally for adoption to the Conference of the states parties. In the latter case, the drafting process would start at the level of the Sub-Commission on Prevention of Discrimination and Protection of

Minorities[32] and then would go up the ladder to the Commission on Human Rights, the Economic and Social Council, and finally the General Assembly. These two courses of action are both possible; the choice seems to be political. The latter has the advantage that the adopted instrument would be applicable, at least politically and morally, if not legally, to 185 member states of the United Nations under the authority of the U.N. General Assembly resolution. But one must pay the cost of ignoring and undermining the ICESCR with its ineffective but still useful reporting and monitoring mechanism. The latter, on the other hand, has the advantage: (a) that the drafting would be conducted by a group of real experts on these rights, *i.e.*, the expert members of the Committee on Economic, Social and Cultural Rights; and (b) that there is an advantage of using the reporting and monitoring mechanism under the ICESCR. On the other hand, this course of action would always be under the limitation of the ICESCR system: debate over the legal nature of the Covenant provisions and the effectiveness of the Economic and Social Committee.

Whichever course one might take, it is quite useful to have a separate, more detailed instrument, clarifying the nature of the rights and obligations involved, establishing or proposing a more effective reporting, monitoring, and information-gathering mechanism, and providing adequate relief and compensation procedures. As we have already a number of separate, more detailed conventions for civil and political rights, such as the 1965 International Convention on the Elimination of All Forms of Racial Discrimination[33] and the 1984 Convention against Torture and Other Cruel, Inhuman or Degrading Treatment or Punishment,[34] we could have similar conventions for economic, social, and cultural rights, such as a convention on the rights to social security and basic human needs, a convention on the right to an adequate standard of living and housing, a convention on the right to education and a convention on cultural rights.

Actually, there already is a large volume of international conventions drafted and adopted by the Conference of the International Labour Organisation (ILO). Since its creation in 1919, the ILO has adopted more than 175 conventions (which are legally binding upon ratifying ILO member states[35]) and more than 180 recommendations (which are not legally binding, but ILO member states still are under

---

32   *See* note 30, *supra*.

33   Concluded, Dec. 21, 1965 (entered into force, Jan. 4, 1969), 660 U.N.T.S. 195 (hereinafter Racial Discrimination Convention), *reprinted in* 3 Weston III.I.1, *supra* note 6.

34   Concluded, Dec. 10, 1984 (entered into force, June 26, 1987), G.A. Res. 39/46 (Annex), U.N. GAOR, 39th Sess., Supp. No. 15, at 197, U.N. Doc. A/39/51 (1985) (hereinafter Torture Convention), *reprinted in* 23 I.L.M. 1027 (1984) *and* 3 Weston III.K.2, *supra* note 6.

35   Art. 19(5)(a) of the Constitution of the International Labour Organisation (ILO) provides that "the Convention will be communicated to all Members for ratification." This means that an ILO Convention is an international treaty "binding upon the Members who ratify it"

a duty to pay adequate respect to the realization of their provisions[36]). Of course, the case of labor rights conventions of the ILO is exceptional, but there is no reason why we cannot look for a similar course in the case of other economic, social, and cultural rights.

The second suggestion is that the Economic and Social Committee should develop a list of targets for each economic, social, or cultural right and begin a negotiation with each state party to the ICESCR to agree on a schedule of achievement for each right. The actual target for a particular right for a particular country would be different. It would have to balance the ideal (maximum attainable level) and the reality (currently available resources). It also would have to provide for needed international assistance and cooperation. Consider, for example, in a country that is a state party to the ICESCR, where a great majority of the rural population may be living under horrific conditions, lacking adequate food, safe water, medicine, and medical care—a clear case of the violation of economic, social, and cultural rights. In this case, the Committee representative would visit the country to negotiate with the government a target for improving the living condition in the following manner:

- *Final objective*: all rural population will be leading an adequate life with minimum necessary supply of food, safe water, medicine and medical care;

- *Stages*: the above objective should be achieved over a span of five years, gradually from district to district; and

- *Involved actors*: governmental departments, international organizations and agencies, and international nongovernmental organizations.

In the actual situation, it is likely that the government involved may not wish to cooperate with the Committee representative in negotiating for this kind of arrangement. In such a case, the Committee could declare that the government is not fulfilling the obligations under the Covenant because: (a) the situation of life in the rural area of the country is in violation of Article 11(1) which stipulates that "[t]he States Parties to the present Covenant recognize the right of everyone to an adequate standard of living for himself and his family, including adequate food, clothing and housing, and continuous improvement of living conditions"; and

---

(Art. 20 of the ILO Constitution). For more detail, see NICOLAS VALTICOS, DROIT INTERNATIONAL DU TRAVAIL 142–46 (1970). For the text of the ILO Constitution as revised through Oct. 9, 1946, see 15 U.N.T.S. 35.

36 Art. 19(6)(a) of the ILO Constitution, *supra* note 35, provides: "the Recommendation will be communicated to all Members, for their consideration with a view to effect being given to it by national legislation or otherwise." Sub-para. (d) of the same paragraph stipulates further that "apart from bringing the Recommendation before the said competent authority or authorities, no further obligation shall rest upon the Members, except that they shall report to the Director-General of the International Labour Office."

(b) noncooperation with the Committee and no action to improve the living condition of the rural population is a violation of Article 2(1) of the Covenant which stipulates that "[e]ach State Party to the present Covenant undertakes to take steps, individually and through international assistance and cooperation, especially economic and technical, to the maximum of its available resources, with a view to achieving progressively the full realization of the rights recognized in the present Covenant by all appropriate means."

The second suggestion is an approach in which the meaning of at least some provisions of the ICESCR would be individually defined, taking into account the actual political, economic, social, historical, and cultural situations of each country and the views and policies of its government. In other words, instead of trying to obtain an agreed, uniform interpretation applicable universally, we should strive for an agreed individual interpretation tailored to the situations and needs of each country.

In this connection, there is an interesting and useful project that has been undertaken by the Philippine Human Rights Information Center (or PhilRights) in the Philippines.[37] After some general description of economic, social, and cultural rights in the context of Philippine history and culture, the report of the project, in Chapter IV ("Newly Articulated or Re-articulated Economic, Social and Cultural Rights and Possible Indicators"), explains in detail possible indicators such rights for each of the following fifteen areas of concern: (1) health; (2) internal refugees; (3) indigenous peoples; (4) work; (5) education; (6) land and peasants; (7) adequate standards of living; (8) cultural rights; (9) environment; (10) fisherfolk; (11) development; (12) Moro rights; (13) women's rights; (14) peace; and (15) governance. Then, for each area, at the beginning, a list of relevant provisions of international treaties and declarations is given to show the international standards applicable to the area under consideration. After this, some articulation of the rights related to the area made, followed by some possible indicators.

Let us look at one representative area as an example. In the Section on Education Rights, first, provisions of the UDHR and ICCPR are given as well as the relevant provision of the 1987 Philippine Constitution. Then, the following articulated rights are listed with some explanations and suggested indicators:

"right to free access to basic education (and accessible education opportunities)" indicators: (a) free and equal access to basic education, (b) availability of free basic education, (c) availability and affordability of higher education, (d) provision and availability of structures for special education, (e) literacy rate, (f) functional literacy, (g) adequate school facilities, (h) an elementary school in each barangay, and (i) availability of books free of charge.

---

[37] *See* PHILIPPINE HUMAN RIGHTS INFORMATION CENTER, MONITORING ECONOMIC, SOCIAL AND CULTURAL RIGHTS: THE PHILIPPINE EXPERIENCE (1997).

As one can see, the list of indicators is not yet complete and needs refinement. However, this is a useful exercise and a good start. It would be extremely helpful if a similar endeavor were attempted for other countries.

IV. Realization of Economic, Social, and Cultural Rights

As Craven writes, "[t]he central issue that dominates the study of the international law of human rights is that of enforcement."[38] This is as true of civil and political rights as it is of economic, social, and cultural rights. Many economic, social, and cultural rights are often not easy to realize, and enforcement, such as through court decisions which are workable in many cases involving the violations of civil and political rights,[39] does not work well to achieve a high level of enjoyment of such rights. The reasons for this particular difficulty in realizing economic, social, and cultural rights are multiple.

First, to realize economic, social, and cultural rights, concerned governments must have the necessary resources, which many in the developing countries do not possess at all or in any significant quantity. The irony is that many governments in the developing world do not always make the best use of the available resources, which are very limited, for improving the general living conditions of people under their rule. Instead, they often misallocate their scarce resources for unnecessarily large military expenditure and personal luxury, and waste them also by corrupt practices. Thus, the excuses often given by the governments of the developing countries, to the effect that they cannot provide adequate food, housing, and clothing to their people for lack of funds and resources, need to be studied and analyzed carefully. In some cases, the governments genuinely need such funds and resources for carrying out a sensible policy to improve the living conditions of the public, particularly the poorest of them. In such a case, it is the responsibility of the international community in general, and the developed countries in particular, to provide such governments truly in need with necessary funds and resources. On the other hand, if the governments of the developing countries are not making sincere efforts to ensure the basic human needs of the people by wasting their resources, the responses of the international community and the developed countries should be cautious.

A second reason for the difficulty of realizing economic, social, and cultural rights is related to the bureaucratic and institutional complexity of implementing the policies necessary to realize them. Whilst there are only limited governmental ministries and departments traditionally involved in civil and political rights, such as the courts, ministries of justice, the police, the military, and ministries of foreign

---

38 CRAVEN, *supra* note 1, at 367.

39 Normally, "courts" means domestic courts; but recently some international courts have started to play this sort of enforcement role, including the European Court of Human Rights, the Inter-American Court of Human Rights, the International Military Tribunal for the Former Yugoslavia, the International Military Tribunal for Rwanda, and the recently agreed-upon International Criminal Court (Rome, July 1998).

affairs, there are many more diverse ministries and departments involved in the realization of economic, social, and cultural rights. In addition to courts, ministries of justice, and ministries of foreign affairs, which are concerned with both categories of human rights, ministries of finance, labor, education, economic development and trade, and health and welfare are also involved at a minimum in respect of economic, social, and cultural rights. The complexity of the institutional set-up of economic, social, and cultural rights is problematic in the following manner: (a) many of these concerned ministries have not been hitherto involved in human rights affairs and therefore are human rights ignorant or insensitive (most such ministries in most countries do not have a section or desk responsible for human rights matters); (b) because of the compartmentalization, the officials in these ministries tend to show an attitude of evading responsibility by saying that the realization of economic, social, and cultural rights are not within their proper jurisdiction or mandate, typical bureaucratic traits all over the world; and (c) there is no central governmental office (or ministry) in charge of the formulation and implementation of a coherent and integrated national policy for economic, social, and cultural rights, which leads to the conclusion that there should be a national institution at the ministerial level to coordinate the activities of various ministries and departments concerned with the realization of economic, social and cultural rights.

A third difficulty is related to the diversity and complexity of the organizations, organs, and agencies involved in the realization of economic, social, and cultural rights. At the global level, there are many and different types of institutions and bodies concerned with this category of human rights. First, there are several U.N. organs generally responsible for human rights, including civil and political as well as economic, social, cultural rights: (a) the General Assembly; (b) the Economic and Social Council (ECOSOC); (c) the Commission on Human Rights; and (d) the Sub-Commission on Prevention of Discrimination and Protection of Minorities.[40] The Commission on the Status of Women, a subsidiary organ of ECOSOC, also deals with economic, social, and cultural rights related to women.[41] Other organs of the U.N. such as the Security Council,[42] the United Nations Development Programme (UNDP) and the United Nations Children's Fund (UNICEF) also are involved in various aspects of economic, social, and cultural rights in relation to their proper mandates which are not limited to human rights.

---

[40]   For concise descriptions of the role of the General Assembly, ECOSOC, the Commission of Human Rights, and the Sub-Commission, see Antonio Cassese, *The General Assembly: Historical Perspective 1945–1989, in* ALSTON, *supra* note 21, at 25; John Quinn, *The General Assembly into the 1990s, in id.* at 55; Declan O'Donovan, *The Economic and Social Council, in id.* at 107; Philip Alston, *The Commission on Human Rights, in id.* at 126; and Eide, *supra* note 30.

[41]   *See generally* Laura Reanda, *The Commission on the Status of Women, in* ALSTON, *supra* note 21, at 265.

[42]   *See* Sydney D. Bailey, *The Security Council, in* ALSTON, *supra* note 21, at 304.

There are several specialized agencies of the United Nations that are concerned with the realization of economic, social, and cultural rights.[43] The obvious and most involved, of course, is the International Labour Organization (ILO). The United Nations Educational, Scientific and Cultural Organization (UNESCO) deals with human rights such as those that are related to education, science, and culture. UNESCO plays also an important role in human rights education including education about economic, social, and cultural rights. The World Health Organization (WHO) and the United Nations Food and Agriculture Organization (FAO) are engaged in activities related to the right to health, food, and safe drinking water. The World Bank Group,[44] whose functions have traditionally been regarded as strictly economic and financial, has in recent years been paying more and more attention to human rights dimension of its activities.[45] In addition, the World Bank Group is a major source of funding for various development projects which are intended to contribute to the economic development of the developing countries, a process indispensable for the enjoyment of a higher level of economic, social, and cultural rights.

---

[43] The specialized agencies are the intergovernmental organizations which were created by separate charters to achieve a specific purpose of a global nature, and which have entered into a special relationship with the United Nations. Art. 57 of the U.N. Charter provides as follows:

1. The various specialized agencies, established by intergovernmental agreement and having wide international responsibilities, as defined in their basic instruments, in economic, social, cultural, educational, health, and related fields, shall be brought into relationship with the United Nations in accordance with the provisions of Article 63.

2. Such agencies thus brought into relationship with the United Nations are hereinafter referred to as specialized agencies.

For a detailed explanation of the specialized agencies, see *Specialized Agencies within the UN System, in* ENCYCLOPEDIA OF THE UNITED NATIONS AND INTERNATIONAL AGREEMENTS 772–74 (Edmund Jan Osmanczyk ed., 1985) [hereinafter Osmanczyk].

[44] The World Bank Group comprises the International Bank for Reconstruction and Development (IBRD, or World Bank), the International Finance Corporation (IFC), the International Development Association (IDA), the International Centre for Settlement of Investment Disputes (ICSID), and the Multilateral Investment Guarantee Agency (MIGA).

[45] In fact, the World Bank is required under its charter, formally the Articles of Agreement of the International Bank for Reconstruction and Development, July 22, 1944, 2 U.N.T.S. 134, *reprinted in* 4 INTERNATIONAL LAW AND WORLD ORDER BASIC DOCUMENTS IV.A.2 (Burns H. Weston ed., 5 vols., 1994–), to pay regard only to economic considerations and not to political considerations. Art. 4(10) of the Bank's Articles of Agreement provides:

The Bank and its officers shall not interfere in the political affairs of any member; nor shall they be influenced in their decisions by the political character of the member or members concerned. Only economic considerations shall be relevant to their decisions, and these considerations shall be weighed impartially in order to achieve the purposes stated in Article 1.

See Yozo Yokota, *Non-Political Character of the World Bank,* 20 JAPANESE ANN. INT'L L. 39 (1978).

Another category of international institutions concerned with the realization of economic, social, and cultural rights is the so-called "treaty bodies" or "Organs Monitoring Treaty Compliance."[46] They are a body of individual experts (not governmental representatives) whose functions include study and research on situations related to the rights and obligations provided for in their respective human rights conventions, and monitoring their compliance by states parties through reporting and communications procedures. Such a treaty body exists for the ICCPR[47] (the Human Rights Committee), the ICESCR[48] (the Committee on Economic, Social and Cultural Rights[49]), the 1965 International Convention on the Elimination of All Forms of Racial Discrimination[50] (the Committee on the Elimination of Racial Discrimination[51]), the 1979 Convention on the Elimination of All Forms of Discrimination against Women[52] (the Committee on the Elimination of Discrimination against Women[53]), the 1984 Convention against Torture and Other Cruel, Inhuman or Degrading Treatment or Punishment[54] (the Committee against Torture[55]), and the Convention on the Rights of the Child[56] (the Committee on the Rights of the Child). Among them, the bodies particularly pertinent to the economic, social, and cultural rights are the Committee on Economic, Social and Cultural Rights, the Committee on the Elimination of Discrimination against Women, and the Committee on the Rights of the Child.

The last category of international institutions concerned with economic, social, and cultural rights is the so-called international nongovernmental organizations (NGOs).[57] They are the organizations of volunteers, independent from governments, to tackle issues of global nature affecting the whole of humankind, such as human

---

46   This term is used in Karl Josef Partsch, *The Committee on the Elimination of Racial Discrimination, in* ALSTON, *supra* note 21, at 337.

47   ICCPR, *infra* Appendix III.

48   ICESCR, *infra* Appendix II.

49   *See* Philip Alston, *The Committee on Economic, Social and Cultural Rights, in* ALSTON, *supra* note 21, at 473.

50   Racial Discrimination Convention, *supra* note 33.

51   *See* Partsch, *supra* note 46, at 339.

52   Concluded, Dec. 18, 1979, 1249 U.N.T.S. 13, *reprinted in* 3 Weston III.C.13, *supra* note 6.

53   Roberta Jacobson, *The Committee on the Elimination of Discrimination against Women, in* ALSTON, *supra* note 21, at 444.

54   Torture Convention, *supra* note 34.

55   Andrew Byrnes, *The Committee Against Torture, in* ALSTON, *supra* note 21, at 509.

56   Concluded, Nov. 20, 1989 (entered into force, Sept. 2, 1990), G.A. Res. 44/25 (Annex), U.N. GAOR 44th Sess., Supp. No. 49, at 166, U.N. Doc. A/44/49 (1990), *reprinted in* 3 Weston III.D.3, *supra* note 6.

57   *See Non-Governmental Organizations, NGO, in* Osmanczyk, *supra* note 43, at 565. *See also* Julie Mertus, *Human Rights and the Promise of Transnational Civil Society, infra* in this

rights, the human environment, development, disarmament, and cultural and sports activities. Among them, there are many that are concerned with human rights, particularly economic, social, and cultural rights.

Thus, there is a large number of international organizations, agencies, bodies, or institutions involved in activities related to economic, social, and cultural rights. They are of different nature with different mandates, powers, functions, and resource bases. This is a good thing in a way because there are so many different actors working for the realization of economic, social, and cultural rights. However, it also causes a problem of coordination of their activities. Especially in international society where a central governing authority is lacking, the coordination of the activities of actors so diverse and independent is not an easy task. It seems that the United Nations, particularly the General Assembly and the ECOSOC, could play a major role for the coordination of such activities.[58]

There remains one important issue that must be briefly mentioned relative to the realization of economic, social and cultural rights: how to monitor the level of respect for such rights. The monitoring under the reporting procedure of the ICE-SCR is widely known, with both its advantages and shortcomings. In addition, we are equally interested in the question of how to assess the level of enjoyment of such rights. Some attempts have already been made to the indexing of these rights. In sum, we consider that more efforts should be made to: (a) improve the present monitoring procedure under the ICESCR, including the development of individual communications procedure for economic, social, and cultural rights; (b) develop a method of evaluation of the achievement of economic, social, and cultural rights; and (c) improve a mechanism for coordination of the activities of various actors in the field of economic, social, and cultural rights.

V. The Relationship Between Economic, Social, and Cultural Rights and Economic Development

As has been mentioned already, to realize economic, social, and cultural rights fully, it is essential that the governments that have the primary responsibility to ensure the enjoyment of such rights have adequate resources. In principle, the availability of resources is not and should not be a problem for the developed countries, or the countries with an annual per capita GDP of more than us$10,000. However, for poorer countries, particularly those with an annual per capita GDP of less than us$ 1,000, it is not easy for the governments to ensure the full enjoyment of these rights to their

---

volume at p. 433; Laurie S. Wiseberg, *Human Rights Nongovernmental Organizations, in* HUMAN RIGHTS IN THE WORLD COMMUNITY: ISSUES AND ACTION 372 (Richard P. Claude & Burns H. Weston eds. & contribs., 2d ed.1992).

[58] The coordination of the activities of various organs and specialized agencies of the U.N. has been a legal and practical difficulty from the beginning of the U.N.'s birth. *See* Nessim Shalon, *Co-ordination of the Programs of Specialized Agencies*, 1949 ANN. REV. U.N. AFF. 69.

peoples. It is here that the role and responsibility of the international community as a whole and of the developed countries more specifically come onto the scene.

As Article 3(3) of the Declaration on the Right to Development[59] provides, "States have the duty to co-operate with each other in ensuring development and eliminating obstacles to development." Its Article 4(1) further provides that "States have the duty to take steps, individually and collectively, to formulate international development policies with a view to facilitating the full realization of the right to development." Paragraph 2 of the same article reads: "As a complement to the efforts of developing countries, effective international co-operation is essential in providing these countries with appropriate means and facilities to foster their comprehensive development."

These provisions of the Declaration on the Right to Development suggest that states must cooperate in order that all states and peoples, including individuals, may enjoy the right to development. The right to development in this context is defined in Article 1(1) of the Declaration as "an inalienable human right by virtue of which every human person and all peoples are entitled to participate in, contribute to, and enjoy economic, social, cultural and political development, in which all human rights and fundamental freedoms can be fully realized."

In sum, we may conclude from the provisions of the Declaration on the Right to Development that: (a) for all persons and peoples to enjoy fully economic, social, and cultural rights, the right to development must be assured; and (b) an effective international cooperation among states is essential for the right to development to be enjoyed. What this boils down to is that international development assistance is one of the key elements for the enjoyment of economic, social, and cultural rights. However, after careful analyses of the development assistance programs carried out by international organizations and agencies—such as the World Bank and its affiliates—and bilateral aid agencies of the industrial countries—such as the United States Agency for International Development (USAID) and the Japanese Overseas Economic Development Fund (OECF)—we have come to the conclusion that these international development agencies, which have traditionally been concerned mainly with development from an economic point of view, must develop a new policy and strategy to advance the enjoyment by the peoples of the recipient developing countries of economic, social, and cultural rights.[60] In this connection, there are five considerations to be given by such aid agencies.

First, economic development in general is a welcome occurrence in a given developing country from the standpoint of the realization of economic, social, and cultural rights because the country would be able to use the fruit of economic development. In other words, economic development can create resources which can be

---

[59] *Supra* note 6.

[60] In fact, the World Bank, which had been reluctant to talk about human rights, has squarely dealt with them in its welcome publication, DEVELOPMENT AND HUMAN RIGHTS: THE ROLE OF THE WORLD BANK (1998).

utilized for the people of the country to enjoy economic, social, and cultural rights. In this sense, the increase in quantity of international development assistance should be encouraged, both multilaterally as well as bilaterally. However, as was pointed out earlier, it is not always the case that the governments of the recipient countries will make the best use of the fruit of development for the realization of economic, social, and cultural rights. Thus, international development agencies should pay attention to governmental policy and strategy for using the resources made available as a result of economic development with such international assistance.

Second, the international aid agencies should study the level of enjoyment of economic, social, and cultural rights of a country which they are to assist, and draw up conditions to improve such levels with concrete objectives to be achieved. For instance, in a loan or credit agreement between an aid agency and a recipient country, the agency could require the country, in the form of a conditionality, to improve the income distribution by setting higher income tax for the rich and lower income tax for the poor.

Third, the international aid agencies should propose to finance more projects which will affect positively the level of enjoyment of economic, social, and cultural rights. For example, more projects for creating local jobs (thus improving the enjoyment of the right to work), schools (thus improving the enjoyment of the right to education), water supply and sewerage systems (thus improving the enjoyment of the right to clean drinking water and health), and hospitals (thus improving the enjoyment of the right to medical care).

Fourth, in all the projects to be financed by the international aid agencies, there should be some elements of improving the level of enjoyment of economic, social, and cultural rights. For instance, in a textile project to be financed by an international aid agency, there should be one component of employing two hundred workers in a factory to be built under the project. This would create jobs allowing two hundred workers to enjoy the right to work. There also should also be a requirement that half of such workers should be women. This would allow more women to work, thus leading to the achievement of equal treatment of women in the workplace. Another requirement should be that work conditions, including wages, work hours, paid holidays, and safety at work place, should be in accordance with the provisions of the ICESCR.

Fifth, all projects assisted by the international aid agencies should be appraised from the standpoint of economic, social, and cultural rights, and, if it is found that some projects would have an negative impact upon the enjoyment of economic, social, and cultural rights, then such projects must be adjusted to avoid such adverse effects. For example, a dam project might require relocation of a local village. If the project is planned without due regard to the life of the affected villagers, it might hamper the villagers' enjoyment of the rights to an adequate standard of living, to work, to housing, to family, and to cultural life. In such a case, the project should be changed either to avoid such relocation of the village or, alternatively, to provide another place to live with accompanying compensation for any material loss and mental suffering involved in such relocation.

For international aid agencies to be more human rights-conscious so that they will take adequate consideration of all of the five points mentioned above, there should be a group of human rights experts within the staff of such agencies. One natural development in this direction would be the creation of a human rights section composed of a number of lawyers specializing in human rights, particularly economic, social, and cultural rights, within their respective legal departments. Such lawyers would formulate a general policy along the lines described above, appraise all projects from the aspect of enjoyment of human rights by the peoples of the recipient countries, draw up projects specifically intended to improve the level of enjoyment of human rights, particularly economic, social, and cultural rights, and conduct studies on the relationship between development and human rights.

VI. Summary Remarks on the Future of Economic, Social, and Cultural Rights

This year, we are celebrating the fiftieth anniversary of the Universal Declaration of Human Rights.[61] It is noteworthy that the UDHR contains a full range of economic, social, and cultural rights in its provisions, together with detailed provisions for civil and political rights. Although the Declaration does not distinguish the two sets of human rights in any way except that the two categories are more or less grouped together so that we find most of the civil and political rights in Articles 1 to 21 and most of the economic, social, and cultural rights in Articles 22 to 26, the subsequent treatment of the two categories has been uneven. While civil and political rights have been attracting most people's attention, economic, social and cultural rights have been neglected.

In the next fifty years, it is certain from the current international trend that more focus must be placed upon economic, social, and cultural rights, without of course sacrificing civil and political rights. To make this change of emphasis more meaningful, the following developments are likely or desirable.

First, the provisions of economic, social, and cultural rights recognized by international documents such as the UDHR and ICESCR will have to be elaborated preferably in the form of detailed commentaries prepared either by the Committee on Economic, Social and Cultural Rights or by the Sub-Commission on Prevention of Discrimination and Protection of Minorities.

Second, efforts should be made to draft and adopt a new declaration and conventions on specific rights in the field of economic, social, and cultural rights. We already have an unevenly large number of labor rights conventions and recommendations adopted by the International Labour Conference. Similar efforts should

---

61   UDHR, *infra* Appendix I.

be devoted to other economic, social, and cultural rights, such as the rights to education, to health, to social security and welfare, and to a minimum standard of living adequate for health and well-being.

Third, there should be an agreed list of targets for each economic, social, or cultural right for each country with a schedule of achievement in stages. This could be attempted in the process of reporting and monitoring by the Committee on Economic, Social and Cultural Rights or by a newly created working group under the U.N. Sub-Commission on Prevention of Discrimination and Protection of Minorities.

Fourth, for the full realization of economic, social, and cultural rights in each state, there should be established a mechanism to coordinate and oversee the activities of different governmental ministries and departments concerned with economic, social, and cultural rights. There should also be an effective mechanism to guard against the misallocation of funds and resources in the form of corruption and over allocation to military and other unnecessary expenses.

Fifth, better coordination of activities of various international actors involved in the realization of economic, social, and cultural rights, including NGOs, is absolutely necessary. ECOSOC should regain its original mandate under the U.N. Charter to coordinate the activities of specialized agencies and NGOs.

Finally, international aid agencies should become more human rights-conscious and guide their activities in the direction of the full realization of economic, social, and cultural rights. For this purpose, there should be created a new unit of lawyers in their respective legal departments who are specialists in human rights law to study and review the relationship between development projects or programs and the enjoyment of economic, social, and cultural rights.

Reflections on the Future of Civil and Political Rights

Rein Müllerson*

I. Introduction

Civil rights are rights necessary for the establishment of individual autonomy, including liberty of the person; freedom of speech, thought, and faith; the right to own property and to enter into contracts; and the right to be treated equally with others before the law.[1] Political rights are rights empowering individual participation in the political processes of a country. The right to elect and to be elected, equal access to civil service, and related civil rights such as freedom of association and speech are human rights without which no democratic political system can thrive.

But it is impossible to think of such rights in isolation from the future of human rights generally, and not only because of various interdependencies between categories of human rights. There are some general tendencies and developments in the world and in individual societies that have an impact on all the categories of human rights. This impact may differ depending on the nature of the rights and freedoms involved as well as on the character of the society where rights are to be implemented. Moreover, the division of human rights into categories (or "generations") is far from strict. For example, the prohibition of various forms of discrimination, the right to own property, and a whole set of minority rights cross the boundaries of the traditional divide between civil-political and socio-economic rights.

Still, it often is said that civil and political rights are absolute while social and economic rights are conditional, and certainly there is some truth in this. The realization of social and economic rights often is directly and greatly dependent on the socio-economic development of a society. However, in a very real sense civil and political rights also are conditional. A poor country with high illiteracy and infant mortality rates in which the population "enjoys" civil and political rights simply would be a contradiction in terms.

Thus it would be naive to expect that, in the foreseeable future, civil and political rights will thrive in all societies. While there has been progress in many countries in recent decades, the level of enjoyment of basic civil and political rights will continue to differ greatly from one region of the world to another. It is not possible

* I thank Professor Burns H. Weston for valuable comments on my manuscript.

1 See DAVID HELD, DEMOCRACY, AND THE GLOBAL ORDER: FROM THE MODERN STATE TO COSMOPOLITAN GOVERNANCE 65 (1995).

to speak of the future of civil and political rights without taking into account immense dissimilarities between societies. Though the world will become more and more interrelated and interdependent in the years to come, dissimilarities between societies will not disappear quickly.

In any event, the future of civil and political rights is in no way predetermined. It will depend on at least three categories of factors which influence the future of civil and political rights: (1) the desire and will of individuals, nongovernmental organizations, states, and inter-governmental organizations to seek civil and political rights and to influence the future in relation to them; (2) current observable tendencies in individual societies and in the world as a whole that may be either conducive to the realization of civil and political rights or, *vice versa*, antithetical thereto; (3) developments of which we know nothing or, if already discernible, the impact of which we are not yet able to determine. Understandably we can say nothing about the last category of factors except that, in our predictions, we must be always open-minded and never categorical. It is not easy to foresee what tendencies will affect civil and political rights and even more difficult to predict how they will do so.

One may assume that individuals will continue to need and want existing rights and that they will continue to struggle for their full implementation. It also is safe to predict that, even if there may not be desires or needs for completely new rights (though this possibility is not excluded), existing rights are likely to evolve and extend to new areas (for example, gender equality in some societies has begun to mean also equality of sexual orientation). Of course, it may be that some rights lose their topicality. For example, freedom of movement in ex-communist countries, including the right to leave one's own country, was especially topical prior to the collapse of communism because in those formerly closed societies the opportunity to travel abroad generally was denied. Now, in those parts of the former communist bloc where peoples' freedom of movement is not restricted any more, other rights have acquired greater topicality.

One may assume also that, in most countries, civil and political rights, like social and economic rights, will be affected by various historical developments among which the processes of globalization and fragmentation may be paramount. Ian Clark observes:

> There remains . . . considerable consensus that future world politics will be shaped by the contradictory, but interrelated, forces of globalisation and fragmentation. The first trend emphasises the expansion of integrated functional activities—particularly in the economy, communications, and aspects of socialisation—towards a genuinely global system. The second trend, and at least in part as a reaction to the other, reasserts claims to national or ethnic identities, individual cultures, regional trading blocs, and smaller forms of political association. There is a surprisingly wide recognition of the existence of these integrative and disintegrative forces: transnational-

ism versus ethno-nationalism; political federalism and intergovernmentalism versus separatism; cosmopolitan culture versus multi-faceted individual identities; and modernism versus its resisters.[2]

Thus, though the processes of globalization may be affecting economic and social rights more directly than civil and political rights, the latter will not be unaffected and fragmentation may have greater impact on minority rights. My comments and remarks will reflect these probabilities even while they will at times relate to human rights as a whole.

Finally, while remaining convinced that both civil-political and socio-economic rights embrace values without which modern (or "post-modern," whatever that may mean) life would be impossible, I nevertheless believe that it is not true that all human rights are equally important and or that they all play the same role in all societies at all times. Certainly there are some rights (such as the right to life or freedom from torture or slavery) that are more important than some other rights (for example, the requirement that adult and juvenile detainees should be confined separately). Moreover, depending on concrete circumstances and levels of development, some rights may at different periods acquire special value (for example, in ethnically or religiously plural societies freedom from discrimination may be more important than other rights).

II. Culture, Societal Development, and Evolution of Civil and Political Rights

It is difficult, if not impossible, to reflect on the future of human rights without addressing first the question of whether human rights are immutable (natural rights deriving either from human nature or God) or a function of history, changing over space and time from sixth century B.C. Greece to twenty-first century United States.

In my view, the whole history of humankind seems to prove that human rights are neither immutable nor natural at all. Alan Gerwith's assertion, that "legal rights may not be morally justified, such as the past legal rights to own slaves,"[3] needs some clarification. The past legal right to own slaves is certainly morally reprehensible from the standpoint of our present-day mores. For Aristotle, however, it was quite natural that the Hellenes should be born free and that the "barbarians" who revolted against them were destined by nature to be slaves. And rebellious slaves, like Spartacus, fought for *their* freedom, not for the freedom of all.

That contemporary human rights standards do not reflect immutable values can be illustrated also by the fact that Western countries, and others as well, came to accept these values through a lengthy historical process. David Selbourne traces the

---

2   IAN CLARK, GLOBALISATION AND FRAGMENTATION: INTERNATIONAL RELATIONS IN THE TWENTIETH CENTURY 174 (1997).

3   ALAN GEWIRTH, THE COMMUNITY OF RIGHTS 10 (1996).

historical widening of claims-to-rights in liberal democratic civic orders as follows:

From claims made by seventeenth-century property owners to the concomitant political rights to which they believed themselves entitled by virtue of their ownership; to claims made by non-property-owners in the nineteenth century to a variety of civic rights which should owe nothing to wealth or position; to claims made by all citizens (and even non-citizens) in the twentieth century to rights of protection from the consequences of misfortune, including the consequences of unemployment, old age, homelessness, and sickness.[4]

In other words, the emergence and development of human rights are a consequence of the advancement of material conditions of societal life as well as of the intellectual and even emotional evolution of mankind.[5] Human rights are historically contingent. They depend on material circumstances (economic development, the social and political structures of society, etc.) as well as on the development of ideas. Also, one should not underestimate (or for that matter overestimate) the role of cultural factors in the development of human rights.

A. Culture, Religion, and Human Rights

It has been asserted that some religions—Christianity and Judaism, for example—evidence stronger human rights roots than others do—Islam, for another example. However, while international human rights standards protect freedom of religion, and while different religions or individual clergymen often have contributed to the protection of human rights, there is no religion that has been always friendly to human rights and none that has never had pernicious effect on human freedoms and dignities. The Spanish inquisition is probably the most violent example in Europe of how religion can be used for inhumane purposes. Torquemada as the Grand Inquisitor, torturer of Moors, Jews, Protestants, and other "heretics" was a fruit of Christianity.

Even in contemporary Western Europe, religion is not unambiguously supportive of human rights. For example, the 1993 Church of England decision to allow the ordination of women, quite natural from a human rights point of view, was

---

4   DAVID SELBOURNE, THE PRINCIPLE OF DUTY 57 (1994).

5   Richard Rorty believes that people who do not respect human rights are deprived not so much of truth or moral knowledge, but of "two more important things: security and sympathy." See Richard Rorty, Human Rights, Rationality, and Sentimentality, in ON HUMAN RIGHTS: OXFORD AMNESTY LECTURES 1993, at 128 (Stephen Shue & Susan L. Hurley eds., 1993). Rorty's view that security for oneself and sympathy for others go together makes sense. When life is a constant struggle for survival, the sufferings of others cease to be of interest.

adopted far from unanimously and has alienated many of the followers of that faith. As Arthur Schlesinger Jr., rightly observes:

As an historian, I confess to a certain amusement when I hear the Judeo-Christian tradition praised as the source of our concern for human rights. In fact, the great religious ages were notable for their indifference to human rights in the contemporary sense. They were notorious not only for acquiescence in poverty, inequality, exploitation and oppression but also for enthusiastic justifications of slavery, persecution, abandonment of small children, torture and genocide. Religion enshrined and vindicated hierarchy, authority and inequality.[6]

Thus, one should not be surprised by Adamantia Pollis finding that in Eastern Orthodox theology "woman is considered morally inferior" or that her "inexorable conclusion is that individual human rights cannot be derived from Orthodox theology."[7] More surprising is the notion that human rights may be derived from a particular religion. Fred Halliday is correct that "no derivation from any religion is ultimately possible."[8]

At the same time, religion, an important—often the most important—element of practically every culture, traditionally has had considerable impact on human rights, particularly in the West. While it is impossible to anchor contemporary human rights in any particular religion or culture, practically all religions and cultures contain premises upon which human rights ideas and practices can be and often are built. There are traditions in all nations, including religious traditions, that can be and are supportive of human rights ideas. I believe, indeed, that, though human rights ideas and their realization in practice originated in Western Europe, human rights are universal, at least the core ones, because they protect values that are shared by the Buddhists, Christians, Jews, Muslims, and atheists alike.[9]

---

[6]   Arthur M. Schlesinger, Jr., *The Opening of the American Mind*, N.Y. TIMES BOOK REV., July 23, 1989, at 26.

[7]   Adamantia Pollis, *Eastern Orthodoxy and Human Rights*, 15 HUM. RTS. Q. 344, 353 (1993). Will Durant's comparison of the two branches of Christianity is rather different from that of Pollis: "While Western Europe was shrouded in darkness, misery, and ignorance of the ninth and tenth centuries . . . , the Greek Church drew strength and pride from the revived wealth and power of the Byzantine state. . . . To the Greeks of this age the Germans, Franks, and Anglo-Saxons of the contemporary West seemed crude barbarians, an illiterate and violent laity led by a worldly and corrupt episcopate." WILL DURANT, 4 AGE OF FAITH: THE STORY OF CIVILIZATION 544 (1950).

[8]   FRED HALLIDAY, ISLAM AND THE MYTH OF CONFRONTATION: RELIGION AND POLITICS IN THE MIDDLE EAST 140 (1996).

[9]   The last British Governor of Hong Kong, Chris Patten, is only a bit too categorical when he writes: "Values are universal. So, too, is the case for market economics, which work every-

Often it is the format, wording or details of international human rights standards rather than their substance that sound Western. The terminology of Article 14 of the International Covenant on Civil and Political Rights,[10] for example, which contains detailed rules of fair trial, is certainly Western, having been drafted by Western lawyers. But the logic of these rules is simple and universal: to guarantee, as far as possible, that no innocent person is behind bars or, worse still, executed, and that there be no unnecessary suffering for those who may have committed crimes. Jack Donnelly correctly observes that, while human rights—inalienable entitlements of individuals held in relation to state and society—have not been a part of most cultural traditions or even the Western tradition until quite recently, there is a striking similarity in many of the basic values of most cultures that today we seek to protect through human rights, particularly when these values are expressed in relatively general terms: "Life, social order, protection from arbitrary rule, prohibition of inhuman and degrading treatment, the guarantee of a place in the life of the community, and access to an equitable share of the means of subsistence are central moral aspirations in nearly all cultures."[11] This viewpoint is substantiated by a table published in *The Independent* of London in June 1995 demonstrating the attitude of different religions (the Church of England, the Catholic Church, Judaism, Islam, Hinduism, and Buddhism) as well as today's secular consensus towards issues such as blasphemy, the nonobservance of religious events, murder, adultery, theft, lying, premarital sex, homosexual practices, divorce, masturbation, suicide, and cruelty to animals.[12] The attitudes were categorized in terms of "sin," "wrong," "harmful," "permitted," "not a sin," "not harmful," "accepted," "not mentioned." Some of the practices (for example, murder, lying, adultery, and theft) were considered as a sin, wrong, or harmful by *all* religions just as they are condemned by secular morals. Others (for example, premarital sex, homosexual practices, suicide, and blasphemy) were considered wrong by *all or most* religions. Generally the overlap in attitude between religions and between religions and today's secular consensus was considerable. It also should be noted that even if some practices are not considered wrong or sinful, especially by today's secular morals, they often are tolerated and not encouraged or considered completely normal by the majority of people in different societies. In any event, these comparisons prove that there is much more in common among different societies than cultural relativists usually assume.

---

where better than any other economic system, and free and open economies perform most effectively in plural societies. Liberal economics and liberal democracy go hand in hand. Freedom, democracy, the rule of law, stability and prosperity are found most frequently in one another's company." CHRIS PATTEN, EAST AND WEST 4 (1998).

10   *See infra* Appendix III.

11   Jack Donnelly, *Cultural Relativism and Human Rights*, 6 HUM. RTS. Q. 400, 414–15 (1984).

12   THE INDEPENDENT (London), June 8, 1995, at 15.

At the same time, one hardly can deny that there are cultural differences and different historical or religious traditions that make the implementation of at least some human rights problematic in certain countries. The equality of men and women and the freedom to choose or change one's religion are obvious examples of rights that are difficult to realize in some, particularly Muslim, societies. Nor are historical traditions always supportive of the acceptance of the basic assumption of democracy: the one person-one vote principle.[13] Therefore, it would be wrong to ignore religious or other cultural differences when speaking of human rights in a particular country. Indeed, these differences should be kept in mind by individual states and international organizations when trying to promote human rights. But culture is capable of changing, even if more slowly than the economic and political structures of society. Francis Fukuyama notes that "we see evidence of cultural change all around us. Catholicism, for example, has often been held to be hostile to both capitalism and democracy . . . , yet there has been a 'Protestantization' of Catholic culture that makes differences between Protestant and Catholic societies much less pronounced than in times past."[14] Moreover, societies themselves change. As Eric Hobsbawm observes, "in the 1980s, socialist Bulgaria and non-socialist Ecuador had more in common than either had with the Bulgaria or Ecuador of 1939."[15] A similar comment could be made about many societies. Previously human rights were an unfamiliar concept in most Asian societies, for example. Today, the peoples of Asia are taking human rights more and more seriously.

B. Individualism, Collectivism, and Human Rights

The rise of the nation state, individualism (as a philosophical doctrine), and human rights ideas are linked in their genesis. Both individualism and human rights ideas were aimed at liberating human beings from oppression by the state and church, and at getting rid of feudal hierarchies that not only kept individuals in shackles but also stifled social development as a whole. The advocates of "Asian values," less vocal than before, often have argued that as individualism is a Western concept, so are human rights also Western.

---

13 The one-man-one-vote system is not the only principle of democratic elections. In many modern plural (*i.e.*, multi-ethnic or multi-religious) societies, some combination of elements of consociational democracy may be needed (*e.g.*, governments including political elites of all the main ethnic or religious groups, mutual veto on vital minority issues, proportionality as the principal standard of political representation, high degree of autonomy for each segment to run its own affairs). These elements need not all be present. Their choice depends on concrete circumstances and is always political. However, without some form of power-sharing and some degree and form of autonomy, it is difficult to achieve integration in a plural society by democratic means.

14 FRANCIS FUKUYAMA, TRUST: THE SOCIAL VIRTUES AND THE CREATION OF PROSPERITY 41 (1995).

15 ERIC J. HOBSBAWM, AGE OF EXTREMES 9 (1994).

This is not true. Simply put, the West has not always been individualistic. Some influential Western schools of thought (Rousseau, Marx, and fascism) are in fact quite communitarian. Anthony Giddens observes that "a collectivist attitude has also long been part of Christian democratic ideology in Continental countries"[16] Currently, many Western thinkers are more concerned with societal cohesion than with individual liberties. The former U.S. Ambassador to the United Kingdom, Raymond Seitz, speaking of the U.K. and the U.S., recently wrote: "If a democracy becomes only a matter of asserting rights—merely an excuse for licence—then society can rapidly become a *melee* of self-indulgence."[17] The recent report of the Commission on Global Governance also stresses that "rights need to be joined with responsibilities" and that "the tendency to emphasise rights while forgetting responsibilities has deleterious consequences."[18] Indeed, as Nobel laureate Aung San Suu Kyi has rightly emphasized, excessive individualism may lead to the destruction of civic bonds in society. She writes: "[g]ross individualism and cut-throat morality arise when political and intellectual freedoms are curbed on the one hand while on the other fierce economic competitiveness is encouraged by making material success the measure of prestige and progress. The result is a society where cultural and human values are set aside and money value reigns supreme."[19] The comment applies to the East and the West equally. Excessive individualism can be counterproductive to human rights, and it is a threat that exists in both Eastern and Western societies. This does not mean, however, that Communitarianism is the answer. I tend to agree with Hamish McRae who concludes that "maybe the real message is that all modern industrial societies have to find a way of striking a balance between individualism and social control, and that somehow the democratic process has to maintain that balance, making the costs and benefits clear."[20]

In short, societies usually need more of that in which they are relatively lacking. If many Western societies need to emphasise the importance of individual responsibility or community, most Asian societies (though not only Asian societies, of course) must come to see individual liberties as among their main concerns.

C. Societal Development and Human Rights

More than the cultural practices that influence the perception and implementation of human rights and that sometimes is confused with the cultural or historical traditions of a given society, the level of a society's economic, social, political, and cultural development provides, in my view, a realistic explanation of different human

---

16   ANTHONY GIDDENS, THE THIRD WAY 34 (1998).

17   THE TIMES, June 3, 1995, at 8.

18   THE REPORT OF THE COMMISSION ON GLOBAL GOVERNANCE, OUR GLOBAL NEIGHBOURHOOD 56 (1995).

19   AUNG SAN SUU KYI, FREEDOM FROM FEAR 24 (1995).

20   HAMISH MCRAE, THE WORLD IN 2000: POWER, CULTURE AND PROSPERITY: A VISION OF THE FUTURE 204 (1994).

rights situations around the world. How people are executed (electrocuted, hanged, stoned, guillotined) or tortured typically depends on the specific culture. Whether people are executed or tortured at all depends more on the stage or level of societal development.

However, there are no direct or inevitable dependencies between the economic development of society and civil and political rights. Sometimes rapid economic growth has gone hand-in-hand with political repression (*e.g.*, Chile, South Korea). On the other hand, the evidence does suggest that economic well-being is, at the end of the day, conducive to the expansion of civil liberties and democracy. Chile and South Korea would appear to be illustrations of this point. Chris Patten, the last British Governor of Hong Kong, explains developments in Hong Kong:

> To be fair, until the 1970s there was no great pressure for change; people were too occupied by making their way in the world, earning a living, getting a roof over their heads, putting their children into school, finding the security that stormy times had so far denied them, to worry too much about democracy. Proconsuls ordained; officials administered; buildings rose; trade flourished; bank accounts burgeoned.[21]

However, things began gradually to change:

> By the late 1970s education, prosperity and travel had produced the same effects in Hong Kong as elsewhere. Those young men and women brought up in Hong Kong, and increasingly born there too, who at universities at home, or in Britain, Canada and the United States, had been encouraged to read Locke, Hume, Paine, Mill and Popper, those who had been examined in the histories of Britain's and America's struggles for freedom, could hardly be expected that in Britain's last colonial redoubt the full panoply of civil liberties they had been taught to cherish should be denied them.[22]

Of course, democracy and human rights do not follow automatically from economic prosperity. Human rights always have emerged and developed in the struggle for them. Yet, education, economic prosperity, and the institutional development of society—themselves all interrelated—make the soil fertile for democracy and human rights.

As human rights are not immutable, they should not be seen in terms of "being" but, rather, in terms of "becoming." This means that, to a great extent, the future of civil and political rights will depend on the character of the changes that are taking place in individual societies and in the world as a whole.

---

[21] PATTEN, *supra* note 9, at 25.

[22] *Id.* at 26.

III. Commonalities Influencing the Future of Civil and Political Rights

A. The End of the Cold War

There is no doubt that the demise of communism and the collapse of the Soviet Empire have had an impact on human rights discourse in the world. This impact, however, has been more noticeable and direct in the countries that belonged to the former East bloc than in other parts of the world. Also, it is possible to exaggerate the importance of these historical watersheds insofar as human rights are concerned. Taking the long view, the "real socialism" (communism) may prove to be but a blip in the history of humankind—and, if so, its demise is not likely to have many long-term effects on the future of civil and political rights.

More influential, I believe, has been the end of the East-West confrontation; the end of the Cold War has helped clear the way for the development of processes that previously were suppressed by the overwhelming East-West political and ideological struggle. Some of these developments have had a negative effect on civil and political rights. Others have facilitated their promotion and protection. The upsurge of nationalism and spread of inter-ethnic conflict is at least partly due to the end of the discipline that was imposed by the East-West conflict. The rapid spread of the market economy and democratization, however, generally has had a positive impact on civil and political rights.

Still, the collapse of Soviet communism has had some concrete influences. For instance, the *raison d'être* of the exaggerated divide between civil and political rights, on the one hand, and economic and social rights, on the other, seems to be diminishing. Serious attention to social and economic rights cannot justify neglect or violation of civil and political rights, and it would be completely inapposite and out of date to assert or insist as much today. The two categories of rights must be seen as fundamentally interdependent.

The Soviet Union was the chief proponent of so-called socialist doctrine of human rights, which, though not exactly fitting present-day concepts of cultural relativism, was a relativist approach to human rights that undermined their breadth and universality, a kind of ideological relativism. The collapse of the Soviet Union has revealed that this relativistic doctrine was used to justify political repression, paralleling some claims to so-called Asian values. The "socialist doctrine of human rights," which in reality was not about human rights at all but, rather, a tool in the ideological struggle between capitalism and communism, accused Western human rights doctrines and practices of being "formal," not backed up by material conditions that would allow equal access to the enjoyment of civil and political rights. This denigrating attack was not generated by any concern for human rights. Rather, it was to justify the absence of these "formal bourgeois rights" in communist societies where legislative confirmation of them would have given individuals an opportunity to demand them.

Now, however, that the East-West confrontation over human rights is a thing of the past, we are at liberty to recognize that sometimes and for some people some civil and political rights, even in advanced democracies, may be in a sense formal. The full enjoyment of at least certain civil and political rights often is dependent on material conditions that are far from equal, with some people having the "right" to sleep under a bridge and others to sleep in a Hilton. Existing poverty in some highly developed countries or poor education standards in many inner-city areas are among the conditions that make the enjoyment of some civil and political rights for many people impossible, and thus, there still is some room for improvement in civil and political rights even in rich democratic countries in the sense of making the enjoyment of these rights real to everyone.

Likewise, in so-called transitional societies (*e.g.*, some ex-communist states, the countries of Latin America and Asia) there often is a hiatus between declared rights and their real meaning for every individual. Corruption, the criminalization of society, and increasing gaps between the rich and poor mean that, though the rights may be declared in the constitution and though a part of the population may even enjoy some of them in fact, the majority of the citizens do not have the means to benefit from these rights. Anthony Giddens, who defines equality as inclusion and inequality as exclusion, believes that inclusion "refers in its broadest sense to citizenship, to the civil and political rights and obligations that all members of a society should have, *not just formally, but as reality of their lives.*"[23]

Generally speaking, the collapse of the Soviet Union and the end of the Cold War has helped separate some wheat from the chaff in the human rights field. Although human rights will remain in many cases a sensitive political issue, they must and can be "de-ideologized" both at the international level (as an issue of the East-West or North-South ideological struggle) and domestically (as an issue in the struggle between Left and Right[24]).

B. The State, Market Economy, and Human Rights

Democracy and human rights are closely related to the state. Democracy, be it in ancient Greece and Rome or in the contemporary Western liberal democracies, always has been confined to a particular society, be it the city-state or nation-state. To a great extent, human rights emerged as a counterweight to the omnipresence of the nation-state; in a sense, human rights and the state are like Siamese twins whose individual existence is not complete without the other. One says "human rights" and one implies "the state" in its capacity either as a human rights violator or as an entity charged to promote and protect human rights.

The rise of civil and political rights is linked not only to the emergence of the nation-state but also to the development of the capitalist market economy. David Held writes:

---

[23] GIDDENS, *supra* note 16, at 103.

[24] *See* ANTHONY GIDDENS, BEYOND LEFT AND RIGHT: THE FUTURE OF RADICAL POLITICS (1994).

[T]he emerging economic classes often became the reforming classes of the eighteenth and nineteenth centuries, seeking to conjoin the struggle for representative government. The chief connecting mechanism was the attempt to establish civil and political rights. For what was at issue in the establishment of these rights was the attempt to uphold "freedom of choice" in areas as diverse as personal, family, business and political affairs.[25]

A market economy requires agents who are free to buy and sell; economic freedom presupposes at least a degree of personal freedom. Slaves or peasants bonded to the land owned by landlords could not be effective agents of a market economy; at least a degree of basic civil rights was essential to a competitive capitalist market. The new rights allowed each person who enjoyed them the power to engage as an independent agent in economic competition; they created individuals who were "free and equal in status," a status that was the foundation of modern contract.[26]

Political rights, even more than civil rights, are anchored to the state. "Citizenship rights embody a conception of empowerment that is strictly limited to the framework of the nation-state."[27] But there are developments that are putting considerable strain on the bonds between the state and market economy, on the one hand, and democracy and human rights, on the other.

C. Globalization, the State, Democracy, and Human Rights

The nation-state and national market economy being the cradle of human rights and democracy are both in the process of radical change. The world market is not any more a sum-total of national markets; it is becoming more and more a real common market. The state has lost not only its ability to control world financial markets but also its ability to protect its own population from the negative effects of fluctuations in the world market.

However, the process of globalization has changed not only economic and financial realities. At least to an extent, it has affected the ability of the state to control and be responsible for human rights and democracy as well, and, like the process of globalization itself, this loss of control has both positive and negative aspects. Worldwide information flows are opening up more and more societies to each other, and the fact that it has become more difficult for leaders of some countries to mistreat their nationals surely is a positive development. At the same time, governments often are powerless *vis-à-vis* the negative effects of globalization, which typically have greater impact on economic and social rights than on civil and political rights. The unfettered global market tends to drag down the protection of

---

25 HELD, *supra* note 1, at 67.

26 *Id.*

27 *Id.* at 223.

economic and social rights to the level of the lowest common denominator (*e.g.* cheap labor and longer working hours in many Asian societies certainly are affecting employment and social protection in the OECD countries). But civil and especially political rights are not unaffected. First, the inability of democratically elected governments to protect their constituencies from negative global effects (*e.g.* from the crash of financial markets in the Far East or Russia or from cheap child labor in some Asian countries) means that democracy has become less effective and political rights less important. Second, in the longer perspective, if no purposeful efforts are made to stop the negative effects, some civil rights will likely exist at the level of the lowest common denominator in their definition and protection.

Globalization, limiting the effectiveness of governments, including democratically elected governments, thus raises the issue of the relationship between democracy and human rights, between democracy and liberalism. Can one exist without the other? Fareed Zakaria observes that "half of the 'democratizing' countries in the world today are illiberal democracies."[28] I would add that elections in these countries could be called only semi-democratic at best. Without freedom of the press and without an absence of discrimination based on race, ethnicity, gender, religion, or political opinion, there cannot be genuine democracy.

But can there be civil liberties and civil rights without democracy? Writing in 1997, Zakaria observes that "Indonesia, Singapore and Malaysia are examples of liberalizing autocracies, while South Korea [prior to Kim Dae Jung], Taiwan, and Tailand are liberal semi-democracies."[29] Also Hong Kong, although more an aberration than a norm, seems to have shown, when it was a British colony, that there can be at least a modicum of human rights and liberties without democracy, having enjoyed human rights because Great Britain was a liberal democracy that had extended its international human rights obligations to all its dependent territories; and had it not been returned to China, Hong Kong would have become, in my view, democratic as well as liberal. Its prosperous people, enjoying most civil and political rights, would not long have tolerated that they enjoyed their rights and liberties at the sufferance of another. Sooner or later, they would have decided to govern themselves and through representatives elected by them. There is, I believe, a necessary link between democracy and human rights. Recent developments in Indonesia and Malaysia show how "liberalizing democracies," trying to cope with economic and political crises, withdraw civil liberties whenever their political elites perceive a threat to their power. "Granted rights" are not real rights. Human rights cannot thrive in the absence of democracy.

James Dale Davidson and Lord William Rees-Mogg welcome globalization without qualification;[30] indeed, they seem especially to welcome those aspects of

---

28   Fareed Zakaria, *The Rise of Illiberal Democracy*, FOREIGN AFF. 24 (Nov./Dec. 1997).

29   *Id.* at 27.

30   JAMES DALE DAVIDSON & WILLIAM REES-MOGG, THE SOVEREIGN INDIVIDUAL (1997).

it that I believe constitute its most negative effects. In the world they see emerging, they welcome the fact that there will be no citizens, only customers.[31] Among these customers will be a small minority of "sovereign individuals" and other "rational individuals" who will flee jurisdictions that try to tax them.[32] The nation-state— "the main parasite and predator upon the individual at the end of the twentieth century"[33]—will become feeble. The United Nations will be liquidated sometime soon after the turn of the millennium,[34] and it will be a "winners take all world" where most people are losers and only "sovereign individuals" will be winners. "[D]emocracy as it has been known in the nineteenth and twentieth centuries is destined to disappear."[35]

True, much of this reads as social science fiction. Also, as in many a "sci-fi" novel, Davidson and Rees-Mogg grasp well some of the world's potentially dangerous tendencies. But the point is that these authors not only do not see any ethical or moral problems in welcoming their predicted paradise for "sovereign individuals" (obviously hell for the rest), they do not think of the possible responses of those of us who are not lucky (clever, talented, ruthless, unscrupulous) enough to belong to the chosen. Domestically, the unfettered market's opposite has been state socialism and communism; the welfare state in the West and totalitarian communism in the East were two solutions (outcomes) to unregulated eighteenth and nineteenth century capitalism, although the welfare state and its associated economic and social rights was a response also of capitalism to the specter of communism haunting Europe.[36] What may be the responses to the negative effects of untamed global market?

The negative consequences of globalization can be avoided or their effect mitigated, I believe, only through purposeful international efforts on the part of governments. As the state becomes less omnipresent and omnipotent, it is not Orwell's 1984[37] that, at least for the Western world, is the most realistic and immediate danger; as recently we have seen in many parts of the world, the failure or total collapse of states, not their strength and stability, has been the main cause of massive human suffering. The clear and present danger is, rather, that the unfettered global market, without any democratic control, may become a "big brother" whose inter-

---

31   *Id.* at 320.

32   *Id.* at 229.

33   *Id.* at 273.

34   *Id.* at 252.

35   *Id.* at 331.

36   The British welfare state, writes Giddens, was "created partly to dispel the socialist menace." GIDDENS, *supra* note 16, at 111. This does not mean, however, that the traditional welfare state as it is known in Europe is a proper answer to new challenges. In many cases, the welfare state has turned into what is sometimes called a "nanny state" in need of substantial reforms.

37   *See* GEORGE ORWELL, NINETEEN EIGHTY-FOUR (1949).

ference with individual liberties, though more anonymous and less direct than that of the state, may prove equally or more nefarious. It may be that, in some societies at least, freedom from the negative effects of globalization could become more important than traditional civil and political rights (freedom of movement, fair trial, personal security, etc.). Accordingly, purposeful, mitigating efforts of some international kind are needed from governments without delay.

From my point of view, the most important task of the state (or at least the "post-modern" state) is the management of global issues such as the globalized economy, the prevention of environmental degradation, the maintenance of national and international security, and the promotion of democracy and human rights. It is sometimes said that states are too big for small things and too small for big things. However, if there exist entities ready to take over some of the smaller things, there is nothing yet available to resolve the big things. To manage these issues successfully, states must pool their resources and power, not surrender them. The world needs strong and stable states working together to respond to human needs. States must simultaneously take advantage of processes of globalization and try to minimize, as far as possible, their negative effects. In so doing, the state must cooperate with sub-national and with inter- or supra-national entities, often the main hub of this cooperation. As Giddens observes:

> The state must respond structurally to globalization. The democratising of democracy first of all implies decentralisation—but not as a one-way process. Globalization creates a strong impetus and logic to the downward devolution of power, but also upward devolution. Rather than merely weakening the authority of the nation-state, this double movement—a movement of double democratisation—is the condition of reasserting that authority, since this movement can make the state more responsive to the influences that otherwise outflank it all around.[38]

In any event, without strong, stable, and cooperating states, there will be no human rights either.

Currently there is much discourse about "the third way" between unfettered capitalism and state interventionism. Actually, most liberal democracies already have developed a kind of third way over the years as a result of their vacillation between the Scylla of unbridled markets and deregulation and the Charybdis of state interference and nationalization. Whether it will be possible to steer a more sensible course instead of having things result principally from left-to-right and right-to-left vacillations is not clear. The nature of politics in liberal democracies, or the nature of politics in general, makes the implementation of any of such third ways problematic. Both the right and the left naturally attack the idea of a third way. In this era of globalization, however, such a course will require international cooper-

---

[38] GIDDENS, *supra* note 16, at 72.

ation and, as an aspect of it, equal attention to civil-political and socio-economic rights worldwide.

Indeed, when it comes to international co-operation on human rights, more important than ever before, the forms and methods of this cooperation must change. International human rights discourse is moving from a predominantly standard-setting phase to one that is concerned predominantly with implementation. In this context, it is important to tailor responses to specific problems, situations, and countries. All of which means that international efforts must be principled and differentiated at the same time. There is no universal remedy available for all human rights violations. What may work in El Salvador or Haiti may be completely inappropriate in Iraq or Saudi Arabia.

But does not a differentiated approach to violations mean that inevitably there will be double standards? Probably the threat of double standards is serious, but it seems that there are two categories of double standards. One category is dictated, first of all, by objective differences. For example, one can stop violations of human rights in Haiti through military intervention sanctioned by the Security Council, but a similar operation in Afghanistan would be a disaster. Equally, the world community as a whole or states separately are not able to prevent or stop all violations, and this makes for hard choices. If the world community has done little in respect of one particular humanitarian crisis, this does not mean that, for the sake of consistency, it should refrain from intervening in other instances. However, when responses to human rights violations are different because some dictators are friends or clients while others are deemed pariahs, we enter another domain of double standards, unacceptable double standards. Such double standards are serious indeed, as they erode confidence in the impartiality and therefore the credibility of human rights enforcement.

For the international community represented by the United Nations and its sister organizations, it is necessary to concentrate on the eradication of gross and massive violations of human rights mainly in pre-modern and modern states.[39] This means dealing with the root causes of such violations and the creation of conditions for the implementation of civil and political rights. The response of the international community to different human rights situations and violations must be calibrated according to the requirements of concrete situations. Some human rights violations may be for treaty-bodies; others should concern the Security Council; and still other situations may require the attention of the IMF or World Bank.

D. Fragmentation and Human Rights

The process of globalization finds its nemesis in the process of fragmentation that also is taking place in various parts of the world. Like globalization, fragmentation has both positive and negative aspects, and its impact on civil and political rights may differ from society to society. Nationalist sentiments are becoming stronger in

---

[39]   *See infra* § IV.

many ethnically plural societies, and in the 1990s this led to the emergence of several new states. In some cases, new states that have emerged in the place of communist dictatorships are on the way to becoming stable liberal democracies and have achieved satisfactory progress on civil and political rights. Processes of devolution of autonomy, territorial and otherwise, are sometimes solutions that help to mitigate inter-ethnic tension and protect human rights. Often, however, the reverse is true. Ethnic minorities prefer to interpret the right to self-determination as supporting their claims to independence (a right to fragmentation) rather than the right of everyone to political participation. Moreover, once becoming majorities in new states, former minorities often are not liberal at all. The civil and political rights (*e.g.*, freedom of expression, liberty, and security of person) of the whole population are not guaranteed in some of the new states (*e.g.*, Croatia, Belarus, Serbia, Slovakia, the central Asian republics of the former Soviet Union).

There is a strange relationship between nationalism and democracy. As discussed above, democracy developed together with and within the nation-state, and nationalism played a significant role in the development of both. However, nationalism, especially in its extreme forms, can also threaten or erode democracy. Nowadays, especially in ethnically plural societies, "national democracy" sounds a bit like slave-owners' democracy or national socialism. The exclusions in democracy that were quite normal in ancient Greece and Rome or even in the eighteenth century United States are not acceptable in the twenty-first century. Contemporary notions of democracy assume equal inclusion in the political participation of the whole population without exception. The former High Representative in Bosnia, Carl Bildt, writes, that challenges stemming from inter-ethnic (religious) conflicts "cannot be met by setting up new national states, which tend sooner or later towards the destructive, illiberal and inhumane ideal of ethnic purity. In the longer term, the only way forward is to extend to the Balkans the frameworks and institutions of European integration."[40] It is certain that processes of fragmentation have and will continue to have significant impact on civil and political rights.

IV. The Diversity of the World and the Future of Civil and Political Rights

States, like the societies they represent, are unequal. The principle of sovereign equality mitigates only some of the effects of this factual inequality. Robert Cooper distinguishes three categories of states existing side by side in the contemporary world: pre-modern, modern, and post-modern.[41] Prominent examples of pre- modern states would be Afghanistan, Liberia, and Somalia, but many others are struggling in this post- imperial chaos also. Most states still belong to the modern world with its balance of power politics, its noninterference principle, and other traditional attributes of sovereignty. The post-modern world, to which the Western European states belong,

---

40   Carl Bildt, *Holbrook's History*, 40 Survival 190 (1998) (review essay).
41   Robert Cooper, The Post-Modern State and the World Order (1996).

is characterized by a breakdown in distinctions between domestic and foreign affairs; by mutual interference in (traditional) domestic affairs; by the rejection not only of the use force but of the very idea of the use of force to resolve disputes among themselves; by the growing irrelevance of borders; by security based on transparency, openness, and interdependence. In the "post-modern" space, to which many Central and Eastern European states aspire, human rights problems are quite different from those found in modern or pre-modern states. As was stressed earlier, an important way of advancing civil and political rights in post-modern societies as well as in many modern societies is not so much to create new rights or even deepen the interpretation of existing rights but to create the conditions that are conducive to the *de facto* enjoyment of declared rights by all citizens and noncitizens alike. It is not sufficient for governments simply to abstain from interference in the civil rights and liberties of individuals. Approaching civil and political rights as "negative" rights does not guarantee their full and equal enjoyment by all individuals. The poor, the illiterate, and the unemployed are not able to enjoy civil and political rights to the same extent as their rich and well-educated fellow citizens. Once again, there is a mutual interdependence between civil-political and socio-economic rights.

Other human rights issues that may become topical in advanced "post-modern" states (liberal democracies) are the further extension of rights to immigrants, special attention to the delicate problems of ethnic and religious minorities, as well as concern for human rights in other parts of the world. Processes of economic globalization have exacerbated the problem of immigration inasmuch as free capital movement and restrictions on the movement of labor do not fit well together. As Saskia Sassen writes, "current immigration policy in the highly developed countries is increasingly at odds with other major policy frameworks in the international system. There is a combination of drives to create border-free economic spaces yet intensify border control to keep immigrants and refugees out."[42] The European Union's experience, where nationals of one EU country enjoy practically the same range of rights in all the other EU countries, may show the way for other post-modernizing states. Giddens believes that "the citizenship laws need to be changed and major cultural shifts made."[43]

In "modern" states (Brazil, Argentina, Malaysia, South Korea, etc.), where material conditions for civil and political rights usually are significantly evolved, the development of human rights cultures and democratic traditions will be the most important tasks. In some of these societies, human rights must compete with religious and historical traditions hostile to human rights culture. There are countries, especially in the Middle East, which, while being rich in monetary terms, are socially and politically backward (rich underdeveloped societies). The exhaustion of their oil resources may quite possibly be accompanied by a social implosion that could negatively affect human rights not only in these countries.

---

42   SASKIA SASSEN, LOSING CONTROL: SOVEREIGNTY IN AN AGE OF GLOBALISATION 85 (1996).
43   GIDDENS, *supra* note 16, at 137.

In "pre-modern" states, the main task should be the creation of elementary conditions for the introduction of basic civil and political rights. In some cases, this will mean trying to end civil wars and inter-ethnic conflicts. Without the eradication of extreme forms of poverty, the elevation of education standards, and the resolution of the most acute health problems, it will be impossible to speak of real civil and political rights. At the same time, it would be wrong to justify all the violations of human rights by reference to poverty. The corruption of local political elites and repressions are also responsible.

V. Conclusions

The struggle for fuller implementation of civil and political rights will continue in the twenty-first century, and economic globalization and information flows will globalize human rights discourse. However, globalization will sometimes undermine the capacity of states to promote and protect human rights. Fragmentation, being a reaction to globalization at least in part, means that people will try to find some familiar anchors in a world full of unfamiliar influences, frantically searching for identity within smaller—usually ethnic or religious—communities. The extreme nationalism and religious extremism that often accompany such searches are both inimical to civil and political rights.

The enjoyment of civil and political rights will differ from society to society and from region to region. For some societies, progress probably will be marked by a fuller and more equal enjoyment of civil and political rights that already are well-entrenched in society and, as well, their re-interpretation or possible expansion to new areas in the light of the evolution of society. For other societies, the main task will be the creation and development of institutions such as independent and impartial judiciaries as well as strong civil society organizations. There also are societies that must create, usually with the assistance of the outside world, basic material conditions for the introduction of civil and political rights. Without the eradication of extreme poverty, illiteracy, and dangerous disease, there can be no real enjoyment of civil and political rights.

It is not unreasonable to believe that there will be general progress in the enjoyment of civil and political right in the twenty-first century. However, such progress is not inevitable. Indeed, without purposeful efforts to promote and protect civil and political rights and to face new challenges to the enjoyments of human rights, it is chaos that is inevitable. And there are no human rights in chaos. Richard Falk is right, I believe, that "neither optimism, nor pessimism about the future can be convincingly validated, and neither seems appropriate, as compared to acting on the basis of bounded conviction and personal engagement in political struggle to overcome concrete circumstances of cruelty and deprivation."[44] This means, of course, that the future of civil and political rights depends on, more than anything else, our commitment to them.

---

[44]   RICHARD A. FALK, ON HUMANE GOVERNANCE: TOWARD A NEW GLOBAL POLITICS 43 (1995).

Strengthening the Norms of International Humanitarian Law to Combat Impunity*

M. Cherif Bassiouni

I. Introduction

The year 1998 marked the fiftieth anniversary of the Universal Declaration of Human Rights[1] and the Convention on the Prevention and Punishment of the Crime of Genocide,[2] respectively adopted on the tenth and ninth of December 1948. The year 1998 marked also the birthdate of the Treaty on the Establishment of an International Criminal Court adopted in Rome on July 17, 1998. On this occasion, it is important to take stock of international law's progress, to assess how much its veneer has thickened, and to determine what needs to be done to make more effective its goals of prevention and control. Since most of the world's victimization occurs in violation of international law's proscriptions against war crimes, crimes against humanity, and genocide, this article will deal with the weaknesses of the normative framework of these three *jus cogens* crimes. My purpose is to eliminate, or at least substantially narrow, the legal loopholes through which the perpetrators of war crimes, crimes against humanity, and genocide are able, with impunity, to escape accountability for their international crimes and widespread violations of fundamental human rights.

International humanitarian law is that body of norms that protects certain categories of persons and property and prohibits attacks against them during the course of armed conflicts be they of an international or noninternational character.[3] These norms derive from conventional and customary international law which are respec-

<hr>

* An earlier version of this essay was published under the title *The Normative Framework of International Humanitarian Law: Overlaps, Gaps and Ambiguities* in 8 TRANSNAT'L L. & CONTEMP. PROBS. 199 (1998). Reprint permission granted.

1   *See infra* Appendix I [hereinafter UDHR].

2   Dec. 9, 1948, 78 U.N.T.S. 277 (entered into force Jan. 12, 1951) (entered into force with respect to the United States Nov. 25, 1989) [hereinafter Genocide Convention], *reprinted in* 28 I.L.M. 763 (1989), *and* 3 INTERNATIONAL LAW AND WORLD ORDER: BASIC DOCUMENTS III.J.1 (Burns H. Weston ed., 5 vols., 1994–) [hereinafter 3 Weston].

3   *See generally* THE LAW OF WAR: A DOCUMENTARY HISTORY (Leon Friedman ed., 2 vols., 1972); THE LAWS OF ARMED CONFLICTS: A COLLECTION OF CONVENTIONS, RESOLUTIONS AND OTHER DOCUMENTS (Dietrich Schindler & Jiří Toman eds., 1988); HOWARD S. LEVIE, TERRORISM IN WAR: THE LAW OF WAR CRIMES (1993); and HOWARD S. LEVIE, THE CODE OF INTERNATIONAL ARMED CONFLICT (2 vols., 1986).

tively referred to as "the Law of Geneva" (for the conventional law of armed conflicts) and "the Law of The Hague" (for the customary law of armed conflicts). "The Law of The Hague" is not, however, exclusively customary law because it is in part treaty law and the "the Law of Geneva" is also not exclusively treaty law because it includes customary law. Thus, the traditional distinction between conventional and customary law is substantially eroded. Additionally, the treaty law that applies to weapons derives from customary as well as conventional law, and some of its specific norms have become part of customary law. In sum, in the last one hundred years, the evolution of the dual sources of international humanitarian law, namely conventional and customary law, have become so intertwined and so overlapping that they can be said to be two sides of the same coin. The nomenclature "the Law of Geneva" and "the Law of The Hague" is therefore only a useful shorthand label.

In addition to this historic dual-track evolution of the law of armed conflicts, two additional developments have expanded the general scope of the term "international humanitarian law," namely, the proscriptions against crimes against humanity[4] and genocide.[5] The first originated as an outgrowth of war crimes even though it subsequently evolved into a distinct category of international crimes; the second, though originally intended to encompass crimes against humanity, also evolved into a distinct and separate category of international crimes. The norms contained in these three major international crimes—war crimes, crimes against humanity, and genocide—have become part of *jus cogens*.[6] Deriving from multiple legal sources,

---

[4]   *See generally* M. Cherif Bassiouni, Crimes Against Humanity in International Criminal Law (1992) (2d rev. ed., 1998) [hereinafter Bassiouni, Crimes Against Humanity].

[5]   *See, e.g.*, Pieter N. Drost, The Crime of State (2 vols., 1959); Matthew Lippman, *The Drafting of the 1948 Convention on the Prevention and Punishment of the Crime of Genocide*, 3 B.U. Int'l L.J. 1 (1984); and Matthew Lippman, *The Convention on the Prevention and Punishment of the Crime of Genocide, in* 1 International Criminal Law (M. Cherif Bassiouni ed., 2d ed., 1998).

[6]   *See* M. Cherif Bassiouni, *International Crimes: Jus Cogens and Obligatio Erga Omnes*, 59 Law & Contemp. Probs. 63 (1996). The *Tadić* majority opinion dealt with several aspects of international humanitarian law in an overlapping manner when it held:

The second aspect, determining which individuals of the targeted population qualify as civilians for purposes of crimes against humanity, is not, however, quite as clear. Common Article 3, the language of which reflects "elementary considerations of humanity" which are "applicable under customary international law to any armed conflict," provides that in an armed conflict "not of an international character" Contracting States are obliged "as a minimum" to comply with the following: "Persons taking no active part in the hostilities, including members of armed forces who have laid down their arms and those placed *hors de combat* by sickness, wounds, detention, or any other cause, shall in all circumstances be treated humanely. . . ." Protocol Additional to the Geneva Conventions of 12 August 1949, and Relating to the Protection of Victims in International Armed Conflicts

they overlap relative to their context, content, purpose, scope, application, perpetrators, and protected interests.[7]

These norms also contain certain ambiguities and gaps, the existence of which is due essentially to two factors. The first is the haphazard evolution of international criminal law.[8] The second is that governments, which control the international legislative processes, are not, for a variety of reasons, though mostly for political reasons, desirous of eliminating the overlaps, closing the gaps, and removing the

---

(Protocol I) defines civilians by the exclusion of prisoners of war and armed forces, considering a person a civilian in case of doubt. However, this definition of civilians contained in Common Article 3 is not immediately applicable to crimes against humanity because it is a part of the laws or customs of war and can only be applied by analogy. The same applies to the definition contained in Protocol I and the *Commentary*, Geneva Convention IV, on the treatment of civilians, both of which advocate a broad interpretation of the term "civilian." They, and particularly Common Article 3, do, however, provide guidance in answering the most difficult question: specifically, whether acts taken against an individual who cannot be considered a traditional "non-combatant" because he is actively involved in the conduct of hostilities by membership in some form of resistance group can nevertheless constitute crimes against humanity if they are committed in the furtherance or as part of an attack directed against a civilian population.
Prosecutor v. Duško Tadič, May 7, 1997 (IT–94–I–T), *reprinted in* 36 I.L.M. 908, 939–40 (1997) (citations and footnotes omitted). It is unclear, in the understanding of the majority, what are the legal boundaries between the customary law of armed conflicts applicable to conflicts of a non-international character and, respectively, Common Article 3 of the 1949 Geneva Conventions. *See infra* Annex, at 283. *See also* Protocol II, *infra* note 86, *reprinted in* 2 INTERNATIONAL LAW AND WORLD ORDER: BASIC DOCUMENTS II.B.11 (Burns H. Weston ed., 5 vols., 1994–) [hereinafter 2 Weston]. *See also* Theodor Meron, *International Criminalization of Internal Atrocities*, 89 AM. J. INT'L L. 554 (1995).

[7] For example, the International Criminal Tribunal for the Former Yugoslavia, in the *Tadič* majority opinion, erroneously applied the standards of "state responsibility" reflected in the I.C.J.'s *Nicaragua v. U.S.* to determine whether a conflict is of an international or noninternational character. *See* Military and Paramilitary Activities (Nicar. v. U.S.), 1986 I.C.J. 14, 331–47 (June 27). The majority also did not contribute to clarity when it concluded, very broadly, that:

International humanitarian law applies from the initiation of such armed conflicts and extends beyond the cessation of hostilities until a general conclusion of peace is reached; or, in the case of internal conflicts, a peaceful settlement is achieved. Until that moment, international humanitarian law continues in the whole territory of the warring States or, in the case of internal conflicts, the whole territory under the control of a party, whether or not actual combat takes place there.

Tadič, *supra* note 6. *See also* Theodor Meron, *Classification of Armed Conflict in the Former Yugoslavia: Nicaragua's Fallout*, 92 AM. J. INT'L L. 236 (1998).

[8] *See* M. CHERIF BASSIOUNI, INTERNATIONAL CRIMINAL LAW CONVENTIONS AND THEIR PENAL PROVISIONS 21–31 (1997) [hereinafter BASSIOUNI, ICL CONVENTIONS].

ambiguities[9]; not a surprising fact given that two of the three categories of crimes, crimes against humanity and genocide, occur with deliberate state action or policy, and that governments are not particularly inclined to criminalize the conduct of their high officials.[10] War crimes can also be a product of state action or policy, but frequently are committed by individual combatants acting on their own, which probably explains why there is less reluctance to criminalize this type of individual criminal conduct.[11]

Crimes against humanity and genocide are essentially crimes of state, as are sometimes war crimes, because they need the substantial involvement of state organs, including the army, police, paramilitary groups, and the state's bureaucracy.[12] These crimes generate significant victimization and must be strenuously deterred. Nevertheless, governments are reluctant to remove the ambiguities in the relevant normative provisions applicable to crimes against humanity and genocide, and to fill the existing gaps in these proscriptions.[13] The individual criminal responsibility of soldiers and others in the lower echelons of state power is much more

---

[9]   This is evidenced by the position of different governments in the Preparatory Committee on the Establishment of an International Criminal Court. *See Report of the Preparatory Committee on the Establishment of an International Criminal Court*, U.N. Doc. A/CONF.183/2/Add.1 (1998) [hereinafter *Report of the PrepCom*].

[10]   One reason will be the fact that international crimes involving state action or policy potentially reach all the way to the top of the military and civilian hierarchy. *See* M. Cherif Bassiouni, *From Versailles to Rwanda in Seventy-Five Years: The Need to Establish a Permanent International Criminal Court*, 10 HARV. HUM. RTS. J. 11 (1997) [hereinafter Bassiouni, *From Versailles to Rwanda*] (describing the history of international criminal investigatory bodies and international criminal tribunals). With respect to the limits of command responsibility, see INTERNATIONAL CRIMINAL LAW, *supra* note 5, at 21–74.

[11]   The regulation of armed conflicts benefits from the fact that regular armies are usually well-disciplined and have a tight command structure that controls discipline and the observance of the laws of armed conflicts. Furthermore, regular armies have a shared interest in the observance of the laws of armed conflicts because violations by one side to a conflict can result in actions by the other side, even though reprisals are limited. *See* FRITS KALSHOVEN, BELLIGERENT REPRISALS (1971). Conversely, however, when genocide or crimes against humanity occur, the same constraints that exist in armies arising out of the considerations stated above, are not usually present in the course of genocide and crimes against humanity.

[12]   Genocide and crimes against humanity, as discussed below, are, however, also applicable to non-state actors. The problem of non-state actors, acting by themselves or in concert with state actors, nevertheless remains, as the definitions of genocide and crimes against humanity do not specifically contemplate non-state actors, particularly when there is no concert of action with state actors. By implication, however, it should be clear that genocide and crimes against humanity apply to non-state actors as well.

[13]   The most recent example of such governmental reluctance to remove ambiguities and fill gaps is that of the ICC Diplomatic Conference in Rome, June 15–July 17, 1998, whose statute has not removed the overlaps, gaps, and ambiguities with respect to genocide, crimes against humanity, and war crimes. *See Rome Statute of the International Criminal Court*, U.N. Doc. A/Conf.183/9 (1998), arts. 6–8 [hereinafter ICC Statute], *reprinted in* 1

easily accepted by governments than that of political leaders and senior government officials and, as well, those in the governmental bureaucracy who carry out, execute, and facilitate the policies and practices of crimes against humanity, genocide, and even war crimes. Indeed, the articulation of relevant international norms effectively shields them from criminal responsibility; existing international norms of criminal responsibility relative to crimes against humanity, crimes of genocide, and even war crimes, are too ambiguous to reach effectively into this category of violators. This renders their prosecution virtually impossible.

Since World War II, there have been an estimated 250 conflicts of an international, noninternational, and purely internal legal character. The estimates of the resulting casualties reach as high as 170 million.[14] Most of that victimization occurred at the hands of tyrannical regimes and by non-state actors during internal conflicts. This tragic new dimension in world victimization requires a reexamination of international humanitarian law to make it unambiguously applicable to non-state actors, and to reconcile their overlapping application, fill in their gaps, and clarify their ambiguities so as to render their enforcement sufficiently effective to prevent, deter, and punish the perpetrators of such crimes. This article discusses these questions.

II. Crimes Against Humanity

Crimes against humanity originated after World War I[15] in the concept of "crimes against the laws of humanity," a term found in the Preamble to the 1907 Hague Convention.[16]

INTERNATIONAL LAW AND WORLD ORDER: BASIC DOCUMENTS I.H.13 (Burns H. Weston ed., 5 vols 1994–) [hereinafter 1 Weston].

14   This estimate is, by some accounts, for all conflicts since World War I and, by others, for all victimization since World War II. *See* Jennifer L. Balint, *An Empirical Study of Conflict, Conflict Victimization and Legal Redress*, 14 NOUVELLES ÉTUDES PÉNALES 101 (Christopher C. Joyner, special ed. & M. Cherif Bassiouni, general ed., 1998); M. Cherif Bassiouni, *Searching for Peace and Achieving Justice: The Need for Accountability*, 59 LAW & CONTEMP. PROBS. 9 (1996); *see, e.g.,* R.J. RUMMEL, STATISTICS OF DEMOCIDE, GENOCIDE AND MASS MURDER SINCE 1900 (1997); Margareta Sollenberg & Peter Wallensteen, *Major Armed Conflicts in 1995, in* SIPRI YEARBOOK 1996 (1996). There were two studies reported in the PIOOM Newsletter and Progress Report in 1994 and 1995: A. J. Jongman & A. P. Schmid, *Contemporary Conflicts: A Global Survey of High and Lower Intensity Conflicts and Serious Disputes,* 7 PIOOM NEWSL. & PROGRESS REP. 14 (Winter, 1995) and *Study,* 6 PIOOM NEWSL. & PROG. REP. 17 (1994). *See also* Alex P. Schmid, *Early Warning of Violent Conflicts: Causal Approaches, in* VIOLENT CRIME & CONFLICTS 47 (ISPAC 1997); "PIOOM World Conflict and Human Rights Map 1998" (visited Oct. 30, 1998) <http://www.fsw. leiden.univ.nl>.

15   BASSIOUNI, CRIMES AGAINST HUMANITY, *supra* note 4.

16   Convention Respecting the Laws and Customs of War on Land [Second Hague, IV], Oct. 18, 1907, 36 Stat. 2277, 1 Bevans 631 (entered into force Jan. 26, 1910) (entered into

Until a more complete code of laws of war has been issued, the High Contracting Parties deem it expedient to declare that, in cases not included in the Regulations adopted by them, the inhabitants and the belligerents remain under the protection and the rule of the principles of the law of nations, as they result from the usages established among civilized peoples, from the laws of humanity, and from the dictates of the public conscience.[17]

After the war, in 1919, the Allies established a Commission to investigate war crimes[18] which thereafter found that the killing of Armenians by the Turks around 1915[19] constituted "crimes against the laws of humanity." The United States and Japan strongly objected to the concept and insisted on having their dissenting positions reflected in the Report.[20] In 1923, after the failure of ratification of the 1919 Treaty of Sèvres,[21] which required that the Turkish government turn over to the Allies those responsible for such crimes, the Treaty of Lausanne[22] excluded such a provision and a protocol was attached, giving amnesty to the Turks who had committed the crime irrespective of whether they acted as state actors or non-state actors.[23] By 1942, the Allies realized that they would have to revisit that crime,[24] and in 1945 the London Charter provided, in Article 6(c), for the prosecution of those who committed "crimes against humanity"[25]:

---

force with respect to the United States Jan. 26, 1910) [hereinafter 1907 Hague Convention], *reprinted in* 2 Weston II.B.1, *supra* note 6.

[17] *Id.*, pmbl.

[18] Commission on the Responsibility of the Authors of the War and on Enforcement of Penalties, *Report Presented to the Preliminary Peace Conference, March 29, 1919*, 14 AM. J. INT'L L. 95 (1920).

[19] VAHAKN N. DADRIAN, THE HISTORY OF THE ARMENIAN GENOCIDE: ETHNIC CONFLICT FROM THE BALKANS TO ANATOLIA TO THE CAUCASUS (1985).

[20] *See Memorandum of Reservations Presented by the Representatives of the United States to the Report of the Commission on Responsibilities*, Annex II, April 4, 1919, *reprinted in* 14 AM. J. INT'L L. 127, 144–51 (1920); *Reservation by the Japanese Delegation*, Annex III, April 4, 1919, *reprinted in* 14 AM. J. INT'L L. 151 (1920).

[21] Treaty of Peace Between the Allied Powers and Turkey, Aug. 10, 1920 (Treaty of Sèvres), *reprinted in* 15 AM. J. INT'L L. 179 (Supp. 1921).

[22] Treaty with Turkey and Other Instruments Signed at Lausanne, July 24, 1923, Final Act, *reprinted in* 18 AM. J. INT'L L. 1 (Supp. 1925).

[23] JAMES F. WILLIS, PROLOGUE TO NUREMBERG: THE POLITICS AND DIPLOMACY OF PUNISHING WAR CRIMINALS OF THE FIRST WORLD WAR (1982).

[24] THE PUNISHMENT OF WAR CRIMINALS: RECOMMENDATIONS OF THE LONDON INTERNATIONAL ASSEMBLY (Report of Commission I) (1944).

[25] Agreement by the Government of the United Kingdom of Great Britain and Northern Ireland, the Government of the United States of America, the Provisional Government of the French Republic, and the Government of the Union of the Soviet Socialist Republics for the

Crimes against humanity: namely, murder, extermination, enslavement, deportation, and other inhumane acts committed against any civilian populations, before or during the war; or persecutions on political, racial or religious grounds in execution of or in connection with any crime within the jurisdiction of the Tribunal, whether or not in violation of the domestic law of the country where perpetrated.

But that article linked Article 6(c) crimes to "crimes against peace" (the initiation and conduct of war) as defined in Article 6(a) and to "war crimes" as defined in Article 6(b). This meant that all "crimes against humanity" committed before the initiation of the war, between 1932 and 1939, were not prosecutable.[26]

The war-connecting link was removed in a 1950 Report of the International Law Commission (ILC).[27] The question that remained, however, was the legally binding effect of such a report.[28] On its face, a report of the ILC has no binding effect, unless it is deemed to be the embodiment of customary international law, in which case the ILC report can be seen as the progressive codification of customary international law and therefore binding as to its content. However, the practice of states remains an important element in addition to the element of *opino juris* to establish customary international law,[29] and this practice seems to be somewhat wanting because there are few states that have prosecuted persons for such crimes.[30] Moreover, no convention on crimes against humanity has been developed since 1945,[31] even though many other conventions on various international crimes have

---

Prosecution and Punishment of the Major War Criminals of the European Axis and the Charter of the International Military Tribunal, Aug. 8, 1945, 59 Stat. 1544, 1546, 82 U.N.T.S. 279, 3 Bevans 1238 (entered into force Aug. 8, 1945) [hereinafter London Charter], *reprinted in* 2 Weston II.E.1, *supra* note 6. *See also* Special Prosecution Establishing an International Military Tribunal for the Far East and Charter of the International Military for the Far East, Jan. 19, 1946, T.I.A.S. No. 1589, at 3, 4 Bevans 20 [hereinafter IMTFE], *reprinted in* 2 Weston II.E.2 *supra* note 6. Article 5(c) is similar to Article 6(c) of the London Charter, as is Article II(c) of Control Council No. 10, though it removes the war connecting requirement.

[26] Lucy S. Dawidowicz, The War Against the Jews: 1933–1945 (1975).

[27] *See* Principles of International Law Recognized in the Charter of the Nuremberg Tribunal and in the Judgment of the Tribunal, 5 U.N. GAOR Supp. (No. 12), at 11, U.N. Doc. A/1316 (1950), 44 Am. J. Int'l L. 126 (1950) [hereinafter 1950 ILC Report], *reprinted in* 2 Weston II.E.4, *supra* note 6.

[28] Hans-Heinrich Jescheck, *Development and Future Prospects, in* International Criminal Law 83 (M. Cherif Bassiouni ed., 1986).

[29] *See* Michael Akehurst, *Custom as a Source of International Law*, 47 Brit. Y.B. Int'l L. 1 (1974–75); Anthony A. D'Amato, The Concept of Custom in International Law (1971).

[30] The states that have done so are Canada, France, and Israel.

[31] *See* Bassiouni, Crimes Against Humanity, *supra* note 4.

been adopted since that time.[32] There is no rational explanation for this gap other than the lack of political will by governments.

The next opportunity to reaffirm the London Charter's "crimes against humanity" arose in 1993 when the Security Council adopted the Statute of the International Criminal Tribunal for the former Yugoslavia (ICTY).[33] In this statute, however, the connection to an armed conflict was preserved[34] with Article 5 requiring that

---

[32] BASSIOUNI, ICL CONVENTIONS, *supra* note 8.

[33] *See Statute of the International Tribunal (for the Prosecution of Persons Responsible for Serious Violations of Humanitarian Law Committed in the Territory of the Former Yugoslavia), May 25, 1993, S.C. Res. 827, U.N. SCOR, 48th Sess., 3217th mtg., U.N. Doc. S/RES/827 (1993) [hereinafter ICTY Statute], reprinted in* 32 I.L.M. 1159 *and* 2 Weston II.E.10 *supra* note 6 at 908.

[34] *Tadić* (1997), *supra* note 6, at 908. *See also* ICTY Statute, *supra* note 33, at art.5. Concerning the war-connecting link, the *Tadić* decision stated:

> Article 5 of the Statute, addressing crimes against humanity, grants the International Tribunal jurisdiction over the enumerated acts "when committed in armed conflict." The requirement of an armed conflict is similar to that of Article 6(c) of the Nürnberg Charter which limited the Nürnberg Tribunal's jurisdiction to crimes against humanity committed "before or during the war," although in the case of the Nürnberg Tribunal jurisdiction was further limited by requiring that crimes against humanity be committed "in execution of or in connection with" war crimes or crimes against peace. Despite this precedent, the inclusion of the requirement of an armed conflict deviates from the development of the doctrine after the Nürnberg Charter, beginning with Control Council Law No. 10, which no longer links the concept of crimes against humanity with an armed conflict. As the Secretary-General stated: "Crimes against humanity are aimed at any civilian population and are prohibited regardless of whether they are committed in an armed conflict, international or internal in character." In the Statute of the International Tribunal for Rwanda the requirement of an armed conflict is omitted, requiring only that acts be committed as part of an attack against a civilian population. The Appeals Chamber has stated that, by incorporating the requirement of an armed conflict, "the Security Council may have defined the crime in Article 5 more narrowly than necessary under customary international law," having stated earlier that "[s]ince customary international law no longer requires any nexus between crimes against humanity and armed conflict . . . Article 5 was intended to reintroduce this nexus for the purposes of this Tribunal." Accordingly, its existence must be proved, as well as the link between the act or omission charged and the armed conflict. The Appeals Chamber, as discussed in greater detail in Section VI.A of this Opinion and Judgment, stated that "an armed conflict exists whenever there is resort to armed force between States or protracted armed violence between governmental authorities and organized armed groups or between such groups within a State." Consequently, this is the test which the Trial Chamber has applied and it has concluded that the evidence establishes the existence of an armed conflict.

"crimes against humanity" take place in the context of "an armed conflict" of an international or internal character. The difference between the war-connecting link of the London Charter's Article 6(c) and the ICTY's Article 5 is the addition in Article 5 of a conflict of an internal character.

In 1994, however, when the same Security Council adopted the Statute for the International Criminal Tribunal for Rwanda (ICTR),[35] it did not include any war-connection whatsoever.[36] Why the change? One explanation is that the ICTY's

---

The next issue which must be addressed is the required nexus between the act or omission and the armed conflict. The Prosecution argues that to establish the nexus for a violation of Article 5 it is sufficient to demonstrate that the crimes were committed at some point in the course or duration of an armed conflict, even if such crimes were not committed in direct relation to or as part of the conduct of hostilities, occupation, or other integral aspects of the armed conflict. In contrast the Defence argues that the act must be committed "in" armed conflict.

The Statute does not elaborate on the required link between the act and the armed conflict. Nor, for that matter, does the Appeals Chamber Decision, although it contains several statements that are relevant in this regard. First is the finding, noted above, that the Statute is more restrictive than custom in that "customary international law no longer requires any nexus between crimes against humanity and armed conflict." Accordingly, it is necessary to determine the degree of nexus which is imported by the Statute by its inclusion of the requirement of an armed conflict. This, then, is a question of statutory interpretation.

The Appeals Chamber Decision is relevant to this question of statutory interpretation. In addressing Article 3 the Appeals Chamber noted that where interpretative declarations are made by Security Council members and are not contested by other delegations "they can be regarded as providing an authoritative interpretation" of the relevant provisions of the Statute. Importantly, several permanent members of the Security Council commented that they interpret "when committed in armed conflict" in Article 5 of the Statute to mean "during a period of armed conflict." These statements were not challenged and can thus, in line with the Appeals Chamber Decision, be considered authoritative interpretations of this portion of Article 5.

The Appeals Chamber, in dismissing the Defense argument that the concept of armed conflict covers only the precise time and place of actual hostilities, said: "It is sufficient that the alleged crimes were closely related to the hostilities occurring in other parts of the territories controlled by the parties to the conflict." Thus it is not necessary that the acts occur in the heat of battle.

Tadić (1997), *supra* note 6, at 937.

[35] *See Resolution 955 (1994) Establishing the International Tribunal for Rwanda,* Nov. 8, 1994, S.C. Res. 955, U.N. SCOR, 49th Sess., 3453d mtg., U.N. Doc. S/RES/955 (1994) [hereinafter ICTR Statute], *reprinted in* 33 I.L.M. 1598 (1994) *and* 2 Weston II.E.12, *supra* note 6.

[36] *See id.* art. 3.

formulators sought to preserve the London Charter's requirement, though expanding it to internal conflicts, to offset arguments that Article 5 of the ICTY departed from existing customary law.[37] Since there was no convention on crimes against humanity, that category of crimes had to be deemed as falling within customary law.[38] But with respect to the ICTR, the Government of Rwanda was not expected to challenge the absence of such a requirement.[39] To have included such a war-connecting requirement in the ICTR statute would have meant that prosecutions for such crimes would have been impossible because that conflict was purely internal.[40]

An examination of the contents of crimes against humanity as defined in Article 6(c) of the Nuremberg Charter reveals that it covers the following acts: "murder, extermination, enslavement, imprisonment, deportation or other inhumane acts," and "persecution."[41] The ICTY and ICTR added "rape" for specificity.[42] However, the ICTR also added the restrictive requirement not present in the ICTY; that the acts constituting the crime must be the result of "widespread or systematic" practices.[43] Furthermore, some of the terms used in the London Charter's Article

---

[37] *See, e.g.*, M. CHERIF BASSIOUNI & PETER MANIKAS, THE LAW OF THE INTERNATIONAL TRIBUNAL FOR THE FORMER YUGOSLAVIA 199–235 (1996) (ch. 2, "Establishment of the Tribunal and Legislative History"). The Appeal Chamber in the *Tadić* case noted that "it is by now a settled Rule of customary international law that crimes against humanity do not require a connection to international armed conflict. Indeed . . . customary international law may not require a connection between crimes against humanity and any conflict at all." Decision in Prosecutor v. Duško Tadić, (IT–94–1–AR72), *reprinted in* 35 I.L.M. 32 (1996), at 72. Further, the *Tadić* decision stated:

> If customary international law is determinative of what type of conflict is required in order to constitute a crime against humanity, the prohibition against crimes against humanity is necessarily part of customary international law. As such, the commission of crimes against humanity violates customary international law, of which Article 5 of the Statute is, for the most part, reflective. As stated by the Appeals Chamber: "There is no question . . . that the definition of crimes against humanity adopted by the Security Council in Article 5 comports with the principle of *nullum crimen sine lege.*"

Tadić (1997), *supra* note 6, at 937. The Appeal Chamber in the *Nikoli* case noted that a crime against humanity must be shown to have been committed in the course of an armed conflict. *Nikoli Rule 61 Hearing*, (IT–95–2–R61).

[38] *See, e.g.*, Bassiouni, *supra* note 6.

[39] *See* Bassiouni, *From Versailles to Rwanda, supra* note 10, at 46–49.

[40] For an insight into the establishment of the ICTR, see VIRGINIA MORRIS & MICHAEL P. SCHARF, THE INTERNATIONAL CRIMINAL TRIBUNAL FOR RWANDA (2 vols., 1998).

[41] *See* London Charter, *supra* note 25, art. 6(c).

[42] *See* ICTY Statute, *supra* note 33, art. 5(g); ICTR Statute, *supra* note 35, art. 3(g).

[43] *See* ICTR Statute, *supra* note 35, art. 3. It is interesting to note that Article 5 of the ICTY does not refer to the words "widespread or systematic" contained in Article 3 of the ICTR. Yet, in the *Tadić* opinion the Trial Chamber referred to the words "widespread or systematic" using the disjunctive. *See generally* MICHAEL P. SCHARF, BALKAN JUSTICE (1997).

6(c), the ICTY's Article 5, and the ICTR's Article 3 may be deemed to lack sufficient specificity to satisfy the "principles of legality" required in the world's major legal systems.[44] For example, "other inhuman acts" can be deemed vague, "murder" overlaps with "extermination," and "imprisonment" and "deportation" can be lawful. Of course, careful judicial interpretation can avoid such vagueness and ambiguity, but that presupposes the existence of a judicial process that can develop a clear and precise jurisprudence, and in that respect much is expected from the ICTY and ICTR.

Another issue concerning "crimes against humanity" is whether it is essentially a category of mass victimization crimes, which is predicated on the existence of state-action or state-policy, or whether it is but a catch-all category for mass crimes even when committed by non-state actors.[45] The formulation of Article 6(c) raises that issue relative to whether "persecution" is a required policy element or simply another *genre* of the specific crimes listed in Article 6(c), or indeed, whether it is both a specific type of prohibited act as well as a policy element applicable to state and non-state actors alike.[46] In this writer's judgment, "crimes against humanity" as set forth in Article 6(c) is no mere catch-all category for mass victimization, but rather a category of international crimes, distinguishable from other forms of mass victimization by the jurisdictional policy element of a "state action or policy." But when the ICTR's Article 3 was made to qualify Article 6(c)'s policy of persecution by the addition of the terms "widespread *or* systematic,"[47] the drafters, while doubtless seeking to tailor the definition of "crimes against humanity" to the Rwandan conflict, brought about a progressive development. This is evidenced in the disjunctive "or" as opposed to the conjunctive "and." If the mass victimization can be only "widespread" and not also "systematic," then it can be the spontaneous consequence of a given conflict[48] and not necessarily a reflection of "state action or policy."

The statute of the ICC adopted in Rome on July 17, 1998, follows the ICTR's precedent in that it states in its Article 7 that "[f]or the purpose of this statute, 'crimes against humanity' means any of the following acts when committed as part of a widespread *or* systematic attack directed against any civilian population with knowledge of the attack. . . ."[49] At the same time, the ICC Statute's Article 7(h)

---

44   See BASSIOUNI, CRIMES AGAINST HUMANITY, *supra* note 4 (ch. 4, "The Principles of Legality").

45   See *id.* ch. 5.

46   See *id.* See also Roger S. Clark, *Crimes Against Humanity at Nuremberg, in* THE NUREMBERG TRIAL AND INTERNATIONAL LAW 177 (George Ginsburgs & Vladimir N. Kudriavtsev eds., 1990); Egon Schwelb, *Crimes Against Humanity,* 23 BRIT. Y.B. INT'L L. 178 (1946).

47   ICTR Statute, *supra* note 35, at art. 3 (emphasis added).

48   Surely the terms "widespread or systematic" as used in Article 3 of the ICTR cannot be interpreted as characteristic of the specific crimes listed in the definition because, for example, there can be no particular crime called "widespread extermination."

49   ICC Statute, *supra* note 13, at art. 7 (emphasis added).

makes "persecution" specifically prohibited conduct;[50] and while it is one of the forms of carrying out an "attack directed against any civilian population," the persecution of a group of persons is by its very nature possible only as a consequence of state action or policy carried out by state actors or non-state actors, or the product of policy carried out by non-state actors. In fact, most of the specific crimes listed within the meaning of this definition can occur only as a result of state action or policy carried out by state actors or non-state actors: "(b) extermination; (c) enslavement; (d) deportation or forcible transfer of population; . . . (j) the crime of Apartheid."[51] The other specifically listed crimes presumably can be committed by individuals without the existence of state action or policy. But clearly if such crimes are directed against a "civilian population," they are necessarily the product of state action or policy carried out by state actors or the product of policy of non-state actors. These specific crimes are:

(a) murder; . . . (e) imprisonment or other severe deprivation of physical liberty in violation of fundamental rules of international law; (f) torture; (g) rape, sexual slavery, enforced prostitution, forced pregnancy, enforced sterilization, or any other form of sexual violence of comparable gravity; . . . (i) enforced disappearance of persons; . . . (k) other inhumane acts of a similar character intentionally causing great suffering, or serious injury to body or to mental or physical health.[52]

Thus, the element of state policy for state actors and that of policy for non-state actors is dominant throughout this latest definition of "crimes against humanity."

The element of state action or policy is not the only distinguishing international jurisdictional characteristic of crimes against humanity;[53] it carries with it also certain implications concerning the criminal responsibility of a state's agents who contribute to the overall execution of the state's plan or policy. Thus, if it is established that a state has developed a policy, or carried out a plan, or engaged in acts whose outcomes include the crimes contained in the definition of crimes against human-

---

50　Article 7 states:

　　Persecution against any identifiable group or collectivity on political, social, national, ethnic, cultural, religious, gender as defined in paragraph 3, or other grounds that are universally recognized as impermissible under international law, in connection with any act referred to in this paragraph or any crime within the jurisdiction of the Court. . . .

　　Id.

51　*Id.*

52　*Id.*

53　For example, genocide requires a specific "intent to eliminate in whole or in part," while war crimes, no matter how widespread or systematic or both, do not require any element of state action or policy in connection with the commission of these crimes.

ity, then those persons in the bureaucratic apparatus who brought about, or contributed to, that result could be charged with complicity to commit crimes against humanity. Further those who intended to carry out the policy could be charged with the commission of that crime, or at least, with complicity to commit that crime.[54] The responsibility of state agents arises in this case irrespective of whether their conduct was lawful under national law. However, it is important to note that the policy element, whether developed or carried out by state actors or non-state actors, is the jurisdictional element that makes "crimes against humanity" a category of international crimes and that distinguishes it from other forms of mass victimization which otherwise are within national criminal jurisdiction.

Between the Nuremberg formulation of Article 6(c) in 1945 and the ICTR's formulation of Article 3 in 1994, "crimes against humanity" have shifted from a category of crimes applicable only to situations involving state policy or action to situations involving non-state actors. This shift has been evidenced in the ICTR and ICC Statutes which provide the requirements of "widespread or systematic" and "attack against any civilian population." The combination of the two requirements makes the crime applicable to both state and non-state actors; and also applicable in time of peace and war, without any connecting link to the initiation or conduct of war or to war crimes.

Other than these two formulations, "crimes against humanity" never have been the subject of a specialized international convention, thus leaving some doubt as to some of the specific contents of that category of international crimes and as to their applicability to non-state actors.[55] This is evident in the eleven international instruments that have been elaborated between 1907 and 1998 and that define, in different though similar ways, "crimes against humanity." Thus, "crimes against humanity" remain part of customary law, with a mixed baggage of certainty as to some of its elements, and uncertainty as to others and to their applicability to non-state actors.

A textual comparison of these formulations, which are contained in Appendix I, evidences the slight differences between them. It also evidences the overlap that exists between genocide and war crimes relative to the protected targets and prohibited conduct.

III. Genocide

In defining protected groups the Convention on the Prevention and Punishment of the Crime of Genocide, specifies only three, namely: national, ethnic, and

---

54   This was the case with the *Touvier* and *Papon* cases in France. *See generally* sources cited *infra* notes 137–139. *See also* SORJ CHALANDON & PASCALE NIVELLE, CRIMES CONTRE L'HUMANITÉ: BARBIE, TOUVIER, BOUSQUET, PAPON (1998).

55   *See generally* M. Cherif Bassiouni, *"Crimes Against Humanity": The Need for a Specialized Convention*, 31 COLUM. J. TRANSNAT'L L. 457 (1994). *See also* BASSIOUNI, CRIMES AGAINST HUMANITY, *supra* note 4, ch. 7.

religious groups. This enumeration excludes political and social groups,[56] an omission that was no accident. The Convention was elaborated in 1948, and at that time the USSR was not desirous of having political and social groups included in those being given protection because Stalin and his regime already had begun their purges which targeted these very groups.[57] As a consequence of this omission, the killing of an estimated one million persons in Cambodia by the Khmer Rouge between 1975 and 1985, almost 40 percent of the population, can be argued to have not constituted genocide because the perpetrators and victims were of the same ethnic group and because the targeted victim group was a political group which is not covered by the convention.[58]

This gap in the Genocide Convention is well known, but at no time since 1948 was there any effort to fill it. In fact, three opportunities were never seized. The Statutes of the ICTY[59] in 1993 and the ICTR[60] in 1994 were adopted with the same formulation as Article II of the Genocide Convention. Later, in connection with the elaboration of the Statute of the International Criminal Court, the Preparatory Committee failed to support any changes to Article II of the Genocide Convention.[61]

As stated, the Genocide Convention protects three groups: national, ethnic, and religious.[62] It also specifies that there must be a specific "intent to destroy [the protected group] in whole or in part."[63] This requirement makes it appear that the criminal responsibility befalls essentially those who plan, initiate, or carry out the policy that is specifically intended to produce the result of destroying the protected group "in whole or in part," and leaves open the questions of the responsibility of those in the lower echelons of the execution of such a policy and the legal standards required to prove it.[64] The requirement of specific intent in the criminal laws of most legal systems is more difficult to prove than that of general intent. General intent can be proven inferentially by the legal standard of what the ordinary rea-

---

[56]   *See generally* the Genocide Convention, *supra* note 2. *See also* Lippman, *supra* note 5.

[57]   *See, e.g.,* ROBERT CONQUEST, THE GREAT TERROR: STALIN'S PURGE OF THE THIRTIES (1973). *See also* CHALANDON & NIVELLE, *supra* note 54.

[58]   *See generally* JASON S. ABRAMS & STEVE R. RATNER, STRIVING FOR JUSTICE: ACCOUNTABILITY AND THE CRIMES OF THE KHMER ROUGE (1995); DAVID P. CHANDLER ET AL., POL POT PLANS THE FUTURE: CONFIDENTIAL LEADERSHIP DOCUMENTS FROM DEMOCRATIC KAMPUCHEA (1988); GENOCIDE AND DEMOCRACY IN CAMBODIA (Ben Kiernan ed., 1993). *See also* CENTURY OF GENOCIDE: EYEWITNESS ACCOUNTS AND CRITICAL VIEWS (Samuel Totten et al. eds., 1997).

[59]   *See* ICTY Statute, *supra* note 33, at art. 4.

[60]   *See* ICTR Statute, *supra* note 35, at art. 2.

[61]   *See* ICC Statut, *supra* note 13, at art. 6.

[62]   *See* Genocide Convention, *supra* note 2, at art. II.

[63]   *Id.*

[64]   *See generally* BASSIOUNI, CRIMES AGAINST HUMANITY, *supra* note 4 (ch. 8, "Elements of Criminal Responsibility").

sonable person would have known under existing circumstances.[65] This difficulty is especially true of lower echelons of executors where typically there exists no "paper trail." But to prove specific intent by higher echelons may also be arduous if there is no paper trail. The reason is that the Genocide Convention was drafted with the Nazi experience in mind; the Germans, who were meticulous in everything, left behind a detailed paper trail.[66] But this situation never has been repeated. In the Yugoslav[67] and Rwandan[68] conflicts, for example, a paper trail, if it exists, has yet to be found, and it may never be made public by those who have the information.[69] The same is true of other conflicts such as Cambodia.[70] There are, moreover, conflicts where a paper trail exists but has not been made public.[71]

In addition to the issue of specific genocidal intent, which is fraught with evidentiary difficulties, there is the question of whether the protected group can be identified differently. For example, can it be based on gender, or limited to a group in a given area? The Commission of Experts Established Pursuant to Security Council Resolution 780 (1992), which investigated violations of international humanitarian law in the former Yugoslavia, concluded that these two questions can

---

[65] That standard exists in the criminal laws in those legal systems influenced by the Romanist-Civilist Germanic legal traditions, as well as those legal systems influenced by the Common Law tradition.

[66] *See* Telford Taylor, The Anatomy of the Nuremberg Trials 57 (1992).

[67] *See* M. Cherif Bassiouni, *The Commission of Experts Established Pursuant to Security Council Resolution 780: Investigating Violations of International Humanitarian Law in the Former Yugoslavia,* 5 Crim. L.F. 279–340 (1994). *See also Final Report of the Commission of Experts Established Pursuant to Security Council Resolution 780* (1992), U.N. SCOR, 49th Sess. (Annex), U.N. Doc. S/1994/674 (1994).

[68] *See generally* Gérard Prunier, The Rwanda Crisis: History of Genocide (1995). *See also* Morris & Scharf, *supra* note 40; Madeline H. Morris, *The Trials of Concurrent Jurisdiction: The Case of Rwanda,* 7 Duke J. Comp. & Int'l L. 349 (1997).

[69] It is also believed that in the Yugoslav conflict the U.S. has satellite and other air-reconnaissance pictures and probably recorded air-waves and telephone communications that would establish certain facts constituting any one of the three major crimes mentioned, but for political reasons has elected not to make them available to the ICTY Prosecutor.

[70] *See* sources cited *supra* note 58, particularly Abrams & Ratner.

[71] In the Arabian Gulf, the U.S. has amassed substantial documentation of war crimes committed by the Iraqi regime against Kuwaiti, Iraqi Kurds and Shià, and Iranians, but the documentation has not yet been made public. *See Indictment and Prosecution of Saddam Hussein,* S. Con. Res. 78, 105th Cong. (March 13, 1998). *See also* 144 Cong. Rec. Nos. 12–13 (daily ed. Feb. 23, 1998) (Senate Resolution 179, Relating to the Indictment and Prosecution of Saddam Hussein for War Crimes and Other Crimes Against Humanity). *See also War Crimes: Hearing before the Subcommittee on International Law, Immigration, and Refugees of the Committee on the Judiciary, House of Representatives,* 102d Cong., 1st Sess. (Mar. 13, 1991); *International Criminal Court,* S. Rep. No. 103–71 (1993); S. J. Res. 93, 103d Cong. (1993); S. J. Res. 32, 103d Cong. (1993).

be answered in the positive.[72] In the French trial of Papon who was convicted on April 2, 1998 of complicity for "crimes against humanity" as defined in French criminal law,[73] the central issue, where "genocide" was frequently referred to though the charge was only "crimes against humanity," was how to prove complicity in these types of crimes by agents of the state. When a person charged is a bureaucrat operating in a large bureaucracy,[74] it is so far unclear how individual criminal responsibility can be established for such a person where no specific criminal act is accomplished, but whose administrative function aids in the ultimate conduct.[75] These questions remain unanswered by the norms applicable both to "genocide" and to "crimes against humanity."

Lastly, a question arises as to "genocide," and that is the nature and size of the "group" targeted for elimination "in whole or in part." Is it the entire group as it exists in the world, or a smaller portion of that group which is identified and targeted by the perpetrators? Could it be, for example, that portion of the group that inhabits a certain area, or a given town, or a segment of that group such as the intellectuals or the women in that group? That was the issue that faced the Commission of Experts[76] in determining whether "ethnic cleansing"[77] could be deemed a form of genocide. Similarly, the issue arose with respect to the policy of systematic rape of the women of a certain identifiable group.[78]

The Genocide Convention leaves these questions unanswered, but it would be valid to consider the Genocide Convention as susceptible of progressive interpretation in light of the new techniques that nefarious planners devise to achieve their

---

[72] See Final Report of the Commission of Experts Established Pursuant to Security Council Resolution 780 (1992), U.N. SCOR, 49th Sess. (Annex), U.N. Doc. A/1994/674 (1994); Annexes to the Final Report, U.N. SCOR, 49th Sess., U.N. Doc. S/1994/674/Add.2 (1994); Bassiouni, supra note 67.

[73] Craig R. Whitney, Vichy Official Found Guilty of Helping Deport Jews, N.Y. Times, Apr. 2, 1998, at A8.

[74] See generally Jacques Francillon, Crimes de guerre, Crimes contre l'humanité, Juris-Classeur, Droit Int'l, Fascicule 410 (1993); Leila Sadat Wexler, National Prosecutions for International Crimes: The French Experience, in 3 International Criminal Law (M. Cherif Bassiouni ed., 2d ed. 1999) [hereinafter 3 International Criminal Law]; Leila Sadat Wexler, Prosecutions for Crimes Against Humanity in French Municipal Law: International Implications, in ASIL Proceedings 270–76 (1997).

[75] See, e.g., Mark J. Osiel, Ever Again: Legal Remembrance of Administrative Massacre, 144 U. Pa. L. Rev. 463 (1995).

[76] See Final Report, supra note 72.

[77] Id.

[78] Id. See also M. Cherif Bassiouni, Investigating Serious Violations of International Humanitarian Law in the Former Yugoslavia (DePaul University, Occasional paper); Meron, supra note 6. See also the indictment of Karadžić and Mladić, in which the judge referred to "ethnic cleansing" as a form of genocide (IT–95–18–I).

evil goals. The Genocide Convention justifies an evolving interpretation that fulfills its goals and purposes.[79]

Since 1948, "genocide," as defined in the Genocide Convention,[80] has been embodied in three international instruments, to wit, the statutes of the ICTY,[81] ICTR,[82] and the Statute of the International Criminal Court,[83] and the incorporation of Article II of the Genocide Convention into these three instruments has been without change.[84] Accordingly, none of the problems evident since 1948 have been addressed to date.

IV. War Crimes

The regulation of armed conflicts has two sources: (1) conventional law, also referred to as the "Law of Geneva," consisting of the four Geneva conventions of 1949[85] plus two additional protocols of 1977[86] relating to "conflicts of an international character" and to "conflicts of a non-international character"; and (2) cus-

---

[79] *See* Lippman, *supra* note 5.

[80] *See* Genocide Convention, *supra* note 2, at art. II.

[81] *See* ICTY Statute, *supra* note 33, at art. 4.

[82] *See* ICTR Statute, *supra* note 35, at art. 2.

[83] ICC Statute *supra* note 13, at art. 2.

[84] *See, e.g.,* Annex, at 283.

[85] Geneva Convention for the Amelioration of the Condition of the Wounded and Sick in Armed Forces in the Field, Aug. 12 1949, 6 U.S.T. 3114, 75 U.N.T.S. 31, 4 Bevans 853, (entered into force Oct. 21, 1950), (entered into force with respect to the United States Feb. 2, 1956), *reprinted in* 2 Weston II.B.11, *supra* note 6; Geneva Convention for the Amelioration of the Condition of Wounded, Sick and Shipwrecked Members of Armed Forces at Sea, Aug. 12, 1949, 6 U.S.T. 3217, 75 U.N.T.S. 85 (entered into force Oct. 21, 1950) (entered into force with respect to the United States Feb. 2, 1956) *reprinted in* 2 Weston, II.B.12, *supra* note 6; Geneva Convention Relative to the Treatment of Prisoners of War, Aug. 12, 1949, 6 U.S.T. 3316, 75 U.N.T.S. 135, 47 Am. J. Int'l L. 119 (1953) (entered into force Oct. 21, 1950) (entered into force with respect to the United States Feb. 2, 1956), *reprinted in* 2 Weston II.B.13, *supra* note 6; 53 Geneva Convention Relative to the Protection of Civilian Persons in Time of War, Aug. 12, 1949, 6 U.S.T. 3516, 75 U.N.T.S. 287, 50 Am. J. Int'l L. 119 (1956) (entered into force Oct. 21, 1950) (entered into force with respect to the United States Feb. 2, 1956), *reprinted in* 2 Weston II.B.14, *supra* note 6.

[86] Protocol Additional to the Geneva Conventions of 12 August 1949, and Relating to the Protection of Victims of International Armed Conflicts of 8 June 1977 [hereinafter 1977 Protocol I], *opened for signature at Berne*, Dec. 12, 1977, U.N. Doc. A/32/144 (1977), Annex I (entered into force Dec. 7, 1978), *reprinted in* 16 I.L.M. 1391 (1977) *and* 2 Weston II.B.20, *supra* note 6; Protocol Additional to the Geneva Conventions of 12 August 1949, and Relating to the Protection of Victims of Non-International Armed Conflicts [hereinafter 1977 Protocol II], Dec. 12, 1977, U.N. Doc. A/32/144 (1977), Annex II (entered into force Dec. 17, 1978), *reprinted in* 16 I.L.M. 1391 (1977) *and* 2 Weston II.B.21, *supra* note 6.

tomary law, also referred to as the "Law of The Hague," which refers to the customary practices of states.[87]

As stated above, however, the "Law of The Hague" is not exclusively customary law because it is in part treaty law and the "Law of Geneva" is also not exclusively treaty law because it incorporates customary law. Thus, the traditional distinction between conventional and customary law is substantially eroded. Additionally, the treaty law that applies to weapons derives from both customary and conventional law, and that body of treaty law, as well as some of its specific norms, has become part of customary law. Customary law, however, is binding only on the states that share in the custom and that express their will to be bound by it unless it becomes a general custom that is binding on all states. Consequently, states that do not follow the custom, unless it is a general custom, are not bound by it as a legal obligation. Nevertheless, a custom can rise to such a level of general acceptance that it may become binding even on those states that do not share in the custom or that may express their will not to be bound by it. This applies to those general customs that rise to a higher level of acceptance and which reflect a universal sense of opprobrium, namely *jus cogens* or a peremptory norm of international law.[88] Among the international crimes that fall within this category are: aggression, genocide, "crimes against humanity," war crimes, slavery and slave-related practices, torture, and piracy. In time, other international crimes[89] may rise to that level and be deemed *jus cogens* crimes.

---

[87] Customary international law consists of the practice of states confirmed by their intention to be legally bound by the practice. *See* Akehurst, *supra* note 29; Hiram E. Chodosh, *An Interpretive Theory of International Law: The Distinction Between Treaty and Customary Law*, 28 VAND. J. TRANSNAT'L L. 973 (1995); D'AMATO, *supra* note 29; Jordan J. Paust, *Customary International Law: Its Nature, Sources and Status as Law of the United States*, 12 MICH. J. INT'L L. 59, 61 (1990); JORDAN J. PAUST, INTERNATIONAL LAW AS LAW OF THE UNITED STATES (1996). *But see* Curtis A. Bradley & Jack L. Goldsmith, *Customary International Law as Federal Common Law: A Critique of the Modern Position*, 110 HARV. L. REV. 815 (1997).

[88] *See* Bassiouni, *supra* note 6, and the authorities cited therein.

[89] At present, there are twenty-five categories of international crimes. They are: (1) aggression; (2) genocide; (3) crimes against humanity; (4) war crimes; (5) crimes against United Nations and associated personnel; (6) unlawful possession or use or emplacement of weapons; (7) theft of nuclear materials; (8) mercenarism; (9) apartheid; (10) slavery and slave-related practices; (11) torture and other forms of cruel, inhuman, or degrading treatment; (12) unlawful human experimentation; (13) piracy; (14) aircraft hijacking and unlawful acts against international air safety; (15) unlawful acts against the safety of maritime navigation and the safety of platforms on the high seas; (16) threat and use of force against internationally protected persons; (17) taking of civilian hostages; (18) unlawful use of the mail; (19) unlawful traffic in drugs and related drug offenses; (20) destruction and/or theft of national treasures; (21) unlawful acts against certain internationally protected elements of the environment; (22) international traffic in obscene materials; (23) falsification and coun-

In 1899 and then again in 1907, the customary law of armed conflicts was "codified" in the Hague Convention Respecting the Laws and Customs of War on Land.[90] But that codification was applicable only to states and only when a conflict was between states—in other words, a "conflict of an international character," as that term was developed subsequently in the 1949 Geneva conventions. Contrary to general belief, the 1907 Hague Convention did not establish the principle of individual criminal responsibility for the enunciated violations, but only the principle of compensation, which was incumbent upon the violating state. It was only in time, starting with the aftermath of World War I, but more particularly in the aftermath of World War II, that the principles of individual criminal responsibility, and of command responsibility under international law, were made part of customary law.[91]

In addition to this original customary law of armed conflicts, a number of international instruments have been executed. Most of these cover the use or prohibition of use of certain weapons in time of war, the prohibition of certain weapons at all times, and the prohibition of emplacement of weapons in certain places at any time;[92] as well as the protection from destruction and pillage of cultural property

---

terfeiting; (24) unlawful interference with submarine cables; and (25) bribery of foreign public officials. These crimes are reflected in 323 international instruments elaborated between 1815–1997. *See* BASSIOUNI, ICL CONVENTIONS, *supra* note 8.

[90]   *See* Hague Convention, *reprinted in* 2 Weston II.B.1, *supra* note 6.

[91]   *See* Bassiouni, *From Versailles to Rwanda, supra* note 10.

[92]   There are 35 treaties on the control of weapons. *See* BASSIOUNI, ICL CONVENTIONS, *supra* note 8: (1) 1868 Declaration Renouncing the Use, in Time of War, of Explosive Projectiles Under 400 Grammes Weight (St. Petersburg Declaration); (2) 1899 Declaration Concerning the Prohibition, for the Term of Five Years, of the Launching of Projectiles and Explosives from Balloons or Other New Methods of a Similar Nature (First Hague, IV, 1); (3) 1899 Declaration Concerning the Prohibition of the Use of Projectiles Diffusing Asphyxiating Gases (First Hague, IV, 2); (4) 1899 Declaration Concerning the Prohibition of the Use of Expanding Bullets (First Hague, IV, 3); (5) 1907 Convention Respecting the Rights and Duties of Neutral Powers and Persons in Case of War on Land (Second Hague, V); (6) 1907 Convention Relative to the Laying of Automatic Submarine Contact Mines (Second Hague, VIII); (7) 1907 Convention Concerning Bombardments by Naval Forces in Time of War (Second Hague, IX); (8) 1907 Convention Concerning the Rights and Duties of Neutral Powers in Naval War (Second Hague, XIII); (9) 1907 Declaration Relative to Prohibiting the Discharge of Projectiles and Explosives from Balloons (Second Hague, XIV); (10) 1921 Convention Relating to the NonFortification and Neutralisation of the Aaland Islands; (11) 1922 Treaty in Relation to the Use of Submarines and Noxious Gases in Warfare; (12) 1925 Protocol for the Prohibition of the Use in War of Asphyxiating, Poisonous or Other Gases, and of Bacteriological Methods of Warfare; (13) 1943 Protocol No. III on the Control of Armaments (Treaty for Collaboration in Economic, Social and Cultural Matters and for Collective Self-Defence; (14) 1959 Antarctic Treaty; (15) 1963 Treaty Banning Nuclear Weapon Tests in the Atmosphere, in Outer Space and Under Water; (16) 1967 Treaty on Principles Governing the Activities of States in the Exploration and Use of Outer Space, including the Moon and Other Celestial Bodies; (17) 1967 Treaty for the Prohibition of

in the time of war.[93] There is a divergence of views among governments and experts as to which of these treaties rise to the level of a general custom and which do not. Nevertheless, a general custom has evolved from the cumulative effect of these treaties that weapons that "cause unnecessary pain and suffering" are prohibited even though what these weapons are is still the subject of debate.[94]

The "Law of Geneva" (four Geneva conventions of 1949 and portions of protocols I and II which embody customary law) are also deemed to have risen to the level of a general custom.[95] They are therefore binding on all states irrespective

---

Nuclear Weapons in Latin America (Treaty of Tlatelolco) (Inter-American); (18) 1967 Additional Protocol I to the Treaty of 14 February 1967 for the Prohibition of Nuclear Weapons in Latin America (Inter-American); (19) 1967 Additional Protocol II to the Treaty of 14 February 1967 for the Prohibition of Nuclear Weapons in Latin America (Inter-American); (20) 1968 Treaty on the Non-Proliferation of Nuclear Weapons; (21) 1971 Treaty on the Prohibition of the Emplacement of Nuclear Weapons and Other Weapons of Mass Destruction on the Sea-bed and the Ocean Floor and in the Subsoil Thereof; (22) 1972 Convention on the Prohibition of the Development, Production and Stockpiling of Bacteriological (Biological) and Toxin Weapons and Their Destruction; (23) 1974 Treaty Between the United States of America and the Union of Soviet Socialist Republics on the Limitation of Underground Nuclear Weapon Tests (Threshold Test Ban Treaty, TTBT); (24) 1976 Treaty Between the United States of America and the Union of Soviet Socialist Republics on Underground Nuclear Explosions for Peaceful Purposes (Peaceful Nuclear Explosions Treaty, PNET); (25) 1977 Convention on the Prohibition of Military or Any Other Hostile Use of Environmental Modification Techniques (ENMOD); (26) 1979 Agreement Governing the Activities of States on the Moon and Other Celestial Bodies; (27) 1980 Convention on Prohibitions and Restrictions on the Use of Certain Conventional Weapons Which May be Deemed to be Excessively Injurious or to have Indiscriminate Effects; (28) 1980 Protocol on Non-Detectable Fragments to the Convention on Prohibitions or Restrictions on the Use of Certain Conventional Weapons (Protocol b; (29) 1980 Protocol on Prohibitions or Restrictions on the Use of Mines, Booby Traps and Other Devices to the Convention on Prohibitions or Restrictions on the Use of Certain Conventional Weapons, Appendix C, (Protocol II); (30) 1980 Protocol on Prohibitions or Restrictions on the Use of Incendiary Weapons to the Convention on Prohibitions or Restrictions on the Use of Certain Conventional Weapons (Protocol III) (not yet in force); (31) 1995 Protocol on Blinding Laser Weapons (Protocol IV); (32) 1985 South Pacific Nuclear-Free Zone Treaty (Treaty of Rarotonga); (33) 1993 Convention on the Prohibition of the Development, Production, Stockpiling and Use of Chemical Weapons and on their Destruction; (34) 1995 Treaty on Southeast Asia Nuclear Weapon-Free Zone; and (35) 1996 African Nuclear-Weapon-Free Zone Treaty.

93   See BASSIOUNI, ICL CONVENTIONS, supra note 8, Hague Convention for the Protection of Cultural Property in the Event of Armed Conflict and Regulations for the Execution of the Convention for the Protection of Cultural Property in the Event of Armed Conflict, 14 May 1954, 249 U.N.T.S. 240 (entered into force Aug. 7, 1956) reprinted in 2 Weston, II.B.15, supra note 6.

94   For example, the U.S. takes the position that incendiary and laser weapons and land mines are not included in that category.

95   See 3 INTERNATIONAL CRIMINAL LAW, supra note 74; Paust, supra note 87. See also, e.g.,

of whether a given state has or has not ratified one of them.[96] But it should be noted that some states maintain that not all of protocols I and II codify customary international law and therefore some of their provisions are still deemed to be part of conventional law which is applicable only to states parties. As a result, there is an overlap in the binding legal effect of these conventions since they are first binding on their signatories, then also binding on the same signatories and on all other states because they are part of customary law. But some governments, like the United States, argue that only portions of protocols I and II, which the United States has not yet ratified, have risen to the level of a general custom. Selecting what is and what is not part of custom is not only a challenging legal exercise, but one that is fraught with political considerations.[97]

As earlier noted, the "Law of Geneva" is divided into two categories: (1) "conflicts of an international character" where violations (war crimes) are referred to as "grave breaches"[98]—well defined, but applicable only to armed conflicts taking place between states; and (2) "conflicts of a non-international character" where violations are not referred to as "grave breaches"—involving a foreign element, according to some, but applicable mainly to armed conflicts between a state and a belligerent or insurgent group within that state. There are, therefore, two regimes applicable to war crimes within the "Law of Geneva": the "grave breaches" regime of the four Geneva conventions of 1949 and protocol I, in addition to the "violations" regime of common Article 3 of the four Geneva conventions of 1949 and Protocol II. Within the first "grave breaches" regime, war crimes are not limited to

---

Meron, *supra* note 6; Theodor Meron, *The Continuing Role of Custom in the Formation of International Law*, 90 Am. J. Int'l L. 238 (1996).

[96] *See* Geneva Conventions of 12 August 1949 and Additional Protocols of June 1977: ratifications, accessions and successions (Oct. 5, 1998) <http://www.icrc.org/unicc/icrnews>. *See also* Bassiouni, ICL Conventions, *supra* note 8, at, respectively, pp. 416–17, 426–27, 434–35, 440–41, 457–60 and 486–87. This position is bolstered by the number of ratifications for these conventions. They are:

The First Geneva Convention of 1949:	188
The Second Geneva Convention of 1949:	188
The Third Geneva Convention of 1949:	188
The Fourth Geneva Convention of 1949:	188
Protocol I of 1977:	152
Protocol II of 1977:	144

See supra note 85 for the full citation to the first four Geneva Conventions. *See supra* note 86, for the citations to Protocol I and Protocol II.

[97] This was obvious in the 1997 Preparatory Committee for an International Criminal Court at its second and third sessions.

[98] *See* arts. 50 and 51 of the First and Second Geneva Conventions, *supra* note 85, *reprinted in* 2 Weston II.B.11–12, *supra* note 6, and arts. 130 and 147 of the Third and Fourth Conventions, respectively, *supra* note 85, *reprinted in* 2 Weston II.B.13–14, *supra* note 6; 1977 Protocol I, *supra* note 86.

"grave breaches" but extend to other transgressions of norms contained in these codifications which also incorporate customary law. Within the second "violations" regime there is lingering reluctance to consider all the transgressions of norms contained in Protocol II as war crimes. In that regime, "violations" of common Article 3 are deemed war crimes and require no foreign element to make common Article 3 applicable; but, Protocol II, which applies to this regime, precludes the application of common Article 3 to conflicts between dissident groups within a given state. Thus, the two regimes of the "Law of Geneva" exclude most of those conflicts that may be deemed purely internal conflicts, including tyrannical regime victimization, even though these types of conflicts have since caused most of the world's wartime victimization since World War II.

As noted, conflicts of a "non-international character" are regulated in the 1949 Geneva conventions by a single article, common to all four conventions—common Article 3.[99] Protocol II expands upon common Article 3[100] relative to what that article deems to be "violations" and not "grave breaches." But, common Article 3 and Protocol II are limited in scope and do not have the specificity or detail contained in the articles defining "grave breaches." The "grave breaches" contained in common Articles 50, 51, 130, and 147 of the 1949 Geneva conventions embrace nine categories of war crimes:

1. wilful killing (I–IV conventions);

2. torture or inhuman treatment, including biological experiments (I–IV conventions);

3. wilfully causing great suffering or serious injury to body or health (I–IV conventions);

4. extensive destruction and appropriation of property, not justified by military necessity and carried out unlawfully and wantonly (I, II, and IV conventions);

5. compelling a prisoner of war or a protected person to serve in the forces of the hostile Power (III and IV conventions);

6. wilfully depriving a prisoner of war or a protected person of the rights of fair and regular trial prescribed in the Convention (III and IV conventions);

7. unlawful deportation or transfer of a protected person (IV convention);

8. unlawful confinement of a protected person (IV convention); and

9. taking of hostages (IV convention).

To be considered a "grave breach," each of the categories listed above must be committed against persons or property protected by the relevant conventions.

---

[99] *See* Common Article 3 of the four Geneva Conventions, *supra* note 85.

[100] *See* 1977 Protocol II, *supra* note 86.

Common Article 3 of the four Geneva conventions does not categorically establish that "violations" of that provision are war crimes, but scholars have interpreted common Article 3 violations as constituting war crimes.[101] Article 4(2) of Protocol II, expanding on Article 3 of the four Geneva conventions, provides:

> Without prejudice to the generality of the foregoing, the following acts against the persons referred to in paragraph 1 are and shall remain prohibited at any time and in any place whatsoever:
>
> (a) violence to the life, health and physical or mental well-being of persons, in particular murder as well as cruel treatment such as torture, mutilation or any form of corporal punishment;
>
> (b) collective punishments;
>
> (c) taking of hostages;
>
> (d) acts of terrorism;
>
> (e) outrages upon personal dignity, in particular humiliating and degrading treatment, rape, enforced prostitution and any form of indecent assault;
>
> (f) slavery and the slave trade in all their forms;
>
> (g) pillage; and
>
> (h) threats to commit any of the foregoing acts.

Cognate provisions[102] further provide that certain fundamental protections be observed: (1) humane treatment for detained persons, such as protection from violence, torture, and collective punishment; (2) protection from intentional attack, hostage-taking, and acts of terrorism of persons who take no part in hostilities; (3) special protection for children to provide for their safety and education and to preclude their participation in hostilities; (4) fundamental due process for persons against whom sentences are to be passed or penalties executed; (5) protection and appropriate care for the sick and wounded, and medical units which assist them; and (6) protection of the civilian population from military attack, acts of terror, deliberate starvation, and attacks against installations containing dangerous forces. However, Article 4(2) of Protocol II is narrow in scope: (1) it applies only to internal conflicts in which dissident armed groups are under responsible command and exercise control over such a part of the national territory as to carry out sustained and concerted military operations; (2) it has the effect of excluding many internal conflicts in which dissident armed groups occupy no significant territory but conduct sporadic guerrilla operations over a wide area; (3) it does not guarantee all the

---

[101] See generally LEVIE (1933), supra note 3; Meron, supra note 6.

[102] See arts. 5 and 6 of the four Geneva Conventions, supra note 85.

protections of the Conventions for international armed conflicts, *e.g.*, prisoner-of-war treatment for captured combatants; and (4) it does not contain provisions to punish offenders—noninternational conflicts are not covered by the definition of "grave breaches" contained in the 1949 Geneva Conventions and its Protocol I.

The essential differences between the explicit obligations arising from the two normative regimes deemed "grave breaches" and "violations" arise with respect to the duties and rights associated with their enforcement. For "grave breaches" the duties are: (1) to investigate; (2) to prosecute; (3) to extradite; and (4) to assist through judicial cooperation of investigations; and the rights include: (1) the right for any state to rely on universal jurisdiction to investigate, prosecute and punish; and the rights include: (2) the nonapplicability in national or international processes of statutes of limitations;[103] (3) the nonapplicability of the defense of "obedience to superior orders,"[104]; and (4) the nonapplicability of immunities including that of Head of State.[105] The same duties and rights are not explicit relative to "violations" of common Article 3, and thus a normative gap exists with respect to the enforcement consequences that arise out of transgressions of these two regimes.[106] There is, however, a notable trend among legal experts to consider such formalism as historically *dépassé* and to consider the same enforcement consequences applicable to both legal regimes.

The formal distinctions discussed above, and the gaps that exist in their scope, application, protection, and enforcement are no longer tenable. The "writings of the

---

103 Convention on the Non-Applicability of Statutory Limitations to War Crimes and Crimes Against Humanity, *opened for signature* Nov. 26, 1968, 754 U.N.T.S. 73 (entered into force Nov. 11, 1970), *reprinted in* 8 I.L.M. 68 (1969) *and* 2 Weston II.E.16, *supra* note 6; European Convention on the Non-Applicability of Statutory Limitations to Crimes Against Humanity and War Crimes (Inter-European), Jan. 25, 1974, Europ. T.S. No. 82, *reprinted in* 13 I.L.M. 540 (1974) (not yet in force). *See also* Christine van den Wyngaert, *War Crimes, Crimes Against Humanity and Statutory Limitations, in* 3 INTERNATIONAL CRIMINAL LAW, *supra* note 74.

104 Article 8 of the London Charter removed the defense of "obedience to superior orders." *See* London Charter, *supra* note 25, art. 8. Further, Article 7 of the ICTY and Article 6 of the ICTR both removed the defense of "obedience to superior orders" as well. *See* ICTY Statute, *supra* note 33, art. 7; ICTR Statute, *supra* note 35, at art. 6. For a historical evolution of the defense, see Leslie C. Green, *Superior Orders and Command Responsibility*, 27 CAN. Y.B. INT'L L. 167 (1989); Major William H. Parks, *Command Responsibility for War Crimes*, 62 MIL. L. REV. 1 (1973). *See also* Leslie C. Green, *The Defence of Superior Orders in the Modern Law of Armed Conflict*, 31 ALBERTA L. REV. 320 (1993).

105 Article 7 of the London Charter removed the defense of immunity for "head of state." *See* London Charter, *supra* note 25, art. 7. Further, Principle III of the "Nuremberg Principles" removed the defense of immunity for heads of state. *See* 1950 ILC Report, *supra* note 27, Principle III. The defense was also removed in the statutes for the ICTY and the ICTR. *See* ICTY Statute, *supra* note 33, at art. 7; ICTR Statute, *supra* note 35, art. 6.

106 *Compare* Common Article 3 *with* "grave breaches" of the Third and Fourth Conventions, respectively arts. 130 and 147, *supra* note 85.

most distinguished publicists"[107] agree that there should be no distinctions between "grave breaches" and "violations" of common Article 3 and Protocol II; they agree that both contain equally enforceable prohibitions carrying the same enforcement consequences.[108] They do so at least in part because the overwhelming majority of post-World War II conflicts have been of a "non-international character,"[109] and because these conflicts have produced an overwhelming number of victims. As noted above, there have been, since World War II, some 250 conflicts and internal tyrannical regime victimizations that have produced an estimated 170 million casualties.[110] Thus, to maintain a distinction between these two legal regimes and their enforcement consequences ignores the purpose of these regimes, which is to protect innocent victims from harm.

For purposes of war crimes, however, the distinction between types of conflicts and the legal regimes applicable to them does not apply with respect to crimes against humanity and genocide. These two categories of crimes are deemed applicable in time of peace as well as in time of war. The most significant problems arising out of overlaps and gaps in the law of armed conflict are the legal standards applicable in distinguishing between conflicts of an international and noninternational character, and in ascertaining the relevant parts of conventional and customary law of armed conflicts applicable to these contexts, considering that the two sets of norms mirror one another.[111] Another layer of confusion originates in doctrines of international law from which improvident extrapolations are made into the law of armed conflicts; legal interpretation and analysis of these two overlapping areas are thus frequently more confusing than they are elucidating.

---

[107] One of the sources of international law as stated in Article 38 of the Statute of the International Court of Justice. *See* Statute of the International Court of Justice, June 26, 1945, 59 Stat. 1055, U.N.T.S. No. 993, *reprinted in* 1 Weston I.H.2, *supra* note 13.

[108] *See generally* Meron, *supra* note 6.

[109] *See* Bassiouni, *supra* note 14. *See also, e.g.*, sources cited *supra* note 14.

[110] *See* Balint, *supra* note 14. *See generally* sources cited *supra* note 14 and accompanying text.

[111] These difficulties were evident in the work of the General Assembly's Preparatory Committee for the Establishment of an International Criminal Court on the Definition of War Crimes. *See Report of the Preparatory Committee on the Establishment of an International Criminal Court*, U.N. GAOR, 51st Sess., Supp. No. 22, U.N. Doc. A/51/22 (1996); *Report of the Inter-Sessional Meeting From 19 to 30 Jan. 1998 in Zutphen, The Netherlands*, U.N. Doc. A/AC.249/1998/L.13 (1998); *Report of the PrepCom, supra* note 9. *See also* the Commentaries of Jordan Paust in 13 NOUVELLES ÉTUDES PÉNALES (M. Cherif Bassiouni ed., 1997) and 13*bis* NOUVELLES ÉTUDES PÉNALES (M. Cherif Bassiouni ed., 1998). *See* the text of the *Report of the PrepCom* and its correlation to conventional and customary law norms.

The foregoing observations were evidenced in two related judgments by the ICTY. The first was in connection with the Tadič jurisdictional appeal case.[112] Commenting on that judgment Professor Meron notes:

> The appeals chamber's expansive interpretation that "laws or customs of war" in Article 3 of the Tribunal's Statute reach noninternational armed conflicts largely avoided the worst possible consequences. However, the chamber refused to use Article 3 of its Statute (laws and customs of war) as a conduit to bring in as customary law conduct comprising grave breaches of the Geneva Conventions (grave breaches are the subject of Article 2 of the Statute; these can be regarded as customary law whose content parallels the pertinent provisions of these Conventions). The grave breaches are the principal crimes under the Conventions. Thus deprived of the core of international criminal law in cases deemed to be noninternational, the Tribunal can only raise the level of actionable violations to crimes against humanity and perhaps, in the future, genocide. Not only does this handicap the Tribunal's ability to carry out its mandate, but some commentators also criticize the resort to such heavy artillery against evil, but relatively minor, actors. Disregarding considerations of judicial economy, the appeals chamber has therefore enabled the creation of a crazy quilt of norms that would be applicable in the same conflict, depending on whether it is characterized as international or noninternational. No less, the potential for unequal and inconsistent treatment of the accused is great. Fortunately, until *Tadič* . . . , the decisions of the trial chambers on indictments pursuant to Article 61 of the Tribunal's Rules of Procedure and Evidence found that the situations involved international armed conflicts and that the grave breaches provisions were therefore applicable, avoiding potential chaos.[113]

Meron then further notes that the decision was not inevitable, as the proposition that the fighting was part of an international armed conflict—a proposition advanced by the Commission of Experts, the U.S. Government, and many scholars—was a position known to the majority of the appeals chamber though one they chose not to adopt. Further, Meron notes, Judge Georges Abi-Saab proposed terming the fighting as part of noninternational armed conflicts, but including "grave breaches" within the applicable customary law.[114]

The fact remains, however, that the ICTY eschewed this reasoning. Worse, the subsequent *Tadič* judgment on the merits erroneously applied another international

---

112   *Tadič*, (1977), *supra* note 6. For a critical appraisal, see George H. Aldrich, *Jurisdiction of the International Criminal Tribunal for the Former Yugoslavia*, 90 AM. J. INT'L L. 64 (1996).

113   Meron, *supra* note 7, at 238.

114   *Id.*

law standard to the issue presented.[115] In that decision, the *Tadić* majority erroneously applied the international law standard of state responsibility to determine whether a conflict is or is not of an international character. In so doing, the Tribunal relied on the opinion of the International Court of Justice in *Military and Paramilitary Activities In and Against Nicaragua (Nicaragua v. U.S.).*[116] The Court, however, failed to appreciate that the agency relationship needed to establish state responsibility, essentially for the purposes of civil damages, is distinguishable from the legal standard required to establish whether a given conflict is of an international or noninternational character. Meron, aptly commenting on this confusion, writes:[117]

> [The *Tadić* case] was not an issue of (state) responsibility at all. Identifying the foreign intervenor was . . . only the question of state responsibility. Conceptually, it cannot determine whether a conflict is international or internal. In practice, applying the *Nicaragua* test to the question in produces artificial and incongruous conclusions.

> Indeed, even a quick perusal of international law literature would establish that imputability is not a test commonly used in judging whether a foreign intervention leads to the internationalization of the conflict and the applicability of those rules of international humanitarian law that govern armed conflicts of an international character.

This decision led several government experts at the ICC Diplomatic Conference to express their fear that, unless the war crimes provision of Article 8 was clearly and unambiguously drafted, that judges may, in the future, interpret Article 8 in a confusing or expansive manner, and thus create new law by judicial fiat. Such concern for strict judicial interpretation did not however produce the desired lack of

---

[115] *Tadić* (1977), *supra* note 6. *See also, e.g.,* SCHARF, *supra* note 43.

[116] *Supra* note 7.

[117] Meron, *supra* note 7, at 237, 239. Professor Dinstein agrees that intervention by a foreign state on behalf of the insurgents turns a civil war into an interstate war. Specifically with regard to Yugoslavia Meron writes:

> The *Tadić.* . . . trial chamber has already accepted that, before the announced withdrawal of JNA forces from the territory of Bosnia-Herzegovina, the conflict was an international armed conflict. The facts of the situation and the rules of international humanitarian law should determine whether the JNA continued to be involved after that date and during the period pertinent to the indictments; if so, the international character of the conflict would have remained unchanged. The provisions of the Fourth Geneva Convention on termination of the application of the Convention, including Article 6, are relevant, not the legal tests of imputability and state responsibility. Finally, the appeals chamber would also be well-advised to abandon its adherence to the literal requirements of the definition of protected persons and help adapt it to the principal challenges of contemporary conflicts.

Meron, *supra* note 7, at 242.

ambiguity. On the contrary, it gave, in my opinion, more opportunities for non-strict interpretative approaches.

Thus, in these two judgments, which are the first of an international jurisdiction since the close of World War II and the subsequent proceedings at Nuremburg[118] and in the Far East,[119] we find more confusion than clarity regarding the following issues:

A. *Generally*

1. What norms of conventional law of armed conflicts have become part of customary law, and how is that evidenced?

2. What norms of customary law have been codified in conventional law, and how is that evidenced?

B. *Specifically*

1. Does customary law include all the "grave breaches" of the 1949 Geneva conventions?

2. Does customary law include all or some of the "grave breaches" of Protocol I, and, if so, which ones?

3. Does customary law include common Article 3 of the 1949 Geneva conventions?

4. Does customary law include all or some of the provisions of Protocol II, and, if so, which ones?

---

[118] *See* London Charter, *supra* note 25. For the proceedings before the IMT, see International Military Tribunal sitting at Nuremberg, *reported in* TRIAL OF THE MAJOR WAR CRIMINALS BEFORE THE INTERNATIONAL MILITARY TRIBUNAL (1949) (commonly known as the "Blue Series"). For the subsequent proceedings of the IMT, see TRIALS OF WAR CRIMINALS BEFORE THE NUREMBERG MILITARY TRIBUNALS UNDER CONTROL COUNCIL LAW NO. 10 (1949) (commonly known as the "Green Series").

[119] *See* Special Proclamation Establishing an International Military Tribunal for the Far East and Charter of the International Military Tribunal for the Far East, Jan. 19, 1946, T.I.A.S. No. 1589, at 3, 4 Bevans 20 (IMTFE Proclamation), *reprinted in* 2 Weston II.E.2, *supra* note 6. On the same day General MacArthur issued his proclamation, the Charter for the IMTFE was adopted. Pursuant to a policy decision by the Far Eastern Commission, the Charter was later amended by General's Order No. 20, issued by MacArthur. *See* Charter for the International Military Tribunal for the Far East, Apr. 29, 1946, T.I.A.S. No. 1589, at 11, (IMTFE Charter), *reprinted in* 2 Weston II.E.2, *supra* note 6. *See generally* THE TOKYO WAR CRIMES TRIAL: THE COMPLETE TRANSCRIPTS OF THE PROCEEDINGS OF THE INTERNATIONAL MILITARY TRIBUNAL FOR THE FAR EAST IN TWENTY-TWO VOLUMES (R. John Pritchard & Sonia Magbanua Zaide eds., 1981); THE TOKYO WAR CRIMES TRIAL: COMPREHENSIVE INDEX AND GUIDE TO THE PROCEEDINGS OF THE INTERNATIONAL MILITARY TRIBUNAL FOR THE FAR EAST IN FIVE VOLUMES (R. John Pritchard & Sonia Magbanua Zaide eds., 1981); YUKI TANAKA, HIDDEN HORRORS: JAPANESE WAR CRIMES IN WORLD WAR II (1996).

5. What other treaties on the regulation of armed conflicts, particularly those concerning the prohibition and use of certain weapons, have become part of customary law,[120] and on what basis?

C. *Legal Standards*

1. Are the standards applicable to state responsibility applicable also to the determination of whether a conflict is of an international or non-international character; and, if applicable, is it exclusively applicable or simply applicable as one of several legal standards?

2. Is the determination of the nature of a given armed conflict based on one or more standards deemed part of customary law, and, if so, to what extent does customary law rely on legal standards that derive from:

(a) Common Article 3 of the 1949 conventions; and

(b) Protocol II.

These and other questions still loom large in the law of armed conflicts; and, as stated above, they are reflected in the range of governmental positions on the definition of war crimes in the draft statute of the ICC.[121]

In 1995, the United Nations General Assembly established an *Ad Hoc* Committee for the Establishment of an International Criminal Court.[122] In 1996, it established a Preparatory Committee for an International Criminal Court.[123] Subsequently, during three-and-a-half-years of deliberations, the question of defining war crimes became the subject of detailed discussions. Questions were raised, in particular, about whether all of the contents of Protocols I and II have risen to the level of customary law, about the specific contents of customary law, and still more particularly, about the rules governing conflicts of a noninternational character and the prohibitions of the use of certain weapons in all categories of conflicts. While there was no dispute that the "grave breaches" provisions of the 1949 Geneva conventions are applicable, and substantial agreement that most of the "grave breaches" in Protocol I are included, there was less agreement that some of the Protocol II prohibitions can be deemed part of custom. In fact, the texts proposed, and the one adopted reflects, a partial regression from the norms contained in Protocol I and a substantial regression from the norms contained in Protocol II. The draft provision submitted to the diplomatic conference evidences these divergent views,[124] as set forth in the chart contained in Appendix V detailing the sources

---

120 *See* BASSIOUNI, ICL CONVENTIONS, *supra* note 8.

121 *See Report of the PrepCom Committee, supra* note 9.

122 *Report of the Ad Hoc Committee on the Establishment of an International Criminal Court*, U.N. GAOR, 50th Sess., Supp. No. 22, U.N. Doc. A/50/22 (1995).

123 *See Report of the PrepCom Committee, supra* note 9.

124 *Id.*

of law for war crimes. The chart was developed and circulated at the Preparatory Committee for the Establishment of an International Criminal Court[125] and, in setting forth the various sources for the provisions, highlights the overlaps and gaps.

The ICC adopted a similar text, contained in Appendix V, but the distinction between conflicts of an international and non-international character is reflected in the distinction between "grave breaches" and other violations of common Article 3 in this instance. Protocols I and II are neither specifically nor entirely applied, but norms are taken selectively therefrom and are listed under what can be termed "war crimes" under customary law. Subparagraph 2(a) of Article 8 refers specifically to the "Grave Breaches of the Geneva Conventions of 12 August 1949, . . ." and lists eight such under this heading:

(i)   Wilful killing;

(ii)   Torture or inhuman treatment, including biological experiments;

(iii)   Wilfully causing great suffering, or serious injury to body or health;

(iv)   Extensive destruction and appropriation of property, not justified by military necessity and carried out unlawfully and wantonly;

(v)   Compelling a prisoner of war or other protected person to serve in the forces of a hostile Power;

(vi)   Wilfully depriving a prisoner of war or other protected person of the rights of fair and regular trial;

(vii)   Unlawful deportation or transfer or unlawful confinement;

(viii) Taking of hostages.[126]

Subparagraph 2(b) of Article 8 refers to "Other serious violations of the laws and customs applicable in international armed conflict. . . ."[127] It incorporates the customary law of armed conflict and some of the provisions of Protocol I.

In subparagraphs 2(c) and 2(d) of Article 8, the ICC Statute then focuses on the distinction between conflicts of an international character and those of a non-international character. In so doing, it invokes the domain of common Article 3 of the four 1949 Geneva conventions. Subparagraph 2(c), focusing on "the case of armed conflict not of an international character," refers to the serious violations of

---

[125] Non-paper circulated at the December 1997 session of the Preparatory Committee for the Establishment of an International Court, entitled *Synopsis on War Crimes Relating to the Informal Working Paper on War Crimes* (A/AC.249/1997/WG.1/CRP.7) (Dec. 3, 1997). See *infra* Annex, at 283.

[126] ICC Statute, *supra* note 13, art. 8, para. 2(a).

[127] *Id.* para. 2(b).

Article 3 common to the four Geneva Conventions of 12 August 1949,"[128] thus adding the limitation of "serious" to the "violations" of common Article 3 for the exclusive purposes of the ICC's statute. Subparagraph 2(c), like subparagraph 2(a), embodies the contents of the 1949 Geneva conventions, the former relative to "grave breaches" and the latter relative to the prohibitions contained in common Article 3. The latter prohibits the following acts:

> (i) violence to life and person, in particular murder of all kinds, mutilation, cruel treatment and torture; (ii) committing outrages upon personal dignity, in particular humiliating and degrading treatment; (iii) taking of hostages; (iv) the passing of sentences and the carrying out of executions without previous judgment pronounced by a regularly constituted court, affording all judicial guarantees which are generally recognized as indispensable.[129]

Subparagraph 2(d) of Article 8 emphasizes, like Protocol II, that subparagraph 2(c) "does not apply to situations of internal disturbances and tensions, such as riots, isolated and specific acts of violence or other acts of a similar nature."[130] The specificity contained herein by far exceeds what Protocol II contains and it is therefore specific to this statute.

Subparagraph 2(e) of Article 8 is the counterpart of subparagraph 2(b) and it applies customary law to armed conflicts not of an international character. What follows is an extensive list that includes most of the provisions of Protocol II and overlaps in part with common Article 3. It also adds several specifics that Protocol II does not contain, but which have come to be recognized as part of customary law. Further, it is progressive when it comes to sexual violence in (vi) and to the protection of children in (vii). It reads as follows:

> (e) Other serious violations of the laws and customs applicable in armed conflicts not of an international character, within the established framework of international law, namely, any of the following acts:
>
> > (i) intentionally directing attacks against the civilian population as such or against individual civilians not taking direct part in hostilities;
> >
> > (ii) intentionally directing attacks against buildings, material, medical units and transport, and personnel using the distinctive emblems of the Geneva conventions in conformity with international law;

---

[128] *Id.* para 2(c).

[129] *Id.*

[130] *Id.* para 2(d).

(iii) intentionally directing attacks against personnel, installations, material, units or vehicles involved in a humanitarian assistance or peacekeeping mission in accordance with the Charter of the United Nations, as long as they are entitled to the protection given to civilians or civilian objects under the law of armed conflict;

(iv) intentionally directing attacks against buildings dedicated to religion, education, art, science or charitable purposes, historic monuments, hospitals and places where the sick and wounded are collected, provided they are not military objectives;

(v) pillaging a town or place, even when taken by assault;

(vi) committing rape, sexual slavery, enforced prostitution, forced pregnancy, as defined in Article 7, paragraph 2, enforced sterilization, and any other form of sexual violence also constituting a serious violation of Article 3 common to the four Geneva Conventions;

(vii) conscripting or enlisting children under the age of fifteen years into armed forces or groups using them to participate actively in hostilities;

(viii) ordering the displacement of the civilian population for reasons related to the conflict, unless the security of the civilians involved or imperative military reasons so demand;

(ix) killing or wounding treacherously a combatant adversary;

(x) declaring that no quarter will be given;

(xi) subjecting persons who are in the power of another party to the conflict to physical mutilation or to medical or scientific experiments of any kind which are neither justified by the medical, dental or hospital treatment of the person concerned nor carried out in his interest, and which cause death to or seriously endanger the health of such person or persons;

(xii) destroying or seizing the property of an adversary unless such destruction or seizure be imperatively demanded by the necessities of the conflict;

(f) Paragraph 2(e) applies to armed conflicts not of an international character and thus does not apply to situations of internal disturbances and tensions, such as riots, isolated and sporadic acts of violence or other acts of a similar nature. It applies to armed conflicts that take place in a territory of a State when there is protracted armed conflict between governmental authorities and organized armed groups or between such groups.

The structure of the foregoing formulation of "war crimes" is thus divided into four parts, reflecting the different sources of applicable law, conventional and customary, and the two relevant contexts, of international and noninternational conflicts. Regrettably, these distinctions were maintained even though the overlaps are glaringly evident. Suffice it to compare subparagraphs 2(b) and 2(e), which incorporate what the drafters believed to be customary law, even though it also clearly reflects existing conventional law, to wit, Protocol II.[131] The ICC missed the opportunity to eliminate these distinctions and to focus on the protected persons and protected targets irrespective of the conflicts' context. But, then, the ICC was an exercise in political feasibility, not progressive codification. From this perspective, it must be said that the definition of "war crimes" is as good as can be achieved at the present time, taking into account the diversity of concerns and interests.

V. Conclusion

Not only are there overlaps in some applications of the sources of law relevant to war crimes, crimes against humanity, and genocide, there also are gaps and ambiguities in their content and scope. So far, however, there is no political will to close the gaps and eliminate the ambiguities. Thus, it is necessary to examine these sources of law separately in order to establish which source applies to which context and then to determine whether the legal elements contained in the applicable sources apply to the facts.[132]

Some 188 states have so far embodied "war crimes" in their military codes. This is a requirement of the Geneva conventions and therefore every state party must domesticate their provisions and criminalize "grave breaches" violations. However, prosecutions for "war crimes" or "grave breaches" or an equivalent term (such as violations of the military code) have, with the exception of the prosecutions arising out of World War II,[133] been few and far between. Since 1949, Germany has prosecuted an estimate of 60,000 cases mostly in the categories of genocide and war crimes, but the United States, in relation to the Vietnam War, prosecuted only two cases for war crimes—the *Calley*[134] and *Medina*[135] cases. It is

---

[131] The United States did not ratify either Protocol and wanted to avoid any references to these Protocols, insisting that whatever norms were derived therefrom should be drafted as part of customary law. In a sense, the United States' position is defensible because the Protocols essentially embody customary law, and that too evidences the overlap between the two sources of applicable law.

[132] For a distinction between humanitarian law norms and human rights law norms as customary law, see THEODOR MERON, HUMAN RIGHTS AND HUMANITARIAN NORMS AS CUSTOMARY LAW (1989).

[133] *See* Bassiouni, *From Versailles to Rwanda, supra* note 10.

[134] U.S. v. Calley, C.M. 426402, 46 C.M.R. 1131 (1971); 48 C.M.R. 19 (1973); 22 C.M.A. 534 (1973).

[135] U.S. v. Medina, 20 C.M.A. 403; 43 C.M.R. 243 (1971).

noteworthy, too, that the only case brought against one of the World War II Allies for war crimes, by Japanese citizens for the use by the United States of atomic weapons against Japan, which killed and injured an estimated 225,000 innocent civilians,[136] was dismissed by the Supreme Court of Japan on technical jurisdictional grounds.[137]

With respect to "crimes against humanity," Canada, France, and Israel have been the only countries to have carried out prosecutions. In Israel, the *Eichmann*[138] and *Demjanjuk*[139] cases were carried out, both for crimes not committed in the territory of the prosecuting state. Demjanjuk was acquitted because he turned out to be the wrong person. In France, prosecutions have occurred for Barbie,[140] Touvier,[141] and Papon.[142] In 1989, Canada prosecuted the first case under a 1987

---

[136]   29 THE NEW ENCYCLOPEDIA BRITANNICA 1022 (1990).

[137]   Shimoda v. The State, 355 HANREI JIHŌ (Sup. Ct., Dec. 7, 1963); also quoted in part in 2 Friedman, *supra* note 3, at 1688. *See also* Richard A. Falk, *The* Shimoda *Case: A Legal Appraisal of the Atomic Attacks Upon Hiroshima and Nagasaki*, 59 AM. J. INT'L L. 759 (1965). The claim in that case was against the United States of America for dropping atomic bombs on Nagasaki and Hiroshima in violation of the laws and customs of war.

[138]   *See* Attorney General of Israel v. Eichmann (Israel Dist. Court of Jerusalem, 1961), 36 I.L.R. 5 (1962), (Supreme Court of Israel 1962), 36 I.L.R. 277 (1962). *See also, e.g.*, GIDEON HAUSNER, JUSTICE IN JERUSALEM (1966).

[139]   *See* Demjanjuk v. Petrovsky, 776 F.2d 571 (6th Cir. 1985), *cert. denied*, 475 U.S. 1016 (1986).

[140]   The *Barbie* judgments: Matter of Barbie, GAZ. PAL. JUR. 710 (Cass. Crim. Oct. 6, 1983); Judgment of Oct. 6, 1983, Cass. Crim., 1984 D.S. Jur. 113, Gaz. Pal. Nos. 352–54 (Dec. 18–20, 1983), 1983 J.C.P. II G, No. 20107, J.D.I. 779 (1983); Judgment of Jan. 26, 1984, Cass. Crim., 1984 J.C.P. II G, No. 20197 (Note Ruzié), J.D.I. 308 (1984); Judgment of Dec. 20, 1985, Cass. Crim., 1986 J.C.P. II G, No. 20655, 1986 J.D.I.; Judgment of June 3, 1988, Cass. Crim., 1988 J.C.P. II G, No. 21149 (Report of Counselor Angevin). For information on the *Barbie* case, see generally LADISLAS DE HOYAS, KLAUS BARBIE (Nicholas Courtin trans., 1985); BRENDAN MURPHY, THE BUTCHER OF LYON (1983).

[141]   The *Touvier* judgments: Judgment of Feb. 6, 1975, Cass. Crim., 1975 D.S. Jur. 386, 387 (Report of Counselor Chapan), 1975 Gaz. Pal. Nos. 124–26 (May 4–6, 1975); Judgment of Oct. 27, 1975, Chambre d'accusation de la cour d'appel de Paris, 1976 D.S. Jur. 260 (Note Coste-Floret), 1976 Gaz. Pal. Nos. 154–55, at 382; Judgment of June 30, 1976, Cass. Crim., 1977 D.S. Jur. 1, 1976 Gaz. Pal. Nos. 322, 323, 1976 J.C.P. II G, No. 18435; Judgment of Nov. 27, 1992, Cass. Crim., 1993 J.C.P. II G, No. 21977; Judgment of Apr. 13, 1992, Cour d'appel de Paris, Première chambre d'accusation, at 133–62, *reprinted in part in* 1992 Gaz. Pal. 387, 387–417; Judgment of June 2, 1993, Cour d'appel de Versailles, Première chambre d'accusation 31. For information on the *Touvier* case, see generally ÉRIC CONAN & HENRY ROUSSO, VICHY, UN PASSÉ QUI NE PASSE PAS (1994); ALAIN JAKUBOWICZ & RENÉ RAFFIN, TOUVIER HISTOIRE DU PROCÈS (1995); ARNO KLARSFELD, TOUVIER UN CRIME FRANCAIS (1994); JACQUES TRÉMOLET DE VILLERS, L'AFFAIRE TOUVIER, CHRONIQUE D'UN PROCÈS EN IDÉOLOGIE (1994).

[142]   The *Papon* case: Papon was indicted on September 18, 1996; the indictment was confirmed on January 23, 1997; Judgment of Sept. 18, 1996, Chambre d'accusation de la cour

statute that permits retrospective application of international law.[143] This writer served as Canada's chief legal expert in testifying on what constituted "crimes against humanity" before 1945. *Regina* resulted in the acquittal of Hungarian Gendarmerie Captain Finta on the facts but the judgment recognized the existence of "crimes against humanity" under international law before 1945. Prosecutions before the ICTY and ICTR have included "war crimes," "crimes against humanity," and "genocide," but when the opportunity arose to prosecute Pol Pot for such crimes in Cambodia, it was not seized.[144]

---

d'appel de Bordeaux (unpublished), affirmed Judgment of Jan. 23, 1997, Cass. Crim., 1997 J.C.P. II G, No. 22812. In April 1998, Maurice Papon was convicted for "crimes against humanity" and sentenced to ten years imprisonment. *See* Craig R. Whitney, *Ex-Vichy Aide Is Convicted and Reaction Ranges Wide*, N.Y. TIMES, Apr. 3, 1998, at A1; Craig R. Whitney, *Vichy Official Found Guilty of Helping Deport Jews*, N.Y. TIMES, Apr. 2, 1998, at A8; and Charles Trueheart, *Verdict Nears in Trial of Vichy Official*, WASH. POST, Apr. 1, 1998, at A21.

For information on the *Papon* case, see generally Laurent Greilsamer, *Maurice Papon, la vie masquée*, LE MONDE, Dec. 19, 1995, *available in* LEXIS, Nexis Library, Monde File; Barry James, *The Final Trial for Vichy? A Model French Bureaucrat Accused*, INT'L HERALD TRIB., Jan. 6–7, 1996, at 2.

For additional information on these cases and French prosecution of war criminals in general, see generally Leila Sadat Wexler, *National Prosecutions for International Crimes: The French Experience, in* 3 INTERNATIONAL CRIMINAL LAW, *supra* note 74; Leila Sadat Wexler, *Prosecutions for Crimes Against Humanity in French Municipal Law: International Implications, in* ASIL PROCEEDINGS 270–76 (1997); Leila Sadat Wexler, *The Interpretation of the Nuremberg Principles by the French Court of Cassation: From Touvier to Barbie and Back Again*, 32 COLUM. J. TRANSNAT'L L. 289 (1994); Leila Sadat Wexler, *Reflections on the Trial of Vichy Collaborator Paul Touvier for Crimes Against Humanity in France*, 20 L. & SOC. INQUIRY 191 (1995); Leila Sadat Wexler, *Prosecutions for Crimes Against Humanity in French Municipal Law: International Implications* (Working Paper No. 97–4–3, Washington University School of Law, 1997). *See also* CHALANDON & NIVELLE, *supra* note 54; Jacques Francillon, *Crimes de guerre, Crimes contre l'humanité*, JURIS-CLASSEUR, DROIT INT'L, FASCICULE 410 (1993).

[143] Regina v. Finta, [1994] 1 S.C.R. 701 (Can). *See* Irwin Cotler, *Bringing Nazi War Criminals in Canada to Justice: A Case Study, in* ASIL PROCEEDINGS 262–69 (1997); Leslie C. Green, *Canadian Law, War Crimes and Crimes Against Humanity*, 59 BRIT. Y.B. INT'L L. 217 (1988); Michèle Jacquart, *La notion de crime contre l'Humanité en droit international contemporain et en droit canadien*, 21 REVUE GÉNÉRALE DE DROIT 607 (1990). *See also* Barry H. Dubner, *The Law of International Sea Piracy*, 11 N.Y.U. J. INT'L L. & POLITICS 471 (1979); REPORT OF THE COMMISSION OF INQUIRY ON WAR CRIMINALS (Jules Deschênes ed., 1986); Sharon A. Williams, *Laudable Principles Lacking Application: The Prosecution of War Criminals in Canada, in* THE LAW OF WAR CRIMES 151 (Timothy L. H. McCormack & Gerry J. Simpson eds., 1997).

[144] *See* sources cited *supra* note 58. *See also* Seth Mydans, *Death of Pol Pot: Pol Pot, Brutal Dictator Who Forced Cambodians to Killing Fields, Dies at 73*, N.Y. TIMES, Apr. 17, 1998, at A14.

Many of the specific acts deemed criminal are contained within the definitions of "war crimes," "crimes against humanity," and "genocide." That is where the overlap exists. Thus, legal questions arise as to when the same acts constitute one or the other of these three crimes. At this point, a jurist must examine the other legal elements required in the sources of law applicable to these three categories of crime. The "grave breaches" of the 1949 Geneva conventions[145] and Protocol I[146] are the clearest enunciation of what the elements of "war crimes" are, but that is because they apply to the context of conflicts of an international character. This is not quite the case with respect to common Article 3 of the 1949 Geneva conventions[147] and Protocol II,[148] which apply to conflicts of a noninternational character, but with the exclusion in Protocol II of conflicts between internal dissident groups. Still, the gap between normative proscriptions applicable to the two contexts of conflicts exists, as does the overlap between these violations. The overlaps essentially are aimed at individual deviant conduct, the same type of criminal conduct that falls also within the scope of crimes against humanity and genocide, since the latter two crimes apply to all contexts of armed conflicts as well as to other non-armed conflicts contexts and to tyrannical regime victimization. Clearly, such a situation need not exist since it would be easy to articulate the elements of each of these three categories of crimes clearly, in a way that prevents these unnecessary overlaps and gaps. So far, however, the political will to do so is nonexistent.

Because there is a connection between the rigors of evidentiary requirements to prove "war crimes," "crimes against humanity," and "genocide," and access to that evidence, the major governments who have the capacity to obtain such evidence remain in control of its use, and thereby in control of any eventual prosecution. This leaves such governments with the option to barter the pursuit of justice in exchange for political settlements.[149] An examination of what happened in all types of post-World War II conflicts clearly indicates that the pursuit of justice has been almost always bartered away for the pursuit of political settlements.[150] Consequently, the pursuit of justice has become part of the toolbox of political settlement negotiations.[151] This is true for all three major crimes, essentially because they are committed by armies, police, and paramilitary groups which act pursuant to orders from the state's highest authorities. The need for an integrated codification of these three categories of crimes is self-evident. But when that opportunity arose in con-

---

145 *Supra* note 85.

146 *See* 1977 Protocol I, *supra* note 86.

147 *Supra* note 85.

148 *See* 1977 Protocol II, *supra* note 86.

149 *See* Bassiouni, *supra* note 14.

150 *See id. See also* Bassiouni, *From Versailles to Rwanda, supra* note 10; TRANSNATIONAL JUSTICE (Neil Kritz ed., 3 vols., 1995).

151 W. Michael Reisman, *Institutions and Practices for Restoring and Maintaining Public Order*, 6 DUKE J. COMP. & INT'L L. 175 (1995).

nection with the establishment of a permanent international criminal court, it was carefully avoided for lack of political will by many governments, including the major powers.

The road ahead is arduous and the same hurdles that have long existed continue to bar the way for the effective protection of the victims of these three major crimes. The voices of millions of victims since World War I continue to cry unheard by the politicians of this world, and the sway of conscience represented by civil society is insufficient to overcome the steadfastness of *realpolitik*. To recall the words of a popular ballad of the sixties: "When will they ever learn."

Impunity for international crimes, and systematic and widespread violations of fundamental human rights, is a betrayal of our human solidarity with the victims of conflicts to whom we owe a duty of justice, remembrance, and redress. To remember and to bring perpetrators to justice is a duty we owe also to our own humanity and to the prevention of future victimization.[152] To paraphrase George Santayana, if we cannot learn from the lessons of the past and stop the practice of impunity, we are condemned to repeat the same mistakes and to suffer their consequences. The reason for our commitment to this goal can be found in the eloquent words of John Donne:

No man is an island, entire of itself;

every man is a piece of the continent, a part of the main . . .

Any man's death diminishes me because I am involved in mankind, and therefore never send to know for whom the bell tolls;

it tolls for thee. . . .[153]

---

[152] To paraphrase the classic and profoundly insightful characterization of George Orwell, "Who controls the past, controls the future; who controls the present, controls the past." GEORGE ORWELL, 1984 (2d ed. 1977). Thus, to record the truth, educate the public, preserve the memory, and try the accused, it is possible to prevent abuses in the future. *See* Stanley Cohen, *State Crimes of Previous Regimes: Knowledge, Accountabitlity and the Policy of the Past*, 20 L. & Soc. INQUIRY 7, 49 (1995).

[153] JOHN DONNE, DEVOTIONS UPON EMERGENT OCCASIONS xvii (1624).

Annex

Non-paper circulated at the December 1997 session of the Preparatory Committee for the Establishment of an International Criminal Court, entitled Synopsis on War Crimes Relating to the Informal Working Paper on War Crimes (A/AC.249/1997/WG.1/CRP.7), 3 December 1997.

Draft article as contained in A/AC.249/1997WG.1/CRP.7	Sources	Reference to A/AC.249/ 1997/L.5
A. Grave breaches of the Geneva Conventions of 12 August 1949, namely, any of the following acts against persons or property protected under the provisions of the relevant Geneva Convention:		A
(a) wilful killing; Art. 51 GC II; Art. 130 GC III; Art. 147 GC IV	Art. 50 GC I;	A (a)
(b) torture or inhuman treatment, including biological experiments; II; Art. 130 GC III; Art. 147 GC IV	Art. 50 GC I; Art. 51 GC	A (b)
(c) wilfully causing great suffering, or serious injury to body or health; II; Art. 130 GC III; Art. 147 GC IV	Art. 50 GC I; Art. 51 GC	A (c)
(d) extensive destruction and appropriation of property, not justified by military necessity and carried out unlawfully and wantonly;	Art. 50 GC I; Art. 51 GC II; Art. 147 GC IV	A (d)
(e) compelling a prisoner of war or other protected person to serve in the forces of a hostile Power;	Art. 130 GC III; Art. 147 GC IV	A (e)

(f) wilfully depriving a prisoner of war or other protected person of the rights of a fair and regular trial;	Art. 130 GC III; Art. 147 GC IV	A (f)
(g) unlawful deportation or transfer or unlawful confinement;	Art. 147 GC IV	A (g)
(h) taking of hostages. GC IV	Art. 147	A (h)
B. Other serious violations of the laws and customs applicable in international armed conflict within the established framework of international law, namely any of the following acts:		B
(a) intentionally directing attacks against the civilian population as such, as well as individual civilians not taking direct part in hostilities;[154]	Art. 51 paras. 2 and 3 Add. Prot. I; Art. 85 para. 3 (a) Add. Prot. I	B 4. (m); cf. also B 1. (a)
[(b) Intentionally launching an attack with the knowledge that such attack will cause incidental loss of life or injury to civilians or damage to civilian objects [or widespread, long-term and severe damage to the natural environment] which is not justified by military necessity;][155]	cf. Art. 57 para. 2 (a) (iii) Add. Prot. I as well as Art. 35 para. 3 Add. Prot. I; Art. 85 para. 3 (b) Add Prot. I	B 1. (b)
(c) attacking or bombarding, by whatever means, towns, villages, dwellings or buildings which are undefended;	Art. 25 Hague IV 1907	B 1. (d)

---

[154] The view was expressed that attacks against civilian objects should be considered in this context.

[155] It has been accepted that it will be necessary to insert a provision, probably in the general principles section, which sets out the elements of knowledge and intent which must be found to have existed for an accused to be convicted of a war crime. For example, "in order to conclude that an accused had the knowledge and the criminal intention required to be convicted of a crime, the Court must first determine that, taking account of the relevant circumstances of, and information available to, the accused at the time, the accused had the requisite knowledge and intent to commit the crime."

(d) killing or wounding a combatant who, having laid down his arms or having no longer means of defence, has surrendered at discretion;	Art. 23 para. 1 (c) Hague IV	B 1. (e)
(e) making improper use of flag of truce, of the flag or of the military insignia and uniform of the enemy or of the United Nations, as well as of the distinctive emblems of the Geneva Conventions, resulting in death or serious personal injury;	*cf.* Art. 2 3 para. 1 (f) Hague IV	B 4. (d); *cf. also* B 1. (f)
[(f) the transfer by the Occupying Power of parts of its own civilian population into the territory it occupies;]	Art. 49 subpara. 6 GC IV; Art. 85 para. 4 (a) Add. Prot. I	B 2. (a)
(g) intentionally directing attacks against buildings dedicated to religion, art, science or charitable purposes, historic monuments, hospitals and places where the sick and wounded are collected, provided they are not being used at the time for military purposes;	*cf.* Art. 27 Hague IV	B 2. (d)
(h) subjecting persons who are in the power of an adverse Party to physical mutilation or to medical or scientific experiments of any kind which are neither justified by the medical, dental or hospital treatment of the person concerned nor carried out in his interest, and which causes death to or seriously endangers the health of such person or persons;	*cf.* Art. 11 para. 1 and 4 Add. Prot. I	B 3.
(i) killing or wounding treacherously individuals belonging to the hostile nation or army;	Art. 23 para. 1 (b) Hague IV	B 4. (a)
(j) declaring that no quarter will be given;	Art. 23 para. 1 (d) Hague IV	B 4. (c)
(k) destroying or seizing the enemy's property unless such destruction or seizure be imperatively demanded by the necessities of war;	Art. 23 para. 1 (g) Hague IV	B 4. (e)

(l) declaring abolished, suspended or inadmissable in a court of law the rights and actions of the nationals of the hostile party;	Art. 23 para. 1 (h) Hague IV	B 4. (f)
(m) compelling the nationals of the hostile party to take part in the operations of war directed against their own country, even if they were in the belligerent's service before the commencement of the war;	Art. 23 para 2 Hague IV	B 4. (g)
(n) pillaging a town or place, even when taken by assault;	Art. 28 Hague IV	B 4. (i)
(o) employing the following weapons, projectiles and material and methods of warfare which are calculated to cause superfluous injury or unnecessary suffering;	cf. Art. 35 para. 2 Add. Prot. I	B 4. (k)
(i) poison or poisoned weapons;	Art. 23 para. 1 (a) Hague IV	B 4. (j)
(ii) asphyxiating, poisonous or other gases, and all analogous liquids, materials or devices,	Geneva Protocol 1925	B 4. (k) (i)
(iii) bullets which expand or flatten easily in the human body, such as bullets with a hard envelope which does not entirely cover the core or is pierced with incisions,	Declaration of 1899	B 4. (k) (ii)
(iv) bacteriological (biological) agents or toxins for hostile purposes or in armed conflict,	Conv. On Biological Weapons 1972	B 4. (k) (iii)
(v) chemical weapons as defined in and prohibited by the 1993 Convention on the Prohibition of the Development, Production, Stockpiling and Use of Chemical Weapons and On Their Destruction;	Conv. On Chemical Weapons	B 4. (k) (iv)
(p) [committing] outrages upon personal dignity, in particular humiliating and degrading treatment, including rape, enforced prostitution and other sexual violence of comparable gravity;	Art. 76 para. 1 Add. Prot. I; Art. 77 para. 1 Add. Prot. I	B 4. (n)

(q) utilizing the presence of a civilian or other protected person to render certain points, areas, or military forces immune from military operations;	Art. 51 para. 7 Add. Prot. I	B 4. (o)
(r) intentionally directing attacks against buildings, material, medical units and transport, and personnel using, in conformity with international law, the distinctive emblems of the Geneva Conventions;		B 4. (q)
(s) intentionally using starvation of civilians as a method of warfare by depriving them of objects indispensable to their survival, including wilfully impeding relief supplies as provided for under the Geneva Conventions;	cf. Art. 54 para. 1 and 2 Add. Prot. I; cf. also Art. 23 GC IV	B 4. (r)
[(t) [forcing] [recruiting] children under the age of fifteen years to take direct part in hostilities;]	Art. 77 para. 2 Add. Prot. I; Art. 38 Conv. Rights of Child	B 4. (s)
***** Sections C and D of this Article apply to armed conflicts not of an international character and thus do not apply to situations of internal disturbances and tensions, such as riots, isolated and sporadic acts of violence or other acts of a similar nature.	Cf. Art. 1 para. 2 Add. Prot. II	
[C. Serious violations of Article 3 common to the four Geneva Conventions of 12 August 1949 in the case of an armed conflict not of an international character, namely any of the following acts committed against persons taking no active part in the hostilities, including members of armed forces who laid down their arms and those placed *hors de have combat* by sickness, wounds, detention or any other cause:		C
(a) violence to life and person, in particular murder of all kinds, mutilation, cruel treatment and torture;	Art. 3 para. 1 sent. 1 (a) GC I-IV	C 1. (a)

(b) [committing] outrages upon personal dignity, in particular humiliating and degrading treatment [including rape, enforced prostitution and other sexual violence of comparable gravity];	Art. 3 para. 1 sent. 1 (c) GC I-IV; [cf. Also Art. 4 para 2 (e) Add. Prot. II]	C 1. (c)
(c) taking of hostages;	Art. 3 para. 1 sent. 1 (b) GC I-IV	C 1. (b)
(d) the passing of sentences and the carrying out of executions without previous judgment pronounced by a regularly constituted court, affording all judicial guarantees which are generally recognized as indispensable.]	Art. 3 para. 1 sent. 1 (d)	C 1. (d)
[D. Other serious violations of the laws and customs applicable in armed conflicts not of an international character, within the established framework of international law, namely any of the following acts:		C 2.
(a) intentionally directing attacks against the civilian population as such, as well as individual civilians not taking direct part in hostilities;[156]	Art. 13 para. 2 sent. 1 and para. 3 Add. Prot. II	C 2. (i)
(b) intentionally directing attacks against buildings, material, medical units and transports, and personnel using, in conformity with international law, the distinctive emblems of the Geneva Conventions;		C 2. (m)
(c) intentionally directing attacks against buildings dedicated to religion, art, science or charitable purposes, historic monuments, hospitals and places where the sick and wounded are collected, provided they are not being used at the time for military purposes;	cf. Art. 27 Hague IV	C 2. (n)
(d) pillaging a town or place, even when taken by assault;	cf. Art. 28 Hague IV	C 2. (h)

---

[156] The view was expressed that attacks against civilian objects should be considered in this context (cf. 12).

(e) [committing] outrages upon personal dignity, in particular humiliating and degrading treatment, including rape, enforced prostitution and other sexual violence of comparable gravity;	*cf.* Art. 4 para. 2 (e) Add. Prot. II	C 1. (c)
[(f) [forcing] [recruiting] children under the age of fifteen years to take direct part in hostilities;]	*cf.* Art. 4 para. 3 (c) Add. Prot. II; Art. 38 Rights of the Child Conv.	C 2. (p)
(g) ordering the displacement of the civilian population for reasons related to the conduct, unless the security of the civilians involved or military reasons so demand;	Art. 17 para. 1 Add. Prot. II	C 2. (q)
(h) killing or wounding treacherously a combatant adversary;	*cf.* Art. 23 para. 1 (b) Hague IV	C 2. (r)
(i) declaring that no quarter will be given;	*cf.* Art. 23 para. 1 (d) Hague IV	C 2. (s)
(j) subjecting persons who are in the power of another Party to the conflict to physical mutilation or to medical or scientific experiments of any kind which are neither justified by the medical, dental or hospital treatment of the person concerned nor carried out in his interest, and which cause death to or seriously endanger the health of such person or persons;	*cf.* Art. 5 para. 2 (e) Add. Prot. II	new
(k) destroying or seizing the property of an adversary unless such destruction or seizure be imperatively demanded by the necessities of the conflict.]	*cf.* Art. 23 para. 1 (g) Hague IV	new

***** [Elsewhere in the Statute: The jurisdiction of the Court shall extend to the most serious crimes of concern to the international community as a whole. The Court shall have jurisdiction in respect of the crimes listed in Article X [war crimes] only when committed as part of a plan or policy or as part of a large-scale commission of such crimes.][157]		chapeau before A

---

[157] The view was expressed that the substance and placement of this proposal should be considered.

The United Nations and Human Rights: The Promise of Multilateral Diplomacy and Action

Stephen P. Marks*

> *"[W]hat we must offer is a vision of human rights
> that is foreign to no one and native to all."*
>
> —Kofi Annan[1]

I. Introduction: The "Spirit of Our Age"

The principal institutional framework for furthering human rights in the fifty years since the adoption of the Universal Declaration of Human Rights (UDHR)[2] and for charting a path for human rights for the beginning decades of the new millennium is the United Nations, the only structure with a general mandate for realizing all human rights in all countries.[3] The role of the United Nations as a force for the realization of human rights in the coming decades is determined by three world order dimensions that are both constraining and liberating. Consider each.

First, the *neoliberal paradigm* (*i.e.*, the general acceptance of the neoliberal premise that free markets go hand-in-hand with a free society) is constraining because it tends to leave the realization of economic, social, and cultural rights to the vagaries of market forces, the essential outcome of which is maximization of gain rather than satisfaction of human needs. It is liberating insofar as democratic modes of exercising power (as opposed to authoritarian ones associated with antiliberal regimes) allow demands for social justice to be heard and acted upon in the legislative and political process.

The second dimension—*the dominant role of a single superpower*—limits much of the potential of other nations and of popular movements to achieve change

---

* The author gratefully acknowledges the research assistance of Brian D. Grogan and especially the wise intellectual advice, fine editing, and infinite patience of his co-editor, Professor Burns H. Weston.

1 Kofi Annan, *Ignorance, Not Knowledge, Makes Enemies of Man* (statement delivered Oct. 18, 1997, to the Communications Conference of the Aspen Institute, Colo.) U.N. Doc. SG/SM/6366 (Oct. 20, 1997).

2 *See infra* Appendix I [hereinafter UDHR].

3 For the official history of the U.N.'s human rights program since the founding of the United Nations, see THE UNITED NATIONS AND HUMAN RIGHTS 1945–1995 (Blue Books Series, 1995).

in the interests of human rights unless the change is consistent with U.S. national interest and capacity, which frequently has proved to be contrary to the human rights of many people in the U.S. (immigrants, prisoners, minorities) and abroad (victims of repressive regimes strategically allied with the U.S. and people suffering from deprivation due to practices of multinational corporations and intentional financial institutions supported by U.S. policy). At the same time human rights continues to be a genuine foreign policy objective of the U.S., making it possible for people's human rights movements and enhanced mandates of international institutions to receive official support from the U.S. government.

The third dimension characterizing post-Cold War international relations is the *weakening of the state*. The first principle guiding the action of the U.N. and its members is "the sovereign equality of all its Members."[4] Today, the principle of state sovereignty has been challenged not only by secessionist nationalism and religious fundamentalism but also—and more measurably—by the vast power of multinational business interests. The potential for effective human rights progress through the U.N. is thus limited to the extent that multinational business interests wield power superior to many states and act in the interests of return on investment, which is indifferent at best to human rights concerns and often hostile to them. Non-state actors who seek the destruction of the state out of religious or nationalistic zeal similarly jeopardize efforts to guarantee human rights. The state thus remains an indispensable agency for human rights. At the same time, the interests of the state are less important and often contrary to those within civil society who would base legitimacy of those who govern on the degree to which they respect and protect the rights of the governed. The emergence of a global civil society, embracing nongovernmental organizations (NGOs) of all kinds[5] and capable of collaborating or contending with states and intergovernmental structures, has proved to be the most prominent influence on the progressive development of human rights norms and action in international relations.[6] From this perspective, the Leviathan state must be resisted and constantly held in check by a global movement of peoples pursuing the human interest.

---

4   U.N. CHARTER art. 2(1), *reprinted in* 1 INTERNATIONAL LAW AND WORLD ORDER: BASIC DOCUMENTS I.A.1 (Burns H. Weston ed., 5 vols., 1994–   ).

5   I use the term "nongovernmental organizations" or "NGOs" because it is used in the U.N. Charter and is the most common way of referring to associations independent of the state that animate civil society. However, more positive appellations have been proposed, such as People's Movements, Voluntary Independent Movements, Civil Society Associations, and Voluntary Civil Societies. For a proposal to change the U.N. terminology, see SWEDISH PEACE ACADEMY, "WE THE PEOPLES OF THE UNITED NATIONS . . .": EMPOWERMENT OF PEOPLES MOVEMENTS IN THE UNITED NATIONS 7 (Feb. 1995).

6   Some valuable reflections on the meaning of civil society may be found in JOHN W. HARBESON, DONALD ROTHCHILD & NAOMI CHAZAN, CIVIL SOCIETY AND THE STATE IN SOUTH AFRICA (1994) and ALFRED STEPHAN, RETHINKING MILITARY POLITICS: BRAZIL AND THE SOUTHERN CONE (1988).

These, then, are among the most salient dimensions of world order that determine the potential for multilateral diplomacy and action at century's end, and a major consequence of them is the persistent impoverishment of much of Africa, Asia, Latin America, and especially the former Soviet Union, as well as increased inequality in the U.S., with predictable implications for human rights. In 1945, the impact on Africa and Asia could be attributed in large part to colonialism. Today a mix of misguided internal policies, harsh demands by international financial institutions, and unfavorable terms of trade are more relevant causal factors than colonialism of Third World poverty. The U.N.'s potential for progress in human rights is, regrettably, diminished by the impact of impoverishment of the economies of the political South, resulting in a dialogue of the deaf such as often characterizes debates in the U.N. General Assembly, the Commission on Human Rights, and other of the U.N.'s political organs. Delegates from developing countries seek symbolic victories against the human rights policies and practices of the developed countries with little or nothing being done to advance human rights in the process.

Also noteworthy is the status of human rights as a U.N. concern from the U.N.'s beginnings. The founders of the United Nations, not content merely to add human rights as one among many common objectives for U.N. members, articulated a theory of peace according to which respect for human rights and fundamental freedoms was a necessary condition for peace within and among nations. Having in mind the atrocities of the Second World War, they doubtless sincerely believed in such a theory of peace. Yet, they did not apply it to the political power arrangement of the Charter. Instead, the human rights provisions are relegated to the authorization of nonbinding studies and recommendations of the General Assembly[7] and to the setting up by the Economic and Social Council of a commission—the U.N. Commission on Human Rights—to promote human rights.[8] The Charter language was deliberately weak, emphasizing "promotion" (as opposed to "protection"), which can be limited to rhetoric. The real power was vested in the Security Council, authorized to render binding decisions and require states to modify their aggressive behavior under threat of enforcement action, including the use of armed force.[9] No such power was envisaged to promote, much less "protect" (or enforce) human rights.

In fact, human rights were not among the purposes of the future Organization nor among the specific functions of various organs proposed at Dumbarton Oaks. The Big Four did allow one reference to the promotion of human rights within the framework of economic and social cooperation; and, under pressure from Latin American delegations and nongovernmental organizations (NGOs), the U.S. eventually agreed to support the human rights provisions now contained in Articles 1

---

7   U.N. CHARTER, *supra* note 4, art. 13.
8   *Id.* art. 68.
9   *Id.* arts. 41–43.

and 55 of the Charter and the human rights functions of the General Assembly and ECOSOC in Chapters IV and X thereof. But proposals made during the San Francisco Conference to grant enforcement powers were defeated. The final language, as a historian of the Commission on Human Rights has put it, "provides for something more than mere promotion of human rights, but does not propose United Nations protection."[10] He quotes Edwin Borchard, a U.S. State Department official, who wrote in 1946:

> [T]he times seem hardly propitious for the much greater advance involved in affording the individual protection for the enforcement or international guarantee of his rights against his own state. . . . [T]he chances that the United Nations will implement their promises and hopes by provisions of positive law, and especially that they will enforce these provisions effectively are rather less than rosy.[11]

The Charter stipulates that the member states "pledge themselves to take joint and separate action in cooperation with the Organization for the achievement of . . . universal respect for and observance of human rights."[12] This "pledge" (a legally ambiguous term) remains the core human rights obligations of member states. Most of the human rights energies of the Organization were taken up, during the first years, with the drafting of the UDHR and its progeny, resulting today in a considerable body of international human rights law. As Erskine Childers and Brian Urquhart observed, "if nothing more had been done in forty-five years . . . this alone would fully justify the existence of the organization."[13] But the codification, though impressive, involved the establishment largely of paper rights, and a second area of accomplishment under the general "promotion" mandate of the Charter that resulted in studies and public information also has been useful but at the same time innocuous to governments who considered their freedom to mistreat their population as an attribute of sovereignty.

In the 1970s and 1980s, the United Nations undertook human rights investigations through a system of special rapporteurs on specific countries and themes. Timidly at first, these rapporteur bodies and individuals have carried out several thorough investigations or studies leading now to resolutions that denounce governments by name and call for specific changes. Indeed, the practice of exposing facts and naming names has reached a point that even the hardiest delegate in San

---

10 HOWARD TOLLEY, JR., THE U.N. COMMISSION ON HUMAN RIGHTS 5 (1987).

11 Edwin Borchard, *Historical Background of International Protection of Human Rights*, ANNALS AM. ACAD. POL. & SOC. SCI. 116–17 (Jan. 1946), *as quoted in* TOLLEY, *supra* note 10, at 8.

12 U.N. CHARTER, *supra* note 4, arts. 55 and 56.

13 ERSKINE CHILDERS WITH BRIAN URQUHART, RENEWING THE UNITED NATIONS SYSTEM 105 (1994).

Francisco would not have imagined to be accommodated by the term "promotion." Nevertheless, the U.N. was hampered during its first forty-five years by the limitations that arose both from Cold War rivalry and the prevailing view that the U.N. was not free to challenge the internal policies and practices of its members. The progress made was remarkable considering these constraints. It was woefully inadequate when one considers the frequency and intensity of human rights violations in all parts of the world.

However, the pace of change accelerated rapidly in the late 1980s, to the point that the then head of the Centre for Human Rights noted by 1990 "a dramatic reduction in sterile ideological confrontation,"[14] symbolized in extraordinary fashion by the unanimous observance of one minute of silence by the Commission on Human Rights for Andrei Sakharov, a man whose fate was championed by the West for a decade in the same meeting room to the consternation of the Soviet Union and its allies. Events such as this one placed the international community on a new threshold of opportunity.

In the euphoria of that first phase of the post-Cold War, it was proposed to hold a second World Conference on Human Rights, which was to take place symbolically in Berlin. Already, however, aftershocks of the transformation of world order were being felt. Immigration had become a delicate issue in Germany and xenophobia was on the rise. Ethnic conflict was erupting in the Yugoslav Federation and in the former Soviet republics. Economic dislocations and inequalities were troubling countries that had tried to leap with both feet from state socialism to a free market economy. Developing countries, no longer constrained by Cold War loyalties, were tiring of being preached to about free and fair elections and about accountability for human rights violations. When the World Conference on Human Rights finally did take place in Vienna in June 1993, it was not certain that it would rise above the resurgence of state power. In an eloquent appraisal by Upendra Baxi, who chaired the NGO meeting that preceded the Conference,

> [i]t would not be unjust to the plenipotentiaries (whom Shakespeare would have, with deadly accuracy, described as human beings dressed in little, brief authority) to maintain that the Vienna Declaration derives its vision and vitality from solidarity in struggle of world's peoples against perishable state sovereignties. That is testified by the Declaration all through, which stresses equal responsibilities of *peoples* of the world as well as of the states to secure active enjoyment of *all* human rights and fundamental freedoms. People's solidarity signifies the "spirit of our [age]"; the recalcitrant power of the state constitutes the "realities of our times." The Vienna Declaration registers this dialectic and accentuates the tendencies

---

14 Jan Mårtenson, *in* 27 U.N. MONTHLY CHRON. No. 3, at 39 (Sept. 1990).

towards new cultures of governance which will assail the micro- and macro-fascism of state power nationally and globally.[15]

The aim of this essay is to reexamine the potential for U.N. action in the field of human rights in light of the limitations on that action as they are emerging since the end of the Cold War. Borrowing from Baxi's apt distillation of the Vienna Declaration, I will suggest the possibilities and limitations of U.N. action in the "spirit of our age" and the "realities of our times." Has the end of the Cold War created new opportunities for the U.N. to act in new ways "in the spirit of our age" (*i.e.*, people's solidarity)? Has it placed new constraints on the Organization to take greater account of "the realities of our times" (*i.e.*, state power)? After reflecting on these questions, I will identify some priority issues for U.N. action in the field of human rights as the fiftieth anniversary of the UDHR ends and the dawn of a new millennium breaks. Finally, I will consider the means and methods for making this action more effective.

II. Constraints on U.N. Human Rights Diplomacy and Action in the Post-Cold War Era

Four trends characteristic of the post-Cold War period limit the potential for United Nations action in the field of human rights. All are characteristic of international relations in the twentieth century in general, but raise particular problems and opportunities in the post-Cold War era. The first is the continued claim that human rights are an imported and alien ideology for much of the world. The second is the geopolitics of state sovereignty according to which the U.N. is barred from intervening in the matters between the government of a state and the people within that state's borders. The third is the unleashing of violent passions based on national, ethnic, or religious identity in disregard of traditional state sovereignty or for concepts of global governance. The fourth concerns the internal constraints on the U.N. as an institution.

A. A Fragile Consensus on the Content of Human Rights

Throughout the cold war, the terms "democracy," "freedom," and "human rights" were employed in the West in opposition to communism. Until the early 1990s, the human rights policy of the United States was officially described as part of the struggle against communism as opposed to expressing any intrinsic value. With the end of the Cold War, conservatives in the U.S. and elsewhere claim, simplistically, the end of ideology. The political philosophy of liberalism is deemed to be the basis of human rights and democracy, uncontested by any credible alternative. The for-

---

15   Upendra Baxi, *The Spirit of Our Age, the Realities of Our Time: The Vienna Declaration on Human Rights, in* UPENDRA BAXI, MAMBRINO'S HELMET? HUMAN RIGHTS FOR A CHANGING WORLD 1–2 (1994).

eign policy aim to support democracy and human rights is no longer a smoke screen to justify the flow of military and economic aid to anti-leftist governments. With the de-linking of human rights and ideology, words take on new meaning and a new consensus became possible.

Thus, in spite of its shortcomings, the Vienna Declaration adopted at the conclusion of the World Conference on Human Rights in June 1993[16] confirmed the universality of human rights standards as defined by the U.N. and by and large rejected the counterclaims of cultural relativism.[17] The consensus reached there was a fragile bridging of the very real divide between perceptions of human rights by different governments and peoples' movements. Many Western countries, chiefly the United States, do not take economic, social, and cultural rights seriously and countries that have moved rapidly from communist-party states and planned economies to multiparty democracies with a market economy are discovering the extreme social dislocations and hardship that follow the abandonment of these rights. States whose societies value respect for authority at all levels tend to equate their economic prosperity with the virtues of authoritarian rule, challenge human rights as Western-imposed, and seek to define their own approach to democracy and human rights.[18] Part of this apparent lack of universality can be explained by the abusive attitudes of authoritarian governments to justify control over their population. As Upendra Baxi describes it, paragraph 5 of the Vienna Declaration (which affirmed human rights as "universal, indivisible and inter-dependent and inter-related") "places beyond controversy, at least till such time that the Declaration is renegotiated and revised, both the trans-state constituted nature of rights and freedoms and their universality." After referring to the challenge to that universality, especially at the Bangkok Asian regional preparatory conference, he writes:

> One suspects that this contestation had more to do with diplomacy of human rights negotiations and less with the ontological grounding ("birthright") of rights and freedoms. After all, most decolonized nations

---

[16] The Vienna Declaration and Programme of Action may be found in REPORT OF THE WORLD CONFERENCE ON HUMAN RIGHTS, U.N. Doc. A/CONF.157/24 (pt. I) (Oct. 13, 1993), at 20–46, *reprinted in* 32 I.L.M. 1661 *and* 3 INTERNATIONAL LAW AND WORLD ORDER: BASIC DOCUMENTS III.U.2 (Burns H. Weston ed., 5 vols., 1994–) [hereinafter 3 Weston].

[17] For a new approach to the debate between the universality of human rights and cultural relativism, see Burns H. Weston, *The Universality of Human Rights in a Multicultured World: Toward Respectful Decision-Making, supra* in this volume, at p. 65.

[18] On the subject of Asian positions critical of "Western" ideas of democracy and human rights, see Edward Friedman, *Democratization: Generalizing the East Asian Experience, in* EDWARD FRIEDMAN, THE POLITICS OF DEMOCRATIZATION: GENERALIZING EAST ASIAN EXPERIENCES 19–57 (1994); Bilahari Kausikan, *Asia's Different Standard*, 92 FOR. POL'Y 24 (Fall 1993); Kim Dae Jung, *Is Culture Destiny? The Myth of Asia's Anti-Democratic Values*, 73 FOR. AFF. 189 (Nov./Dec. 1994); Minxin Pei, *The Puzzle of East Asian Exceptionalism*, 5 J. DEMOCRACY 90 (Oct. 1994).

asserted the universality of rights in their struggle for self-determination against the imperial power. . . . It was odd that the learned Indian representative at Bangkok should have chosen to inveigh against "universality" enunciation, coming as he did from a history of freedom struggle. . . .[19]

In much the same spirit, former human rights activist, now South Korean President Kim Dae Jung rejected the "Asian values" argument of former Prime Minister of Singapore Lee Kuan Yew, which he found "not only unsupportable but self-serving."[20] Kim considered that "[t]he biggest obstacle [to establishing democracy and strengthening human rights in Asia] is not its cultural heritage but the resistance of authoritarian rulers and their apologists."[21] The UDHR, he wrote, "reflects basic respect for the dignity of people, and Asian nations should take the lead in implementing it."[22]

The 1993 consensus on universality was confirmed, *inter alia*, in the Declaration of the Fourth World Conference on Women held in Beijing in 1995[23] and the resolution on the fiftieth anniversary of the UDHR[24] However, it remains fragile at the diplomatic level and each major enunciation is the result of considerable negotiating effort. It is much less so at the level of popular movements and civil society.

Discussion in the Commission on Human Rights or the General Assembly used to be a sparing match between Western and Soviet bloc diplomats over denial of freedom of expression and the right to leave, on one side, and racial discrimination and denial of basic needs to the population, on the other. Developing countries, far from monolithic, would express various views on the importance of development, the need to eliminate *apartheid*, and to combat colonialism and racism. But now the East-West counter-accusations are gone, as is the regime of *apartheid* in South Africa.

Human rights is now falsely perceived by some as an exclusively Western cause. There is no doubt that, for reasons related to educational opportunities, legal capacity to operate independently of governments, access to means of mass communication and transportation, NGOs tend to be located in Western capitals and to

---

[19] Baxi, *supra* note 15, at 5.

[20] Kim Dae Jung, *supra* note 18, at 190.

[21] *Id*. at 194.

[22] *Id*.

[23] *Beijing Declaration and Platform of Action: Report of the Fourth World Conference on Women,* Beijing, Sept. 1995, U.N. Doc. A/CONF.177/22, *reprinted in* 35 I.L.M. 401 (1996). *See also* Anne Orford, *Contesting Globalization: A Feminist Perspective on the Future of Human Rights, supra* in this volume, at p. 157 (text accompanying note 92).

[24] Commission on Human Rights Res. 1998/56, U.N. ESCOR, Supp. No. 3, at 181, U.N. Doc. E/CN. 4/1998/177 (adopted Apr. 17, 1998) (declaring "solemnly its commitment to the fulfillment of the Universal Declaration of Human Rights as a common standard of achievement for all peoples and all nations. . . .").

draw upon Western methods of mobilizing civil society. However, the rapidly expanding networks of human rights NGOs based outside of the West and involvement of persons from non-Western cultures in major human rights NGOs and in U.N. human rights work are creating a more accurate image of the common human rights struggle across cultures. But to be effective in enhancing the potential for more effective U.N. human rights diplomacy and action, this consensus must operate in a new climate regarding domestic jurisdiction.

B. The Persistence of the "Domestic Jurisdiction" Limitation

The inclusion of human rights among the purposes and principles of the United Nations[25] marked a major innovation compared to the League of Nations and appears to contradict the principle of nonintervention by the U.N. "in matters which are essentially within the domestic jurisdiction of any state."[26] A simple way of illustrating the shifting trend over the last fifty years is to note the changing perception of the tension between the principles of human rights and nonintervention. In the minds of the participants in the 1945 San Francisco Conference, there was no real contradiction: the U.N.'s role was to promote abstract principles, not to scrutinize how governments apply or disregard those principles. Today, governments are well aware of the real contradiction between the claim of states to be left alone and the U.N.'s responsibility to further human rights everywhere, through rigorous fact-finding and forthright denunciation, leading, in exceptional cases, to enforcement action under Chapter VII of the Charter. The end of the Cold War has encouraged a new climate in which it is increasingly acceptable to regard human rights as an exception to the rule that the U.N. may not intervene in the internal affairs of states. In fact, the human rights exception had gained considerable ground before the transformation of East Central Europe. The range of action by the U.N. to respond to human rights situations without violating the "domestic jurisdiction" clause has expanded over time in three directions.

The first, which I call "soft intervention," is rendered possible by the contraction of the scope of Article 2(7) and the expansion of that of the Article 56 obligation of every member state of the U.N. to cooperate with the U.N. to achieve universal respect for and observance of human rights for all.[27] Numerous actions by the U.N. that would have been deemed "intervention" by most states a few decades ago, such

---

[25] Article 1(3) of the U.N. Charter, *supra* note 4, includes among the purposes of the U.N. "promoting and encouraging respect for human rights and . . . fundamental freedoms for all without distinction as to race, sex, language, or religion."

[26] Article 2(7) of the U.N. Charter, *supra* note 4, provides that "[n]othing contained in the present Charter shall authorize the United Nations to intervene in matters which are essentially within the domestic jurisdiction of any state or shall require the Members to submit such matters to settlement under the present Charter. . . ."

[27] *See* U.N. CHARTER, *supra* note 4, arts. 55 and 56. For the concepts of "soft," "hard," and "intrusive" intervention, see Stephen P. Marks, *Preventing Humanitarian Crises Through*

as investigation of abuse, adoption of resolutions explicitly denouncing countries by name, sending special envoys and rapporteurs, and addressing complaints to a government, are now common practices of the General Assembly and the Commission on Human Rights. As the balance between nonintervention and action to further human rights has tipped progressively in favor of the latter, these bodies have authorized on-site visits, the collection of information (especially from NGOs) the hearing of witnesses, receiving of complaints, communicating complaints to governments, and reporting to their parent bodies with detailed factual reports and recommendations. Thus, what was regarded as intolerable intervention a few decades ago is deemed acceptable today in the normal operation of the human rights bodies of the UN. This "soft intervention" is based on the consent of the accused state obtained under the political pressure that the Commission, the General Assembly, individual governments, and NGOs are willing to bring to bear.

The second significant evolution regarding U.N. responses to human rights situations has to do with "hard intervention"—that is, the use of coercive or enforcement measures pursuant to Chapter VII of the Charter. Enforcement action under Chapter VII, through economic sanctions or use of military force, is an explicit exception to the prohibition of intervention in domestic affairs.[28] Therefore, when the Security Council authorized "Member States to form a multinational force under unified command and control and . . . to use all necessary means to facilitate the departure from Haiti of the military leadership,"[29] it was acting under Chapter VII and fell within this exception to the rule against intervention. Prior to the Haiti resolution, "hard intervention" was not used for purely humanitarian purposes, even in the case of the repression of the Kurds. The Security Council never authorized military protection of the Kurds. Instead, it found the flow of transborder refugees to be a threat to international peace and security, and insisted that Iraq allow immediate access by international humanitarian organization to all those in need of assistance in all parts of Iraq.[30] As one commentator has pointed out, the debate over this resolution "was both a response to urgent human needs and a wide-ranging philosophical discussion of the purpose and limits of the Security Council," including the "meaning and contemporary significance of" the nonintervention principle.[31] The eventual establishment of no-fly zones and Operation Provide Comfort were not, at least as far as the U.N. was concerned, based on the Security Council

---

Peace-Building and Democratic Empowerment: Lessons from Camodia, 1 MED. & GLOBAL SUVIVAL 208 (1994). *See also* the similar formulation in Fernando R. Tesón, *Collective Humanitarian Intervention,* 17 MICH. J. INT'L L. 323, 325–28 (1996).

28 The nonintervention principle of Article 2(7), *quoted in, supra* note 26, according to the same text, "shall not prejudice the application of enforcement measures under Chapter VII."

29 S.C. Res. 940, U.N. SCOR, 49th Sess., Supp. No. 49, at 51, U.N. Doc. S/INF/50 (1994).

30 S.C. Res. 688, U.N. SCOR, 46th Sess., 2082d mtg., at 31, U.N. Doc. S/INF/47 (1993), *reprinted in* 30 I.L.M. 858 (1991) and 3 Weston II.F.3, *supra* note 16.

31 Jane E. Stromseth, *Iraq's Repression of its Civilian Population: Collective Responses and Continuing Challenges, in* LORI F. DAMROSCH, ENFORCING RESTRAINT: COLLECTIVE INTERVENTION IN INTERNAL CONFLICTS 86 (1993).

resolution. In Haiti, contrary to Iraq, the Security Council did invoke Chapter VII and authorized military action with respect to a purely internal situation.[32] Although the resolution stresses the "unique character" of the Haitian situation, it is nevertheless, a precedent for military intervention to redress a humanitarian crises due to an antidemocratic coup and massive human rights violations.

A third U.N. response to the domestic jurisdiction obstacle to human rights action is *intrusive action based on invitation or consent* by the territorial state to carry out tasks designed to restore or establish the conditions for a peaceful society—in U.N. parlance, "peacekeeping" and "peace-building." When consent is given by the territorial state to a multicomponent peace operation, the role of the U.N. is couched in terms of "cooperation" with whatever is left of a sovereign state rather than "intervention." But the form of action—despite consent to the agreement and to the presence of the international military and civilian personnel—is clearly an intrusive one. U.N. action affects some of the most basic matters of domestic jurisdiction, including the functioning of government and the security forces. As defined by former Secretary-General Boutros Boutros-Ghali in *An Agenda for Peace,* "peace-building" refers to "comprehensive efforts to identify and support structures which will tend to consolidate peace and advance a sense of confidence and well-being among people."[33] Peace-building tasks should involve, in the words of the Secretary-General, "disarming the previously warring parties and the restoration of order, the custody and possible destruction of weapons, repatriating refugees, advisory and training support for security personnel, monitoring elections, advancing efforts to protect human rights, reforming or strengthening governmental institutions and promoting formal and informal processes of political participation."[34] This

---

[32] *See* DAVID MALONE, DECISION MAKING IN THE U.N. SECURITY COUNCIL: THE CASE OF HAITI (1998). Haiti was not the first case of the Security Council using Chapter VII powers with respect to an internal situation affecting human rights. Violations of human rights were regarded as a threat or possible threat to international peace and security by the Council in its actions with respect to the Portuguese territories of Africa (language close to but not fully a determination of such a threat), the Unilateral Declaration of Independence of Southern Rhodesia, Namibia (without a formal determination under Chapter VII), South Africa, and the U.S. hostages in Iran (language close to but not fully a determination of such a threat). *See* Sidney D. Bailey, *The Security Council, in* THE UNITED NATIONS AND HUMAN RIGHTS: A CRITICAL APPRAISAL 304, 306–15 (Philip Alston ed., 1992). Human rights issues have also been addressed by the Security Council with respect to the application of the Geneva Conventions, military intervention to rescue or protect nationals, and supervising elections and plebiscites, *id.* at 315–24, but without authorizing coercive measures under Chapter VII.

[33] BOUTROS BOUTROS-GHALI, AN AGENDA FOR PEACE 32 (1992). Gareth Evans defines the term as "action taken after a conflict or crisis in order to help ensure that there is no recurrence of the problem: it may involve rehabilitation and reconstruction assistance generally, support for various kinds of institution-building, and specific practical programs like demining." GARETH EVANS, COOPERATING FOR PEACE: THE GLOBAL AGENDA FOR THE 1990S AND BEYOND 39 (1993).

[34] BOUTROS-GHALI, *supra* note 33, at 32.

function can entail also "support for the transformation of deficient national structures and capabilities, and for the strengthening of new democratic institutions."[35] The potential impact of the U.N.'s efforts is considerable, whether through an explicit human rights program or through the promotion of the rule of law and good governance, is clear.

There is an obvious connection between democratic practices—such as the rule of law and transparency in decision-making—and the achievement of lasting peace and security in any new and stable political order. As part of its post-Cold War role, the U.N. has defined these elements of good governance at all levels of international and national political communities.[36] Peace-building, including the "good governance" function, has been a little understood part of several multicomponent peace-keeping operations in the early 1990s, especially, UNTAC in Cambodia and ONUSAL in El Salvador.

Thus, "intervention " by the U.N. in human rights situations, where normal rules of state sovereignty would otherwise preclude it, has been resorted to either through "soft intervention" to express international concern with the human rights situation, "hard intervention" through the peace-enforcement exception of Chapter VII, or through the peace-keeping and peace-building exceptions based on consent. Through U.N. protective action, as Richard Falk puts it, the "basic social contract between States and the United Nations is . . . being rewritten."[37] Acceptance by the international community of these three encroachments on the *"domaine réservé"* constitute a major shift in international relations that enhance considerably opportunities for the U.N. to investigate and improve the human rights situation inside member states. That capacity has proved of little effect when confronted with xenophobic nationalism and ethnic conflict.

C. Nationalism and Ethnic Conflict

One of the most dangerous features of post-Cold War politics is the challenge to the sanctity of the principle of sovereignty of the nation-state and the resurgence of ethnic nationalism. For the United Nations human rights agenda, this development is full of contradictions. Self-determination had attained the status of a peremptory norm during the period of decolonization and was attached to the international bill of human rights as common Article 1 of the two international covenants of 1966,[38]

---

[35] *Id.* at 34–35.

[36] *Id.* at 34. The point has been made that democratic practices tend to increase rather than decrease instability and the propensity for political violence at the early stages. *See* Jack Snyder, *Nationalism and the Crisis of the Post-Soviet State*, 20 Survival 5 (Summer 1995); Edward Mansfield and Jack Snyder, *Democratization and War*, 74 Foreign Aff. 79 (May/Jun. 1995); Fareed Zakaria, *The Rise of Illiberal Democracy*, 76 Foreign Aff. 23 (Nov./Dec. 1997).

[37] Richard A. Falk, *The United Nations and the Rule of Law*, 4 Transnat'l L. & Contemp. Probs. 630 (1994).

[38] *See* International Covenant on Economic, Social and Cultural Rights, *infra* Appendix

which constitute the basic catalogue of internationally recognized human rights. It was in the name of self-determination that colonial empires were dissolved and the majority of the U.N.'s members gained independence and admission to the Organization. And it was in its name that the Baltic states attained or regained independence, followed by nations whose claims overturned the presumption in favor of the integrity of existing states.[39] The passion of the principle's basic premise overran this traditional state-centric limitation and produced the breakup of the Soviet Union and the Yugoslav Federation. The international human rights system, no more than the international security system, had not anticipated this development and was ill-prepared to respond to it, whether the massive human rights violations perpetrated by the Serbs in Bosnia and Kosovo and the Russians in Chechnya, or the even more massive atrocities resulting from the breakdown of all authority in Somalia, Rwanda, Zaire/D.R.C. and Sierra Leone.

Whether, against this backdrop, the U.N. can find an acceptable meaning of self-determination for the twenty-first century is doubtful. The tragedy of the Balkans is likely to provoke serious hesitation before recognizing similar claims in the future.[40]

D. Bureaucratic Constraints

Alongside these external ideological and political constraints on United Nations human rights diplomacy action are internal constraints resulting from the nature of the bureaucracy and the pressures placed on it by member states. These constraints have an impact on leadership, the quality and morale of staff, and on the availability of resources.

After the Vienna Conference in 1993, there occurred a major breakthrough with the creation of the post of U.N. High Commissioner for Human Rights.[41] The post

---

II [hereinafter ICESCR]; International Covenant on Civil and Political Rights, *infra* Appendix III [hereinafter ICCPR].

[39] *See Declaration on Principles of International Law Concerning Friendly Relations and Co-operation Among States in Accordance with the Charter of the United Nations*, G.A. Res. 2625 (XXV), 25 U.N. GAOR, Supp. No. 28, at 122, U.N. Doc. A/8028 (1971), *reprinted in* 9 I.L.M. 1292 (1970) *and* 1 INTERNATIONAL LAW AND WORLD ORDER: BASIC DOCUMENTS I.D.7 (Burns H. Weston ed., 5 vols., 1994–) [hereinafter 1 Weston], adopted by the General Assembly on Oct. 24, 1970 (excluding from the principle of self-determination anything that would authorize or encourage "any action which would dismember or impair, totally or in part, the territorial integrity or political unity of sovereign and independent States conducting themselves in compliance with the principle of equal rights and self-determination of peoples as described above and possessed of a government representing the whole people belonging to the territory without distinction as to race, creed or colour").

[40] *See* Hurst Hannum, *Rethinking Self-Determination*, 34 VA. J. INT'L L. 1, 17–28 (1993). *See also* Upendra Baxi's essay in this volume, *supra* p. 99.

[41] The position was created by General Assembly resolution 48/141, U.N. GAOR, 48th Sess., Supp. No. 49, at 261, U.N. Doc. A/48/49 (1993) (laying out the mandate).

was long an ideal of NGO activists and visionary government delegates who saw in it a high-level figure with potential for effective intervention on behalf of victims of human rights violations. The idea may be traced back to a proposal from René Cassin of France to establish a position of "Attorney-General for Human Rights,"[42] but it was not until the renewed hopes for an enhanced U.N. after the Cold War that the idea gained political momentum. After contentious debates and long night negotiations, the idea was finally endorsed by the World Conference on Human Rights in Vienna[43] and created by the General Assembly on December 20, 1993.[44] The following February, Secretary-General Boutros Boutros-Ghali appointed as the first U.N. High Commissioner for Human Rights, Mr. José Ayala Lasso, the Ecuadorian diplomat who had successfully chaired the working group that found the compromise language for the High Commissioner's mandate.

From the start, leadership was problematic. In appointing Ayala-Lasso to the new post, the Secretary-General, who was never favorable to its creation in the first place, appointed a person who, as chair of an ECOSOC working group, was successful in the negotiations for the mandate of the Office of the High Commissioner (OHCHR), but had no special credentials in the field. Also, his diplomatic skills were not necessarily the best credentials for the job, and he soon entered an "uneasy cohabitation" with another candidate for the job, the Assistant Secretary-General for Human Rights and the Director of the Centre for Human Rights, Ibrahima Fall of Senegal, who had solid human rights credentials and remained as director of the Centre. The two often seemed to be working at cross-purposes.[45] In 1997, both left the human rights scene.[46]

While an explicit role for the Commissioner in controlling the conditionality of development aid and explicit reference to fact-finding were dropped, the final mandate alludes to the obligation "to respect the sovereignty, territorial integrity and domestic jurisdiction of States." It also calls on the High Commissioner "to promote and protect the effective enjoyment by all of all civil, cultural, economic, political and social rights" and "to play an active role in removing the current obstacles and in meeting the challenges to the full realization of all human rights and in preventing the continuation of human rights violations throughout the world"—

---

[42] Andrew Clapham, *Creating the High Commissioner for Human Rights: The Outside Story*, 4 EUR. J. INT'L L. 556 (1994). *See also* ROGER S. CLARK, A UNITED NATIONS HIGH COMMISSIONER FOR HUMAN RIGHTS (1972).

[43] *See* Vienna Declaration and Programme of Action, *supra* note 16, para. 18.

[44] G.A. Res. 48/141, *supra* note 41.

[45] The tension between the two is described in A GLOBAL AGENDA: ISSUES BEFORE THE 51ST GENERAL ASSEMBLY OF THE UNITED NATIONS 176 (John Tessitore & Susan Woolfson eds., 1996).

[46] Mr. Ayala-Lasso accepted an Ecuadorian government appointment as Minister of Foreign Affairs. Mr. Fall took over responsibilities for Africa in the U.N.'s Department of Political Affairs in New York.

without awaiting, as proposals from the non-aligned countries would have required, a mandate from the Commission on Human Rights. The issue for the future is how the High Commissioner will interpret this "active role."

The day after Ayala-Lasso took up his position on April 5, 1994, the Presidents of Rwanda and Burundi were killed, setting off the massive bloodletting in Rwanda with the risk of engulfing Burundi in the process. Ayala-Lasso visited the area, called for a special session of the Commission on Human Rights, attempted to field a team of human rights monitors in Rwanda, and set up a "human rights assistance program" for Burundi.[47] This first reaction to human rights violations shows both the strength and weakness of the High Commissioner. It certainly is to Ayala-Lasso's credit that he moved rapidly to visit the area, urged a special session of the Commission, and sought practical measures to prevent further violations. At the same time, the fact that his means of action was an assistance program under Advisory Services indicates an interpretation of the "active role" provision of the mandate that is quite a few cautious steps away from the idea of an Attorney General for Human Rights. The extreme difficulties encountered in funding the human rights mission to Rwanda and in developing working methods, coordinating with the Prosecutor's office of the *ad hoc* tribunal, and directing operational activity from the Centre for Human Rights reveal both inherent defects in the mandate and the necessary process of adapting to a complex bureaucracy and the relatively unfamiliar world of human rights. A person with a different profile—less a diplomat and more a highly visible and pro-active world figure—might well have made a significant difference at this early stage of the Office of the High Commissioner. Reed Brody has argued that, "with the right person in the position and a mandate providing sufficient independence," the High Commissioner "could energize the entire U.N. human rights program."[48] It would indeed be a great stride forward if this position could become an effective vehicle of high level intervention capable of raising the stakes for persistent violators and an effective stimulus for the entire system. The potential for the position is considerable.

The new Secretary-General, Kofi Annan, appointed Ireland's President, Mary Robinson, as High Commissioner on June 12, 1997[49] and she was confirmed by the General Assembly on June 17.[50] Secretary-General Annan called this appointment "one of the most important . . . I will probably have the opportunity of mak-

---

[47]   *See Report of the United Nations High Commissioner for Human Rights*, U.N. Doc. A/49/36 (1995), paras. 60–66. *See also* Clapham, *supra* note 42, at 565–66.

[48]   Reed Brody, *Improving U.N. Human Rights Structures, in* HUMAN RIGHTS: AN AGENDA FOR THE NEXT CENTURY 297, 303 (Louis Henkin & John L. Hargrove eds., 1994).

[49]   Barbara Crossette, *U.N. Chief Picks Irish President to Be Top Aide on Human Rights*, N.Y. TIMES, June 13, 1997, at 11, col. 1.

[50]   *General Assembly Approves Appointment of Mary Robinson, President of Ireland, as High Commissioner for Human Rights*, Press Release, at 1, U.N. Doc. GA/9254 (June 17, 1997).

ing during my term, and it is very important for the entire international community."[51] By naming a woman with a reputation for courage and integrity who also
knows a great deal about human rights, Mr. Annan gave the post of High
Commissioner a higher profile than before. She changed the name to the Office of
the High Commissioner for Human Rights (OHCHR), absorbed the Centre into it
and benefitted from Kofi Annan's reform, which upgraded the New York office of
the High Commissioner and placed her on all four executive committees (dealing
with peace and security; economic and social affairs; development cooperation;
humanitarian affairs).[52] She also wisely chose a Latin American as deputy, Enrique
Ter Horst, a Venezuelan, although that relation did not last. More promising was
her appointment of veteran U.N. official and highly regarded scholar and activist,
Bertie Ramcharan of Guyana. The relationship between the two high officials has
already proved to be a vast improvement in the OHCHR.

A related issue is the perception and reality of a disproportionate number of
Western staff in the OHCHR.[53] Although an effort was made to micro-manage this
issue, the 1997 Commission decided to defer consideration of a draft resolution—
"composition of the staff of the Centre for Human Rights"—to the 54th session
of the Commission in 2001.[54] The new High Commissioner also inherited an elaborate plan to restructure the six branches of the Centre and meld them into three:
the Right to Development, Research and Analysis branch, with about 25 percent of
the regular budget and around 15 percent of extra-budgetary funding; the Support
Services branch, servicing meetings of various bodies, with about 25 percent of the
regular budget and 4.5 percent of extra-budgetary funds; and the Advisory Services,

---

[51] Transcript of Press Conference by Secretary-General Kofi Annan at United Nations
Headquarters, June 12, 1997, Press Release, at 9, U.N. Doc. SG/SM/6255, at 9 (June 12, 1997).

[52] *Report of the Secretary-General to the General Assembly, Renewing the United Nations:
A Programme for Reform,* U.N. Doc. A/51/950, para. 28 (July 14, 1997).

[53] U.N. reports at the time Mary Robinson took up as U.N. High Commissioner indicated
twelve American, two British, three Dutch, seven French, two German, six Italian, and five
Spanish (including staff temporarily placed in professional posts subject to geographical distribution), with the remaining thirty-three posts spread among some twenty-three developing countries. *See* U.N. Docs. A/51/641, A/51/650, and E/CN.4/1997/45 (1997). The
Commission's resolution on "Strengthening the Office of the United Nations High
Commissioner for Human Rights/Centre for Human Rights," Commission on Human Rights
Res. 1997/76, U.N. ESCOR, Supp. No. 3, at 255, U.N. Doc. E/CN.4/1997/150 (1997), echo-
ing G.A. Res. 51/90, U.N. GAOR, Supp. No. 49, at 233, U.N. Doc. A/51/49 (1996), asked
the High Commissioner to submit annual reports reflecting grade, nationality, and gender of
staff, including nonregular staff. The Commission reaffirmed the importance of ensuring
universality, objectivity, and nonselectivity in the consideration of human rights issues and,
expressing concern that earlier requests for a substantial increase in resources for the human
rights program had not met the level of need, requested that increase now, to come from
the existing regular U.N. budget.

[54] The draft resolution is contained in U.N. Doc. E/CN.4/1997/ L.47 (1997).

Technical Cooperation, and Support to Human Rights Fact-finding Procedures and Field Activities branch, including the various decades, special rapporteurs, and working groups, with about 50 percent of the regular budget and 80 percent of extra-budgetary funds.[55]

Ms. Robinson has the gargantuan task of restoring morale and ensuring the efficient functioning of her staff under the reformed structure. To make her task more difficult, the Commission seems bent on micro-managing the restructuring. Despite its decision in 1997 to defer consideration of "composition of the staff of the Centre for Human Rights" until 2001,[56] the Commission decided that it was necessary "to change the currently prevailing geographical distribution of the staff of the Office, in favour of a more equitable geographical distribution of posts."[57] It is not in the interest of a strong human rights program of the U.N. for the High Commissioner and her staff to be perceived as Western and Ms. Robinson has clearly understood the need for all geo-cultural groups to believe that her Office serves them all and that it will be even-handed in playing "the active role" in removing obstacles to, and preventing violations of, human rights.

III. The Potential for U.N. Human Rights Diplomacy and Action at Century's End

Four challenges merit priority attention to enhance the effectiveness of the U.N.'s as the principal instrument for multilateral diplomacy and action to advance human rights.

A. Listening to New Voices

While it is true that the claim of universality of human rights draws on both international law and the experience of peoples, the U.N. political organs began only a few decades ago to take seriously the voices of those who are not represented in diplomatic circles, where mainly men from dominant social groups working for governments draft texts and determine policies. Today, the struggle by women and indigenous peoples—to name but two significant examples—for recognition of their rights have made inroads into multilateral diplomacy at the U.N. In addition, the democratization of the U.N. through the increased involvement of "global civil society" in the U.N.'s decision-making and implementation processes is gaining strength. As argued by Upendra Baxi, these and other voices need to be heard if the U.N.'s human rights agenda is to be responsive to the new challenges of coming decades.[58]

---

55 *Proposed Programme Budget for the Biennium 1998–1999*, U.N. Doc. A/52/6, sect. 22, May 13, 1997, at 2–3.

56 *See* the Commission's draft resolution contained in U.N. Doc. E/CN.4/1997/ L.47.

57 Commission on Human Rights Resolution 1998/46, U.N. ESCOR, Supp. No. 3, at 156, U.N. Doc. E/CN.4.1998/177 (1998).

58 *See* Upendra Baxi, *Voices of Suffering, Fragmented Universality, and the Future of Human Rights, supra* in this volume, at p. 101.

1. Women

The U.N.'s record on improving the status of women and protecting their rights is, like human rights generally, one of timid beginnings and immense potential. The Commission on the Status of Women (CSW) was created at the same time as the Commission on Human Rights as a functional commission of ECOSOC. It has to its credit the drafting of the 1953 Convention on the Political Rights of Women,[59] the 1957 Convention on the Nationality of Married Women,[60] the 1962 Convention on Consent to Marriage, Minimum Age for Marriage, and Registration of Marriages,[61] the 1967 Declaration on the Elimination of Discrimination Against Women,[62] and the 1979 Convention on the Elimination of All Forms of Discrimination Against Women (CEDAW).[63] CEDAW is remarkable in that it not only obliges states parties "to take all appropriate measures to eliminate discrimination against women in the political and public life of the country"[64] and in other areas, but it requires them also to undertake to adopt measures "to modify the social and cultural patterns of conduct of men and women, with a view to achieving the elimination of prejudices and customary and all other practices which are based on the idea of inferiority or the superiority of either of the sexes or on stereotyped roles for men and women."[65] The Convention also allows affirmative action in the form of "temporary special measures aimed at accelerating *de facto* equality between men and women."[66]

The CSW's role in standard-setting is, however, diminished by its failure to adopt a system for examining complaints of violations of women's rights.[67]

---

[59] Convention on the Political Rights of Women, Mar. 31, 1953, 193 U.N.T.S. 135, *reprinted in* 3 Weston III.C.9, *supra* note 16.

[60] Convention on the Nationality of Married Women, Feb. 20, 1957, 309 U.N.T.S. 65, *reprinted in* 3 Weston III.C.10, *supra* note 16.

[61] Convention on Consent to Marriage, Minimum Age for Marriage, and Registration of Marriages, Dec. 10, 1962, 521 U.N.T.S. 231, *reprinted in* 3 Weston III.C.11, *supra* note 16.

[62] *Declaration on the Elimination of Discrimination Against Women*, Nov. 7, 1967, G.A. Res. 2263, U.N. GAOR, 22d Sess., Supp. No. 16, at 35, U.N. Doc. A/6716 (1968), *reprinted in* 3 Weston III.C.12, *supra* note 16.

[63] Convention on the Elimination of All Forms of Discrimination Against Women, Dec. 18, 1979, 1249 U.N.T.S. 13 [hereinafter CEDAW], *reprinted in* 3 Weston III.C.13, *supra* note 16.

[64] *Id.* art. 7.

[65] *Id.* art. 5(a).

[66] *Id.* art. 4(1).

[67] Until 1983, the CSW received "communications" concerning violations of women's rights, but was not allowed to take action. By ECOSOC Resolution 1983/27, U.N. ESCOR, Supp. No. 1, at 21, U.N. Doc. E/1998/83 (1983), the CSW was empowered to appoint a sessional working group to review the confidential communications for patterns of injustice or discrimination and report the categories of abuse to the Commission, which then may make

Moreover, the implementation of CEDAW is the responsibility of the Committee on the Elimination of Discrimination Against Women, and the drafting of the Declaration on the Elimination of Violence Against Women[68] (an issue not covered by CEDAW) and the appointment of a Special Rapporteur on that subject were the work of the Commission on Human Rights rather than the CSW. The CSW's efforts have focused more on the World Conference on Women in Mexico City in 1975, the Decade of Action on Women, the mid-decade review conference in Copenhagen in 1980, and the end-of-decade conference in Nairobi in 1985, which adopted the "Forward-Looking Strategies." On the other hand, the CSW has not played a significant role in the reports and programs deriving from these events.[69] It was the General Assembly and ECOSOC rather than the CSW that established the International Research and Training Institute for the Advancement of Women (INSTRAW) and the United Nations Development Fund for Women (UNIFEM), with the CSW playing only a peripheral role.

Laura Reanda finds in the CSW's history a "familiar dilemma" in the struggle for women's rights.[70] She explains:

> The creation of separate institutional mechanisms and the adoption of special measures for women are often necessary in order to rectify existing situations of discrimination. The danger of creating a "women's ghetto" endowed with less power and resources, attracting less interest and commanding lower priority than other national policy goals is latent in this approach. On the other hand, efforts to improve the situation of women through general measures addressed to the population as a whole often result in the struggle for equality becoming submerged in global concerns.[71]

In the 1990s, women's NGOs have taken the lead in moving women's human rights to a much more visible position on the U.N.'s human rights agenda. Resisting opposition from countries favoring traditional roles for women, U.N. conferences have altered the landscape for women's human rights. At the Vienna Conference on

---

recommendations to ECOSOC for possible action by that body. The procedure has rarely been used and reforms have been proposed. *See* Laura Reanda, *The Commission on the Status of Women, in* THE UNITED NATIONS AND HUMAN RIGHTS: A CRITICAL APPRAISAL 265, 295 (Philip Alston ed., 1992).

68   Declaration on the Elimination of Violence Against Women, Dec. 20, 1993, G.A. Res. 48/104, U.N. GAOR, 48th Sess., Supp. No. 49, at 261, U.N. Doc. A/RES/48/104, *reprinted in* 33 I.L.M. 1049 (1994) *and* 3 Weston III.C.12, *supra* note 16.

69   *See* Reanda, *supra* note 67, at 293.

70   *Id.* at 267.

71   *Id.* (citing her previous article, *Human Rights and Women's Rights: The United Nations Approach*, 3 HUM. RTS. Q. 12 (1961)).

Human Rights in 1993 and the Cairo Conference on Population and Development in 1994, the governments participating recognized that key to coping with population issues is the empowerment of women through education and economic opportunity. One observer, Upendra Baxi, considered the section on equal status and human rights of women in the Vienna Declaration as "the cornerstone of the Vienna Declaration."[72] After reviewing the full range of provisions concerning women, Baxi concludes:

> From rigorous feminist perspectives, assessment of the Vienna achievements, and their future trajectories, is bound to vary enormously. This is as it should be, as combating patriarchy at its roots (social foundations) represents a millennial marathon which can only be imperfectly flagged off by a United Nations Declaration. What is important, however, is not any form of ideological critique but rather how such a critique can enhance the *telos* which animates the Vienna Declaration.[73]

The Fourth World Conference on Women, held in Beijing in September 1995, moved the agenda forward not only by reaffirming (as the Vienna Declaration had done) that women's rights are human rights, but also by expressing the conviction that "the explicit recognition and reaffirmation of the right of all women to control all aspects of their health, in particular their own fertility, is basic to their empowerment."[74] The member states expressed their determination to "promote and protect all human rights of women and girls" and to "intensify efforts to ensure equal enjoyment of all human rights and fundamental freedoms for all women and girls who face multiple barriers to their empowerment and advancement because of such factors as their race, age, language, ethnicity, culture, religion, or disability, or because they are indigenous people."[75] They adopted the Platform for Action, which reaffirmed "the fundamental principle set forth in the Vienna Declaration and Programme of Action . . . that the human rights of women and of the girl child are an inalienable, integral and indivisible part of universal human rights."[76] The Platform is "an agenda for action [that] seeks to promote and protect the full enjoyment of all human rights and the fundamental freedoms of all women throughout their life cycle."[77] The text uses the expression "human rights" over forty times. Although women activists were disappointed in not achieving all they had hoped

---

[72] Baxi, *supra* note 15, at 12.

[73] *Id.* at 15.

[74] *U.N. Report of the Fourth World Conference on Women* (Beijing, Sept. 4–15, 1995), para. 17, U.N. Doc. A/CONF.177/20 (1995) and U.N. Doc. A/CONF.177/20/Add.1 (1995), *reprinted in* 35 I.L.M. 405 (1996).

[75] *Id.* para. 32.

[76] *Id.* para. 9.

[77] *Id.* at 2.

from this U.N. event, there was general satisfaction over the linkage between women's rights and human rights and the acknowledgment that women had rights related to their sexuality and reproduction.[78]

The potential for the United Nations does not lie in overcoming patriarchy, which is a "millennial marathon," but in a strategy of three parts. The first is to continue, at the normative level, to reflect the voices of women and "acknowledge the history of women's economic and political invisibility, the misuse of custom and culture as impediments, and the tradition of structural inequality."[79] The second is to strengthen the implementation of CEDAW, empowering the CEDAW Committee, through an optional protocol, to receive communications alleging violations[80], by programs that effectively include CEDAW in development planning and education, and by encouraging more interaction between the CEDAW Committee and NGOs, as occurs informally already. The third is to increase the resources and political significance of the work of the CSW by adopting a more credible complaints procedure dealing with specific situations and cases leading to the CSW's addressing recommendations directly to governments, by taking the lead in "mainstreaming" women's rights concerns throughout the U.N. system, and by working effectively with the Commission on Human Rights to give greater political attention to neglected issues such as violence against women. In addition, as many have suggested, the U.N. should overcome obstacles to bringing its own internal employment practices in line with the principles of CEDAW.[81]

---

[78] For example, the Platform affirms that

[t]he human rights of women include their right to have control over and decide freely and responsibly on matters related to their sexuality, including sexual and reproductive health, free of coercion, discrimination and violence. Equal relationships between women and men in matters of sexual relations and reproduction, including full respect for the integrity of the person, require mutual respect, consent and shared responsibility for sexual behaviour and its consequences.

Id. para. 97.

[79] Marcha A. Freeman & Arvonne S. Fraser, *Women's Human Rights: Making the Theory a Reality, in* HUMAN RIGHTS: AN AGENDA FOR THE NEXT CENTURY 124 (Louis Henkin & John Lawrence Hargrove eds., 1994).

[80] Pursuant to a recommendation of the Vienna Conference on Human Rights and drawing on a draft proposed by an expert meeting at the University of Maastricht in 1994, the CSW worked for three years on a draft protocol, which it adopted on March 12, 1999, for final adoption by the General Assembly at its 54th session. *See* U.N. Doc. E/CN.6/1999/WG/ L.2 (Mar. 10, 1999). For the background, see A. Byrnes and J. Connors, *Enforcing the Human Rights of Women: A Complaints Procedure for the Women's Convention*, 21 BROOK. J. INT'L L. 679–797 (1996) and Suzanne Spears, *Optional Protocol to the Convention on the Elimination of All Forms of Discrimination Against Women*, __ COLUM. HUM. RTS. L. REV. __ (forthcoming). While some NGOs regret that proposals on standing were not accepted, the text makes progress regarding the inquiry procedures, interim measures, and exclusion of reservations.

[81] *See, e.g.*, Freeman & Fraser, *supra* note 79, at 125.

2. Indigenous Peoples

Indigenous populations—peoples whose identity with the land antedates the arrival of the dominant population—are affected by the asset deprivation resulting from unequal land distribution, increased mechanization, and depressed markets, as well as the loss of cultural identity to the point of cultural and physical extinction. Development may threaten their traditional culture while land use and mining, cattle grazing, logging, hydroelectric power and other industries often eliminate traditional forms of land ownership and use and production of distribution patterns. Indigenous populations have an attachment to the land antedating the arrival of the dominant population and possess a distinct history, customs, religion and language.[82] As one U.N. reform proposal notes, "[s]ome 300 million indigenous people now demand an end to the long denial of their identity."[83]

Since states tend to deal with such populations as an internal matter, their voice is not likely to be heard in intergovernmental deliberations. However, several states, concerned about the problems affecting their own indigenous populations (*e.g.*, Australia, Canada, Norway, and Finland), supported NGO initiatives during the 1970s to bring these concerns before the U.N. In 1982, the Working Group on Indigenous Populations was established within the Sub-Commission on Prevention of Discrimination and Protection of Minorities to review developments and standards. The General Assembly made 1993 the International Year of the World's Indigenous People and proclaimed the decade beginning December 10, 1994 the International Decade of the World's Indigenous People with the aim of "strengthening international cooperation for the solution of problems faced by indigenous people in such areas as human rights, the environment, development, education and health."[84] Finally, the Commission on Human Rights, while endorsing the Decade, recognized "the value and the diversity of the cultures and the forms of social organization of the world's indigenous people."[85]

The U.N. has generated a considerable body of research and official statements on the human rights problems of indigenous peoples.[86] States, protective of their

---

[82]   *See* Asbjørn Eide, *The Sub-Commission on Prevention of Discrimination and Protection of Minorities, in* THE UNITED NATIONS AND HUMAN RIGHTS: A CRITICAL APPRAISAL 211, 235–39 (Philip Alston ed., 1992). *See also* JAMES ANAYA, INDIGENOUS PEOPLES IN INTERNATIONAL LAW (1996); INDIGENOUS PEOPLES, THE UNITED NATIONS AND HUMAN RIGHTS (Sarah Pritchard ed., 1999); Russel L. Barsh, *Indigenous Peoples: An Emerging Object of International Law*, 80 AM. J. INT'L L. 369 (1986); Russel L. Barsh, *Indigenous Peoples in the 1990s: From Object to Subject of International Law?*, 7 HARV. HUM. RTS. J. 33 (1994).

[83]   CHILDERS & URQUHART, *supra* note 13, at 107.

[84]   G.A. Res. 48/163, U.N. GAOR, 48th Sess., Supp. No. 49, at 381, U.N. Doc. A/48/49 (1993).

[85]   Commission on Human Rights Res. 1994/26, U.N. ESCOR, 49th Sess., Supp. No. 49, U.N. Doc. E/CN.4/1994/132 (1994).

[86]   *See* JOSÉ MARTINEZ COBO, STUDY OF THE PROBLEM OF DISCRIMINATION AGAINST INDIGE-

sovereignty, are not naturally inclined to support successionist claims at home or in international institutions. They are, therefore, cautious to ensure that the use of the term "peoples" in relation to indigenous peoples does not imply acceptance on their part that such peoples enjoy a right of succession. The U.N. has provided the diplomatic setting where, over many years, states and indigenous peoples could work out the appropriate normative language on this complex issue.

After ten years of drafting, the Sub-commission on Prevention of Discrimination and Protection of Minorities adopted the Declaration on the Rights of Indigenous Peoples in August 1994.[87] A remarkable feature of the functioning of the Working Group and the Commission's consideration of the International Year and the Decade is the strong participation of representatives of indigenous peoples. The mandate of the Working Group, requiring that it include such representatives in its work and a Voluntary Fund, plus support from foundations and other sources, have made this participation an effective precursor to including global civil society the work of the U.N.[88] The Working Group is a small cog in the giant wheels of the U.N., but it is a relatively successful experiment in people's participation.

The participation of indigenous peoples in the U.N. human rights system requires more than the opportunity to address the Working Group. Several U.N. reform proposals call for the transformation of the Trusteeship Council into some type of council responsible for minorities and indigenous peoples.[89] Such an arrangement would make sense. The issues of indigenous peoples require system-wide action as well, considering the role of the International Labour Organisation regarding its Convention (No. 169) Concerning Indigenous and Tribal Peoples in

---

NOUS POPULATIONS, U.N. Doc. E/CN.4/Sub. 2/21 and Add. 1–7 (1983) and more recent reports by Special Rapporteur Asbjørn Eide; AMNESTY INTERNATIONAL, THE AMERICAS: HUMAN RIGHTS VIOLATIONS AGAINST INDIGENOUS PEOPLES (1992); Reports of the Working Group on Indigenous Populations.

[87] *See Draft Declaration on the Rights of Indigenous Peoples*, adopted by the U.N. Commission on Human Rights Sub-Commission on the Prevention of Discrimination and Protection of Minorities, Aug. 26, 1994, U.N. Doc. E/CN.4/1995/2, E/CN.4/Sub.2/1994/56 (Oct. 28, 1994), *reprinted in* 34 I.L.M. 541 (1989) *and* 3 Weston III.F.4, *supra* note 16.

[88] *See* United Nations Commission on Human Rights Resolution 1995/32 (1995), *reprinted in* 34 I.L.M. 535 (1995).

[89] One such proposal is for a "Council on Diversity, Representation and Governance" in CHILDERS & URQUHART, *supra* note 13, ch. VIII. Hurst Hannum has proposed the establishment of a "permanent office or institution to deal with minorities questions" but appears to consider that the Working Group on Indigenous Populations should "continue to review current developments relevant to indigenous peoples and, ultimately, monitor implementation of the declaration on indigenous rights after it is adopted by the General Assembly." Hurst Hannum, *Minorities, Indigenous Peoples, and Self-Determination, in* HUMAN RIGHTS: AN AGENDA FOR THE NEXT CENTURY 12 (Louis Henkin and John Lawrence Hargrove eds., 1994).

Independent Countries of 1989[90] and the impact of development projects by other specialized agencies and the international financial institutions (IFIs) on indigenous peoples. The IFIs tend to support agents of globalization and place structural adjustment and export-driven development projects ahead of the needs of indigenous peoples.[91] The interest of the latter requires, therefore, that the voices of indigenous peoples be heard through a more powerful body than the Sub-Commission on Prevention of Discrimination and Protection of Minorities. The proposal to create a permanent forum in the U.N., possibly as an ECOSOC body with competence over human rights, environmental, and development issues affecting indigenous peoples, is a step in the right direction.

3. Civil Society

The meaning of "civil society" has evolved in the history of Western political thought and has been used in post-Cold War political discourse to refer to those organizations and movements that stand between society·and the state and seek to define and monitor the norms by which the latter may be held accountable to the former.[92] In a 1994 Secretariat assessment of the "role of non-state actors in contemporary society," the U.N. linked the emergence of civil society to globalization:

> With the revolution in communications and information technology and the profound transnationalization of the economy, events, issues and processes in one part of the world immediately reverberate across regions with a resulting transformation of the perceptions that communities everywhere form about the evolution of the world as a whole.[93]

---

[90]   International Labour Organisation Convention (No. 169) Concerning Indigenous and Tribal Peoples in Independent Countries, June 27, 1989, International Labour Conference Draft Report of the Committee on Convention No. 107, App. I, C.C. 1–7/D 303 (June 1989), *reprinted in* 28 I.L.M. 1382 (1989) *and* 3 Weston III.F.2, *supra* note 16.

[91]   The World Health Organization has begun to deal with the issue through such activities as a conference on the health of indigenous peoples held in New Zealand in February 1998. Also, the World Bank has demonstrated a certain sensitivity to the issue of indigenous people in recent years. *See, e.g.,* INDIGENOUS PEOPLE AND POVERTY IN LATIN AMERICA: AN EMPIRICAL ANALYSIS (George Psacharopoulos and Harry Anthony Patrinos eds., 1994); TRADITIONAL KNOWLEDGE AND SUSTAINABLE DEVELOPMENT: PROCEEDINGS OF A CONFERENCE SPONSORSHIP BY THE WORLD BANK'S ENVIRONMENT AND THE BANKWIDE TASK FORCE ON THE INTERNATIONAL YEAR OF THE WORLD'S INDIGENOUS PEOPLE (Shelton Davis and Katrinka Ebbe, 1995).

[92]   *See supra* note 6.

[93]   *General Review of Arrangements for Consultations with Non-Governmental Organizations,* Report of the U.N. Secretary-General, U.N. Doc. E/AC.70/1994/5, para. 7 (May 26, 1994).

The norm-setting role of the United Nations, acknowledged as "one of the United Nations' great accomplishments,"[94] provided the basis for challenges of repressive regimes by civil society. The vitality and courage of independent human rights groups has animated the human rights movement since the founding of the U.N.[95] In recent years, they have contributed in significant measure to the end of centralized authoritarian regimes, whether in the pre-1989 right wing militaristic model of Central and South America and South Africa or the communist police states of East Central Europe. The human rights provisions of the Helsinki Final Act and the "human dimension" component of the Helsinki process were truly empowering for the emerging civil society of East Central Europe.[96] In this connection, Richard Falk writes that

> the foundations for a greatly enhanced system of global governance lie dormant, but these latent potentialities are unlikely to be activated by leading governments, unless they are prodded by mobilized and focused social forces associated with transnational democratic initiatives. The plausibility of such mobilization is established by reference to the impressive NGO role in relation to the implementation and extension of human rights (for instance, with particular reference to women and indigenous peoples) and environmental standards, as well as regionally, during the 1980s with respect to the human rights provisions of the Helsinki Accords.[97]

In the United Nations, where human rights NGOs had been behind the procedures of "soft intervention" mentioned above, the new dogma of civil society was integrated into official discourse at seminars and in publications of the OHCHR, in debates of the Commission on Human Rights, and in human rights aspects of field operations. The U.N. has experience with participation of NGOs in the determination of policy and implementation of programs, although most government officials are not comfortable with such involvement. The World Conference on Human

---

[94]   Hurst Hannum, *Human Rights, in* 1 UNITED NATIONS LEGAL ORDER 319, 345 (Oscar Schachter & Christopher Joyner eds., 1995).

[95]   The literature on human rights NGOs is vast. A major recent work is WILLIAM KOREY, NGOs AND THE UNIVERSAL DECLARATION OF HUMAN RIGHTS: A CURIOUS GRAPEVINE (1998). *See also* DIVERSE PARTNERS: NON-GOVERNMENTAL ORGANIZATIONS IN THE HUMAN RIGHTS MOVEMENT (Henry Steiner ed., 1991); THE CONSCIENCE OF THE WORLD: THE INFLUENCE OF NON-GOVERNMENTAL ORGANIZATIONS IN THE U.N. SYSTEM (Peter Willetts ed., 1996); Felice D. Gaer, *Reality Check: Human Rights NGOs Confront Governments at the U.N.*, in NGOs, THE U.N., AND GLOBAL GOVERNANCE 51 (Thomas G. Weiss & Leon Gordenker eds., 1996); Julie Mertus, *Human Rights and the Promise of Transnational Civil Society, infra* in this volume, at p. 433.

[96]   *See, e.g.*, in this connection, WILLIAM KOREY, THE PROMISES WE KEEP: HUMAN RIGHTS, THE HELSINKI PROCESS AND AMERICAN FOREIGN POLICY (1993).

[97]   Falk, *supra* note 37, at 639–40.

Rights in June 1993 recognized "the important role of non-governmental organizations in the promotion of all human rights and in humanitarian activities at national, regional and international levels."[98] The Conference, while not particularly resounding about NGO rights, did acknowledge that they "should be free to carry out their human rights activities, without interference," adding immediately that such activities are "within the framework of national law and the Universal Declaration of Human Rights."[99]

In fact, the rights of NGOs have been on the agenda of the Commission on Human Rights since 1984, when a working group was established to draft a declaration on human rights defenders.[100] After almost a decade and a half of laborious and often stalled negotiations, and with the urging of High Commissioner, Mary Robinson, and the recent fiftieth anniversary of the UDHR, the Commission's working group on the Declaration finished its work in Winter 1998 and the Commission adopted it on March 4, 1998.[101] In spite of its weakness, the text was welcomed by NGOs and was adopted by the General Assembly on December 9, 1998.[102]

Constitutionally, the interactions between this global civil society and the intergovernmental structures of the U.N. are the responsibility of the Economic and Social Council.[103] In 1946, ECOSOC created an NGO committee of five members (now nineteen) to deal with consultative status. The criteria for admission to this status were established in 1968[104] and were revised in 1996.[105] The impetus for this review came from the effective participation of NGOs to the 1992 U.N. Conference on Environment and Development in Rio,[106] followed by similarly significant NGO

---

[98] Vienna Declaration and Programme of Action, *supra* note 16, at para. 38.

[99] *Id.*

[100] *See* Allan McChesney & Nigel Rodley, *Human Rights Defenders: Drafting a Declaration, in* 48 INT'L COMM. JUR., THE REVIEW 50 (1992). *See also* Michael H. Posner & Candy Whittome, *The Status of Human Rights NGOs*, 25 COLUM. HUM. RTS. L. REV. 269 (1994).

[101] Commission on Human Rights Res. 1998/7, U.N. ESCOR , Supp. No. 3, at 47, U.N. Doc. E/CN.4/1998/177 (1998).

[102] *Declaration on the Rights and Responsibilities of Individuals, Groups and Organs of Society to Promote and Protect Universally Recognized Human Rights and Fundamental Freedoms*, Dec. 9, 1998, G.A. Res. 53/144, U.N. GAOR, 53d Sess., Supp No.__, U.N. Doc.__ (known unofficially as "the U.N. Declaration on Human Rights").

[103] U.N. Charter article 71 provides that the Council "may make suitable arrangements for consultation with non-governmental organizations which are concerned with matters within its competence."

[104] ECOSOC Res. 1296 (XLIV), U.N. ESCOR, 44th Sess., Supp. No. 1, at 21, U.N. Doc. E/4548 (1968).

[105] ECOSOC Res. 1996/31, U.N. ESCOR, 47th Sess., Supp. No. 1, at 53, U.N. Doc. E/1996/96 (1996)

[106] Chapter 27 of Agenda 21, "strengthening the role of non-governmental organizations:

presence at the 1993 Vienna Conference on Human Rights, the 1994 Cairo Conference on Population and Development, the 1995 Copenhagen World Summit on Social Development, and the 1995 Beijing Conference on Women. Efforts to expand NGO participation to open access to national NGOs from the South and to enhance the rights of NGOs ran up against resistance from state-centric G-77 countries, and the revised rules continue to require human rights NGOs to meet a condition not required of other NGOs, namely, that they "pursue the goals of promotion and protection of human rights in accordance with the spirit of the Charter of the United Nations, the Universal Declaration of Human Rights and the Vienna Declaration and Programme of Action."[107] Proposals to involve global civil society in more general U.N. affairs beyond ECOSOC have been motivated by the best of intentions as they give meaning to the words "We, the Peoples . . ." with which the Charter opens. The Commission on Global Governance, for example, proposed that a Forum of Civil Society meet in the Plenary Hall of the General Assembly just prior to each annual session.[108] However, the efforts of a working group to explore NGO participation in non- ECOSOC U.N. activities (galvanized by governments that welcomed NGO criticism of major powers in the fields of peace and security or trade and finance) floundered, precisely because the U.S. and other powerful countries wanted to keep NGOs out of these areas.

In addition to the expansion of NGO rights in the U.N., whether for human rights or other purposes, the problem of representation and m.anipulation by interest groups must be addressed. As Chadwick Alger points out,

[international NGOs] have often been dominated by cosmopolitan élites in national capitals and . . . cities in the North. But there is no doubt that the growth of participation by local and grass-roots people in both the North and the South has made citizen efforts . . . more reflective of the global population, particularly in the South. We vitally need comprehensive assessments of the actual and potential respresentativeness of these efforts.[109]

Presumably, it would be in the interest of a stronger U.N. human rights program for pro-human rights "cosmopolitan élites" and grass-roots activists to have greater access to U.N. decision-making bodies and to be able to make oral and writ-

---

partners for sustainable development," refers to their role with respect to participatory democracy, provision of expertise, monitoring environmental impacts and global networking. *See* Report of the U.N. Conference on the Environment and Development at Rio de Janeiro, June 3–14, 1992, Agenda 21, U.N. Doc A/CONF.151/26 (Vols. I–III) (1992).

[107] *Supra* note 105, para. 25.

[108] Commission on Global Governance, Our Global Neighborhood 258–59 (1995).

[109] Chadwick F. Alger, *Citizens and the U.N. System in a Changing World, in* Yoshikazu Sakamoto, Global Transformation: Challenges to the State System 301, 325 (1994).

ten submissions and otherwise lobby the U.N. for more accountability by governments and stronger multilateral enforcement of human rights. However, there is a potential danger for human rights if such expanded rights were genuinely empowering and the repressive regimes and economic interests that support them were to manipulate that access to create so-called independent NGOs with neutral or pro-U.N. sounding names that would in practice undermine the human rights regime of the U.N. One can imagine a group calling itself the "Association for Human Rights in a Pluralistic World" which would challenge the universality of human rights or a "League for Human Rights and Economic Opportunities" that would lobby for full payment of foreign debts. The criteria for admission to NGO status under ECOSOC Resolution 1996/31 allows ECOSOC to suspend or withdraw consultative status if an organization "either directly or through its affiliates or representatives acting on its behalf, clearly abuses its status by engaging in a pattern of acts contrary to the purposes and principles of the Charter of the United Nations including unsubstantiated or politically motivated acts against Member States of the United Nations incompatible with those purposes and principles" or if "there exists substantiated evidence of influence from proceeds resulting from internationally recognized criminal activities such as the illicit drugs trade, money-laundering or the illegal arms trade."[110] It is not difficult to imagine how highly professional lobbyists pursuing an agenda favorable to statist, financial or industrial interests contrary to human rights would avoid these sanctions.

Therefore, while there is merit in the proposition that global civil society holds the key to reinvigorating the U.N.'s human rights program, we must be cautious lest the current window of opportunity for empowerment be massively occupied by those forces of globalization that are hostile to the human rights agenda. Nevertheless, the process of listening to the voices of the global civil society, including those of women and indigenous peoples, is gaining momentum and will be a prominent feature of the U.N.'s human rights agenda as the century draws to a close.

B.   Peace Operations

The entry of human rights into the U.N.'s mandate in international peace and security has been one of the most promising of post-Cold War developments, although fraught with risks and political misgivings. The most dramatic human rights link with peace and security has been the use of enforcement powers for expanded human rights purposes, including prosecution of individuals responsible for genocide, crimes against humanity, and war crimes. The second salient dimension of this link has been the creation of human rights components of multidimensional peace operations. The third aspect—related to, but different from, the second—is the

---

110   ECOSOC Res. 1996/31, *supra* note 105, para. 57. A third ground for suspension or withdrawal of status is the failure, during the preceding three years, of the organization to "make any positive or effective contribution to the work of the United Nations and, in particular, of the Council or its commissions or other subsidiary organs." *Id.*

human rights dimension of post-conflict peace-building, including human rights field operations.

1. Peace Enforcement

The Gulf War brought human rights into the purview of the Security Council when it characterized internal repression as a threat to international peace and security. The willingness of Russia and China to let such a determination pass was a major turning point in the post-Cold War. A determination of the existence of such a threat is a precondition for Security Council action under its peace enforcement powers,[111] and technically the Council did not determine that the repression of the Kurds constituted a threat to international peace and security. But it did conclude, per Resolution 688, that the consequences of that repression had that effect, and this was enough for it to demand that Iraq allow access by international humanitarian organizations and to appeal to member states to contribute to this humanitarian effort.[112] The resolution was interpreted by the U.S., UK, and French governments as providing the basis for them to station troops in, and send NATO aircraft over, Northern Iraq to protect the Kurdish population from further abuse by the Baghdad authorities. Baghdad, in turn, agreed to let the U.N. set up "humanitarian centres" in the Kurdish region of the North and the Shi'ite region of the south with U.N. guards.[113] Human rights made an ambiguous entry into U.N. peace enforcement.

The next major precedent was set when the Security Council decided to authorize the United States to command a multinational force to secure the departure of the *de facto* regime in Port-au-Prince and the return of the democratically elected president Jean-Bertrand Aristide.[114] In this case the Council did not feel the need to allude to the "international consequences" of the internal situation. The violation of human rights and suppression of democracy were sufficient, it appears, to justify the authorization of the use of the multinational force (MNF) and to authorize the MNF "to use all necessary means to facilitate the departure from Haiti of the military leadership, consistent with the Governors Island Agreement, the prompt return of the legitimately elected President and the restoration of the legitimate authorities of the Government of Haiti, and to establish and maintain a secure and stable environment. . . ."[115] While the Council expressed grave concern over "the significant further deterioration of the humanitarian situation in Haiti, in particular the continuing escalation by the illegal *de facto* regime of systematic violations of

---

[111] *See* U.N. CHARTER, *supra* note 4, art. 39. For precedents during the Cold War, *see supra* note 32.

[112] S.C. Res. 688, *supra* note 30.

[113] *See Letter Dated May 19, 1991, from the Permanent Representative of Iraq to the United Nations Secretary-General,* U.N. Doc. S/22623 (1991).

[114] S.C. Res. 940, U.N. SCOR, 49th Sess., 3413th mtg., at 51, U.N. Doc. S/INF/50 (1994).

[115] *Id.*

civil liberties, the desperate plight of Haitian refugees. . . .",[116] the avoidance of the language of human rights reflects the divergent approaches of the Special Representative of the Secretary-General and the director for human rights of the civilian mission, and the reality was incontestably one of violation of human rights redressed by a Security Council-authorized use of force.

The Bosnian crisis has been less explicitly a case of human rights violations *stricto sensu*, since the Security Council has tended to focus on "ethnic cleansing" and violations of international humanitarian law. It should be clear, however, that ethnic cleansing is shorthand for a particularly violent set of human rights violations based on the religious or national origin of the victims: arbitrary detention, torture, summary execution, disappearance, deportation, and forcible displacement.[117] Furthermore, international humanitarian law is in fact human rights law applied in times of armed conflict.[118] In any event, the intensity of the human rights tragedy in Bosnia convinced the Commission on Human Rights to convene its first special session in 1992, which resulted in the appointment of a Special Rapporteur to investigate first-hand the human rights situation in the territory of the former Yugoslavia, in particular within Bosnia and Herzegovina.[119] Former Polish foreign minister Tadeusz Mazowiecki was appointed to the position and subsequently submitted detailed reports of massive and systematic violations of human rights and humanitarian law.[120] The UNPROFOR mandate, however, was not a human rights mandate, but rather one "to create the conditions of peace and security required for the negotiation of an overall settlement of the Yugoslav crisis,"[121] expanded to provide protection for humanitarian deliveries, protected areas, pink areas, and eventually close air support in defense of UNPROFOR personnel.[122] The contradictions between the logic and dynamic of the UNPROFOR mandate and the imperative of human rights led the Special Rapporteur to resign in disgust in July 1995 when he realized that the U.N. could do nothing to prevent flagrant violations of human rights

---

[116] *Id.*

[117] *See* HUMAN RIGHTS WATCH, THE LOST AGENDA: HUMAN RIGHTS AND U.N. FIELD OPERATIONS 77 (1993).

[118] The International Committee of the Red Cross prefers to think of human rights law and humanitarian law as "related but distinct [and] complementary." *See* JEAN PICTET, INTERNATIONAL HUMANITARIAN LAW: DEFINITION xxii (1988, 1998).

[119] Commission on Human Rights Res. 1992/S–1/1, U.N. ESCOR, 47th Sess., Supp. No. 2A, at 4, U.N. Doc. E/1992/22/Add.1 (1992).

[120] See the following Periodic Reports on the Situation of Human Rights in the Territory of the Former Yugoslavia Submitted by Mr. Tadeusz Mazowiecki, Special Rapporteur of the Commission on Human Rights Pursuant to Paragraph 32 of Commission Resolution 1993/7 of 23 February 1993: U.N. Doc. S/26383 (1993); U.N. Doc. S/26415 (1993); U.N. Doc. S/26469; U.N. Doc. A/49/641–S/1994/1252; U.N. Doc. A/50/69–S/1995/79; and U.N. Doc. A/50/71–S/1995/80.

[121] S.C. Res. 743, U.N. SCOR, 47th Sess., 3055th mtg., at 8, U.N. Doc. S/RES/743 (1992).

[122] S.C. Res. 908, U.N. SCOR, 49th Sess., 3356th mtg., at 4, U.N. Doc. S/RES/908 (1994).

and that he could not "continue to participate in the pretense of the protection of human rights."[123]

The enforcement function of the U.N. without a human rights dimension can be disastrous for human rights. When the Security Council decided to establish the "safe areas" in eastern Bosnia, military advisors determined that 34,000 troops would be needed to enforce them. After weeks, only a few thousand were authorized and fewer still actually deployed. Bosnian Serbian forces are suspected of having slaughtered some 8,000 unarmed Muslims in July 1995, while the U.N. forces were outnumbered and powerless to do anything about it, according to the Dutch minister of defense, responding the criticism of the Dutch battalion.[124] On July 10, when the U.N. military observers warned that air strikes alone could prevent the impending massacre, the Force Commander rejected the advice. As a result, massive human rights violations, constituting war crimes, were committed, and the vastly outnumbered Dutch peacekeepers did nothing to prevent it. An American military observer to NATO remarked that the U.N. peacekeepers "didn't have the firepower. The truth is the safe areas were always a myth."[125]

In Bosnia, Somalia, and elsewhere, not only was the U.N. unable to protect human rights, but some of its forces actually committed human rights violations themselves. It has been recommended, for example, that "[i]n Bosnia and elsewhere, for instance, states and international organizations (U.N. and NATO) can further the international rule of law by recognizing appropriate applications of current human rights law."[126] Cases of rape, torture, and even murder—all human rights violations—have been added to smuggling, prostitution, and other crimes U.N. forces are known to have committed.[127] Theoretically, the rules of international humanitarian law apply by virtue of the commitments of the international legal obligations of the troop-contributing countries, and therefore every soldier should be trained to respect the rules of humanitarian law and be submitted to the discipline of her or

---

[123] *Quoted in* Marcus Kabel, *U.N. Yugoslavia rights sleuth resigns over Bosnia*, REUTERS WORLD SERV., July 27, 1995. Mazowiecki has been replaced by Elisabeth Rehn, the former Finish defense minister. She submitted her final report in January 1998 and was replaced by Mr. Jirí Dienstbier of the Czech Republic. *See* 41–42 HUM. RTS. MONITOR 90–92 (International Service for Human Rights 1998) [hereinafter International Service for Human Rights].

[124] Tony Barber, *Dutch Deny They Betrayed Srebrenica; Bosnia Outrage; Report Absolved Troops of Blame for Incident that Led to Massacre of 8,000*, THE INDEPENDENT, Oct. 31, 1995, at 13.

[125] *Srebrenica: A U.N. "Safe Haven" That Soon Was Not*, N.Y. TIMES, Oct. 29, 1995, at A14, col. 1.

[126] Robert O. Weiner and Fionnuala Ni Aolain, *Beyond the Laws of War: Peacekeeping in Search of a Legal Framework*, 27 COLUM. HUM. RTS. L. REV. 293, 351 (1996).

[127] Lucia Mouat, *Rights Groups to U.N. Troops: Police Thyself*, CHRISTIAN SCI. MONITOR, Jan. 27, 1994, at 6.

his own military justice. The reality is quite different for lack of training and lack of interest on the part of commanders. These obligations of troop-contributing countries must, of course, be reinforced through more effective training and severe disciplinary measures. Beyond that, however, the U.N. should make it part of the guidelines to troop-contributing countries and status-of-forces agreements that all serving the U.N.—international and local civilians, military under U.N. command, and military under multinational forces authorized by the U.N.—must know, respect, and ensure respect by others of U.N. human rights standards. John Ruggie observes that "a doctrinal basis for 'robust' U.N. peace operations must be formulated if the U.N. is to have a future in the terrain between traditional peacekeeping and warfighting."[128] If this doctrine does not include a human rights protection role with adequate force to back it up, the U.N. and the troop-contributing countries will confront more situations where U.N. forces will allow serious human rights violations to occur without acting to stop them and where some of these forces will commit abuses themselves.

2. Human Rights Components of Multidimensional Peace Operations Rights

It requires a humanitarian emergency and intense diplomatic pressure before the Security Council will use its enforcement powers, and as a consequence the Council has moved in fits and starts to use those powers for human rights purposes. The Council is much more willing to support deployment of U.N. personnel in the context of a comprehensive political settlement to a long-festering conflict, and the doctrine applicable in such cases has been called "second generation" or "expanded" peacekeeping.[129] The first such mission was the United Nations Advisory Group in Namibia. The peace agreements in Cambodia and El Salvador built upon this experience. In all these cases, the U.N. painstakingly engineered peace negotiations towards the conclusion of a comprehensive political settlement, in which human rights was an integral part, and the relative success of UNTAC and ONUSAL influenced the setting up of human rights components in Haiti, Rwanda, and Angola. However, the lessons of previous missions are not always well-studied. The Aspen Institute brought together the heads of the human rights components of the U.N. operations in Cambodia, El Salvador, and Haiti to compare experiences and draw lessons.[130] That study recommends standardized terms of reference for human rights missions, more careful advanced missions, collaboration with other components, early and more professional recruitment, improved staff training and advanced brief-

---

[128] JOHN G. RUGGIE, CONSTRUCTING THE WORLD POLITY 249 (1998).

[129] *See, e.g.*, EVANS, *supra* note 33; STEVEN R. RATNER, THE NEW U.N. PEACEKEEPING: BUILDING PEACE IN LANDS OF CONFLICT AFTER THE COLD WAR (1995); John Mackinlay & Jarat Chopra, *Second Generation Multinational Operations*, 15 WASH. Q. 113, 113–129 (Summer 1992).

[130] *See* HONORING HUMAN RIGHTS AND KEEPING THE PEACE: LESSONS FROM EL SALVADOR,

ing, application of a code of conduct for mission staff, utilization of standard reporting formats, improved security, and public reporting.[131] It further supports building human rights protection and verification, as well as long-term institution-building, legal reform, and human rights education into peace agreements.[132] Finally , the study proposes that the U.N. "create a specialized unit to coordinate and institutionalize human rights field work in the context of peacekeeping operations," with the capacity to assess missions, debrief staff, professionalize recruitment, and develop training and reporting procedures.[133] These are sound recommendations. They have been further developed by the High Commissioner's advisor in this area, Ian Martin, who is one of the most knowledgeable and experienced of experts, having been Secretary-General of Amnesty International and director of the human rights operations in Haiti and Rwanda. More improvement is needed along the lines recommended by the Aspen meetings and the advisor.[134]

3. Democratic Institution Building and Constitutionalism

Beyond the investigative and educational tasks of human rights components of peacekeeping, U.N. field operations are called upon to contribute to the institutionalization of key democratic institutions, without which whatever progress is made to ensure human rights during a peace operation will be short-lived. Judicial reform, constitution drafting, professionalization and demilitarization of the police—all are tasks that the U.N. has been given and about which its capacity to produce lasting results has not been adequately tested.

The U.N.'s role in this area has to be seen in a broader context of trends towards democratization, although the General Assembly has been somewhat schizophrenic on the question of democracy. On the one hand, it asserts that elections and democratization are the sole prerogative of the state,[135] and, on the other, it asserts that all

---

CAMBODIA, AND HAITI—RECOMMENDATIONS FOR THE UNITED NATIONS (The Aspen Institute Justice and Society Program, Alice Henkin ed., 1995).

[131] *Id.* at 19–23.

[132] *Id.* at 24–28.

[133] *Id.* at 28–29.

[134] *See* International Service for Human Rights, *supra* note 123, at 100. It should be noted that Ian Martin has left the service of the OHCHR to be Director of Human Rights in the Office of the High Representative for Bosnia and Herzegovina.

[135] *See, e.g.,* G.A. Res. 48/124, U.N. GAOR, 48th Sess., Supp. No. 49, at 243, U.N. Doc. A/48/49 (1993) (reaffirming "that it is the concern solely of peoples to determine methods and to establish institutions regarding the electoral process, as well as to determine the ways for its implementation according to their constitution and national legislation, and that, consequently, States should establish the necessary mechanisms and means to guarantee full popular participation in those processes.")

states must have periodic and genuine elections.[136] Many members resist the push for internationally supervised elections, holding firm to the view, justified in traditional international law, that the way they govern is purely an internal matter over which the U.N. has no authority or legitimate interest.

At the same time, the U.N.'s Division of Electoral Assistance receives scores of requests to help with elections, many of which it has to decline. The Security Council, for its part, has centered multicomponent peace operations around elections and democratic transition in Angola, Cambodia, El Salvador, Mozambique, Namibia, Western Sahara, and elsewhere; and in the case of Haiti, the commitment to preserve the outcome of a free and fair election, which the U.N. had observed, was firm enough to reject the *coup d'état*, support the exiled president, impose sanctions, and eventually authorize the use of force.

There is a much deeper form of support for democratic change that the U.N. undertook in Cambodia, El Salvador, and elsewhere—namely, "peace-building," which refers to "comprehensive efforts to identify and support structures which will tend to consolidate peace and advance a sense of confidence and well-being among people."[137] Peace-building tasks should involve, in the words of the Secretary-General, "disarming the previously warring parties and the restoration of order, the custody and possible destruction of weapons, repatriating refugees, advisory and training support for security personnel, monitoring elections, advancing efforts to protect human rights, reforming or strengthening governmental institutions and promoting formal and informal processes of political participation."[138] This function also can entail "support for the transformation of deficient national structures and capabilities, and for the strengthening of new democratic institutions."[139]

The building of democratic societies is a task of generations. However, there is a window of opportunity during U.N. multicomponent peace operations and their aftermath where many processes can receive a "kick-start." Since the decline of peacekeeping in the mid-1990s, many of these human rights tasks have been pursued by field operations under the responsibility of the High Commissioner for Human Rights, which have grown from one in 1992 to twenty-two in 1998.[140] These

---

[136] *See, e.g.,* G.A. Res. 46/137, U.N. GAOR, 46th Sess., Supp. No. 49, at 209, U.N. Doc. A/46/49 (1991) (underscoring "the significance of the Universal Declaration of Human Rights and the International Covenant on Civil and Political Rights, which establish that the authority to govern shall be based on the will of the people, as expressed in periodic and genuine elections. . . .").

[137] BOUTROS-GHALI, *supra* note 33, at 32. *See* EVANS, *supra* note 33, for the author's definition of the term.

[138] BOUTROS-GHALI, *supra* note 33, at 32.

[139] *Id.* at 33–34.

[140] The countries where the High Commissioner has field offices are: Abkhazia, Angola, Burundi, Cambodia, Central African Republic, Colombia, Democratic Republic of the Congo, El Salvador, Gaza, Georgia, Guatemala, Indonesia, Liberia, Malawi, Mongolia, Rwanda,

offices operate under difficult conditions with inadequate resources. More effective and better-supported offices would make a significant difference in the extent to which societies in transition benefit from international support in integrating human rights into their institutions and political culture and thereby consolidate democracy. The positive experiences of Cambodia and El Salvador deserve to be improved upon and adapted elsewhere.[141]

C. Responding to Violations

Responses to human rights violations have always been the cutting edge between absolute state sovereignty and international accountability. While the long-term, preventive strategy calls for the creation of a culture in which rights are respected as a matter of course, the curative strategy requires that human rights violations be detected, that victims be protected, and that the perpetrators be held accountable. The U.N. can improve the effectiveness of all of its procedures for dealing with human rights violations in the coming years, whether treaty-based or Charter-based.

1. Treaty-Based Procedures for Dealing with Violations of Human Rights

Of the sixty or so major U.N. human rights treaties,[142] six have functioning monitoring bodies that examine states parties' reports on progress made and problems encountered and three (ICCPR,[143] the Torture Convention,[144] and the Racial

---

Sierra Leone, South Africa, Southern Africa, Togo, and "ex-Yugoslavia." Source: Office of the High Commissioner for Human Rights, Geneva.

141 On these two cases, see MICHAEL W. DOYLE, IAN JOHNSTONE & ROBERT C. ORR, KEEPING THE PEACE: MULTIDIMENSIONAL UN OPERATIONS IN CAMBODIA AND EL SALVADOR (1997); Stephen P. Marks, *Preventing Humanitarian Crises Through Peace-Building and Democratic Empowerment: Lessons from Cambodia*, 1 MED. & GLOBAL SURVIVAL 208 (Dec. 1994); IAN JOHNSTONE, RIGHTS AND RECONCILIATION: U.N. STRATEGIES IN EL SALVADOR (1995). On these experiences as well as those in Guatemala, Haiti, Rwanda, and Bosinia, see HONORING HUMAN RIGHTS: FROM PEACE TO JUSTICE (Alice Henkin ed., 1998) (including significant recommendations at 27–37).

142 *See* Chart of Ratifications issued twice a year by the Office of the High Commissioner for Human Rights, available on their web site at <http://www.unhchr.ch>. For the texts of the treaties, along with other human rights instruments, updated every five years, see HUMAN RIGHTS: A COMPILATION OF INTERNATIONAL INSTRUMENTS, U.N. Doc. ST/HR/Rev.5 (1994). *See also* 3 Weston, *supra* note 16.

143 *Supra* note 38.

144 *Convention Against Torture and Other Cruel, Inhuman or Degrading Treatment or Punishment*, Dec. 10, 1984, G.A. Res. 39/46 (Annex), U.N. GAOR, 39th Sess., Supp. No. 51, at 197, U.N. Doc. A/RES/39/51 (1985), [hereinafter Torture Convention], *reprinted in* 23 I.L.M. 1027 (1984) *and* 3 Weston III.K.2, *supra* note 16.

Convention[145]) have procedures for handling individual complaints of alleged violations.[146]

The three principal concerns for the effectiveness of the treaty system are:

(a) universal ratification without crippling reservations;

(b) timely presentation and proper consideration of reports with follow-up on recommendations; and

(c) availability of a complaints procedure for individual cases of violation of human rights treaties.

(a) Universal Ratification

Universal ratification has been endorsed as a major objective of the High Commissioner.[147] The dilemma of universal ratification is that, at the drafting stage, the norms risk dilution in order to accommodate countries that might hesitate to ratify high standards and, at the accession stage, as countries impose reservations to avoid the higher standards. In an insightful study of the issues, Anne Bayefsky has cautioned against overemphasizing the goal of universal ratification. Her recommendations seek to reconstitute the system "in a manner that renders universal membership secondary, which has as its focus the integrity of the treaties, and its chief object adherence to the treaty obligations," and to include rules for expelling states parties that do not comply with key implementation provisions, to empower the treaty bodies to judge reservations and exclude states that do not withdraw incompatible reservations, to replace the system of state reporting with country rapporteurs for each ratifying state, and to establish a judicialized petition system for each treaty and enhanced publicity through media coverage.[148] Reservations, understandings, and declarations by the U.S. upon ratification of human rights treaties,

---

[145] *International Convention on the Elimination of all Forms of Racial Discrimination*, Dec. 21, 1965, 660 U.N.T.S. 195 [hereinafter Racial Convention], *reprinted in* 5 I.L.M. 352 (1966) *and* 3 Weston III.I.1, *supra* note 16.

[146] The six conventions with treaty-monitoring bodies are the 1965 Racial Convention, *supra* note 145, the 1966 ICCPR and 1966 ICESCR, *supra* note 38; the 1979 CEDAW, *supra* note 63; the 1989 Convention on the Rights of the Child, G.A. Res. 44/25 (Annex), U.N. GAOR, 44th Sess., Supp. No. 49, at 166, U.N. Doc. A/44/49 (1990), *reprinted in* 3 Weston III.D.3, *supra* note 16, and the 1984 Torture Convention, *supra* note 144. The Convention on the Suppression and Punishment of the Crime of Apartheid, Nov. 30, 1973, 1015 U.N.T.S. 243, *reprinted in* 3 Weston III.I.2, *supra* note 16, provided for a Group of Three to monitor its implementation, but that work has been suspended since the end of *apartheid* in South Africa.

[147] *See* International Service for Human Rights, *supra* note 123, at 79.

[148] *See* Anne Bayefsky, *Making the Human Rights Treaties Work, in* HUMAN RIGHTS: AN AGENDA FOR THE NEXT CENTURY 246 (Louis Henkin and John Lawrence Hargrove eds., 1994). Bayefsky has identified fourteen areas in which the treaty-monitoring bodies could do more.

particularly the ICCPR, reservations by Islamic countries upon ratification of CEDAW, the purported (although illegal) withdrawal from the ICCPR by North Korea, and the denunciation by Jamaica of the first optional protocol to the ICCPR are significant cases of backsliding on the universality of the treaty regime.

At the request of the General Assembly in 1988, the Secretary-General appointed Philip Alston, Chair of the Committee on Economic, Social and Cultural Rights, to identify ways to improve the effective functioning of the U.N. human rights treaty system.[149] He has reported twice to the General Assembly[150] and submitted his final report to the Commission on Human Rights in 1997.[151] Alston sets out detailed lessons and recommendations to achieve universal ratification, to resolve the problem of overdue reports and delays in submitting and processing reports, and to improve public information. He also explores some valuable reform options, including consolidated reports, creation of a single treaty body, treaty amendments, and the creation of special *bureaux* on ratification with the High Commissioner's office. These are sound suggestions, which have support among NGOs, in the secretariat and among several members states. The effectiveness of the treaty system would be greatly enhanced if they were fully implemented.

(b) The Reporting Process

The second weakness of the treaty monitoring system is the failure of states parties to submit their reports on time, if at all, and to utilize the process as an opportunity to rethink and reform national policies. The public is rarely involved in the process of preparing and reviewing national reports. The treaty monitoring bodies themselves are not always willing to point out deficiencies in reports and to keep after governments that either fail to provide adequate information or fail to take the committee's recommendations seriously.[152] Alston proposes the examination of country situations by the competent treaty monitoring body in the absence of an overdue report. Several countries support this innovation, while Israel, against whom the practice was applied in the Committee on Economic, Social and Cultural Rights, opposes it for lack of any legal basis.[153] Governments and the treaty bodies need to publicize much more than they do the drafting and reviewing of reports and provide greater assistance to governments through advisory services and the creation of regional advisors similar to those of the ILO.[154] However, NGOs should not wait

---

[149] *See* G.A. Res. 43/115, U.N. GAOR, 43d Sess., Supp. No. 49, at 191, U.N. Doc. A/43/49 (1988) (on reporting obligations of states parties to international instruments on human rights and effective functioning of bodies established pursuant to such instruments).

[150] *See* U.N. Doc. A/44/668 (1989) and A/Conf.157/PC/62/Add.11/Rev.1 (1991).

[151] *See* U.N. Doc. E/CN.4/1997/74 (1977).

[152] Bayefsky, *supra* note 148, at 264–65.

[153] *See* International Service for Human Rights, *supra* note 123, at 79.

[154] *Id.* at 80 (indicating that the Secretary-General was favorable to the recommendation for regional advisors).

for such initiatives; they can (and do in some cases) volunteer information to governments, hold public discussion of the content of the reports, alert the media to discrepancies between what is reported and reality, prepare "shadow reports" setting out their views regarding government claims, provide information and suggest questions to the treaty bodies, and track the follow-up to recommendations those bodies make at the conclusion of the consideration of reports. With respect to NGO-sponsored "shadow reports" critiquing the official government reports, it already is the case that they often are the principal source of information for the experts on the treaty bodies.

The Human Rights Commission has asked the Secretary-General to continue to collect the views of governments, U.N. bodies, and NGOs on Alston's report, and to present his views in the year 2000.[155] The General Assembly regularly addresses the issue of effective implementation of international instruments on human rights, including reporting obligations under international instruments on human rights, and has reaffirmed that the full and effective implementation of these instruments "is of major importance" to the U.N.'s human rights tasks.[156] The Assembly stressed the need for "securing sufficient financial, human and information resources" so that the treaty bodies function effectively, recognizing the importance of NGOs to the effective implementation of human rights instruments.

The serious backlog of reports can best be remedied by discontinuing the current periodic reporting under each treaty and replacing it with a consolidated report, prepared in an exhaustive manner by each state party for all the human rights treaties to which it is a party. This would allow for the rescheduling of submission of reports and for providing for subsequent period reports to focus on specified issues identified in the committees' comments and concluding observations.[157] The Committee on the Elimination of Discrimination Against Women and the Commission Against Torture (CAT) already allow states parties to submit overdue reports in a single document, although leading scholars and practitioners such as Anne Bayefsy and Rosalyn Higgins find this practice contrary to the treaty obligations of the states parties who thus avoid the duty of catching up with the separate overdue reports.[158]

It has also been proposed to consolidate the six committees into one mega-committee or super- committee which would examine all reports. The disadvantage is that such a committee would not be able to give the same level of attention or

---

[155] *See* Commission on Human Rights Res. 1998/27.

[156] *See* G.A. Res. 51/87, U.N. GAOR, 51st Sess., Supp. No 49, at 29, U.N. Doc A/51/49 (vol. 1) (1996) (concerning "Effective implementation of international instruments on human rights, including reporting obligations under international instruments on human rights").

[157] *See* International Service for Human Rights, *supra* note 123, at 80.

[158] Bayefsky, *supra* note 148, at 235 and notes 30 & 36 therein (citing Rosalyn Higgins, *The United Nations: Some Questions of Integrity*, 52 MOD. L. REV. 1, 19 (1989)).

provide the same degree of expertise as the current six committees.[159] A possible solution would be to constitute a committee of the whole, consisting of all six committees, subdivided into six chambers. Thus, the "Child Rights Chamber" would meet to examine special reports on child rights, and so on for each committee/treaty. The precedent for doing so would be the meetings of the chairpersons of the treaty bodies, which began informally and held their ninth annual meeting in 1998. At the eighth meeting, the chairpersons debated the idea of a consolidated committee and views were divided.[160] The advantages to states parties who are behind in reporting are obvious: their backlog would be wiped out as they present a consolidated report to the larger committee. Maintaining the existing committees could avoid the necessity of amending the six treaties.[161] It may not even be necessary to convene a meeting of the states parties because the meetings of the mega-committee would not be an exception to the annual or semiannual meetings of the committee as determined by convention in question. Moreover, convening a meeting of all chairpersons and members could be interpreted as falling within the "facilities" that the Secretary-General is required to provide for the effective performance of the committees' functions.[162] Alternatively, the arrangements could be formalized by a meeting of all the states parties. A single meeting of parties to all six conventions would be the most efficient way to settle the matter. While the creation of such a large body of over one hundred members would be admittedly cumbersome, a more streamlined version would be possible, with the larger committee being a pool from which general meetings to examine consolidated reports would be constituted by a limited number selected by each committee.[163] Whether such an arrangement is made or not, it is urgent that the idea of consolidated reports and rescheduling of overdue reports be implemented.

(c) Individual Complaints Procedures

The third area in which the human rights treaty system could be strengthened is with regard to the availability of individual complaints procedures. Currently three human rights treaties have such procedures: the 1965 Racial Convention,[164] the 1966

---

[159] Some of these objections were voiced at the 1998 session of the Commission on Human Rights. *See* International Service for Human Rights, *supra* note 123, at 80.

[160] *Id.*

[161] The treaties provide that the duration of meetings shall be reviewed by, if necessary, a meeting of the states parties, subject to the approval of the General Assembly. *See, e.g.*, Convention on the Rights of the Child, *supra* note 146, art. 43(10).

[162] The treaties provide that the Secretary-General "shall provide the necessary staff and facilities for the effective performance of the functions of the Committee under the present Convention." *Id.* art. 43(11).

[163] For example, if three were selected from each committee, the larger committee would be approximately the same size as each of the current committees.

[164] *Supra* note 145.

ICCPR,[165] and the 1984 Torture Convention.[166] Under the Optional Protocol to the ICCPR, the Human Rights Committee examines and expresses its final views on individual cases brought to it by alleged victims of violations occurring within states parties to the protocol. As of January 6, 1999, 844 cases had been opened and 308 had resulted in decisions on the merits, 237 of them finding a violation (principally by Canada, Colombia, Democratic Republic of the Congo, Ecuador, Jamaica, Peru, Surinam, Trinidad and Tobago, and Uruguay).[167] Fewer cases have been brought before the Committee against Torture and the Committee on the Elimination of All Forms of Racial Discrimination. Under Article 22 of the Torture Convention, 122 complaints had been registered as of January 7, 1999, of which twenty-nine led to decisions on the merits, fifteen of which found a violation (by Austria, Canada, the Netherlands, Spain, Sweden, Switzerland, and Venezuela). As for complaints under Article 14 of the Racial Discrimination Convention, only eight cases have been considered, of which four led to a decision on the merits, three of which found a violation (two by the Netherlands and one by Norway).[168]

The Committee on Economic, Social and Cultural Rights has been discussing an optional protocol for the ICESCR[169] since 1990. In 1991 the adoption of such a protocol was expressly recommended by Danilo Türk, the Special Rapporteur of the Sub-Commission on Prevention of Discrimination and Protection of Minorities.[170] Subsequently, at the Committee's request, Philip Alston prepared four separate reports, and a report containing the text of the draft optional protocol was submitted to the Commission at its 1997 session.[171] The Commission asked the Secretary-General to transmit the text of the draft optional protocol to the ICESCR to governments, intergovernmental organizations, and NGOs for comments.[172] The Optional Protocol to CEDAW was adopted by the Commission on the Status of Women in 1999.[173]

---

[165] *Supra* note 38.

[166] *Supra* note 144.

[167] The statistics for this and the other two conventions mentioned below are provided by the web site of the Office of the High Commissioner for Human Rights (visited Feb. 1, 1999) <http://www. unhchr.ch>.

[168] The fact that countries with good human rights records have been found in violation is more a reflection of their willingness to set an example by submitting to the procedure than an indication of the state of human rights worldwide.

[169] *Supra* note 38.

[170] *See* U.N. ESCOR, 38th Sess., Supp. No. 38, at 211, U.N. Doc. E/CN.4/Sub.2/1992/16 (1992).

[171] *See Draft Optional Protocol to the International Covenant on Economic, Social and Cultural Rights at its Fiftieth Session*, U.N. Doc. E/CN.4/1997/105 (1997).

[172] Press Release of Mar. 21, 1997, U.N. Doc. HR/CN/808 (1997).

[173] *See supra* note 80 and accompanying text.

2. Charter-Based Procedures for Dealing with Violations of Human Rights

The procedures for dealing with violations that are based on the U.N. Charter rather than separate treaties include complaints procedures and special procedures.

(a) Complaints Procedures

For thirty years, the U.N. has had two non-treaty procedures for dealing with complaints or petitions addressed to it and alleging human rights violations. The first is the so-called "public" procedure, which has existed since 1967, when the Economic and Social Council authorized the Commission to examine as a regular agenda item violations of human rights.[174] In appropriate cases, the Commission was authorized, per ECOSOC Resolution 1235, to "make a study of situations which reveal a consistent pattern of violations of human rights, as exemplified by the policy of apartheid . . . and racial discrimination . . . and report, with recommendations thereon, to the Economic and Social Council."[175] Although conceived as a means of attracting attention to *apartheid* in southern Africa and other situations characterized by colonialism and racism, the "1235 procedure" (as it has come to be called) is now used to examine all types of situations and usually involves appointing a Special Rapporteur to visit the country under scrutiny. The Rapporteur's report of relevant findings is the basis for the Commission's resolution on that country. These country situations are examined under caption: "Question of the violation of human rights and fundamental freedoms, with particular reference to colonial and other dependent countries and territories."

The second extra-conventional complaints procedures is a "confidential procedure" according to which the Sub-commission on Prevention of Discrimination and Protection of Minorities and the Commission examine in private session the petitions sent by victims or their representatives that reveal a pattern of violations in any country in the world. In 1970, the Commission, pursuant to ECOSOC Resolution 1503, adopted a procedure now known as the "1503 procedure" to examine in closed session complaints sent to the Organization revealing "a consistent pattern of gross and reliably attested violations of human rights."[176] These com-

---

[174] Commission on Human Rights Res. 8, U.N. ESCOR, 42d Sess., Supp. No. 6, at 131, U.N. Doc. E/CN.4/940 (1967) (authorizing the Commission to consider the "Question of the violation of human rights and fundamental freedoms, including policies of racial discrimination and segregation and of apartheid, in all countries, with particular reference to colonial and other dependent countries and territories").

[175] ECOSOC Res. 1235, U.N. ESCOR, 42d Sess., Supp. No. 1, at 17, U.N. Doc. E/4393 (1967), *reprinted in* 3 Weston III.T.3, *supra* note 16.

[176] ECOSOC Res. 1503, U.N. ESCOR, 48th Sess., Supp. No. 1A, at 8, U.N. Doc. E/4382/Add.1 (1970), *reprinted in* 3 Weston III.T.6, *supra* note 16.

plaints may be referred to the Commission by the Sub-Commission, both of which have established working groups to deal with such violations. The Commission "received" its first situations in 1974; in 1978, the Chair of the Commission began announcing the countries under discussion; and in 1984 the Chair began providing the names of countries kept under consideration and those that had been dropped. Between 1974 and 1998, a total of seventy-five country situations had been placed before the Commission under the procedure, as indicated in Table 1. This confidential, cumbersome and inconclusive procedure has been justly criticized by NGOs and by independent scholars and diplomats.[177] Philip Alston has concluded that the procedure should be either radically reformed or abolished since "its shortcomings are so considerable, its tangible achievements so scarce, the justifications offered in its favour so modest, and the need for an effective and universally applicable petition procedure so great. . . ."[178]

(b) Special Procedures of Thematic and Country Rapporteurs

Since 1980, when the Commission created a Working Group on enforced or involuntary disappearances, it has appointed numerous working groups or Special Rapporteurs, Representatives, and Experts to examine a general phenomenon (theme) of particular significance to ensuring respect for human rights. These "thematic mechanisms," as they are called, include special procedures to collect information directly from victims and to communicate with governments—not only to request a clarification of the situation concerning the alleged victim but also to apply an "urgent action" or "prompt intervention" procedure when the case is recent and a representation to the government might have an impact on the treatment of the victim, her or his family, witnesses, or NGOs involved, and to facilitate on-site visits. The reports of the Special Rapporteurs constitute a mode of accountability that many governments take quite seriously. The list of thematic mechanisms appears in Table 2.

Similar special procedures have developed for the country rapporteurs, who have also developed the practice of communicating with victims, their representatives, NGOs, and governments. The effectiveness of these special procedures has been enhanced by the annual meetings of the special rapporteurs, representatives, experts, and chairpersons of working groups since 1993. By the fourth meeting, the Special Rapporteurs had formulated an impressive set of recommendations, but the Chairperson of the meeting expressed considerable frustration and irritation at the lack of follow-up by the OHCHR.[179] The list of country procedures appears in Table 3 below.

---

177   *See, e.g.*, Philip Alston, *The Commission on Human Rights, in* THE UNITED NATIONS AND HUMAN RIGHTS: A CRITICAL APPRAISAL 151 (Philip Alston ed., 1992).

178   *Id.* at 154.

179   International Service for Human Rights, *supra* note 123, at 98. The High Commissioner under criticism was the predecessor to Ms. Robinson, the Ecuadorian diplomat José Ayala-Lasso.

Table 1
States Examined under the "1503 Procedure" by the
Commission on Human Rights (up to 1998)

Afghanistan	Grenada	Pakistan
Albania	Guatemala	Paraguay
Antigua-et-Barbuda	Guyana	Peru
Argentina	Haiti	Philippines
Armenia	Honduras	Portugal
Azerbaijan	Indonesia (and East Timor)	Rwanda
Bahrain		Saudi Arabia
Benin	Iran	Sierra Leone
Bolivia	Iraq	Slovenia
Botswana	Israel	Somalia
Brazil	Japan	Sudan
Brunei Darussalam	Kampuchea, Democratic (Cambodia)	Syrian Arab Republic
Burma (Myanmar)		Thailand
Burundi	Kenya	Turkey
Central African Republic	Korea, Republic of	Uganda
Chad	Kuwait	United Kingdom
Chile	Kyrgyzstan	United Republic of Tanzania
Czech Republic	Lao People's Democratic Republic	
El Salvador	Latvia	United States of America
Equatorial Guinea	Lebanon	Uruguay
Estonia	Lithuania	Uzbekistan
Ethiopia	Malawi	Venezuela
Gabon	Malaysia	Viet Nam
Gambia	Mali	Yemen
German Democratic Republic	Moldova	Zaire (the Democratic Republic of the Congo)
Germany	Mozambique	
	Nepal	

Source: Office of the U.N. High Commissioner for Human Rights, Geneva.

The problems for the special procedures are in part technical, including the need for better coordination of missions and for changing the structure of the OHCHR so that support for special procedures may be separated from the technical cooperation role of that office. The special rapporteurs have expressed concern over the lack of coordination of visits and appeals between the High Commissioner, the thematic rapporteur, and the country rapporteur when all three are dealing with the same country.[180]

These difficulties are easier to remedy than the political ones. Countries seeking to avoid international scrutiny of their own practices have pursued several initiatives to weaken these procedures and, in the name of "rationalization" and of avoiding duplication, challenged the special procedures through resolutions on non-selectivity, impartiality, and objectivity.[181] The legitimate concern with efficiency and effectiveness must not be allowed to justify ending the mandate of rapporteurs or working groups whose investigations or urgent appeals would not be covered adequately by other mechanisms.[182] As the head of International Service for Human Rights, a leading Geneva-based NGO, which assists NGOs in accessing the U.N.'s human rights machinery, correctly observed: "it must not be forgotten that the aim of the process [of review of the special procedures] is to improve effectiveness and not to weaken it."[183] Even though the Commission has requested the Secretary-General "to ensure the availability of such resources as are necessary for the effective implementation of all thematic mandates, including any additional tasks entrusted to the thematic special rapporteurs and working groups by the Commission,"[184] it still is conducting a politically-motivated review of the special

---

[180] *Id.* at 81–82 (citing the recommendations of the fourth meeting of special rapporteurs in Geneva, May 20–23, 1997).

[181] *See, e.g.,* G.A. Res. 51/105, U.N. GAOR, 51st Sess., Supp. No. 49, at 251, U.N. Doc. A/51/49 (1996) (entitled "Strengthening of United Nations actions in the field of human rights through the promotion of international cooperation and the importance of non-selectivity, impartiality and objectivity" and affirming the importance of "objectivity, independence and discretion of the special rapporteurs and representatives on thematic issues and countries, as well as of the members of the working groups, in carrying out their mandates " and asserting that "promotion, protection and full realization of human rights . . . should not be used for political ends.").

[182] As of 1999, the Commission's Bureau made numerous and valuable proposals in *Report of the Bureau of the Fifty-Fourth Session of the Commission on Human Rights Submitted Pursuant to Commission Decision 1998/112: Rationalization of the Work of the Commission,* U.N. Doc. E/CN.4/1999/104 (Dec. 23, 1998). A group of self-appointed "like-minded countries" responded with more restrictive proposals, thus prolonging the debate into the early 2000s.

[183] Adrien-Claude Zoller, *U.N. Commission on Human Rights "Signs of Hope": Analytic Report of the 54th Session,* 41–42 HUM. RTS. MONITOR 115 (1998).

[184] Commission on Human Rights Res. 1997/37, U.N. ESCOR, Supp. No. 3, at 123, U.N. Doc. E/CN.4/1997/150 (1997).

procedures. Of particular concern are recent cases of lawsuits against Dato' Param Cumaraswamy, the thematic rapporteur on the independence of lawyers and judges (examined by the International Court of Justice[185]) and censorship of part of the report by the thematic rapporteur on contemporary forms of racism, as well as reprisals against individuals who cooperate with the special rapporteurs.[186]

The political clout of special rapporteurs needs to be raised so that people like Mazowiecki do not resign in disgust, that recommendations like those of the Special Rapporteur on human rights in Iraq, Max van der Stoel, do not remain dead letters; and that governments do not sue them, as in the case of Special Rapporteur on the independence of judges and lawyers. More publicity and political attention should be paid to the recommendations of the truly independent and courageous country rapporteurs. With respect to thematic rapporteurs, they need far more human and financial resources (especially for research and site visits to locations of large-scale violations), revised mandates allowing them to examine country situations on their own initiative, and wide publicity relative to the failure of governments to respond to requests for information as well as other forms of noncooperation.[187]

The innovation of the special procedures stands as one of the most valuable human rights achievements of the political organs of the U.N. and the NGOs that have lobbied them. The threats against them are not a reaction to a "Western" agenda or approach, since many of them were initiatives of developing countries. They are more the result of certain governments clinging to a state-centered mode of multilateral diplomacy and action rather than one that seeks to preserve and protect human beings from abuses committed by states.

D. The Human Rights Approach to the Development Gap

Development has been a major challenge to the community of nations, and the end of the Cold War did not change the situation in any significant way, except with respect to models of development. The free market has been widely accepted for better or worse as the sole model for countries aspiring to rise out of poverty. The failure of development models, including those based on the free market, has left the U.N. in confusion, as can be readily seen by reading *An Agenda for Development*.[188] Former Secretary-General Boutros-Ghali begins by stating that

---

[185] *Difference Relating to Immunity From Legal Process of a Special Rapporteur of the Commission on Human Rights*, 1998 General List No. 100. (Advisory Opinion of 29 April 1999, affirming that "Dato' Param Cumaraswamy is entitled to immunity from legal process of every kind for the words spoken by him" during the interview for which he was sued.)

[186] International Service for Human Rights, *supra* note 123, at 82–83.

[187] *See* Brody, *supra* note 48, at 312.

[188] BOUTROS BOUTROS-GHALI, AGENDA FOR DEVELOPMENT 1995, WITH RELATED U.N. DOCUMENTS (1995).

Table 2

Thematic Procedures

Contemporary forms of racism, racial discrimination and xenophobia	Mr. Maurice Glêlê-Ahanhanzo (Benin)	Special Rapporteur
Extrajudicial, summary or arbitrary executions	Mrs. Asthma Jahangir (Pakistan)	Special Rapporteur
Freedom of opinion and expression	Mr. Abid Hussain (India)	Special Rapporteur
Impact of armed conflict on children	Mr. Olara Otunnu (Côte d'Ivoire)	Special Representative
Independence of judges and lawyers	Mr. Param Cumaraswamy (Malaysia)	Special Rapporteur
Internally displaced persons	Mr. Francis Deng (Sudan)	Representative of the Secretary-General
Mercenaries	Mr. Enrique Bernales Ballesteros (Peru)	Special Rapporteur
Religious intolerance	Mr. Abdelfattah Amor (Tunisia)	Special Rapporteur
Sale of children, child prostitution and child pornography	Ms. Ofelia Calcetas-Santos (Philippines)	Special Rapporteur
Torture and other cruel, inhuman or degrading treatment or punishment	Mr. Nigel Rodley (United Kingdom of Great Britain and Northern Ireland)	Special Rapporteur
Illicit movement and dumping of toxic waste	Ms. Fatma Zohra Ksentini (Algeria)	Special Rapporteur

Violence against women, its causes and consequences	Ms. Radhika Coomaraswamy (Sri Lanka)	Special Rapporteur
Effects of foreign debt	Mr. Reinaldo Figueredo (Venezuela)	Special Rapporteur
Restitution, compensation and rehabilitation for victims of grave violations of human rights	Mr. Cherif Bassiouni (Egypt/USA)	Expert
Extreme poverty	Ms. Anne-Marie Lizin (Belgium)	Independent Expert
Education	Ms. Katarina Tomaševski (Croatia)	Special Rapporteur
Right to development	Mr. Arjun. Sengupta (India)	Independent Expert
Structural adjustment	Mr. Ismail-Sabri Abdalla (Egypt)	Independent Expert
Working Group on Arbitrary Detention	Mr. Kapil Sibal (India)	Chairman
Working Group on Enforced or Involuntary Disappearances	Mr. Ivan Tosevski (The former Yugoslav Republic of Macedonia)	Chairman

Source: Office of the U.N. High Commissioner for Human Rights, Geneva.

Table 3

Country Specific Procedures

Afghanistan	Mr. Choong-Hyun Paik (Republic of Korea)	Special Rapporteur
Burma (Myanmar)	Mr. Rajsoomer Lallah (Mauritius)	Special Rapporteur
Burundi	Mr. Paolo Pinheiro (Brazil)	Special Rapporteur
Democratic Republic of the Congo (former Zaire)	Mr. Roberto Garretón (Chile)	Special Rapporteur
Chad	Ms. Emma Aouij (Tunisia)	Independent Expert
Equatorial Guinea	Mr. Alejandro Artucio (Uruguay)	Special Rapporteur
Iraq	Mr. Max van der Stoel (Netherlands)	Special Rapporteur
Iran (Islamic Republic of)	Mr. Maurice Copithorne (Canada)	Special Representative
Nigeria	Mr. Soli J. Sorabjee (India)	Special Rapporteur
Palestinian territories occupied since 1967	Mr. Hannu Halinen (Finland)	Special Rapporteur
Rwanda	Mr. Michel Moussalli (Switzerland)	Special Representative
Sudan	Mr. Leonardo Franco (Argentina)	Special Rapporteur
Territory of the former Yugoslavia	Mr. Jiri Dienstbier (Czech Republic)	Special Rapporteur
Technical Cooperation Programme		
Cambodia	Mr. Thomas Hammarberg (Sweden)	Special Representative
Haiti	Mr. Adama Dieng (Senegal)	Independent Expert
Somalia	Ms. Mona Rishmawi (Jordan)	Independent Expert

Source: Office of the U.N. High Commissioner for Human Rights, Geneva.

"[d]evelopment is a fundamental human right."[189] He expanded the definition of "development" by embracing five dimensions: peace, the economy (*i.e.*, growth to generate resources), the environment (*i.e.*, policies to make development sustainable), society (*i.e.*, healthy social conditions), and democracy (*i.e.*, creativity, good governance, and stability).[190] His successor, Kofi Annan, asserts the positive role of human rights, which, he says, "propel[s] peace and development, reinforce[s] the rule of law and release[s], without inhibitions, the creativity of individuals and societies alike. . . . It [is] only gradually beginning to be understood how much our approach to . . . sustainable development [will] be altered and enriched by taking in the human rights factor."[191]

The recognition through policy rather than rhetoric that human rights are part of the development process is a recent phenomenon in the U.N. system. Human rights have been absent from previous U.N. development strategies, although the link between human rights and development has been a feature of U.N. studies on the realization of economic, social, and cultural rights for quite some time; it is the essence of the concept of the right to development, and resulted in the late 1990s in initiatives to "mainstream" human rights into development and financial agencies of the U.N. system. The agendas of the Commission and Sub-Commission now cover numerous items dealing with the impact of economic and development processes on economic, social, and cultural rights. Studies and resolutions cover critical issues of structural adjustment policies and foreign debt,[192] extreme poverty,[193] and the right to food.[194] Somewhat more controversial have been the resolutions on unilateral coercive measures[195] and toxic wastes.[196] There are now rapporteurs or experts on the right to education, on extreme poverty, foreign debt and structural adjustment. The politicization of these issues is inevitable and will increase as the negative impacts of globalization of the world economy are brought into sharper focus.[197]

Parallel to the emergence of these issues on the human rights agenda of the U.N. are thirty years of efforts to make sense of the concept to a human right to development. Indeed, the right to development has become the principal concept

---

[189]   *Id.* at 17.

[190]   *Id.* at 20–49.

[191]   *As quoted in* International Service for Human Rights, *supra* note 123, at 16.

[192]   *See, e.g.*, Commission on Human Rights Res. 1998/24 and Decision 1998/102.

[193]   *See, e.g.*, Commission on Human Rights Res. 1998/25.

[194]   *See, e.g.*, Commission on Human Rights Res. 1998/23.

[195]   *See, e.g.*, Commission on Human Rights Res. 1998/11.

[196]   *See, e.g.*, Commission on Human Rights Res. 1998/12.

[197]   On the negative impacts of globalization on human rights, see Kamal Hossain, *Globalization and Human Rights: Clash of Universal Aspirations and Special Interests, supra* in this volume, at p. 187.

on which developing countries draw to advance the claim that human rights should serve the cause of development. The idea of the right to development emerged in the early 1970s. The Commission had become highly charged with ideological positioning on practically every issue: the socialist countries pushed for peace and disarmament; developing countries pushed for development, non-discrimination, and the end of *apartheid*; and Western countries exercised damage control or favored machinery to scrutinize violations of civil and political rights, often as part of an anti-communist foreign policy. As the socialist countries launched the idea of the right of societies to live in peace, the Non-Aligned Movement (NAM) countries picked up on the idea of declaring development itself a human right. Moreover, the momentum for a New International Economic Order (NIEO)[198] and a Charter on the Economic Rights and Duties of States (CERDS)[199] had not been lost yet, and NAM countries continued to have faith in the U.N. system to allow majority decisions of the General Assembly to establish the normative basis and the blueprint for the creation of a more just international economic order. The hope was that a declaration on the right to development would use the categorical imperatives of human rights to oblige the countries that dominate the international economy to accept greater responsibility for eliminating the causes of poverty and maldevelopment and to pay more for raw materials extracted from developing countries, provide more aid, and improve the terms of trade in favor of developing countries.

The Commission on Human Rights began formal consideration of the idea in 1977. A comprehensive report by the U.N. Secretary-General in 1979 presented the principal ideas and issues considered.[200] However, by the time the drafting got started, Ronald Reagan was in the White House and Margaret Thatcher was at 10 Downing Street. While their governments could accept a general moral (not legal) commitment to human development, under no circumstances would they allow a text to affirm any legal obligation to transfer resources from North to South or to codify any specifics regarding any of the issues contained in the declaration. The U.N. General Assembly proclaimed the Declaration on the Right to Development in 1986.[201] The United States cast the only negative vote; eight other countries abstained. A considerable body of commentary has appeared in support of the dec-

---

[198] *See Programme of Action on the Establishment of a New International Economic Order*, May 1, 1974, G.A. Res. 3202, U.N. GAOR, 6th Spec. Sess., Supp. No. 1, at 5, U.N. Doc. A/9559 (1974), *reprinted in* 13 I.L.M. 720 (1974) *and* 4 INTERNATIONAL LAW AND WORLD ORDER: BASIC DOCUMENTS IV.F.4 (Burns H. Weston ed., 5 vols., 1994–) [hereinafter 4 Weston].

[199] *Charter of Economic Rights and Duties of States*, Dec. 12, 1974, G.A. Res. 3281, U.N. GAOR, 29th Sess., Supp. No. 31, at 50, U.N. Doc. A/9631 (1975), *reprinted in* 14 I.L.M. 251 (1975) *and* 4 Weston IV.F.5, *supra* note 198.

[200] *See* U.N. Doc. E/CN.4/1334.

[201] *Declaration on the Right to Development*, Dec. 4, 1986, G.A. Res. 41/128 (Annex), U.N. GAOR, 41st Sess., Supp. No. 53, at 186, U.N. Doc. A/41/53 (1987) [hereinafter DRD], *reprinted in* 3 Weston III.R.2, *supra* note 16.

laration, mainly in human rights publications, but critical and skeptical views have also emerged in legal and political writings.[202]

The Vienna Declaration and Programme of Action called the right to development "a universal and inalienable right and an integral part of fundamental human rights."[203] Besides the high priority in the Vienna text, the right has been given prominence in the mandate of the High Commissioner, other international conferences and summits, the structure of the OHCHR, and the annual resolutions of the General Assembly and the Commission. However, all these decisions seem to be based on the misguided assumption that they must constitute a victory for the poor countries, a precious surviving feature of the NIEO. The Declaration on the Right to Development does mention that "states should realize their rights and fulfil their duties in such a manner as to promote a new international economic order,"[204] which is then rendered rather vague insofar as it is "based on sovereign equality, interdependence, mutual interest and co-operation among all states, as well as to encourage the observance and realization of human rights."[205] That compromise language is rather far removed from mandating an altered international division of labor or terms of trade or aid. Nevertheless, the right to development is used rhetorically to amplify "Third World" demands on the industrialized world for a transfer of resources in the form of foreign aid and debt forgiveness.

Regularly reaffirmed in the General Assembly and the Commission (with Washington usually but not always abstaining or opposing), the right to development has been the object of protracted debate. At the 1996 Commission, the resolution on the right to development was passed by consensus for the first time. This resolution established an intergovernmental group of ten experts with a two- year mandate to elaborate a strategy for implementing the Declaration on the Right to

---

202   Among the most frequently cited are Mohammed Bedjaoui, *The Right to Development, in* INTERNATIONAL LAW: ACHIEVEMENTS AND PROSPECTS 1178 (Mohammed Bedjaoui ed., 1991); IAN BROWNLIE, THE HUMAN RIGHT TO DEVELOPMENT (1989); SUBRATA R. CHOWDHURY, ERIK M.G. DENTERS & PAUL J.I.M. DE WAART, THE RIGHT TO DEVELOPMENT IN INTERNATIONAL LAW (1992); YASH GHAI AND Y. R. RAO, WHOSE HUMAN RIGHT TO DEVELOPMENT (1989); Philip Alston, *Making Space for Human Rights: The Case of the Rights to Development*, 1 HARV. HUM. RTS. Y.B. 1 (1988); Philip Alston, *Conjuring Up New Human Rights: A Proposal for Quality Control*, 78 AM. J. INT'L L. 607 (1984); Upendra Baxi, *The Development of the Right to Development, in* BAXI, *supra* note 15, at 22; Paul H. Brietzke, *Consorting with the Chameleon, or Realizing the Right to Development*, 15 CAL. W. INT'L L.J. 560 (1985); Jack Donnelly, *In Search for the Unicorn: The Jurisprudence and Politics of the Right to Development*, 15 CAL. W. INT'L L.J. 4723 (1985); James C. N. Paul, *The Human Right to Development: Its Meaning and Importance*, 25 J. MARSHALL L. REV. 235 (1992).

203   Vienna Declaration and Programme of Action, *supra* note 16, pt. I, para. 10.

204   DRD, *supra* note 201, pmbl.

205   *Id.*

Developmet.[206] In 1998, the Commission established a follow-up mechanism on the subject, initially for a period of three years, consisting of an open-ended working group to meet for five working days each year with a mandate to monitor and review progress, review reports and other information, and present a sessional report to the Commission; also the appointment by the Chairman of the Commission of an independent expert to present to the working group at each of its sessions a study on the current state of progress in implementation of the right to development.

The confusion regarding the scope and meaning of the right as defined in the Declaration concerns both the normative pronouncements in the text and the potential modes of its implementation. Regarding the normative content, there are at least five myths that need to be dispelled.

Myth 1: Development takes priority over respect for human rights. The right, as defined in the 1986 Declaration, supports the opposite position, namely, that all human rights, including civil and political rights, must be respected in development planning and implementation and that, consequently, underdevelopment and lack of resources cannot be a pretext for violation of human rights.[207]

Myth 2: States determine whatever development policy suits them. The Declaration in fact implies a limitation on states' determination of their development policy because it establishes the duty of states "to formulate appropriate national development policies that aim at the constant improvement of the well-being of the entire population and of all individuals, on the basis of their active, free and meaningful participation in development and the fair distribution of the benefits resulting therefrom."[208] The right to development could thus be interpreted to mean that development policies should be revised to meet the human-centered and participatory elements of the definition contained in the Declaration.

Myth 3: Support for development is a separate issue from human rights violations. It is understood that the promotional approach to human rights in the context of development is more appropriate than the violations approach. The Declaration on the Right to Development specifies that "states *shall*[209] take resolute steps to eliminate the massive and flagrant violations of human rights of peoples and human beings affected by situations such as apartheid, racism," etc.[210] Moreover, "states should take steps to eliminate obstacles to development resulting from failure to observe civil and political rights, as well as economic, social and cultural rights."[211] Thus, the Declaration makes clear that violations of civil and political rights are an obstacle to development and that the removal of such violations are a necessary part of development.

---

[206]   *See* Commission on Human Rights Res. 1996/15.

[207]   DRD, *supra* note 201, art. 6(3).

[208]   *Id.* art. 8(1).

[209]   *I.e.*, not the hortatory "should" as used elsewhere in the Declaration.

[210]   DRD, *supra* note 201, art. 5.

[211]   *Id.* art. 6(3).

Myth 4: Equity and distributive justice are not a necessary part of development. Reference to "fair distribution of the benefits" of development[212] and nondiscrimination in development[213] are part of the right and, if taken seriously, could be invoked to block or reduce support for projects that fail on either of these grounds.

Myth 5: Whether and how civil society is involved in the development process is not part of the right to development. The duty of states to ensure "active, free, and meaningful participation"[214] and "encourage popular participation in all spheres as an important factor in development"[215] could have a profound effect on democratization and the empowerment of civil society. If national policy and development agencies took seriously these principles, the result would not be the reinforcement of prerogatives of authoritarian states or of the claims of poor countries against rich ones, as some seem to fear.

In short, the Declaration is a more balanced text than the politicized debate would suggest. It is not "neutral" on the model of development but defines the essence of the "human" in sustainable human development. As the High Commissioner told the Commission on March 19, 1998,

> [t]he rights based approach will enhance the human dimension of UNDP strategies that, among others, focus on eliminating poverty, helping groups that require special protection, and strengthening institutions of governance and democracy. The right to development is all-encompassing, demanding the realisation of all human rights: civil, economic, political and social, and this approach understands the role of human rights as empowering individuals and communities. By protecting these rights, we can help prevent the many conflicts based on poverty, discrimination and exclusion that continue to plague humanity and destroy decades of development efforts."[216]

Her position echoes the recommendation of the Working Group on the Right to Development in 1994 that "the right to development is more than development itself; it implies a human rights approach to development, which is something new."[217]

The United Nations Development Programme (UNDP) was the first major institution in the U.N. system to attempt to mainstream human rights and estab-

---

[212] *Id.* art. 2(3).

[213] *Id.* arts. 6(1) & 8(1).

[214] *Id.* art. 2(3).

[215] *Id.* art. 8(2).

[216] Statement by Mary Robinson, United Nations High Commissioner for Human Rights, to the 54th Session of the Commission on Human Rights, Geneva (Mar. 19, 1998) (visited Mar. 1, 1999) <http://www.unhchr.org>.

[217] E/CN.4/1995/11 (Sept. 4, 1994), para. 44.

lish close cooperation with the High Commissioner. In November 1997, it developed a policy too integrate human rights into sustainable human development.[218] The Administrator of UNDP sent the policy to all resident representatives in which he suggested that UNDP engage in human rights advocacy that "may include encouragement of the country's acceding to international human rights treaties and/or the development of capacity to implement its treaty obligations";[219] and on March 4, 1998, he signed a Memorandum of Understanding (MOU) with High Commissioner Mary Robinson. In a subsequent document addressed to the Intergovernmental Group of Experts on the Right to Development, UNDP acknowledged that its four critical sustainable development programs (eliminating poverty and sustaining livelihoods, promoting the advancement of women, protecting and regenerating the environment, and developing the capacities for good governance) "will greatly benefit from a more explicit human rights approach."[220] Thus, at the level of policy and planning, the collaboration between the OHCHR and UNDP is a promising development for the future of human rights, particularly with respect to the right to development[221] and the implementation of human rights treaties.[222]

The transformation of this policy into effective practice by a large agency with little experience in the field beyond its governance program will be slow and resisted in many quarters. Several measures could facilitate this process and accelerate the realization of a human rights-based approach to development:

---

[218] *See* UNITED NATIONS DEVELOPMENT PROGRAMME, INTEGRATING HUMAN RIGHTS WITH SUSTAINABLE HUMAN DEVELOPMENT: A UNDP POLICY DOCUMENT (Jan. 1998).

[219] "Direct Line 17" of Jan. 30, 1998 (internal document on file with the author).

[220] E/CN.4/1998/28 (Feb. 16, 1998), para. 33.

[221] On this point, the High Commissioner agrees, in the MOU (on file with the author), to "facilitate close cooperation between UNDP and the human rights organs, bodies and procedures, as well as [to] examine with UNDP the possibilities of joint initiatives aimed at implementing the human right to development, in particular through defining indicators in the area of economic and social rights and designing other relevant methods and tools for their implementation."

[222] On the subject of international human rights treaties, this MOU (on file with the author) stipulates, *inter alia*, that "UNDP and HCHR shall closely co-operate with a view to promote universal ratification and implementation of international human rights treaties. Through its country offices, UNDP shall inform the governments seeking assistance or advice on ratification of human rights instruments or on reporting obligations under these instruments about the availability of assistance under the Technical Co-operation Programme of HCHR in this respect." The MOU goes on to announce that "the High Commissioner shall examine with UNDP and the treaty-monitoring bodies ways to facilitate further substantive participation by UNDP in the work of the treaty bodies. Subject to the rules of confidentiality of specific procedures and documents, an exchange of country reports, profiles and situation analyses, treaty monitoring bodies' reports and comments, and other relevant information from UNDP and HCHR should be established. Participation of UNDP representatives in the meetings of the treaty-monitoring bodies shall be encouraged."

(1) UNDP could *"adopt"* the *Committee on Economic Social and Cultural Rights* in much the same way the UNICEF had "adopted" the Committee on the Rights of the Child, so as to establish a more secure resource base for the Committee's work and more systematic exchanges.

(2) The current short-term *training of UNDP staff* could be expanded so that staff can learn how UNDP could integrate the rights perspective into the discourse of sustainable human development and development planning, including many of the specific recommendations of the Intergovernmental Group of Experts of the Right to Development.[223]

(3) UNDP could develop a program of support for the *education and training about the Declaration on the Right to Development*, particularly of stake holders in field offices (government officials responsible for human rights reporting, development and human rights NGOs, other development agencies, including Specialized Agencies, etc.) about the requirements of the DRD that development be participatory, people-centered, equitable, and respectful of all human rights. The challenge here is to get beyond the rhetorical invocation of the right to development and to examine real development policies and practices that would be altered if the right to development were taken seriously.

(4) UNDP could co-operate with the OHCHR to *integrate understanding and interpretation of the relevant human rights treaties into development planning* at the country level. The objective of this suggestion is that UNDP staff and all interlocutors in the field expand their understanding of the Declaration on the Right to Development in light of the two 1966 covenants[224] and the racial convention,[225] the Women's Convention (CEDAW),[226] the children's, convention,[227] and the torture convention.[228] UNDP could draw specifically on the general comments and final observations of the various treaty committee, as well as on commentaries on the treaties, in negotiating its Country Co-operation Framework (CCF) at the country level.

(5) Drawing on articles 2(1) and 22 of the ICESCR,[229] UNDP could adopt as a matter of policy a *priority in allocating resources* to projects in countries where, for reasons of unavailability of resources, the "core minimum obligations to ensure the satisfaction of, at the very least, minimal essential levels of each of the rights" as defined in General Comment No. 3 of

---

223 E/CN.4/1998/29 (Nov. 7, 1998).
224 *Supra* note 38.
225 *Supra* note 145.
226 *Supra* note 63.
227 *Supra* note 146.
228 *Supra* note 144.
229 *Supra* note 38.

the Committee on Economic, Social and Cultural Rights[230] are not being met, thus assisting them in achieving the elimination of poverty within the normative framework of the Covenant.

(6) UNDP could *provide the OHCHR with documentation, suggestions, and explanations regarding the relevance and reliability of various indicators and benchmarks* that could assist the OHCHR and the government in drawing up its reports and especially in re-assessing policies and measures taken to implement the various human rights treaties.

(7) UNDP could *prepare country profiles*, as suggested in the March 4, 1998, MOU with High Commissioner Robinson. The OHCHR could include these profiles in the various reports and thus facilitate the work of the treaty bodies. In addition, UNDP could be present during the consideration of the reports in New York and Geneva to provide technical explanations and suggestions as appropriate.

(8) UNDP could adjust its current *support for good governance in consultation with the OHCHR* to maximise the overlap between the development perspective on governance and the rights-based approach to governance. Specifically, much closer co-ordination between the OHCHR and UNDP could lead to long-term planning on the judiciary, the parliament, the bar, etc., in ways that meet human rights objectives explicitly. UNDP supports judicial training, publishing legislation, and judicial decisions in several countries. Such efforts appear to be an excellent initiative but could be made relevant to UNDP's rights-based approach to governance by including a digest system specifically linked to human rights norms under constitutional and international law. Major projects requiring significant capital investment, such as support for national institutes for judicial training, could be considered in this context.

A similar reflection is called for with respect to each of the other agencies and program of the U.N. system, including the international financial institutions, whose contribution to sustainable human development (or whatever other term may capture their particular approach) would benefit from integrating the unique normative perspective of human rights in the policy determination, program planning, and project implementation.

IV. Conclusions

The observations contained in this essay only scratch the surface of the complex web of U.N. institutions and bodies and their vast potential to contribute, through multilateral diplomacy and action, to the realization of human rights. The human rights movement in the U.N. began with an educational mission whose revolution-

---

[230] Committee on Economic, Social and Cultural Rights, General Comment No. 3, U.N. Doc. E/1991/23, Annex III (1990).

ary potential has been and still is generally underestimated. It began with the proclamation of the UDHR "to the end that every individual and every organ of society, keeping this Declaration constantly in mind, shall strive *by teaching and education* to promote respect for these rights. . . ."[231]

We are now in the middle years of the U.N. Decade for Human Rights Education. In proclaiming the Decade, the General Assembly acknowledged that human rights education "involves more than providing information but rather is a comprehensive life-long process by which people at all levels of development and in all strata of society learn respect for the dignity of others and the means and methods of ensuring that respect within a democratic society."[232] Perceived as innocuous by most governments and as "weak-kneed" by many activists, these words and the concept of a transformative pedagogy of human rights they represent hold out the potential for upsetting the power structure behind most forms of oppression and repression. Indeed, if people everywhere commit to and build a political culture based on the right and responsibility of everyone to respect, ensure, and fulfill the human rights of everyone, the space for abuse of public trust, violence against the physical and mental integrity of others, and exploitation of the vulnerable will retract.

What is the role of the U.N. in such a millennial quest? It is a tool of governments purporting to represent "We the people of the United Nations" in whose name the U.N. Charter was ratified. The Secretariat and the member states are required by the Charter to "achieve international co-operation in . . . promoting and encouraging respect for human rights. . . ."[233] The means are multilateral diplomacy (the legislative role of the Commission on Human Rights, the General Assembly, and all the subsidiary bodies and international conferences that address human rights issues) and multilateral action (the treaty mechanisms, Charter mechanisms, field programs and missions, and the myriad ways resources are applied by the U.N. system to change reality). I have outlined a few of the new opportunities and new challenges facing the U.N.'s human rights agenda as we enter upon a new century and millennium.[234] These thoughts may be summarized as follows:

> (1) State sovereignty is less than ever an insurmountable obstacle to U.N. action to pursue the Charter objective of universal respect for human rights. The traditional limitations based on Article 2(7) are receding in three ways. *First,*

---

[231] UDHR, *supra* note 2, pmbl. (emphasis added).

[232] *United Nations Decade for Human Rights Education*, G.A. Res. 49/184, 49th Sess., Supp. No. 49, at 202, U.N. Doc. A/49/49 (vol. 1) (1994). *See* HUMAN RIGHTS: UNITED NATIONS DECADE FOR HUMAN RIGHTS EDUCATION 1995–2004 (U.N. pub. HR/PUB/DECAOR/1998/1) (1998).

[233] U.N. CHARTER, *supra* note 4, art. 1(3).

[234] The temptation to refer to the millennium is irresistible, although one should bear in mind that the year 2000 is a somewhat arbitrary milestone, based as it is on the questionable dating of a birth on a calendar of one of the world's great religions.

"soft" intervention through the machinery of the Commission and Sub-commission has progressively expanded and, despite resistance from authoritarian states, will continue to do so. *Second,* "hard" intervention through peace enforcement and international criminal prosecutions has begun to provide an option for responding decisively to the most brutal forms of human rights violence. The peace enforcement option unfortunately is dependent too often on U.S. political will and military might, which is not a valid basis for the systematic and evenhanded application of this possibility. The criminal prosecution dimension of this option, after the adoption of the Rome Statute, shows more promise of even-handed treatment. *Third,* democratic empowerment has made considerable progress through consent-based peace-building and other field operations that affect basic institutions of the state and the expectations and aspirations of the society. In all these ways, the margin of action by the U.N. expanded in the early years of the 1990s and retracted in mid-decade. The year 2000 is likely to see a return of an expanded U.N. role.

(2) Transitions to democracy in former communist-party states and in former military dictatorships, as well as through U.N. peace-building and democratic empowerment have released the potential for the participation of civil society in transformative processes and in the consolidation of democracy in ways that the U.N. can nurture. The forces of civil society are in large part represented by NGOs, but these are not the only forces. The free press, the labor movement, religious organizations allied with people's interests, and even the private economic sector can be essential to maintaining viable democratic institutions respectful of human rights. The U.N. can capture and nurture this trend by recognizing greater participation of NGOs in its work, providing more voice to representative groups, and supporting various forces of the civil society "on the ground."

(3) The principal structural innovation in the U.N. human rights world is the OHCHR, which is coming of age and enjoying the well-deserved reputation of the incumbent and the sincere and politically effective support of the Secretary-General. It is nevertheless a fragile institution not yet endowed with resources sufficient to the tasks it has been mandated to fulfill. The renewed hopes in that Office risk being disappointed if rhetorical commitment is not transformed into a significant commitment of resources.

(4) The nature of conflict in the post-Cold War era has created radically new challenges for the U.N.'s human rights program. Massive violations occur in the course of internal armed conflict, especially when fed by ethnic nationalism. The self-determination framework of U.N. human rights thinking has been inadequate to respond to this type of conflict. The combatants tend to commit war crimes, crimes against humanity, and genocide. Two responses of the U.N. show promise. First, as already mentioned, the

international community seems willing, for the first time since the Nuremberg and Tokyo trials, to hold the perpetrators and their commanders criminally responsible. Support from the U.N. for the effective implementation of the Rome Statute of the International Criminal Court[235] is a priority to advance accountability for human rights violations and eliminate the scourge of impunity. Second, preventive diplomacy and peacemaking by the U.N. have demonstrated the value of integrating the human rights dimension into comprehensive peace agreements, and the High Commissioner for Human Rights can encourage this practice as a member of the Secretary-General's Executive Committee on peace and security. This function, about which many governments and international officials remain reserved, needs to be nurtured and sustained so that human rights becomes an inseparable element of U.N. efforts to achieve and maintain peace.

(5) The creation of a "human rights culture" has been a rhetorical appeal of the U.N. for decades. Responding to NGO initiatives, the U.N. finally launched a Decade for Human Rights Education in 1994, with a plan of action that has the potential for empowering people at the local level in numerous practical ways. This can be carried out as other U.N. decades, that is, by generating lots of paper, many resolutions, and numerous meetings. Or the U.N. can make the Decade a success if it acts to legitimize and support nongovernmental and local educational efforts, especially through well-targeted financial support to NGOs. The potential value of human rights education to democratic empowerment cannot be over-stressed. In the broader sense, it is the key to the creation of a political culture based on human rights, which is clearly a more effective and satisfying basis for human security than the accumulation of weapons and military strength. Military defense will continue to lay claim to the resources of nations and to provide the primary strategic option. A new doctrine of human security based on a holistic approach to human rights deserves to capture the imagination of people who can think beyond the military option. The U.N. is necessarily the principal framework for the development and expansion of this idea.

(6) A major challenge to the U.N. is to give practical meaning to economic, social, and cultural rights and the right to development. One dimension of the ideological confrontation of the Cold War—admittedly an oversimplified one—was the opposition between Western insistence on civil and political rights, on the one hand, and socialist countries emphasis on eco-

---

[235] The text of the Rome Statute is reprinted in 37 I.L.M. 999 (1998). For pertinent commentary, see THE STATUTE OF THE INTERNATIONAL CRIMINAL COURT—A DOCUMENTARY HISTORY (compiled by M. Cherif Bassiouni, 1999). *See also* M. Cherif Bassiouni, *Strengthening the Norms of International Humanitarian Law to Combat Impunity, supra* in this volume, at p. 243.

nomic, social, and cultural rights, on the other. Today, Central and Eastern European countries have embraced civil and political rights and market economy, and suffer the most rapid rise in social inequalities, organized crime, unemployment, and general deterioration of social conditions of any region in the world. Ordinary people are paying a high price for the abandonment of economic, social, and cultural rights. The U.S. has been particularly impervious to these rights, but now no longer has the excuse that they are merely propagandistic tools of Soviet bloc countries. These rights are legitimate claims of people against the harmful consequences of free market economies. Through multilateral diplomacy, the U.N. should be the leader in promoting wider acceptance of these rights and, through multilateral action, in pursuing exemplary ways of defining and implementing a human rights-based approach to development. Without such diplomacy and action these concepts are likely to remain little more than pious aspirations.

These are but a few of many challenges facing the U.N. in its human rights program. The deeper question is whether the UN, as an intergovernmental institution, can be expected to make any meaningful contribution in this area that so challenges state prerogatives. Stanley Hoffmann has written that "[t]he promotion of human rights to the agenda of international politics is part of an effort at moving beyond Machiavellian statecraft."[236] When treatment of individuals and groups within states becomes a matter of legitimate concern to the world community and gradually more and more resolute forms of U.N. action are taken, then, Hoffmann explains, "the notion of sovereignty, the very cornerstone of the 'Westphalian Order' . . . has been breached."[237] Hoffmann also correctly predicted that "an effective international order of human rights [would not only] require as a precondition a decline in the role of states and the emergence of powerful collective mechanisms or regimes, but it would also, in the long run, amount to a revolution in the nature of most political regimes."[238] Multilateral diplomacy and action through the U.N. holds out the promise of more "breaches" in that order and of advancing that "revolutionary" agenda. If it can live up to that promise, hundreds of millions of people stand to benefit in the next century.

---

[236] Stanley Hoffmann, *Human Rights as a Foreign Policy Goal*, 112 DAEDALUS 19, 20 (Fall 1983).

[237] *Id.* at 21.

[238] *Id.* at 33.

The Promise of Regional Human Rights Systems

Dinah Shelton

I. Introduction

Scholars of international law and relations frequently speak of *systems*[1] or *regimes*.[2] In describing the international protection of human rights, the term "system" seems best to encompass the interdependence, complexity,[3] and punctuated

---

1   *See, e.g.*, COVEY OLIVER ET AL., THE INTERNATIONAL LEGAL SYSTEM (4th ed. 1995); ORAN R. YOUNG, A SYSTEMIC APPROACH TO INTERNATIONAL POLITICS (Princeton Research Monograph No. 33, 1968); Alexandre Kiss & Dinah Shelton, *Systems Analysis of International Law: A Methodological Inquiry*, 17 NETH. Y.B. INT'L L. 45 (1986). On systems analysis of law generally, see Lynn M. LoPucki, *The Systems Approach to Law*, 82 CORNELL L. REV. 479 (1997). A system is "a regularly interacting or interdependent group of items forming a unified whole." WEBSTER'S NINTH NEW COLLEGIATE DICTIONARY, s.v. "System." Social systems are characterized by an additional criterion of purposefulness. MICHAEL L. GIBSON & CARY T. HUGHES, SYSTEMS ANALYSIS AND DESIGN 5 (1994) ("a system is a set of interrelated and interactive elements that work together to accomplish specific purposes"). *See also* C. WEST CHURCHMAN, THE SYSTEMS APPROACH 11 (2d ed. 1979).

2   *See* Burns H. Weston et al., *Regional Human Rights Regimes: A Comparison and Appraisal*, 20 VAND. J. TRANSNAT'L L. 586 (1987); Jack Donnelly, *International Human Rights: A Regime Analysis*, 40 INT'L ORG. 599 (1986); Nicholas G. Onuf & V. Spike Peterson, *Human Rights from an International Regimes Perspective*, 38 J. INT'L AFF. 329 (1984). For an overview of basic concepts of regime theory, see Kenneth W. Abott, *Modern International Relations Theory: A Prospectus for International Lawyers*, 14 YALE J. INT'L L. 335 (1989). A regime has been defined as the "principles, norms, rules, and decision-making procedures around which actor expectations converge in a given issue-area." Friedrich Kratochwil & John G. Ruggie, *International Organization: A State of the Art on an Art of the State*, 40 INT'L ORG. 753, 754 (1986). Keohane similarly describes international regimes as "[f]ormal international organizations and codified rules and norms." ROBERT O. KEOHANE, INTERNATIONAL INSTITUTIONS AND STATE POWER vii (1989).

3   Complexity theory has been described as the study of the behavior of macroscopic collections of interacting units that are endowed with the potential to evolve over time. PETER COVENEY & ROGER HIGHFIELD, FRONTIERS OF COMPLEXITY: THE SEARCH FOR ORDER IN A CHAOTIC WORLD 7 (1995). Complexity theory looks at nonlinear dynamical systems, suggesting that law and society coexist interdependently and dynamically, inevitably leading to unpredictable, unanticipated behavior that is necessary for the system to thrive and adapt in a dynamically fit manner. *See* J. B. Ruhl, *Complexity Theory as a Paradigm for the*

equilibrium[4] that characterize the norms, institutions, and procedures that are particular to this field. Systems share certain fundamental characteristics, yet each is unique.[5] Accordingly, based on an understanding of the attributes of systems, especially their inherent complexity, regional human rights systems can be evaluated in light of the aims, structures, and surrounding environments of each, and on their flexibility to move between rigidity on the one hand and chaos on the other. The flexibility to evolve is particular important: systems analysis suggests that those systems that balance stasis and change are the most successful in maintaining themselves in the long run, however much they are challenged by unforeseen developments in their surrounding environments.[6]

A human rights system can be said to consist of: (1) a list or lists of internationally-guaranteed human rights; (2) permanent institutions; and (3) compliance or enforcement procedures. In addition, each system is composed of various subsystems.[7] At the global level, the United Nations system consists in large part of many interacting organs and specialized agencies concerned with human rights. Regional human rights systems contribute to the global system, as well as forming their own interdependent systems. Subsystems of actors also exist: states, intergovernmental organizations, nongovernmental organizations, business enterprises, labor unions, and networks of individuals.

This essay evaluates the promise of regional human rights systems to contribute to respect for human rights in the coming decades. A brief survey of the reasons

---

Dynamical Law and Society System: A Wake-Up Call for Legal Reductionism and the Modern Administrative State, 45 Duke L.J. 849 (1996).

[4] *See* J. B. Ruhl, *The Fitness of Law: Using Complexity Theory to Describe the Evolution of Law and Society and its Practical Meaning for Democracy*, 49 Vand. L. Rev. 1407 (1996). *Punctuated equilibrium* is taken from biology and describes the evolutionary process whereby periods of minute variations in genetic makeup are interrupted by episodes of major change, many of which are random in nature rather than responsive to pressures for natural selection (the "science of surprises"). In addition, ecosystem dynamics indicate that evolution takes place in the context of complex, chaotic environments with which it is interdependent. Where gradualism does not explain the full dynamics of evolution, punctuated equilibrium does. The theory is seen to be applicable to all dynamical systems. *Id.* at 1414–16, 1440.

[5] System characteristics include: (1) self-generation, self-regulation and self-reproduction; (2) the tendency for systems to become more structured, more capable and more vulnerable with age; (3) the tendency for systems to accumulate information over time; and (4) entropy, the tendency for systems to dissipate. Purposefulness is also inherent. Paul Licker, Fundamentals of Systems Analysis 5 (1987) ("A system is defined as a set of elements that are related and that, through this set of relationships, aim to accomplish goals."). Waltz describes a system as having a structure that consists of an ordering principle, differentiation and functional specification of the units, and the distribution of capabilities across units. The behavior of actors in the system is dictated by the structure. Kenneth N. Waltz, Theory of International Politics 99 (1979).

[6] Ruhl, *supra* note 4, at 1410.

[7] *See* LoPucki, *supra* note 1.

behind the creation of regional systems and their consequent stated aims precedes this discussion. The convergences and divergences of regional systems provide the focus for evaluating the unique contributions of regional systems to human rights law and practice. The similar and different challenges facing them complete the analysis. The conclusion asserts that regional systems are indispensable to achieving effective compliance with international human rights law, performing as they do a necessary intermediary function between state domestic institutions that violate or fail to enforce human rights and the global system which is so far incapable of providing redress to individual victims of human rights violations. They have the necessary ability and flexibility to change as conditions around them change, and sometimes they do so quickly. As their norms and procedures converge, yet are applied in response to regionally-specific problems, they achieve an equilibrium between uniform enforcement of global norms and regional diversity. With both cooperation and competition among them, they advance the substantive understanding of human rights guarantees through their jurisprudence, reinforcing the law and inspiring each other.

II. The Origins of Regional Systems

The promise of regional systems can be understood initially by considering why regional systems exist. First, regional systems are a product of the global concern for human rights that emerged at the end of the Second World War. Given the widespread movement for human rights that followed, it should not be surprising that regional organizations created or reformed after the war should have added human rights to their agendas. All of them drew inspiration from the human rights provisions of the United Nations Charter and the Universal Declaration of Human Rights.[8]

Second, historical and political factors encouraged each region to focus on human rights issues. The Americas had a tradition of regional approaches to international issues, including human rights that grew out of regional solidarity developed during the movements for independence. Pan American Conferences had taken action on several human rights matters well before the creation of the United Nations,[9] and this

---

8   See infra Appendix I [hereinafter UDHR].

9   For a history of the Inter-American system, see THOMAS BUERGENTHAL & DINAH SHELTON, PROTECTING HUMAN RIGHTS IN THE AMERICAS 37–44 (4th ed. 1995). At the International American Conference of War and Peace, held at Chapultepec, Mexico in March 1943, twenty-one American states asked for a bill of human rights to be included in the Charter of the United Nations. Three of these countries (Cuba, Chile, and Panama) were the first ones to submit a draft for such a bill. At the San Francisco Conference, they lobbied for the inclusion of a bill of rights in the Charter. Other Latin American countries prepared drafts that became part of the background to the drafting of the UDHR, supra note 8. The text submitted by the Inter-American Juridical Committee was particularly influential. The Chilean draft and the work of the Chilean delegate, Hernan Santa Cruz, were also important.

history led the Organization of American States to refer to human rights in its Charter[10] and to adopt the American Declaration on the Rights and Duties of Man[11] some months before the United Nations completed the Universal Declaration of Human Rights.[12]

Europe had been the theater of the greatest atrocities of the Second World War, and felt compelled to press for international human rights guarantees as part of European reconstruction. Faith in western European traditions of democracy, the rule of law, and individual rights inspired the belief that a regional system could be successful in avoiding future conflict and stemming post-war revolutionary impulses supported by the Soviet Union.[13]

Somewhat later, in Africa, claims to self-determination became a recognized part of the human rights agenda as African states emerged from colonization and continued struggles for national cohesion. Resistance to human rights abuses in South Africa also contributed to regional efforts for all of Africa.[14] A former president of the African Commission traces a history of concern with human dignity in African culture, history, and values, and notes that

---

[10] Charter of the Organization of American States, Apr. 30, 1948, 2 U.S.T. 2394, U.N.T.S. 48 [hereinafter OAS Charter], *reprinted in* 1 INTERNATIONAL LAW AND WORLD ORDER: BASIC DOCUMENTS I.B.14 (Burns H. Weston ed., 5 vols., 1994–) [hereinafter 1 Weston]. The OAS Charter was amended by the Protocol of Buenos Aires (1967), and the Protocol of Caragena de Indias (1985). The Protocol of Washington (1992) and the Protocol of Managua (1993) have been adopted, but are not yet in force.

[11] American Declaration of the Rights and Duties of Man (1948) [hereinafter American Declaration], *in* OAS, BASIC DOCUMENTS PERTAINING TO HUMAN RIGHTS IN THE INTER-AMERICAN SYSTEM [hereinafter BASIC DOCUMENTS], OAS Res., OAS Off. Rec., OEA/Ser. L/V/I.4 Rev. (1965), OEA/Ser.L/VII.92, doc. 31, rev. 3 at 17, (1996), *reprinted in* 3 INTERNATIONAL LAW AND WORLD ORDER: BASIC DOCUMENTS III.B.23 (Burns H. Weston ed., 5 vols., 1994–) [hereinafter 3 Weston].

[12] *Supra* note 8.

[13] In the preamble to the European Convention on Human Rights, the contracting parties declared that they were "reaffirming their devotion to the spiritual and moral values which are the common heritage of their peoples and the true source of individual freedom, political liberty and the rule of law, the principles which form the basis of all genuine democracy." *See* J.G. Merrills, *The Council of Europe (I): The European Convention on Human Rights, in* AN INTRODUCTION TO THE INTERNATIONAL PROTECTION OF HUMAN RIGHTS 221 (Raija Hanski & Markku Suksi eds., 1997) [hereinafter HANSKI & SUKSI] ("Many statesmen of the immediate post-war epoch had been in resistance movements or in prison during the Second World War and were acutely conscious of the need to prevent any recrudescence of dictatorship in Western Europe."). Merrills also views the emergence of the East-West conflict as a stimulus to closer ties in Western Europe.

[14] The United Nations had also abandoned its earlier opposition to the creation of a regional human rights system and actively supported the creation of a system in Africa. *See* Weston et al., *supra* note 2.

the "youth" of the African system does not mean it is less valuable or important than other regional systems.[15]

A third impulse to regionalism came from frustration at the long-stalled efforts of the United Nations to produce a human rights treaty that would complete the international bill of rights. Indeed, it took nearly two decades to finalize and adopt the two United Nations covenants.[16] During the process, it became clear that the compliance mechanisms at the global level would not be strong[17] and that any judicial procedures to enforce human rights would have to be on the regional level. As a result, beginning with Europe, regional systems focused on the creation of procedures of redress,[18] establishing control machinery to supervise the implementation and enforcement of the guaranteed rights. The functioning European and Inter-American courts are among the great contributors to the protection of human rights by regional systems. A June 8, 1998 protocol to the African Charter,[19] which will create a court in the African system, promises to add to the regional protections.

---

[15] Isaac Nguema, *L'Afrique, les droits de l'homme et le developpement*, 1 REV. COMM. AF. DHP. 16, 26 (1991). The author quotes two African proverbs: (1) to be the first in a family to marry does not necessarily mean one is the richest and to be the last to marry does not necessarily mean one is the poorest; (2) to be the eldest child does not make one the most intelligent and to be the last born does not make one the most stupid. In other words, he views the chronology of concern with human rights, even assuming it can be established, as distinct from the maturity and excellence of the present systems.

[16] International Covenant on Economic, Social and Cultural Rights, *infra* Appendix II [hereinafter ICESCR]; International Covenant on Civil and Political Rights, *infra* Appendix III [hereinafter ICCPR].

[17] The U.N. legal advisor held in 1949 that the U.N. could not consider human rights complaints.

[18] "We desire a Charter of Human Rights guaranteeing liberty of thought, assembly and expression as well as the right to form a political opposition; We desire a Court of Justice with adequate sanctions for the implementation of this Charter." *Message to Europeans*, adopted by the Congress of Europe, May 8–10, 1948, *quoted in* COUNCIL OF EUROPE, REPORT ON THE CONTROL SYSTEM OF THE EUROPEAN CONVENTION ON HUMAN RIGHTS 4 (H (92)14) (Dec. 1992). A Resolution adopted by the Congress stated that it "is convinced that in the interest of human values and human liberty, the (proposed) Assembly should make proposals for the establishment of a Court of Justice with adequate sanctions for the implementation of this Charter, and to this end any citizen of the associated countries shall have redress before the Court, at any time and with the least possible delay, of any violation of his rights as formulated in the Charter." *Id.* at 4.

[19] The African Charter, officially known as the African Charter on Human and Peoples' Rights, was concluded June 27, 1981, and entered into force Oct. 21, 1986. OAU Doc. CAB/LEG/67/3, Rev. 5, *reprinted in* 21 I.L.M. 58 (1982) *and* 3 Weston III.B.1, *supra* note 11. The 1998 protocol may be found at "African States Establish Human Rights Court," AFRONET File (visited Dec. 5, 1998) <http://www.zamnet.zm/zamnet/afronet/a_file/ i6_pg8.htm>.

Thus, regional systems have elements of uniformity and diversity in their origins. All of them began as the global human rights system was developing and each was inspired by the agreed universal norms. At the same time, each region had its own issues and concerns. As the systems have evolved, the universal framework within which they began, together with their own interactions, have had surprisingly strong influence, leading to converging norms and procedures in an overarching interdependent and dynamic system. In many respects they are thinking globally and acting regionally. Each uses the jurisprudence of the other systems and amends and strengthens its procedures with reference to the experience of the others. In general, their mutual influence is highly progressive, both in normative development and institutional reform.

III. Regional Human Rights Systems

As noted, regional human rights systems exist in Europe, the Americas, and Africa. The Arab League has assisted a nascent system in the Middle East, having adopted the Arab Charter for Human Rights in 1994.[20] Continuing efforts are underway to create a regional system or systems within the Asia-Pacific region.[21] All of the systems have experienced important recent changes in membership and enacted new normative instruments and procedural reforms.

A. The European System

The European system, the first to be fully operational, began with the creation of the Council of Europe by ten Western European states in 1949.[22] It has since expanded to include Central and Eastern European countries, bringing the total membership to forty.[23] Article 3 of the Council's Statute provides that every member state must accept the principles of the rule of law and of the enjoyment by all persons within its jurisdiction of human rights and fundamental freedoms; membership in the Council is conditioned *de facto* upon adherence to the European

---

[20]   Arab Charter on Human Rights, Sept. 15, 1994, Council of the League of Arab States, 102d Sess., Res. 5437. An unofficial translation of the Charter appears in 56 REV. INT'L COMM. JURISTS 57 (1996) and 4 INT'L HUM. RTS. REP. 850 (1997), *reprinted in* 3 Weston III.B.27, *supra* note 11.

[21]   *See* Vitit Muntarbhorn, *Asia, Human Rights, and the New Millennium: Time for a Regional Human Rights Charter?*, 8 TRANSNAT'L L. & CONTEMP. PROBS. 407, 413 (1998).

[22]   The Statute of the Council of Europe was signed in London on May 5, 1949, on behalf of Belgium, Denmark, France, Ireland, Italy, Luxembourg, the Netherlands, Norway, Sweden, and the United Kingdom. Statute of the Council of Europe, May 5, 1949. Europ. T.S. No. 1, Gr. Brit. T.S. No. 51 (Cmnd. 8969), *reprinted in* 1 Weston II.B.4, *supra* note 10.

[23]   Five other states have applied for membership: Armenia (Mar. 8, 1996), Azerbaijan (July 13, 1996), Belarus (Mar. 12, 1993), Bosnia-Herzegovina (Apr. 10, 1995) and Georgia (July 14, 1996). Russia joined in 1996.

Convention on Human Rights and Fundamental Freedoms (ECHR) and its eleven protocols.[24]

As the first of its kind, the ECHR began with a short list of civil and political rights, to which additional guarantees have been added over time. The European system was the first to create an international court for the protection of human rights and to create a procedure for individual denunciations of human rights violations.[25] But the jurisprudence of the European Court of Human Rights has been relatively conservative compared to that of other systems, reflecting an early concern for maintaining state support in light of the innovations of the European system and the then-optional nature of the Court's jurisdiction. The role of the victim was initially very limited and admissibility requirements were stringent. As the system has matured, however, the institutional structures and normative guarantees have been considerably strengthened. Although most of the changes result from efforts to improve the effectiveness of the system and add to its guarantees, some of the evolution reflects a responsiveness to the activities of other regional organizations both within and outside Europe, while still other changes have resulted from the impact of expanding membership in the Council of Europe.

The evolution of the European system is in fact characterized by the adoption of numerous treaties and protocols. Through its Parliamentary Assembly, the Council has drafted a series of human rights instruments.[26] The most significant of these are the 1950 ECHR and its eleven protocols,[27] the 1961 European Social

---

24   Concluded Nov. 4, 1950 [hereinafter ECHR] (entered into force, Sept. 3, 1953, Europ. T.S. No. 5, 213 U.N.T.S. 221, *reprinted in* 3 Weston III.B.2, *supra* note 11, as completed by Protocol No. 2, Europ. T.S. No. 44, and amended by Protocol No. 3, Europ. T.S. No. 45; Protocol No. 5, Europ. T.S. No. 55; and Protocol No. 8, Europ. T.S. No. 118. In addition, the following protocols have been adopted: Protocol to the Convention, EUROP. T.S. No. 9; Protocol No. 4 (Securing Certain Rights and Freedoms), Europ. T.S. No. 46; Protocol No. 6 (Concerning the Abolition of the Death Penalty), Europ. T.S. No 114; Protocol No. 7, Europ. T.S. No. 117; Protocol No. 9, Europ. T.S. No. 140; Protocol No. 10, Europ. T.S. No. 146; and Protocol No. 11 (Restructuring the Control Machinery), Europ. T.S. No 155. All protocols to the ECHR are reprinted in 3 Weston, *supra* note 11.

25   An earlier, more limited effort was made in 1907 with the creation of the Central American Court of Justice. The court had jurisdiction over cases of "denial of justice" between a government and a national of another state if the cases were of an international character or concerned alleged violations of a treaty or convention. *See* MANLEY O. HUDSON, PERMANENT COURT OF INTERNATIONAL JUSTICE 49 (1943).

26   It is worth noting that the Assembly also adopts recommendations on human rights, some of which are influential in shaping the laws and policies of member states. In some cases, the Committee of Ministers requests governments to inform it of measures they have taken to implement specific recommendations

27   ECHR, *supra* note 24. *See* Committee of Ministers, *Declaration on Compliance with Commitments Accepted by Member States of the Council of Europe*, adopted Nov. 10, 1994, *reprinted in* Council of Europe, Information Sheet No. 35 (July–Dec. 1994) (1995), App. I,

Charter (ESC) with its protocols,[28] the 1987 European Convention for the Prevention of Torture and its protocols,[29] the European Charter for Regional or Minority Languages,[30] the 1995 Framework Convention for the Protection of National Minorities,[31] and the 1997 Convention on Human Rights and

---

146. All forty member states of the Council of Europe have ratified the Convention, as restructured by Protocol 11, *supra* note 24, and all but Lithuania have ratified or acceded to the European Convention for the Prevention of Torture and Inhuman and Degrading Treatment or Punishment, Nov. 26, 1987, Europ. T.S. No. 126, *reprinted in* 27 I.L.M. 1152 (1987) *and* 3 Weston III.K.4, *supra* note 11 [hereinafter European Torture Convention]. Russia was the last state to ratify the 1950 European Convention, on May 5, 1998. Lithuania signed the 1987 European Torture Convention on Sept. 14, 1995, but had not ratified it as of May 5, 1998.

[28] Europ. T.S. No. 35, *reprinted in* 3 Weston III.B.4, *supra* note 11. The Charter entered into force on February 26, 1965, and had twenty-three contracting parties as of June 22, 1998. An Additional Protocol to the Charter, adopted May 5, 1988, imposes legal obligations in regard to additional economic and social rights. It entered into force Sept. 4, 1992. *See* Europ. T.S. No. 128, *reprinted in* 3 Weston III.B.12, *supra* note 11. It has been ratified by eight of the twenty-two states parties to the Social Charter (Denmark, Finland, Greece, Italy, the Netherlands, Norway, Slovakia, Sweden). A 1991 Turin Protocol, Europ. T.S. No. 142, *reprinted in* 3 Weston III.B.15, *supra* note 11, is not yet in force, as it requires the ratification of all parties to the Charter. A further Protocol, adopted Nov. 9, 1995, to provide for a system of collective complaints, is now in force, having seven ratifications among the twenty-two states parties to the Charter. *See* Europ. T.S. No. 158, *reprinted in* 3 Weston III.B.16c, *supra* note 11. Finally, as of July 15, 1998, only one state, Sweden, had accepted the revised Charter, Europ. T.S. No. 163, *reprinted in* 3 Weston III.B.16d, *supra* note 11.

[29] *Supra* note 27. Protocol 1 widens the geographical scope of the Convention by enabling states not members of the Council of Europe to accede to it by invitation. Europ. T.S. No. 151. Protocol 2 makes technical changes to the arrangements for elections of the members of the European Committee for the Prevention of Torture and Inhuman and Degrading Treatment or Punishment. Europ. T.S. No. 152. Neither of the two protocols is in force because they must be ratified by all states parties to the Convention. The texts of the protocols are reprinted in 1 INT'L HUM. RTS. REP. 339 (1994). *See* Antonio Cassese, *A New Approach to Human Rights: The European Convention for the Prevention of Torture*, 83 AM. J. INT'L L. 128 (1989); Malcolm Evans & Rod Morgan, *The European Convention for the Prevention of Torture: Operational Practice*, 41 INT'L & COMP. L.Q. 590 (1992).

[30] European Charter for Regional or Minority Languages (entered into force Mar. 1, 1998), Europ. T.S. No. 148. It has seven ratifications, five of them from Western Europe (Finland, Liechtenstein, the Netherlands, Norway and Switzerland) and two from Central Europe (Hungary and Croatia).

[31] Framework Convention on the Protection of National Minorities (entered into force Feb. 1, 1998). Europ. T.S. No. 15, *reprinted in* 2 INT'L HUM. RTS. REP. 217 (1995) *and* 3 Weston III.I.7, *supra* note 11. The Convention has been accepted by just over half of the member states of the Council of Europe, equally among Western European states and those of Central and Eastern Europe. Each of the first four states to ratify has significant minority issues: Spain, Hungary, Romania, and Slovakia. One non-member state, Armenia, has also ratified

Biomedicine,[32] with its protocol banning human cloning.[33] Together these instruments form a network of mutually reinforcing human rights protections in Europe.

B. The Inter-American System

The Inter-American system began with the transformation of the Pan American Union into the Organization of American States (OAS), the Charter of which proclaims the "fundamental rights of the individual" as one of the Organization's basic principles.[34] The 1948 American Declaration on the Rights and Duties of Man[35] gives definition to the Charter's general commitment to human rights.[36] Over a decade later, in 1959, the OAS created a seven member Inter-American Commission of Human Rights with a mandate to further respect for human rights among the OAS member states.[37] In 1965, the Commission's competence was expanded to accept communications, request information from governments, and make recommendations to bring about the more effective observance of human rights.[38] In 1969,

---

the Convention. The term "framework," widely used in environmental agreements, indicates that the Convention sets forth general principles and objectives but does not specify the details of implementation by states parties. Supervision is by means of periodic state reports, to be reviewed by the Committee of Ministers with the assistance of an expert advisory committee. The Convention requires ratification by twelve members of the Council of Europe. Work is underway also on a protocol to the European Convention on Human Rights which would add some minority protections to the Convention, allowing cases to be brought to the European Court.

[32]   European Convention on the Protection of Human Rights and Dignity of the Human Being with Regard to the Application of Biology and Medicine: Convention on Human Rights and Biomedicine, Apr. 4, 1997, Europ. T.S. No. 164, *reprinted in* 36 I.L.M. 817 (1997) *and* 3 Weston III.K.6, *supra* note 11.

[33]   Draft Additional Protocol to the European Convention on Human Rights and Protection of Human Rights and Dignity of the Human Being with Regard to the Application of Biology and Medicine on the Prohibition of Cloning Human Beings (with Explanatory Report and Parliamentary Assembly Opinion), C.E. Doc. DIR/JUR (97) 9 (July 4, 1997), *reprinted in* 36 I.L.M. 1415 (1997) *and* 3 Weston III.K.7, *supra* note 11.

[34]   OAS Charter, *supra* note 10, art. 3.

[35]   American Declaration, *supra* note 11.

[36]   *See* Interpretation of the American Declaration of the Rights and Duties of Man Within the Framework of Article 64 of the American Convention, 10 Inter-Am. Ct. H.R. (Ser. A) (1989).

[37]   *Id.* at 7–9. The Statute of the Commission described it as an autonomous entity of the OAS having the function to promote respect for human rights. *See* 1960 Statute, art. 1. In 1967, the Protocol of Buenos Aires amended the Charter to make the Commission a principal organ of the OAS.

[38]   *Id.* at 10.

the American Convention of Human Rights[39] which entered into force in 1978, conferred additional competence on the Commission to oversee compliance with the Convention.[40]

The Commission's jurisdiction extends to all thirty-five OAS member states.[41] The twenty-five states that have ratified the Convention are bound by its provisions, while other member states are held to the standards of the American Declaration. Communications may be filed against any state; the optional clause applies only to interstate cases. Standing for non-state actors to file communications is broad.[42]

The Commission may also prepare country reports and conduct on-site visits to examine the human rights situations in individual countries and make recommendations to the government in question. Country reports have been prepared on the Commission's own initiative and at the request of the country concerned. The Commission may also appoint special rapporteurs to prepare studies on hemisphere-wide problems.

The American Convention also created the Inter-American Court of Human Rights. The Court has jurisdiction over contentious cases submitted against states that accept its jurisdiction and it may issue advisory opinions.

Like the European system, the Inter-American system has expanded its protections over time through the adoption of additional human rights prescriptions. The major instruments are: the 1985 Inter-American Convention to Prevent and Punish Torture;[43] the 1988 Additional Protocol to the American Convention on Human Rights in the Area of Economic, Social and Cultural Rights;[44] the 1990

---

[39]   Concluded, Nov. 22, 1969 (entered into force, July 18, 1978), OASTS No. 36, OAS Off. Rec. OEA/Ser. L/V/IL.23, Doc. 21, Rev. 6 (1979), 1144 U.N.T.S. 123, *reprinted in* 9 I.L.M. 673 (1970) *and* 3 Weston III.B.24, *supra* note 11.

[40]   *Id.* arts. 33–51.

[41]   Virtually the entire Western Hemisphere is included: Antigua and Barbuda, Argentina, The Bahamas, Barbados, Belize, Bolivia, Brazil, Canada, Chile, Colombia, Costa Rica, Cuba, Dominica, Dominican Republic, Ecuador, El Salvador, Grenada, Guatemala, Guyana, Haiti, Honduras, Jamaica, Mexico, Nicaragua, Panama, Paraguay, Peru, St. Kitts and Nevis, Saint Lucia, Saint Vincent and the Grenadines, Suriname, Trinidad and Tobago, the United States, Uruguay, and Venezuela.

[42]   Article 44 of the American Convention, *supra* note 39, states that "[a]ny person or group of persons, or any non-governmental entity legally recognized in one or more member states of the Organization, may lodge petitions with the Commission containing denunciations or complaints of violation of this Convention by a State Party." The Commission's Regulations provide the same extensive standing for complaints to be filed against OAS member states that are not party to the Convention.

[43]   Concluded, Dec. 9, 1985 (entered into force, Feb. 28, 1987), OASTS No. 67, *reprinted in* 25 I.L.M. 519 (1986) *and* 3 Weston III.K.3, *supra* note 11.

[44]   Concluded, Nov. 17, 1988, OASTS No. 69, OAS Doc. OEA/.Ser.A/42 (SEPF), *reprinted in* 28 I.L.M. 156 (1989), BASIC DOCUMENTS, *supra* note 11, *and* 3 Weston III.B.25, *supra* note 11. The Protocol is not yet in force.

Second Additional Protocol to the American Convention on Human Rights to Abolish the Death Penalty;[45] the 1994 Inter-American Convention on the Prevention, Punishment, and Eradication of Violence against Women;[46] the 1994 Inter-American Convention on Forced Disappearance of Persons;[47] and the 1998 Declaration of the Rights of Indigenous Peoples.[48]

C. The African System

The regional promotion and protection of human rights in Africa is established by the African Charter on Human and Peoples' Rights (African Charter),[49] designed to function within the framework of the Organization of African Unity (OAU). The OAU Assembly of Heads of State and Government adopted the African Charter on June 27, 1981, and as of January 1, 1998 it had been ratified by fifty-two of the fifty-three OAU member states.[50]

The African Charter differs from other regional human rights treaties in its inclusion of "peoples' rights." It also includes economic, social, and cultural rights to a greater extent than either the European or the American conventions. Like its European and American counterparts, however, it establishes a human rights commission, the African Commission on Human and Peoples' Rights, comprising eleven independent members elected for a renewable period of six years. The Charter confers four functions on the Commission: the promotion of human and peoples' rights; the protection of those rights; interpretation of the Charter; and the performance of other tasks that may be entrusted to it by the OAU Assembly of Heads of State and Government. In addition, the Commission may undertake studies, perform training and teaching functions, convene conferences, initiate publication programs, disseminate information, and collaborate with national and local institutions concerned with human and peoples' rights. Unlike the other regional systems, the African system envisages not only interstate and individual communications procedures, but a special procedure for the handling of gross and systematic violations of human rights.

---

[45] Protocol to the American Convention on Human Rights to Abolish the Death Penalty, *reprinted in* BASIC DOCUMENTS, *supra* note 11, at 83. The Protocol, approved June 8, 1990, at Asuncion, Paraguay, entered into force Aug. 28, 1991. It has four state parties (Brazil, Panama, Uruguay and Venezuela).

[46] Concluded, June 9, 1994 (entered into force, Mar. 5, 1995), *reprinted in* BASIC DOCUMENTS, *supra* note 11, at 109.

[47] Concluded June 9, 1994 (entered into force, Mar. 28, 1996), *reprinted in* BASIC DOCUMENTS, *supra* note 11, at 99.

[48] IACHR, Press Communique of 3/97, *reprinted in* OAS, ANNUAL REPORT OF THE INTER-AMERICAN COMMISSION ON HUMAN RIGHTS 1997, OAS Doc. OEA/Ser.L/V/II.98, Doc.7 rev., at 1081 (1998).

[49] African Charter, *supra* note 19.

[50] Only Eritrea has not yet ratified the Charter.

D. The Nascent Middle East System

On September 15, 1994, building on earlier texts adopted by regional nongovern-mental[51] and inter-governmental organizations,[52] the League of Arab States, which did not mention human rights in its founding charter,[53] approved an Arab Charter on Human Rights.[54] The Charter requires acceptance by seven states before it will enter into force;[55] until then there are no Middle Eastern regional institutions or procedures for monitoring human rights. The Charter foresees the election by its states parties of a seven-member independent Committee of Experts to serve for three years, subject to the possibility of a single re-election. Article 41 foresees peri-

---

[51]   On September 19, 1981, for example, the Islamic Council, a nongovernmental organi-zation consisting of representatives from countries in the Middle East, adopted the Universal Islamic Declaration of Human Rights, 4 EUROP. HUM. RTS. REP. 433 (1982), *reprinted in* 3 Weston III.B.26, *supra* note 11.

[52]   A larger organization of all Islamic states, the Islamic Conference, endorsed human rights in its 1972 Charter, reaffirming the commitment of Islamic states to the U.N. Charter and fundamental human rights. On August 5, 1990, at a meeting of foreign ministers of the Conference, member states adopted the Cairo Declaration on Human Rights in Islam. For an English translation, see *World Conference on Human Rights*, U.N. GAOR, 4th Sess., Agenda Item 5, U.N. Doc. A/CONF.157/PC/62/Add.18 (1993). For a critique of the Declaration, see Ann Elizabeth Mayer, *Universal Versus Islamic Human Rights: A Clash of Cultures or a Clash with a Construct?*, 15 MICH. J. INT'L L. 307 (1994). For background on the Islamic Conference, see HASSAN MOINUDDIN, THE CHARTER OF THE ISLAMIC CONFERENCE AND LEGAL FRAMEWORK OF ECONOMIC COOPERATION AMONG ITS MEMBER STATES (1987).

[53]   The Pact of the League of Arab States, 70 U.N.T.S. 238, *reprinted in* 1 Weston I.B.16, *supra* note 10, was adopted on March 22, 1945, and entered into force on May 10, 1945. On September 12, 1966, the Council of the League of Arab States adopted its first resolution on human rights, calling for the establishment of a steering committee to elaborate a program for the celebration of Human Rights Year in 1968. The Committee recommended the estab-lishment of a permanent Arab Committee on Human Rights and the convening of an Arab Conference on Human Rights. The latter was held in December 1968 in Beirut. *See* Mohamed Noman Galal, *The Arab Draft Charter for Human Rights, in* HUMAN RIGHTS: EGYPT AND THE ARAB WORLD 37 (17 Cairo Papers in Social Science 1994).

[54]   Arab Charter, *supra* note 20. The Arab Charter was adopted by Resolution 5437 of the Council of the League of Arab States, which was approved after a motion by Kuwait to adjourn discussion of the Charter was defeated. The defeat was interpreted by the Jordanian Chairman as an endorsement of the Charter. A Standing Committee on Human Rights in 1968 began drafting the Charter in 1970 and completed its work in 1985. *See* Report and Recommendations of the Arab Standing Committee on Human Rights at its eleventh session held at Cairo during January 10–14, 1993, E/CN.4/1993/90 (1993). For a history of the draft-ing of the Arab Charter, see Galal, *supra* note 53. For early background on the League and its human rights activities, see Stephen P. Marks, *La commission permanente arabe des droits de l'homme*, 3 REV. DROIT DE L'HOMME [HUM. RTS. J.] 101 (1970).

[55]   As of January 1, 1998, only Egypt had ratified the Charter. Iraq signed it on February 5, 1996.

odic reporting by the states parties and implies that the Committee may request a report by submitting inquiries to a state party, with the Committee studying the reports and distributing its own report to the Human Rights Committee of the Arab League. No other functions of human rights promotion or protection are specified in the Charter.

The emerging Middle East system is marked probably more than other regional systems by the great division among its states in their willingness to accept and give effect to international human rights law. These divisions have slowed progress in achieving a true human rights system.

E. Asia

No human rights system exists in Asia, despite efforts by nongovernmental organizations and the United Nations to create one.[56] In 1993, over one hundred Asia-Pacific nongovernmental organizations adopted an Asia-Pacific Declaration of Human Rights supporting the universality of human rights and the creation of a regional system,[57] but governments have been slow to respond. At a 1996 UN-sponsored workshop on the issue, the thirty participating governments[58] concluded that "it was premature, at the current stage, to discuss specific arrangements relating to the setting up of a formal human rights mechanism in the Asian and Pacific region." The participating governments agreed, however, to explore "the options available and the process necessary for establishing a regional mechanism."[59]

---

[56] One of the early regional efforts in Asia resulted in a 1983 document entitled "The Declaration of Basic Duties of ASEAN Peoples and Governments." LAWASIA, a regional nongovernmental organization, and the ASEAN Law Association have supported the creation of a regional human rights mechanism. The United Nations Center for Human Rights has sponsored a series of government workshops (Manila-1990, Jakarta-1993, Seoul-1995, Katmandu-1996, Amman-1997, and Teheran-1998) for officials from countries in the Asia-Pacific region. *See, e.g.,* United Nations, *Fourth Workshop on Regional Human Rights Arrangements in the Asian and Pacific Region,* HR/PUB/96/3 (1996) [hereinafter United Nations, *Fourth Workshop*].

[57] Bangkok Declaration on Human Rights (Asian Cultural Forum on Development), Mar. 29–Apr. 3, 1993, U.N. Doc. A/CONF/93, *reprinted in* 14 HUM. RTS. L.J. 370 (1993). The support of the universality of human rights was equivocal, however.

[58] Afghanistan, Australia, Bangladesh, Bhutan, China, Democratic People's Republic of Korea, Fiji, India, Indonesia, Iran, Iraq, Japan, Jordan, Malaysia, Maldives, Micronesia, Myanmar, Nepal, New Zealand, Papua New Guinea, Philippines, Republic of Korea, Saudi Arabia, Singapore, Solomon Islands, Sri Lanka, Syrian Arab Republic, Thailand, United Arab Emirates, and Vietnam.

[59] United Nations, *Fourth Workshop, supra* note 56, at 3. The rejection of a regional system continued at the 1997 and 1998 regional meetings. At the 1997 meeting in Amman, participants agreed on incremental steps, some of which are positive, others seemingly intended to slow the implementation of human rights in the region. The steps include ratification of

There are many hurdles to creating an Asian-Pacific regional system. First, there is far greater diversity of language, culture, legal systems, religious traditions, and history in the Asia-Pacific region than in other regions of the world. Second, the geographic limits of the region are as unclear as they are vast.[60] These two factors suggest that the region may be better served by "sub-regional" mechanisms that could be more easily and quickly developed on the basis of the closer ties and geographic proximity of states in smaller areas.[61] A third factor hindering the development of an Asian regional system is that, in general, governments in the region have been unwilling to ratify human rights instruments,[62] a reluctance that makes it unlikely that an effective regional system can garner widespread support in the near future.

Finally, recent economic crises in Asia have put additional pressures on governments trying to survive in the wake of growing unrest; the crises create risks of

---

human rights instruments, the promotion of national institutions, the recognition of nongovernmental organizations and the role of civil society, promotion of the right to development, advocacy against human rights conditionality, attention to vulnerable groups, support for universality, "objectivity and non-selectivity" of human rights, more technical cooperation, information-sharing, capacity-building, and programs for regional cooperation. Clarence Dias, *From Building Blocks to Next Steps: The Task Ahead at Teheran* (background paper for the Sixth Workshop on Regional Arrangements for the Promotion and Protection of Human Rights in the Asian and Pacific Region, 1998), at 15. The 1998 workshop in Teheran reaffirmed the universality, indivisibility and interdependence of human rights "in a region proud of its rich cultures, religions and diversities," and pledged commitment to the Vienna Declaration and Program of Action.

60   "Asian" members of the U.N. Human Rights Commission have included not only China, Japan, the Philippines and Indonesia, but India, Pakistan and Cyprus. The U.N. lists forty countries in the region. *See* E/CN.4/1998/50, at 10 (1998).

61   ASEAN member states created working groups for a human rights mechanism. In 1997, members met in Kuala Lumpur and adopted conclusions supporting the development of a regional human rights mechanism, including the possibility of drafting an ASEAN Convention on Human Rights. According to U.N. classifications, the Arab Charter, *supra* note 20, represents an Asian regional instrument.

62   Among the thirty Asian countries that participated in the 1996 workshop, only Australia, Nepal, New Zealand, the Philippines and the Republic of Korea have ratified both covenants and the Optional Protocol to the ICCPR (on individual communications), Dec. 16, 1966, 999 U.N.T.S. 171, 302, *reprinted in* 3 Weston III.A.4, *supra* note 11. As of March 1998, twenty-seven states in the region, including virtually all the Pacific island states, had not signed or ratified either of the U.N. covenants, *supra* note 16, or the Convention on Torture and Other Cruel, Inhuman or Degrading Treatment or Punishment, Dec. 10, 1946, G.A. Res. 39/46 (Annex), U.N. GAOR, 39th Sess., Supp. No. 15, at 197, U.N. Doc. A/39/51 (1985), *reprinted in* 23 I.L.M. 1027 (1984) and 3 Weston III.K.2, *supra* note 11 [hereinafter U.N. Torture Convention] : Bahrain, Bangladesh, Bhutan, Brunei, Comoros, Cook Islands, Fiji, Indonesia, Laos, Malaysia, Maldives, Marshall Islands, Micronesia, Myanmar, Nauru, Neiu, Oman, Pakistan, Palau, Papua New Guinea, Qatar, Samoa, Singapore, Tonga, Tuvalu, United Arab Emirates, and Vanuatu.

repression in the short term. "Asian values," observes Thai human rights scholar Vitit Muntarbhorn, may become even more "a tool of some authoritarian regimes to suppress individual rights, especially freedom of expression and association which are at the heart of democratic aspirations."[63] On the other hand, the regional economic and political crises have led many to question the concept of "Asian values" as a means to progress. Political movements and nongovernmental organizations have renewed efforts to ensure greater respect for human rights in the region. If the crisis continues and the economic justification often given for limiting civil and political rights disappears, the opportunity to create a regional system may improve quickly and dramatically, as it did in Central and Eastern Europe.

IV. Universality and Regional Diversity

The seemingly endless debate over universality and diversity in human rights law is inescapable when evaluating regional systems. The issue of normative diversity is complex. Virtually all the legal instruments creating the various regional systems refer to the Universal Declaration of Human Rights (UDHR)[64] and to the Charter of the United Nations, providing a measure of uniformity in the fundamental guarantees and a reinforcement of the universal character of the Declaration.[65] Also, the rights contained in the regional human rights treaties reflect the human rights norms set forth in global human rights declarations and conventions, in particular the United Nations Covenant on Economic, Social and Cultural Rights (ICESCR)[66] and its companion Covenant on Civil and Political Rights (ICCPR).[67] In addition, as each successive system has been created, it has looked to the normative instruments and jurisprudence of the systems that were founded earlier. Yet there are clear differences in the regional instruments within the framework of the universal norms, although the differences may be less pronounced than appears at first reading because of provisions regarding choice of law and canons of interpretation con-

---

[63] Vitit Muntarbhorn, *Protection of Human Rights in Asia and the Pacific: Think Universal, Act Regional?, in* COLLECTION OF LECTURES, TWENTY-NINTH STUDY SESSION, INTERNATIONAL INSTITUTE OF HUMAN RIGHTS 1 (1998). According to the author, "Asian values" are now seen as comprising "profligate expenditure, over-borrowing, excessive investment in the real estate sector, inadequate regulation, and an admixture of vested interests and cronyism." He argues that this could be a blessing in disguise because it enables the region to question the legitimacy of the region's economic and political bases. *Id.* at 3.

[64] UDHR, *supra* note 11.

[65] Only the American Declaration, *supra* note 11, does not mention the UDHR, because it was adopted prior to the completion of the UDHR. However, the Preamble to the American Convention on Human Rights, *supra* note 39, indicates the Convention's origin "in the Charter of the Organization of American States, in the American Declaration of the Rights and Duties of Man, and in the Universal Declaration of Human Rights."

[66] ICESCR, *supra* note 16.

[67] *Id.*

tained in the regional instruments. The application of these provisions has led to a jurisprudential cross-referencing and mutual influence that is producing some convergence in fundamental human rights principles.

A. Universal Norms

The Preamble to the European Convention provides that the "like-minded" governments of Europe, "considering the Universal Declaration of Human Rights," have resolved "to take the first steps for the collective enforcement of certain of the rights stated in the Universal Declaration."[68] The Preamble to the American Convention likewise cites the UDHR and, as well, refers to the OAS Charter, the American Declaration of the Rights and Duties of Man, and other international and regional instruments not referred to by name.[69] The drafting history of the American Convention shows that the states involved utilized the European Convention, the UDHR and the Covenants in deciding upon the Convention's guarantees and institutional structure.[70]

The African Charter mentions the pledge made by the African States in the OAU Charter to promote international cooperation "having due regard to the Charter of the United Nations and the Universal Declaration of Human Rights."[71] In the African Charter's Preamble, in sweeping fashion, the African States also reaffirm "their adherence to the principles of human and peoples' rights and freedoms contained in the declarations, conventions and other international instruments adopted by the Organization of African Unity, the Movement of Non-Aligned Countries and the United Nations."[72]

The Preamble to the Arab also explicitly reaffirms the principles of the United Nations Charter, the Universal Declaration of Human Rights, the provisions of the two United Nations covenants, and the Cairo Declaration on Human Rights in Islam.[73] The Arab Charter further expresses the belief of the participating states in the rule of law and the proposition "that mankind's enjoyment of freedom, justice and equal opportunity is the hallmark of the profound essence of any society."[74]

---

[68] ECHR, *supra* note 24.

[69] *See* note 65, *supra*.

[70] For the drafting history of the American Convention, see Conferencia Especializada Interamericana Sobre Derechose Humanos, San José, Costa Rica, 7–22 Noviembre 1969, Actas & Documentos, OEA/Ser.K/XVI/1.2 (1973). *See also* THOMAS BUERGENTHAL & ROBERT NORRIS, HUMAN RIGHTS: THE INTER-AMERICAN SYSTEM (1982).

[71] African Charter, *supra* note 19, pmbl., para. 4.

[72] *Id.* para. 10.

[73] Arab Charter, *supra* note 20, pmbl. For the Cairo Declaration on Human Rights in Islam, see *supra* note 52.

[74] Arab Charter, *supra* note 20, pmbl.

The various regional instruments not only mention the global instruments, they contain similar guarantees and in many instances use language identical to that contained in other instruments. The economic, social, and cultural rights proclaimed in the Universal Declaration of Human Rights are found also in the American Declaration, and in the African and Arab charters.[75] The Arab Charter and the African Charter include the principle of self-determination from Article 1 of the two U.N. covenants,[76] a right perhaps understandably omitted from their European and American counterparts. In the Arab Charter, virtually all of the rights contained in the ICCPR[77] are included, in some cases with more or less detail. The Arab Charter also iterates ICCPR articles 2(1) and 3 in its affirmation of the duty of the states parties to ensure the guaranteed rights without discrimination, including as between men and women. It further echos the Article 27 minority rights provision of the ICCPR in its Article 37. Other regional treaties do not refer to minority rights. The duties of individuals, included in Article 29 of the UDHR[78] are found in the African Charter,[79] the American Declaration,[80] and the American Convention.[81]

B. Regional Diversity

While basing themselves on universal norms, regional instruments also contain different guarantees and emphases; indeed the preambles of all the regional instruments refer to their regional heritages.[82] The European Convention focuses on civil

---

[75] The Arab Charter, *supra* note 20, includes the rights to work, equal employment opportunities, equal pay, trade union freedoms, an adequate standard of living, social security, education, and the right to participate in cultural life and to be "given the chance to advance his artistic thought and creative talent." Article 26 of the American Convention, *supra* note 39, calls for progressive realization of the economic, social and cultural standards set forth in the OAS Charter, *supra* note 10. In Europe, only the right to education and the right to property are guaranteed by the European Convention, Protocol 1, *supra* note 24. Other economic and social rights are specified in the European Social Charter, *supra* note 28, while cultural rights are guaranteed within the new Framework Convention on National Minorities, *supra* note 31.

[76] Article 2 of the Arab Charter, *supra* note 20, duplicates the language of Article 1 of the covenants, while Article 20 of the African Charter, *supra* note 19, is more lengthy and detailed than the comparable provisions of the other instruments.

[77] ICCPR, *supra* note 16.

[78] UDHR, *supra* note 8.

[79] African Charter, *supra* note 19, arts. 27–29.

[80] American Declaration, *supra* note 11, arts. 29–38.

[81] American Convention, *supra* note 39, art. 32.

[82] The Preamble to the ECHR, *supra* note 24, refers to the "common heritage of political traditions, ideals, freedom and the rule of law." The resolution adopting the American Declaration, *supra* note 11, refers not only to prior meetings and actions of the American states, but to "evolving American law," while the American Convention, *supra* note 39, reaf-

rights, especially due process. The American system is strongly concerned with democracy and the rule of law, having experienced repeated military coups in the region. Its preamble begins with a reference to democratic institutions and its guarantees emphasize the right to participate in government and the right to judicial protection. The Arab Charter is deistic, taking religion as its starting point, referring in its preamble to God, monotheistic religions, the Islamic Shari'a and "other divine religions."[83] It refers both in its Preamble and in its Article 1 to rejecting racism and Zionism and to the close link between human rights and world peace. The Preamble to the African Charter contains similar language on racism and Zionism. The African Charter focuses on economic development, calling it essential to pay particular attention to the right to development. It also is unique in its inclusion of peoples' rights, although the Preamble suggests that they are viewed as instrumental to the achievement of individual rights rather than goals in and of themselves, recognizing "that the reality and respect of peoples' rights should necessarily guarantee human rights."

Among the pronounced differences, the Arab Charter is unique in omitting explicit mention of slavery, although it prohibits forced labor which could be intended to include slavery, and it has few guarantees of political rights, leaving out the right to free and fair elections and specifying only the right of citizens to occupy public office.[84] The Arab Charter is also less protective of the rights of aliens, limiting to citizens the right to leave and not to be expelled, the right of political asylum, the right to private property, the right to freedom of assembly and association, the right to work and to social security, the right to equal opportunity in employment and equal pay for equal work, political rights, and the right to education.[85] However, the Arab Charter expands on the right of political asylum, adding that "political refugees shall not be extradited,"[86] and in its regulation of the death penalty it uniquely prohibits the execution of a nursing mother until two years have

---

firms the intention of the states parties to consolidate a system of rights "within the framework of democratic institutions." The African Charter, *supra* note 19, states that it takes into consideration the virtues of African historical tradition and "the values of African civilization." The Preamble of the Arab Charter, *supra* note 20, states that it stems "from the Arab Nation's faith in the dignity of man; from when God favored it by making the Arab nation the cradle of monotheistic religions and the birthplace of civilization; which has reaffirmed man's right to a life of dignity based on freedom, justice and peace."

83   Arab Charter, *supra* note 20, pmbl.

84   Article 19 of the Charter adds that "[t]he people are the source of authority. Political capacity is a right for every citizen of a legal age to be exercised in accordance with the law."

85   It is worth noting that the ICESCR allows states to limit economic rights for aliens. All human rights treaties limit political rights to citizens. Civil rights guarantees for aliens have provoked a number of reservations to the ICCPR. *See* Dinah Shelton, *State Practice on Reservations to Human Rights Treaties*, 1 CAN. Y.B. HUM. RTS. 205 (1983).

86   Arab Charter, *supra* note 20, art. 23.

passed from the date of the birth of her child.[87] Additionally, the prohibition on torture specifies that it extends to both physical and psychological torture and mandates criminal penalties for performing or participating in an act of torture.

Other regional systems, since their inception, have added rights, and in no case has a right been limited or withdrawn by a later instrument. In Europe, for example, even before the signing of the ECHR, the European Parliamentary Assembly proposed the inclusion of additional rights, added by Protocol 1. The evolutionary character of the European system, reflected in its eleven protocols and related human rights treaties, is not unique. Regional systems appear to have added new rights in a kind of feedback process of mutual inspiration, including such specific guarantees as abolition of the death penalty, action to combat violence against women, the right to a satisfactory environment, and strengthened guarantees relative to economic, social, and cultural rights. The right to a satisfactory environment, for example, was first enunciated in the African Charter.[88] Subsequently, in the Additional Protocol of San Salvador on Economic, Social and Cultural Rights,[89] the American system added a similar guarantee. The dynamic interplay of the systems is characteristic of the nonlinear complexity and evolution of modern systems.

All the regional instruments contain limitations clauses, using similar language,[90] based on the UDHR.[91] Limitations clauses allow state parties to restrict

---

[87] *Id*. art. 12.

[88] African Charter, *supra* note 19, art. 24.

[89] *Supra* note 44, art. 11.

[90] Compare the limitations clauses regarding freedom of thought, conscience and religion. The ECHR, *supra* note 24, art. 9(2), provides that "freedom to manifest one's religion or beliefs shall be subject only to such limitations as are prescribed by law and are necessary in a democratic society in the interests of public safety, for the protection of public order, health or morals, or for the protection of the rights and freedoms of others." The American Convention, *supra* note 39, art. 12(3), similarly states, "freedom to manifest one's religion and beliefs may be subject only to the limitations prescribed by law that are necessary to protect public safety, order, health, or morals, or the rights or freedoms of others." Article 30 adds that "the restrictions that, pursuant to this Convention, may be placed on the enjoyment or exercise of the rights or freedoms recognized herein may not be applied except in accordance with laws enacted for reasons of general interest and for the purpose of which the restrictions have been established." The African Convention, *supra* note 19, art. 8, says that the freedom of conscience and religion is "subject to law and order."

[91] UDHR, *supra* note 11. *Compare* Arab Charter, *supra* note 20, art. 4A ("It is prohibited to impose limitations on the rights and freedoms guaranteed by virtue of this Charter unless where prescribed by law and considered necessary to protect national and economic security, or public order, or public health, or morals, or the rights and freedoms of others") *with* UDHR, art. 29(2) ("In the exercise of his rights and freedoms, everyone shall be subject only to such limitations as are determined by law solely for the purpose of securing due recognition and respect for the rights and freedoms of others and of meeting the just requirements of morality, public order and the general welfare in a democratic society"). The Arab Charter

the exercise of guaranteed rights, but specify the legal grounds and requirements for valid restrictions. Regional instruments also contain "clawback" clauses that are similar to limitations clauses insofar as they permit national law to specify the scope of the right guaranteed. However, "clawback" clauses are less constraining of the state's discretion. The European Convention, for example, allows a state to limit by law the right to respect for privacy and family life, home and correspondence if "necessary in a democratic society in the interests of national security, public safety or the economic well-being of the country, for the prevention of disorder or crime, for the protection of health or morals, or for the protection of the rights and freedoms of others."[92] In contrast, the right to marry and to found a family is subject to a "clawback" clause that subsumes it unreservedly "to the national laws governing the exercise of this right."[93] The African and Arab charters contain extensive "clawback" clauses[94] that could undermine the effectiveness of both systems, although the developing jurisprudence of the African system is encouraging in insisting on the effective enjoyment of the rights prescribed.[95]

Some of the greatest differences among the regional instruments are found in their derogations provisions, which govern the exercise of rights during periods of national emergency. The bases for derogating differ, as do the lists of nonderogable rights. The European Convention limits the grounds for suspending rights to "time or war or other public emergency threatening the life of the nation," making it hard to justify a suspension of rights.[96] In contrast, in the American system states may suspend guarantees "in times of war, public danger, or other emergency that threatens the independence or security" of the state,

---

is the only human rights text to specify economic security as a basis for limiting rights and creates a considerable loophole for states in the region.

[92]   ECHR, *supra* note 24, art. 8.

[93]   *Id.* art. 12.

[94]   The African Charter, *supra* note 19, states, for example, that "everyone shall have the right to free association provided that he abides by the law" (art. 10). The Arab Charter, *supra* note 20, similarly provides that political capacity is a right "to be exercised in accordance with the law" (art. 19). Freedom of movement and trade union rights are also to be exercised "within the limits of the law."

[95]   *See, e.g.,* Case 101/93, Civil Liberties Organization in re Nigerian Bar Association v. Nigeria (Merits), adopted at the 17th Ordinary Session of the Commission, Lomé, Togo, March 1995, *in* Eighth Annual Activity Report of the African Commission on Human and Peoples' Rights, 1994–1995, ACHPR/RPT/8th/XVIII, Rev. 1 [hereinafter Eighth Annual Report], Annex IX, at 9–10 (1995). *See generally,* Chidi Anselm Odinkalu, *The Individual Complaint Procedures of the African Commission on Human and Peoples' Rights: A Preliminary Assessment,* 8 Transnat'l L. & Contemp. Probs. 359 (1998).

[96]   ECHR, *supra* note 24, art. 15. In both the European and the Inter-American systems, the measures taken must be temporary, "strictly required by the exigencies of the situation" and compatible with other international obligations. The American Convention, *supra* note 39, art. 27(1), adds a nondiscrimination requirement.

making it easier to do so.[97] On the other hand, the list of nonderogable rights is much longer in the Inter-American system, so that the ease of derogation is balanced by greater human rights protections in periods of emergency. Africa has no general derogation clause, but "clawback" provisions may make it unnecessary. Article 4 of the Arab Charter[98] is close to the language of the ICCPR, referring to public emergencies which threaten the life of the nation and requiring that the measures be "strictly required by the circumstances;" but the nonderogable rights in the Arab Charter are unusual, applying to the right to be free from torture and degrading treatment, the right to return to one's country, the right of political asylum, the right to trial, a prohibition on double jeopardy, and "the principle of the legality of the crime and punishment." It is unclear if the reference to trial would include due process guarantees, but the emphasis on the rule of law suggests that it might.

C. Enhancing Protections

The protections of the various legal instruments are enhanced by canons of interpretation or choice of law principles that call for states and tribunals to apply the rule most favorable to the individual. The European Convention affirms that measures taken by a state in derogation of the Convention cannot be "inconsistent with [that state's] other obligations under international law;"[99] Article 1 of Protocol I contains a similar reference to international law,[100] which the European Court of Human Rights apparently considers to embrace the traditional rules of customary international law on state responsibility.[101] More generally, Article 60 of the European Convention provides that nothing in the Convention "shall be construed as limiting or derogating from any of the human rights and fundamental freedoms which may be ensured under the laws of any High Contracting Party or under any other agreement to which it is a Party."

The American Convention, implicitly referring to customary as well as conventional international law, is particularly broad. It provides that no provision of the Convention can be interpreted to restrict a right recognized in the national or international law applicable to a state party.[102] Article 60 of the African Charter, man-

---

[97]   American Convention, *supra* note 39, art. 27.

[98]   Arab Charter, *supra* note 20.

[99]   ECHR, *supra* note 24, art. 15(1).

[100]   ECHR, Protocol 1, art.1 ("Every natural or legal person is entitled to the peaceful enjoyment of his possessions. No one shall be deprived of his possessions except in the public interest and subject to conditions provided for by law and by the general principles of international law.").

[101]   The Case of James, 98 Eur. Ct. H.R. (ser. A) at 9 (1985); the Case of Lithgow, 102 Eur. Ct. H.R. (ser. A) at 4 (1984).

[102]   The American Convention, *supra* note 39, also provides for possible application of the American Declaration, *supra* note 11, and "other international acts of the same nature" as

dates its Commission to "draw inspiration from international law on human and peoples' rights," explicitly citing the U.N. Charter, the UDHR, and other instruments adopted by the U.N. and its specialized agencies. Article 61 then lists "subsidiary measures to determine principles of law," thus indicating the primary nature of international human rights law as a source of law for interpreting and applying the Charter.[103] Also, the future African court is directed in Protocol Article 7 to apply the provisions of the African Charter and "other human rights instruments." Finally, the Arab Charter specifies that there can be no restriction of any basic human right that is recognized in any state party "by virtue of law, treaties or custom" and, according to Article 3A, nothing in the Charter can be used to derogate from these guarantees.

In sum, there is diversity within diversity. The basic texts of each regional system can be read to reaffirm the universal norms. Yet, there are sufficient references to regional divergences that the states and the supervisory organs of each system could choose to focus on their differences instead of their similarities. Thus it is important to study the normative evolution of the systems as it is reflected in the jurisprudence of the regional commissions and courts.

V. Normative Evolution

As observed, the regional human rights systems have evolved through a complex interplay of environmental pressures, institutional changes, and inter-regional contacts. Perhaps most importantly, the dynamic reading given human rights guarantees by the regional supervisory organs has prevented a rigid formalism from reducing the relevance of regional systems as circumstances change and new problems arise. Judicial power in the regional systems is very significant, created in large part by the character of human rights conventions. Written in general terms, they leave ample scope for judges and commissioners to apply and creatively interpret their provisions. The European Court of Human Rights has confirmed that "the Convention is a living instrument which . . . must be interpreted in the light of the present-day conditions."[104] The Inter-American Court has similarly emphasized the notion of "evolving American law."[105]

---

well as "other rights or guarantees that are inherent in the human personality or derived from representative democracy as a form of government." *Id.* art. 29 (c), (d).

[103] The subsidiary measures specified are other general or special international conventions, African practices "consistent with international norms on human and peoples' rights," customs generally accepted as law, general principles of law recognized by African States, as well as legal precedents and doctrine. *See* art. 61.

[104] Tyrer v. United Kingdom, 26 Eur. Ct. H.R. (ser. A) at 10 (1978).

[105] *See* Interpretation of the American Declaration of the Rights and Duties of Man, *supra* note 36, paras. 37–38.

All of the systems have a growing case law detailing the rights and duties enunciated in the basic instruments. The jurisprudence of the regional human rights bodies has thus become a major source of human rights law. In many instances, this case law reflects a convergence of different substantive protections in favor of broad human rights protections. In other instances, differences in treaty terms or approach have resulted in a rejection of precedent from other systems.[106] In general, however, the judges and commissioners have been willing to substantiate or give greater authority to their interpretations of the rights guaranteed by referencing not only their own prior case law but the decisions of other regional and even global bodies.

Some decisions cross-reference specific articles of other regional and global instruments. The European Court of Human Rights, for instance, has utilized Article 19(2) of the ICCPR[107] to extend the application of Article 10 of the European Convention to cover freedom of artistic expression.[108] It has referred to the U.N. Convention on the Rights of the Child[109] relative to education[110] and to both the ICCPR and American Convention[111] to ensure the right to a name as part of Article 8 of the European Convention.[112] Best known is the *Soering* case, wherein the Court found implicit in Article 3 of the European Convention the obligation of Article 3 of the U.N. Torture Convention[113] not to extradite someone who might face torture.[114]

The Inter-American Court frequently uses other international decisions and human rights instruments to interpret and apply inter-American norms. It has

---

106 *E.g.*, the European and Inter-American courts take very different approaches to their remedial powers based on the different languages of their respective treaties. In its case law, the Inter-American Court also has rejected the European doctrine of "margin of appreciation."

107 ICCPR, *infra* Appendix III.

108 Muller, et al., 133 Eur. Ct. H.R. (ser. A) para. 27 (1988).

109 *Convention on the Rights of the Child*, Nov. 20, 1989, G.A. Res. 44/25 (Annex), U.N. GAOR, 44th Sess., Supp. No. 49, at 166, U.N. Doc. A/44/49 (1990), *reprinted in* 3 Weston III.D.3, *supra* note 11.

110 Costello-Roberts v. United Kingdom, 247C Eur. Ct. H.R. (ser. A) para. 27 (1993).

111 American Convention, *supra* note 39.

112 Burghartz v. Switzerland, 280B Eur. Ct. H.R. (ser. A) para. 24 (1994).

113 U.N. Torture Convention, *supra* note 62.

114 Soering v. United Kingdom, 161 Eur. Ct. H.R. (ser. A) para. 88 (1989). Referring to the U.N. Torture Convention, *supra* note 62, the Court said "The fact that a specialized treaty should spell out in detail a specific obligation attaching to the prohibition of torture does not mean that an essentially similar obligation is not already inherent in the general terms of Article 3 of the European Convention." The Commission has also stated that it finds it useful in interpreting the provisions of the Convention to refer to provisions contained in other international legal instruments for the protection of human rights, especially those which contain broader guarantees. *See* Case 210/92, Gestra v. Italy, 80A Dec. & Rep. 93 (1995).

referred to the European Convention,[115] the ICCPR[116] and other United Nations treaties, and to decisions of the European Human Rights Commission and the Court.[117] It has stated explicitly that it will use cases decided by the European Court and the ICCPR Human Rights Committee when their value is to augment rights protection,[118] and has indicated a commitment to the nonincorporation of restrictions from other systems.[119] In turn, Inter-American Commission and Court decisions provide extensive jurisprudence on due process, conditions of detention and treatment of detainees, legality of amnesty laws, rape as torture, disappearances, obligations to ensure respect for rights, direct applicability of norms, exhaustion of local remedies, burden and standard of proof, admissibility of evidence, and general doctrine on the interpretation of human rights treaties. In addition, the Inter-American court has emphasized the importance of an independent judiciary.

The decisions of the African Commission also show the influence of other regional systems, having adopted several doctrines established in European and Inter-American case law: presumption of the truth of the allegations from the silence of government,[120]

---

[115] *See e.g.* Compulsory Membership in an Association Prescribed by Law for the Practice of Journalism, 5 Inter-Am. Ct. H.R. (ser. A) para. 43–46 (1985); Enforceability of the Right to Reply or Correction, 7 Inter-Am. Ct. H.R. (ser. A) para. 25 (1986).

[116] *Id.* Proposed Amendments to the Naturalization Provisions of the Constitution of Costa Rica, 4 Inter-Am. Ct. H.R. paras. 50–51 (1984).

[117] The Effect of Reservations on the Entry into Force of the American Convention, 2 Inter-Am. Ct. H.R. (ser. A) para. 29 (1983); Proposed Amendments, *supra* note 116, para 56; The Word "Laws" in Article 30 of the American Convention on Human Rights, 6 Inter-Am. Ct. H.R. (ser. A) para 20 (1986); Compulsory Membership, *supra* note 115, paras. 43–46, 69; In the Matter of Viviana Gallardo et al. v. Government of Costa Rica, Decision of Nov. 13, 1981, Inter-Am. Ct. H.R. 12, OEA/ser. L/V/III.7, Doc. 13, Ser. A and B, No. G/101/81, paras. 26–27 (1982); Gangaram Panday Case, 16 Inter-Am. Ct. H. R. (ser. C) para. 39 (1994); Caballero Delgado and Santa Case (Preliminary Objections), 17 Inter-Am. Ct. H.R. (ser. C) (1994).

[118] Compulsory Membership in an Association Prescribed by Law for the Practice of Journalism, *supra* note 115, para. 52 ("if in the same situation both the American Convention and another international treaty are applicable, the rule most favorable to the individual must prevail.").

[119] *Id.* para. 51 ("the comparison of the American Convention with the provisions of other international instruments" should never be used to read into the "Convention restrictions that are not grounded in its text.").

[120] *See, e.g.*, the Commission's decisions in Communications 59/91, 60/91, 87/93, 101/93 and 74/92. "The African Commission . . . has set out the principle that where allegations of human rights abuse go uncontested by the government concerned, even after repeated notifications, the Commission must decide on the facts provided by the complainant and treat those facts as given. This principle conforms with the practice of other human rights adjudicatory bodies and the Commission's duty to protect human rights." Comms. 25/89/47/90, 56/91, 100/93, Free Legal Assistance Group, Lawyers' Committee for Human Rights, Union Interafricaine des Droits de l'Homme, Les Temoins de Jehovah v. Zaire. Adopted at the 19th

the notion of continuing violations,[121] continuity of obligations despite a change of government,[122] state responsibility for failure to act,[123] and the presumption that states are responsible for custodial injuries.[124] In regard to the admissibility of communications, the African Commission, like other regional bodies, has found that some so-called remedies are "not of a nature that requires exhaustion" because they are discretionary and nonjudicial.[125] The African Commission, like the Inter-American Court, emphasizes the

Ordinary Session of the Commission, Ouagadougou, Burkina Faso, March 1996, *in* NINTH ANNUAL ACTIVITY REPORT OF THE AFRICAN COMMISSION ON HUMAN AND PEOPLES' RIGHTS, 1995/96, AHG/207 (XXXII) [hereinafter NINTH ANNUAL REPORT], Annex VIII, at 7. Article 42 of the Regulations of the Inter-American Commission allows it to presume the facts in the petition are true if the government fails to respond to the complaint.

[121] *See, e.g.*, Comm. 142/94, Muthuthurin Njoka v. Kenya, at 13. Case 39/90, Annette Pagnoulle on behalf of Abdoulaye Mazou v. Cameroons, is another continuing violations case. *See also* Case 39/90, Decision adopted by the Commission at its 21st Ordinary Session, April 1997, *in* TENTH ANNUAL ACTIVITY REPORT OF THE AFRICAN COMMISSION ON HUMAN AND PEOPLES'S RIGHTS, ACHPR/DOC/OS/XXII [hereinafter TENTH ANNUAL REPORT], Annex 10 (1997). In a communication against Malawi, the Commission held: "[p]rinciples of international law stipulate . . . that a new government inherits the previous government's international obligations, including the responsibility for the previous government's mismanagement. The change of government in Malawi does not extinguish the present claim before the Commission. Although the present government of Malawi did not commit the human rights abuses complained of, it is responsible for the reparation of these abuses." Comm. 64/92, *in* EIGHTH ANNUAL REPORT, *supra* note 95, Annex IX, at 4, *reprinted in* 18 HUM. RTS. L.J. 29 (1997).

[122] Joined cases 83/92, 88/93, 91/93, Jean Yaovi Degli, Union Interafricaine des Droits de l'Homme, Commission International de Juristes v. Togo, *in* EIGHTH ANNUAL REPORT, *supra* note 95, Annex XI. The Commission sent a delegation to Togo and determined that the acts of the prior regime were being remedied by the present government

[123] In Comm. 74/92, Commission Nationale des Droits de l'homme et des Libertes v. Chad, the Commission expounded on the state duty specified in Article 1 to give effect to the rights and freedoms guaranteed by the Charter. According to the Commission, "if a state neglects to ensure the rights in the African Charter, this can constitute a violation, even if the State or its agents are not the immediate cause of the violation." Decision adopted at the 18th Ordinary Session of the Commission, Praia, Cape Verde, October 1995, *in* NINTH ANNUAL REPORT, *supra* note 120, Annex VIII, at 12. The Commission found that Chad had failed to provide security and stability in the country, thereby allowing serious and massive violations of human rights. In language reminiscent of the *Velasquez Rodriguez* case, the Commission said, "Even where it cannot be proved that violations were committed by government agents, the government had a responsibility to secure the safety and the liberty of its citizens, and to conduct investigations into murders. Chad therefore is responsible for the violations of the African Charter." *Id.* at 15.

[124] In the European system, see Tomasi v. France, 241 Eur. Ct. H.R. (ser. A) para. 40, 41 (1992).

[125] *See* Comm. 60/91, Constitutional Rights Project v. Nigeria, *in* EIGHTH ANNUAL REPORT, *supra* note 95, Annex IX, at 3.

need for independence of the judiciary and the guarantees of a fair trial, having called attacks on the judiciary "especially invidious, because while it is a violation of human rights in itself, it permits other violations of rights to go unredressed."[126]

In its first country report, concerning Nigeria, the African Commission made use of regional precedents.[127] After Nigeria complained of the lack of a hearing, the Commission noted that Nigeria never had responded to communications and that

> for the Commission to postpone decisions indefinitely while waiting for the government to send a representative would make the communications procedure hostage to governments, and effectively place in the government's hands the ability to prevent any decisions. These consequences have been recognized by other international human rights bodies such as the Inter-American Commission on Human Rights, and the African Commission was inspired by their example.[128]

The African Commission also has given "clawback" clauses in the African Charter[129] a narrow reading, using other international human rights texts. A case against Nigeria[130] involved the government's retroactive decree creating a new institution to control the bar association and its lawyer members. The Commission held that both Article 7 (the right to fair trial) and Article 10 (freedom of association) had been violated. The latter is significant because Article 10 contains one of the African Charter clawback clauses ("Every individual shall have the right to free association provided he abides by the law. . . ."). According to the Commission, the right enunciated in article 10 entails "first and foremost a duty for the State to abstain from interfering with the free formation of association."[131] The government

---

126 Comm. 129/94, Civil Liberties Organization v. Nigeria, *in* NINTH ANNUAL REPORT, *supra* note 120, Annex VIII, at 17. The Commission deemed the ousting of the jurisdiction of courts in Nigeria in this case "an attack of incalculable proportions on Article 7." *Id.* at 19. The Commission refers not only to article 7, but to Article 26, which enshrines the duty of the state to guarantee independence of the judiciary. According to the Commission, Article 26 "clearly envisions the protection of the courts which have traditionally been the bastion of protection of the individual's rights against the abuses of State power." *Id.* Compare the Inter-American Court's opinions Habeas Corpus in Emergency Situations, 8 Inter-Am. Ct. H.R. (ser. A) (1987) and Judicial Guarantees in States of Emergency, 9 Inter-Am. Ct. H.R. (ser. A) (1987).

127 *Human Rights Report on the Situation in Nigeria*, Doc.II/ES/ACHPR/3 Add.1 (1995).

128 *Id.* at 5–6.

129 African Charter, *supra* note 19.

130 Case 101/93, Civil Liberties Organization in re Nigerian Bar Association v. Nigeria, *supra* note 95, at 9–10.

131 *Id.* at 11.

action was found "inconsistent with the preamble of the African Charter in conjunction with the U.N. Basic Principles on the Independence of the Judiciary[132] and thereby constitutes a violation of Article 10 of the African Charter."[133]

While the mutual influence of the systems is clear, there are regional differences in the nature of cases filed that have limited the relevance of precedents from other systems. In Europe, until recently, virtually all cases raised questions of law on agreed facts. In addition, a large percentage concerned procedural guarantees in civil and criminal proceedings. In contrast, nearly all of the Inter-American cases have concerned factual determinations of state responsibility for the death, disappearance, or other mistreatment of individuals. The result has been an Inter-American focus on issues of standard of proof and burden of proof that has arisen in the European system only rarely; for this reason, Inter-American references to European jurisprudence are found mainly in the Inter-American Court's advisory opinions on questions of law and not in its opinions that have decided contentious cases. The Inter-American Commission also has had to be concerned with widespread civil strife and internal armed conflicts in the region. As a result, it has begun to document human rights violations by non-state actors, making an important contribution to international human rights law.[134]

Matters submitted in Africa thus far have involved varied issues, including trade union freedoms, arbitrary detention, killings, and the right to health.[135] While the African Commission has adopted established doctrines from the other systems, it also has used some of the unique provisions of the African Charter to apply its guarantees progressively. In *Commission Nationale des Droits de l'Homme et des Libertées v. Chad*, for example, the Commission held that the absence of a derogation clause in the African Charter means the Charter as a whole remains in force

---

[132] Basic Principles on the Independence of the Judiciary, adopted by the Seventh United Nations Congress on the Prevention of Crime and the Treatment of Offenders, U.N. Doc. A/CONF.121/22/Rev.1, at 58–62, U.N. Sales No. E/86/IV.1 (1986); welcomed by the U.N. General Assembly in G.A. Res. 40/146, U.N. GAOR, 40th Sess., Supp. No. 53, at 254, U.N. Doc. A/40/53 (1985) (inviting governments to respect them and take them into account within the framework of their national legislation and practice) and G.A. Res. 40/32, U.N. GAOR, 40th Sess., Supp. No. 53, at 205, U.N. Doc. A/40/53 (1985).

[133] *Id.*

[134] International Responsibility for the Promulgation and Enforcement of Laws in Violation of the Convention, 14 Inter-Am. Ct. H.R. (ser. A) (1994).

[135] *See, e.g.* Comm. 64/92, Krischna Achutan (on behalf of Aleke Banda), Comm. 68/92, Amnesty International on behalf of Orton and Vera Chirwa; and 78/92, Amnesty International on Behalf of Orton and Vera Chirwa v. Malawi, *in* EIGHTH ANNUAL REPORT, *supra* note 95, Annex XI, at 4. These were political cases involving opposition political leaders. The Commission found violations of the right to life, the right to be free from torture, and the right to liberty in violation of Charter articles 4, 5, 6, and 7.

even during periods of armed conflict.[136] In *Katangese Peoples' Congress v. Zaire*,[137] a unique case in which the Commission was asked to recognize the right of Katangese independence, the Commission balanced international legal principles, calling for an exercise of the right of self-determination "that accords with the wishes of the people but [is] fully cognizant of other recognized principles such as sovereignty and territorial integrity." It then held that it was obligated to uphold the sovereignty and territorial integrity of Zaire *"in the absence of concrete evidence of violations of human rights to the point that the territorial integrity of Zaire should be called into question and in the absence of evidence that the people of Katanga are denied the right to participate in government as guaranteed by Article 13(1) of the African Charter."*[138] While this balancing of human rights and territorial integrity relative to self-determination corresponds to the U.N. Declaration of Principles of International Law,[139] it is surprising that the African Commission, as a relatively young institution, would make such a forthright statement on such a controversial issue.

In addition to differences that stem from variance in the nature of the cases filed, there also is divergence in treaty interpretation.[140] One evident difference is found in the law concerning derogations from enunciated rights and the protection of nonderogable rights. The relative conservatism of the European Court of Human Rights is particularly evident in this regard.[141] Where national interests are at stake, the Court appears to be concerned that a state condemned for wrongfully suspend-

---

[136] *See* Comm. 74/92, Commission Nationale des Drtois de l'homme et des Libertes v. Chad, *in* NINTH ANNUAL REPORT, *supra* note 120, Annex VIII, at 12, 16 ("The African Charter . . . does not allow for states parties to derogate from their treaty obligations during emergency situations. Thus, even a civil war in Chad cannot be used as an excuse by the State for violating or permitting violations of rights in the African Charter.").

[137] Case 75/92, Katangese Peoples' Congress v. Zaire, *in* EIGHTH ANNUAL REPORT, *supra* note 95, Annex IX, at 6.

[138] *Id.* (emphasis added).

[139] *Declaration of Principles of International Law Concerning Friendly Relations and Cooperation Among States in Accordance with the Charter of the United Nations*, Oct. 24, 1970, G.A. Res. 2625, U.N. GAOR, 25th Sess., Supp. No. 28, at 121, U.N. Doc. A/8028 (1971), *reprinted in* 9 I.L.M. 1292 (1970) *and* 1 Weston I.D.7, *supra* note 10 ("Nothing in the [principle of self-determination] shall be construed as authorizing or encouraging any action which would dismember or impair, totally or in part, the territorial integrity or political unity of sovereign and independent States conducting themselves in compliance with the principle of equal rights and self-determination of peoples as described above and thus possessed of a government representing the whole people belonging to the territory without distinction as to race, creed or color.").

[140] Fionnuala Ni Aolain, *The Emergence of Diversity: Differences in Human Rights Jurisprudence*, 19 FORDHAM INT'L L.J. 101 (1995).

[141] *See id.* at 108–26. *See also* Joan F. Hartman, *Derogation from Human Rights Treaties in Public Emergencies*, 22 HARV. INT'L L.J. 1 (1981).

ing rights might withdraw from the Convention. Another difference in interpretation can be seen in the approach each institution takes to the issue of its implied or inherent powers to create remedies for violations of human rights. In contrast to the European Court's restrictive view, the African and Inter-American Commissions, and the American Court, have often used doctrines of implied powers. In Africa, for example, after Nigeria complained that the Commission had directed the annulment of certain domestic decrees, the Commission found that issuing such a directive was within its inherent powers, being "surely implied in all the decisions where the Commission finds that a system of special tribunals, or the ouster of the courts, is incompatible with the African Charter.[142]

Despite the differences in treaty interpretation and norm application, there is a progressive convergence in these respects and it is in large part stimulated by the victims and their lawyers. They submit memorials that draw attention to the relevant case law of other systems and help to expand human rights protections by obtaining a progressive ruling in one system, then invoking it in another, a pattern that is enhanced by the liberal (standing) rules of the Inter-American and African systems. Many complaints are filed by nongovernmental organizations (NGOs) familiar with, and operating in, more than one system. Most of the communications submitted to the African system, for example, have come thus far from groups such as Amnesty International, the International Commission of Jurists, and the Lawyers Committee for Human Rights. In the European system, briefs submitted *amicus curiae* by NGOs similarly draw attention to regional and global norms and jurisprudence. The epistemic community of NGOs has its parallel in the regular meetings of the commissioners and judges of the regional systems. All of which strongly suggests that no human rights lawyer should rely solely on the jurisprudence of a single system in pleading a case.

VI. Procedural and Institutional Evolution

Regional human rights procedures and institutions have evolved perhaps to an even greater extent than have substantive human rights guarantees. While some changes result from amendments to the basic legal instruments, at least as much change is due to regional bodies developing their own implied powers. A serious commitment to giving effect to regional protections is evident in the evolution of the functions and procedures of regional human rights bodies.

---

[142] The Commission was clear on its power: "When the Commission concludes that a communication describes a real violation of the Charter's provisions, its duty is to make that clear and indicate what action the government must take to remedy the situation." *Human Rights Report on the Situation in Nigeria, supra* note 127, at 6. The report had an impact. At the session where the Nigerian report was considered, the government extended an invitation to the Commission for an on-site visit.

A. Individual Complaints Procedures

One of the greatest contributions of the regional systems is the establishment of individual complaint mechanisms for judicial or quasi-judicial redress of human rights violations. Europe was the first to create a commission and court that could hear such complaints, followed by the Americas and now Africa. Over the years, the regional commissions and courts have gradually strengthened their procedures for handling complaints.

In Europe, a slow evolution toward individual standing first allowed individuals to appear before the court in the guise of assistants to the Commission. A protocol later permitted them to appear by right.[143] With the entry into force of Protocol 11, individual complainants will now have sole standing.[144]

The European Social Charter also has been strengthened through amendment and through practice.[145] Additional rights have been added by a 1988 Protocol and a second Protocol radically revises the system of supervision.[146] Although the latter Protocol is not yet in force, most of its provisions have been implemented by the supervisory organs.[147] An even greater change is underway with a 1995 Additional Protocol that provides for collective complaints from trade unions and employers' organizations and from nongovernmental organizations.[148]

From its creation in 1960, the Inter-American Commission on Human Rights interpreted its powers broadly to include the ability "to make general recommen-

---

[143]   Protocol 9 to the ECHR, *supra* note 24.

[144]   Protocol 11 to the ECHR (Restructuring the Control Machinery Established by the Convention), *supra* note 24.

[145] For a general review of the evolution of the European Social Charter, see David Harris, *The Council of Europe (II): The European Social Charter, in* HANSKI & SUKSI, *supra* note 13, at 243.

[146]   *See supra* note 28.

[147]   Although interim application of treaty commitments is common in the environmental field, it is extremely rare in international human rights law. This may, in fact, be a unique example. Among the changes implemented prior to the entry into force of the Protocol, the Committee of Ministers agreed to expand the Committee of Independent Experts (CIE) that reviews state reports from seven to nine members. The Amending Protocol also codifies the practice of the CIE in assessing from a legal standpoint the compliance of national law and practice with the obligations imposed on states parties by the Charter. *See* art. 24(2), Amending Protocol. Finally, there has already been implementation of the provisions of the Amending Protocol that provide for meetings between the CIE and representatives of a state party at the request of either. This brings the CIE process of reviewing state reports into conformity with the practice of U.N. treaty-monitoring bodies such as the Human Rights Committee. One difference, however, is that the CIE reviews of state reports during meetings with state representatives are generally *in camera*. For additional provisional application of the Amending Protocol, see *supra* note 24.

[148]   Europ. T.S. No. 158. The Protocol requires five ratifications to enter into force.

dations to each individual state as well as to all of them,"[149] and to include the power to take cognizance of individual petitions and use them to assess the human rights situation in a particular country, based on the normative standards of the American Declaration. The Inter-American system was thus the first to make the complaints procedure mandatory against all member states. Still, the Inter-American Commission has taken steps to improve the processing of cases, having begun recently to determine admissibility before evaluating the merits of the claim and to hold hearings on admissibility or the merits at the request of either party or on the Commission's initiative. Additionally, restructuring of the case system in the Inter-American system has involved greater use of provisional measures, registration of petitions, creating chambers for hearings, and more on-site visits to gather evidence. The Commission also has developed a structured "friendly settlement" procedure and stronger means to protect confidentiality. In the absence of standing for victims at the Inter-American Court until the reparations phase, the Commission has consistently appointed petitioners or their legal representatives as Commission legal advisors, a practice first developed in the European system.

The African system has evolved quickly through the African Commission's interpretation of its powers and revision of its rules of procedure.[150] The African Commission, like the Inter-American Commission, may "give its views or make recommendations to Governments"[151] and it has read this mandate to include the formulation of principles and rules for the resolution of human rights problems in specific states. In 1990, the Commission decided to publish its annual reports. Also, while the African Commission, like its European and Inter-American counterparts, negotiates friendly settlements,[152] it is developing its own follow-up actions as evidenced in various Nigerian cases, wherein the Commission recommended the release of persons it decided were wrongfully detained and decided "to bring the file to Nigeria for the planned mission in order to verify that . . . [the victims] had been released."[153] In its procedures on communications, however, the African Commission has benefited from the experience of the other systems. It follows the usual two-stage process of considering a communication for admissibility and on the merits and has added a three-month time limit within which states must reply

---

[149] INTER-AMERICAN COMMISSION ON HUMAN RIGHTS, FIRST REPORT 1960, OAS Doc. OEA/ser. L/V/II.1, Doc. 32 (1961).

[150] *See generally* Odinkalu, *supra* note 95.

[151] African Charter, *supra* note 19, art. 45(1)(a).

[152] Afr. Comm. 44/90, Peoples' Democratic Organization for Independence and Socialism v. Gambia, concerned voter registration irregularities. A new government acknowledged the problem and expressed its intent to correct the problem by establishing an independent electoral commission and team of experts to review the electoral law.

[153] Case 60/91, *in* EIGHTH ANNUAL REPORT, *supra* note 95, Annex IX, at. 4. *See also* Case 87/93, The Constitutional Rights Project *in* In re Zamani Lakwot & Others v. Nigeria, *id.* at 7–9.

to requests for information and make observations regarding the admissibility of communications, then giving the states an additional three months to submit explanations or statements regarding the case if it determines the petitions to be admissible. Further, despite the lack of explicit Charter authorization, the Commission has adopted and strengthened rules on conflict of interest and agreed on the possibility of requesting provisional measures. The African Commission's rule on provisional measures is almost identical to Article 63(2) of the American Convention.

In general, all of the regional systems have enhanced their complaints procedures by providing means for greater participation by victims and their representatives. In most cases, these changes have occurred through action by the supervisory bodies rather than through amending the basic texts.

B.   Other Functions and Powers

The exercise of implied powers has not only improved complaint procedures, but has strengthened other functions of regional institutions, especially evident in the case of Africa. The ability of the African Commission to write its own rules of procedure[154] has enhanced its functioning and allowed it to expand its role considerably. Its rules allow it to hold sessions anywhere and to convene extraordinary as well as regular sessions. They also provide the greatest openness and transparency of proceedings among the regional bodies. Nongovernmental organizations may submit items for inclusion in the Commission's agenda and they must be informed of the provisional agenda of each session. According to Rule 72, the Commission may invite any informed organization or persons to participate in its deliberations without voting rights.[155] NGOs with observer status may appoint representatives to participate in public sessions of the Commission and its subsidiary bodies.[156]

NGO participation has strengthened the African Commission's role in promoting human rights. During its seventeenth session, held in Togo, and on the basis of a document prepared by a Togolese NGO, three members of the Commission met with the President of Togo and his aides, discussing questions of enhanced democracy, human rights, amnesty, by-elections and the establishment of more constitutional structures.[157] African Commission sessions include very active NGO and

---

[154] *See* Rules of Procedure of the African Commission on Human and Peoples' Rights, Doc. ACHPR/RP/XIX (1996).

[155] The African Charter, *supra* note 19, gives the Commission considerable authority to develop its practice of consulting observers or experts. Article 46 provides that "the Commission may resort to any appropriate method of investigation, it may hear from the Secretary General of the Organization of African Unity or any other person capable of enlightening it."

[156] Rule 32 calls for open meetings unless the Commission decides otherwise or the Charter requires it.

[157] Eighth Annual Report, *supra* note 95, ACHPR/8th/ACT/RPT/SVII.

government participation.[158] More than 200 NGOs have observer status and NGO interventions have focused on human rights violations in the region, including in Senegal, Guinea-Bissau, Djibouti, Nigeria and Burundi.[159] The interventions can be effective; after severe public criticism of the special rapporteur on summary and extra-judicial executions and of the independence and impartiality of some members of the Commission, the Commission amended its rules of procedure to strengthen standards to avoid conflicts of interest.

African Commission Rules of Procedure also take an open view of the publication of Commission proceedings. Although Article 59 of the African Charter[160] provides that "all measures taken within the provisions of the present chapter shall remain confidential until such a time as the Assembly of Heads of State and Government shall otherwise decide," the Commission presumes that publication is permitted unless directed otherwise. Interstate communications, for example, while communicated to the Assembly of the OAU in a report that is confidential, "shall be published by the Chairman of the Commission after reporting unless the Assembly directs otherwise."[161]

The African Commission has also developed a periodic reporting system to match the procedure followed by the U.N. Human Rights Committee. The Commission determines the required contents of the report, invites states to appear for discussion, and addresses observations to reporting states when it finds that they have not discharged any of their obligations under the Charter. Also, the Commission may determine that a report does not contain adequate information and it may request the state to furnish the information by a specific date. Still, though the procedures are progressive, the reporting system has not been a success. Many reports are more than ten years overdue and thirty-three of the fifty-three states parties have not submitted any reports. On the other hand, ironically, the lack of reports probably has enhanced the effectiveness of the African Commission, given its limited resources and meeting time, by leaving it more time to focus on individual communications and situations of gross and systematic violations.

The Inter-American and African Commissions have adopted, in addition, the procedure of thematic rapporteurs, giving them broad mandates to address problems specific to their regions. In 1998, the Inter-American Commission had rapporteurs studying women's rights, indigenous populations, migrant workers, prison conditions, and freedom of expression. The African Commission has appointed rapporteurs on extra-judicial executions, prisons, and women. The rapporteur on extra-

---

158 *See* Rachel Murray, *Report on the 1996 Sessions of the African Commission on Human and Peoples' Rights*, 18 HUM. RTS. L.J. 16 (1997).

159 TENTH ANNUAL REPORT, *supra* note 121, at 8.

160 African Charter, *supra* note 19.

161 Rules of Procedure, *supra* note 154, Rule 77.

judicial executions[162] has consulted the U.N. special rapporteur on the same topic, to avoiding duplicating the U.N.'s work. The African rapporteur decided to pay specific attention to wars and ethnic conflicts in Africa and announced a program of cooperation with the International Criminal Tribunal for Rwanda[163] gather information for prosecutions. In this instance, the regional system thus has served to supplement and enhance the effectiveness of U.N. human rights efforts.[164]

The evolution of the regional systems demonstrates their dynamic nature and their ability to respond to new demands, through cases brought, through NGO pressure, and through inter-regional meetings. In some instances, the need for change has been sudden, in the face of an unexpected crisis. The Inter-American system's action in Haiti, where it cooperated with the United Nations to restore the democratically-elected government, is a case in point.[165] The smaller size of the regional systems relative to the U.N. system, may make the change easier to achieve than at the U.N., where bureaucratic inertia often seems overwhelming.

C. On-Site Visits

The trust and cooperation that develops in regional systems can lead to highly effective mechanisms apart from the individual communications procedures. The ability to make on-site visits to study the human rights situation in member states is particularly significant. The Inter-American Commission has long claimed this power and exercised it frequently.[166] More recently, the European Committee for the Prevention of Torture and Inhuman or Degrading Treatment was given the power

---

[162] Hatem Ben Salem, *Report on Extra-judicial, Summary or Arbitrary Executions, in* TENTH ANNUAL REPORT, *supra* note 121, Annex VI, at 2.

[163] The International Criminal Tribunal for the Prosecution of Persons Responsible for Genocide and Other Serious Violations of International Humanitarian Law Committed in the Territory of Rwanda and Rwandan Citizens Responsible for Genocide and Other Such Violations Committed in the Territory of Neighboring States, between January 1, 1994 and December 31, 1994, was created by S.C. Res. 995, U.N. SCOR, 49th Sess., 3453d mtg. at 15, U.N. Doc. S/RES/955 (1994), *reprinted in* 33 I.L.M. 1598 (1994) *and* 2 INTERNATIONAL LAW AND WORLD ORDER: BASIC DOCUMENTS II.E.12 (Burns H. Weston ed., 5 vols., 1994–).

[164] *See also* Report of the Special Rapporteur on Prisons and Conditions of Detention in Africa, *in* TENTH ANNUAL REPORT, *supra* note 121, Annex VII, whose mandate is to examine prison conditions in Africa and recommend improvement, pushing relevant international human rights norms and standards. The mandate also extends to creating a special communications procedure for persons deprived of their liberty and taking preventive measures. The rapporteur initiated his work with an on-site visit to Zimbabwe, where he met with NGOs and prison officials.

[165] *See* BUERGENTHAL & SHELTON, *supra* note 9, at 537–59.

[166] The Commission has issued country reports, usually on the basis of on-site visits, in regard to Argentina, Bolivia, Brazil, Chile, Colombia, Cuba, Dominican Republic, Ecuador, El Salvador, Guatemala, Haiti, Nicaragua, Panama, Paraguay, Peru, Suriname, and Uruguay.

to visit prisons and other places of detention,[167] making both periodic visits for which it gives notice and *ad hoc* visits which are not announced but made whenever the Committee deems it necessary. The Committee decides where to visit on the basis of information supplied by nongovernmental organizations.

As suggested above, the African Commission has developed its procedures on communications to include country reports and on-site visits to countries suspected of systematic violations of human rights, with on-site missions sent to Nigeria, Sudan, Mauritania, Burundi,[168] and Rwanda,[169] and a mission to Senegal to offer the Commission's good offices in the aftermath of an armed clash with separatists.[170]

The technique of the on-site visit is an invaluable instrument in human rights protection and promotion. On-site visits enable regional bodies to gather information and verify the information they have received. At the same time, they allow governments to indicate the context and complexities of situations, giving officials as well as private persons the opportunity to be heard, and increase public knowledge of the regional system. Finally, they can deter violations by the mere presence of an outside human rights group. As such, a principal advantage to on-site visits is preventive. Unlike communications procedures that begin only after a violation has occurred and local remedies have been exhausted, the visits of the European Torture Committee and of the Inter-American and African Commissions can occur whenever indications are received that violations may take place, or where a state seeks assistance in evaluating and improving its human rights performance. Visits

---

167   The Committee is not a judicial body. It studies the places visited, reports on its findings, and makes recommendations. Reports are normally confidential, but can be published at the request of a party or if a two-thirds majority of the Committee members decides that a state has failed to cooperate with the Committee or refused to act on its recommendations. European Torture Convention, *supra* note 27, art. 10(2). The publication sanction was used against Turkey in 1992, when the Committee found that its recommendations regarding serious police abuse had been persistently ignored.

168   The resolution on Burundi expressed concern with the "serious violations" and "abuses" in Burundi, "considering that impunity is one of the main causes of the worsening situation." It referred to "hate media" in the country and urged the government to conduct transparent and impartial investigations into the violations and abuses, guarantee the independence of the judiciary, and allow on-site investigations by several international organizations, including the African Commission. The resolution also asked the U.N. to send a commission of inquiry.

169   *See* NINTH ANNUAL REPORT, *supra* note 120, at 7, para. 20.

170   The Commission's mission included fact-finding to establish the basis of future negotiations between the separatists and the government. After its one-week trip, the Commission found that "in sum the arguments developed to support the separatist positions lack pertinence. They cannot justify the grave attacks against human rights in the course of the conflict." The Commission also rejected some of the government's arguments and made recommendations to both sides to assist in resolving the dispute.

can be cooperative rather than confrontational and as such can offer the same advantages as the "constructive dialogue" entered into through U.N. reporting mechanisms, but with better information. On-site visits are particularly important in avoiding regression during periods of transition and in dealing with gross and massive violations of rights where it may be impracticable to open individual cases. Given the importance of on-site visits, it is not surprising that the Inter-American Commission has visited the large majority of OAS member states and that the practice of on-site visits is becoming the rule, not the exception, in Africa.

D. Institutional Changes

The European and the African systems are poised to undertake major changes in their institutional structures. European Convention Protocol 11[171] is an example of the punctuated equilibrium predicted by systems analysis.[172] Rather than continuing to make *ad hoc* incremental changes in procedure to improve the functioning of the complaints process, the European system has reworked its institutional structure entirely. A new full-time Court of Human Rights replaces the former Commission and Court[173] and will consist largely of new judges. The full-time nature of the court will preclude judges from holding any other office, a mandatory retirement age of seventy has been added, and the time in office has been reduced from nine to six years.[174] In a further and substantial change, a merit selection process has been instituted, requiring all judicial candidates to appear before a panel of the Parliamentary Assembly for an individual interview and evaluation prior to the election of the judges.

Protocol 11 also fundamentally changes the procedures of the European system,[175] giving individuals direct access to the Court to bring actions against any

---

[171] ECHR Protocol 11, *supra* note 24.

[172] *See* Ruhl, *supra* note 4.

[173] The number of judges on the new Court is equal to the number of parties to the Convention. The Court will sit in Committees of three judges to decide on admissibility. If the Committee is not unanimous in declaring a case inadmissible, the issue will be decided by a Chamber of seven judges. Chambers will also decide most cases on the merits, but may decide to relinquish jurisdiction in favor of a Grand Chamber of seventeen judges.

[174] Judges can be re-elected without limit, however.

[175] Protocol 11, however, retains some elements of the prior system. The conditions of admissibility are unchanged, although with an entirely new court there may be differences of interpretation. Friendly settlement is still encouraged and can be seen as comparable to pre-trial settlement conferences that exist in national legal systems. More controversially, the judge of the nationality of the defendant state will sit *ex officio* as a member of a Chamber or Grand Chamber, maintaining a sense of special pleading and deference to state interests. While national judges have not generally sought to restrict application of human rights guarantees in favor of their state or had obvious influence on the outcome of cases, the presence of new judges from countries with little or no tradition of an independent judiciary could pose problems for the future.

state party to the Convention—that is, acceptance of individual communications is no longer optional. In addition, a limited appellate procedure is introduced.[176] A Grand Chamber of seventeen judges has jurisdiction to review decisions of any seven member Chamber if the case raises a "serious question affecting the interpretation or application of the Convention or protocols thereto, or a serious issue of general importance"[177] and if a panel of five judges of the Grand Chamber decides that it is appropriate to do so after a request from one of the parties.[178] Although there is no explicit reference to intra-Chamber conflicts in interpreting and applying the Convention, the Grand Chamber could serve to ensure consistency of jurisprudence by resolving any conflicts that may arise. The Grand Chamber will conduct *de novo* review of cases referred to it, including admissibility if the issue is raised.

The African system also is scheduled to undergo dramatic change with the approval of an African Court on Human Rights. The Protocol creating the Court was adopted on June 8, 1998 by the OAU Assembly of Heads of State and Government and signed by thirty of the fifty-three member states.[179] Fifteen ratifications are required to bring the protocol into force and when this occurs the Court will have jurisdiction over all cases and disputes submitted to it concerning the Charter, the Protocol, and "any other applicable African human rights instrument."[180] Cases can be submitted by the Commission or a state party involved in a

---

[176] Technically, the case is not on appeal because the judgment of the Chamber is not final until the period for referring the case to the Grand Chamber has expired. *See* art. 44. A full right to appeal decisions was unacceptable to some states, while others insisted on the importance of a larger number of judges deciding important cases. The result in Protocol 11 represents a compromise between the two positions. *See* Rudolf Bernhardt, *Reform of the Control Machinery under the European Convention on Human Rights: Protocol No. 11*, 89 AM. J. INT'L L. 145, 152 (1995).

[177] ECHR Protocol 11, *supra* note 24, art. 43.

[178] Note that the Chamber cannot refer a case on its own motion. Moreover, a Chamber may only relinquish jurisdiction in favor of the Grand Chamber prior to judgment if none of the parties to the case object. These innovations place more control over the litigation in the hands of the parties. According to Judge Bernhardt, *supra* note 176, at 152–53, this is not necessarily positive, as the parties may be unaware of conflicts within the court regarding matters before it: "The experience of the present Court, acquired over some decades, indicates that relinquishment may be advisable before the chamber has taken a firm stand in cases where the matter is complex or the opinions of the chamber's members diverge." He adds that the new system "will seriously endanger the coherence of the case law of the future Court." *Id.* It is likely, however, that most losing parties to cases will feel that the issue is one of importance and should be referred to a Grand Chamber. The other party cannot block a request for referral. If the Chamber has failed to follow prior case law in making its decision, the requesting party should find five judges of the Grand Chamber willing to review the case.

[179] AFRONET, *supra* note 19.

[180] Protocol to the African Charter, *supra* note 19, art. 3.

case as complainant or defendant, but Article 6, highlighting the "leapfrogging" effect of regional systems, provides for broader standing than other regional courts allow by also opening the African Court to public interest litigation by individuals and by NGOs with observer status. They may submit to the court urgent cases and those involving serious, systematic or massive violations of human rights against states that file a declaration accepting Article 6. In support of access, the *travaux preparatoires* indicate that "it was in fact pointed out that the statutes of the Inter-American Court on Human Rights were now being amended to allow individuals and NGOs to have access to the Court without any hindrance."[181] The procedure could by-pass the Commission, but the Court can transfer the case in its discretion.

The Protocol is also progressive in giving the African Court the broadest remedial jurisdiction of any human rights tribunal. If the court finds that there has been a violation of a human or people's right "it shall make appropriate orders to remedy the violation, including the payment of fair compensation or reparation."[182] No other court is expressly given the power to issue orders, although the Inter-American Court has directed the release of a prisoner held in violation of the Convention,[183] and the drafting history of Article 26 indicates no controversy over the Court's remedial powers. Instead, the drafters focused on the provision permitting non-state actors to file cases. In this connection, those who appear before the African Court are entitled to legal representation.[184] Free representation may be provided where the interests of justice require, something also provided in the European system, but not in the Inter-American system.

Those drafting the African Charter Protocol benefitted from being able to evaluate the divergent procedural practices of the earlier constituted regional systems. The African system also seems to have noted the gender imbalance among judges of the previously-created courts, the African Charter Protocol being the only regional instrument that requires states to pay due consideration to adequate gender representation in nominating and electing judges.[185]

VII. Changing Memberships and Changing Problems

All the regional systems have seen dramatic changes in their geopolitical environments, especially from democratic transitions in South Africa, Central and Eastern

---

[181] *See Report of the Secretary-General on the Draft Protocol on the Establishment of an African Court on Human and Peoples' Rights*, CM/2020(LXVI), Annex II, at 6, OAU/LEG/EXP/AFC/HPR/RPT (2). The statement regarding the Inter-American system is erroneous; individuals have standing at the Court only during the reparations phase of a case.

[182] Protocol to the African Charter, *supra* note 19, art. 26.

[183] Loayza Tamayo v. Peru, Order of the Court of July 2, 1996, Inter-Am. Ct. H.R. (ser. C) (1997).

[184] Protocol to the African Charter, *supra* note 19, art. 27.

[185] There has been considerable criticism of the European and Inter-American Court on this ground. The Inter-American Court has had one female judge in its history, as is also the

Europe, and much of Latin America. There has been a breakdown of authoritarian, repressive regimes and a resulting dramatic decrease in the worst governmental abuses: disappearances, summary executions, and other forms of brutal repression. New member states have joined all the regional systems, bringing with them both new possibilities and new problems. Countries in transition pose enormous challenges as they attempt to build democratic institutions that go beyond elections, such as independent judicial systems, professional police and military, a free press, and accountability for violations. Regional systems also face unprecedented problems from the resurgence of minority nationalism and ethnic tensions, often leading to massive violations of human rights by non-state as well as state actors. Still, the response of regional institutions suggest a "mainstreaming" of human rights, as regional bodies are occupied increasingly with issues of democracy, armed conflict, transnational crime, environmental protection, economic development, science and technology, and, indeed, the full range of human activities. In Europe, this "mainstreaming" may be seen in the proliferation of intra-regional institutions concerned with human rights, a development that has had an impact on regional norms and procedures. Regional systems are attempting to broaden their human rights activities without reducing their emphasis on the individual complaint procedures, their major contribution to the development of human rights law. Unfortunately, limited time and resources require that hard choices be made to accomplish the enormous tasks of prevention as well as protection. The promise of regional systems is conditioned on the willingness of member states to increase resources for regional institutions in the future.

A. Changes in Membership

Efforts to strengthen human rights protections on the regional level have succeeded in large part because of the cultural, geographic, economic, and historical proximity of the states involved.[186] In Europe, it has been claimed that "one of the explanations for the success of the Convention is that European States make up a culturally identifiable unit and their like-mindedness has meant easier agreement

---

case with the much larger European Court. The new European Court has a somewhat better composition. The Committee of Ministers adopted a Declaration at their 593rd meeting on May 28, 1997 on balanced representation of women and men in the new court. In spite of this, of the thirty-one judges elected to the Court in January 1998, only six are women, four of them from northwestern Europe (Belgium, the Netherlands, Norway, Sweden), and two from among the new member states (Slovakia and Macedonia).

[186] Weston et al. set forth three basic elements favoring the appearance and growth of regional human rights systems: (1) "regions (by which we mean geographical areas or units marked by relatively high socioeconomic, cultural, political and juridical commonalities) tend toward homogeneity"; (2) the first element helps create "reciprocal tolerance and mutual forbearance"; and (3) it is more likely that violations of the rules will be investigated and remedied. Weston et al., *supra* note 2, at 589, 590.

on what are considered to be basic human rights."[187] Also, such relative homogeneity has fostered a sense of trust among the member states that has made them sometimes less sensitive to criticism of their human rights performance.

Changes in membership in the regional systems, which have been significant, are not altogether positive to regional cohesion. The Inter-American and African systems have benefitted from the recent adherence of large and important states in the region. In the Inter-American system, Canada joined in 1989 and played a major role in events in Haiti. The transition to democracy in South Africa brought it into the African system where its resources and example of peaceful change can contribute to the future effectiveness of the system.

But, with its expansion into Central and Eastern Europe, some question whether the European system can continue to be successful.[188] Somewhat less than half the members states of the Council of Europe have joined since 1990, all of them in Central and Eastern Europe. If all that have applied for membership are admitted, the Council will be almost evenly divided between former Central and Eastern European countries and those of Western Europe, a change of membership will affect the culture of the system and the nature of cases that are brought to it. To date, "[t]he problems which come to Strasbourg, important as they may be for the individuals concerned, are with few exceptions of only marginal significance when compared with the massive and flagrant violations of human rights which occur in other parts of the world."[189] The new European Court will likely face unprecedented situations of widespread violations where factual determinations of responsibility will be crucial; future European cases may be comparable to those found in the Inter-American and the African systems. Both the character of the system and its effectiveness will be challenged. There is a risk that the new Court may narrow the interpretation of the principles embedded in the Convention and that the new states may disregard prior jurisprudence, deliberately or from lack of knowledge.

---

[187] RALPH BEDDARD, HUMAN RIGHTS AND EUROPE 1 (3d ed. 1993). Similarly, Rudolph Bernhardt, a judge of the European Court, says that "[t]he main reason for the effectiveness of the European Convention and Court is the considerable measure of homogeneity among European states. The member states of the Council of Europe and the parties to the Convention have recognized that the interpretation and the application of the European Convention can contribute to uniform European standards. . . . There is a feeling among the member states that there exists a common European standard and that this standard should be further developed." Rudolph Bernhardt, *Commentary: The European System*, 2 CONN. J. INT'L L. 299, 299–300 (1987).

[188] *See, e.g.*, Peter Leuprecht, *Innovations in the European System of Human Rights Protection: Is Enlargement Compatible with Reinforcement?*, 8 TRANSNAT'L L. & CONTEMP. PROBS. 313 (1998); David Seymour, *The Extension of the European Convention on Human Rights to Central and Eastern Europe: Prospects and Risks*, 8 CONN. J. INT'L L. 243 (1993).

[189] Merrills, *supra* note 13, at 240.

B. Institutional Proliferation

In contrast to other regions, Europe is faced also with an institutional proliferation that creates problems and possibilities for advancing human rights protections. In addition to the European system, which was created by the Council of Europe (Council), the Organization on Security and Cooperation in Europe (OSCE) and the European Community (EC) are engaged in human rights activities. Their existence and work constitute a fundamental change in the European human rights environment and have helped to transform the region in relation to the promotion and protection of human rights.

The 1975 Helsinki Final Act,[190] which is at the origin of the OSCE, brought human rights into the context of peace and security in the region and the various follow-up meetings to the Helsinki Conference have helped to strengthen human rights protections, sometimes adding details not found in other regional or global instruments.[191] The OSCE has tended to focus on human rights issues primarily through diplomatic intervention for conflict-prevention and mediation and, in this context, various meetings have made specific references to and commitments regarding national minorities. The OSCE has been engaged also in developing regional democracy, linking it with human rights. An Office for Democratic Institutions and Human Rights, established in Warsaw, assists the democratization process in OSCE states and monitors the implementation of OSCE commitments regarding "the human dimension." Parallel to the OSCE efforts, the Council of Europe created a program in 1990 to strengthen genuine democracy and to facilitate the integration of new member states into the Council of Europe.[192]

---

[190] Final Act of the Conference on Security and Co-operation in Europe, Aug. 1, 1975, *reprinted in* 14 I.L.M. 1292 (1975) *and* 1 Weston I.D.9, *supra* note 10.

[191] Follow-up conferences have been held in Madrid (1983), Vienna (1989), Copenhagen (1990) and Budapest (1994). The Madrid meeting focused on the issue of trade union freedoms in light of the advent of the Solidarity movement in Poland. Specific and detailed guarantees regarding freedom of religion, nondiscrimination, minority rights, freedom of movement, conditions of detention and capital punishment were added at the Vienna meeting. *See* Concluding Document of the Vienna Meeting 1986 of Representatives of the Participating States of the Conference on Security and Co-operation in Europe, Jan. 17, 1989, *reprinted in* 328 I.L.M. 527 (1989) *and* 1 Weston I.D.11, *supra* note 10. The 1990 meeting in Copenhagen also resulted in considerable standard-setting in several areas of human rights protections, especially concerning national minorities. *See* Document of the Copenhagen Meeting of the Conference on the Human Dimension of the Conference on Security and Co-operation in Europe, June 29, 1990, *reprinted in* 29 I.L.M. 1305 (1990) *and* 3 Weston III.B.20, *supra* note 11. It was also one of the first documents to refer to the right of conscientious objection to military service, a right not contained in the European Convention on Human Rights.

[192] *See* Andrew Drzemczewski, *The Council of Europe's Cooperation and Assistance Programmes with Central and Eastern European Countries in the Human Rights Field*, 14 Hum. Rts. L.J. 229 (1993).

The European Community (EC), in its transformation into the European Union, has also been concerned with human rights, although it was comprised originally of institutions of economic integration. Since the 1970s, the European Court of Justice has held that respect for basic rights is an integral part of Community law.[193] Over time, both the basic legal instruments and the jurisprudence of the Court have evolved to expand the rights of individuals not just in the economic field, but in respect to political rights as well.[194] The Court has been particularly active in enforcing equal rights in employment.[195] The Court refers to the European Convention in its jurisprudence and has expressly recognized the right to respect for private life[196] and the right to pursue a trade.[197] Its decisions are reflected in Article F(2) of the Treaty of European Union which contains an explicit reference to the European Convention on Human Rights.[198]

Other Community institutions also act in regard to human rights. The EC signs OSCE documents through its president[199] and EC employees sometimes participate in OSCE meetings as delegation members. The European Parliament has adopted

---

[193] Case 11/70, International Handelsgesellschaft mbH v. Einfuhr-und Vorratsstelle fur Getreide und Futtermittel, 1970 E.C.R. 1125.

[194] Article 8(b) of the Treaty on European Union, Feb. 7, 1992, *reprinted in* 31 I.L.M. 253 (1992) *and* 1 Weston I.B.13a, *supra* note 10, creates citizens' rights to vote and stand as a candidate in European elections throughout the Union. There is also a right to petition the European Parliament. Treaty on European Union, Aug. 31, 1992 O.J. (C 224) 31. EC documents on environmental protection stress rights of information, public participation and redress. *See, e.g.*, the "Seveso" Directive, Directive 84/501/EEC, O.J. (L 230) 1; Council Directive 85/337/EEC on assessment of the effects of certain public and private projects on the environment, 1985 O.J. (L 175) 40; and Directive 90/313/EEC on freedom of access to information on the environment, 1990 O.J. (L 158) 56.

[195] *See, e.g.*, Case 152/84, M. H. Marshall v. Southampton and South-West Hampshire Area Health Authority (Teaching), 1986 E.C.R. 723. The case is based on the EC Equal Treatment Directive.

[196] Case 165/82, Commission of the European Communities v. United Kingdom of Great Britain and Northern Ireland, 1983 E.C.R. 3431.

[197] Case 249/83, Vera Hoeckx v. Openbaar Centrum voor Maatschappelijk Welzijn Kalmthout, 1985 E.C.R. 973.

[198] Nold, Kohlen-und Baustoffsgrosshandlung v. Commission, 1974 E.C.R. 491. The Preamble to the 1989 Single European Act, Feb. 17, 1986, L169 OJEC 1 (1987) and Corr. L304 OJEC 46 (1987), *reprinted in* 25 I.L.M. 503 (1987) and 1 Weston I.B.12, *supra* note 10, also refers to the "fundamental rights recognized in the constitutions and laws of the Member States and in the Convention for the Protection of Human Rights and Fundamental Freedoms." Like the Council of Europe, the EC now considers respect for human rights a condition of membership.

[199] Erika Schlager, *The Procedural Framework of the CSCE: From the Helsinki Consultations to the Paris Charter, 1972–1990*, 12 Hum. Rts. L.J. 221, 230 (1991).

a Declaration of Fundamental Rights,[200] which has broader guarantees than the European Convention and, in addition, the Parliament's Human Rights Sub-Committee produces an annual report on human rights in countries throughout the world.

The result of multiple regional institutions can be both positive and negative. On the positive side, the mutual influence that can be seen inter-regionally also can occur intra-regionally, leading to greater human rights protections. Under the influence of the Helsinki process, for example, which has set high standards for minority protections,[201] the Council has taken action to meet the challenges of ethnic tensions in the region, important since the enlargement of the Council of Europe, by adopting new treaties to protect minority rights.[202]

Multiple regional institutions can manifest areas of specialization. The OSCE has a comparative advantage in conflict prevention because the Council of Europe is not a security organization and its mandate is thus more limited. The OSCE has also taken action on some situations where the Council of Europe and the U.N. have been inactive, such as with regard to citizenship and language laws in Estonia and Latvia, and the language law in Slovakia. On the other hand, the complaints procedure of the European Convention has no parallel in the OSCE. The political character of the OSCE commitments precludes judicial enforcement or complaints procedures, but consequently allows rapid response in periods of crisis. It can thus be seen to supplement, but not replace the pre-existing European system. More generally, the various regional bodies can reinforce the views and messages of the others provided there is good cooperation and careful coordination to avoid forum shopping by governments and contradictory messages from European institutions.

On the other hand, multiple institutions can lead to divergent jurisprudence, which is more problematic within a region than between regions because it places states in a position of conflicting obligations. For example, the European Court of Justice has held that the right to privacy in Article 8 of the European Convention, does not extend to business premises whereas the European Court of Human Rights

---

[200] May 16, 1989 O.J. (C 120) 51.

[201] The OSCE High Commissioner on National Minorities was created as an instrument of security to work on conflict prevention. Notably, the High Commissioner may receive information regarding national minority issues and a violation of OSCE commitments from any sources, including individuals and groups involved in situations of tension which could lead to conflict. The work involves direct contacts to promote dialogue, confidence building and cooperation. The broad mandate of the High Commissioner is at the intersection of peace, security, human rights, democracy and the rule of law. *See* Max Van der Stoel, *The Role of the OSCE High Commissioner on National Minorities in CSCE Preventive Diplomacy, in* THE CHALLENGE OF PREVENTIVE DIPLOMACY: THE EXPERIENCE OF THE OSCE 33 (Staffan Carlsson ed., 1994).

[202] European Charter for Regional or Minority Languages, *supra* note 30; Framework Convention on the Protection of National Minorities, *supra* note 31.

has held that it does.[203] In addition, the competition between institutions can create a risk of diluting human rights protections. It was due in part to concern that the Council of Europe human rights system would lose its significance after the OSCE expanded its activities in the Paris Charter[204] that the Council rushed to admit the new members before they were truly democratic and committed to human rights.

C. Mainstreaming of Human Rights: Old and New Problems

All the regional systems are expanding their efforts to consider issues of democracy, conflict prevention and resolution, environmental protection, and other problems related to human rights. The Council of Europe has adopted, for example, a Convention on Human Rights and Biomedicine[205] and a 1997 Protocol on the Prohibition of Cloning Human Beings,[206] the first legally binding international text on cloning.[207] The Inter-American and African systems have increasingly become involved in internal armed conflicts and democratic institution-building.

Ethnic conflicts are a particular concern. A 1988 study found that ninety-nine of 111 armed conflicts were linked either to separatism or to autonomy.[208] In 1993, the United Nations High Commissioner for Refugees identified twenty-five ongoing ethnic conflicts involving armed force.[209] The Parliamentary Assembly of the Council of Europe has acted by adopting a set of basic principles on minority rights and declared commitment to these principles a precondition of membership in the Council of Europe.[210] Three bilateral treaties between Hungary-Slovakia (March

---

[203] *Compare* Hoechst AG v. E.C. Commission, 4 C.M.L.R. 410 (1991) *and* Orkem v. Commission of the European Communities, 1989 E.C.R 3283 *with* Niemetz v. Germany, 251B Eur. Ct. H.R. (1992) *and* Funke v. France, 256A Eur. Ct. H.R. (1993).

[204] Charter of Paris for a New Europe and Supplement Document to Give Effect to Certain Provisions Contained in the Charter of Paris for a New Europe, Nov. 21, 1991, 30 I.L.M. 190 (1991), *reprinted in* 1 Weston I.D.13, *supra* note 10.

[205] *Supra* note 32.

[206] *Supra* note 33.

[207] The Protocol prohibits without reservation or derogation any intervention intended to create a human being genetically identical to another, whether living or dead. States are to legislate criminal or other sanctions, license revocation for laboratories or clinics, and bans on research or medical practice in case of offense.

[208] PETER WALLENSTEEN, STATES IN ARMED CONFLICT (Uppsala: Dep't of Peace and Conflict Researches, Report No. 30, 1989)

[209] David Levinson, *Ethnic Conflicts and Refugees*, REFUGEE—UNHCR REV. AUG. 1993, at 4.

[210] *See* Order No. 175 (1993) (Slovakia); Order No. 176 (1996) (Romania); Order No. 183 (1994) (Latvia); Order No. 188 (1995) (Moldavia); Order No. 189 (1995) (Albania); Order No. 190 (1995) (Ukraine); Order No. 191 (1995) (Macedonia, FYROM); Order No. 193 (1996) (Russia).

19, 1995), Hungary-Croatia (April 5, 1996) and Hungary-Romania (Sept. 16, 1996) are based on the Assembly principles.

Increasingly, the regional systems are similarly facing problems of wide disparity of economic development, civil war or repeated military coups, and terrorism and organized criminal associations. Coordination, cooperation, and competition among them may help produce some solutions to these seemingly intractable issues.

D. Threats to Regional Systems

The regional systems suffer from expanding work and diminishing resources. Their success is in part responsible for the difficulties they face.

Beginning in the early 1980s, the caseload of the European system began to double every five years on average.[211] During its first eighteen years, the European Court rendered twenty-six judgments while the next eighteen years brought 472 decisions. At the end of 1993, the system had a backlog of 3100 cases. The caseload is not likely to decrease; dissemination of knowledge about the Convention has encouraged more frequent recourse to the regional system. The question is whether even a full-time court can cope.

The Inter-American Commission's caseload is also expanding. As of January 20, 1998, it had 976 cases under consideration and a staff of twelve lawyers to handle them.

In Africa, the Commission has repeatedly complained of shortage of staff and equipment. An OAU budgetary crisis has meant several projects of the Commission have had to be suspended and one session of the Commission was cut from two weeks to eight days. As of June 2, 1998, OAU member states owed more than US$48 million in contributions, an amount that represented one-and-one-half times the annual budget of the organization.[212] Only twenty of the fifty-three members are up to date in their assessments. Two states have not paid for twelve years, two others not for ten years.[213]

Finally, there is always the risk of "backsliding." In the Caribbean, in 1999, Barbados, Guyana, Jamaica, and Trinidad intend to establish a Caribbean Court of

---

[211] In 1982, the Commission registered more than 500 applications for the first time; in 1988, more than 1000 applications were registered. By 1992, the number of registered applications reached 2,037. EUROPEAN COMMISSION OF HUMAN RIGHTS, SURVEY OF ACTIVITIES AND STATISTICS (1993). The number of court judgments has similarly risen. During its first fifteen years, it issued seventeen judgments in regard to eleven cases. During the next ten years, fifty-nine judgments were adopted. From 1984 to 1993, the number jumped to 372.

[212] Sidy Gaye, *OAU Owed 48 Million by Member States*, PAN AFRICAN NEWS AGENCY, June 2, 1998.

[213] *See id.*

Justice in large part out of disagreement with Inter-American standards on due process in death penalty cases.[214] On May 26, 1998, Trinidad and Tobago denounced the Inter-American Convention on Human Rights, the only state ever to do so. It also denounced the Optional Protocol to the ICCPR.[215] In January 1998, Jamaica withdrew from the ICCPR Optional Protocol on the death penalty and Barbados announced that it was considering denouncing the American Convention. While these events challenge both regional and global standards, the regional system can continue to supervise the states' behavior. So long as the states remain members of the OAS, they are bound by regional norms and subject to the jurisdiction of the Inter-American Commission.

VIII.   Conclusions

The evolution in regional norms and procedures does not address the fundamental question of whether regional systems actually have had a positive impact on respect for human rights, but there can be little doubt in this regard. While compliance is not as good as it should be and while much remains to be done, there is considerable evidence that states have responded to judgments of the regional tribunals, changing their laws and practices as a result. In Europe it is relatively easy to demonstrate the effect of the Convention and Court judgments: Austria, for example, has modified its Code of Criminal Procedure;[216] Belgium has amended its Penal Code, its laws on vagrancy, and its Civil Code;[217] France has strengthened the protection for privacy of telephone communications;[218] Germany has modified its Code of Criminal Procedure regarding pretrial detention, given legal recognition to transsexuals, and taken action to expedite criminal and civil proceedings;[219] The Netherlands has modified its Code of Military Justice and the law on detention of mental patients;[220] Ireland created a system of legal aid;[221] Sweden introduced rules

---

[214]   *4 Nations Shedding Curbs on Executions*, Chicago Sun-Times, July 5, 1998, at 45. Trinidad and Tobago is to be the seat of the new Court, which will replace the Privy Council as the last court of appeal for death row cases in the four countries. *Trinidad and Tobago to be Centre for Caribbean Court*, The Lawyer, Aug. 4, 1998, at 36.

[215]   ICCPR Optional Protocol, *supra* note 62.

[216]   *See* Neumeister, 8 Eur. Ct. H.R. (ser. A) (1968); Stogmuller, 9 Eur. Ct. H.R. (ser. A) (1969); Matznetter, 10 Eur. Ct. H.R. (ser. A) (1969); Ringeisen, 13 Eur. Ct. H.R. (ser. A) (1971); and Bonisch, 92 Eur. Ct. H.R. (ser. A) (1985).

[217]   De Wile, Ooms and Versyp (Vagrancy Cases), 12 Eur. Ct. H.R. (ser. A) (1970) and Marckx, 31 Eur. Ct. H.R. (ser. A) (1979) (discrimination between legitimate and illegitimate children).

[218]   Kurslin and Huvig, 176 Eur. Ct. H.R. (ser. A) (1990) (wiretapping).

[219]   *See, e.g.*, Luedicke, Belkacem and Koc, 29 Eur. Ct. H.R. (ser. A) (1978) (interpreters fees).

[220]   Engel, 22 Eur. Ct. H.R. (1976) (military penal code) and Winterwerp, 33 Eur. Ct. H.R. (ser. A) (1979) (mentally ill).

[221]   Airey, 32 Eur Ct. H.R. (ser. A) (1979).

on expropriation and legislation on building permits;[222] Switzerland amended its Military Penal Code and completely reviewed its judicial organization and criminal procedure applicable to the army;[223] France has strengthened the protection for privacy of telephone conversations.[224] According to Buergenthal,

> the decisions of the European Court are routinely complied with by European governments. As a matter of fact, the system has been so effective in the last decade that the Court has become, for all practical purposes, Western Europe's constitutional court. Its case law and practice resembles that of the United States Supreme Court.[225]

The impact of the European human rights system is relatively easy to demonstrate because of the follow-up procedure which requires states to report to the Committee of Ministers on their compliance with decisions of the European Court. In a similar fashion, the Inter-American Court maintains open files on cases until the defendant state carries out the judgment. It has closed a number of cases following compliance. The impact of the decisions of the Inter-American Commission is harder to measure, but in the field of criminal justice there have been significant changes in laws and practices throughout the hemisphere—for example, in regard to amnesty for human rights violators. According to a former member of the Inter-American Commission,

> [i]n many ways the Inter-American system has not been as efficient as the European regional system, though its mandate is notably broader. The challenges the Inter-American system has faced are, however, severe and make its accomplishments all the more impressive. The fact that government leaders, diplomats, commission and court members, and many non-governmental organizations in the Americas have been able, often in an ongoing adversarial collaboration, to fashion and implement a useful human rights instrument may be of particular importance to those interested in establishing regional human rights systems.[226]

Even without undertaking a detailed empirical analysis of the impact of the regional human rights systems, it is clear that they contribute to the functioning and improvement of the global human rights system. All systems are strengthened by

---

[222] Sporrong and Lonnroth, 88 Eur. Ct. H.R. (ser. A) (1985).

[223] Eggs v. Switzerland, Committee of Ministers, 1980.

[224] Guzzardi, 39 Eur. Ct. H.R. (ser. A) (1980).

[225] BUERGENTHAL & SHELTON, *supra* note 9, at 34.

[226] W. Michael Reisman, *Practical Matters for Consideration in the Establishment of a Regional Human Rights Mechanism: Lessons from the Inter-American Experience*, 1995 ST. LOUIS-WARSAW TRANSNAT'L 89 (1995).

the variety of subsystems that interact and even compete as parts of them.[227] As each subsystem attempts to optimize its functioning, the interaction of the subsystems at various meeting points changes the nature of the problems to be solved by them. The adaptive moves by each further modify the problems, stimulating additional co-evolution. The variety of responses leads to overall sustainability and resistence to threats, just as a diverse ecosystem is more resilient to challenge than a monocultural system because each component can respond as it is differently adapted. Each subsystem benefits from the response of the others, learning and evolving in an on-going interdependent process.

Human rights law has been enhanced through the developing jurisprudence and evolution of regional human rights systems, wherein the various systems reinforce global norms while responding to the particular problems of each region. In particular, regional systems continue to reaffirm the Universal Declaration of Human Rights on which each of them is based. The convergence of regional jurisprudence confirms the universality of the rights proclaimed in the Declaration and the wisdom of its authors. Through the participation of NGOs in various ways and through their own interactions, regional systems learn from each other about the meaning of the Declaration and its on-going relevance to regional human rights instruments, enhancing the legitimacy of their decisions by relying on it and on precedents from other systems.

Regional systems thus are interconnected with each other, with the larger global system of which they are components and smaller systems of which they are products. They also are engaged in constant exchanges with their geopolitical and technological environments and thus never reach equilibrium. As a result, their operations never will be completely consistent with their goals; there almost always will be some malfunction or inefficiency in the process. Nonetheless, it is possible to seek reform and greater efficiency to achieve the aim of promoting and protecting international human rights. That is the promise of the regional systems.

---

[227] STUART KAUFFMAN, AT HOME IN THE UNIVERSE: THE SEARCH FOR LAWS OF SELF-ORGANIZATION AND COMPLEXITY 247 (1995).

Reconciliation and Justice: The South African Experience*

John Dugard

I. Introduction

When the Universal Declaration of Human Rights was adopted on 10 December 1948, to give expression to the rights proclaimed in Articles 55 and 56 of the United Nations Charter, no one could have contemplated the enforcement of these rights by criminal sanctions. States still viewed the treatment of their own nationals as a matter of exclusive domestic concern, protected by Article 2(7) of the Charter, and the only enforcement procedures anticipated were reports by states on their compliance with the rights proclaimed and, perhaps, the hearing of individual complaints by an international body. In the years that followed, regional conventions, such as the European Convention on Human Rights, and universal conventions, notably the International Covenant on Civil and Political Rights, gave legal force to the rights proclaimed in the Universal Declaration of Human Rights. They established machinery to receive reports from signatory states, to provide for the settlement of disputes between states over the question of compliance with their obligations, and, in the final resort, to allow individuals to petition international monitoring bodies when their human rights were violated. The idea that state officials might be punished under international law for grave human rights violations perpetrated on their own nationals in time of peace or internal conflict remained a utopian dream. It is true that the Nuremberg tribunals had tried the leaders of the Nazi regime for atrocities committed against their own nationals, but that was for crimes associated with an international armed conflict. Furthermore, the failure of the United Nations to create a permanent international criminal court seemed to reinforce the view that the international community was not prepared to resort to criminal prosecution to enforce human rights.

Today, the situation has changed dramatically in response to the genocidal conflicts in the former Yugoslavia and Rwanda. Two *ad hoc* tribunals, the International Criminal Tribunal for the Former Yugoslavia[1] and the International Tribunal for

---

* This essay was published earlier under the same title in 8 TRANSNAT'L LAW & CONTEMP. PROBS. 277 (1998). Reprint permission granted.

1 *See International Criminal Tribunal for the Former Yugoslavia*, U.N. SCOR, 48th Sess., 3217th mtg., U.N. Doc. S/RES/827 (1993), *reprinted in* 2 INTERNATIONAL LAW AND WORLD ORDER: BASIC DOCUMENTS II.E.11 (Burns H. Weston ed., 5 vols., 1994–) [hereinafter 2 Weston].

Rwanda[2] have been created to try persons charged with international crimes arising out of the ethnic conflicts in those territories; and, on July 17, 1998, the dream
of a permanent international criminal court was realized when a diplomatic conference in Rome gave its approval to a statute to establish such a court.[3] Both the
ad hoc tribunals and the International Criminal Court are given jurisdiction over
crimes unconnected with international armed conflict—genocide, crimes against
humanity and war crimes committed in noninternational armed conflict—that is,
acts constituting the most serious violation of human rights, including the practices
of *apartheid*. In addition, it is now argued that states are not only permitted but
obliged in law to try persons for these crimes before their own domestic courts.

In 1948, South Africa was one of eight states that abstained from voting on the
Universal Declaration of Human Rights. Thereafter, it pursued a policy of systematic racial discrimination, backed by political repression, known as *apartheid*, which
violated virtually every right proclaimed in the Universal Declaration. In 1990, this
policy was abandoned, and in 1994, following a process of negotiation between the
National Party government and opposition political groupings, culminating in a
democratic election, South Africa became a democratic state constitutionally committed to racial equality and respect for human rights.

Inevitably the question arose in South Africa as to how to deal with its own
dark past, and what to do about the crimes that had been committed in the name of
apartheid. The United Nations, greatly relieved that a matter had been settled that
had been featured on its agenda since its very inception, did not suggest or even
consider the establishment of an *ad hoc* tribunal to try *apartheid's* criminals despite
the fact that many of the acts in question constituted international crimes, particularly crimes against humanity. On the contrary, the United Nations left it to South
Africa completely to decide on the course to adopt. Within South Africa, suggestions ranged from total amnesty to conditional amnesty accompanied by an inquiry
into the past by a truth and reconciliation commission, modeled on commissions of
this kind established in Latin-American countries following the overthrow of military regimes in the late 1980s. The decision to adopt the latter course was warmly
welcomed by the international community, thereby casting doubts on the existence
of an obligation upon successor regimes to prosecute those suspected of having
committed international crimes.

The present study examines whether the South African way of dealing with the
past by conditional amnesty and the "truth and reconciliation process" is compatible with international law. It also considers the wisdom of pursuing such a course

---

2   *See International Tribunal for Rwanda*, U.N. SCOR, 49th Sess., 3453d mtg., U.N. Doc.
S/RES/955 (1994), *reprinted in* 2 Weston II.E.12, *supra* note 1.

3   *See Rome Statute of the International Criminal Court, adopted by the United Nations
Diplomatic Conference of Plenipotentiaries on the Establishment of an International Court*,
U.N. Doc. A/CONF. 183/9 (1998), [hereinafter Statute of International Criminal Court],
reprinted in 37 I.L.M. 999 (1998) *and* 1 INTERNATIONAL LAW AND WORLD ORDER: BASIC
DOCUMENTS I.H.13 (Burns H. Weston ed., 5 vols., 1994–   ) [hereinafter 1 Weston].

in a world increasingly committed to the punishment of those responsible for gross human rights violations. I start with an examination of the experience of other countries, and the norms and guidelines of international law applicable to a successor regime in respect of past human rights violations. I then turn to the South African truth and reconciliation process and consider whether it complies with the norms of international law and whether it has served, or will serve, to advance respect for human rights in South Africa.

II. International Norms and Guidelines for Dealing with Crimes of the Past

In some instances, the international community has not been content to allow successor regimes to deal with the crimes of their predecessors and has itself established machinery to prosecute and punish the wrongdoers. This has happened where the delinquent regime has engaged in an aggressive or genocidal war and the successor regime lacks the institutions or resources to try the wrongdoer itself.[4] In most instances, however, particularly where the crimes in the form of egregious human rights violations have occurred within the territory of a state, the international community has left it to the successor regime to decide on the measures to be taken in the context of its own political realities. Some have chosen to prosecute the criminals of the previous regime, as in the case of the 1975 trials of leaders of the military junta that ruled Greece from 1967 to 1974,[5] the prosecution of East German border guards after German unification,[6] the trials of leaders of the Mengistu regime in Ethiopia,[7] and the prosecution of Hutus in Rwanda following the genocidal war of 1993. Others have granted complete amnesty, as in the case of post independence Zimbabwe,[8] while still other regimes, such as Chile and South Africa, have coupled amnesty with truth and reconciliation commissions.

Although the decision on what measures to take against the officers of the predecessor regime generally is left to the successor regime without outside interference, this is not a matter that falls entirely within the protected domestic domain of the state. Nor is it ungoverned by international law. The violation of human rights is no longer a purely domestic issue. Moreover, many of the crimes that form the basis of the charges in such cases have a dual character as national and international

---

4   In broad terms, this covers the Nuremberg and Tokyo trials and the *ad hoc* tribunals for the former Yugoslavia and Rwanda.

5   *See* Naomi Roht-Arriaza, *Overview, in* IMPUNITY AND HUMAN RIGHTS IN INTERNATIONAL LAW AND PRACTICE 73, 78 (Naomi Roht-Arriaza ed., 1995).

6   *See* Susanne Walther, *Problems in Blaming and Punishing Individuals for Human Rights Violations: The Example of the Berlin Wall Shootings, in* IMPUNITY AND HUMAN RIGHTS IN INTERNATIONAL LAW AND PRACTICE 99 (Naomi Roht-Arriaza ed., 1995).

7   *See* Roht-Arriaza, *supra* note 5, at 224.

8   *See* Richard Carver, *Zimbabwe: Drawing a Line Through the Past, in* IMPUNITY AND HUMAN RIGHTS IN INTERNATIONAL LAW AND PRACTICE 252 (Naomi Roht-Arriaza ed., 1995).

crimes. Torture is normally a crime under both national and international law; while multiple murders become genocide if committed "with intent to destroy, in whole or in part, a national, ethnical, racial or religious group"[9] or a crime against humanity "when committed in a systematic manner or on a large scale and instigated or directed by a government or by any organization or group."[10] Consequently states do not enjoy absolute freedom of choice in deciding upon the measures to be taken. They must take account of international norms and expectations.

In the past decade, there have been major developments in this field resulting from the repudiation of military dictatorships in Latin America, the fall of communism and the dissolution of the Soviet Union, the genocidal conflicts in Yugoslavia and Rwanda, and the demise of *apartheid*. The options to be followed have spawned an immense legal literature[11] and been subjected to scrutiny at a host of conferences. Firm opinions are held in many quarters on the correct procedures to be applied, but treaty law and state practice lag behind. Thus it is difficult to identify mandatory rules of international law to govern the conduct of the successor regime. The best one can do is to identify trends that probably qualify as emergent norms. These norms appear from recent state practice.

A. Prosecution

It is argued today with growing conviction that the rule of *aut dedere aut judicare* (extradite or prosecute) is part of customary international law and that it requires states (as represented by the successor regime) to ensure that those responsible for egregious violations of human rights are tried and punished.[12] Certainly such an obligation is to be found in a number of treaties.

The 1949 Geneva Conventions oblige High Contracting Parties

> to search for persons alleged to have committed, or to have ordered to be committed, . . . grave breaches, and shall bring such persons, regardless of

---

[9]   Convention on the Prevention and Punishment of the Crime of Genocide, Dec. 9, 1948, art. 2, 78 U.N.T.S. 277 (entered into force, Jan. 12, 1951) [hereinafter Genocide Convention], *reprinted in* 3 INTERNATIONAL LAW AND WORLD ORDER: BASIC DOCUMENTS III.J.1 (Burns H. Weston ed., 5 vols., 1994–) [hereinafter 3 Weston].

[10]   *Draft Code of Crimes Against the Peace and Security of Mankind, Report of the International Law Commission on the Work of Its Forty-Eighth Session*, 51st Sess., Supp. No. 10, art. 18, U.N. Doc. A/51/10 (1996) [hereinafter *Code of Crimes Against the Peace and Security of Mankind*].

[11]   *See, e.g.*, the three-volume study on the topic, TRANSITIONAL JUSTICE: HOW EMERGING DEMOCRACIES RECKON WITH FORMER REGIMES (Neil J. Kritz ed., 3 vols., 1995) [hereinafter TRANSITIONAL JUSTICE].

[12]   *See generally* M. CHERIF BASSIOUNI & EDWARD M. WISE, AUT DEDERE AUT JUDICARE: THE DUTY TO EXTRADITE OR PROSECUTE IN INTERNATIONAL LAW (1995).

their nationality, before its own courts . . . [or] hand such persons over for trial to another High Contracting Party. . . .[13]

"Grave breaches" under these conventions include "wilful killing, torture or inhuman treatment, including biological experiments, wilfully causing great suffering or serious injury to body or health, unlawful deportation or transfer or unlawful confinement."[14] This provision, however, applies only to international armed conflicts.[15] The 1948 Genocide Convention likewise contains an absolute obligation to prosecute offenders.[16] The 1984 Torture Convention is less strict in this regard; it requires a state party to submit a case of torture to its competent authorities "for the purpose of prosecution" or to extradite the alleged offender.[17] Whether the International Covenant on Civil and Political Rights[18] imposes a duty on states to punish violations of the rights contained in the treaty is the subject of debate.[19] The Covenant itself is silent on this matter, but several comments of the Human Rights Committee, established to monitor compliance with the Covenant, give

---

[13]   Geneva Convention Relative to the Protection of Civilian Persons in Time of War, *opened for signature Aug. 12, 1949,* art. 146, 6 U.S.T. 3516, 75 U.N.T.S. 287 [hereinafter Protection of Civilian Persons], *reprinted in* 2 Weston II.B.14, *supra* note 1.

[14]   *Id.* art. 147. *See also* Geneva Convention for the Amelioration of the Condition of the Wounded and Sick in Armed Forces in the Field, *opened for signature* Aug. 12, 1949, arts. 49–50, 6 U.S.T. 3114, 3146, 75 U.N.T.S. 31, 62, *reprinted in* 2 Weston II.B.11, *supra* note 1; Geneva Convention for the Amelioration of the Condition of Wounded, Sick and Shipwrecked Members of Armed Forces at Sea, *opened for signature* Aug. 12, 1949, art. 51, 6 U.S.T. 3217, 3250, 75 U.N.T.S. 85, 116, *reprinted in* 2 Weston II.B.12, *supra* note 1; Geneva Convention Relative to the Treatment of Prisoners of War, *opened for signature* Aug. 12, 1949, arts. 129–130, 6 U.S.T. 3316, 3318, 75 U.N.T.S. 135, 236, *reprinted in* 2 Weston, II.B.13, *supra* note 1.

[15]   *See* Protection of Civilian Persons, *supra* note 13, art. 2.

[16]   *See* Genocide Convention, *supra* note 9, art. 4.

[17]   *Convention against Torture and other Cruel, Inhuman or Degrading Treatment or Punishment, opened for signature* Feb. 4, 1985, arts. 5, 7, 39 U.N. GAOR, Supp. No. 51, at 197, U.N.Doc. A/139/51 (1984) (entered into force June 26, 1987), *reprinted in* 23 I.L.M. 102 (1984) *and* 2 WESTON II.K.2, *supra* note 9.

[18]   International Covenant on Civil and Political Rights, *infra* Appendix III [hereinafter ICCPR].

[19]   *See, e.g.,* Naomi Roht-Arriaza, *Sources in International Treaties of an Obligation to Investigate, Prosecute and Provide Redress, in* IMPUNITY AND HUMAN RIGHTS IN INTERNATIONAL LAW AND PRACTICE 24, 28–30 (Naomi Roht-Arriaza ed., 1995); Diana F. Orentlicher, *Settling Accounts: The Duty to Prosecute Human Rights Violations of a Prior Regime,* 100 YALE L.J. 2537, 2568 (1991); Michael Scharf, *The Letter of the Law: The Scope of the International Legal Obligation to Prosecute Human Rights Crimes,* 59 LAW & CONTEMP. PROBS. 41, 47 (1996).

support to this notion.[20] The strongest statement of the Human Rights Committee, however, states that amnesties covering acts of torture "are *generally* incompatible with the duty of States to investigate such acts,"[21] which suggests that some amnesties—for example, those accompanied by a truth and reconciliation process— are acceptable. The case for prosecution under the American Convention on Human Rights[22] is stronger. Although it too is silent on the obligation to prosecute offenders, both the Inter-American Court of Human Rights and the Inter-American Commission of Human Rights have interpreted the Convention to require prosecution of violators of the rights contained in the Convention. In the *Velásquez Rodríguez Case*, the Court interpreted Article 1(1) of the Convention obliging member states to "ensure" the rights set forth in the Convention as imposing an obligation on states to "prevent, investigate and punish any violation of the rights recognized by the Convention and, moreover, if possible to attempt to restore the rights violated and provide compensation as warranted for damages resulting from the violation."[23] Later the Commission found that the amnesties granted by Uruguay[24] and Argentina[25] following the fall of military dictatorships in those countries, were incompatible with the Convention's right to a remedy (Article 25) and right to judicial process (Article 8,) read together with Article 1's obligation to "ensure" the rights in the Convention.

Customary international law presents greater difficulties as a source of obligation to prosecute for the violation of international crimes. Here the debate focuses on crimes against humanity, the most authoritative definition of which is that given by the International Law Commission in its Draft Code of Crimes against the Peace and Security of Mankind of 1996:

---

20   *See* Muteba v. Zaire, Comm. No. 124/1982, 39 U.N. GAOR Supp. (No. 40) Annex XIII, U.N. Doc. A/39/40 (1984); Boaboeram v. Surinam, Comm. Nos. 146/1983 and 148–154/1983, 40 U.N. GAOR Supp. (No. 40), Annex X, U.N. Doc. A/40/40 (1985); Quinteros v. Uruguay, Comm. No. 107/1981, 38 U.N. GAOR Supp. (No. 40) Annex XXII, U.N. Doc. A/38/40 (1983).

21   General Comment No. 20 (44) (art. 7), U.N. Doc. CCPR/C21/REV.I/Add.3, para. 15 (Apr. 1992) (emphasis added).

22   *See* American Convention on Human Rights, *opened for signature* Nov. 22, 1969, art. 46, 1144 U.N.T.S. 123, 9 I.L.M. 673 (adopted Jan. 7, 1970), *reprinted in* 3 Weston III.B.24, *supra* note 9.

23   *See* Velásquez Rodríguez Case, Judgment of July 29, 1988, Inter-Am. C.H.R. (ser. C) No. 4, para. 166, *reprinted in* 3 Transitional Justice, *supra* note 11, at 586–90 [hereinafter Velásquez Case].

24   *See* Inter-American Commission on Human Rights, Report No. 29/92 (Uruguay), 82d Sess., OEA/ser. L/V/II.82, Doc. 25 (Oct. 2, 1992), *reprinted in* 3 Transitional Justice, *supra* note 11, at 605–12.

25   *See* Inter-American Commission on Human Rights, Rep. No. 24/92 (Argentina), 82d Sess., OEA/ser. L/V/II. 82, Doc. 24 (Oct. 2, 1992), *reprinted in* 3 Transitional Justice, *supra* note 11, at 533–39.

A crime against humanity means any of the following acts, when committed in a systematic manner or on a large scale and instigated or directed by a Government or by any organization or group:

(a) murder;

(b) extermination;

(c) torture;

(d) enslavement;

(e) persecution on political, racial, religious or ethnic grounds;

(f) institutionalized discrimination on racial, ethnic or religious grounds involving the violation of fundamental human rights and freedoms resulting in seriously disadvantaging a part of the population;

(g) arbitrary deportation or forcible transfer of population;

(h) arbitrary imprisonment;

(i) forced disappearance of persons;

(j) rape, enforced prostitution and other forms of sexual abuse;

(k) other inhumane acts which severely damage physical and mental integrity, health or human dignity such as mutilation and severe bodily harm.[26]

This crime covers a multitude of sins, including *apartheid*.[27] Indeed the 1998 Rome Statute of the International Criminal Court expressly describes *apartheid* as a species of crimes against humanity.[28] If acts proscribed by this definition constitute acts in respect of which there is an obligation under international law to extradite or prosecute, this will place severe restraints on the power of a successor regime to grant amnesty to members of the previous regime. This explains why the debate over the existence of such an obligation is of such importance when it comes to measuring transitional justice arrangements that do not involve prosecution.

Several academic writers argue that states are obliged under customary international law to prosecute crimes against humanity.[29] Support for this view is to be

---

[26] *Code of Crimes Against the Peace and Security of Mankind, supra* note 10, at 93–94. The Statute of the recently adopted International Criminal Court contains a substantially similar definition. *See* Statute of International Criminal Court, *supra* note 3, art. 7.

[27] The commentary on (f) describes it as "in fact the crime of apartheid under a more general denomination." *Code of Crimes Against the Peace and Security of Mankind, supra* note 10, at 99.

[28] *See* Statute of International Criminal Court, *supra* note 3, art. 7(j).

[29] *See, e.g.*, M. Cherif Bassiouni, *Searching for Peace and Achieving Justice: The Need for Accountability*, 59 Law & Contemp. Probs. 9, 17 (1996); Carla Edelenbos, *Human Rights Violations: A Duty to Prosecute?*, 7 Leiden J. Int'l L. 5, 15 (1994); Ziyad Motala, *The Constitutional Court's Approach to International Law and its Method of Interpretation in the "Amnesty Decision": Intellectual Honesty or Political Expediency?*, 21 S. Afr. Y.B. Int'l

found in the 1996 International Law Commission's Draft Code of Crimes against the Peace and Security of Mankind, which obliges states to try or extradite those alleged to have committed crimes against humanity,[30] a nonbinding resolution of the General Assembly,[31] the Final Declaration and Programme of Action of the 1993 World Conference on Human Rights,[32] and the Convention on the Non-Applicability of Statutory Limitations to War Crimes and Crimes against Humanity of 1968[33] (which has not been widely ratified). State practice, however, hardly confirms the existence of such a customary rule. On the contrary, modern history is replete with examples of cases in which successor regimes have granted amnesty to human rights violators of the previous regime rather than prosecute them.[34] In these circumstances it is difficult to disagree with the statement of Michael Scharf that

[c]ustomary international law recognizes permissive jurisdiction to prosecute persons responsible for crimes against humanity either nationally or before an international tribunal. Yet, despite a large collection of General Assembly Resolutions calling for prosecution of crimes against humanity, and notwithstanding the forceful arguments of several international legal scholars, state practice does not yet support the existence of an obligation under international law to refrain from conferring amnesty for crimes against humanity. That the United Nations, itself, has felt free of legal constraints in endorsing recent amnesty for peace deals underscores this conclusion.[35]

L. 29, 57–58 (1996); Ziyad Motala, *The Promotion of National Unity and Reconciliation Act, the Constitution and International Law*, 28 COMP. INT'L L.J. S. AFR. 338, 353–57 (1995); Orentlicher, *supra* note 19, at 2549; Naomi Roht-Arriaza, *Nontreaty Sources of the Obligation to Investigate and Prosecute, in* IMPUNITY AND HUMAN RIGHTS IN INTERNATIONAL LAW AND PRACTICE 39, 50–56 (Naomi Roht-Arriaza ed., 1995).

30   *See Code of Crimes Against the Peace and Security of Mankind, supra* note 10, art. 6.

31   *See Principles of International Cooperation in the Detection, Arrest, Extradition and Punishment of Persons Guilty of War Crimes and Crimes Against Humanity*, G.A. Res. 3074, U.N. GAOR, 28th Sess., Supp. No. 30, at 78, U.N. Doc. A/9030 (1973) [hereinafter Principles of International Cooperation], *reprinted in* 13 I.L.M. 230 (1974) *and* 2 Weston II.E.7, *supra* note 1.

32   This Declaration stipulates that "[s]tates should abrogate legislation leading to impunity for those responsible for grave violations of human rights such as torture and prosecute such violations." *World Conference on Human Rights, Declaration and Programme of Action*, U.N. Doc. A/Conf./157/23 (1993).

33   Convention on the Non-Applicability of Statutory Limitations to War Crimes and Crimes Against Humanity, *opened for signature* Nov. 26, 1968, 754 U.N.T.S. 73 (entered into force Nov. 11, 1970) [hereinafter Convention on the Non-Applicability of Statutory Limitations], *reprinted in* 8 I.L.M. 68 (1969) *and* 2 Weston II.E.6, *supra* note 1.

34   For a description of these cases, see Scharf, *supra* note 19, at 52. *See also* Douglass Cassel, *Lessons from the Americas: Guidelines for International Response to Amnesties for Atrocities*, 59 LAW & CONTEMP. PROBS. 196, 197–203 (1996).

35   Scharf, *supra* note 19, at 56.

State practice accords with political reality.[36] Where the new regime has cause to fear a military uprising if its members are prosecuted, it would obviously be wise to avoid such a course and to seek some alternative method of acknowledging the crimes of the past. The history of Chile[37] and Argentina[38] illustrates this point. Alternatively, the new regime may, as in the case of South Africa, have come to power as a result of a political compromise, following negotiation with its predecessor, and be compelled both constitutionally and morally to pursue a policy of reconciliation that excludes prosecution. A host of other reasons may make prosecution unwise, ranging from an inadequate judicial system to difficulties of presenting sufficient evidence to secure the conviction of the officers of the previous regime. This was a factor alluded to by the South African Constitutional Court when it upheld the validity of the South African amnesty legislation. In *Azapo and Others v. President of the Republic of South Africa* Mahomed D.P. (Deputy President of the Constitutional Court) declared:

Most of the acts of brutality and torture which have taken place have occurred during an era in which neither the laws which permitted the incarceration of persons or the investigation of crimes, nor the methods and the culture which informed such investigations, were easily open to public investigation, verification and correction. Much of what transpired in this shameful period is shrouded in secrecy and not easily capable of objective demonstration and proof. Loved ones have disappeared, sometimes mysteriously, and most of them no longer survive to tell their tales. Others have had their freedom invaded, their dignity assaulted or reputations tarnished by grossly unfair imputations hurled in the fire and the cross-fire of a deep and wounding conflict. The wicked and the innocent have often both been victims. Secrecy and authoritarianism have concealed the truth in little crevices of obscurity in our history. Records are not easily accessible, witnesses are often unknown, dead, unavailable or unwilling. All that often effectively remains is the truth of wounded memories of loved ones sharing instinctive suspicions, deep and traumatising to the survivors but otherwise incapable of translating themselves into objective and corroborative evidence which could survive the rigours of the law. The [Promotion of National Unity and Reconciliation] Act seeks to address this massive problem by encouraging these survivors and the dependants of the tortured and the wounded, the maimed and the dead to unburden their grief publicly, to

---

[36] *See, e.g.*, Stephan Landsman, *Alternative Responses to Serious Human Rights Abuses: Of Prosecution and Truth Commissions*, 59 LAW & CONTEMP. PROBS. 81, 84–87 (1996).

[37] *See generally* Jorge Correa Sutil, *"No Victorious Army Has Ever Been Prosecuted . . .": The Unsettled Story of Transitional Justice in Chile, in* TRANSITIONAL JUSTICE AND THE RULE OF LAW IN NEW DEMOCRACIES 123 (A. James McAdams ed., 1997).

[38] *See generally* Carlos S. Nino, *Response: The Duty to Punish Past Abuses of Human Rights Put into Context: The Case of Argentina*, 100 YALE L.J. 2619 (1991).

receive the collective recognition of a new nation that they were wronged, and, crucially, to help them to discover what did in truth happen to their loved ones, where and under what circumstances it did happen, and who was responsible. That truth, which the victims of repression seek so desperately to know is, in the circumstances, much more likely to be forthcoming if those responsible for such monstrous misdeeds are encouraged to disclose the whole truth with the incentive that they will not receive the punishment which they undoubtedly deserve if they do. Without that incentive there is nothing to encourage such persons to make the disclosures and to reveal the truth which persons in the positions of the applicants so desperately desire. With that incentive, what might unfold are objectives fundamental to the ethos of a new constitutional order. The families of those unlawfully tortured, maimed or traumatised become more empowered to discover the truth, the perpetrators become exposed to opportunities to obtain relief from the burden of a guilt and an anxiety they might be living with for many long years, the country begins the long and necessary process of healing the wounds of the past, transforming anger and grief into a mature understanding and creating the emotional and structural climate essential for the "reconciliation and reconstruction" which informs the very difficult and sometimes painful objectives of the amnesty articulated in the epilogue.

The alternative to the grant of immunity from criminal prosecution of offenders is to keep intact the abstract right to such a prosecution for particular persons without the evidence to sustain the prosecution successfully, to continue to keep the dependants of such victims in many cases substantially ignorant about what precisely happened to their loved ones, to leave their yearning for the truth effectively unassuaged, to perpetuate their legitimate sense of resentment and grief and correspondingly to allow the culprits of such deeds to remain perhaps physically free but inhibited in their capacity to become active, full and creative members of the new order by a menacing combination of confused fear, guilt, uncertainty and sometimes even trepidation.[39]

B. Civil Sanctions

Clearly it is undesirable that persons responsible for gross human rights violations should continue to hold public office under a successor democratic regime. Consequently some successor regimes, particularly in Eastern Europe after the fall of communism, have enacted lustration laws prohibiting members of the previous

---

[39] Azapo and Others v. President of the Republic of South Africa, 1996 (4) SALR 671, 683–85 (CC).

government from holding elected or appointed office for a fixed period.[40] In practice, the net often has been spread very wide to cover officials whose involvement in the activities of the previous regime were minimal. Moreover, the sanctions of exclusion from public office generally is imposed by administrative means which raises serious questions of due process of law. Consequently, there has been criticism of lustration laws and practices from human rights groups.[41] As there is no multilateral treaty giving support to lustration it remains a questionable method of dealing with the past.

C. Truth Commissions

There is wide support for the Truth Commission as an alternative to prosecution. Priscilla Hayner has identified fifteen truth commissions established during the period 1974 to 1994,[42] and to this figure there must now be added the South African Truth and Reconciliation Commission of 1995 and the Guatemala Clarification Commission of 1996. Most of these commissions were set up by the government of the successor regime but in some instances they have been created by a political party or nongovernmental organization. In 1991 the United Nations established a truth commission for El Salvador.[43] Although truth commissions vary considerably in respect of their powers, they share in common the commitment to providing a clear picture of human rights abuses committed by a previous regime over a fixed period of time.

If the truth commission is to provide a genuine alternative to prosecution, it is essential that it be given powers and resources that will enable it to ascertain and publicize events of the past. At the same time, it is necessary to bear in mind that the very circumstances that prevent prosecution will place restrictions on the powers of the truth commission. This is illustrated by comparing the truth commissions of Argentina and Chile. The truth commission for Argentina[44]—the National

---

[40] *See generally* Mark S. Ellis, *Purging the Past: The Current State of Lustration Laws in the Former Communist Bloc*, 59 LAW & CONTEMP. PROBS. 176 (1996).

[41] *See* Naomi Roht-Arriaza, *Conclusion: Combating Impunity, in* IMPUNITY AND HUMAN RIGHTS IN INTERNATIONAL LAW AND PRACTICE 281, 288 (Naomi Roht-Arriaza ed., 1995). The Hungarian Constitutional Court had great difficulty in reconciling Hungary's lustration laws with the rule of law: see Gábor Halmai & Kim Lane Scheppele, *Living Well is the Best Revenge: The Hungarian Approach to Judging the Past, in* TRANSITIONAL JUSTICE AND THE RULE OF LAW IN THE NEW DEMOCRACIES 155, 171 (A. James McAdams ed., 1997).

[42] *See* Priscilla B. Hayner, *Fifteen Truth Commissions—1974 to 1994: A Comparative Study*, 16 HUM. RTS. Q. 597, 600 (1994).

[43] *See From Madness to Hope: The 12 Years War in El Salvador: Report of the Commission on the Truth for El Salvador*, U.N. SCOR, 48th Sess., Annexes, U.N. Doc. 2/25500 (1993).

[44] *See* COMISIÓN NACIONAL SOBRE LA DESAPARICION DE PERSONAS, NUNCA MÁS: THE REPORT OF THE ARGENTINE NATIONAL COMMISSION OF THE DISAPPEARED (1st Am. ed. 1986).

Commission for the Disappeared—was set up by President Raúl Alfonsin in 1983 *after* the fall of the military junta and was able to carry out thorough investigations into torture and disappearances. Although it did not make judgments on individual responsibility, it did not refrain from naming members of the military who had committed atrocities. Moreover it held public hearings. The Truth Commission for Chile[45]—the National Commission on Truth and Reconciliation—on the other hand, was established by President Aylwin while the military, under General Pinochet, was still in power. It therefore met *in camera*, confined its investigations to deaths and disappearances (excluding torture not resulting in death), and failed to name members of the military regime responsible for deaths and disappearances.

Although the powers of a truth commission will be influenced by the political realities of the society in which it operates, certain minimum qualifications must be met if it is to be considered an acceptable alternative to prosecution. Failing this, the truth commission will become simply an instrument for avoiding the emerging norm of international law requiring action to be taken by a successor government against the perpetrators of gross human rights violations acting in the name of a previous regime. At present, there are serious attempts to prepare guidelines[46] for the operation of truth commissions, which provide some assistance in determining the minimum requirements for acceptable truth commissions. On the basis of these guidelines and the experience of truth commissions from different parts of the world, it is suggested that the following minimum requirements be met:

(1) The commission should be established by the legislature or executive of a democratically elected regime.

(2) Members of the truth commission should be elected or appointed so as to ensure broad representation of the different political and ethnic groups of society.

(3) The commission should be an independent body and its members should be independent of the government.

(4) The commission should be adequately financed and resourced to enable it to make a full and effective investigation into the crimes of the past.

---

45 *See* 1–2 REPORT OF THE CHILEAN NATIONAL COMMISSION ON TRUTH AND RECONCILIATION (Phillip E. Berryman trans., 1994). Excerpts from the Report appear in 3 TRANSITIONAL JUSTICE, *supra* note 11, at 105.

46 *See Set of Principles for the Protection and Promotion of Human Rights Through Action to Combat Impunity*, U.N. Subcommission for Prevention of Discrimination and Protection of Minorities, 48th Sess., Annex II, Agenda Item 10, at 12, U.N. Doc. E/CN.4/Sub.2/1996/18 (1996) (Special Rapporteur Louis Joinet); Landsman, *supra* note 36, at 83–84; Neil J. Kritz, *Coming to Terms with Atrocities: A Review of Accountability Mechanisms for Mass Violations of Human Rights*, 59 LAW & CONTEMP. PROBS. 122, 136–39 (1996); Priscilla B. Hayner, *International Guidelines for the Creation and Operation of Truth Commissions: A Preliminary Proposal*, 59 LAW & CONTEMP. PROBS. 173, 178–81 (1996).

(5) The commission should have a broad mandate to enable it to make a thorough investigation. It should not, for example, be restricted to deaths and disappearances (as with Chile) but should be permitted instead to investigate all forms of gross human rights violations.

(6) The commission should hold public hearings at which victims of human rights abuses are permitted to testify.

(7) The perpetrators of gross human rights violations should be named, provided adequate opportunity is given to them to challenge their accusers before the commission.

(8) The commission should have the competence to recommend payment of compensation to victims of gross human rights abuses.

(9) The commission should be required to submit a comprehensive report of the abuses of human rights and recommendations aimed at preventing the repetition of such abuses.

(10) The commission should be required to complete its report within reasonable time.

(11) Amnesty should be denied to perpetrators of gross human rights abuses who refuse to co-operate with the commission in providing a comprehensive picture of the wrongs of the past.

III. The South African Truth and Reconciliation Process

A. Background of the Amnesty Legislation

Before 1990, when the South African national liberation movements[47] and the South African *apartheid* regime were locked in a conflict, both political and military, it was widely believed that, if the liberation movements were victorious in their effort to overthrow the apartheid regime by force, the leaders of the regime would be tried in the same way that Nazi leaders had been tried at Nuremberg. The spectre of Nuremberg was held out as a threat by the liberation movements in exile, and steps were taken to implement this goal should the regime be overthrown. The 1973 International Convention on the Suppression and Punishment of the Crime of Apartheid[48] declared *apartheid* to be a crime against humanity,[49] defined the crime to cover the principal practices of *apartheid*,[50] provided for individual criminal

---

[47] These liberation movements were spearheaded principally by the African National Congress [hereinafter ANC] and Pan-Africanist Congress [hereinafter PAC].

[48] *See International Convention on the Suppression and Punishment of the Crime of Apartheid*, Nov. 30, 1973, G.A. Res. 3068, U.N. GAOR, 28th Sess., Supp. No. 30, at 75, U.N. Doc. A/9030 (1974) [hereinafter Apartheid Convention], *reprinted in* 13 I.L.M. 50 (1974) *and* 3 Weston III.I.2, *supra* note 9.

[49] *See id.* art. 1.

[50] *See id.* art. 2.

responsibility for those who committed the acts constituting the crime of *apartheid*,[51] and empowered the United Nations Commission on Human Rights to prepare "a list of individuals, organizations, institutions and representatives of states which are alleged to be responsible for the crimes enumerated in Article II of the Convention."[52] The Convention also provided for the trial of such persons and organizations before the domestic courts of state parties or before an international penal tribunal,[53] and required states to extradite suspects whom they did not prosecute.[54] Although the primary purpose of this Convention was to authorize the trial of *apartheid* criminals outside South Africa, should they come within the jurisdiction of state parties, it also laid the foundation for prosecutions *à la* Nuremberg. *Apartheid* was criminalized under international law and the expectation was held out of a trial before an international penal tribunal.[55]

This plan was thwarted, however, by the abandonment of *apartheid* by the National Party regime. In February 1990, President Frederik W. de Klerk announced the end of *apartheid*, withdrew the ban on the African National Congress (hereinafter ANC) and Pan-Africanist Congress (hereinafter PAC), released Nelson Mandela from prison, and initiated a process of negotiation aimed at the establishment of a just political order in South Africa.[56] To facilitate negotiations between the National Party regime and the ANC, the principal liberation movement, the National Party itself released political prisoners and granted temporary indemnity from prosecution to members of the ANC in exile for crimes committed in the course of their struggle against *apartheid*.[57] The National Party government then attempted to extend this indemnity to its own security forces—a measure that proved to be ineffectual.[58] Consequently it was left to constitutional negotiations to decide on the question of dealing with the crimes of the past.

---

[51]   *See id.* art. 3.

[52]   *Id.* art 10.

[53]   *See* Apartheid Convention, *supra* note 48, arts. 4–5.

[54]   *See id.* art. 11.

[55]   The United Nations Commission on Human Rights commissioned Professor M. Cherif Bassiouni to prepare a Draft Statute for such a court, but no action was taken to implement the plan. *See Draft Statute for the Creation of an International Criminal Jurisdiction to Implement the International Convention on the Suppression and Punishment of the Crime of Apartheid*, U.N. Doc. E/CN.4/1416 (1980); M. Cherif Bassiouni & Daniel H. Derby, *Final Report on the Establishment of an International Criminal Court for the Implementation of the Apartheid Convention and Other Related International Instruments*, 9 HOFSTRA L. REV. 523 (1981).

[56]   *See generally* Debates of Parliament *Hansard* 2 Feb 1990 Cols. 1–18.

[57]   *See* Indemnity Act 35 of 1990. *See also* Government Notice R2625, GOV'T GAZETTE 12834 of Nov. 7, 1990 (Regulation Gazette 4584).

[58]   Further Indemnity Act 151 of 1992. For further scholarly analysis on this statute, see Peter Parker, *The Politics of Indemnities, Truth Telling and Reconciliation in South Africa*, 17 HUM. RTS. L.J. 1 (1996); Lyn Berat, *South Africa: Negotiating Change, in* IMPUNITY AND

B. The Amnesty Legislation

Although *apartheid* was an international crime there was no suggestion from the United Nations, following the peaceful transition from *apartheid* to democracy between 1990 and 1994, that those responsible for the worst features of *apartheid* should be brought to international justice. By 1994, the South African situation was no longer seen as a threat or potential threat to international peace, and it would have been impossible to justify the establishment of an international criminal tribunal along the lines of those established for the Former Yugoslavia and Rwanda under Chapter VII of the United Nations Charter. The new ANC-led South African government could have decided to prosecute members of the former regime for the atrocities of *apartheid*, at least in theory, but political reality made this impossible. The National Party government had participated actively in the transition from *apartheid* to democracy and, in terms of the constitutional compact, it was to be rewarded with places in a government of national unity to rule South Africa under an interim Constitution.

Politically there were only two options open to the negotiators of the new political order: unconditional, blanket amnesty, which understandably was favored by the National Party, or conditional amnesty for individual applicants. The latter was chosen.

South Africa's interim Constitution,[59] to apply from 1994 to 1996, was drafted by the representatives of South Africa's main political groupings, numbering twenty-six in all, at the World Trade Centre in Kempton Park on the outskirts of Johannesburg. After months of heated negotiations, a constitutional blueprint was agreed upon, to be given final constitutional endorsement by the South African Parliament under which South Africa had been ruled by the National Party for forty-five years. This Draft Constitution contained no provision for amnesty. In the period between the approval of the Draft Constitution at Kempton Park and its adoption by Parliament at the end of 1993, the ANC and the National Party hammered out a postscript to the Draft Constitution on the subject of amnesty behind closed doors. The postscript, generally known as the "epilogue" or "postamble" to the Constitution, which appears in the interim Constitution, commits post-*apartheid* South Africa to a policy of reconciliation, to "a need for understanding but not for vengeance;"[60] and in pursuance of this goal it provides:

HUMAN RIGHTS IN INTERNATIONAL LAW AND PRACTICE 267, 271–74 (Naomi Roht-Arriaza ed., 1995); Raylene Keightley, *Political Offences and Indemnity in South Africa*, 9 S. AFR. J. HUM. RTS. 334 (1993).

[59]   S. AFR. CONST. (Interim Constitution, Act 200 of 1993) [hereinafter Act 200]. The full text of Act 200 may be found at the home page of the South African Parliament at (visited Sept. 29, 1998) <http://www.parliament.gov.za/legislation/1993/constitution.txt>.

[60]   *Id.* at epilogue.

In order to advance such reconciliation and reconstruction, amnesty shall be granted in respect of acts, omissions and offences associated with political objectives and committed in the course of conflicts of the past. To this end, Parliament, under this Constitution, shall adopt a law determining a firm cut-off date, which shall be a date after 8 October 1990 and before 6 December 1993, and providing for the mechanisms, criteria and procedures, including tribunals, if any, through which such amnesty will be dealt with at any time after the law has been passed.[61]

In 1995, Parliament enacted the Promotion of National Unity and Reconciliation Act[62] which gives effect to the policy of conditional amnesty. Its preamble identifies the principal goals and the procedures to be followed: reconciliation, amnesty, reparation, and the search for truth.[63] On the search for truth it declares that

it is deemed necessary to establish the truth in relation to past events as well as the motives for and circumstances in which gross violation of human rights have occurred, and to make the findings known in order to prevent a repetition of such acts in future.[64]

The Act provides for the creation of a Truth and Reconciliation Commission (TRC) of seventeen members, appointed by the President in consultation with the Cabinet, to establish, by means of hearings and investigations, a complete picture of "the gross violations of human rights" committed between March 1960 (the time of the massacre at Sharpeville) and 1993, to facilitate the granting of amnesty, to restore the human dignity of victims by providing them with an opportunity to relate their own accounts of the human rights violations of which they were victims, to recommend reparation to the victims of human rights abuses, and to prepare a report containing recommendations of measures to prevent the future violations of human rights.[65] A Commission broadly representative of the peoples of South Africa, presided over by Desmond Tutu, Nobel Peace Laureate and former Archbishop of Cape Town, was appointed early in 1996 and commenced the task of conducting public hearings into human rights violations. Although several members of the TRC are lawyers by training, the majority are drawn from church or community service backgrounds, emphasizing the fact that the TRC is not and does not purport to be a judicial body. The TRC is assisted by a Committee on Human Rights Violations,

---

[61] *Id.*

[62] Promotion of National Unity and Reconciliation Act 34 of 1995, 1 JSRSA 2–385 (1995) [hereinafter Act 34 of 1995].

[63] *Id.* at pmbl.

[64] *Id.*

[65] *See id.* §§ 2, 3.

responsible for investigating "gross violations of human rights,"[66] a Committee on Amnesty,[67] a Committee on Reparation and Rehabilitation[68] and an investigating unit.[69]

The TRC has wide powers of investigation, including the power of search and seizure[70] and the power to subpoena persons to appear before it.[71] Its hearings are public unless special circumstances require an *in camera* hearing.[72] It also has the power to conduct investigative hearings in private,[73] known as "section 29 hearings." Any person subpoenaed to appear before the TRC is entitled to legal representation.[74] However, the TRC is empowered to place reasonable restrictions on the length of cross-examination.[75]

The "Committee on Amnesty," unlike the TRC, is a quasi-judicial body. According to the Promotion of National Unity and Reconciliation Act enacted in 1995, it was to comprise only five members, of whom the chairperson is to be a judge.[76] However, the workload of the Committee has resulted in its membership being increased to nineteen, and it now sits as several committees of three, with several members of these committees being judges while others are practicing lawyers. Consequently, it is more correct to speak of amnesty committees. Entrusted with the task of granting or refusing amnesty, they occupy a pivotal role in the truth and reconciliation process. An amnesty committee considers applications for amnesty and may grant amnesty if it is satisfied that the applicant has committed an act constituting "a gross violation of human rights," and made "a full disclosure of all relevant facts," and that the act to which the application relates is "an act associated with a political objective committed in the course of conflicts of the past."[77] The criteria to be employed for deciding whether the act is one "associated with a political objective" are drawn from the principles used in extradition law for deciding whether the offense in respect of which extradition is sought is a political offense. The criteria include, *inter alia*, the motive of the offender; the context in which the act took place and, in particular, whether it was committed "in the course of or as part of a political uprising, disturbance or event;" the gravity of the act; the

---

66   *Id.* §§ 3(3)(a), 12–15.

67   *See* Act 34 of 1995, *supra* note 62, §§ 3(3)(b), 16–22.

68   *See id.* §§ 3(3)(c), 23–27.

69   *See id.* §§ 3(3)(d), 28.

70   *See id.* § 32.

71   *See id.* § 29.

72   *See* Act 34 of 1995, *supra* note 62, § 33.

73   *See id.* § 29.

74   *See id.* § 34.

75   *See id.*

76   *See id.* § 17.

77   Act 34 of 1995, *supra* note 62, §§ 10(1), 19(3)(b)(iii).

objective of the act, and in particular, whether it was "primarily directed at a political opponent or State property or personnel or against private property or individuals;" and the relationship between the act and the political objective pursued, and "in particular the directness and proximity of the relationship and the proportionality of the act to the objective pursued."[78] A person granted amnesty shall not be criminally or civilly liable in respect of the act in question.[79]

The Amnesty Committees, like the TRC, conduct their hearings in public. Both applicants and victims are entitled to legal representation.

In 1996 the interim Constitution of 1993 was replaced by the Constitution of the Republic of South Africa.[80] A Schedule to the 1996 Constitution dealing with transitional arrangements provides that all the provisions relating to amnesty contained in the 1993 interim Constitution are deemed to be part of the new Constitution.[81]

C. Special Features of the Legislation

The South African Truth and Reconciliation process has a number of unusual features that require special mention, the most unusual feature being that the inquiry into the events of the past is not limited to acts committed in furtherance of the *apartheid* state. Members of the liberation movements, notably the ANC, and PAC, together with officers of the *apartheid* regime, fall within the terms of reference of the Commission.[82]

The ANC and PAC, inevitably, were guilty of "the gross violation of human rights" in the course of their attempts to overthrow the *apartheid* regime by force. Innocent civilians were killed and maimed by acts of violence directed at civilian targets.[83] Moreover, suspected spies were brutally tortured in the military camps of the liberation movements in neighboring territories.[84] Despite this, the ANC had every right to claim that it occupied the moral high ground as it was engaged in a

---

78 *Id.* § 20(3).

79 *See id.* § 20(7)(a).

80 S. Afr. Const. (Act 108 of 1996) [hereinafter Act 108]. The full text of the Act 108 can be found at the home page of South Africa's Parliament at (visited Sept. 29, 1998) <http://www.parliament.gov.za/legislation/>.

81 *See id.* at sched. 6, § 22.

82 *See id.* § 4(a)(iv).

83 For example, see the tavern bombing carried out by ANC member Robert McBride in 1986, which killed three and injured sixty-nine others. *See* Mark Gerisser, *The Witness*, N.Y. Times, June 22, 1997, at 32.

84 Between 1992 and 1993, three nongovernmental commissions of inquiry, two appointed by the ANC itself, examined allegations of human rights violations committed by the ANC in military camps and found that the ANC had indeed been guilty of torture and other forms of mistreatment. *See* Berat, *supra* note 58, at 274–75.

war of national liberation, legitimized or condoned by the United Nations,[85] against a government whose policies and practices had been condemned by the United Nations as an international crime against humanity.[86] The Promotion of National Unity and Reconciliation Act, however, fails to distinguish between the moral culpability of the opposing sides and subjects the agents of both sides to the amnesty process. Unfortunately this even-handedness, which was a necessary consequence of the political compromise that led to the adoption of the amnesty law, and which aimed at dispelling accusations of victors' justice, has been construed by supporters of the *apartheid* regime as recognition of the "moral equality" of those who promoted and those who opposed *apartheid*. Such a conclusion takes no account of the nature of *apartheid*, ranked with slavery and Nazism as the grossest manifestations of racial cruelty in modern history.

Another surprising feature of the Promotion of National Unity and Reconciliation Act is that it fails to provide for an investigation into the injustices of *apartheid*, i.e., its systematic racial discrimination and domination, or to require the functionaries of the *apartheid* state to seek amnesty for their complicity in the crime of *apartheid*. The "gross violations of human rights" investigated by the TRC and the Committee on Amnesty are confined, in terms of the definition of this phrase in the Act, to the "killing, abduction, torture or severe ill-treatment of any person."[87] Clearly the phrase "severe ill-treatment of any person" is to be narrowly interpreted to mean physical ill-treatment, as this accords with the categories of crimes that precede it. Thus, "gross human rights violations" are limited to acts that were crimes under the *apartheid* legal order—such as murder, culpable homicide, kidnapping, and assault. There is no attempt to bring within the ambit of the inquiry acts that constituted a crime under international law but were not criminal under the law of *apartheid*.[88] Although this interpretation has been disputed,[89] the TRC has made little effort to examine the impact of discriminatory laws that seriously

---

[85]   *See* KADER ASMAL ET AL., RECONCILIATION THROUGH TRUTH: A RECKONING OF APARTHEID'S CRIMINAL GOVERNANCE 15, 42, 180, 188 (1996). For scholarly treatment of national liberation movements, see generally HEATHER A. WILSON, INTERNATIONAL LAW AND THE USE OF FORCE BY NATIONAL LIBERATION MOVEMENTS (1988).

[86]   Numerous resolutions of the U.N. General Assembly labelled apartheid a crime against humanity. *See, e.g., Policies of Apartheid of the Government of South Africa*, G.A. Res. 39/72, 99th mtg. (1984) (visited Oct. 24, 1998) <gopher://gopher.un.org/00/ga/recs/39/72>; *see also* Apartheid Convention, *supra* note 48. For further commentary, see ASMAL, *supra* note 85, at 189–91.

[87]   Act 34 of 1995, *supra* note 62, § 1.

[88]   Many of the lawfully prescribed practices of *apartheid* relating to systematic discrimination and persecution on racial grounds, but not involving physical violence to the person, might be categorized as crimes against humanity under customary international law or as crimes of *apartheid* under the 1973 Convention on the Suppression and Punishment of the Crime of Apartheid. *See* Apartheid Convention, *supra* note 48.

[89]   *See, e.g.*, ASMAL, *supra* note 85, at 25.

violated the human rights of black South Africans but did not involve acts of physical violence. Moreover, the Committee on Amnesty has not received applications for amnesty from the functionaries of *apartheid* responsible for administering the laws governing race classification, social segregation, influx control, or population removals.[90] To bring such acts within the purview of the truth and reconciliation process, it would have been necessary to denounce the validity of the laws of *apartheid* with retrospective effect, and this the legislature was not prepared to do out of respect for the political compromise that constituted the foundation of the process, the Rule of Law and the principle of legality.

D. The Truth and Reconciliation Process in Practice

The TRC has completed its hearings but still has to produce its report and recommendations. The Committee on Amnesty is behind schedule due to an extension of the cut-off date for crimes qualifying for amnesty from December 6, 1993 to May 10, 1994 (to include atrocities committed by members of the right-wing white Afrikaner Weerstandsbeweging (AWB) and the Azanian People's Liberation Movement (APLA, the military wing of the PAC) and an extension of the deadline for the submission of applications from December 6, 1996, to September 30, 1997. Consequently it seems unlikely that this part of the process will be completed before mid-1999.

Hearings held by the TRC and its committees on Human Rights Violations and Reparation and Rehabilitation have been public, and televised throughout the country on a wide field of subjects ranging from particular atrocities to contextual themes designed to explain the nature of *apartheid* and its impact on South African society: on the sufferings of the victims of *apartheid* (at which victims and their families have given graphic accounts of systematic police torture); on the conduct of the security forces; on the impairment of human dignity; on prison conditions; on the conflict between the Inkatha Freedom Party (IFP) and the ANC in Kwa Zulu/Natal; on the shooting of ANC demonstrators by the Ciskei police at Bisho in 1992; and on the activities of Winnie Madikizela-Mandela and her notorious "football club." In pursuit of its objective to make known the fate or whereabouts of victims the TRC's investigating unit has been able to find, and exhume, the bodies of some of the disappeared. In addition, all the major political parties have appeared before it, with TRC exploring such themes as the complicity of the media, business, the legal and medical professions, and the churches in the *apartheid* state. Despite repeated requests, the TRC failed to secure the presence of former President, Pieter W. Botha, to answer questions about the role of the State Security Council under his presidency in the gross violation of human rights. Botha is, however, presently

---

[90] *See generally* JOHN DUGARD, HUMAN RIGHTS AND THE SOUTH AFRICAN LEGAL ORDER (1978) (providing an account of these laws).

on trial on charges of contempt of the Commission arising out of his refusal to appear before it.[91]

Undoubtedly the two-week hearing in November 1997 on the allegations of kidnapping, murder, torture and assault against Mrs. Winnie Madikizela-Mandela received the most media attention.[92] Other hearings were, however, of greater historical importance as they provided the South African people with a picture of human suffering and police brutality that had been withheld from the public during the *apartheid* years. The hearings on the role of the judiciary succeeded in showing the extent to which judges had collaborated with the *apartheid* state by their acquiescent enforcement of the discriminatory and repressive laws of *apartheid*; and the refusal of judges to testify in person before the TRC did little to restore public confidence in the judiciary.[93]

Fears that the proceedings before the TRC would be judicialized were soon realised when alleged perpetrators challenged their names being mentioned to their detriment in proceedings before the TRC or its Committee on Human Rights Violations without being given reasonable and timeous notice.[94] After several contradictory judicial decisions had been given on this challenge,[95] the Appellate Division of the Supreme Court of South Africa held that the TRC and the Committee on Human Rights Violations were "under a duty to act fairly towards persons implicated to their detriment by evidence or information coming before the Committee in the course of its investigations and/or hearings" because the Committee's findings might lead to criminal or court proceedings against such persons—if they were not granted amnesty.[96] The court accordingly found that

procedural fairness demands not only that a person implicated be given reasonable and timeous notice of the hearing, but also that he or she is at the same time informed of the substance of the allegations against him or her, with sufficient detail to know what the case is all about.[97]

---

91 Section 36 of Act 34 of 1995, *supra* note 62, gives the Commission broad contempt powers similar to those enjoyed by courts of law.

92 *See generally* Terry Anderson, *Winnie Madikizela-Mandela Should Be Denied Any Public Role*, THE TIMES UNION (Albany, N.Y.), Dec. 14, 1997, at e3; Gwynne Dyer, *Winnie: Africa's Most Dangerous Woman?*, JAKARTA POST, Dec. 13, 1997, at 5.

93 *But see The Truth and Reconciliation Commission, and the Bench: Legal Practitioners and Legal Academics*, 115 S. AFR. L.J. 15 (1998).

94 Challenges were brought by Du Preez and Janse Van Rensberg, some of the most notorious members of the security police, and by Gideon Nieuwoudt, who played a major part in many of the police atrocities committed in the Eastern Cape. Du Preez and Janse van Rensburg have been linked with the poisoning and disappearance of activist Phil Mtimkulu.

95 *See* Truth and Reconciliation Comm'n v. Du Preez and Another, 1996 (3) SALR 997 (C); Nieuwoudt v. Truth and Reconciliation Comm'n, 1997 (2) SALR (SECLD) 70.

96 Du Preez and Another v. Truth and Reconciliation Comm'n, 1997 (3) SALR 204, 233 (A).

97 *Id.* at 234.

This decision fails to distinguish between TRC hearings designed to provide victims with an opportunity to tell their stories and amnesty hearings in which the culpability of a perpetrator is the issue.[98] The result is that TRC hearings have come to resemble criminal trials, with both victims or their families and the alleged perpetrators of human rights violations represented by lawyers determined to drag out the examination and cross-examination of witnesses.

In theory, the decision of the Appellate Division might be interpreted to mean that no perpetrator of a gross human rights violation could be named in a TRC hearing unless he or she had been timeously notified. In practice, this has not happened and the TRC has been unable to prevent victims from naming perpetrators in the course of hearings.[99]

Amnesty committees faced with the task of considering some 8,000 applications, have made little progress, as the judicial nature of the proceedings has resulted in time-consuming "trials." While members of the military generally have refused to apply for amnesty, their counterparts in the *apartheid* security police clearly have decided that amnesty offers them the most secure future. This has resulted in a succession of hearings in which members of the security police have confessed to the assassination and torture of anti-*apartheid* activists in pursuance of superior orders to "eliminate" or "remove" such persons or because of their own perception as to what would best advance the interest of the *apartheid* state. The coldly clinical testimony of the planning and execution of the assassinations has clearly shaken many white South Africans who believed the explanation of the National Party regime that allegations of police brutality during the *apartheid* era were simply "communist propaganda." The amnesty hearings of members of APLA, the military wing of the PAC, have been equally distressing. Here "soldiers" have testified of their orders to kill whites in churches and night clubs in the months before the 1994 democratic elections and of the savage manner in which these orders were executed.

As shown above, amnesty is conditional and not automatic. An applicant must satisfy the Committee that he or she committed the crime "with a political objective" and has made a full disclosure of the relevant facts. To date, with some 2,000 applications still to be heard, amnesty committees have upheld 125 applications and dismissed about 4571 applications, on the grounds of incomplete disclosure, the absence of a political objective, the disproportionality of the act to the objective pursued or failure to meet other requirements of the legislation.[100] Unfortunately, the committees have failed to give clear guidelines as to how the amnesty tests are to be interpreted. While this might have been acceptable when there was only one

---

[98] *See* Nieuwoudt v. Truth and Reconciliation Comm'n, 1997 (2) SALR 70, at 74–75 (SECLD) (discussing the remarks of A.J. Buchanan).

[99] *See* Jeremy Sarkin, *The Trials and Tribulations of South Africa's Truth and Reconciliation Commission*, 12 S. AFR. J. HUM. RTS. 617, 634 (1996).

[100] For reference to these statistics, see the South African newspapers CITY PRESS, Aug. 2, 1998, at 2; BUSINESS DAY, Aug. 3, 1998, at 2; SUNDAY INDEPENDENT, Aug. 2, 1998, at 10.

amnesty committee there now are several committees in operation which, inevitably, gives rise to a risk that inconsistent interpretations may be given to the concepts of "political objective" and nondisclosure.

E. Prosecutions

Many guilty of gross human rights violations have chosen not to apply for amnesty in the belief that evidence of their wrongdoing will not be forthcoming. Undoubtedly the acquittal of the former Minister of Defence, Magnus Malan, and his generals, for murder arising from the KwaMakutha massacre, has strengthened their conviction that they are untouchable. (In this case, thirteen civilians, mainly woman and children, were killed in KwaZulu by IFP soldiers trained by the South African Defence Force. Magnus Malan and his generals were tried for their role in training and equipping the soldiers.)[101]

Subsequent events have called the approach into question. Major Eugene de Kock, a member of the notorious Vlakplaas Unit responsible for counter insurgency operations was found guilty in August 1996 of six counts of murder and some thirty other charges, ranging from attempted murder to fraud, and sentenced to 212 years of imprisonment.[102] He has applied for amnesty, but it seems unlikely that all of his crimes will fall within the generous provisions of the amnesty legislation. Another member of this Unit, Ferdi Barnard, presently is facing charges of murder arising out of the assassination in 1989 of academic activist David Webster.[103] He did not apply for amnesty before the cut-off date. Prosecutors in several of the provinces are now bringing charges against other members of the Vlakplaas Unit. This emphasizes the fact that South African law does not confer blanket amnesty on *apartheid's* criminals.

For many, it is now too late to apply for amnesty and they will have to live with the fear of possible prosecution. This applies to former cabinet ministers, senior police, and military officers, most of whom have not applied for amnesty. Inevitably the "foot soldiers" of the *apartheid* state, who have applied for amnesty, have blamed their superiors for issuing orders to kill, which they simply executed. If they produce evidence of this complicity, the leaders of the *apartheid* state will come to regret their decision not to ask for amnesty.

Amnesty in South Africa is conditional. An applicant must satisfy an amnesty committee that the crime was committed with a political objective, that the crime was proportionate to this objective, and that a full disclosure has been made. Those

---

[101] *See* Mary Braid, *Moments that Made the Year: Divisions of the Past Still Cloud the Rainbow Nation: Abolished in Theory, Apartheid is Everywhere*, THE INDEPENDENT (London), Dec. 26, 1996, at 14.

[102] *See* Alec Russell, *Apartheid's Assassin*, THE DAILY TELEGRAPH, May 3, 1997, at 22.

[103] *See* Stephane Bothma, *Will Pillow Talk be This Man's Undoing?*, BUSINESS DAY (South Africa), May 21, 1998, at 18.

who fail to do this will remain in prison if they have already been convicted (as in the case of Eugene de Kock and other members of the security forces already convicted and sentenced to imprisonment) or face prosecution for the crimes for which they were refused amnesty.

F. Reparations

The Promotion of National Unity and Reconciliation Act established a Committee on Reparation and Rehabilitation to consider the question of reparation[104] and empowers the full TRC

> to make recommendations with regard to the policy which should be followed or measures which should be taken with regard to the granting of reparation to victims or the taking of other measures aimed at rehabilitating and restoring the human and civil dignity of victims.[105]

Although this subject will be dealt with more fully in the final report, the TRC has unveiled an ambitious reparations policy, in terms of which some 22,000 victims of *apartheid* will each be paid annual amounts of R24,000 (approximately US$4,000) for six years.[106] The plan will cost the state R3 billion. Appeals have, however, been made to the business sector to contribute substantially to this sum, in order to atone for its collaboration with the *apartheid* state.

IV. Does South Africa's Truth and Reconciliation Process Comply with International Norms?

The international community has given its full support to South Africa's truth and reconciliation process. It has been hailed as a creative method of dealing with the past and there have been no calls for the prosecution of *apartheid* criminals before a specially constituted international tribunal or South Africa's own courts. On the contrary, the world has applauded the generosity of the majority government personified by President Nelson Mandela and the commitment to reconciliation displayed by Desmond Tutu.

In South Africa itself the granting of amnesty from criminal prosecution and civil claims, albeit conditional, has not been so well received. The families of many tortured and killed by the agents of the *apartheid* regime have protested that they should be brought to trial and punished. Consequently many applications for amnesty, notably those of the killers of Steve Biko, Griffith Mxenge, Mathew

---

104 *See* Act 34 of 1995, *supra* note 62, §§ 23–27.

105 *Id.* § 4(f)(i).

106 The South African unit of currency, the Rand, is presently worth about $1.80. It has depreciated substantially in the past year.

Goniwe and Chris Hani, have been challenged by the families of the deceased on the ground that they fail to make a full disclosure of what happened or that the crimes were not committed with a political objective. Moreover an unsuccessful attempt was made to set aside the amnesty legislation itself on constitutional grounds.

In *Azanian Peoples Organization (AZAPO) v. President of the Republic of South Africa,*[107] AZAPO and the relatives of some of apartheid's best-known victims—Steve Biko, Griffith and Victoria Mxenge and Dr. and Mrs. Fabian Ribeiro—sought to set aside section 20(7) of the Promotion of National Unity and Reconciliation Act,[108] providing for amnesty from criminal and civil proceedings, on the ground that it was inconsistent with section 22 of the interim Constitution which provides that every person shall have the right to have justifiable disputes settled by a court of law or, where appropriate, another independent or impartial forum. In support of this challenge the applicants argued that "the State was obliged by international law to prosecute those responsible for gross human rights violations and that the provisions of section 20(7) which authorised amnesty for such offences constituted a breach of international law."[109]

In *AZAPO*, the Constitutional Court held, in an eloquent and expressive judgment[110] written by Mahomed D.P., that the epilogue to the Constitution trumped section 22 and that section 20(7) of the Promotion of National Unity and Reconciliation Act authorising criminal and civil amnesty was therefore constitutional.[111] Policy considerations, notably the importance of amnesty to the 1993 political settlement and the incentive it provided for truth-telling,[112] weighed heavily with Mahomed D.P. in his beautifully scripted judgment.

From the perspective of international law, the judgment is disappointing because it fails to address adequately the question of whether conventional and customary international law oblige a successor regime to punish the officials and agents of the prior regime for violations of international law it thus gave support to the constitutional challenge advanced by the applicants.

As shown above, it is today convincingly argued that both treaties and customary international law oblige a successor regime to punish members of the previous regime for acts that constitute crimes under international law. The treaties

---

[107] Azanian Peoples Organization (AZAPO) v. President of the Republic of South Africa, (4) SALR 671, 683–85 (CC).

[108] *See* Act 34 of 1995, *supra* note 62, § 20(7).

[109] Azanian Peoples Organization (AZAPO), (4) SALR, at 687, para. 25.

[110] Although Didcott J. concurred in the order proposed by Mahomed D.P., he wrote a separate opinion. As this opinion does not deal with the question of international law, no reference is made to it.

[111] Azanian Peoples Organization (AZAPO), (4) SALR, at 698, para. 50.

[112] *Id.* at 683–85, paras. 17–19.

claimed to have this consequence—such as the Genocide Convention,[113] the International Convention on the Suppression and Punishment of the Crime of Apartheid,[114] the Convention against Torture and Other Cruel, Inhuman or Degrading Treatment or Punishment,[115] and, possibly, the International Covenant on Civil and Political rights[116]—were, *as treaties*, inapplicable because South Africa was not a party to any of them at the time the acts in question were committed. The decision of the Committee Against Torture in 1989 that the Convention Against Torture did not oblige Argentina to prosecute members of the military for acts of torture committed before Argentina became a party to the convention is apposite here.[117] This left the 1949 Geneva Conventions on the Laws of War,[118] which oblige signatory states to punish those guilty of grave breaches of the Conventions, as the only treaties to be considered. South Africa became a party to these Conventions in 1952. Although they have not been incorporated into municipal law by an Act of Parliament it has been argued that they have been incorporated by the exercise of the prerogative power.[119]

Whether customary international law requires South Africa to prosecute members of the previous government for international crimes is a more difficult question. To answer this question for the purposes of the challenge to the amnesty legislation, it is necessary to establish, first, whether any of the acts alleged to have been committed by members of the previous regime falling within the jurisdiction of the Amnesty Committees (that is acts that were crimes under South African law) constitute international crimes and, secondly, whether South Africa is required to prosecute the perpetrators of such crimes. Although it has been argued that the conventional prohibitions on genocide and torture have attained the status of customary law and may be applicable to acts of the functionaries of *apartheid*, I shall confine my enquiry to crimes against humanity.

That customary international law recognises crimes against humanity today is beyond serious dispute.[120] It is likewise clear that crimes against humanity do not

---

[113]   *See* Genocide Convention, *supra* note 9.

[114]   *See* Apartheid Convention, *supra* note 48.

[115]   *See* Convention against Torture and Other Cruel, Inhuman or Degrading Treatment or Punishment, *supra* note 17.

[116]   *See* ICCPR, *infra* Appendix III.

[117]   *See Decision on Admissibility, dated November 23, 1989, Regarding Communications Nos. 1/1988, 2/1988 and 3/1988 (O.R., M.M. and M.S. v. Argentina): Report of the Committee Against Torture*, U.N. GAOR, 45th Sess., Supp. No. 44, Annex VI, at 111, U.N. Doc. A/45/44 (1990).

[118]   *See supra* notes 13–14.

[119]   *See generally* JOHN DUGARD, INTERNATIONAL LAW: A SOUTH AFRICAN PERSPECTIVE 55–57 (1994).

[120]   *See generally* M. CHERIF BASSIOUNI, CRIMES AGAINST HUMANITY IN INTERNATIONAL LAW (1992).

require a connection to international armed conflict.[121] The customary international law definition of the crime contained in the Nuremberg Charter[122] has been refined in instruments such as the Statute of the International Tribunal for the Former Yugoslavia,[123] the Statute of the International Tribunal for Rwanda[124] and the International Law Commission's Draft Code of Crimes against the Peace and Security of Mankind,[125] the Rome Statute of the International Criminal Court[126] to include systematic murder, torture, persecution on political, racial, religious or ethnic grounds, and forced disappearance of persons. In the *Barbie* case the French Court of Cassation held that the crime against humanity also covered:

> Inhumane acts and persecution committed in a systematic manner in the name of a state practising a policy of ideological supremacy, not only against persons by reason of their membership of a racial or religious community, but also against the opponents of that policy, whatever the form of their opposition.[127]

These definitions, which encompass many of the acts of the functionaries of *apartheid*, and the fact that *apartheid* has been labeled as a crime against humanity by resolutions of the General Assembly,[128] the 1973 International Convention on the Suppression and Punishment of the Crime of Apartheid[129] and the 1968 Convention on the Non-Applicability of Statutory Limitations to War Crimes and Crimes against Humanity,[130] and the Rome Statute of the International Criminal Court[131] have lead to widespread acceptance that the practices of *apartheid* constituted crimes against humanity.[132] Moreover the acts in question cover acts that

---

[121] *See* Prosecutor v. Tadič. No. IT–94–1–AR72 (Oct. 2, 1995) (appeal on jurisdiction), *reprinted in* 35 I.L.M. 32 (1996).

[122] *See* Charter of the International Military Tribunal, *annexed to* Agreement for the Prosecution and Punishment of the Major War Criminals of the European Axis, Aug. 8, 1945, 59 Stat. 1544, 1547, 82 U.N.T.S. 279, 288.

[123] *See International Criminal Tribunal for the Former Yugoslavia, supra* note 1.

[124] *See International Tribunal for Rwanda, supra* note 2.

[125] *See Code of Crimes Against the Peace and Security of Mankind, supra* note 10.

[126] *See* Statute of International Criminal Court, *supra* note 3.

[127] Féderation National des Déportes et Internés Rèsistants et Patriotes and others v. Barbie, Cass. crim. 1983–85, in 78 INT'L L. REP. 125 (1988).

[128] *See e.g., Policies of Apartheid of the Government of South Africa*, G.A. Res. 39/72A (1984) (visited Oct. 24, 1998) <gopher:// gopher.un.org/00/ga/recs/39/72>.

[129] *See* Apartheid Convention, *supra* note 48.

[130] *See* Convention on the Non-Applicability of Statutory Limitations, *supra* note 33.

[131] *See* Statute of International Criminal Court, *supra* note 3.

[132] *See generally* Roger S. Clark, *The Crime of Apartheid, in* 1 INTERNATIONAL CRIMINAL LAW 299 (M. Cherif Bassiouni ed., 1986).

were both crimes under South African law (systematic murder, torture, disappearances) and those that were authorised by the laws of *apartheid* (racial persecution).

State practice gives little support to the view that a successor regime is required to prosecute members of the previous regime for crimes against humanity.[133] However, as shown above,[134] jurists have argued persuasively in favor of such an obligation. In these circumstances it was incumbent on the South African Constitutional Court to give serious consideration to this argument.

In *AZAPO*, both the lower court and the Constitutional Court confined their judgments largely to the question of whether there was an obligation to prosecute those guilty of grave breaches of the Geneva Conventions, despite the fact that articles by Diane Orentlicher[135] and Ziyad Motala,[136] which stress the obligation to prosecute crimes against humanity, were before the courts.

The lower court[137] held that the Geneva Conventions of 1949 and its two Additional Protocols did not prohibit the granting of amnesty. The question whether there is an obligation under customary international law to prosecute those alleged to have committed crimes against humanity was not considered as the court appeared to equate crimes against humanity with crimes under the 1973 International Convention on the Suppression and Punishment of the Crime of Apartheid for all purposes and held that such acts were not criminal under South African law at the time they were committed and therefore did not require amnesty.

The Constitutional Court took a similar line.[138] It held that the 1949 Geneva Conventions and 1977 Protocols were not applicable to the internal conflict in South Africa and that if Protocol II, which deals with noninternational armed conflicts, was applicable, it was no bar to amnesty as Article 6(5) of this Protocol encourages the granting of the broadest possible amnesty.[139] Consequently, there was nothing in the Promotion of National Unity and Reconciliation Act which could properly

---

[133] *See supra* notes 34–35 and accompanying text.

[134] *See supra* note 29 and accompanying text.

[135] *See* Orentlicher, *supra* note 19.

[136] *See* Motala, *supra* note 29.

[137] The judgment of the lower court, the Cape Provincial Division, is reported in Azanian Peoples Organization v. Truth and Reconciliation Comm'n, 1996 (4) SALR 562 (C).

[138] *See* Azanian Peoples Organization (AZAPO) v. President of the Republic of South Africa, (4) SALR 671 (CC).

[139] It seems that the Constitutional Court erred in its interpretation of art. 6(5) of Protocol II. According to Douglass Cassel, "Article 6(5) seeks merely to encourage amnesty for combat activities otherwise subject to prosecution as violations of the criminal law of the states in which they take place. It is not meant to support amnesties for violations of international humanitarian law." Cassel, *supra* note 34, at 212. *See also* Naomi Roht-Arriaza, *Combating Impunity: Some Thoughts on the Way Forward*, 59 LAW & CONTEMP. PROBS. 87, 91 (1996). Both writers rely on personal communication with Dr. Toni Pfanner, the Head of the Legal Division of the International Committee of the Red Cross, for this view.

be said to be a breach of the obligations of South Africa in terms of the instruments of public international law relied on by the applicants.[140] No mention was made of the possible obligation under customary international law to prosecute in case of crimes against humanity.

The Constitutional Court acknowledged that the problem of transitional justice was not unique to South Africa. It briefly described the establishment of truth commissions in Argentina, Chile, and El Salvador, but it failed to mention the judgment of the American Court of Human Rights in the *Velásquez Rodríguez* case,[141] involving a successor regime in Honduras, or the decisions of the Inter- American Commission of Human Rights in cases involving successor regimes in Uruguay and Argentina,[142] which held under the American Convention on Human Rights that a successor regime is obliged to investigate international human rights violations and to prosecute those responsible. Nor did it consider the two recent African precedents that support prosecution: Ethiopia and Rwanda. While Mahomed D.P. was correct in stating that "there is no single or uniform international practice in relation to amnesty"[143] it is unfortunate that the court did not embark on a wider survey of comparative precedents.

Richard Goldstone was appointed to the South African Constitutional Court when it was established in 1994. When, shortly afterwards, he was appointed Prosecutor for the *ad hoc* international criminal tribunals for the former Yugoslavia and Rwanda, he was given leave of absence from the Constitutional Court. Consequently he was not a member of the Court in the *AZAPO* case. It is interesting to speculate whether his presence might have made any difference to the court's decision as he was clearly sensitive to the debate among international lawyers over the question of the existence of an obligation to prosecute persons suspected of having committed crimes against humanity. Indeed, in March 1996, several months before the *AZAPO* decision was handed down, he declared that "fundamental to all forms of justice is official acknowledgment of what happened, whether by criminal process or by truth commission."[144]

My objection to the judgment of the Constitutional Court in *AZAPO* is not that it was wrong in law. I believe that state practice at this time is too unsettled to support a rule of customary international law obliging a successor regime to prosecute those alleged to have committed crimes against humanity in all circumstances and that the present state of international law does not bar the granting of conditional amnesty in circumstances of the kind prevailing in South Africa.[145] Instead, my

---

140 *See* Azanian Peoples Organization (AZAPO), (4) SALR, at 691, para 32.

141 *See* Velásquez Case, *supra* note 23.

142 *See supra* notes 24–25 and accompanying text.

143 Azanian Peoples Organization (AZAPO), (4) SALR, at 687, para. 24.

144 ASMAL, *supra* note 85, at 13.

145 *See supra* text accompanying notes 34–36.

objection is that the court failed to address an important question that was before it, namely whether South Africa's truth and reconciliation process offers an internationally acceptable alternative to prosecution. It thus missed an opportunity to show that although there may be an emergent norm in favor of prosecution, it is not absolute, provided that the course followed in lieu of prosecution meets internationally accepted standards.

In my view the South African truth and reconciliation/amnesty process does comply with internationally accepted standards.[146] It is the result of a political compact included in a liberal Constitution[147] that was given form by a statute enacted by a democratically elected Parliament.[148] The TRC and its amnesty committees are independent of government and are broadly representative of the peoples of South Africa.[149] The process is sufficiently funded and resourced to enable both TRC and amnesty committees to make a full and thorough investigation into the crimes of the past. The TRC has a broad mandate that empowers it to investigate "the gross violations of human rights" over a period of thirty-four years and to receive testimony at public hearings from the victims of such violations.[150] The perpetrators of these violations may be named, but adequate safeguards are provided to ensure that their procedural rights are protected.[151] The TRC is required to recommend the payment of compensation to victims[152] and is obliged to submit its final report within a reasonable time[153]—less than three years. Amnesty is not unconditional. No person will be given amnesty unless he or she applies for amnesty, makes a full disclosure of the crimes, and establishes that they were committed with a political objective.[154] Wrongdoers who fail to follow this course will be, and indeed are being, prosecuted.

Both international human rights law and international humanitarian law demand that those responsible for the gross violation of human rights should be held accountable for their crimes. For this reason the granting of unconditional, blanket amnesty is unacceptable. On the other hand, political realities often prevent a successor regime from prosecuting members of the previous regime for gross

---

[146] *See supra* note 46 and accompanying text.

[147] *See* Act 200, *supra* note 59.

[148] *See* Act 34 of 1995, *supra* note 62.

[149] *See id.* §§ 2, 3.

[150] *See id.* § 3(3)(a), 12–15.

[151] See Du Preez and Another v. Truth and Reconciliation Comm'n, 1997 (3) SALR 204, 234 (A) (noting that "procedural fairness demands not only that a person implicated be given reasonable and timely notice of the hearing, but also that he or she is at the same time informed of the substance of the allegations against him or her, with sufficient detail to know what the case is all about.").

[152] *See* Act 34 of 1995, *supra* note 62, §§ 4(f)(i), 23–27.

[153] *See id.* §§ 2, 3.

[154] *See id.* §§ 10(1), 20(3), 19(3)(b)(iii).

human rights violations constituting international crimes. In these circumstances it is unlikely that international law will develop sufficiently, by means of treaty or custom, to impose an obligation on successor regimes to prosecute those guilty of international crimes. The truth commission accompanied by conditional amnesty offers a viable alternative to prosecution. Here the South African model provides a helpful precedent. It is not without flaws but it does provide a mechanism other than prosecution that ensures that wrongdoers are held accountable, and that crimes of the past are not forgotten.

V. The Truth and Reconciliation Process and the Protection of Human Rights

The fact that South Africa's truth and reconciliation amnesty process, or similar processes, may comply with international law does not mean that it is the best method for achieving reconciliation or that it is the most effective method for securing respect for human rights in a society that has experienced a systematic violation of human rights for many years. I consider these questions in closing.

The healing of a society that has suffered requires knowledge of the past. The trial of selected individuals from the previous regime will not necessarily achieve this goal, as inevitably such trials will focus on individual guilt and not attempt to provide a comprehensive picture of the atrocities of the past or to expose the social and political context of the crimes. The truth and reconciliation process, on the other hand, examines patterns, policies, and episodes in their broad socio-political setting without neglecting incidents and individual crimes. It is a better medium therefore for explaining not only who did what and when, but also why.

Reconciliation, however, does not follow automatically or even easily from knowledge. On the contrary, knowledge may produce bitterness and a desire for revenge on the part of victims, or, on the part of unknowing supporters of the previous regime, resentment that blame is attached to silent acquiescence. Understanding and forgiveness, the hallmarks of reconciliation, are rare qualities. Some individuals may achieve this, but a collective display of understanding and forgiveness—reconciliation—on the part of a nation is more difficult to attain.

Reconciliation is hard to achieve and difficult to sustain. For this reason, it is necessary to strive for the rebuilding of the society to ensure that the crimes of the past are not repeated while at the same time continuing the pursuit of reconciliation. This is where human rights come in. The ultimate goal of any truth and reconciliation process must be the structuring of society to accord human rights to all and to put in place legal institutions that will obstruct the recurrence of the events that gave rise to the process. In this sense, the truth and reconciliation process becomes an instrument for the advancement and enforcement of human rights—one not foreseen by the Universal Declaration of Human Rights in 1948, but an evolutionary extension of the methods adopted by states and the international community to secure the rights proclaimed in the Universal Declaration.

The protection of human rights and the development of as human rights culture are, however, difficult to achieve without paying greater attention to justice in the form of the trial of the worst offenders of the past regime. Here trial and punishment serve not only as an expression of society's condemnation of the crimes committed but as a warning to others, to future leaders in particular, that they can expect no mercy for certain crimes. This is the moral basis for the *ad hoc* tribunals for the former Yugoslavia and Rwanda and for the projected permanent international criminal court. This is the philosophy that has persuaded the international community, after years of inaction, to establish international criminal tribunals to try the most egregious human rights violations—crimes against humanity, war crimes, and genocide.

The South African truth and reconciliation process is unusual in that is provides not only for amnesty, based on knowledge, but also for the prosecution of those unwilling to seek amnesty. Inevitably the question arises whether it has succeeded, or is likely to succeed, in its quest for truth, reconciliation, and justice.

Together the TRC and amnesty committees have succeeded in revealing more truth about the activities of the *apartheid* regime than was originally contemplated. Fears that evidence of the actions of the security forces had effectively been destroyed or suppressed and that there would therefore be no incentive on their part to apply for amnesty have been dispelled. Today, the killers of many of the martyrs of the anti-*apartheid* struggle—Biko, Goniwe, Griffith Mxenge, Mthimkulu and Bopape—are before the amnesty committees and have made startling disclosures of how they assaulted, tortured, kidnapped and killed activists.

The mandate of the TRC and the amnesty committees, however, is to uncover the crime—*under South African law of the* apartheid *era*—committed by the functionaries of *apartheid*, and not to investigate the evils of *apartheid* itself and the acts of those who planned and executed the policies of *apartheid*. The decision not to examine in detail acts that were lawful under *apartheid's* own abhorrent legal order has resulted in a failure to expose the political, social, and economic practices and policies that gave rise to the gross human rights violations committed by the security forces. Although it is expected that the final report of the TRC will provide a history of *apartheid*, it is unfortunate that the TRC was not directed to probe the actions of the bureaucrats, outside the security forces, who executed the inhuman racial policies of the *apartheid* regime *and* those who conceived and ordered the implementation of these policies. It is true that the acts of the security forces charged with the task of promoting and defending the *apartheid* state were sometimes brutal and criminal, but ultimately it was *apartheid* itself—the systematic repression of the majority black population in order to ensure white racial domination—that constituted the worst crime.

The hearings have provided an opportunity for killers in both the security forces and the liberation movements to seek public forgiveness from the families of their victims. In one of the many moving moments of the process, the parents of murdered American human-rights worker, Amy Biehl, publicly forgave the APLA killers of their young daughter.[155] Television and radio brought these revelations and acts of reconciliation into the homes of South Africa. Knowledge of the past, backed by the appeals of President Mandela and Archbishop Tutu has done much to heal the wounds of the past. But it would be naive to contend that truth has brought reconciliation with it. Many victims demands retribution. APLA remains largely unrepentant for it actions. The IFP has consistently refused to co-operate with the TRC. And the white community, which stands to benefit most from the process, has failed to respond positively. The National Party has accused the TRC of bias, following the dismay it expressed in response to former President de Klerk's denial of knowledge of the atrocities committed by the security forces. Moreover, there has been widespread sympathy among whites for the obstinate refusal of De Klerk's predecessor, P.W. Botha, to appear before the TRC. Resentment that the past should be uncovered, rather than remorse for their acquiescence in the wrongs of *apartheid*, seems to characterize the response of the white community.

These conclusions are tentative. The final report of the TRC will provide further evidence of the success or failure of the exercise. But only time will tell whether knowledge of the past has achieved reconciliation within South African society.

In these circumstances it is premature to hail the South African experiment as a model for future societies emerging from the darkness of repression. The prosecution and punishment of the leaders of such societies may be more effective, particularly where trial is before an international tribunal. The impact of the decisions of such tribunals must therefore be studied alongside the truth and reconciliation processes of South Africa, Chile, and Argentina. Possibly the two could be combined to allow the principal offenders to be tried for international crimes before an international tribunal while a domestic truth and reconciliation commission seeks to heal the wounds of its own society by uncovering the past. The present attempt to initiate a truth and reconciliation process in Bosnia while the *ad hoc* tribunal for the former Yugoslavia continues to try those responsible for the commission of international crimes is a step in this direction.

In 1998, we commemorate the fiftieth anniversary of the Universal Declaration of Human Rights. Although there is today general consensus on the rights to be protected and on the need for their protection, methods of enforcement lag behind. State reports and individual petitions are effective methods for addressing individual human rights violations, but they fail to provide a remedy for systematic, large-scale violations. While truth and reconciliation commissions and the international criminal court will not halt such violations, the knowledge that such crimes will not go unpunished or uncovered may help to deter the leaders of future regimes. No solution is complete but the truth and reconciliation commission and the prospect of justice before an international tribunal hold out some hope for the more effective enforcement of the rights proclaimed in the Universal Declaration of Human Rights.

---

[155] *See* Renee Tawa, *Life After Death: For Amy Biehl's Parents, Path to Forgiveness Leads to South Africa*, L.A. Times, Aug. 1, 1998, at A1.

Human Rights and the Promise of Transnational Civil Society

Julie Mertus*

I. Introduction: Transnational Civil Society and the Universal Declaration of Human Rights

Today's political and legal geography presents opportunities and challenges not faced by the drafters of the Universal Declaration of Human Rights (UDHR)[1] some fifty years ago. The shape, direction, and nature of state responses to human rights problems have been dramatically altered. Non-state actors[2] and transnational networks[3] now play a greater role in the promotion and protection of human rights. At the same time, the challenges faced by the international community have shifted

* This essay benefited greatly from conversations with Richard Falk, Jack Donnelly, Ilene Grabel and Dan Wessner at a SSRC/MacArthur-sponsored workshop in Hanoi, Vietnam in April 1998. I also appreciate the comments and suggestions of Janet Lord, Keith Krause, and the participants in the 1997 Halle Faculty Seminar series at Emory University, as well as the research support of the Halle Center for International Studies and my skilled research assistants Katherine Guernsey and Barbara Wilson.

1   See infra Appendix I [hereinafter UDHR].

2   Note that Rosalyn Higgins' term "participant," derived from the methodology of her Yale Law School mentors, the late Myres S. McDougal and Harold D. Lasswell, refers to all who participate in international legal process and that this essay uses the term "nonstate actor" to refer to those participants who are not formally answerable to the state. See ROSALYN HIGGINS, PROBLEMS AND PROCESS: INTERNATIONAL LAW AND HOW WE USE IT 94 (1994); John Spanier, Who Are the "Non-State Actors"?, in THE THEORY AND PRACTICE OF INTERNATIONAL RELATIONS 43 (William C. Olson ed., 1991).

3   See RONALD INGLEHARDT, MODERNIZATION AND POSTMODERNIZATION: CULTURE, ECONOMIC AND POLITICAL CHANGE IN FORTY-THREE SOCIETIES 188–90 (1997) (on the importance of organizational networks); Victor Perez-Diaz, The Possibilities of Civil Society: Transitions, Character and Challenges, in CIVIL SOCIETY: THEORY, HISTORY, COMPARISON 80, 90 (John Hall ed., 1995) (noting emerging economic, social, and informational networks); Timothy W. Luke, New World Order or Neo-World Orders: Power, Politics and Ideology in Informationalizing Glocalities, in GLOBAL MODERNITIES 91 (Mike Featherstone et al. eds., 1995) (discussing emerging local/global "webs"); Patricia Chilton, Mechanics of Change: Social Movements, Transnational Coalitions, and the Transformation Process in Eastern Europe, in BRINGING TRANSNATIONAL RELATIONS BACK IN: NON-STATE ACTORS, DOMESTIC STRUCTURES AND INTERNATIONAL INSTITUTIONS 189, 225 (Thomas Risse-Kappen ed., 1995)

from localized national security concerns to matters of a more global nature, such as the environment, mass migration, and the human rights of women. It is in this context that the UDHR assumes even greater relevance as a guiding source for human rights advocates.

The increased participation of non-state actors and the emergence of transnational civil society opens a new space within which the rights enumerated in the UDHR can be realized. Variously called "world,"[4] "global,"[5] "international,"[6] or "transnational" civil society,[7] this space is distinguishable from traditional spaces within which sovereign states and international regimes have considered human rights. Transnational civil society in this context refers to "a set of interactions among an imagined community to shape collective life that are not confined to the territorial and institutional spaces of states."[8] The voluntary associations of transnational civil society include such entities as nongovernmental advocacy organizations, humanitarian service organizations, unions, religious groups, civic and neighborhood associations, political and social movements, information and news media, educational associations, and certain forms of economic organization.[9] The

---

(explaining how "transnationalism takes account of coalitions of non-state actors across national borders").

[4]   *See, e.g.*, RALF DAHRENDORF, THE MODERN SOCIAL CONFLICT 181 (1988).

[5]   *See, e.g.*, RICHARD FALK, ON HUMANE GOVERNANCE: TOWARD A NEW GLOBAL POLITICS 17 (1995).

[6]   *See, e.g.*, Dianne Otto, *Nongovernmental Organizations in the United Nations System: The Emerging Role of International Civil Society*, 18 HUM. RTS. Q. 107, 125 (1996).

[7]   I choose to use the term "transnational" throughout because civil society is much more uneven and issue-specific than the terms "world" or "global" imply, and because the term "international" can be too easily conflated with inter-state regimes. I also like the term "transovereign" inasmuch as it emphasizes a lack of obedience to any particular sovereign and not merely the crossing of national borders. However, "transnational" has, by some commentators, been narrowed to include only structures that embody a moral commitment that requires "a more fundamental commitment to an organization's values and agenda than the ordinary NGO would involve." Timothy P. Terell & Bernard L. McNamee, *Transovereignty: Separating Human Rights from Traditional Sovereignty and the Implications for the Ethics of International Law Practice*, 17 FORDHAM J. INT'L L. 459, 460 n.3 (1994) (naming as examples of transovereigns "the Catholic Church, the environmental 'Green' movement, fundamentalist Islam, international communism, and in many ways the United Nations. . . .").

[8]   *See* Richard Price, *Reversing the Gun Sights: Transnational Civil Society Targets Land Mines*, 52 INT'L ORG. 613, 615 (1998).

[9]   One debate that will not be resolved here is whether nongovernmental business associations should be considered part of civil society. Hegel and his followers define civil society as that which is apart from the state. Many theorists writing today see civil society as the space "mediating between private markets and . . . government." BENJAMIN BARBER, JIHAD VS. MCWORLD 285 (1995). A more nuanced view is that civil society may encompass certain economic institutions such as worker organizations and consumer cooperatives that function

state boundary-crossing of such associations makes them transnational;[10] their voluntary, non-state natures make them part of "civil society."[11]

The idea of civil society can be explained through various political and philosophical lenses.[12] For the purpose of examining the promise of transnational civil society for human rights, however, a definitional focus on relational networks helps to sharpen our inquiry. One proponent of this focus, Michael Walzer, writes that "[t]he words 'civil society' name the space of uncoerced human association and also the set of relational networks—formed for the sake of family, faith, interest and ideology—that fill this space."[13] Ideally, the associational life of civil society is pluralistic and encouraging of diverse participation. A primary measure of the strength of civil society is its capacity simultaneously to *resist* subordination to state authority and to *demand inclusion* into state political structures.[14] The opportunity for human rights advocates is that civil society can create a "setting of settings"[15] in which the human rights norms embodied in the UDHR and its progeny are worked out, tested, and applied. Hence the importance of relational networks.

The rise of civil society presents a paradox to human rights advocates. On the one hand, civil society can promote human rights norms and raise the concerns of unheard voices, including those of people oppressed due to violations of the core principles of the UDHR. The inclusive and pluralistic nature of associational groups promotes what has been seen as the "emerging right to democratic governance."[16]

---

in private markets but that have their origins outside the market. *See* Michael Walzer, *A Better Vision: The Idea of Civil Society: A Path to Social Reconstruction*, DISSENT 293, 300 (Spring 1996). *See also* DAVID HELD, MODELS OF DEMOCRACY 300 (1987) (arguing that democratic civil society is incompatible with unrestricted private ownership).

10   *Cf.* Gordon A. Christenson, *Federal Courts and World Civil Society*, 6 J. TRANSNAT'L L. & POL. 405, 412 (1997).

11   *See generally* ERNEST GELLNER, CONDITIONS OF LIBERTY: CIVIL SOCIETY AND ITS RIVALS (1994).

12   *See generally* THOMAS JANOSKI, CITIZENSHIP AND CIVIL SOCIETY (1998); PAUL BARRY CLARKE, DEEP CITIZENSHIP (1996); JUSTINE ROSENBERG, THE EMPIRE OF CIVIL SOCIETY (1994); Guyora Binder, *Post-Totalitarian Politics*, 91 MICH. L. REV. 1491 (1993); JEAN L. COHEN & ANDREW ARATO, CIVIL SOCIETY AND POLITICAL THEORY (1992); and ADAM B. SELIGMAN, THE IDEA OF CIVIL SOCIETY (1992); Charles Taylor, *Modes of Civil Society*, 3 PUB. CULTURE 95 (1990); Daniel Bell, *"American Exceptionalism" Revisited: The Role of Civil Society*, PUB. INTEREST 38 (Spring 1989); JOHN KEANE, DEMOCRACY AND CIVIL SOCIETY (1988).

13   Michael Walzer, *The Civil Society Argument, in* DIMENSIONS OF RADICAL DEMOCRACY 89, 89 (Chantal Mouffe ed., 1992).

14   Philip Oxhorn, *Controlled Inclusion to Coerced Marginalization, in* CIVIL SOCIETY: THEORY, HISTORY AND COMPARISON 250, 252 (John Hall ed., 1995).

15   *Id.* at 98.

16   Thomas M. Franck, *The Emerging Right to Democratic Governance*, 86 AM. J. INT'L L. 46 (1992). *See also* Gregory H. Fox, *The Right to Political Participation in International Law*, 17 YALE J. INT'L L. 539 (1992).

Indeed, the very existence of a robust civil society may be seen as a precondition to democratic governance and to the realization of human rights.[17] On the other hand, transnational civil society may undermine this norm of democratic governance because voluntary associations may be wholly unaccountable to any sovereign or constituency and, thus, they may act in a manner contrary to democratic principles, such as transparency, accountability, and participation.

To understand the nature and implications of this paradox, we must grapple with the ways in which the world has changed since the UDHR was adopted. Accordingly, I divide this essay into three analytical parts. First, I outline transformations pertaining to globalization and the roles of state and non-state actors. A discussion of these changes exposes the increasing importance of transnational civil society. Second, I outline transformations pertaining to methodology and ideas, introducing the concepts of "governance" and the right to "democratic governance." In so doing, I unpack the changed focus from government to governance and explain this phenomenon as interconnected with the promotion of human rights. I outline the role played by NGOs in transnational civil society, explain why their actions may rU.N. contrary to democratic norms and suggest how their participation in transnational civil society could be improved to promote human rights better. Ultimately I seek to provide insight into the evolution of international human rights law and practice and the challenges that lie ahead.

II. Transformed Space: Globalization and the Roles of State and Nonstate Actors

The rise of non-state participation and networks is a product of the complex phenomenon known as "globalization." Richard Falk has drawn a distinction between globalization from above and globalization from below to identify two interrelated tendencies: "[T]he restructuring of the world economy on a regional and global scale through the agency of the transnational corporation and financial markets from above, and the rise of transnational social forces concerned with environmental protection, human rights, and peace and human security from below."[18] The impact of globalization from below is the creation of a transnational civil society, "the thin and uneven public sphere that can coalesce at the global level where individuals interact for common purposes and shape collective life."[19]

Globalization represents four interrelated and seemingly contradictory dimensions.[20] First, globalization speaks to increasing interdependence at the world level,

---

[17]   See GELLNER, *supra* note 11, at 188. *See also* COHEN & ARATO, *supra* note 12, at 80 (civil society as "locus of democratization").

[18]   Richard Falk, *The Right to Self-Determination Under International Law: The Coherence of Doctrine Versus the Incoherence of Experience, in* SELF-DETERMINATION AND SELF-ADMINISTRATION: A SOURCEBOOK 47, 335 (Wolfgang F. Danspeckgruber & Arthur Watts eds., 1997).

[19]   Price, *supra* note 8, at 627.

[20]   These are drawn from Zdravko Mlinar, *Individuation and Globalization: The*

wherein the activities of people in specific areas have repercussions that go beyond local, regional, or national borders. Human rights problems in an interdependent world increasingly cross state borders.[21] For example, products that present environmental hazards endanger the health of people in numerous states; and the interdependence of markets reverberates in cross-border explosions when markets go bad, resulting in mass migrations and widespread threats to economic and social rights. To find solutions to such issues, human rights advocates must find a way to gather information and conduct transborder advocacy.

Second, globalization results in the fragmentation of states and peoples into autonomous groups and areas. As a survival tactic in an increasingly interconnected world, economic networks form to promote their own collective interests.[22] Associations form around identity markers such as culture, kinship, and language. Identity groups place new demands for their own rights to association, culture, and language. In addition, the formation of identity groups may, by design or unintentional by-product, threaten the human rights of other identity groups—for example, the formation of ethnic Hungarian groups in Romania may be perceived as threatening by ethnic Romanians.[23] The markers chosen by identity groups cross state boundaries, but within a demarcated territory or population (*e.g.*, Romania). The rise of the identity groups is experienced as fragmentary because it emphasizes the division of an imagined larger identity (*e.g.*, the people of Romania) into smaller pieces (*e.g.*, ethnic Romanian versus all other minority ethnicity). In such situations, human rights advocates become concerned about protecting and promoting the human rights of ethno-national minorities. The situation may even erupt into an intra-state conflict, raising a whole host of human rights concerns.

Third, to some extent globalization results in a homogenization of the world wherein, "instead of differences among territorial units which were mutually exclusive, there is now a *uniformity*."[24] Two branches to this process of unification can be identified.

The first branch, which has tremendous implications for human rights advocates, has been described as "a growing element of global consciousness in the way

---

Transformation of Territorial Social Organization, in GLOBALIZATION AND TERRITORIAL IDENTITIES 15, 20–22 (Zdravko Mlinar ed., 1992).

[21] For early articulations of the interdependence theory, see TRANSNATIONAL RELATIONS AND WORLD POLITICS (Robert O. Keohane & Joseph S. Nye, Jr. eds., 1972).

[22] *See, e.g.*, Sol Picciotto, *Networks in International Economic Integration: Fragmented States and the Dilemmas of Neo-Liberalism*, 17 NW. J. INT'L L. & BUS. 1014 (1996–1997).

[23] This example is drawn from the author's Fulbright-sponsored research in Romania during 1995–96. For an interesting discussion of the importance of this kind of fragmentation in Romania for the construction of civil society, see KATHERINE VERDERY, WHAT WAS SOCIALISM AND WHAT COMES NEXT? 115–126 (1996).

[24] Mlinar, *supra* note 20, at 21 (emphasis added).

the members of global civil society act."[25] Participants in civil society are progressively agreeing on norms for their own participation, including diplomatic language and systems of representation[26] and norms of democratic governance, as described in more detail herein. The domination of liberal norms in international politics dislocates the social construction of the world as anarchical and makes possible emerging social constructions based on a more cooperative, problem-solving civil society.[27]

The second branch of unification, which has limited utility for human rights advocates is the so-called "McDonaldization" of the world. This form of outside, consumer-oriented homogenization does not necessarily minimize the competing cultural perspectives that threaten to diminish the prospects for developing truly universal standards of human rights and more effective mechanisms for achieving them.[28] On the contrary, the forced imposition of outside ideas on a local circumstance may result in retrenchment and reactive nationalism which can spell a human rights disaster for minority groups. Furthermore, the view of globalization as homogenization discounts the complex way in which the local interacts with the international.[29] Much of what is described as "local culture" in opposition to "outside ideas" is in fact already a reflection of the global; conversely, the "local" influences and is reflected in the global.[30] Aggressive forms of contemporary nationalism, for example, are made within global terms of identity shaped by local particularities. Human rights advocates must be sensitive to the local conditions that give rise to human rights abuses and the ways in which local societies adapt and apply human rights norms.

A fourth dimension of globalization also undercuts homogeneity. Globalization produces diversification within territorial communities. The easing of borders in previously restrictive states, bowing to the pressures of globalization, results in an inward flow of goods, information, ideas, and peoples, including peoples with new and challenging ideas on human rights. Exposure to outsider ideas increases the variety of ideas in local spaces. This can have a positive impact for human rights

---

25   Ronnie D. Lipschutz, *Reconstructing World Politics: The Emergence of a Global Civil Society*, 21 MILLENIUM J. INT'L STUD. 389, 399 (1992).

26   *See* Albert Bergesen, *Turning World System Theory on Its Head, in* GLOBAL CULTURE: NATIONALISM, GLOBALIZATION AND MODERNITY 76 (Mike Featherstone ed., 1990).

27   *See* Lipschutz, *supra* note 25, at 407.

28   *See* Abdulahi Ahmed An-Na'im, *Introduction, in* HUMAN RIGHTS IN CROSS-CULTURAL PERSPECTIVES: A QUEST FOR CONSENSUS 1 (Abdulahi An-Na'im ed., 1992).

29   *See* Arjun. Appardurai, *Disjuncture and Difference in the Global Cultural Economy, in* GLOBAL CULTURE: NATIONALISM, GLOBALIZATION AND MODERNITY 295–310 (Mike Featherstone ed., 1990).

30   Roland Robertson calls this phenomenon "glocalization." *See* Roland Robertson, *Glocalization: Time–Space and Homogeneity–Heterogeneity, in* GLOBAL MODERNITIES 25, 26 (Mike Featherstone et al. eds., 1995).

as it may result in an increased willingness to accept human rights norms within a local context. At the same time, new human rights concerns may arise where local power structures perceive a threat and fortify themselves against outside influences.

Where is the state in this new global geography? The state is still active and inter-state activities pertaining to human rights issues still are important, but the shape, direction, and nature of state action has changed. All of these changes have an impact on the ways in which we think about and work on human rights problems and on how we approach the progressive realization of the principles of the UDHR.

In today's political geography, the state interacts with a wider array of state and non-state actors than existed fifty years ago. Participants in the human rights decision-making process include not only individual states but also individual participants, nongovernmental organizations (NGOs) and other voluntary associational groups, and intergovernmental organizations (IGOs). The formulation of human rights standards and their implementation now involves more than the state. They involve many non-state interests as well.[31]

The direction of inter-state interaction has been altered by an increased emphasis on cross-boundary linkages, to wit, non-state actors in state A may interact directly with state and non-state actors in states B and C regardless of the attitude of state A or whether or not state A actually relates to states B and C. In the past, the most important decisions were made with states directly connecting with other states on a one-to-one basis. Today, non-state actors interact directly with each other and with states, and the lines of communication may "cross" in unusual and unexpected ways.

The direction of inter-state interaction has been altered further by an increasing growth of international and regional networks operating at the sub-state level. Importantly, there has been a rise in direct contacts between national regulators with similar functional responsibilities, such as between environmental regulatory groups in states A, B, and C. Similarly, there has been a rise in direct contacts between nongovernmental organizations with similar human rights concerns, such as between women's human rights groups in states A, B, and C.[32]

Technological changes have been instrumental in promoting the kinds of cross-linkages that foster burgeoning transnational social movements. Many participants in transnational civil society today depend on public communication and discourse; in addition, the realms of public communication and discourse are themselves a site of transnational civil society.[33] Internet user groups, bulletin boards, and Web sites

---

[31] Spanier, *supra* note 2, at 43. International organizations may be comprised of representatives of state, and, thus, their "non-state" nature may be of a different quality than that of nongovernmental organizations.

[32] *See generally* MARGARET KECK AND KATHRYN SIKKINK, ACTIVISTS BEYOND BORDERS: ADVOCACY NETWORKS IN INTERNATIONAL RELATIONS (1998); Kathryn Sikkink, *Human Rights, Principled Issue-Networks, and Sovereignty in Latin America*, 47 INT'L ORG. 411 (1993).

[33] *See generally* JOHN KEANE, THE MEDIA AND DEMOCRACY (1991).

have constructed a new arena wherein political and social norms are proposed, debated, and determined.[34] Communication on the Internet creates a community of informed activists who are unbounded by hierarchy or territory—anyone, anywhere can be an activist on the Internet. As Leon Gordenker and Thomas Weiss note, "[e]lectronic means have made it possible to ignore boundaries and to create the kinds of communities based on common values and objectives that were once the almost exclusive prerogative of nationalism."[35]

The reaction of transnational participants to the war in Bosnia-Herzegovina illustrates the mobilization of transnational civil society in response to human rights and humanitarian crises. A global network of state and non-state actors watched the crises develop; slowly, they decided whether to take action. The network included transnational professionalized bodies designed to manage, control, and respond to such crises, such as the OSCE and NATO. Media and information sources, including the Internet, publicized information about human rights abuses and humanitarian conditions, drawing attention to the widespread use of rape as a strategic weapon of war and to the deliberate targeting of civilian groups based on their ethno-national background. NGOs monitored abuses and suggested action to professionalized international bodies, including the state-based Helsinki Committees and Amnesty International, as well as trans-state and sub-state service organizations such as the United Nations High Commissioner for Refugees (UNHCR), Croatian Red Cross, and Save the Children. Also, NGOs successfully pushed for the issuance of U.N. Security Council resolutions authorizing various forms of humanitarian and/or military intervention and for the establishment of international war crimes tribunals. States were involved in this response, both as members or supporters of the various types of bodies named above and as actors responding in their own names. The states that were most effective in addressing human rights questions were the ones that adjusted to the shifting global landscape and, in particular, worked with non-state actors.[36]

This simplified rendition of the actors responding to the crisis in the former Yugoslavia serves to illustrate the changing role of the state and the importance of non-state actors. A primary lesson of the new political geography is that transnational civil society has become an increasingly important space in which human rights norms may be given the force of law. Another key lesson, well-illustrated by the former Yugoslavia, is that state and non-state actors must work together to promote and protect human rights.

---

34   RONALD DEIBERT, PARCHMENT, PRINTING, AND HYPERMEDIA: COMMUNICATION IN WORLD ORDER TRANSFORMATION 163 (1997).

35   Leon Gordenker & Thomas Weiss, *Pluralizing Global Governance: Analytical Approaches and Dimensions*, 16 THIRD WORLD Q. 357 (1995).

36   In making this observation, the author draws from her two years in Yugoslavia during the war.

III. Transformed Methodologies and Ideas: Governance and the Right to Democratic Governance

Within the new political geography, state and non-state actors have at their disposal methodologies and ideas for addressing human rights issues that were not at the forefront fifty years ago. The rise of non-state actors and the changed role of the state are intertwined with a shift from "government" to "governance." We have moved away from the building of international organizations that generate and administer rules (a "world" government)[37] toward governing, without sovereign authority, relationships that transcend national frontiers. James Rosenau distinguishes governance from government as follows:

> [G]overnment suggests activities that are backed by formal authority, by police powers to insure the implementation of duly constituted policies, whereas governance refers to activities backed by shared goals that may or may not derive from legal and formally prescribed responsibilities and that do not necessarily rely on police powers to overcome defiance and attain compliance. . . . [Governance] embraces governmental institutions, but it also subsumes informal, nongovernmental mechanisms whereby those persons and organizations within its purview move ahead, satisfy their needs, and fulfill their wants.[38]

Some environmental activists, to give one illustration, have argued in favor of good environmental governance[39] while at the same time not pushing for the creation of a uniform government on the environment.[40] Good environmental governance would reflect such values as transparency, accountability, and accessibility in a "more or less formalized bundle of rules, roles, and relationships that define the social practice of states and nonstate participants interacting in various issue areas [such as the environment], rather than formal interstate organizations with budgets and buildings and authority to make rules and impose sanctions."[41]

---

[37] For a reformist call for global governance that still embodies an institutional focus, see COMMON RESPONSIBILITY IN THE 1990S: THE STOCKHOLM INITIATIVE ON GLOBAL SECURITY AND GOVERNANCE 35–42 (1991).

[38] James N. Rosenau, *Governance, Order and Change in World Politics, in* GOVERNANCE WITHOUT GOVERNMENT: ORDER AND CHANGE IN WORLD POLITICS (James Rosenau & Ernst-Otto Czempiel eds., 1992).

[39] *See, e.g.*, ORAN R. YOUNG, INTERNATIONAL GOVERNANCE: PROTECTING THE ENVIRONMENT IN A STATELESS SOCIETY (1994).

[40] *See, e.g.*, Daniel C. Esty, *Stepping up to the Global Environment Challenge*, 8 FORDHAM ENVTL. L.J. 103 (1996).

[41] David Kennedy, *New Approaches to Comparative Law: Comparativism and International Governance*, 1997 UTAH L. REV. 545, 549 n.4 (1997). *See also* Benedict Kingsbury, *The Tuna Dolphin Controversy, the World Trade Organization, and the Liberal Project to Reconceptualize International Law*, 5 Y.B. INT'L ENVTL. L. 1, 27–28 (1994).

Governance embraces two distinct components. The first component is characterized by an increase in the delegation of public functions to particularized bodies operating on the basis of professional technique and with stated goals of greater transparency, accountability, and more inclusive participation. Environmental regulatory bodies, formed on either an interstate or sub-state level, provide one illustration of groups composed of professionals who open their day-to-day policy deliberations and operations to public comment and scrutiny. The second component is characterized by an increasing growth of nongovernmental norm-promoting and norm-monitoring organizations, and reflects a reaction to the dangers posed by the delegation of public functions to particularized bodies, which may not easily be held accountable. Operating on both transnational and sub-state levels, these organizations act as "watch" organizations and push for the realization of human rights norms.

In addition to regulating who gets what, when, and how, governance has a constitutive function.[42] In this sense, global governance can be conceptualized as multiple and overlapping processes of decision for defining and distributing authority and power worldwide.[43] Global governance structures our world by determining what constitutes relevant political behavior and which dimensions of collective life are most significant. By creating the very terrain in which authority and power are exercised, the constitutive function of governance has great importance for states and non-state actors who try to exert some influence or control over human rights issues; for it is the constitutive function of "governance" that provides a source and marker for legitimacy of state governments and international organizations,[44] and legitimacy is central to the enforcement of human rights. Only human rights processes and bodies perceived as legitimate will be taken seriously; only states perceived as legitimate can enforce human rights norms successfully.[45]

A key idea arising out of the connection between legitimacy and governance is the "right to democratic governance." An "emerging right" that finds its ground-

---

[42]   Keith Krause made this point at the 1997 ACUNS/ASIL meeting on global governance at Brown University.

[43]   Philip Allott explains the constitutive nature of this kind of power as "a power over consciousness itself, through its control of society's reality-forming, as well as the power to embody the values derived from such reality-forming in legal relations and to interpret and apply those legal relationships authoritatively." PHILIP ALLOTT, EUNOMIA: NEW ORDER FOR A NEW WORLD 210 (1990).

[44]   See Franck, supra note 16, at 50 ("Legitimacy . . . is the quality of the rule, or a system of rules, or a process for making or interpreting rules that pulls both the rule makers and those addressed by the rules towards voluntary compliance"); David Caron, Governance and Collective Legitimation in the New World Order, 6 RECUEIL DES COURS (Hague Acad. Int'l L.) 29 (1993). See generally THOMAS M. FRANCK, FAIRNESS IN INTERNATIONAL LAW AND INSTITUTIONS (1995); THOMAS M. FRANCK, THE POWER OF LEGITIMACY AMONG NATIONS (1990).

[45]   W. Michael Reisman, Sovereignty and Human Rights in Contemporary International Law, 84 AM. J. INT'L L. 866, 867 (1990).

ing in the words of Article 21 of the UDHR: "the will of the people shall be the basis of the authority of government."[46] As Thomas Franck argues, "the radical vision [that governments should rule with the consent of the governed and that governments that acted in such a manner would be perceived as legitimate] is rapidly becoming, in our time, a normative rule of the international system."[47] Franck terms this rule a right of "democratic governance" or a "democratic entitlement," and its supporters variously argue that it is essential for the legitimacy of states, for peace, and for the enforcement of human rights.[48]

Although the elements of the right to democratic goverance have not been clearly defined, it appears to encompass both procedural and participation-oriented theories about what constitutes a democracy.[49] One component of the right to democratic governance focuses on the electoral process. The 1990 Paris Charter of the Organization on Security and Cooperation in Europe (OSCE) illustrates this focus where it recognizes the right of every individual, without discrimination "to participate in free and fair elections."[50] The 1990 Copenhagen Document of the OSCE spells out the substantive elements of what could be seen as a "right to elections," such as "free elections that will be held at reasonable intervals by secret ballot or by equivalent free voting procedure, under conditions which ensure in practice the free expression of opinion of the electors of their choice of representatives."[51]

Another process-based component of the right to democratic governance is the bundle of rights that help to ensure free and open elections, such as association and speech rights. Rights such as speech and association are valued by participation-oriented theorists as they enable more individuals and groups to take part in political life. Process-oriented theorists underscore an independent norm of participation. As Eric Dannemaier observes, "[a] true democracy . . . must . . . feature transpar-

---

[46] UDHR, *supra* note 1, art. 21.

[47] Franck, *supra* note 16, at 26.

[48] For both sides of the "democratic peace" argument, see DEBATING THE DEMOCRATIC PEACE (Michael E. Brown et al. eds., 1996). For an early prediction that democracies are not prone to aggression, see IMMANUEL KANT, PERPETUAL PEACE 107–39 (Ted Humphrey rev. ed., 1983) (1795).

[49] *See* COHEN & ARATO, *supra* note 12, at 4–8.

[50] Charter of Paris for a New Europe and Supplementary Document to Give Effect to Certain Provisions Contained in the Charter of Paris for a New Europe, *reprinted in* 30 I.L.M. 190 (1991) *and* 1 INTERNATIONAL LAW AND WORLD ORDER: BASIC DOCUMENTS I.D.13 (Burns H. Weston ed., 5 vols., 1994–). *See also* Article 25 of the International Covenant on Civil and Political Rights, *infra* Appendix III [hereinafter ICCPR].

[51] Document of the Copenhagen Meeting of the Conference on the Human Dimension of the Conference on Security and Co-operation in Europe, June 29, 1990, para. 5 [hereinafter Copenhagen Document], *reprinted in* 29 I.L.M. 1305 (1990) *and* 3 INTERNATIONAL LAW AND WORLD ORDER: BASIC DOCUMENTS III.B.20 (Burns H. Weston ed., 5 vols., 1994–) [hereinafter 3 Weston].

ent and participatory decision-making and a government that is in constant dialogue with its citizens to shape and direct fundamental policies. It is pluralistic decision-making that is at the heart of democracy. . . ."[52] The provisions of the UDHR and its progeny can be read as "embody[ing] rights of free and equal participation in governance."[53] In conjunction with recognizing the importance of fair and open elections, the OSCE has recognized "the importance of pluralism with regard to political organizations."[54]

In any event, whether conceived as a right unto itself or as a bundle of rights, the notion of democratic entitlement has at its core one coherent purpose: to create the opportunity for all persons to assume responsibility for shaping the kind of world in which they live and work.[55] In practice, democratic governance norms also reflect such values as change and progress over tradition, growth over distribution, and so forth.[56]

All participants in international human rights discourse—weak states, strong states, non-state actors— have had to answer to these ideas of governance and democratic entitlement. Small and weak states in particular are said to have much to gain from the right to democratic governance. Ideally, norms of democratic participation provide an important role for small and weak states so that they can participate in international society on their own terms. Democratic rights are said also to facilitate order in "anarchical societies"[57] by providing legal norms and mechanisms that prevent powerful states from forcing less powerful states to acquiesce with their interests and values.[58]

But rules about democratic participation in transnational civil society, are intended to apply to strong as well as weak states, and for strong states there exist at least four types of incentives to adhere to norms of democratic governance.[59] Above all, the substance of such norms may benefit both sides, and thus adhering to them may serve a state's self-interest. Second, following norms of participation may avoid transaction costs, that is, reduce the costs of doing business. Third, acquiescing to participatory rules, even if the state does not benefit from the rules themselves, can facilitate the striking of a deal on another issue (trade, security, the

---

52 Eric Dannemaier, *Democracy in Development: Toward a Legal Framework for the Americas*, 11 TUL. ENVTL. L.J. 1, 3 (1997).

53 Franck, *supra* note 16, at 79.

54 Copenhagen Document, *supra* note 51, para. 3.

55 Franck, *supra* note 16, at 79.

56 I am indebted to Keith Krause for these examples.

57 *See* HEDLEY BULL, THE ANARCHICAL SOCIETY: A STUDY OF WORLD ORDER IN POLITICS (2d ed. 1977).

58 I am indebted to Jack Donnelly for this argument.

59 For setting forth these arguments, I am indebted to Jack Donnelly once again.

environment, etc.).[60] Finally, assuming the democratic norms have the force of law, states can avoid developing reputations as lawbreakers by respecting them.

Despite the purported advantages for all participants in international life of adhering to norms of democratic governance, however, the idea of democratic governance has manifestly yet to be fully defined and realized. Many commentators critique ways in which the right to democracy has been implemented on the state level.[61] On the transnational level, too, commentators see a democratic deficit. Somewhat paradoxically, Janet Lord notes that "it is by now characteristic for discussions concerning the democratic entitlement to refer also to the democratic deficit evident in some international institutions, the very ones which are responsible for advancing democratic principles and for promoting the establishment of democracy within States."[62] As the former Secretary-General of the United Nations has argued, norms of democratic participation "should be extended to the international arena."[63] He added: "[I]f the international community encourages democratic movements within states, it must also attempt to practice democracy itself. Within the international system, all nations—large and small, powerful and weak—should be able to make their voices heard and to participate in decision-making."[64]

But how is this to be accomplished? Exports of democratic governance could backfire. The notion of democratic entitlement, some observers fear, could "create new opportunities for Western imperialism"[65] and "a continuation of humiliating intervention by states bent on 'civilizing' missions."[66] Richard Falk has long seen great promise in a new jurisprudence of transnational civil society, yet he worries that "liberal North American scholars have been, in effect, proclaiming the universal applicability of the U.S. political and legal system, its commitment to consti-

---

[60] As Thomas Buergenthal has noted, "[l]inkage permits the participating States . . . to condition their bilateral and multilateral relations in general upon progress in the human dimension sphere." Thomas Buergenthal, *CSCE Human Dimension: The Birth of System*, 1 COLLECTED COURSES OF THE ACADEMY OF EUROPEAN LAW, No. 2, at 3, 43.

[61] *See, e.g.*, the contributors to THE MULTIVERSE OF DEMOCRACY: ESSAYS IN HONOUR OF RANJNI KOTHARI (D.L. Sheth & Ashis Nandy eds., 1996).

[62] Janet E. Lord, *Due Process in the International Legal Order: Beyond the State-Centered Paradigm* (undated paper for the U.S. Institute for Peace, on file with author).

[63] Boutros Boutros-Ghali, *Democracy: A Newly Recognized Imperative*, 1 GLOBAL GOVERNANCE 1, 9 (1995). Note that while this statement seemingly applies only to the state system, this chapter considers the application of democratic governance to non-state participants.

[64] *Id.*

[65] Dianne Otto, *Challenging the "New World Order": International Law, Global Democracy and Possibilities for Women*, 3 TRANSNAT'L L. & CONTEMP. PROBS. 371, 383 (1993) [hereinafter Otto, *New World Order*].

[66] Franck, *supra* note 16, at 80 (remarking that states with a long history of "civilizing missions" may not take too kindly to pro-democracy imports).

tutionalism, electoral politics, and civil and political rights."[67] Falk suggests that serious questions arise as to whether western style, market-oriented democracy can be transplanted to other countries and to international institutions without violating international human rights norms.[68] The idea of democracy in international human rights law, as stated in the Declaration from the 1993 U.N. World Conference on Human Rights, is "based on the freely expressed will of the people to determine their own political, economic, social and cultural systems."[69] Whenever states or non-state participants coerce weak governments to accept democratic norms, such actions can rU.N. contrary to this notion of democracy.

Both the process of legal transplants (by which politically strong states such as the U.S. persuade weaker states to adopt U.S.-style laws and institutions) and the processes of international law making (through which transnational bodies determine the content and impact of international law) rU.N. the danger of violating democratic norms. The democratic norms of participation, accountability, and transparency may be violated when smaller and politically marginalized voices are effectively kept out of the decision-making process. Weaker states may feel coerced into agreeing to adopt U.S.-style laws, and the process by which those laws are adopted may not be open to public scrutiny.

This "democracy from above"—that is, democracy imposed on states by outside forces—will likely be unsuccessful at affecting positive social change.[70] Human rights norms generally work when they are internalized and not forced on a local body politic by some outside power. One of the most basic lessons of foreign economic development that can be applied to human rights is that any transplants "must support domestically rooted processes of change, not attempt to artificially reproduce pre-selected results."[71] This is in line with Franck's argument that states and processes are unlikely to gain respect and affect compliance if they are not viewed as legitimate.

So, should the norms of democracy be abandoned altogether? No, but the norm of democratic entitlement needs refinement if it is to be seen as relevant to all societies and not merely as a transplant of outside (*i.e.*, Western) values.[72] In rethink-

---

[67] Richard Falk, *The Nuclear Weapons Advisory Opinion and the New Jurisprudence of Transnational Civil Society*, 7 TRANSNAT'L L. & CONTEMP. PROBS. 333 (1997).

[68] *See* Falk, *supra* note 18, at 47.

[69] Vienna Declaration and Programme for Action, para. 5, adopted June 25, 1993, REPORT OF THE WORLD CONFERENCE ON HUMAN RIGHTS, U.N. Doc. A/CONF.157/24 (Pt. I) (Oct. 13, 1993), at 20–46, *reprinted in* 32 I.L.M. 1661 (1993) *and* 3 Weston III.U.2, *supra* note 51.

[70] *See* Yoshikazu Sakamoto, *Introduction: The Global Context of Democratization*, 16 ALTERNATIVES—SOCIAL TRANSAFORMATION AND HUMANE GOVERNANCE 119, 120 (1991).

[71] Thomas Carothers, *The Rule of Law Revisited*, 77 FOREIGN AFF. 95, 104 (March/April 1998).

[72] *Cf.* Martti Koskenniemi, *The Police in the Temple, Order, Justice and the UN: A Dialectical View*, 6 EUR. J. INT'L L. 325, 343 (1995).

ing the universality of human rights law, Dianne Otto suggests a useful approach. Human rights, she argues, should be framed as "a dialogue, in the sense of struggle, rather than a civilizing mission."[73] In other words, the intersections between global ideas of democracy and local practices and adaptations could be viewed as a process of constant "transformative dialogue,"[74] with neither universalism nor democracy being rejected but particularized.[75] We learn about the values of democracy and its meaning for structuring relationships by paying attention "to the ongoing evolution of democratic discourses"[76] in civil society.

Otto's approach to human rights emphasizes both the relational as well as constitutive aspects of human rights. Rights matter because they define relationships; also, the process of defining and enforcing rights is done in the context of relationships. The processes of rights definition and enforcement demonstrate who we are as a society, what we value, how power is distributed, and how relationships are regulated. This focus on relationships makes particular sense in our globalized world where, as described above, the varieties of relationships, the kinds of actors, and the direction of dialogue is complex and changing. It also makes sense in a world transformed by the concept of governance because, as we have seen, this concept has key relational and constitutive components. As explained below, these concepts hold promise for transformed participation in human rights processes.

IV. Toward Transformed Participation in Human Rights Processes

The net result of the transformed political geography and the transformed ideas and methodology described above is the creation of new opportunities and challenges for realizing human rights. The *transformations* have the potential to be *transformative* for human rights advocates; full application of democratic norms in transnational civil society could result in two sets of structural changes. First, it could open a space for restructuring the international human rights system so that the identity of the system itself is altered by democratic norms in a manner receptive to human rights. Second, through ethical engagement in this process, human rights advocates themselves may be changed, as if forced to question "what kind of individuals we would have to become in order to open ourselves to new worlds."[77]

---

73   Dianne Otto, *Rethinking the Universality of Human Rights Law*, 29 COLUM. HUM. RTS. L. REV. 1, 3 (1997).

74   *Id.* at 35.

75   Chantal Mouffe, *Radical Democracy: Modern or Postmodern?*, *in* UNIVERSAL ABANDON? THE POLITICS OF POSTMODERNISM 31, 36 (Andrew Ross ed., 1988).

76   Otto, *New World Order, supra* note 65, at 400.

77   DRUCILLA CORNELL, TRANSFORMATIONS: RECOLLECTIVE IMAGINATION AND SEXUAL DIFFERENCE 1 (1993). Diane Otto employs this definition of transformation in her examination of human rights universals. *See* Otto, *supra* note 73, at 3–4.

In explaining the potential for positive social transformation, I use, as an illustration, the work of human rights NGOs, although the lessons could be applied to other actors participating in transnational civil society as well. I first outline some of the roles played and activities undertaken by human rights NGOs in transnational civil society.[78] I then explain how they may threaten democratic norms even while their existence may promote governance and the right to democratic entitlement. Finally, I suggest how NGOs could apply to their own activity a refined version of Franck's "democratic entitlement." Such a step, I urge, will improve the ability of NGOs to realize the norms of the UDHR.

Transnational civil society is a highly political space for all participants and human rights NGOs are no exception. As Burns Weston has noted, "[t]he debate about the nature and content of human rights reflects, after all, a struggle for power and for favored conceptions of the 'good society.'"[79] Human rights NGOs act within the space of transnational civil society to push for their visions of a good society. In so doing, they "constitute themselves in an assembly of arrangements so that they can express themselves and their interests."[80] NGOs disagree about the nature and scope of human rights and advance contending approaches to public order and scarcity among resources. Nonetheless, "in an increasingly interdependent and interpenetrating global community, any human rights orientation that is not genuinely in support of the widest possible shaping and sharing of all values among all human beings is likely to provoke widespread skepticism."[81] Thus, the trends toward globalization have pushed legitimacy-seeking human rights NGOs to agreement on central issues.[82]

NGOs participate in debates about the nature of human rights through a variety of tactics which allow them to play vital roles in international human rights lawmaking and law implementing at both the domestic and international levels. Local

---

[78] For a more exhaustive discussion, see David Weissbrodt, *The Contribution of International Nongovernmental Organizations to the Protection of Human Rights, in* HUMAN RIGHTS IN INTERNATIONAL LAW: LEGAL AND POLICY ISSUES 406–08 (Theodor Meron 1984). *See also* Steve Harnovitz, *Two Centuries of Participation: NGOs and International Governance,* 18 MICH. J. INT'L L. 183 (1997); Farouk Mawlawi, *New Conflicts, New Challenges: The Evolving Role of Nongovernmental Actors,* 46 J. INT'L AFF. 391 (1993).

[79] Burns H. Weston, *Human Rights,* 20 ENCYCLOPAEDIA BRITANNICA 714 (15th ed. 1997 prtg.), *revised and updated in* ENCYCLOPAEDIA BRITANNICA ONLINE (visited Dec. 1, 1998) <http://www.eb.com:180/cgi-bin/g?DocF=macro/5002/93.html>.

[80] ALFRED STEPHEN, RETHINKING MILITARY POLITICS: BRAZIL AND THE SOUTHERN CONE 3–4 (1988).

[81] Weston, *supra* note 79.

[82] The 1993 U.N. World Conference on Human Rights, to take one illustration, brought an array of human rights NGOs to Vienna, where many advanced their own specific human rights claims based on their own particularistic visions of a good society. Despite divergence among the tactics and substantive arguments of NGO leadership, the Vienna participants managed to work together to push state leaders to adopt a statement reaffirming their commitment to universal human rights. These efforts culminated in the signing of a Declaration and Platform for Action, signed by the representatives of 171 states, which proclaimed that

NGOs learn strategies and substantive information from their participation in international networks and from the teachings of international law that then can be used locally, in efforts to shape the form and operation of domestic law.[83] In some cases, key individuals act as transnational entrepreneurs by playing a critical and persistent role in pushing for normative change on human rights issues.[84] In other cases, domestic and international groups mobilize around key concerns to put pressure on state and international bodies to adopt and enforce a norm. Increasingly, it is "from the NGOs that new ideas, approaches, and solutions are springing forth,"[85] at the local, national, regional, and international levels.

The techniques of human NGOs include: the monitoring and surveillance of human rights problems; notification of emergency situations; the dissemination of information about human rights norms and their violations to the general public; the exchange of such information with other non-state actors in transnational civil society; the reporting of human rights problems to state and international bodies; and ongoing or *ad hoc* consultation with governments or international human rights bodies.[86] By investigating and publicizing human rights norms, NGOs have been extremely influential in shaping domestic and international agendas on such matters as the environment,[87] landmines,[88] women's human rights,[89] and human rights in general.[90]

"[a]ll human rights are universal, indivisible, interdependent and interrelated" and that "[w]hile the significance of national and regional particularities and various historical, cultural and religious backgrounds must be borne in mind, it is the duty of States, regardless of their political, economic and cultural systems, to promote and protect all human rights and fundamental freedoms." Vienna Declaration and Platform for Action, *supra* note 69, para. 5.

83   *See* Nira Bruner Worcman, *Local Groups Think Globally*, 95 Tech. Rev. 36 (Oct. 1992).

84   *See, e.g.*, David Lumsdaine, Moral Vision in International Politics (1993).

85   *See, e.g.*, Kal Raustiala, *The 'Participatory Revolution' in International Environmental Law*, 21 Harv. Envtl. L. Rev. 537 (1997); Patricia Waak, *Shaping a Sustainable Planet: The Role of Nongovernmental Organizations*, 6 Colo. J. Int'l Envtl. L. & Pol'y 345, 346 (1995); A. Dan Tarlock, *The Role of Nongovernmental Organizations in the Development of International Environmental Law*, 68 Chi.-Kent L. Rev. 61 (1992).

86   *See* Peter J. Spiro, *New Global Communities: Nongovernmental Organizations in International Decision Making Institutions*, 18 Wash. Q. 45 (1995). *See generally* Laurie S. Wiseberg, *Human Rights Nongovernmental Organizations, in* Human Rights in the World Community: Issues and Action 372 (Richard Pierre Claude & Burns H. Weston eds., 2d ed. 1992); Pressure Groups in the Global System: The Transnational Relations of Issue-Oriented Non-Governmental Organizations (Peter Willetts ed., 1982).

87   *See generally* Kal Raustiala, *States NGOs, and International Environmental Institutions*, 41 Int'l Stud. Q. 710 (1997); Thomas Princen & Matthias Finger, Environmental NGOs in World Politics (1994).

88   Price, *supra* note 8, at 613.

89   *See* Martha Alter Chen, *Engendering World Conferences: The International Women's Movement and the UN, in* NGOs, the U.N. & Global Governance 139 (Thomas G. Weiss & Leon Gordenker eds., 1996).

90   *See* Felice D. Gaer, *Reality Check: Human Rights NGOs Confront Governments at the*

Also, NGOs contribute to the development of international law through the submission of complaints and, through international litigation, instituting or intervening in cases as parties, serving as court- or party-appointed experts, testifying as witnesses, and participating in proceedings as *amici*.[91] Within the United Nations human rights system, three treaty-based procedures exist that provide possibilities for individuals and NGOs to submit petitions directly to the respective committees.[92] Non-state actor participation in human rights issues is contemplated also under the constitutional authority of international organizations (such as the UNESCO procedure[93] to protect freedom of association developed by the ILO[94]) and in the rules of procedure and evidence for the International Tribunal for the Former Yugoslavia and Rwanda.[95] The regional systems for the protection of human rights also provide, to a greater and lesser extent, mechanisms for non-state actor participation, recognizing in limited cases the ability of non-state actors to raise claims against states.[96]

UN, in NGOs, THE U.N. & GLOBAL GOVERNANCE 51–66 (Thomas G. Weiss & Leon Gordenker eds., 1996).

[91] For a study of the increasingly important role played by NGOs in international litigation, see Diane Shelton, *The Participation of Nongovernmental Organizations in International Judicial Proceedings*, 88 AM. J. INT'L L. 611 (1994).

[92] *See* Optional Protocol to the International Covenant on Civil and Political Rights, Dec. 16, 1966, 999 U.N.T.S. 171, *reprinted in* 3 Weston III. A.4, *supra* note 51; optional Article 14 of the International Covenant on the Elimination of All Forms of Racial Discrimination, Mar. 7, 1966, 660 U.N.T.S. 195, *reprinted in* 5 I.L.M. 352 (1966) *and* 3 Weston III.I.1, *supra* note 51; and optional Article 22 of the *Convention Against Torture and Other Cruel, Inhuman or Degrading Treatment or Punishment*, Dec. 10, 1984, G.A. Res. 39/46, 39 U.N. GAOR, Supp. No. 51, at 197, U.N. Doc. A/39/51 (1985), *reprinted in* 3 Weston III.K.2, *supra* note 51.

[93] *See* Stephen P. Marks, *The Complaint Procedure of the United Nations Educational, Scientific and Cultural Organization, in* GUIDE TO INTERNATIONAL HUMAN RIGHTS PRACTICE 103 (Hurst Hannum ed., 3d ed. 1999).

[94] *See* Lee Sweptson, *Human Rights Complaint Procedures of the International Labour Organization, in* GUIDE TO INTERNATIONAL HUMAN RIGHTS PRACTICE 85 (Hurst Hannum ed., 3d ed. 1999).

[95] *See generally*, Daniel D. Ntanda Nsereko, *Rules of Procedure and Evidence of the International Tribunal for the Former Yugoslavia*, 5 CRIM. L.F. 507 (1994).

[96] *See* Protocol 9 to the European Convention for the Protection of Human Rights and Fundamental Freedoms, Nov. 6, 1990, Europ. T.S. No. 140, *reprinted in* 30 I.L.M. 869 (1991) *and* 3 Weston III.B. 14, *supra* note 51; Articles 44–47 of the American Convention on Human Rights, Nov. 22, 1969, 1114 U.N.T.S. 123, O.A.S.T.S. No. 36, O.A.S. Off. Rec. O.E.A./ser.L?V/II.23 Doc. 21, rev. 6 (1979), *reprinted in* 3 Weston III.B.24, *supra* note 51; African [Banjul] Charter on Human and Peoples' Rights, June 27, 1981, O.A.U. Doc. CAB/LEG/67/3 rev. 5, *reprinted in* 21 I.L.M. 59 (1982) *and* 3 Weston III.B.1, *supra* note 51. *See also* Martin A. Ölz, *Non-Governmental Organizations in Regional Human Rights Systems*, 28 COLUM. HUM. RTS. L. REV. 307 (Winter 1997); Dinah Shelton, *The Promise of Regional Human Rights Systems, supra* in this volume at p. 351.

A separate development within the human rights system concerns an extension of access by non-state actors to the human rights treaty-monitoring bodies. Article 71 of the U.N. Charter grants NGOs consultative status with the Economic and Social Council. In recent years, this provision has been read broadly, and an increasing number of NGOs now are involved in the work of U.N. bodies.[97] The Committee on Economic, Social and Cultural Rights (CESCR), the Committee on the Rights of the Child, and the Committee Against Torture all permit NGOs to make formal interventions on human rights matters.[98] Women's human rights groups have taken the initiative to carve a role for themselves in the monitoring procedure before the Committee on the Elimination of All Forms of Discrimination Against Women, irrespective of any formal grant of permission.[99]

NGOs have made a substantial impact on the development of international human rights laws and policies by channeling proposals to states through their consultative and observer status in treaty bodies and international organizations, multilateral conferences, and in international meetings such as preparatory conferences for international conferences.[100] One sign of the impact of human rights NGOs is the reaction of states and international bodies to their work. As Donna Sullivan has observed, "[a]s more NGOs have come into the decision-making settings, we have seen greater resort to less formal decision-making processes, in other words, we now see that negotiating [on human rights issues] is occurring in informal sessions to which NGOs have no access. . . ."[101]

To guard against such abuses, human rights NGOs actively monitor the workings of state, regional, and international bodies established to address human rights abuses. With respect to the World Conference on Women in Beijing in 1995, NGOs

---

97 *See* Peter Willetts, *Consultative Status for NGOs at the United Nations, in* THE CON-SCIENCE OF THE WORLD: THE INFLUENCE OF NONGOVERNMENTAL ORGANIZATIONS IN THE U.N. SYSTEM 31 (P. Willetts ed., 1996).

98 For including of NGOs in reporting procedures before human rights bodies, see Sandra Colliver & Alice M. Miller, *International Reporting Procedures, in* GUIDE TO INTERNATIONAL HUMAN RIGHTS PRACTICE 175 (Hurst Hannum ed., 3d ed. 1999).

99 *See generally* JULIE MERTUS ET AL., WOMEN, LAW AND DEVELOPMENT: WOMEN'S HUMAN RIGHTS STEP-BY-STEP (Marge Schuler et al. eds., 1996).

100 *See Panel: The Growing Role of Nongovernmental Organization*, 89 AM. SOC'Y INT'L L. PROC. 413 (1995) (remarks of Donna Sullivan). Donna Sullivan discerns different types of NGOs working on human rights that can be said to fall into the following overlapping categories: the "old timers" who have long enjoyed consultative status with the U.N.; NGOs that participate largely through regional networks; NGOs that act as coordinators for international conferences; and NGOs that view themselves as playing the role of technical advisors to other NGOs and movements. *See also* Theo van Boven, *The Role of Non-Governmental Organizations in International Human Rights Standard Setting: A Prerequisite of Democracy*, 20 CAL. W. INT'L L.J. 207 (1990).

101 *Panel: The Growing Role of Nongovernmental Organization, supra* note 100, at 423 (remarks of Donna Sullivan).

were instrumental in exposing the lack of transparency and accountability in the accreditation process. By checking the norms of democratic participation and ensuring some representation by non-state actors, these transnational NGOs "make democracy safe for the world."[102]

But who will make the work safe for transnational NGOs? Without democratic safeguards, there is no guarantee that any actor in transnational civil society will be democratic. In fact, NGOs often violate democratic norms.

The operations of NGOs may be deliberately opaque. The many ways in which NGOs, acting individually and in networks, wield influence on decision-making often are "behind closed doors" and without pluralistic participation. The agenda of women's human rights groups for the U.N. World Conference on Human Rights in Vienna in 1993, for example, was developed largely by an insider group of women. These leaders sought to promote inclusion and transparency by operating on a "caucus basis" through which they did their agenda-setting work while simultaneously trying to educate individuals from other NGOs to participate in that process.[103] Nonetheless, the agenda emerging from this process did not include many minority voices on rights issues and the selection procedure of both participants and agenda items was not transparent to outsiders.[104] Moreover, the deals struck between individual representatives of NGOs and state leaders were the result of quiet lobbying, not the product of a visible and accessible process.

Institutions of, and actors in, civil society exercise considerable power, but there is no civil society parliament, no multi-party electoral process. Accordingly, the institutions of civil society may rU.N. against the most basic rule of democracy: to govern with the consent of the governed. International NGOS that have worked in consultative status with the United Nations over the past ten to twenty years, for example, are among the NGOs least likely to base their policies on the concerns of a well-defined constituency.[105] Studies have found that the closer an NGO is to the grass-roots, the greater its chances at promoting positive social change[106] because it is more likely to represent a highly motivated and engaged constituency.

Civil society groups rU.N. afoul of democracy in another manner: they may violate with impunity specific human rights closely connected with democracy pro-

---

102 Leslie Paul Thiele, *Making Democracy Safe for the World: Social Movements in Global Politics*, 18 ALTERNATIVES—SOCIAL TRANSFORMATION AND HUMANE GOVERNANCE 273 (1993).

103 *Panel: The Growing Role of Nongovernmental Organization, supra* note 100, at 423 (remarks of Donna Sullivan).

104 *See* Julie Mertus & Pamela Goldberg, *A Perspective on Women and International Human Rights After the Vienna Declaration: The Inside/Outside Construct*, 26 N.Y.U. J. INT'L & POL. 201, 221–22 (1994).

105 *Panel: The Growing Role of Nongovernmental Organization, supra* note 100, at 421 (remarks of Donna Sullivan).

106 *See, e.g.*, MANUEL CASTELLS, THE CITY AND THE GRASSROOTS (1983); Oxhorn, *supra* note 14, at 267–69.

motion. Applying Franck's theory of legitimacy, their actions are thus likely to be perceived as undemocratic and illegitimate. As explained above, specific provisions of the U.N. Charter, the UDHR, and other human rights instruments can be said to create a normative canon that embodies "the rights of free and equal participation in governance."[107] Such rights as freedom of opinion and expression (UDHR, art. 19) and peaceful assembly and association (UDHR, art. 20) create, in Franck's words, a "net of participatory entitlements."[108] Nonetheless, the specific entitlements enumerated in the UDHR and its progeny pertain generally to the rights of persons vis-à-vis their governments, not to the rights of persons vis-à-vis non-state or transnational actors.[109] As long as international law fails to articulate a clear and consistent position as to the responsibility of non-state actors, such actors will continue to neglect these rights. Although there is growing international jurisprudence and commentary on non-state actors as subjects of international law,[110] the message to non-state actors in transnational civil society is far from clear.

Another problem with transnational civil society as represented by NGOs is that it often is not strong enough to resist subordination by the state.[111] Many NGOs assume functions that were once the province of states—for example, social service delivery and humanitarian relief.[112] These NGOs must actively promote, or at least not contravene, the agendas of their donors—individual states or international bodies composed of states (particularly the U.N.). Once they become a sort of "public service sub-contractor,"[113] NGOs "are in continual danger of having their local accountabilities and ethnical principles compromised by the financial and discursive capacity of states to shape their agendas."[114] When NGOs are dependent on states, they no longer fulfill their role as non-state counterparts in transnational civil society.

---

[107]   Franck, *supra* note 16, at 79.

[108]   *Id.*

[109]   *See* Claudio Grossman & Daniel D. Bradlow, *Are We Being Propelled Towards a People-Centered Transnational Legal Order?*, 9 AM. U. J. INT'L L. & POL'Y 1 (1993); Benedict Kingsbury, *Claims By Nonstate Groups in International Law*, 25 CORNELL INT'L L.J. 481 (1992); P. K. Menon, *Individuals as Subjects of International Law*, 70 INT'L L.R. 295 (1992).

[110]   *See, e.g.*, CHRISTINE CHINKIN, THIRD PARTIES IN INTERNATIONAL LAW 2, 3 (1993); ANTONIO CASSESE, INTERNATIONAL LAW IN A DIVIDED WORLD 76 (1986); Janet E. Lord, *Taiwan's Right to be Heard by the Security Council, in* THE INTERNATIONAL STATUS OF TAIWAN IN THE NEW WORLD ORDER: LEGAL AND POLITICAL CONSIDERATIONS 133 (Jean-Marie Henckaerts ed., 1996).

[111]   *See* Oxhorn, *supra* note 14, at 252–53.

[112]   For a recent study of this problem, see Antonio Donini, *The Bureaucracy and the Free Spirits: Stagnation and Innovation in the Relationship Between the U.N. and NGOs, in* NGOS, THE U.N. AND GLOBAL GOVERNANCE 67–83 (Thomas G. Weiss & Leon Gordenker eds., 1996).

[113]   *See* BEYOND U.N. SUBCONTRACTING: TASK SHARING WITH REGIONAL SECURITY ARRANGEMENTS AND SERVICE-PROVIDING NGOs (Thomas G. Weiss ed., 1998).

[114]   Otto, *supra* note 73, at 41.

The implications of an undemocratic transnational civil society are far reaching. Undemocratic civil society not only undermines the legitimacy of non-state actors, but threatens also the legitimacy of states and all transnational relationships. Democracy is a "double-sided process" in which the state and civil society "become the condition for each other's democratic development."[115] Democracy on the transnational level is good for democracy on the state level and vice versa. Undemocratic civil society at any level of relationship can act as a contagion that squelches participation and legitimacy and thus undermines the potential for positive social change. The challenge for human rights advocates lies in making transnational civil society democratic and in a manner that can lead to positive social change.

The answer, I suggest, lies in giving content to Franck's "democratic entitlement," shaping it so that it can become *transformative democracy*. Human rights advocates should take steps to ensure more accountability and transparency for non-state actors, especially when they take on state functions. As a first step, the value of participation needs to be better articulated. We know that civil society is underdeveloped where small, participatory, and democratically structured organizations independent of the state are uncommon. We also know that human rights dialogue in transnational civil society provides a good illustration of underdevelopment when it is dominated by large, exclusive, undemocratic organizations.

But how do we refine our understanding of participation to realize transformative democratic goals? One of the main roadblocks lies in the reality that transnational civil society reflects disparities in power that are not recognized. Quite simply, well-financed, Western NGOs are likely to have more power than their poorer and non-Western counterparts, and the lack of transparency and accountability in transnational civil society is likely to keep this power unchecked. There is little incentive for the powerful NGOs to recognize the misbalance, and less powerful groups can be so marginalized that their protests are not heard. Abdullahi An-Na'im recognizes that "ideally participants should feel on equal footing but, given existing power relations, those in a position to do so might seek ways of redressing the imbalance."[116] Diane Otto goes farther in insisting that "transparency of the operations of global networks of power, of exploitation and domination, is a vitally important component of transformative dialogue."[117] Application of democratic principles to transnational civil society would do more than add a dose of pluralism. In addition to opening civil society to more diverse participation, transformative democracy would insist that all actors act ethically by interrogating any privileges they enjoy as a result of structural power imbalances. The most powerful participants of civil society themselves would accept responsibility for developing mechanisms that can enable them to address inequalities in power.

---

[115] HELD, *supra* note 9, at 286.

[116] Abdullahi An-Na'im, *What Do We Mean By Universal?*, 5 INDEX ON CENSORSHIP 10, 122 (1994).

[117] Otto, *supra* note 73, at 33.

A related element of a transformative strategy would be for the more powerful agents of transnational civil society to listen to and value the experiences and wisdom of their less powerful counterparts. While this may be the goal of many human rights advocates, rarely is it carried out in practice. We could draw from our understanding of a participatory norm of democracy in shaping procedures that would bring non-elites into the debate on human rights on their own terms. As a practical matter, at international meetings discussing human rights norms, non-elite groups "might be empowered to have control of agenda-setting, determine the questions of importance, and run meetings according to procedures they understand."[118] These and other like measures would add meaningful context to the norm of participation.

To be transformative, actors in transnational civil society must be committed also to exposing the global economic issues that undermine the ability of some voluntary associations to participate in civil society.[119] Many studies indicate that globalization exacerbates economic disparities. For example, globalization has encouraged, and in some cases demanded, privatization of social services, and researchers have demonstrated, how privatization of key social services in Latin America, such as social security, health care and housing, has exacerbated exclusion of citizens from community life.[120] For the most part, critiques of such changes in the space of transnational civil society have been left to organizations identified as "development" or "economic" groups, and most human rights NGOs have had little say in the matter.[121] To fully realize all of the goals of the UDHR, however this circumstance needs to change. Not only does the failure of human rights NGOs to engage in global economic justice issues result in less attention paid to such matters, but it exacerbates also the conditions that weaken the ability of some individuals and NGOs to participate in *any* human rights dialogue at all. As such, neglect of global justice issues contributes to the democratic deficit in transnational civil society.

A transnational human rights movement that strives to act in line with transformative democratic norms would be better poised to demand that states behave democratically themselves in promoting and protecting human rights. NGOs that are democratic in the sense described in this chapter would be perceived as more legitimate when they call for full realization of the goals of the UDHR. They also would have more credible ground on which to demand that international bodies grant them consultative status on all treaty-monitoring bodies[122] and that states pro-

---

118   *Id.* at 38.

119   *Id.* at 34.

120   Oxhorn, *supra* note 14, at 253

121   Michael Posner & Candy Whittome, *The Status of Human Rights NGOs*, 25 COLUM. HUM. RTS. L. REV. 269, 272–76 (1994).

122   Human rights NGOs may want to follow the model of NGO participation in environmental treaties. *See* Phillipe J. Sands, *The Environment, Community and International Law*, 30 HARV. L.R. 392 (1989). *See generally* PATRICIA BIRNIE & ALAN BOYLE, INTERNATIONAL LAW AND THE ENVIRONMENT (1992).

vide them with a consultative, or at least information-sharing role, on domestic human rights bodies. NGOs need not and cannot take on the role of states in promoting human rights worldwide. Nonetheless, they could do much more in the future if they are perceived as legitimate. Defining and realizing the elements of a transformative democracy would go along way toward addressing these concerns.

V. Conclusion

The human rights concerns motivating the creation of the UDHR are still with us. The good news is that our world has changed in ways that can help to give content and effect to its principles. The new space opened by globalization, the rise of transnational civil society, and the ideas and methodologies represented by governance and the right to democratic entitlement provide new opportunities for non-state actor participation in human rights standard-setting and enforcement. Non-state actors, in particular human rights NGOs, have made tremendous gains in their ability to influence the building of a human rights culture. If they take advantage of the transformations of space and ideas discussed above, they can help restructure the international human rights system. By doing so, the identity of the system itself is altered by democratic norms in a manner receptive to human rights. Therein lies the promise of transnational civil society for the future for the promotion of human rights.

Appendix I
Universal Declaration of Human Rights

Adopted and proclaimed by the United Nations General Assembly December 10, 1948. G.A. Res. 217A, U.N. GAOR, 3d Sess., pt. 1, Resolutions, at 71, U.N. Doc. A/810 (1948), art. 16, reprinted in 3 *International Law and World Order: Basic Documents* III.A.1 (Burns H. Weston., 5 vols., 1994-).

Preamble

Whereas recognition of the inherent dignity and of the equal and inalienable rights of all members of the human family is the foundation of freedom, justice and peace in the world,

Whereas disregard and contempt for human rights have resulted in barbarous acts which have outraged the conscience of mankind, and the advent of a world in which human beings shall enjoy freedom of speech and belief and freedom from fear and want has been proclaimed as the highest aspiration of the common people,

Whereas it is essential, if man is not to be compelled to have recourse, as a last resort, to rebellion against tyranny and oppression, that human rights should be protected by the rule of law,

Whereas it is essential to promote the development of friendly relations between nations,

Whereas the peoples of the United Nations have in the Charter reaffirmed their faith in fundamental human rights, in the dignity and worth of the human person and in the equal rights of men and women and have determined to promote social progress and better standards of life in larger freedom,

Whereas Member States have pledged themselves to achieve, in co-operation with the United Nations, the promotion of universal respect for and observance of human rights and fundamental freedoms,

Whereas a common understanding of these rights and freedoms is of the greatest importance for the full realization of this pledge,

Now, Therefore THE GENERAL ASSEMBLY proclaims THIS UNIVERSAL DECLARATION OF HUMAN RIGHTS as a common standard of achievement for all peoples and all nations, to the end that every individual and every organ of society, keeping this Declaration constantly in mind, shall strive by teaching and education to promote respect for these rights and freedoms and by progressive measures, national and international, to secure their universal and effective recognition and observance, both among the peoples of Member States themselves and among the peoples of territories under their jurisdiction.

Article 1.

All human beings are born free and equal in dignity and rights. They are endowed with reason and conscience and should act towards one another in a spirit of brotherhood.

Article 2.

Everyone is entitled to all the rights and freedoms set forth in this Declaration, without distinction of any kind, such as race, colour, sex, language, religion, political or other opinion, national or social origin, property, birth or other status. Furthermore, no distinction shall be made on the basis of the political, jurisdictional or international status of the country or territory to which a person belongs, whether it be independent, trust, non-self-governing or under any other limitation of sovereignty.

Article 3.

Everyone has the right to life, liberty and security of person.

Article 4.

No one shall be held in slavery or servitude; slavery and the slave trade shall be prohibited in all their forms.

Article 5.

No one shall be subjected to torture or to cruel, inhuman or degrading treatment or punishment.

Article 6.

Everyone has the right to recognition everywhere as a person before the law.

Article 7.

All are equal before the law and are entitled without any discrimination to equal protection of the law. All are entitled to equal protection against any discrimination in violation of this Declaration and against any incitement to such discrimination.

Article 8.

Everyone has the right to an effective remedy by the competent national tribunals for acts violating the fundamental rights granted him by the constitution or by law.

Article 9.

No one shall be subjected to arbitrary arrest, detention or exile.

Article 10.

Everyone is entitled in full equality to a fair and public hearing by an independent and impartial tribunal, in the determination of his rights and obligations and of any criminal charge against him.

Article 11.

(1) Everyone charged with a penal offence has the right to be presumed innocent until proved guilty according to law in a public trial at which he has had all the guarantees necessary for his defence.

(2) No one shall be held guilty of any penal offence on account of any act or omission which did not constitute a penal offence, under national or international law, at the time when it was committed. Nor shall a heavier penalty be imposed than the one that was applicable at the time the penal offence was committed.

Article 12.

No one shall be subjected to arbitrary interference with his privacy, family, home or correspondence, nor to attacks upon his honour and reputation. Everyone has the right to the protection of the law against such interference or attacks.

Article 13.

(1) Everyone has the right to freedom of movement and residence within the borders of each state.

(2) Everyone has the right to leave any country, including his own, and to return to his country.

Article 14.

(1) Everyone has the right to seek and to enjoy in other countries asylum from persecution.

(2) This right may not be invoked in the case of prosecutions genuinely arising from non-political crimes or from acts contrary to the purposes and principles of the United Nations.

Article 15.

(1) Everyone has the right to a nationality.

(2) No one shall be arbitrarily deprived of his nationality nor denied the right to change his nationality.

Article 16.

(1) Men and women of full age, without any limitation due to race, nationality or religion, have the right to marry and to found a family. They are entitled to equal rights as to marriage, during marriage and at its dissolution.

(2) Marriage shall be entered into only with the free and full consent of the intending spouses.

(3) The family is the natural and fundamental group unit of society and is entitled to protection by society and the State.

Article 17.

(1) Everyone has the right to own property alone as well as in association with others.

(2) No one shall be arbitrarily deprived of his property.

Article 18.

Everyone has the right to freedom of thought, conscience and religion; this right includes freedom to change his religion or belief, and freedom, either alone or in community with others and in public or private, to manifest his religion or belief in teaching, practice, worship and observance.

Article 19.

Everyone has the right to freedom of opinion and expression; this right includes freedom to hold opinions without interference and to seek, receive and impart information and ideas through any media and regardless of frontiers.

Article 20.

(1) Everyone has the right to freedom of peaceful assembly and association.

(2) No one may be compelled to belong to an association.

Article 21.

(1) Everyone has the right to take part in the government of his country, directly or through freely chosen representatives.

(2) Everyone has the right of equal access to public service in his country.

(3) The will of the people shall be the basis of the authority of government; this will shall be expressed in periodic and genuine elections which shall be by universal and equal suffrage and shall be held by secret vote or by equivalent free voting procedures.

Article 22.

Everyone, as a member of society, has the right to social security and is entitled to realization, through national effort and international co-operation and in accordance with the organization and resources of each State, of the economic, social and cultural rights indispensable for his dignity and the free development of his personality.

Article 23.

(1) Everyone has the right to work, to free choice of employment, to just and favourable conditions of work and to protection against unemployment.

(2) Everyone, without any discrimination, has the right to equal pay for equal work.

(3) Everyone who works has the right to just and favourable remuneration ensuring for himself and his family an existence worthy of human dignity, and supplemented, if necessary, by other means of social protection.

(4) Everyone has the right to form and to join trade unions for the protection of his interests.

Article 24.

Everyone has the right to rest and leisure, including reasonable limitation of working hours and periodic holidays with pay.

Article 25.

(1) Everyone has the right to a standard of living adequate for the health and well-being of himself and of his family, including food, clothing, housing and medical care and necessary social services, and the right to security in the event of unemployment, sickness, disability, widowhood, old age or other lack of livelihood in circumstances beyond his control.

(2) Motherhood and childhood are entitled to special care and assistance. All children, whether born in or out of wedlock, shall enjoy the same social protection.

Article 26.

(1) Everyone has the right to education. Education shall be free, at least in the elementary and fundamental stages. Elementary education shall be compulsory. Technical and professional education shall be made generally available and higher education shall be equally accessible to all on the basis of merit.

(2) Education shall be directed to the full development of the human personality and to the strengthening of respect for human rights and fundamental freedoms. It shall promote understanding, tolerance and friendship among all nations, racial or religious groups, and shall further the activities of the United Nations for the maintenance of peace.

(3) Parents have a prior right to choose the kind of education that shall be given to their children.

Article 27.

(1) Everyone has the right freely to participate in the cultural life of the community, to enjoy the arts and to share in scientific advancement and its benefits.

(2) Everyone has the right to the protection of the moral and material interests resulting from any scientific, literary or artistic production of which he is the author.

Article 28.

Everyone is entitled to a social and international order in which the rights and freedoms set forth in this Declaration can be fully realized.

Article 29.

(1) Everyone has duties to the community in which alone the free and full development of his personality is possible.

(2) In the exercise of his rights and freedoms, everyone shall be subject only to such limitations as are determined by law solely for the purpose of securing due recognition and respect for the rights and freedoms of others and of meeting the just requirements of morality, public order and the general welfare in a democratic society.

(3) These rights and freedoms may in no case be exercised contrary to the purposes and principles of the United Nations.

Article 30.

Nothing in this Declaration may be interpreted as implying for any State, group or person any right to engage in any activity or to perform any act aimed at the destruction of any of the rights and freedoms set forth herein.

Appendix II
International Covenant on Economic, Social and Cultural Rights

Concluded at New York, December 16, 1966 (entered into force, January 3, 1976), 993 U.N.T.S. 3, reprinted in 6 I.L.M. 360 (1967) and 3 International Law and World Order: Basic Documents III.A.2 (Burns H. Weston ed., 5 vols., 1994-).

The State Parties to the Present Convention,

Considering that, in accordance with the principles proclaimed in the Charter of the United Nations, recognition of the inherent dignity and of the equal and inalienable rights of all members of the human family is the foundation of freedom, justice and peace in the world,

Recognizing that these rights derive from the inherent dignity of the human person,

Recognizing that, in accordance with the Universal Declaration of Human Rights, the ideal of free human beings enjoying freedom from fear and want can only be achieved if conditions are created whereby everyone may enjoy his economic, social and cultural rights, as well as his civil and political rights,

Considering the obligation of States under the Charter of the United Nations to promote universal respect for, and observance of, human rights and freedom,

Realizing that the individual, having duties to other individuals and to the community to which he belongs, is under a responsibility to strive for the promotion and observance of the rights recognized in the present Covenant,

Agree upon the following articles:

PART I

Article I

1. All peoples have the right of self-determination. By virtue of that right they freely determine their political status and freely pursue their economic, social and cultural development.

2. All peoples may, for their own ends, freely dispose of their natural wealth and resources without prejudice to any obligations arising out of international economic

co-operation based upon the principle of mutual benefit, and international law. In no case may a people be deprived of its own means of subsistence.

3.   The States Parties to the present Covenant, including those having responsibility for the administration of Non-Self-Governing and Trust Territories, shall promote the realization of the right of self-determination, and shall respect that right, in conformity with the provisions of the Charter of the United Nations.

PART II

Article 2

1.   Each State Party to the present Covenant undertakes to take steps, individually and through international assistance and co-operation, especially economic and technical, to the maximum of its available resources, with a view to achieving progressively the full realization of the rights recognized in the present Covenant by all appropriate means, including particularly the adoption of legislative measures.

2.   The States Parties to the present Covenant undertake to guarantee that the rights enunciated in the present Covenant will be exercised without discrimination of any kind as to race, colour, sex, language, religion, political or other opinion, national or social origin, property, birth or other status.

3.   Developing countries, with due regard to human rights and their national economy, may determine to what extent they would guarantee the economic rights recognized in the present Covenant to non-nationals.

Article 3

The States Parties to the present Covenant undertake to ensure the equal right of men and women to the enjoyment of all economic, social and cultural rights set forth in the present Covenant.

Article 4

The States Parties to the present Covenant recognize that, in the enjoyment of those rights provided by the State in conformity with the present Covenant, the State may subject such rights only to such limitations as are determined by law only in so far as this may be compatible with the nature of these rights and solely for the purpose of promoting the general welfare in a democratic society.

Article 5

1.   Nothing in the present Covenant may be interpreted as implying for any State, group or person any right to engage in any activity or to perform any act aimed at

the destruction of any of the rights or freedoms recognized herein, or at their limitation to a greater extent than is provided for in the present Covenant.

2. No restriction upon or derogation from any of the fundamental human rights recognized or existing in any country in virtue of law, conventions, regulations or custom shall be admitted on the pretext that the present Covenant does not recognize such rights or that it recognizes them to a lesser extent.

PART III

Article 6

1. The States Parties to the present Covenant recognize the right to work, which includes the right of everyone to the opportunity to gain his living by work which he freely chooses or accepts, and will take appropriate steps to safeguard this right.

2. The steps to be taken by a State Party to the present Covenant to achieve the full realization of this right shall include technical and vocational guidance and training programmes, policies and techniques to achieve steady economic, social and cultural development and full and productive employment under conditions safeguarding fundamental political and economic freedoms to the individual.

Article 7

The States Parties to the present Covenant recognize the right of everyone to the enjoyment of just and favourable conditions of work which ensure, in particular:

(a) Remuneration which provides all workers, as a minimum, with:

    (i) Fair wages and equal remuneration for work of equal value without distinction of any kind, in particular women being guaranteed conditions of work not inferior to those enjoyed by men, with equal pay for equal work;

    (ii) A descent living for themselves and their families in accordance with the provisions of the present Covenant;

(b) Safe and healthy working conditions;

(c) Equal opportunity for everyone to be promoted in his employment to an appropriate higher level, subject to no consideration other than those of seniority and competence;

(d) Rest, leisure and reasonable limitation of working hours and periodic holidays with pay, as well as remuneration for public holidays.

Article 8

1.   The States Parties to the present Covenant undertake to ensure:

   (a)   The right to form trade unions and join the trade union of his choice, subject only to the rules of the organization concerned, for the promotion and protection of his economic and social interests. No restrictions may be placed on the exercise of this right other than those prescribed by law and which are necessary in a democratic society in the interests of national security or public order or for the protection of the rights and freedoms of others;

   (b)   The right of trade unions to establish national federations or confederations and the right of the latter to form or join international trade-union organizations;

   (c)   The right of trade unions to function freely subject to no limitations other than those prescribed by law and which are necessary in a democratic society in the interests of national security or public order or for the protection of the rights and freedoms of others;

   (d)   The right to strike, provided that it is exercised in conformity with laws of the particular country.

2.   This article shall not prevent the imposition of lawful restrictions on the exercise of these rights by members of the armed forces or of the police or of the administration of the State.

3.   Nothing in this article shall authorize States Parties to the International Labour Organisation Convention of 1948 concerning Freedom of Association and Protection of the Right to Organize to take legislative measures which would prejudice, or apply the law in such a manner as would prejudice, the guarantees provided for in that Convention.

Article 9

The States Parties to the present Covenant recognize the right of every one to social security, including social insurance.

Article 10

The States Parties to the present Covenant recognize that:

1.   The widest possible protection and assistance should be accorded to the family, which is the natural and fundamental group unit of society, particularly for its establishment and while it is responsible for the care and education of dependent children. Marriage must be entered into with the free consent of the intending spouses.

2.   Special protection should be accorded to mothers during a reasonable period before and after childbirth. During such period working mothers should be accorded paid leave or leave with adequate social security benefits.

3.   Special measures of protection and assistance should be taken on behalf of all children and young persons without any discrimination for reasons of parentage or other conditions. Children and young persons should be protected from economic and social exploitation. Their employment in work harmful to their morals or health or dangerous to life or likely to hamper their normal development should be punishable by law. States should also set age limits below which the paid employment of child labour should be prohibited and punishable by law.

Article 11

1.   The States Parties to the present Covenant recognize the right of everyone to an adequate standard of living for himself and his family, including adequate food, clothing and housing, and to the continuous improvement of living conditions. The States Parties will take appropriate steps to ensure the realization of this right, recognizing to this effect the essential importance of international co-operation based on free consent.

2.   The States Parties to the present Covenant, recognizing the fundamental right of everyone to be free from hunger, shall take, individually and through international co-operation, the measures, including specific programmes, which are needed:

(a)   To improve methods of production, conservation and distribution of food by making full use of technical and scientific knowledge, by disseminating knowledge of the principles of nutrition and by developing or reforming agrarian systems in such a way as to achieve the most efficient development and utilization of natural resources;

(b)   Taking into account the problems of both food-importing and food-exporting countries, to ensure an equitable distribution of world food supplies in relation to need.

Article 12

1.   The States Parties to the present Covenant recognize the right of everyone to the enjoyment of the highest attainable standard of physical and mental health.

2.   The steps to be taken by the States Parties to the present Covenant to achieve the full realization of this right shall include those necessary for:

(a)   The provision for the reduction of the still birth-rate and of infant mortality and for the healthy development of the child;

(b)   The improvement of all aspects of environmental and industrial hygiene;

    (c) The prevention, treatment and control of epidemic, endemic, occupational and other diseases;

    (d) The creation of conditions which would assure to all medical service and medical attention in the event of sickness.

Article 13

1.   The States Parties to the present Covenant recognize the right of everyone to education. They agree that education shall be directed to the full development of the human personality and the sense of its dignity, and shall strengthen the respect for human rights and fundamental freedoms. They further agree that education shall enable all persons to participate effectively in a free society, promote understanding, tolerance and friendship among all nations and all racial, ethnic or religious groups, and further the activities of the United Nations for the maintenance of peace.

2.   The States Parties to the present Covenant recognize that, with a view to achieving the full realization of this right:

    (a) Primary education shall be compulsory and available free to all;

    (b) Secondary education in its different forms, including technical and vocational secondary education, shall be made generally available and accessible to all by every appropriate means, and in particular by the progressive introduction of free education;

    (c) Higher education shall be made equally accessible to all, on the basis of capacity, by every appropriate means, and in particular by the progressive introduction of free education;

    (d) Fundamental education shall be encouraged or intensified as far as possible for those persons who have not received or completed the whole period of their primary education;

    (e) The development of a system of schools at all levels shall be actively pursued, an adequate fellowship system shall be established, and the material conditions of teaching staff shall be continuously improved.

3.   The States Parties to the present Covenant undertake to have respect for the liberty of parents and, when applicable, legal guardians to choose for their children schools, other than those established by the public authorities, which conform to such minimum educational standards as may be laid down or approved by the State and to ensure the religious and moral education of their children in conformity with their own convictions.

4.   No part of this article shall be construed so as to interfere with the liberty of individuals and bodies to establish and direct educational institutions, subject always to the observance of the principles set forth in paragraph I of this article and to the requirement that the education given in such institutions shall conform to such minimum standards as may be laid down by the State.

Article 14

Each State Party to the present Covenant which, at the time of becoming a Party, has not been able to secure in its metropolitan territory or other territories under its jurisdiction compulsory primary education, free of charge, undertakes, within two years, to work out and adopt a detailed plan of action for the progressive implementation, within a reasonable number of years, to be fixed in the plan, of the principle of compulsory education free of charge for all.

Article 15

1. The States Parties to the present Covenant recognize the right of everyone:

   (a) To take part in cultural life;

   (b) To enjoy the benefits of scientific progress and its applications;

   (c) To benefit from the protection of the moral and material interests resulting from any scientific, literary or artistic production of which he is the author.

2. The steps to be taken by the States Parties to the present Covenant to achieve the full realization of this right shall include those necessary for the conservation, the development and the diffusion of science and culture.

3. The States Parties to the present Covenant undertake to respect the freedom indispensable for scientific research and creative activity.

4. The States Parties to the present Covenant recognize the benefits to be derived from the encouragement and development of international contacts and co-operation in the scientific and cultural fields.

PART IV

Article 16

1. The States Parties to the present Covenant undertake to submit in conformity with this part of the Covenant reports on the measures which they have adopted and the progress made in achieving the observance of the rights recognized herein.

2. (a) All reports shall be submitted to the Secretary-General of the United Nations, who shall transmit copies to the Economic and Social Council for consideration in accordance with the provisions of the present Covenant.

   (b) The Secretary-General of the United Nations shall also transmit to the specialized agencies copies of the reports, or any relevant parts therefrom, from States Parties to the present Covenant which are also members of these specialized agencies in so far as these reports, or parts therefrom relate to any matters which fall within the responsibilities of the said agencies in accordance with their constitutional instruments.

Article 17

1.   The States Parties to the present Covenant shall furnish their reports in stages, in accordance with a programme to be established by the Economic and Social Council within one year of the entry into force of the present Covenant after consultation with the States Parties and the specialized agencies concerned.

2.   Reports may indicate factors and difficulties affecting the degree of fulfillment of obligations under the present Covenant.

3.   Where relevant information has previously been furnished to the United Nations or to any specialized agency by any State Party to the present Covenant, it will not be necessary to reproduce that information, but a precise reference to the information so furnished will suffice.

Article 18

Pursuant to its responsibilities under the Charter of the United Nations in the field of human rights and fundamental freedoms, the Economic and Social Council may make arrangements with the specialized agencies in respect of their reporting to it on the progress made in achieving the observance of the provisions of the present Covenant falling within the scope of their activities. These reports may include particulars of decisions and recommendations on such implementation adopted by their competent organs.

Article 19

The Economic and Social Council may transmit to the Commission on Human Rights for study and general recommendation or, as appropriate, for information the reports concerning human rights submitted by States in accordance with articles 16 and 17, and those concerning human rights submitted by the specialized agencies in accordance with article 18.

Article 20

The States Parties to the present Covenant and the specialized agencies concerned may submit comments to the Economic and Social Council on any general recommendation under article 19 or reference to such general recommendation in any report of the Commission on Human Rights or any documentation referred to therein.

Article 21

The Economic and Social Council may submit from time to time to the General Assembly reports with recommendations of a general nature and a summary of the information received from the States Parties to the present Covenant and the specialized agencies on the measures taken and the progress made in achieving general observance of the rights recognized in the present Covenant.

Article 22

The Economic and Social Council may bring to the attention of other organs of the United Nations, their subsidiary organs and specialized agencies concerned with furnishing technical assistance any matters arising out of the reports referred to in this part of the present Covenant which may assist such bodies in deciding, each within its field of competence, on the advisability of international measures likely to contribute to the effective progressive implementation of the present Covenant.

Article 23

The States Parties to the present Covenant agree that international action for the achievement of the rights recognized in the present Covenant includes such methods as the conclusion of conventions, the adoption of recommendations, the furnishing of technical assistance and the holding of regional meetings and technical meetings for the purpose of consultation and study organized in conjunction with the Governments concerned.

Article 24

Nothing in the present Covenant shall be interpreted as impairing the provisions of the Charter of the United Nations and of the constitutions of the specialized agencies which define the respective responsibilities of the various organs of the United Nations and of the specialized agencies in regard to the matters dealt with in the present Covenant.

Article 25

Nothing in the present Covenant shall be interpreted as impairing the inherent right of all peoples to enjoy and utilize fully and freely their natural wealth and resources.

PART V

Article 26

1. The present Covenant is open for signature by any State Member of the United Nations or member of any of its specialized agencies, by any State Party to the Statute of the International Court of Justice, and by any other State which has been invited by the General Assembly of the United Nations to become a party to the present Covenant.

2. The present Covenant is subject to ratification. Instruments of ratification shall be deposited with the Secretary-General of the United Nations.

3. The present Covenant shall be open to accession by any State referred to in paragraph I of this article.

4. Accession shall be effected by the deposit of an instrument of accession with the Secretary- General of the United Nations.

5. The Secretary-General of the United Nations shall inform all States which have signed the present Covenant or acceded to it of the deposit of each instrument of ratification or accession.

Article 27

1. The present Covenant shall enter into force three months after the date of the deposit with the Secretary-General of the United Nations of the thirty-fifth instrument of ratification or instrument of accession.

2. For each State ratifying the present Covenant or acceding to it after the deposit of the thirty- fifth instrument of ratification or instrument of accession, the present Covenant shall enter into force three months after the date of the deposit of its own instrument of ratification or instrument of accession.

Article 28

The provisions of the present Covenant shall extend to all parts of federal States without any limitations or exceptions.

Article 29

1. Any State Party to the present Covenant may propose an amendment and file it with the Secretary-General of the United Nations. The Secretary-General shall thereupon communicate any proposed amendments to the States Parties to the present Covenant with a request that they notify him whether they favour a conference of States Parties for the purpose of considering and voting upon the proposals. In

the event that at least one third of the States Parties favours such a conference, the Secretary-General shall convene the conference under the auspices of the United Nations. Any amendments adopted by a majority of the States Parties present and voting at the conference shall be submitted to the General Assembly of the United Nations for approval.

2.   Amendments shall come into force when they have been approved by the General Assembly of the United Nations and accepted by a two thirds majority of the States Parties to the present Covenant in accordance with their respective constitutional processes.

3.   When amendments come into force they shall be binding on those States Parties which have accepted them, other States Parties still being bound by the provisions of the present Covenant and any earlier amendment which they have accepted.

Article 30

Irrespective of the notifications made under article 26, paragraph 5, the Secretary-General of the United Nations shall inform all States referred to in paragraph I of the same article of the following particulars:

   (a) Signatures, ratifications and accessions under article 26;

   (b) The date of the entry into force of the present Covenant under article 27 and the date of the entry into force of any amendments under article 29.

Article 31

1.   The present Covenant, of which the Chinese, English, French, Russian and Spanish texts are equally authentic, shall be deposited in the archives of the United Nations.

2.   The Secretary-General of the United Nations shall transmit certified copies of the present Covenant to all States referred to in article 26.

Appendix III
International Covenant on Civil and Political Rights

Concluded at New York, December 16, 1966 (entered into force, March 23, 1976), 999 U.N.T.S. 171, reprinted in 6 I.L.M. 368 (1967) and 3 *International Law and World Order: Basic Documents* III.A.3 (Burns H. Weston ed., 5 vols., 1994–   ).

The State Parties to the Present Convention,

Considering that, in accordance with the principles proclaimed in the Charter of the United Nations, recognition of the inherent dignity and of the equal and inalienable rights of all members of the human family is the foundation of freedom, justice and peace in the world,

Recognizing that these rights derive from the inherent dignity of the human person,

Recognizing that, in accordance with the Universal Declaration of Human Rights, the ideal of free human beings enjoying civil and political freedom and freedom from fear and want can only be achieved if conditions are created whereby everyone may enjoy his civil and political rights, as well as his economic, social and cultural rights,

Considering the obligation of States under the Charter of the United Nations to promote universal respect for, and observance of, human rights and freedom,

Realizing that the individual, having duties to other individuals and to the community to which he belongs, is under a responsibility to strive for the promotion and observance of the rights recognized in the present Covenant,

Agree upon the following articles:

PART I

Article I

1.   All peoples have the right of self-determination. By virtue of that right they determine their political status and freely pursue their economic, social and cultural development.

2.   All peoples may, for their own ends, freely dispose of their natural wealth and resources without prejudice to any obligations arising out of international economic co-operation, based upon the principle of mutual benefit, and international law. In no case may a people be deprived of its own means of subsistence.

3.   The States Parties to the present Covenant, including those having responsibility for the administration of Non-Self-Governing and Trust Territories, shall promote the realizations of the right of self-determination, and shall respect that right, in conformity with the provisions of the Charter of the United Nations.

PART 11

Article 2

1.   Each State Party to the present Covenant undertakes to respect and to ensure to all individuals within its territory and subject to its jurisdiction the rights recognized in the present Covenant, without distinction of any kind, such as race, colour, sex, language, religion, political or other opinion, national or social origin, property, birth or other status.

2.   Where not already provided for by existing legislative or other measures, each State Party to the present Covenant undertakes to take the necessary steps, in accordance with its constitutional processes and with the provisions of the present Covenant, to adopt such legislative or other measures as may be necessary to give effect to the rights recognized in the present Covenant.

3.   Each State Party to the present Covenant undertakes:

   (a) To ensure that any person whose rights or freedoms as herein recognized are violated shall have an effective remedy, notwithstanding that the violation has been committed by persons acting in an official capacity;

   (b) To ensure that any person claiming such a remedy shall have his right thereto determined by competent judicial, administrative or legislative authorities, or by any other competent authority provided for by the legal system of the State, and to develop the possibilities of judicial remedy;

   (c) To ensure that the competent authorities shall enforce such remedies when granted.

Article 3

The States Parties to the present Covenant undertake to ensure the equal right of men and women to the enjoyment of all civil and political rights set forth in the present Covenant.

Article 4

1.   In time of public emergency which threatens the life of the nation and the existence of which is officially proclaimed, the States Parties to the present Covenant may take measures derogating from their obligations under the present Covenant to the extent strictly required by the exigencies of the situation, provided that such measures are not inconsistent with their other obligations under international law and do not involve discrimination solely on the ground of race, colour, sex, language, religion or social origin.

2.   No derogation from articles 6, 7, 8, (paragraphs 1 and 2), 11, 15, 16 and 18 may be made under this provision.

3.   Any State Party to the present Covenant availing itself of the right of derogation shall immediately inform the other States Parties to the present Covenant, through the intermediary of the Secretary-General of the United Nations, of the provisions from which it has derogated and of the reasons by which it was actuated. A further communication shall be made, through the same intermediary, on the date on which it terminates such derogation.

Article 5

1.   Nothing in the present Covenant may be interpreted as implying for any State, group or person any right to engage in any activity or perform any act aimed at the destruction of any of the rights and freedoms recognized herein or at their limitation to a greater extent than is provided for in the present Covenant.

2.   There shall be no restriction upon or derogation from any of the fundamental human rights recognized or existing in any State Party to the present Covenant pursuant to law, conventions, regulations or custom on the pretext that the present Covenant does not recognize such rights or that it recognizes them to a lesser extent.

PART III

Article 6

1.   Every human being has the inherent right to life. This right shall be protected by law. No one shall be arbitrarily deprived of his life.

2.   In countries which have not abolished the death penalty, sentence of death may be imposed only for the most serious crimes in accordance with the law in force at the time of the commission of the crime and not contrary to the provisions of the present Covenant and to the Convention on the Prevention and Punishment of the

Crime of Genocide. This penalty can only be carried out pursuant to a final judgement rendered by a competent court.

3.   When deprivation of life constitutes the crime of genocide, it is understood that nothing in this article shall authorize any State Party to the present Covenant to derogate in any way from any obligation assumed under the provisions of the Convention on the Prevention and Punishment of the Crime of Genocide.

4.   Anyone sentenced to death shall have the right to seek pardon or commutation of the sentence. Amnesty, pardon or commutation of the sentence of death may be granted in all cases.

5.   Sentence of death shall not be imposed for crimes committed by persons below eighteen years of age and shall not be carried out on pregnant women.

6.   Nothing in this article shall be invoked to delay or to prevent the abolition of capital punishment by any State Party to the present Covenant.

Article 7

No one shall be subjected to torture or to cruel, inhuman or degrading treatment or punishment. In particular, no one shall be subjected without his free consent to medical or scientific experimentation.

Article 8

1.   No one shall be held in slavery; slavery and the slave-trade in all their forms shall be prohibited.

2.   No one shall be held in servitude.

3.   (a) No one shall be required to perform forced or compulsory labour;

(b) Paragraph 3(a) shall not be held to preclude, in countries where imprisonment with hard labour may be imposed as a punishment for a crime, the performance of hard labour in pursuance of a sentence to such punishment by a competent court;

(c) For the purpose of this paragraph the term "forced or compulsory labour" shall not include:

(i) Any work or service, not referred to in sub-paragraph (b), normally required of a person who is under detention in consequence of a lawful order of a court, or of a person during conditional release from such detention;

(ii) Any service of a military character and, in countries where conscientious objections is recognized, any national service required by law of conscientious objectors;

    (iii) Any service exacted in cases of emergency or calamity threatening the life or well-being of the community;

    (iv) Any work or service which forms part of normal civil obligations.

Article 9

1. Everyone has the right to liberty and security of person. No one shall be subjected to arbitrary arrest or detention. No one shall be deprived of his liberty except on such grounds and in accordance with such procedure as are established by law.

2. Anyone who is arrested shall be informed, at the time of arrest, of the reasons for his arrest and shall be promptly informed of any charges against him.

3. Anyone arrested or detained on a criminal charge shall be brought promptly before a judge or other officer authorized by law to exercise judicial power and shall be entitled to trial within a reasonable time or to release. It shall not be the general rule that persons awaiting trial shall be detained in custody, but release may be subject to guarantees to appear for trial, at any other stage of the judicial proceedings, and, should occasion arise, for execution of the judgement.

4. Anyone who is deprived of his liberty by arrest or detention shall be entitled to take proceedings before a court, in order that that court may decide without delay on the lawfulness of his detention and order his release if the detention is not lawful.

5. Anyone who has been the victim of unlawful arrest or detention shall have an enforceable right to compensation.

Article 10

1. All persons deprived of their liberty shall be treated with humanity and with respect for the inherent dignity of the human person.

2.   (a) Accused persons shall, save in exceptional circumstances, be segregated from convicted persons and shall be subject to separate treatment appropriate to their status as unconvicted persons;

    (b) Accused juvenile persons shall be separated from adults and brought as speedily as possible for adjudication.

3. The penitentiary system shall comprise treatment of prisoners the essential aim of which shall be their reformation and social rehabilitation. Juvenile offenders shall be segregated from adults and be accorded treatment appropriate to their age and legal status.

Article 11

No one shall be imprisoned merely on the ground of inability to fulfil a contractual obligation.

Article 12

1. Everyone lawfully within the territory of a State shall, within that territory, have the right to liberty of movement and freedom to choose his residence.

2. Everyone shall be free to leave any country, including his own.

3. The above-mentioned rights shall not be subject to any restrictions except those which are provided by law, are necessary to protect national security, public order *(ordre public)*, public health or morals or the rights and freedoms of others, and are consistent with the other rights recognized in the present Covenant.

4. No one shall be arbitrarily deprived of the right to enter his own country.

Article 13

An alien lawfully in the territory of a State Party to the present Covenant may be expelled therefrom only in pursuance of a decision reached in accordance with law and shall, except where compelling reasons of national security otherwise require, be allowed to submit the reasons against his expulsion and to have his case reviewed by, and be represented for the purpose before, the competent authority or a person or persons especially designated by the competent authority.

Article 14

1. All persons shall be equal before the courts and tribunals. In the determination of any criminal charge against him, or of his rights and obligations in a suit at law, everyone shall be entitled to a fair and public hearing by a competent, independent and impartial tribunal established by law. The Press and the public may be excluded from all or part of a trial for reasons of morals, public order *(ordre public)* or national security in a democratic society, or when the interest of the private lives of the parties so requires, or to the extent strictly necessary in the opinion of the court in special circumstances where publicity would prejudice the interests of justice; but any judgement rendered in a criminal case or in a suit at law shall be made public except where the interest of juvenile persons otherwise requires or the proceedings concern matrimonial disputes or the guardianship of children.

2. Everyone charged with a criminal offence shall have the right to be presumed innocent until proved guilty according to law.

3. In the determination of any criminal charge against him everyone shall be entitled to the following minimum guarantees, in full equality:

   (a) To be informed promptly and in detail in a language which he understands of the nature and cause of the charge against him.

   (b) To have adequate time and facilities for the preparation of his defence and to communicate with counsel of his own choosing;

(c) To be tried without undue delay;

(d) To be tried in his presence, and to defend himself in person or through legal assistance of his own choosing; to be informed, if he does not have legal assistance, of this right; and to have legal assistance assigned to him, in any case where the interests of justice so require, and without payment by him in any such case if he does not have sufficient means to pay for it;

(e) To examine, or have examined, the witnesses against him and to obtain the attendance and examination of witnesses on his behalf under the same conditions as witnesses against him;

(f) To have the free assistance of an interpreter if he cannot understand or speak the language used in court;

(g) Not to be compelled to testify against himself or to confess guilt.

4.   In the case of juvenile persons, the procedure shall be such as will take account of their age and the desirability of promoting their rehabilitation.

5.   Everyone convicted of a crime shall have the right to his conviction and sentence being reviewed by a higher tribunal according to law.

6.   When a person has by a final decision been convicted of a criminal offence and when subsequently his conviction has been reversed or he has been pardoned on the ground that a new or newly discovered fact shows conclusively that there has been a miscarriage of justice, the person who has suffered punishment as a result of such conviction shall be compensated according to law, unless it is proved that the non-disclosure of the unknown fact in time is wholly or partly attributable to him.

7.   No one shall be liable to be tried or punished again for an offence for which he has already been finally convicted or acquitted in accordance with the law and penal procedure of each country.

Article 15

1.   No one shall be held guilty of any criminal offence on account of any act or omission which did not constitute a criminal offence, under national or international law, at the time when it was committed. Nor shall a heavier penalty be imposed than the one that was applicable at the time when the criminal offence was committed. If, subsequent to the commission of the offence, provision is made by law for the imposition of a lighter penalty, the offender shall benefit thereby.

2.   Nothing in this article shall prejudice the trial and punishment of any person for any act or omission which, -at the time when it was committed, was criminal according to the general principles of law recognized by the community of nations.

Article 16

Everyone shall have the right to recognition everywhere as a person before the law.

Article 17

1.   No one shall be subjected to arbitrary or unlawful interference with his privacy, family, home or correspondence, nor to unlawful attacks on his honour and reputation.

2.   Everyone has the right to the protection of the law against such interference or attacks.

Article 18

1.   Everyone shall have the right to freedom of thought, conscience and religion. This right shall include freedom to have or to adopt a religion or belief of his choice, and freedom, either individually or in community with others and in public or private, to manifest his religion or belief in worship, observance, practice and teaching.

2.   No one shall be subject to coercion which would impair his freedom to have or to adopt a religion or belief of his choice.

3.   Freedom to manifest one's religion or beliefs may be subject only to such limitations as are prescribed by law and are necessary to protect public safety, order, health, or morals or the fundamental rights and freedoms of others.

4.   The States Parties to the present Covenant undertake to have respect for the liberty of parents and, when applicable, legal guardians to ensure the religious and moral education of their children in conformity with their own convictions.

Article 19

1.   Everyone shall have the right to hold opinions without interference.

2.   Everyone shall have the right to freedom of expression; this right shall include freedom

to seek, receive and impart information and ideas of all kinds, regardless of frontiers, either orally, in writing or in print, in the form of art, or through any other media of his choice.

3.   The exercise of the rights provided for in paragraph 2 of this article carries with it special duties and responsibilities. It may therefore be subject to certain restrictions, but these shall only be such as are provided by law and are necessary

   (a) For respect of the rights or reputations of others;

   (b) For the protection of national security or of public *(ordre public)*, or of public health or morals.

Article 20

1. Any propaganda for war shall be prohibited by law.

2. Any advocacy of national, racial or religious hatred that constitutes incitement to discrimination, hostility or violence shall be prohibited by law.

Article 21

The right of peaceful assembly shall be recognized. No restrictions may be placed on the exercise of this right other than those imposed in conformity with the law and which are necessary in a democratic society in the interest of national security or public safety, public order *(ordre public)*, the protection of public health or morals or the protection of the rights and freedoms of others.

Article 22

1. Everyone shall have the right to freedom of association with others, including the right to form and join trade unions for the protection of his interests.

2. No restrictions may be placed on the exercise of this right other than those which are prescribed by law and which are necessary in a democratic society in the interests of national security, or public safety), public order *(ordre public)*, the protection of public health or morals or the protection of the rights and freedoms of others. This article shall not prevent the imposition of lawful restrictions on members of the armed forces and of the police in their exercise of this right.

3. Nothing in this article shall authorize States Parties to the International Labour Organisation Convention of 1948 concerning Freedom of Association and Protection of the Right to Organize to take legislative measures which would prejudice, or to apply the law in such a manner as to prejudice, the guarantees provided for in that Convention.

Article 23

1. The family is the natural and fundamental group unit of society and is entitled to protection by society and the State.

2. The right of men and women of marriageable age to marry and to found a family shall be recognized.

3. No marriage shall be entered into without the free and full consent of the intending spouses.

4. States Parties to the present Covenant shall take appropriate steps to ensure equality of rights and responsibilities of spouses as to marriage, during marriage and at its dissolution. In the case of dissolution, provision shall made for the necessary protection of any children.

Article 24

1.   Every child shall have, without any discrimination as to race, colour, sex, language, religion, national or social origin, property or birth, the right to such measures of protection as are required by his status as a minor, on the part of his family, society and the State.

2.   Every child shall be registered immediately after birth and shall have a name.

3.   Every child has the right to acquire a nationality.

Article 25

Every citizen shall have the right and the opportunity, without any of the distinctions mentioned in article 2 and without unreasonable restrictions:

(a) To take part in the conduct of public affairs, directly or through freely chosen representatives;

(b) To vote and to be elected at genuine periodic elections which shall be by universal and equal suffrage and shall be held by secret ballot, guaranteeing the free expression of the will of the electors;

(c) To have access, on general terms of equality, to public service in his country.

Article 26

All persons are equal before the law and are entitled without any discrimination to the equal protection of the law. In this respect, the law shall prohibit any discrimination and guarantee to all persons equal and effective protection against discrimination on any ground such as race, colour, sex, language, religion, political or other opinion, national or social origin, property, birth or other status.

Article 27

In those States in which ethnic, religious or linguistic minorities exist persons belonging to such minorities shall not be denied the right, in community with the other members of their group, to enjoy their own culture, to profess and practise their own religion, or to use their own language.

PART IV

Article 28

1.   There shall be established a Human Rights Committee (hereafter referred to in the present Covenant as the Committee). It shall consist of eighteen members and shall carry out the functions hereinafter provided.

2.   The Committee shall be composed of nationals of the States Parties to the present Covenant who shall be persons of high moral character and recognized competence in the field of human rights, consideration being given to the usefulness of the participations of some persons having legal experience.

3.   The members of the Committee shall be elected and shall serve in their personal capacity.

Article 29

1.   The members of the Committee shall be elected by secret ballot from a list of persons possessing the qualifications prescribed in article 28 and nominated for the purpose by the States Parties to the present Covenant.

2.   Each State Party to the present Covenant may nominate not more than two persons. These persons shall be nationals of the nominating State.

3.   A person shall be eligible for renomination.

Article 30

1.   The initial election shall be held no later than six months after the date of the entry into force of the present Covenant.

2.   At least four months before the date of each election to the Committee, other than an election to fill a vacancy declared in accordance with article 34, the Secretary-General of the United Nations shall address a written invitation to the States parties to the present Covenant to submit their nominations for membership of the Committee within three months.

3.   The Secretary-General of the United Nations shall prepare a list in alphabetical order of all the persons thus nominated, with an indication of the States Parties which have nominated them, and shall submit it to the States Parties to the present Covenant no later than one month before the date of each election.

4.   Elections of the members of the Committee shall be held at a meeting of the States Parties to the present Covenant convened by the Secretary-General of the United Nations at the Headquarters of the United Nations. At that meeting, for which two thirds of the States Parties to the present Covenant shall constitute a quorum, the persons elected to the Committee shall be those nominees who obtain the largest number of votes and an absolute majority of the votes of the representatives of States Parties present and voting.

Article 31

1.   The Committee may not include more than one national of the same State.

2.   In the election of the Committee, consideration shall be given to equitable geo-

graphical distribution of membership and to the representation of the different forms of civilization and of the principal legal systems.

Article 32

1. The members of the Committee shall be elected for a term of four years. They shall be eligible for re-election if renominated. However, the terms of nine of the members elected at the first election shall expire at the end of two years; immediately after the first elections, the names of these nine members shall be chosen by lot by the Chairman of the meeting referred to in article 30, paragraph 4.

2. Elections at the expiry of office shall be held in accordance with the preceding articles of this part of the present Covenant.

Article 33

1. If, in the unanimous opinion of the other members, a member of the Committee has ceased to carry out his functions for any cause other than absence of a temporary character, the Chairman of the Committee shall notify the Secretary-General of the United Nations, who shall then declare the seat of the member to be vacant.

2. In the event of the death or the resignation of a member of the Committee, the Chairman shall immediately notify the Secretary-General of the United Nations, who shall declare the seat vacant from the date of death or the date on which the resignation takes effect.

Article 34

1. When a vacancy is declared in accordance with article 33 and if the term of office of the member to be replaced does not expire within six months of the declaration of the vacancy, the Secretary-General of the United Nations shall notify each of the States Parties to the present Covenant, which may within two months submit nominations in accordance with article 29 for the purpose of filling the vacancy.

2. The Secretary-General of the United Nations shall prepare a list in alphabetical order of the persons thus nominated and shall submit it to the States Parties to the present thus nominated and shall submit it to the States Parties to the present Covenant. The election to fill the vacancy shall then take place in accordance with the relevant provisions of this part of the present Covenant.

3. A member of the Committee elected to fill a vacancy declared in accordance with article 33 shall hold office for the remainder of the term of the member who vacated the seat on the Committee under the provisions of that article.

Article 35

The members of the Committee shall, with the approval of the General Assembly of the United Nations, receive emoluments from United Nations resources on such terms and conditions as the General Assembly may decide, having regard to the importance of the Committee's responsibilities.

Article 36

The Secretary-General of the United Nations shall provide the necessary staff and facilities for the effective performance of the functions of the Committee under the present Covenant.

Article 37

1. The Secretary-General of the United Nations shall convene the initial meeting of the Committee at the Headquarters of the United Nations.

2. After its initial meeting, the Committee shall meet at such times as shall be provided in its rules of procedure.

3. The Committee shall normally meet at the Headquarters of the United Nations or at the United Nations Office at Geneva.

Article 38

Every member of the Committee shall, before taking up his duties, make a solemn declaration in open committee that he will perform his functions impartially and conscientiously.

Article 39

1. The Committee shall elect its officers for a term of two years. They may be re-elected.

2. The Committee shall establish its own rules of procedure, but these rules shall provide, *inter alia*, that:

    (a) Twelve members shall constitute a quorum

    (b) Decisions of the Committee shall be made by a majority vote of the members present.

Article 40

1.   The States Parties to the present Covenant undertake to submit reports on the measures they have adopted which give effect to the rights recognized herein and on the progress made in the enjoyment of those rights :

  (a) Within one year of the-entry into force of the present Covenant for the States Parties concerned-

  (b) Thereafter whenever the Committee so requests.

2.   All reports shall be submitted to the Secretary-General of the United Nations, who shall transmit them to the Committee for consideration. Reports shall indicate the factors and difficulties, if any' affecting the implementation of the present Covenant.

3.   The Secretary-General of the United Nations may, after consultation with the Committee, transmit to the specialized agencies concerned copies of such pans of the reports as may fall within their field of competence.

4.   The Committee shall study the reports submitted by the States Parties to the present Covenant. It shall transmit its reports, and such general comments as it may consider appropriate, to the States Parties. The Committee may also transmit to the Economic and Social Council these comments along with the copies of the reports it has received from States Parties to the present Covenant.

5.   The States Parties to the present Covenant may submit to the Committee observations on any comments that may be made in accordance with paragraph 4 of this article.

Article 41

1.   A State Party to the present Covenant may at any time declare under this article that it recognizes the competence of the Committee to receive and consider communications to the effect that a State Party claims that another State Party is not fulfilling its obligations under the present Covenant. Communications under this article may be received and considered only if submitted by a State Party which has made a declaration recognizing in regard to itself the competence of the Committee. No communication shall be received by the Committee if it concerns a State Party which has not made such a declaration. Communications received under this article shall be dealt with in accordance with the following procedure:

  (a) If a State Party to the present Covenant considers that another State Party is not giving effect to the provisions of the present Covenant, it may, by written communication, bring the matter to the attention of that State Party. Within three months after the receipt of the communication, the receiving State shall afford the State which sent the communication an explanation or any other statement in writing clarifying the matters, which should include, to the extent possible and pertinent, reference to domestic procedures and remedies taken, pending, or available in the matter.

(b) If the matter is not adjusted to the satisfaction of both States Parties concerned within six months after the receipt by the receiving State of the initial communication, either State shall have the right to refer the matter to the Committee, by notice given to the Committee and to the other State.

(c) The Committee shall deal with a matter referred to it only after it has ascertained that all available domestic remedies have been invoked and exhausted in the matter, in conformity with the Generally recognized principles of international law. This shall not be the rule where the application of the remedies is unreasonably prolonged.

(d) The Committee shall hold closed meetings when examining communications under this article.

(e) Subject to the provisions of sub-paragraph (c), the Committee shall make available its good offices to the States Parties concerned with a view to a friendly solution of the matter on the basis of respect for human rights and fundamental freedoms as recognized in the present Covenant.

(f) In any matter referred to it, the Committee may call upon the States Parties concerned, referred to in sub-paragraph (b), to supply any relevant information.

(g) The States Parties concerned , referred to in sub-paragraph (b), shall have the right to be represented when the matter is being considered in the committee and to make submissions orally and/or in writing.

(h) The Committee shall, within twelve months after the date of receipt of notice under sub-paragraph (b), submit a report:

(i) If a solution within the terms of sub-paragraph (e) is reached, the Committee shall confine its report to a brief statement of the facts and of the solution reached;

(ii) If a solution within the terms of sub-paragraph (e) is not reached, the Committee shall confine its report to a brief statement of the facts; the written submissions and record of the oral submissions made by the States Parties concerned shall be attached to the report.

In every matter, the report shall be communicated to the States Parties concerned.

2. The provisions of this article shall come into force when ten States Parties to the present Covenant have made declarations under paragraph I of this article. Such declarations shall be deposited by the States Parties with the Secretary-General of the United Nations, who shall transmit copies thereof to the other States Parties. A declaration may be withdrawn at any time by notification to the Secretary-General. Such a withdrawal shall not prejudice the consideration of any matter which is the

subject of a communication already transmitted under this article; no further communication by any State Party shall be received after the notification of withdrawal of the declaration has been received by the Secretary-General, unless the State Party concerned had made a new declaration.

Article 42

1. (a) If a matter referred to the Committee in accordance with article 41 is not resolved to the satisfaction of the States Parties concerned, the Committee may with the prior consent of the States Parties concerned, appoint an *ad hoc* Conciliation Commission (hereinafter referred to as the Commission). The good offices of the Commission shall be made available to the States Parties concerned with a view to an amicable solution of the matter on the basis of respect for the present Covenant;

    (b) The Commission shall consist of five persons acceptable to the States Parties concerned. If the States Parties concerned fail to reach agreement within three months on all or part of the composition of the Commission, the members of the Commission concerning whom no agreement has been reached shall be elected by secret ballot by a two thirds majority vote of the Committee from among its members.

2. The members of the Commission shall serve in their personal capacity. They shall not be nationals of the States Parties concerned, or of a State not party to the present Covenant or of a State Part), which has not made a declaration under article 41.

3. The Commission shall elect its own Chairman and adopt its own rules of procedure.

4. The meetings of the Commission shall normally be held at the Headquarters of the United Nations or at the United Nations Office at Geneva. However they may be held at such other convenient places as the Commission may determine in consultation with the Secretary General of the United Nations and the States Parties concerned.

5. The secretariat provided in accordance with article 36 shall also service the commissions appointed under this article.

6. The information received and collected by the Committee shall be made available to the Commission and the Commission may call upon the States Parties concerned to supply any other relevant information.

7. When the Commission has fully considered the matter, but in any event not later than twelve months after having been seized of the matter, it shall submit to the Chairman of the Committee a report for communication to the States Parties concerned:

    (a) If the Commission is unable to complete its consideration of the matter within twelve months, it shall confine its report to a brief statement of the status of its consideration of the matter.

(b) If an amicable solution to the matter on the basis of respect for human rights as recognized in the present Covenant is reached, the Commission shall confine its report to a brief statement of the facts and of the solution reached:

(c) If a solution within the terms of sub-paragraph (b) is not reached, the Commission's report shall embody its findings on all questions of fact relevant to the issues between the States Parties concerned, and its views on the possibilities of an amicable solution of the matter. This report shall also contain the written submissions and a record of the oral submissions made by the States Parties concerned;

(d) If the Commission's report is submitted under sub-paragraph (c), the States Parties concerned shall, within three months of the receipt of the report, notify the Chairman of the Committee whether or not they accept the contents of the report of the Commission.

8. The provisions of the article are without prejudice to the responsibilities of the Committee under article 41.

9. The States Parties concerned shall share equally all the expenses of the members of the Commission in accordance with estimates to be provided by the Secretary-General of the United Nations.

10. The Secretary-General of the United Nations shall be empowered to pay the expenses of the members of the Commission if necessary, before reimbursement by the States Parties concerned, in accordance with paragraph 9 of this article.

Article 43

The members of the Committee, and of the ad hoc conciliation commissions which may be appointed under article 42, shall be entitled to the facilities, privileges and immunities of experts on mission for the United Nations as laid down in the relevant sections of the Convention on the Privileges and Immunities of the United Nations.

Article 44

The provisions for the implementation of the present Covenant shall apply without prejudice to the procedures prescribed in the field of human rights by or under the constituent instruments and the conventions of the United Nations and of the specialized agencies and shall not prevent the States Parties to the present Covenant from having recourse to other procedures for settling a dispute in accordance with general or special international agreements in force between them.

Article 45

The Committee shall submit to the General Assembly of the United Nations, through the Economic and Social Council, an annual report on its activities.

PART V

Article 46

Nothing in the present Covenant shall be interpreted as impairing the provisions of the Charter of the United Nations and of the constitutions of the specialized agencies which define the respective responsibilities of the various organs of the United Nations and of the specialized agencies in regard to the matters dealt with in the present Covenant.

Article 47

Nothing in the present Covenant shall be interpreted as impairing the inherent right of all people to enjoy and utilize fully and freely their natural wealth and resources.

PART VI

Article 48

1.   The present Covenant is open for signature by any State Member of the United Nations or member of any of its specialized agencies, by any State Party to the Statute of the International Court of Justice, and by any other State which has been invited by the General Assembly of the United Nations to become a party to the present Covenant.

2.   The present Covenant is subject to ratification. Instruments of ratification shall be deposited with the Secretary-General of the United Nations.

3.   The present Covenant shall be open to accession by any State referred to in paragraph I of this article.

4.   Accession shall be effected by the deposit of an instrument of accession with the Secretary-General of the United Nations.

5.   The Secretary-General of the United Nations shall inform all states which have signed this Covenant or acceded to it of the deposit of each instrument of ratification or accession.

Article 49

1.   The present Covenant shall enter into force three months after the date of the deposit with the Secretary-General of the United Nations of the thirty-fifth instrument of ratification or instrument of accession.

2.   For each State ratifying the present Covenant or acceding to it after the deposit of the thirty-fifth instrument of ratification or instrument of accession, the present Covenant shall enter into force three months after the date of the deposit of its own instrument of ratification or instrument of accession.

Article 50

The provisions of the present Covenant shall extend to all parts of federal States without any limitations or exceptions.

Article 51

1.   Any State Party to the present Covenant may propose an amendment and file it with the Secretary-General of the United Nations. The Secretary-General of the United Nations shall thereupon communicate any proposed amendments to the States Parties to the present Covenant with a request that they notify him whether they favour a conference of States Par-ties for the purpose of considering and voting upon the proposals. In the event that at least one third of the States Parties favours such a conference, the Secretary-General shall convene the conference under the auspices of the United Nations. Any amendment adopted by a majority of the States Parties present and voting at the conference shall be submitted to the General Assembly of the United Nations for approval.

2.   Amendments shall come into force when they have been approved by the General Assembly of the United Nations and accepted by a two-thirds majority of the States Parties to the present Covenant in accordance with their respective processes.

3.   When amendments come into force, they shall be binding on those States Parties which have accepted them, other States Parties still being bound by the provisions of the present Covenant and any earlier amendment which they accepted.

Article 52

Irrespective of the notifications made under article 48, paragraph 5, the Secretary-General of the United Nations shall inform all States referred to in paragraph I of the same article of the following particulars:

(a) Signatures, ratifications and accessions under article 48;

(b) The date of the entry into force of the present Covenant under article 49 and the date of the entry into force of any amendments under article 51.

Article 53

1.   The present Covenant, of which the Chinese, English, French, Russian and Spanish texts are equally authentic, shall be deposited in the archives of the United Nations.

2.   The Secretary-General of the United Nations shall transmit certified copies of the present Covenant to all States referred to in article 48.

Index